The Dorsey Series in Sociology

Editor ROBIN M. WILLIAMS, JR. *Cornell University*

AMERICAN DELINQUENCY

Its meaning and construction

LaMar T. Empey

Department of Sociology
University of Southern California, Los Angeles

1978

THE DORSEY PRESS   Homewood, Illinois   60430
Irwin-Dorsey Limited   Georgetown, Ontario   L7G 4B3

ISBN 0-256-01985-1
Library of Congress Catalog Card No. 77–085787

Printed in the United States of America

4 5 6 7 8 9 0 MP 5 4 3 2 1 0

PREFACE

The past two decades have witnessed remarkable changes in the American concepts of delinquency and juvenile justice: the reputation of the juvenile court has been badly tarnished; the rules that define delinquency have been altered; the philosophical foundations, the accuracy, and the policy implications of scientific theories of delinquency have been challenged; faith in the concept of rehabilitation has been seriously eroded; and current efforts at "reform" are being threatened by a resurgent, neoclassical philosophy of retributive justice. In short, we are witnessing changes in our treatment of the young that are every bit as revolutionary as was the invention of the juvenile court in 1899 or the construction of prisons and reformatories almost a century before that.

In writing this book it seemed to me that any attempt to make sense out of these remarkable changes would require more than attention to current concerns over juvenile crime rates or to contemporary debates, theories, and policy changes. Indeed, the scholarly work of the past two decades had indicated all too clearly that "delinquency" should not be conceived merely as the illegal acts of children but as a changing social construction in which rules for behavior, and society's organized reactions to it, as well as the behavior itself, should be the elements of which "delinquency" is comprised. When conceived in these terms, therefore, it became obvious that any full understanding of the phenomenon would require that it be analyzed in terms of the larger cultural and historical contexts out of which it has arisen.

As a part of culture, "delinquency" may be said to include a profoundly complex set of elements:

An evolving body of beliefs about the nature of childhood.

A changing set of rules designed to reinforce prevailing beliefs about childhood.

A social phenomenon in which children not only engage in various forms of illegal behavior but, more often than adults, are the victims of that behavior.

Elaborate bodies of social thought which we call scientific theories.

A welfare-oriented system of justice that is applied only to children.

Each of these products of culture merits considerable attention if we are to put the total mosaic of delinquency together. Hence, each of them is treated in detail and comprises a major segment of this book.

Second, it seemed clear that much would be missed if attention were restricted solely to the impact of contemporary culture for the origins of delinquency. Many of the traditions and practices which have given delinquency its particular character in the United States derive their meaning not merely from the relatively short span of American history but from the much longer history of Western civilization. Hence, even a modest understanding of the delinquency "problem" requires a context which only history can provide. Indeed, when the various elements of delinquency—beliefs, rules, behavior, theories, and legal practices—are analyzed in historical terms, that analysis not only illuminates the past but raises provocative questions about the future. Consider but a few of those that will be examined in this book:

The nature of childhood. The juvenile court was not invented until 1899. This implies a concept of childhood that is relatively recent in the history of Western civilization. How were children perceived and treated in prior centuries? Why were attempts not made until the dawn of the 20th century to provide elaborate legal protections for them, and to circumscribe their moral as well as their criminal behavior? Even more important, how has our concept of childhood changed in recent years so that we now question the assumptions upon which the juvenile court was originally constructed?

Rules that define delinquency. Deviant behavior can only be understood as departure from some set of desirable, conformist standards. What are those standards? How did they evolve? Why did they remain relatively unchanged for most of this century? Why are they now changing?

Delinquent behavior.   Since the rules that define "delinquent" behavior are of recent origin, does that mean that such behavior did not exist in prior centuries? Since it obviously did, how was it perceived? How did society deal with it? Equally important, in what segments of our youth population does it occur today? Who are its perpetrators and its victims?

Theories of delinquency.   Theories of delinquency are more than pristine guides for research. They are influential and evolving bodies of social thought. To what degree, then, do they reflect traditional as well as contemporary values and beliefs, and how might they have altered those beliefs in return? Upon what assumptions about human nature and social order are they based? How have they influenced social policy? In what way have they contributed to the current revolution in juvenile justice?

The juvenile justice system.   The juvenile court was hailed as a triumph of American jurisprudence and benevolence for two thirds of this century. Why, then, has it suddenly been subjected to scathing attacks from almost every quarter? What have been the sources of those attacks? How is justice for children likely to be organized in the future? May current "reforms" be viewed as undeniable steps forward in the progress of humanity?

In short, this book attempts to tell a story. As each element in the mosaic of delinquency is unfolded, its historical evolution, as well as its contemporary state, is analyzed. Attention is paid not only to the content and adequacy of various theories, to the debate over the extent and implications of juvenile crime, or to the way in which the juvenile justice system is run, but to the place of all of these in the larger context and history of American life.

I am indebted to several people for their help in developing this work: to Robin M. Williams, Jr., James F. Short, Jr., and Joseph Sanders for their incisive and extended critiques of the manuscript; to Elaine M. Corry for her invaluable editorial assistance; and to Jacqueline T. Sanchez for typing and retyping draft after draft. Last, but not least, I am grateful to a loving family for their patient understanding of the emotional disorders of a compulsive author.

December 1977   **LaMar T. Empey**

CONTENTS

part three
EXPLANATIONS OF DELINQUENT BEHAVIOR

1

HOW DELINQUENCY IS CONSTRUCTED

This book is about smoking pot, stealing cars, skipping school, joining in a gang fight, mugging an old lady, making out, writing laws, getting busted, going to court, being put on probation and getting locked up—all the many and different things we call "delinquency."

Today, people are preoccupied with delinquency: Why do so many young people misbehave? What can honest people do to protect themselves from young hoods? Why do kids insist on violating rules? Why don't they do the things that parents, teachers, ministers, legislators, police, and judges consider best for them?

These are important questions. They will occupy much of our attention in this book. But they are not the only questions we need to ask. Indeed, if we limit ourselves to questions like these, we will be using tunnel vision. Few people even know, for example, that "delinquency" as we use it is a new word. It was not employed much until the 19th century and the juvenile court was not created until the turn of the 20th century. As something important in the history of civilization, therefore, "juvenile delinquency" is a new phenomenon.

Does this mean, then, that youth did not drink, steal, and fight before the 19th or 20th centuries or that they have only just begun to break the law? Of course not. Young people have always engaged in acts of this type. Behavior that we now define as delinquent has been common among young people throughout history, but it has not always been illegal nor has it always been called "delinquency."

As late as the 17th and 18th centuries, European children continued the medieval practice of wearing and using arms (Ariès, 1962:315–321). Boys as young as five wore swords, and not just as ornaments. The schools of 17th century France were marked by so many duels, mutinies, brawls, and beatings of teachers that regulations were eventually written forbidding pupils to keep firearms, swords, or clubs in their rooms or to bring them to class. But, even then, these weapons were not taken from their youthful owners, just stored in a central place for use outside the school.

The use of arms has obviously declined over time but at different rates in different settings. While student violence and rebellion decreased in France during the 18th century, they increased in England. English schools were often taken over by students, and, in some cases, their rebellions had to be put down by troops armed with bayonets.

Medieval license with regard to wine and sex also carried over into later centuries. Public schoolboys, said Montaigne, "practiced more vices by the age of 16 than anyone else would have by 60" (Ariès, 1962:321–324). A hundred of them had caught the pox before they read their first lesson in Aristotle, and they read Aristotle young! "If I were a woman," wrote one author, "I would rather go with a student than with the most splendid courtiers in France. A student, Ah! He's the pearl of mankind" (Ariès, 1962:321–322).

Similarly, the young were heavy drinkers. Schoolmen tried to control traditional drinking practices, first, by setting up regulations designed to reduce it and, then, by forbidding it entirely. Students, as a result, simply retired to nearby taverns where drinking was not forbidden. French students apparently became somewhat more sober by the 18th century, but English students bravely carried on into the early 19th.

Modern concern over drugs was also unknown until recently even though the use of opium began 4,000 years before the birth of Christ (Ray, 1972:181–191). Although people did not fully understand its chemical properties, they certainly grasped its effects. As a consequence, they used it for recreational as well as medicinal purposes.

In 1805, a London youth bought some laudanum (an opium derivative) for a toothache, reported in ecstacy that he had discovered the secret to happiness, and continued to use and write about it throughout his life (De Quincey, 1907:179). In the second half of the 19th century, opium was introduced into the United States. By the end of the century, there were probably more Americans addicted to it than there have been before or since. Until 1914, it could be purchased legally at the neighborhood drug store, and it was viewed with little concern. But, in contrast to the present, the addict was typically a middle-aged white female, not a young person. (Ray, 1972:189).

It was not until the 19th century that many of the acts which had been entirely acceptable in the Middle Ages and only partially lamented in the 17th and 18th centuries became cause for great alarm. Writing on the evils of sex, an anonymous London author decried the extent to which novels pictured "the dissipated rake, who glories in his debaucheries . . . as humane, generous and benevolent; whilst the heedless female . . . forgets his want of principle, his diseased body, and his rotten heart" (Sanders, 1970:93). And, during an age of unparalleled optimism, 19th century Americans exhibited fright and pessimism over youth behavior. No decent man could safely walk the streets of San Francisco (Bell, 1962:172); the term "hoodlum" was coined to describe the members of teenage gangs (Bruce, 1959:13); young girls, many of them under twelve, were described as "brutalized . . . by premature vice, . . . with harsh laughter and foulness on their lips, . . . with thief written in their cunning eyes and whore on their depraved faces . . ." (Nevins and Thomas, 1952, Vol. II:56); and it was said that the police could enter the central New York area near Broadway only if they were armed and went in pairs (Bell, 1962:171). One author declared that "Crime, especially its more violent forms, and among the young, is increasing steadily and is threatening to bankrupt the nation" (Wasserman, 1965:24).

How should all these past events and descriptions be interpreted? If "delinquency" in our terms, is a recent invention, what should we make of our current preoccupation with it? Two interpretations are possible. Either the behavior of young people has somehow grown worse over the centuries or significant changes have occurred in the way we now define and react to it. History indicates that the latter interpretation is probably the more accurate. "Delinquency" is a social creation of relatively recent times. It is a concept designed to focus our attention upon forms of youthful behavior which, though they have been common throughout history, have become of increasing concern in recent centuries.

The significance of this conclusion is great. People born into a particular society at a particular time tend to take that society for granted, as though its beliefs are timeless and its ways universal. Modern Americans, for example, are inclined to believe that children have always been seen and treated as they are now. Most believe that children are born fragile and innocent. To insure their proper development, therefore, they must be stringently safeguarded by their parents, must receive a long and carefully directed education, and, only after many years of moral and physical quarantine, can they be allowed to join the adults. It is only when this quarantine breaks down that juvenile delinquents are spawned; that is, when parents, schools, and communities fail to do their jobs and when they permit poverty, ignorance, and vice to intrude upon their sacred duty to raise children properly. Thus, it would come as considerable surprise to those who unquestioningly accept such beliefs to find that they have not always prevailed, that children have not always been perceived as delicate and innocent, nor that their departure from innocence has always been defined as legally delinquent.

The point is that while strongly held beliefs and customs are common to all societies the forms they take may differ greatly. Hence, something like delinquency that is seen as a problem in one society, or at one point in time in several societies, may not be defined as such in other times or societies. One cannot understand delinquency, therefore, merely by looking at the illegal behavior of children or by an unthinking concern with the immediate present—whether working mothers ought to stay home with their kids, whether marijuana ought to be legalized, whether more police and judges are needed, or whether everything would be all right if there were just more child guidance clinics. A broader perspective is needed, one that looks not only at the currently undesirable behavior of children, but one that helps to indicate why that behavior is now of overriding concern. Without revealing the whole story, therefore, the remaining sections of this introductory chapter provide a sneak preview of what we will be studying in this book. They will help to spell out the meaning of delinquency in its broader terms.

Creation of childhood and delinquency

The modern juvenile court exists because of widespread beliefs that children are different from adults and therefore require special legal protections and special kinds of care. Throughout the United States and in many countries throughout the world the legal codes now specify that a child can be brought under the jurisdiction of court authorities for one of three major kinds of problems: (1) for cases in which the child has been neglected, exploited, or cruelly treated by adults; (2) for the type of criminal offenses for which adults can be punished, such as robbery, assault, or car theft; or (3) for juvenile "status" offenses that apply only to children because of their age—drinking, truancy, or running away. For any one of these problems, children can be processed legally but are not treated the same as adults.

If they have been neglected or exploited, steps may be taken to insure that children have adequate food, clothing, and shelter; they may actually be removed from their own homes and placed in the care of others; or their parents may be required, under the threat of legal punishment, to change the way they treat their children.

If children are charged with criminal offenses, there are special procedures through which police, court, and correctional agencies must go in dealing with them. The laws stipulate that officials should treat children less formally than adults and should help to solve their problems rather than just punish them.

Finally, children's "status" offenses not only incorporate special treatment of alleged offenders but are different in themselves. They include such things as "incorrigibility," "truancy," "waywardness," "idling," "being in danger of lewd and immoral conduct," or "being beyond reasonable control." Adults cannot be charged with such offenses, but children can. In many states, in fact, status offenses are so broadly defined and so subjective in character that almost any child could be referred to court if some parent or official believed court action was warranted. Why is this? Why are children singled out and treated differently from adults?

The answer is that "childhood," like "adulthood" or "old age," is a social status—a position in the social structure and a phase in the life cycle to which a special set of beliefs and expectations are attached. Most modern cultures imply that children are different from adults, more innocent, less guilty of criminal intent, and more in need of both protection and discipline than grown-ups. The term "status" offense, in fact, implies these many beliefs, indicating that children are to be treated in a special way because of their age. This means, therefore, that if we are to understand the social nature of delinquency, why special laws are written for children, and why the juvenile court was invented, we must first explore the meaning of childhood. We cannot understand why children are singled out for special treatment until we determine how and why their special status developed.

What is a child?

There has been enormous variation, historically and culturally, in the meaning of the term "child." Some of this variation is apparent today. *Webster's Dictionary*, for example, defines a child as "a young person of either sex between infancy and youth." In advancing this definition, it implies that there are at least three periods in the life of a young person: (1) *infancy*—the first few years of life; (2) *childhood*—the period between infancy and youth (or adolescence); and (3) *youth*—the period between the onset of puberty and full adulthood. Yet, *Webster's Dictionary* also agrees with the law in most states by noting that a child is "a person not yet of age," that is, a person who has not reached the legal age of adulthood. In practical terms, this means that anyone who is under 18 must be treated as a "delinquent" rather than a "criminal" for committing a crime and that one cannot assume full responsibility as an adult until age 18 in some states or age 21 in other states.

Childhood, in short, is not a sharply defined status in our society. In one sense, it is defined as ending at puberty while in another it continues on until adulthood. Though such a definition is terribly ambiguous, we can make some sense out of it by considering the assumptions that are made about the development of children (Cf. Skolnick, 1973:316–321):

1.   Children go through several stages of development which are qualitatively different from one another. These stages coincide generally with those described in *Webster's Dictionary* and postpone entrance into full adulthood until the twenties or even later (Coleman, et al., 1974). The developmental process takes that long to complete.

2.   Throughout the various stages of development, children are qualitatively different from adults: "Adults work and are responsible, children play and are irresponsible; adults are controlled and rational, children are emotional and irrational; adults think abstractly, children think concretely; adults are sexual, children are asexual; and so on" (Skolnick, 1973:316).

3.   Until their full emotional, moral, physical, and rational skills have been cultivated, the appropriate place for children is at home, in school with their peers, and in constructive places of recreation. Until they mature fully and until they are well educated, they should be quarantined from adult vices, activities, and responsibilities. Though this quarantine may be reduced gradually as children proceed through

the developmental process, it should not be lifted entirely until adult-hood has been achieved.

In a very real sense, then, we view young people all the way from birth to adulthood as children in different stages of development. Though we certainly do not react to a 6-foot, 200-pound adolescent in the same way we do to an 85-pound 10-year-old, we do not view either of them as fully responsible either. Instead, we see them at different places in the process of growing up. That is why our society is ambiva-lent about granting full rights to young people even of college age. Although we have recently lowered the time at which people can vote to 18, we are reluctant to grant them full recognition as adults until they have completed school and have found regular employment. And, even then, there is a tendency for parents, employers, coaches of professional sports teams, or politicians to call them "kids"—young people who are not quite mature and experienced enough to merit full acceptance as adults.

How old is this concept of childhood?

A series of recent historical works all tend to suggest that our current concept of childhood is a product largely of the past few centuries. Prior to that time, much less attention was paid to the development of chil-dren. Perhaps because death rates were so distressingly high, infants were seen less as human beings than as strange formless little creatures somehow different from people who had survived for a few years and with whom strong emotional ties were to be avoided. Yet, even when they did survive, people we would call children today were regarded more as small or inadequate versions of their parents than as sacred beings in need of special protection. Consequently, many unwanted children, particularly girls, were put to death at birth, were deliberately abandoned, were sold into prostitution, or, at best, were left to be raised by others. Most parents, in short, were simply not much involved with their children except insofar as they could help to preserve the family line or could serve some economic purpose.

For those parents who could afford it, the preferred method for taking care of newborn babies was to send them out to be wet-nursed and to be raised by indifferent women who rented out their milk and services, often with deadly consequences for the babies of the women them-selves. If the wet-nursed baby survived the first few years of life, it was soon apprenticed to another family to be of service and to learn the skills of a trade appropriate to its station in life, whether noble or commoner. Children were not spared, as they are now, from full participation in hard work, lewd jokes, sexual acts, or adult greed and manipulation. At a very early age, all these became a routine part of their lives.

This is not to suggest that young things occupied a status equal to that of adults. They did not. As apprentices they were subject to the whims and demands of their masters and were expected to make a contribution. Further, it was through their apprenticeships and services to others that they gained their educations, not in a classroom organized according to some graded scheme of child development. The modern notion that growing up requires careful guidance through a series of physical, moral, and intellectual stages, in fact, is something that has been totally alien to most people throughout Western history. It did not even occur to them.

It was not until Europe began to awaken from the intellectual hibernation and social stagnation of the Middle Ages that a handful of moral philosophers began to question the customary treatment of children. Over a period of the next two or three centuries, age-old tendencies, either to ignore or to exploit them, were replaced with an ardent concern for their moral welfare: parental care for children became a sacred duty; the school gradually replaced the apprenticeship system as the second most important child-raising institution; and childhood became a transitional period in which protection from, rather than indulgence in, adult activities became the rule.

Out of this process grew the modern concept of childhood—a concept stressing the idea that children have value in their own right and that because of their sweetness and simplicity they require a careful preparation for the harshness and sinfulness of an adult world. Furthermore, it was only after all of these things occurred, only after childhood became a special status in the life cycle, that the concept of a special court for juveniles began to develop. Along with the changing image of childhood, there was an increasing tendency to be less harsh with children charged with crimes. Though they were subject to the same laws and courts as adults, officials were more and more inclined to refrain from holding them fully responsible for their acts and to pardon those who were actually found guilty of crimes. But, as mentioned, it was not until the very last year of the 19th century that the first juvenile court was created and not until the first quarter of the 20th century—just yesterday—that every state created one. The view of delinquency as something uniquely applicable to children had been gaining increased acceptance for many years, but it was not until society had prepared special machinery for dealing with it that its full impact as a unique social creation was actually felt.

Our first task in assessing the meaning of delinquency will be to review this fascinating history in greater detail. By so doing, we will seek to determine what factors led to the discovery of childhood, why juvenile delinquency was invented, and what social reformers sought to accomplish by creating it. Such a background is vitally important because the safeguarding of children is now assumed to be an absolute necessity and the special laws that were written to protect them were originally hailed as a Magna Charta for the young. But are these social creations living up to the great things expected of them?

Many modern critics are not so sure. Even though they might not want to return to the child-raising practices of the Middle Ages, if they know about them, they do not like our current treatment of children either. They would institute new reforms.

Rules that define delinquency

Part of the process of discovering childhood and inventing delinquency involved the gradual evolution of an elaborate set of social rules or norms designed to govern the lives of children. First came a set of informal rules or customs which, before they were ever written into law, assumed a great deal of importance. Indeed, they helped to create an ideal image of childhood toward which parents were expected to strive in raising their children. Though that image is now undergoing change, the social rules that helped to give it its character are still thoroughly familiar to all of us: Children should be obedient, should be hardworking and diligent in their educational and other pursuits, should be submissive to the authorities who guide them in these pursuits, should learn self-control, should be modest, and should avoid the evils of drinking, sex, and other adult vices of this type. That they should avoid the dishonest acts and predatory crimes in which adults engage goes without saying.

There are several things about rules like these that are central to the meaning of delinquency. The first is the fact that they define and set apart undesirable as well as desirable behavior. Not only do they indicate how the ideal child should behave, but they become the standard for indicating when he is out of line. Thus, where there are rules, there is not only conformity but rule breaking. For the young, rule breaking may be relatively innocuous, like talking back to one's parents or failing to do the dishes, or it may be serious like getting kicked out of school or using heroin. Since rules are the standards by which behavior is judged as good or bad, attention must be paid to the nature and character of those rules. To be concerned solely with delinquent behavior, without looking at the rules that define what it is, is like trying to eat soup with a fork. It is not very productive.

Secondly, history reveals that as reformers sought to moralize the young, to protect them from exploitation and to safeguard their premature induction into the corruption of an adult world, they looked at the age-old behaviors in which the young had customarily engaged and discovered immorality. In seeking to foster greater conformity to the ideal image of childhood, they discovered rampant immorality. In seeking to make children more virtuous, they defined more of their acts as deviant. And, in encouraging greater discipline and control, they narrowed the range of acceptable childhood conduct.

It was out of the long and evolutionary process of developing new rules to govern childhood that the invention of delinquency grew. There came a time when the informal controls of home, school, and neighborhood no longer seemed adequate for insuring conformity to the rules thought desirable for children. Thus, formal legal rules were written, and a juvenile justice system was created to enforce them. From vague and informal changes beginning in the 16th century, formal legal structures grew in the 19th and 20th centuries.

Thirdly, history suggests that the ideal image of childhood from which these legal structures developed was a white middle-class image. While that image seemed to the emerging middle class to be particularly well-suited to their interests and aspirations, it overlooked the fact that in Western societies, in general, and in American society, in particular, all people are not cast in the same mold. American society, for example, is a pluralistic society in which a variety of different ethnic and class groups abound. Hence, the social and legal standard by which delinquent as well as conformist behavior is now judged may not be a standard to which all young people are equally socialized and taught how to conform. Opportunities to conform and thereby to escape censure are not equitably distributed.

It is for all of these reasons and many more that a review of the rules by which delinquent behavior is judged will constitute the second main segment of our analysis. On the one hand, organized human society implies the existence of social rules. Without them people cannot do business with one another. On the other hand, existing rules are not necessarily sacred and need not prevent us from asking some important questions: To what extent is there agreement upon, or conflict over, existing rules? Under what circumstances may rules, perhaps more than rule breakers, be at fault? To what degree do existing rules fail to realize the purpose for which they were created?

Rare is the circumstance where the worth of all existing rules is universally hailed and where everyone willingly adheres to them. Is this due to an innate human perversity, or does it signal the need for even greater attention to the rules by which conduct is governed and the worth of people called into question? Conversely, rule violation may become so extensive that human predators are spawned whose acts threaten both the physical and psychological well-being of the many. What should be done about this?

There was a time in more stable societies where rules seemed to take on an immutable quality since they were the product of a relatively unchanging world. That day has passed. Change is rapid and ubiquitous. It is for this and many other reasons that we will be exploring the rules that determine what delinquent behavior is, to what degree they are violated, and how, and upon whom, they are enforced.

Behavior that violates rules

San Francisco is often hailed as one of America's most elegant and civilized cities. But, on a sunny fall afternoon recently, six muggings occurred in stunning succession—all within 30 minutes (*Los Angeles Times*, December 1, 1974).

> In that period, six passengers aboard separate Municipal Railway buses—including a 95-year-old woman—were assailed by groups of youths who clawed for their victims' wallets, tried to pull rings from their fingers, and, in one instance, cut a man's arm in an attempt to slash open his pants pocket.

> Authorities estimate that up to 85 percent of the violence and vandalism aboard city buses and streetcars is committed by juveniles.

Two months later, young vandals caused about $45,000 damage to a shiny, new, and unusually equipped high school in Los Angeles. A fire was set in the security office, school records were destroyed, closed circuit television sets, expensive tape decks, and amplifiers were destroyed, walls were defaced, cafeteria tables were overturned, and food supplies were thrown about (*Los Angeles Times*, January 27, 1975).

Violence and destruction by the young are not confined to California cities. Asphalt-bound citizens of New York are warned not to enjoy the precious pastoral qualities of Central Park; congressmen and senators as well as ordinary mortals are attacked and robbed in the nation's capital; and students are cautioned not to walk alone at night on or near the campus of the University of Chicago. If the rumors about delinquency and crime and media accounts of them are to be believed, the nation is under siege from an army of juvenile and adult felons gone berserk. But are popular accounts and rumor to be believed?

If our attempt to discover the meaning of delinquency is to be successful, we must go beyond rumor and sensational accounts. Lurid accounts not only fail to paint an accurate picture of actual crimes committed by children, but fail as well to acquaint us with the other kinds of behavior called delinquent—the status offenses with which adults cannot be charged or the instances in which children are abused and neglected. In pursuit of a more accurate picture, therefore, we will be looking at delinquent behavior from three perspectives.

The first will utilize reports from official sources, primarily the police and courts. They provide a more systematic method for determining whether official delinquency rates are climbing higher and whether more youth are becoming officially delinquent.

For a view from a second angle, we will turn to the self-reports of children themselves. Instead of relying solely on official accounts, the results of scientific studies will be reported in which young people were asked how many, and in what kinds of, delinquent acts they have engaged. Social scientists began collecting this kind of information for two reasons: because they suspected that most children commit delinquent acts without ever being caught and because official records are often a better indicator of official than of youth behavior—whom officials are lucky enough to catch, upon what segments of the youth population they concentrate their attention, with which kinds of illegal acts they are most concerned, and so on. As might be expected, therefore, official and self-reports differ markedly, sometimes in surprising ways. When young people report what they have done, their accounts do not always conform to many cherished beliefs about who is delinquent and why. Thus, they provide us with a picture of delinquent behavior from a different perspective.

Finally, we will turn to the victims of crime and delinquency for yet a third view. In 1967, the President of the United States appointed a special commission to study crime and delinquency and to make recommendations. As a part of that effort, the commission initiated the first national survey of crime victimization ever conducted (President's Commission on Law Enforcement and Administration of Justice, 1967). The study found that there were far more crime victims than there were crimes being reported by officials or being solved by them. The picture was not a happy one. Since that time, the Law Enforcement Assistance Administration, in collaboration with the Census Bureau, has begun to conduct annual surveys of this type. These newer surveys indicate that the results of the first survey were no fluke. The large gap between official and victim accounts continue to appear. Indeed, when all three views—official, self-report, and victim—are joined together, they provide us with a picture of delinquent behavior that is often in sharp disagreement with the pictures that have been presented heretofore.

Explanations for delinquent behavior

Explanations for delinquent behavior constitute the next major set of factors that must be reviewed in attempting to assess the meaning of delinquency. Some explanations emphasize such things as broken homes, irresponsible parents, and emotional disturbance; others stress poverty and the lack of opportunity; still others focus upon the way delinquent habits might be acquired through associations with the wrong kinds of friends. In order to understand fully these theoretical explanations, we will look not only at their more obvious aspects—at things like home conditions, class membership, or delinquent friends—but at the assumptions about human nature and social order upon which they are based.

Theories of delinquency have changed markedly in the past 200 or 300 years, not because they were always given a thorough test, but because of the changes in the way children (and adults) are viewed. As the basic beliefs of influential philosophers, religious leaders, and other reformers have changed, so have their theories. In fact, it is only in recent times that we have stressed the word "theory" and applied the methods of science in attempts to understand delinquency. In earlier times, few attempts were made to test influential ideas empirically. It is important, therefore, to pay attention to the many beliefs that predate science and to determine in what way they now affect our current thinking.

Thomas Hobbes (1957), a 17th century English philosopher, assumed that the tendency to misbehave is natural in people. Humans are predatory by nature. If there were no enforcement of rules, they would be governed by their passions—the desire for power, self-preservation, and personal gain. If one were seeking to explain delinquent acts, therefore, one would have to look no further than the inborn tendencies of the young. Since they are naturally delinquent, there is nothing to be explained. Rather, the real task is that of finding ways to control their brutish tendencies and to train them to be law-abiding citizens.

By contrast, other philosophers, such as Cesare Beccaria, an Italian, and Jeremy Bentham, an Englishman, emphasized the doctrine of free will and believed that individuals are governed by reason, not passion (Vold, 1958:14–26). In pursuit of their own interests, people seek to maximize pleasure and to minimize pain. Hence, according to this view, delinquency is inherent in the exercise of a rationally directed free will and the desire to maximize personal satisfaction. If a person believes one can gain more pleasure than pain by committing forbidden acts, one will do so. If not, one will refrain from delinquency. So influential were the beliefs of Beccaria and Bentham that long before they could be tested in some systematic way they found their ways into the laws that govern crime and the way people are punished. They became the foundation for what is now called the Classical School of Criminology. Since the causes for rule breaking were assumed to reside in the exercise of free choice, much less attention was paid to why people commit illegal acts than how best to use punishment to convince them that crime does not pay.

Yet a third set of theories has been produced by the same forces that produced the modern concept of childhood and the idea that children must be carefully nurtured if they are to grow up correctly. These theories reject the notion that people are completely free to choose who they will be and how they will behave. Instead, they suggest that behavior is determined by forces over which the individual has little control. The way people perceive the world, the choices available to them, and ultimately their social conduct are products of the process of socialization—the process by which the individual acquires a sense of self and learns how one is expected to behave from those around him.

Theories of this type range all the way from the common sense idea that a child's family, friends, and neighbors will heavily influence his or her final character to highly sophisticated notions advanced by biologists, psychologists, and sociologists. Ultimately, however, all imply that human behavior is determined, not free. Whether people become thieves, famous athletes, or successful lawyers, their careers will be the result of the way they have been raised and with whom they have associated.

The implications of these kinds of theories are profoundly different from Hobbes' idea that people are inherently inclined to be evil at birth or Beccaria's idea that they are free to choose between good and evil. Such differences might be intellectually interesting but relatively unimportant were it not for the fact that elements of all three kinds of theory lie buried in our juvenile justice system today. Hence, it is important that we remain aware of the fact and seek to determine how much they and other traditional beliefs affect our current explanations for delinquent behavior. Besides looking at the more apparent aspects of our modern theories, we will want to ask what kinds of hidden assumptions lie behind them. What assumptions about human nature and social order do they make? Are young people thought to be inherently brutish, inherently rational, or are they thought to be dependent beings whose basic natures are simply the products of the kinds of groups in which they live? Depending upon the basic assumptions upon which modern theories rest, they will vary considerably. Furthermore, these assumptions will greatly affect the construction of social rules or the kinds of social control that are thought necessary to govern behavior. In short, it is imperative that we ask ourselves how much our traditional beliefs about people tend to affect the explanations for delinquent behavior that are currently popular and the ways we react to delinquents.

Society's reaction to delinquent behavior

Society is now organized to react to delinquent behavior in certain ways. The way it does react, in fact, both reflects and influences our explanations for delinquency, how serious it is assumed to be, and whether children are treated differently from adults. As we have seen, there was no separate juvenile justice system in this country prior to the

20th century. Those who upheld the criminal law were officially supposed to react to, and to punish, youthful lawbreakers over age seven in the same way that they punished adults. After the discovery of childhood, however, pressures for change eventually culminated in the creation of a new system. That system today is comprised of police, prosecutors, defenders, courts, probation officers, correctional institutions and personnel, and a host of other public and private agencies all charged with correcting the problems of difficult children. Most of these problems are technically legal, but the law is written in such a way that they might be of almost any conceivable type—emotional, educational, economic, or social. As originally conceived, the juvenile justice system was to become society's superparent.

Whenever there was a breakdown in any other societal institution— the home, school, neighborhood, or world of work—the juvenile justice system was supposed to solve it. How did all this come about? The criminal justice system for adults is designed primarily to deal with crime. Why was the juvenile justice system expected to become a superparent?

The answer lies in the evolution of Western culture and its changing treatment of children. Consider an example. There was a time in American history when children helped to colonize this country and to extend the frontier. Later, they worked on farms and in factories, contributing important sources of inexpensive and much needed labor. The results, at least according to present standards, were both good and bad. On the one hand, youth were seen as economic assets, and their separation from the world of adult work was not so great as now. There was dignity, as well as toil, associated with their contribution to home and community.

On the other hand, children did not always realize much direct benefit from their labors. In our terms, they were exploited, largely because vestiges of the medieval apprenticeship system were present in the settling of America and because the economic system relied upon the use of cheap labor. In the early colonies, they were indentured to farmers and artisans and were required with little choice on their parts to serve the masters to whom they were apprenticed. Later, they were employed in sweatshops, mines, and factories. They were forced to work up to 12 hours a day for a pittance, sometimes under the most miserable of conditions. The children of the poor, in particular, were little more than slaves.

Since there was no juvenile court during this period, there were few legal protections for children. They were expected to be obedient and to accept the subservient role assigned to them. Furthermore, if they got into trouble or disobeyed, the right to punish them was lodged with the persons who were their masters, not in a court of law. Methods of control for children were stern and by no means entirely formal.

Today, by contrast, child labor laws, designed to prevent the exploitation of children, also prevent employment for many of those who would like to work. Several factors have contributed to this state of affairs—the belief that the tender and undeveloped natures of children are harmed by premature toil and responsibility, technological developments which have shrunk the demand for unskilled labor, and a high level of affluence which permits the country to support a large portion of its population, its children, without their having to contribute anything of an economic nature. As a result, participation in economic affairs by the young has dwindled to almost nothing. Apprenticeship, which until the 20th century was the main method by which children learned their future roles and thus gained their educations, is virtually nonexistent. In its stead, the family and particularly the school have assumed greatly increased importance. It is these institutions, rather than apprenticeship, to which society looks to have its newer generations trained.

In part, it is because these institutions often fail that the juvenile justice system was created. While it was clearly expected to get children out of adult jails, courts, and prisons, it was also designed to enforce society's newer view of children. With regard to education, for example, the delinquency laws stipulate that a child can be defined as delinquent for defying school authority, for being truant or for dropping out— something that would have been unheard of in an earlier day. Likewise, instead of requiring that children obey their apprenticeship masters, laws require that they obey their parents. Any child can be brought to court if he or she is "incorrigible" or "beyond reasonable control." If other institutions fail, the legal superparent will step in.

After attempting to fulfill this kind of a function for three quarters of a century, the juvenile justice system is now undergoing changes— changes that are every bit as revolutionary in character as those which led to its initial creation. Modern-day reformers have grown disillusioned with the notion that it can serve effectively as a superparent and are seeking to reduce its power and influence. Whether these "reforms" will somehow produce outcomes that are more desirable than those already being produced is difficult to predict. The desirability and acceptability of social change depends more upon the emergence of new values and beliefs than upon some immutable standard of goodness.

Consequently, the best we can do in preparing ourselves to determine whether we approve of current changes or whether we prefer that the juvenile justice system operate as it has in the past is to examine such issues as the following: how and why society has organized childhood the way it has; what special institutions, particularly legal ones, it has set up to govern their lives; what kinds of people, with what kinds of values, seem to provide leadership in these institutions; what kinds of changes are now being introduced; and how these changes are likely to affect the future. All of these, as well as illegal acts themselves, are factors which help to give delinquency its full meaning.

Summary and conclusions

In summary, this introduction has suggested that delinquency is a social construction comprised not merely of the illegal acts of children but of many other social phenomena as well. Hence, the remainder of this book will be organized to take them into account:

Part I will be concerned with the creation of childhood and delinquency—the discovery of childhood, the invention of delinquency, and how these are defined according to American rules.

Part II will be concerned with the extent and nature of delinquent behavior as indicated by accounts from officials, from young people themselves, and from the victims of delinquent acts.

Part III will be concerned with the evolution of scientific explanations for delinquent behavior, with the philosophical assumptions upon which they are based, and with their implications for the way delinquents are viewed and their offenses treated.

Part IV will be concerned with the legal institutions that society has set up to enforce its beliefs about children. We will examine how, in contrast to scientists and other citizens, the police, courts, and correctional agencies have constructed their own particular views of delinquency. Finally, we will examine the revolutionary changes that the juvenile justice system is now undergoing.

References

Ariès, Philippe
    1962 *Centuries of Childhood* (Trans. by Robert Baldick.) New York: Alfred
        A. Knopf.

Bell, Daniel
    1962   *The End of Ideology* (2nd ed.) New York: Collier Books.

Bruce, Robert V.
    1959   *1877: Year of Violence.* New York: Bobbs-Merrill.

Coleman, James S. et al.
    1974   *Youth: Transition to Adulthood.* Chicago: University of Chicago Press.

Hobbes, Thomas
    1957   *Leviathan.* London: Oxford University Press.

Nevins, Allan and Thomas, Milton H.
    1952   *The Diary of George Templeton Strong.* 4 vols. New York: Macmillan.

President's Commission on Law Enforcement and Administration of Justice
    1967   *Task Force Report: Crime and Its Impact—An Assessment.* Washington, D.C.: U.S. Government Printing Office.

Quincey, Thomas De
    1907   *Confessions of an English Opium Eater.* New York: E. P. Dutton.

Ray, Oakley
    1972   *Drugs, Society and Human Behavior.* St. Louis: C. V. Mosby.

Sanders, Wiley B. (ed.)
    1970   *Juvenile Offenders for a Thousand Years.* Chapel Hill: University of North Carolina Press.

Skolnick, Arlene
    1973   *The Intimate Environment: Exploring Marriage and the Family.* Boston: Little, Brown.

Vold, George B.
    1958   *Theoretical Criminology.* New York: Oxford University Press.

Wasserman, Al
    1965   *NBC White Paper: Terror in the Streets.* Unpublished script for NBC television broadcast, April.

part one

THE CREATION OF CHILDHOOD AND DELINQUENCY

Introduction: Approaching history objectively

In a number of recent and fascinating historical works, several writers have come to the conclusion that the modern concept of childhood in Western civilization is a product largely of the past few centuries (Ariès, 1962; Bremner, 1970; de Mause, 1974; Gillis, 1974; Hunt, 1970; Laslett, 1972; Stone, 1974). These writers are not in total agreement on all the important facts that relate to childhood, nor do they agree on how those facts should be interpreted (Stone, 1974). These differences exist, surprisingly, because historians have just begun to inquire into the history of childhood. Yet, among the important conclusions upon which they all agree is that childhood has not always been a time in life to which much importance has been attached. Indeed, the opposite has often been true. For instance, de Mause (1974:1) says that "The history of childhood [in Western civilization] is a nightmare from which we only recently began to awaken." And, while Stone (1974:29) is somewhat more cautious, he still concludes that the historical treatment of children is a "catalogue of atrocities." How, then, did our modern concern with children come about? Why, today, do we pay so much attention to it?

In order to answer these questions fully, it is necessary that we understand three basic concepts: *culture, childhood,* and *ethnocentrism.*

21

Culture

Anthropologists and sociologists have long been intrigued by the perseverance and continuity of society. If you or I should die tomorrow, society would continue. With scarcely a ripple, most people would rise at their usual times, would eat their usual breakfasts, would go to their usual places of employment or schooling, and would return home at their customary times. Why is this? Why is life in any society broadly predictable?

Social scientists attribute this predictability to *culture*.

> The concept of "culture" is familiar enough to the modern layman. It refers to knowledge, beliefs, values, codes, tasks and prejudices that are traditional in social groups. Our American language, political habits, sex mores, taste for hamburger and cokes, and aversion to horse meat are parts of American culture. We take for granted that the contrasting ways of Hindus, Chinese, and Navahos are for the most part a matter of indoctrination into different culture (Cohen, 1955:12).

An awareness of cultural differences is important to our understanding of childhood because of the unique stamp that American culture with its strong ties to Western civilization has put upon it. We construct and organize childhood in a particular way because of our cultural traditions.

Childhood

In Chapter 1, it was pointed out that childhood in American, and most Western, societies has become a special phase in the life cycle, set apart from adulthood or old age. It is treated as a unique period in life because of prevailing beliefs that children are different from adults, more innocent, less capable of evil intent, and, therefore, more in need of protection, careful direction, and training. Only after many years of physical, moral, and intellectual quarantine in home and school should they be required to confront the harsh realities of adulthood.

Childhood, however, is not a product of nature, like a rock or a tree. Instead, childhood is a product of culture. To be sure, young *Homo sapiens*, like the offspring of other animals, are less well-developed physically, sexually, and intellectually than are adult members of the species. But the notion that they should sleep in a bassinet rather than in a cradle board, that they should be fondled by loving parents rather than wrapped tightly in swaddling clothes, that they should be sent to school rather than farmed out to others as servants or apprentices, or that they require treatment rather than punishment for their misdeeds is man-made.

Childhood, in short, is a social construction. As such, it can be viewed and analyzed as something apart from the young people who are affected by it. Young persons exist in every society, but the values, beliefs, and social institutions that organize their lives vary greatly. Childhood, as we know it, has not been universal throughout history, nor is it universal among all people today. Instead, it is something that is peculiar to our time and place in history. That is why this and other chapters are concerned with the historical factors that have given rise to our particular construction of it. Because it determines the way we view and organize the lives of young people, it leads us to define certain acts as delinquent, to write laws to control those acts, and to organize a juvenile justice system to administer them. As a set of cultural patterns, therefore, childhood provides the context within which the young in our society can best be understood.

Ethnocentrism

One reason that it is important that we be aware of our particular construction of childhood is that most people tend to be *ethnocentric;* that is, to use their own way of life—in this case, their construction of childhood—as a standard for judging other peoples and ways of life. Having been raised according to the dictates of their own culture, they tend to assume that those dictates are, or should be, universal. Hence, any departure from them by another group or person is a sign of inferiority. Such beliefs, however, are a serious impediment to a full understanding of the range and potential of human existence.

In the first place, excessive ethnocentrism even inhibits a full appreciation and comprehension of one's own culture. To the degree that we assume that our own way of life is eternal and immutable, we blind ourselves to reality. Our culture has been anything but eternal and unchanging. Hence, if we ignore its unique development and character, we will be unable to put it into some larger perspective—a perspective that might permit us to ask important questions, to seek out injustices, or to recognize that alternative ways of life are possible.

Excessive ethnocentrism also inhibits an understanding and appreciation of other peoples and cultures. An inclination to brand others as inferior because their way of life is different overlooks the fact that their behavior cannot be judged meaningfully outside the cultural context of which they are a part. Though we may choose eventually to disagree with them and to prefer our ways of doing things, it is important to recognize that those things which they regard as truthful, right, and moral are dependent upon the particular values and beliefs of their culture. Just as our construction of reality tells us we are right, so their construction of it tells them that they are right.

The fact that we are ethnocentric will soon become apparent when we delve into the history of childhood. We will encounter beliefs and practices so different from our own that they will shock and displease us. The fact that historians have called that history a "nightmare" and a "catalogue of atrocities" is evidence of their application of our cultural standards to what they found. But, while according to these standards, shock and disbelief may be merited, we will miss much that is important if that is all we experience. Childhood has been constructed differently in other times and places, not merely because other people were somehow less sensitive to the young than we are, but because of the unique circumstances to which their societies had to adapt. What we seek from our review, therefore, is some understanding of these circumstances in Western civilization so that we may place our own construction of childhood and delinquency into a larger context. Should we be successful in that endeavor, we may be better prepared to approach our own beliefs, as well as those of others, somewhat more rationally.

In order to determine how our own concept of childhood came about, and how delinquency was invented, this part of the book will be divided into four major chapters:

In *Chapter 2*, we will review the general treatment of the young throughout much of Western civilization.

In *Chapter 3*, we will describe the gradual discovery of childhood and the emergence of modern beliefs about it.

In *Chapter 4*, we will assess the transformation that the discovery of childhood brought to modern society, including the invention of delinquency and the creation of a juvenile court.

Finally, in *Chapter 5*, we will analyze the social rules that have defined what delinquent behavior is and how it should be treated.

References

Ariès, Phillippe
  1962 *Centuries of Childhood* (Trans. by Robert Baldick). New York: Alfred
         A. Knopf.
Bremner, Robert H. et al. (Eds.)
  1970 *Children and Youth in America: A Documentary History.* 2 vols. Cam-
         bridge: Harvard University Press.
Cohen, Albert K.
  1955 *Delinquent Boys: The Culture of the Gang.* New York: Free Press.
de Mause, Lloyd (Ed.)
  1974 *The History of Childhood.* New York: Psychohistory Press.
Gillis, John R.
  1974 *Youth and History.* New York: Academic Press.
Hunt, David
  1970 *Parents and Children in History: The Psychology of Family Life in Early
         Modern History.* New York: Basic Books.
Laslett, Peter
  1972 *Household and Family in Past Time.* Cambridge: Cambridge Univer-
         sity Press.
Stone, Lawrence
  1974 "The massacre of the innocents." *The New York Review.* November,
         14:25–31.

2

THE HISTORY OF INDIFFERENCE TO CHILDREN

We are shocked today by occasional reports of child battering and abuse, but if historians are correct, practices we now define as abusive have been a common feature of Western life for much of recorded history. To begin with, infanticide—the deliberate killing of infants—was a regular practice in ancient civilizations and not uncommon as late as the 18th century. Whether in the civilizations of the ancient Middle East, in Greece or Rome, or among the Gauls, the Celts, and Scandinavians in Europe, newborn infants were thrown into rivers, flung into dung heaps, left to be eaten by birds and animals of prey, or sacrificed to the gods in religious rites. The bones of child sacrifices are still being discovered in the walls of buildings constructed all the way from 7000 B.C. to A.D. 1843.

Infanticide

de Mause (1974:25) maintains that the killing of legitimate children was only slowly reduced during the Middle Ages and that the practice of killing illegitimate ones persisted even into the 19th century. In support of this conclusion, he cites historical references suggesting that infanticide may have been only sporadically punished prior to the 16th century and that during the Middle Ages children were still being deliberately suffocated by their mothers or left in the streets to die. He quotes a priest in 1527 who said that "the latrines resound with the cries of children who have been plunged into them" (de Mause, 1974:29). Likewise, Marvick (1974:282) notes that the criminal law of 17th century France enumerated the conditions under which a father had the right to kill an adult son or daughter and indicates that the right to kill an infant may not even have needed official sanction. And, in England during the same period, midwives had to take the following oath (Illick, 1974:306):

> I will not destroy the child born of any woman, nor cut, nor pull off the head thereof, or otherwise dismember or hurt the same, or suffer it to be so hurt or dismembered.

The need to have such an oath for the persons who delivered most of England's babies is some indication that deliberate destruction was still occurring.

The practice of infanticide was apparently rooted in cultural values and beliefs that defined which children should, and should not, survive. In antiquity, any child who was not perfect or seemed to cry too much was generally killed. As the Roman statesman Seneca (1963:145) put it in Christ's time: "Mad dogs we knock on the head, the fierce ox we slay; sickly sheep we put to the knife to keep them from infecting the flock; unnatural progeny we destroy . . . yet, it is not anger, but reason that separates the harmful from the sound."

Throughout history, as we will see again and again, boys were considered to be of much greater value than girls. de Mause (1974:26) says that the few statistics available from antiquity "show large surpluses of boys over girls; for instance, out of 79 families who gained Milesian citizenship about 228–220 B.C., there were 118 sons and 28 daughters." What he is implying, of course, is that more girls than boys were put to death at birth. The first born of any family was usually permitted to live, particularly if it were a boy. Girls, however, were less desirable, as the following advice to parents indicates: "If, as may well happen, you give birth to a child, if it is a boy let it live; if it is a girl expose it [leave it outside to die]" (Cf. de Mause, 1974:26).

Much later in 17th century France, the same sexist themes were perpetuated (Marvick, 1974:283–284). The desire for children even among the upper classes was a desire for boys. Writers of the time noted the "curious" fact that there had been a universal surplus of boys over girls for three centuries, suggesting, of course, that greater efforts were expended on saving boys than girls. One of many contributing factors was the belief that the milk of women who delivered girls was best for boys. Since boys were valued more highly than girls and since many women of the poorer classes hired themselves out as wet nurses, they had an incentive to abandon their own baby girls so they could nurse the boys of wealthier people.

Abandonment

A practice that was closely related to infanticide was abandonment. In some cases, mothers abandoned their children for profit. In antiquity, for example, both boys and girls were sold into slavery or prostitution or used as security to pay debts (de Mause, 1974:33). Likewise, as indicated above, country women throughout much of European history could add to their incomes by abandoning their own children and nursing the offspring of wealthier people.

But, lest any Americans feel smug, it should be recalled that early colonists in this country also traded in children. The first settlements were desperate in their need for laborers. Consequently, large numbers of homeless children were rounded up in the streets of London and other cities and indentured to these settlements as workers. Furthermore, the purchase of black children to act as slaves was common in America until the end of the 19th century. It was not black parents, however, who favored this practice but their white captors of European descent.

In other instances, babies were abandoned because parents could not afford to care for them or simply because all of a couple's children were not equally prized. Infanticide and abandonment, rather than contraception or abortion, were methods of controlling family size. Two sons might be raised, possibly three, but seldom more than one girl (Cf. de Mause, 1974:26). Similarly, orphaned children might experience a sad fate. Rather than raising the orphaned children of a brother or a sister, relatives often abandoned them and sometimes had them killed (Marvick, 1974:284).

In European towns of the Middle Ages and as late as the 17th and 18th centuries, children could be found abandoned and rotting on city streets, on doorsteps, or on garbage dumps. Destitute mothers or the mothers of illegitimate children sometimes brought their children to hospitals or foundling homes, if one were available, but such children were usually filthy and starving and almost inevitably died (Marvick, 1974:286).

In trying to place these practices in some kind of time frame, de Mause (1974:51) says that the practice of outright infanticide was most common prior to the 4th century and that abandonment was more the mode from the 4th to the 13th centuries. During these time periods, relatively few questions were raised about these ways of dealing with the young. The deliberate killing of infants appears to have been re- garded as casually as abortion today. Some people undoubtedly op- posed it, but the prevailing sentiment did not result in its condemna- tion. A high premium was not placed upon the lives of all children, especially if they were thought to be deformed, if they were illegitimate, if they were female, or if they were too costly or troublesome to main- tain. Furthermore, history indicates that infanticide and abandonment were not confined entirely to the periods mentioned above. Long- standing cultural practices do not disappear overnight; rather, they gradually merge into new ones. Thus, infanticide and abandonment continued on into later centuries in guises that appear to have been gradually more acceptable according to our standards.

What all of this means, in short, is that the concept of childhood as we know it did not exist in much of Western history. Not only was the right to life dependent upon the child's sex, his or her economic station in life, or his or her position in the birth order (since first children were pre- ferred over later ones), but those children who were permitted to live were not seen as having a unique right to self-determination, as we believe today, but were treasured because they could serve some eco- nomic, sexual, or family purpose. Since life was organized in ways that differ from those with which we are familiar, the place of children in it took on much different meaning. This different meaning can be illus- trated by delving more deeply into the child-rearing practices of the past.

The care of infants

As older forms of dealing with children began to change, abandon- ment did not always take the form of leaving a child to die or selling it into slavery, nor were such practices confined to the poor and unedu- cated. The reverse was often true. Among the wealthier classes, there were institutionalized and widely accepted patterns for rearing children which, according to modern standards, constituted a form of abandonment. To the people who practiced them, however, these patterns defined the most desirable ways for rearing children.

Wet nursing

The first had to do with the care of small infants. Up to about the 18th century, most children of well-to-do or even average parents spent their earliest years in the care of a wet nurse. Rather than feeding and caring for their own children, mothers who could afford to do so hired other women to perform these tasks (de Mause, 1974:32–34; Illick, 1974:308; Robertson, 1974:410–411; Ross, 1974:195). Soon after birth, a baby was taken from its own home and placed in the home of a wet nurse until it was weaned. And, since human milk was believed to be the most appropriate food for infants, weaning often took a long time—anywhere from a few months to three years. Although the use of wet nurses was confined to families who could afford them, it was apparently widespread nonetheless. "As late as 1780 the police chief of Paris estimated that of the 21,000 children born each year in his city, 17,000 were wet nursed and only 700 were nursed by their mothers" (de Mause, 1974:35).

The practice of using wet nurses was apparently denounced by physicians and moralists from the time of the ancient Greeks and Romans onward, but the hold of custom was great. Hence, although some parents may have loved their babies, the evidence suggests that infants sent to wet nurses died at a far higher rate than did the few who remained in their own homes. Wet nurses were often malnourished and disinterested women who had their own children to care for. Further, these women used other commonly accepted child-raising practices that may have contributed to a distressingly high death rate.

Swaddling

One such practice was the practice of "swaddling." As described by a 19th century physician,

> [swaddling] consists in entirely depriving the child of the use of its limbs, by endlessly enveloping them in an endless bandage . . .; and by which the skin is sometimes excoriated; the flesh compressed, almost to gangrene; the circulation arrested; and the child without the slightest power of motion (de Mause, 1974:37).

The practice of swaddling was believed to serve many functions. Air, sunlight, and soap were thought to be dangerous for a child (Robertson, 1974:410–12). Hence, by keeping the child wrapped tightly, it could be protected. A relatively late 17th century account noted that "when the child is seven months old you may (if you please) wash the body of it twice a week with warm water" (Tucker, 1974:242). The account also advised that the bandages should be shifted often so that the "piss" and the "dung" could be taken care of. But, in terms of our present concerns with constantly changing and washing a child, it can only be imagined what the results of this advice were in terms of an accumulation of excrement and filth on a baby. It is no wonder that infant death rates were appallingly high.

Swaddling was also thought to be a means of protecting the child from hurting itself and of insuring that it would grow straight. But, in addition, it must have been a practice of enormous convenience to wet nurses or mothers who were preoccupied with other tasks. Lacking modern labor-saving devices, they had to devote most of their attention to activities other than cuddling babies or taking them to the zoo. Consequently, while the baby was tied up, it could be left like a parcel in a convenient corner or hanging on the wall. Indeed, both modern research and historical descriptions indicate that "swaddled infants are extremely passive, their hearts slow down, they cry less, they sleep far more and are withdrawn and inert" (de Mause, 1974:37). Clearly, the practice must have survived for centuries (we have all heard about Jesus in swaddling clothes) both because it was believed helpful to infants and because it was practical for adults.

Toughening infants

From a modern perspective, other child-raising practices also revealed practices that we might define as indifference or cruelty to children. Deformed children and children that cried too much were believed to be possessed of the devil (de Mause, 1974:10). The ancient Huns customarily cut the cheeks of newborn males, while adults in Renaissance Italy would burn the necks of babies with a hot iron or hot wax in order to prevent "falling sickness" (de Mause, 1974:31). Some wet nurses starved infants in order to save money or because they had accepted too many babies for their milk supply (Stone, 1974:29). Adults even amused themselves by playing catch with tightly swaddled infants, sometimes with deadly consequences when the pass catcher did not make a good reception (de Mause, 1974:31). Infants were dipped in ice water or rolled in the snow to harden or to baptize them. In other cases they were put to bed wrapped in cold towels. "It is not surprising," concludes de Mause (1974:32), "that the great 18th century pediatrician William Buchan said 'almost one half of the human species perish in infancy by improper management or neglect.' " But was the management improper? Was the neglect deliberate and calculated?

Disease and death

If it could be said that our European ancestors possessed the knowledge of disease that we do or that they shared our cultural perspectives and technology, then the answer could be "Yes." But they did not. Life throughout antiquity and the Middle Ages was often difficult and brutal. Death rates were high; average life expectancy at birth was around 30 years; and the ravages of disease were great (Gillis, 1974:10–11). Indeed, a high death rate among infants and young children may well have been a major reason that childhood as a phase in the life cycle received so little attention—why, from our perspective, people seemed indifferent to children.

Governed by custom and a lack of knowledge by which to control such simple (to us) childhood diseases as measles, pneumonia, or the consequences of malnutrition, few children survived, even among the privileged classes. Paradoxically, such methods as burning the necks of babies or rolling them in the snow—methods which we view as stupid—were used to help children, not to make them suffer. But, because they had an effect that was opposite of the one intended, some babies died needlessly.

As late as the 17th century in England, from one half to two thirds of all children died before the age of 20 (Bremner, 1970, I:3–4; Gillis, 1974:10). In America during a similar period, Cotton Mather went through the trauma of seeing only two of his fifteen children survive. In one measles epidemic in 1713 he lost his wife and three children in a two-week period (Bremner, 1970, I:46). Hence, numerous quotations from writers of both ancient and recent past lend credence to the conclusion that so many young things disappeared early in life that people could not afford to become too attached to them (Ariès, 1962:38; Gillis, 1974:11–12).

Writing to a friend in 1601, a landowner said, "My niece Stukley was lately brought abed of a son, but the joy lasted not longe, for they both vanished soone thereafter" (Bremner, 1970, I:3). Another, a Frenchman, offered a strange bit of consolation to a mother suffering the pangs of childbirth: "Before they are old enough to bother you, you will have lost half of them, or perhaps all of them" (Ariès, 1962:38). Such comments, in short, indicate why many historians cite high infant death rates as one reason people were not preoccupied with children and childhood. As Stone (1974:30) puts it:

> Under these conditions, no parent could retain his or her sanity if he or she became too emotionally involved with such ephemeral creatures as young children. Aloofness, or the acceptance of God's will, or sending one's children away from home were three natural solutions to this problem of how to deal with their deaths.

Reflecting a situation that has been described as a "melancholy procession of cradles and coffins" (Queen and Adams, 1952:211), parents in the 17th century were advised to prepare their own young for the imminence of death, their own as well as that of others. Perhaps that is why when a child did die it did not provoke the grief that the death of an older one would provoke (Gillis, 1974:12).

It is difficult to say with certainty whether the "melancholy procession" of child deaths led to the apparent indifference with which children were treated. Other people, living under equally marginal conditions, have responded differently to children, treating them with greater warmth and attachment. But, whatever the reason, there is evidence that indifference may be the best way to categorize cultural responses to them in Western countries. Ariès (1962:28–29) notes, for example, that various languages did not even include words to describe childhood and the meaning of age:

> In its attempts to talk about little children, the French language of the 17th century was hampered by a lack of words to distinguish them from bigger ones. The same was true of English, where the word "baby" was also applied to big children. . . . People had no idea of what we call adolescence, and the idea was a long time taking shape.

What then, was the nature of family and social life for the children who did survive infancy? What role in the scheme of things did they play?

The lives of children

To begin with, the infant who had been under the care of a wet nurse did not return to the type of home with which we are familiar once it was weaned. Family life during much of recorded history was far more communal than it is today. Today, we live much of our lives in nuclear families where one set of parents live with their children, by themselves, in their own dwellings apart from others. Contact with people from other social classes or even one's blood relatives is often infrequent and sporadic. Parents and children alike live in an environment characterized by greater emotional isolation and interdependence.

In the households of earlier times, by contrast, family life was far less intimate and exclusive. While many poor did live in hovels, those who were servants and the well-to-do whom they served lived in large barn-like dwellings where as many as 25 people were housed (Ariès, 1962:393–394; Ross, 1974:195–196; Bremner, 1970, I:5). A child returning from the home of his wet nurse, therefore, might have to compete for the attention of his mother with a great many other people. Mixed together under one roof were his parents, relatives, servants, apprentices, other little children, even slaves, and a host of visitors flowing in and out.

"There were," says Ariès (1962:393–394), "no professional premises either for the judge or the merchant or the banker or the businessmen. Everything was done in the same rooms with his family." No rooms were set aside specifically for dining, or sleeping, or meeting with guests or clients. Rather, "In the same rooms where they ate, people slept, danced, worked, and received visitors." Even the beds were collapsible. Though pushed aside during the day, they were pulled out at night for everyone—family and servants alike—to sleep on.

The one major exception to this kind of housing and family existence was a large floating lower-class population whose life, if not less communal, was spent in shacks and on the streets or in the fields. What must not be forgotten, however, is that many lower-class people—adults and children—lived and worked in the large homes of wealthier people as servants and apprentices. Hence, many were not unfamiliar with the communal living and life-styles of the better-off. The point is that whether lower or upper class people had little privacy, even in sleeping or making love. There was little segregation of the sexes or of the young and perhaps even less segregation of the classes than today.

In such a setting, the young child might attach himself to an older brother or sister, to an uncle or an aunt, to a female servant, or even to a young slave or apprentice. The social rules of the day apparently did not require that the ties be with his mother. Hence, if he could find someone with whom his physical, social, and psychological needs could be met, all was well. But, if such ties were lacking, then he might suffer. Almost certainly, there were variations in the way children were treated, just as there are today.

Moral rules

Prevailing conditions also meant that the behavioral rules of the time were vastly different from our own. Throughout the 19th and much of the 20th centuries, we have been highly concerned with protecting the moral innocence of children.

> Some months ago I saw two girls, who looked about 12 years old, gaping at and giggling over a magazine in a drugstore. I glanced over their shoulders and saw a color picture of a naked woman holding the penis of a naked man.
>
> You may piously defend the First Amendment, but I would rather you defend the right of children not to have their minds infected by such poison (Letter to the Editor, *Los Angeles Times*, February 18, 1977).

Contrast the moral rules implied in this statement with those that prevailed in the 16th and 17th centuries. Measured by contemporary standards,

> It is easy to imagine the promiscuity which reigned in those rooms where nobody could be alone, which one had to cross to reach any of the communicating rooms, where several couples and several groups of boys or girls slept together (not to speak of the servants, of whom at least some must have slept beside their master, setting up beds which were still collapsible in the room, or just outside the door), in which people foregathered to have their meals, to receive friends or clients, and sometimes to give alms to beggars (Ariès, 1962:394).

This kind of familiarity was not restricted to the poorer classes. It was common among the aristocracy as well. Ariès (1962:100–107) documents its presence with a fascinating series of excerpts taken from the diaries of a man by the name of Heroard, who was the physician of King Henry IV of France. Judged by the rules of modesty that were to develop later, jokes were coarse and gestures obscene. They shocked no one, however, but were taken as perfectly natural.

Consider the treatment of Henry's young son, Louis XIII. According to Heroard's diary, he was apparently seen as a droll little figure by whom adults were amused. "He laughed uproariously when his nanny waggled his cock with her fingers. An amusing trick which the child soon copied. Calling a page, he shouted, 'Hey there!' and pulled up his robe, showing him his cock." Jokes like this were repeated over and over and were made by all members of the extended household: parents and visitors, by lower-class servants as well as royalty.

> [The Marquise de Verneuil] wanted to play with him [Louis] and took hold of his nipples; he pushed her away, saying: "Let go, let go, go away." He would not allow the Marquise to touch his nipples, because his Nanny [a servant] had told him, "Monsieur, never let anyone touch your nipples, or your cock, or they will cut it off!" (p. 101).

Likewise, by our standards, the queen played immodestly with her son. Grasping his penis at one time, she said, "Son, I am holding your cock" (p. 101). Not to be outdone, the king got into the act. While playing in bed with Louis and his sister, the king asked his son: "Son, where is the Infanta's bundle [Louis' penis]." Louis showed it to his father saying, "There is no bone in it, Papa." Then, as it did distend slightly, he said, "There is now, there is sometimes" (p. 101).

Later, when Louis was five or six, familiarity with adult women was permitted. The following took place among Louis, his nanny and Mercier, a female servant, who slept next to Louis. While Mercier was still in bed one morning,

> [Louis] played with her, toyed with her toes and the upper part of her legs. . . . His Nanny asked him: "What have you seen of Mercier?" He replied calmly: "I have seen her arse." "What else have you seen?" He replied calmly and without laughing that he had seen her privates (p. 102).

Louis was married at age 14 and was put into his wife's bed almost by force by his mother, the queen. Young men who were also present had told Louis some ribald stories to encourage him. After making love to his wife twice and sleeping a while, he arrived back in the company to report that his cock was all red. Obviously, this kind of behavior and this kind of familiarity between sexes of all ages was due not just to communal living arrangements but to a set of cultural norms that made them socially acceptable.

Ariès (1962:105–106) cites numerous calenders, church pictures, and other forms of art in which children were commonly shown urinating in public places or mothers were shown breast feeding their children. Neither church nor lay people were offended by such scenes. Likewise, religious iconography commonly depicted the circumcision of young boys "in almost surgical detail." In one church painting, "the scene of the circumcision is surrounded by a crowd of children, some of them with their parents, others climbing the pillars to get a better view" (p. 106). Such scenes may seem shocking to us today, says Ariès, but they were not shocking to people in 16th or early 17th centuries.

Sex and prostitution

This evidence suggests that children had an intimate knowledge of sex and all other bodily functions. Whatever adults did, children knew about. Indeed, children were sometimes treated as sexual objects, as well as becoming early participants in sex like Louis XIII. It is difficult to say how extensive this treatment was, but there is evidence that beginning in antiquity boy brothels may have been fairly common. Men often kept slave boys for their own pleasure. Even in their own homes, it may not have been uncommon for a father's own children to observe him having intercourse with one of these boys (de Mause, 1974). The favorite sexual practice was anal intercourse, not fellatio. In Rome, men preferred boys for this purpose who had been castrated. Castration somehow made the sex act more exciting. While still infants, boys destined for a brothel were castrated by placing them in a tub of hot water. When the testicles were softened, they were squeezed until they disappeared (de Mause, 1974:46). The other alternative, of course, was simply to cut the testicles out.

Better known, of course, is the fact that girls throughout history have been regularly sold into concubinage and prostitution for the satisfaction of men. Like the boys who were castrated, some of these girls suffered clitoridectomies. de Mause (1974:45) describes one recorded instance in which a girl of seven was subjected to intercourse while adult witnesses, both male and female, applauded the procedure. And, even under the regulated ritual of marriage, many girls were contracted out as early as age 12 and had often given birth to several children before finishing the age of adolescence.

The literature of the Middle Ages and the Renaissance is full of statements decrying the sexual abuse of children (de Mause, 1974:47–49). Servants and nursemaids were often criticized for showing "lewd tricks" to children and for carrying out "all sorts of sexual acts" for their (the women's) pleasure. Some people apparently believed as late as 1900 that venereal disease could be cured by having intercourse with children. Hence, it seems likely that while children may have enjoyed the gratifications of sex at an earlier age many of them were also exploited.

Children are also exploited today. There are child molesters; incest occurs; young girls become street walkers at an early age; there are even occasional reports of boy brothels. Consequently, it is not as though the exploitation of children is something that occurred only in ages past. Rather, what is being suggested is that it was probably more the norm the further back in Western history one goes.

We should probably not be too surprised if this were the case. In a population that almost daily witnessed the early death of children, that sometimes observed them lying abandoned and rotting on city streets, that permitted them to be raised by others, that hardly ever washed, and that lived without plumbing amid its own excrement, life was both brutal and cheap. If, as seems likely, children were of relatively less value than now, it follows that their use for the sexual pleasure of adults would also occur. But, even if that practice was not universal, it is almost certain that the norms governing child-raising practices were far different from the ones we now observe.

Training of children

The methods used to train children are also at great odds with contemporary practices. The current emphasis upon formal education and the practice of requiring virtually every child to go to school have been confined largely to recent generations. Prior to that time, children received their preparation for adulthood by leaving their own homes usually at age seven to become apprentices, to work, and to serve in the homes of other people. This was their education. In fact, the day of apprenticeship was a major turning point in the life of a child. "Ready for semidependence, they were dressed as miniature adults and permitted to use the manners and language of adult society" (Gillis, 1974:8). Such was true, says Ariès (1962:365), not only of the poor but of the rich, "for everyone, however rich he may be, sends his children into the houses of others, whilst he, in return, receives those of strangers into his own." Not only did children live elsewhere, but their duty was to serve their masters well and, thereby, to prepare themselves for the adult roles they would occupy whether noble or commoner. After a few short years in their own homes, therefore, boys especially were sent elsewhere.

In judging this practice according to 20th century standards, says Ariès (1962:366–68), we should not become bogged down in trying to determine whether parents were unfeeling or whether the child was merely a servant or an apprentice. Such distinctions would be anachronistic when evaluated in terms of the norms that prevailed. Children learned how they were expected to behave by serving and working in the homes of others. Consequently, family life was not organized to nourish the profound existential attitude between parents and children which we now emphasize. "This did not mean that parents did not love their children, but they cared about them less for themselves, for the affection they felt for them, than for the contributions those children could make to the common task." Consequently, there was simply no repugnance or degradation associated with the services they performed. Such was a custom common to all classes.

American practices

This medieval orientation to childhood carried over into the settling of America. Although, as we will see in the next chapter, significant changes in the concept of childhood were underway during the colonial settlement, older traditions still carried a great deal of weight. Bremner (1970:I:5) notes, for example, that when the English settled the Middle Atlantic colonies in the 17th century, they did so mainly by individuals, not families. And, just as colonial officials sought older artisans or farmers to help in the task, they also sought young children to serve as apprentices. In return for their passage, these children were placed under the total control of new masters.

In some cases, children were signed to indenture contracts by "spirits"—agents who worked in behalf of merchants, shipowners, or settlers to sign up workers. Many young people wished to go to the New World and signed up voluntarily; others, however, were kidnapped. Writing to the Privy Council of England in 1638 the Lord Mayor of London complained that "certain persons called spirits, do inveigle and by lewd subtleties entice away youth against the consent either of their parents, friends, or masters" (Bremner, 1970, I:9). He requested that something be done to control the spirits, as did other people who also placed charges against them.

Because indentured persons, children or adults, could not pay for their passage, they were bound to serve their new masters for at least four years. The masters, in turn, could sell or reassign the contracts for these indentured persons to anyone they pleased. Dependent children from the streets and asylums of England were indentured for even longer periods and were shipped over in large lots. Consider the request in 1619 to the city of London by the Virginia Company for more children (Bremner, 1970, I:5).

> The Treasurer, Council, and Company of Virginia assembled in their great and general Court the 17th of November 1619 have taken into consideration the continual great forwardness of his honorable City in advancing the plantations of Virginia and particularly in furnishing out one hundred children this last year, which by the goodness of God there safely arrived (save such as died in the way).
>
> And foreasmuch as we have now resolved to send this next spring very large supplies for the strength and increasing of the Colony . . . we pray your Lordship and the rest in pursuit of your former so pious actions to renew your like favors and furnish us again with one hundred more [children] for the next spring. Our desire is that we may have them of twelve years and upward . . . They shall be apprentices, the boys till they come to twenty-one years of age, the girls till they be married, and afterwards they shall be placed as tenants upon the public land with best conditions where they shall have houses with stocks of corn and cattle to begin with, and afterward the moiety of all increase and profit whatsoever.

The treatment of lower-class dependent English children in this way was not totally unlike the treatment of black children who were kidnapped in Africa and also shipped to the colonies. While there was little chance that black children would ultimately receive their freedom as would most of their white counterparts, they were considered to be valuable: 3,000 pounds of tobacco for a black child between the ages of 7 and 11 years; 4,000 pounds for a child between 11 and 15, and 5,000 pounds for a young man over 15 (Bremner, 1970, I:16). Some colonists objected to the capture and sale of small black children, but their objections were often monetary rather than humane; that is, such children were considered to be too young to work efficiently. However, given the extent to which white children were also sought as cheap sources of labor, this kind of objection may not seem too strange. Children were not afforded the highly special protection that they are today.

What these few examples reveal is the vestige of European feudalism in the American colonies. In light of the struggle for survival, childhood was paid little deference. While slave children and the children of the poor were the most likely to be exploited, it was not uncommon for the children of the well-to-do to be sold on indenture contracts as well. What is significant, therefore, is that so many children played an important role in settling the colonies and that they were viewed as sources of labor and service, not as fragile, undeveloped beings who required long periods of special care and freedom from responsibility.

Social control of children

The methods that were used to control children throughout the ages and to secure their obedience reveal a legacy of harsh punishment. The evidence, says de Mause (1974:40–42), warrants the conclusion that by present standards a large percentage of the children born to the 18th century could be considered "battered children." With rare exceptions, statements of advice on how to control them from antiquity to modern times approved the use of severe beatings. Even the humanists of the Renaissance, men of relative gentleness and vision, approved of beating children. Beating instruments included whips, heavy rods and cudgels, and the "flapper"—a paddle with holes in it so that it would raise blisters. Beatings began in infancy and were a regular part of a child's life.

Even royalty and other famous figures were not exempt from being beaten or beating others. "Century after century of battered children grew up and in turn battered their own children" (de Mause, 1974:41). The wife of Milton, the poet, complained because she did not like to hear the cries of Milton's nephews as he was beating them; Beethoven used a knitting needle to whip his pupils and sometimes bit them, and Louis XIII, about whose sexual exploits we read earlier, often woke in terror in anticipation of his daily whipping. "I would rather," he said, "do without so much obeisance and honor if they wouldn't have me whipped" (de Mause, 1974:41).

Some attempts to temper the violence of child beating were begun during the Renaissance—the transitional period between the 14th and 17th centuries—but these attempts were relative (de Mause, 1974:42). Rather than attempting to eliminate the practice, reformers urged adults to use lighter instruments than cudgels and to strike children about the body rather than on the head. It was not until the 18th century that significant decreases in child beating began to occur and not until the 19th century that serious whipping began to go out of style. These changes, as we will see, were probably due to the emergence of the modern concept of childhood, but, until that concept emerged, children were not protected.

Psychological controls

Physical beatings were not the only method of control. As now, psychological methods were also used (de Mause, 1974:11–13). Children in antiquity and in medieval times were warned about demons who would eat children alive, would suck their blood, or would steal them away if they were not good. After the Reformation in the 16th century, a vengeful God became the villain. Bad children would be cast into Hell, screaming and burning like loathesome insects if they were not good. In England, ghosts were popular, while elsewhere in Europe children were warned about werewolves and other horrible monsters who stole bad children, mutilated them, and ate their flesh. In America, a horrible Black Man was a common spectre. In each instance, these fictitious specters were used to control children who were disobedient or wanted something they could not have.

It would be misleading to suggest that some children today are not subject to physical punishment. Many people, in fact, are still convinced that it is a necessary means of control. Nonetheless, there are some restrictions on its excessive use. By contrast, there were few special provisions made to protect children from severe punishments in earlier times. The common law in England, like informal practice on the Continent and in America, did not hold children criminally responsible for their acts below the age of seven, but, beyond that, the laws were ambiguous and did permit courts, parents, and apprentice masters to levy severe punishments.

Summary and conclusions

This chapter has indicated that childhood has not always been culturally defined as a special and highly protected phase of the life cycle. "Littlehood," in other words, is not the same thing as "childhood." Until the 12th or 13th centuries, the deliberate killing or abandonment of children was regarded as casually as abortion is today. In later years, as cultural prescriptions began to change, newborn babies were still farmed out to wet nurses, and young children were still sent to the homes of others to serve as apprentices and servants. Compared to the present, the attitude of parents toward their children was one of relative indifference and detachment. Childhood was not noteworthy in its own right; many languages lacked words to distinguish babies from those we now call adolescents or young adults; and young humans were not shielded from adult strength or depravity, work, sex, or death. The emotionally interdependent and highly protective nuclear family of today simply did not exist.

Divergent interpretations

The interpretations placed upon these differences by historians have varied considerably. The two most divergent perspectives have been stated by Ariès (1962) and de Mause (1974). According to Ariès, life in the Middle Ages, if not antiquity, was a happy one for little people. Despite high death rates and exploitation, it was precisely because society was not preoccupied with raising the young and severely restricting their lives that conditions for them were relatively good. The reason is that society was not separated as it is today, by class, age, or ethnic differences. Much of the ambiguity and conflict surrounding the separation of child and adult were absent. Communal living and the apprenticeship system constantly brought people of all ages and ranks together more as natural companions than as uniquely different kinds of beings. In lieu of the intergenerational and class conflicts with which we are familiar, these groups mixed together easily and naturally, wore the same clothes, worked together on common tasks, and enjoyed the same pleasures. Rather than repressing, judging, or attempting to protect children with a special set of moral rules, adults shared all aspects of existence with them. The years of littlehood, as a consequence, were sociable and happy.

de Mause, by contrast, interprets child-raising practices in Freudian psychological terms and concludes that, while some parents in history may have loved children, they were emotionally immature and lodged at a lower stage of human development. Unable to view the child as a person separate from themselves, parents projected or voided on to their children all the evil impulses, the superstitions, the hostilities, and sexual perversions of which they, the parents, were possessed. Thus, parents were both bad and good, loving and unloving, often to the detriment of the child. When they beat children, killed them in infancy, abandoned them to wet nurses, or played with them sexually, it was not the child to whom they were doing these things, but to themselves. In contrast to Ariès, therefore, de Mause believes that the child-raising practices of the past have been a blot on the history of civilization from which, happily, we have begun emerging in the last two or three centuries. In some scheme of human growth, we are at a higher stage of development.

Yet, a third interpretation has been suggested by historians like Gillis (1974) or Stone (1974). First, like most historians, they caution against premature conclusions. The historical study of children has only just begun, good information is sparse, and what sources are available are restricted largely to the wealthier classes. Records chronicling the lives of the poor and such oppressed people as slaves are virtually nonexistent. But, if the children of the better-off were treated with indifference or cruelty, it would not be unreasonable to assume that poor children or those in bondage were subjected to similar, if not worse, treatment.

Beyond that, Stone agrees that we should pay constant attention to the social and cultural contexts in which child-rearing practices occur. To imply, as Ariès does, that life for children used to be happy and sociable but has steadily become more repressive, or to suggest, as de Mause does, that the treatment of children has gotten steadily better is to ignore a host of other issues. For a long time, anthropologists have argued that there is no one natural path from infancy to adulthood, nor one universally best method for raising children (Cf. Skolnick, 1973:326–327). Ways of treating children do not occur in a social vacuum; rather they must be understood in terms of the larger cultural context in which they occur. The biological facts of growing up may be common to all children, but they are altered significantly by the kinds of culture in which those children are raised. What, then, are some of the cultural facts to which we should pay heed?

Cultural adaptions

Perhaps the most important are the demographic facts of life that dominated all Western societies until very recent times. As this chapter has noted, most children were born to die. The odds were two or three to one against a child living until age five, as late as the 18th century (Kessen, 1965). It is not difficult, therefore, to imagine why people in antiquity and in the Middle Ages may have failed to develop strong emotional ties with infants. They could not retain their sanity if they cared too much.

Cultural adaptions to these high death rates seem to have contributed to beliefs which stressed the notion that infants existed "in a sort of limbo, hanging between life and death, more as a kind of animal than a human being, without mental activities or recognizable bodily shape"

(Skolnick, 1973:333). Such beliefs, in turn, may have contributed to child-raising practices which only increased rather than lessened child death rates. Indifference to children made such practices as abandonment, the use of wet nurses, swaddling, and apprenticeship more acceptable. The society in which child mortality is high may find it more difficult to develop a compassionate and valuing attitude toward the young than a society in which life is easier and in which the chances for survival are greater.

If there is merit in these notions, they indicate why it is useful to reserve judgment, to avoid being totally ethnocentric in evaluating the past. Living as we do in a society filled with creature comforts, it is difficult for us to imagine a society in which children are not prized and protected. Yet, as Ariès indicates, there were some things about the lives of children in the Middle Ages that they may lack today—close contacts with members of older generations, common activities from which they are not excluded, and the satisfaction of knowing that they are contributing something to the common good. On the other hand, one can ill-afford to ignore the more difficult side of life during that period. The medieval period in European history has often been called the Dark Ages. Life expectancy was extremely low; the great masses of people were bound into a feudal economic system which, at best, made life relatively easy for only a few; and intellectual growth, education, art, and medicine were at a standstill. That children were often viewed as a burden or were expected to play a contributing role under the circumstances should not be too surprising. To a population that is half-starved, that lives among its own excrement, that hardly ever washes, and that is ravaged by disease, rules of modesty and solicitude are not of overwhelming importance.

Under conditions like these, other cultural prescriptions we consider important were lacking, especially those that make provisions for close ties between parent and child, that stress the importance of the nuclear family, that take delight in the innocence and beauty of children, and that provide long years of total economic support for a phase in the life cycle known as childhood. Perhaps that is why, when judged in terms of these contemporary cultural values, Stone (1974:29) concludes that children have not counted for much throughout much of Western history:

> Everything suggests that in the past most parents have treated their children as the inevitable by-products of sexual pleasure, sometimes barely

tolerated, sometimes useful to be exploited economically, and sometimes cherished and loved. Most frequently, however, the response seems to have been one of relative indifference. The cruel truth . . . may be that most parents in history have not been much involved with their children and have not cared much about them.

References

Ariès, Phillippe
>   1962   *Centuries of Childhood* (Trans. by Robert Baldick). New York: Alfred A. Knopf.

Bremner, Robert H. et al. (Eds.)
>   1970   *Children and Youth in America: A Documentary History.* 2 vols. Cambridge: Harvard University Press.

de Mause, Lloyd
>   1974   *The History of Childhood.* New York: Psychohistory Press.

Gillis, John R.
>   1974   *Youth and History.* New York: Academic Press.

Hunt, David
>   1970   *Parents and Children in History: The Psychology of Family Life in Early Modern History.* New York: Basic Books.

Illick, Joseph E.
>   1974   "Child-rearing in seventeenth century England and America." Pp. 303–350 in Lloyd de Mause (Ed.), *The History of Childhood.* New York: Psychohistory Press.

Kessen, W.
>   1965   *The Child.* New York: John Wiley.

Laslett, Peter
>   1972   *Household and Family in Past Time.* Cambridge: Cambridge University Press.

Marvick, Elizabeth W.
>   1974   "Nature versus nurture: patterns and trends in seventeenth century French child rearing." Pp. 259–302 in Lloyd de Mause (Ed.), *The History of Childhood.* New York: Psychohistory Press.

Queen, Stuart A. and Adams, John B.
>   1955   *The Family in Various Cultures.* New York: J.B. Lippincott.

Robertson, Pricilla
>   1974   "Home as a nest: 'middle-class childhood in nineteenth century Europe," Pp. 407–431 in Lloyd de Mause (Ed.), *The History of Childhood.* New York: Psychohistory Press.

Ross, James B.
 1974 "The middle-class child in urban Italy, fourteenth to early sixteenth century." Pp. 183–228 in Lloyd de Mause (Ed.), *The History of Childhood.* New York: Psychohistory Press.

Seneca
 1963 *Moral Essays* (Trans. by John W. Basone). Cambridge: Harvard University Press.

Skolnick, Arlene
 1973 *The Intimate Environment: Exploring Marriage and the Family.* Boston: Little, Brown.

Stone, Lawrence
 1974 "The massacre of the innocents." *The New York Review.* November, 14:25–31.

Tucker, M. J.
 1974 "The child as beginning and end: fifteenth and sixteenth century English childhood." Pp. 229–258 in Lloyd de Mause (Ed.), *The History of Childhood.* New York: Psychohistory Press.

3

THE DISCOVERY OF CHILDHOOD

We have reviewed historical materials suggesting that in premodern times children were treated, at best, with indifference while, at worst, they were cruelly exploited. Modern Americans, by contrast, have been described as child-centered to an extreme degree (Skolnick, 1973:314). "We have set a new record; no other people seem ever to have been so preoccupied with children" (Goodman, 1970:11).

How did this marked change come about? Why are we so much concerned with children today?

Glimmerings of change

Ariès (1962:33–50) points out that the art of the Middle Ages—the period roughly from A.D. 500 to A.D. 1400—did not even attempt to portray childhood. Instead, when an artist showed children in his paintings, they were simply drawn as small adults having none of the characteristics of young people. In a painting portraying biblical stories, for example, "Isaac is shown sitting between his two wives, surrounded by some fifteen little men who came up to the level of the grown-ups' waists: these are their children" (p. 33). They looked like mature midgets.

As Western civilization began to awaken from the intellectual and social stagnation of the Middle Ages, however, the glimmerings of a new concept of childhood began to emerge. These glimmerings were not marked by a sudden torrent of new ideas and practices. Rather, the changes were gradual. It was not until the 16th and 17th centuries, for example, that art and literature had begun to attribute a special personality to children. Well-to-do persons began to commission portraits of their children which exhibited them in special costumes rather than in the dress of adults. It was as though people had begun to see young humans through a different pair of spectacles. For the first time, children began to look like the children we know rather than miniature adults. There was evidence of a growing tendency to attribute special characteristics to the young and to take increased delight in them.

Besides Ariès, other historians note the presence of change. de Mause (1974:47–48) observes that Christian beliefs and Christian moralists had long stressed the essential innocence and frailty of children although, in practice, people had not paid much attention to them. Christ had advised people to "become as little children," and churchmen had interpreted this to mean that children were inherently free from the contamination of adult guile and sensuality. These ideas, however, did not have much impact until Europe moved into, and beyond, the Renaissance (14th to 17th centuries).

In 14th century Italy, people seem to have become increasingly ambivalent over their treatment of children (Tucker, 1974:231). On the one hand, children still ranked at the bottom of the social scale; on the other hand, there was increasing uncertainty about the wisdom of child-raising practices. Some persons, for example, began to take more seriously the practice of wet nursing. A fashionable mother had not wanted to nurse her baby because it stretched her breasts too much, but now, at least, she began to take greater care in the selection of the woman who would care for her infant. Women "should be prudent, well-mannered, honest, not a drinker or a drunkard, because very often children draw from and resemble the nature of the milk they suck" (Ross, 1974:185).

The essential innocence of children was increasingly symbolized. In 15th and 16th century England, the color "white" was used to symbolize that innocence (Tucker, 1974:232). When they died, children were dressed in white, their coffins were white, and attendants at the funeral wore white. Similarly, children became a symbol of good luck or of Godly qualities. Their images were placed on gravestones or were used to decorate the fringes of frescoes in the form of little angels.

Ariès (1962:33–136) makes an interesting interpretation of developments like these. In addition to an increased emphasis upon the innocence of children, he argues, "a new concept of childhood had appeared in which the child, on account of his sweetness, simplicity, and drollery, became a source of amusement and relaxation for the adults" (p. 129). Young children were still not seen as people who have value in and of themselves, but they were treated somewhat differently.

This new concept began to appear first among the women in upper-class homes, among female servants as well as mothers. They started to cuddle children somewhat more and to be more solicitous of them when they hurt. And the pleasure and amusement that both men and women derived from little children was like that we derive from kittens or puppies today. Ariès believes these newer ways of treating children had begun to spread rather widely by the 17th century. This does not mean, of course, that all the older practices of wet nursing, communal living, apprenticeship, or child exploitation had ceased. Rather, these older practices were simply intermixed with a number of newer ones.

Finally, in the late 16th and the 17th centuries, a growing number of reformers began to criticize the treatment of children and to institute reforms. They objected to the newfound tendency to take amusement and pleasure from children as well as to their exploitation and sexual precociousness. Stressing the essential innocence and dependence of children, they argued that what children required was discipline and careful direction. The premature induction of children into the adult world not only affronted adults but injured children (Ariès, 1962:130; Bremner, 1970,I; de Mause, 1974; Illick, 1974; Marvick, 1974; Robertson, 1974).

Modern concept of childhood

What was emerging was a more modern concept of childhood. Gradually, children were perceived as rather odd creatures—fragile, innocent, and sacred, on one hand, but corruptible, trying, and arrogant on the other: "Unless you give children all they ask for, they are peevish and cry, aye, and strike their parents sometimes; and all this they have from nature. Yet are they free from guilt, neither may we properly call them wicked . . . because wanting the free use of reason they are exempted from all duty" (Hobbes, 1972:100). To insure a child's proper development, therefore, he must be stringently safeguarded, both physically and morally, he must receive a carefully structured and special education, and, only after long years of preparation, will he be properly prepared for adulthood.

It is difficult to overstate the significance of these seminal ideas. While the ideas themselves were obviously well ahead of the actual practices of their day, they signaled the beginning of the end for age-old tendencies, either to ignore children or to view them as existing in limbo until they joined the adults.

Rather, the concept of childhood gradually and increasingly took on unique meaning. The groundwork was laid for the belief that until the child had been given distinctive preparation he was not ready for life, "that he had to be subjected to special treatment, a sort of quarantine, before he was allowed to join the adults" (Ariès, 1962:411–412).

Sources of change

There are many factors that contributed to the emergence and growth of this concept: the Renaissance, the Protestant Reformation, the colonization of the New World, and eventually the Industrial Revolution. Likely, all were important. Insofar as children are concerned, several historians imply that the real innovators were a relatively small band of moralists, schoolmen, and churchmen, both Catholic and Protestant (Ariès, 1962:330–412; Bremner, 1970; Illick, 1974:316–317; Marvick, 1974:261). It was they more than the intellectual humanists of the Renaissance who became specifically concerned with the young and with the corrupting influence of society upon them. A moralization of society was taking place in which the ethical aspects of religion were gradually taking precedence over the sacred. Heretofore, Catholic Church functions had been largely ritualistic; the seriously religious person had withdrawn into a monastery or a nunnery if he or she sought escape from a sinful world. Now, efforts were being made to reshape the world and to do so, in part, through children.

Two Puritan reformers, Robert Cleaver and John Dod, in 1621 reveal both the reformist theme and the mixed perceptions of children; i.e., that they were both wicked and worth saving.

> The young child which lieth in the cradle is both wayward and full of affections; and though his body be but small, yet he hath a reat [wrong-doing] heart, and is altogether inclined to evil. . . . If this sparkle be suffered to increase, it will rage and burn down the whole house. For we are changed and become good not by birth but by education. . . . There-

fore, parents must be wary and circumspect . . . they must correct and sharply reprove their children for saying or doing ill (Cf. Illick, 1974:316–317).

John Winthrope, the first governor of the Massachusetts Bay Colony, justified the Puritan migration to America as a method of carrying the gospel to the New World and of permitting the young to escape the corruption of the Old World. The fountains of learning and religion had been destroyed, he said, such that "most children, even the best wits and of fairest hopes, are perverted, corrupted, and utterly overthrown" (Bremner, 1970, I:18–19).

Besides moral training, it will be noted, the remarks of these reformers stressed the importance of education and learning. An emphasis upon intellectual development also seems to have played a key role in their thinking. In medieval Europe, the school had not occupied a position of much importance. Quite the contrary, this period in European history, especially from the 6th to the 12th or even 14th centuries, was a period in which interest in formal education was virtually nonexistent. The schools that did exist were not intended specifically for children nor did they concern themselves much with moral, intellectual, and social education. Rather, they were a kind of technical school designed to prepare people, young or old, for the clergy (Ariès, 1962:330). This period, as a result, has often been called the Dark Ages because of the intellectual stagnation that occurred. The revival of an interest in education, beginning in about the 15th century, therefore, has been hailed as a significant landmark, as a Renaissance, a rebirth. It marked the time when Western civilization began to come out of the Dark Ages, when an interest in the arts and literature was revived, and when modern science was begun.

The intellectual humanists of the Renaissance are generally given credit for the revival of education, but Ariès (1962:passim) maintains that while they were devoted to the spread of learning they were not particularly interested in children. Learning, the humanists felt, should be available for everyone. Indeed, the schools of the 17th century still bore this stamp. School was not reserved just for children, and pupils were not divided up as they are today according to age and grade. All attended the same classes together. But the various reformers, by contrast, increasingly stressed the need to use formal schooling as a device for preparing children for adult life. They wanted to use it as a mechanism for moral as well as intellectual preparation.

Finally, the new morality stressed the importance of the family and placed special responsibilities upon parents. During the Middle Ages as we have seen, children were a common property, were apprenticed out at an early age, and often lived in large communal households. Under the impact of the forces that introduced the modern concept of childhood, however, all of these slowly began to change.

The emphasis of moralists and churchmen upon protecting the innocence of children led to changes in the norms governing the way they were viewed. These, in turn, seem to have led to a greater stress upon the role of blood parents in raising their own offspring, in seeing that they were educated, and in reducing the chances that they would be subjected to undue influence from nonfamily members. John Elliot, a 17th century American churchman, phrased these sentiments well (Cf. Bremner, 1970,I:33):

> It is a very false and pernicious principle that many people and parents are trained with, viz., that youth must be suffered awhile to take their swing, and sow their wild oats, to travail into the world, to follow the fashions, company, and manner of the time, hoping they will be wiser hereafter. Oh false principle; God speaks fully to the contrary. Prov. 19:18. *Chasten thy son while there is hope, and let not thy soul spare for his crying.* Prov. 13:24. *He that spareth the rod, hateth his son, but he that loveth him, chasteneth him betimes.*

Besides advocating stern methods of control, such injunctions speak of love for children and the importance of attending to their moral welfare —a sharp contrast with the indifference or easy-going attitudes of the Middle Ages. Over a period of two or three centuries, a slow but obvious transformation in the status of children had taken place. The voices of the first 15th century reformers were joined by a veritable chorus by the 17th century, all attesting to the essential dependence of children and demanding that newer standards of morality for them be enforced. By no means had all older practices ceased, but important trends were under way.

The ideal child

The way children were characterized by the religious moralists of the 17th century reflected highly complicated feelings. By no means had the status of children gone from indifference or disregard to complete acceptance and warmth. As the Puritans Cleaver and Dod had suggested, children had "wrong-doing hearts" and were altogether "inclined to evil." If that inclination was not to "rage and burn," it had to be controlled. Therefore, their injunctions to parents were to be "wary" and to "sharply reprove" their children. Although child raising might have entailed some pleasures for parents, it must also have been an onerous duty.

Based upon the precepts of the new morality, many treatises and manuals were written in the 17th and 18th centuries to guide parents. The principles they set forth were important because implicit in them was the image of the ideal child. Such an image became the standard by which not only conformity but deviance among children was judged. Thus, when 19th century Americans became highly concerned over delinquency, this image still retained a great deal of currency. It was the standard by which undesirable conduct by children and failure by unworthy parents was evaluated. Indeed, there is much about the image that is familiar today (Cf. Ariès, 1962:114–119; Bremner, 1970, I:passim).

The first principle emphasized the importance of keeping a close watch over children and never permitting them to be alone. As Benjamin Wadsworth, a clergyman of Boston, put it, "Children should not be left to themselves, to a loose end, to do as they please; but should be under tutors and governors, not being fit to govern themselves" (Cf. Bremner, 1970, I:35).

The second stressed the importance of disciplining rather than pampering or coddling children. It is cruelty to allow children to do as they please, to forbid them nothing, to allow them to laugh when they ought to cry, or to permit them to remain silent when an adult speaks to them. They must learn to exercise self-control and to exhibit appropriate manners.

The third principle stressed the importance of modesty. Children should not be permitted to go to bed in the presence of a person of the opposite sex. Young girls should be completely covered and not lie in an immodest position. Children of different sexes should not sleep together. Songs expressing "dissolute passions" should neither be sung nor heard. Language should be pure and wholesome. Only the most chaste of books should be read. Games, not a part of the educational system, should be avoided. "Ordinary entertainments provided by jugglers, mountebanks, and tightrope walkers [are] forbidden" (Ariès, 1962:118). Even puppet shows are beneath contempt.

Fourth, parents were admonished to "bring up their children to be diligent in some lawful business" (Bremner, 1970, I:110). Work for children was not only morally desirable, but economically necessary. Throughout the 18th and 19th centuries, and well into the 20th, the belief of children in the work ethic was a cardinal virtue.

Finally, a virtue that encompassed all others was respect for, and obedience to, authority. Children were warned to honor, not only their parents, but anyone in authority because disobedience inevitably led to destruction (Cf. Bremner, 1970, I:32; Gillis, 1974:21). Such admonitions may have been softened somewhat during the 19th century but not much. All through the century, in fact, key opinionmakers felt that children who were not being raised according to these principles should be taken from their unworthy parents and placed in an institution where they could be raised properly. Thus, not being able to govern themselves, children should be obedient, submissive to authority, hardworking, self-controlled, modest, and chaste.

The organization of child raising

The new concept of childhood was accompanied by alterations in the way society was organized to raise children. This does not necessarily mean that the discovery of childhood caused these changes; more likely, it means that the forces of change were interactive, being both cause and effect.

The family

Part of the fabric of change was the emergence of the *nuclear* family. The nuclear family is the family with which we are most familiar, where the people living under one roof are confined largely to a set of parents and their own children. The families of the Middle Ages had been *extended* because so many people in addition to parents and children had lived under one roof. Now, however, economic and demographic changes were tending to reduce family size. For example, Peter Laslett (1962:1–89) shows rather conclusively that the English family had become increasingly nuclear during the 17th century. This does not mean, of course, that all the old forms of communal living had suddenly disappeared. But it does represent a trend that increasingly became the model.

Sentiments favoring the nuclear family were carried to the New World by such groups as the Puritans. This particular group apparently emigrated, not only in the interests of preserving their Protestant religious beliefs, but in the interest of liberating their children from the evils of the Old World (Bremner, 1970, I:28–29). So committed were they to this view, in fact, that the Massachusetts Bay Colony passed a law in 1642 designed to broaden and enforce the educational and socialization functions of the family and to insure that parents carried out these responsibilities. The new law required that each family teach its children a trade and how to read. Parents who failed were to be brought before the authorities, while children who disobeyed their parents could be dealt with severely. Further, the law decreed that no single person, especially a young one, could live outside the confines of some family. The family was to be a guardian of the public as well as the private good (Demos, 1970; Farber, 1972).

Despite these innovations, the Puritans did not discard entirely the practices of the apprenticeship system. Rather, the rules governing it were changed. Apprentices were still used as important sources of labor and training. If the new settlements were to survive, everyone had to work. Thus, children were usually put to work at age six. At this age, however, children worked for their own, not other, families. The age at leaving home had gradually gotten older—sometimes as late as 14 or 15 before children were apprenticed to others. But when you put them out to a calling, parents were warned, be sure to see that it is to a lawful calling in a religious home (Bremner, 1970, I:110–111).

Beliefs in the innate depravity of children legitimated severe punishment, as it did in Victorian England. People took very seriously the notion that to spare the rod was to spoil the child. Consequently, the debate was not whether children should be whipped but at which age it should begin (infancy, age three or five?), how the whipping should be administered (a birch or leather thongs?), where it should be administered (bare bottom or covered?), and until what age (fifteen or longer?). Most people preferred such methods to isolating the offender, putting him on bread and water, or tying him up. But even these methods were used (Robertson, 1974:414–420).

As already suggested, the conflicted character of child-raising principles, emphasizing love and affection on the one hand but stern, unyielding punishment for disobedience on the other, seems to have generated considerable ambivalence. Lamenting the death of her eight-year-old granddaughter, an 18th century New England poet by the name of Anne Bradstreet penned the following lines (Illick, 1974:326):

> Farewel dear babe, my heart's too much content,
> Farewel sweet babe, the pleasure of mine eye,
> Farewel fair flower that for a space was lent,
> Then Ta'en away unto Eternity.

But, in another poem, she expressed the prevailing religious belief in child depravity:

> Here sits our Grandame in retired place
> And in her lap, her bloody Cain new born.

Coupled with the high death rates of the times, the new concept of childhood was not without its tensions.

The school

Possibly the greatest consequence of the Renaissance and the efforts of the moralists to reform child-raising practices were the subsequent emphases they placed upon formal schooling for children. Although the colonial schools in America were eventually organized in a way different from European schools, the emphasis upon education was an Old World derivative.

Virtually all of the European schools in the 16th and 17th centuries were privately, not publicly, run and were a mixed lot (Ariès, 1962:269–285). Since not every town or hamlet had a school, school populations were recruited not merely from the towns in which they existed but from other towns and the countrysides as well. As a result, those students who lived too far from the school to return home each night were forced to take up residence in town, either as boarders, as servants on the school premises, or as lodgers in private dwellings. The majority were of the latter type.

The practices surrounding the schools reveal the transitional character of society as it moved from medieval to modern. There is evidence, for example, that in many of the lodgings boys of all classes and ages were housed. Furthermore, the principal source of discipline and control, where it existed, was exercised by the boys themselves. The lodgings sound very much like the communal homes of the medieval period. For a considerable time, little official control over students was exercised, such that their lives could scarcely be distinguished from that of single, unfettered adults. Plumb (1972:83) says that these students "lived like hippies and wandered like gypsies, begging, stealing, fighting; yet they were always hungry for books." "There remained," says Ariès (1962:254), "a great deal of the free and easy attitude of the preceding centuries." But it was not long until both school masters and parents were driven by their philosophy to curb this freedom and to exercise stringent controls over pupils.

Landlords apparently did not feed their lodgers. Hence, on market days, the schools closed down so that pupils could go shopping or collect the money and food their parents had sent to them. They lived from week to week receiving just enough provisions—cheese, bread, fruit, and bacon—to last for that period. Likely, it was in response to circumstances like these that the boarding school system, so common in Europe, developed. Efforts were made to provide means by which pupils could live on school premises and be under the strict supervision of school masters. Under this system, which began to flourish in the 18th century and thereafter, a concerted effort was made to separate pupils from adults and thence to mold them according to the strict moral principles of the reformers.

Reformers in the New World, meanwhile, stressed the importance of schooling, but there were important variations in the way they implemented it (Bremner, 1970, I:72–102). In the English colonies, at first, the responsibility for education was diffused among parents, the masters to whom older children were apprenticed, and clergymen. As the education movement gained steam, however, increasing emphasis was placed upon the immediate family and its new ally, the school. Since parents were often ill-equipped to teach their children, special provision had to be made for educating them. Hence, along with family discipline, education became an important means by which the world was to be shaped into a new, and more moral, pattern.

Besides the 1642 law passed in Massachusetts by which attempts were made to coerce parents and masters into exercising their educational responsibilities, the General Court of that state also took the first step in 1647 toward the establishment of a public educational system (Bremner, 1970, I:72–73). Connecticut and New Hampshire followed suit: towns of 50 households were supposed to provide a schoolmaster for elementary training while larger towns of 100 were expected to have a grammar school. In actual practice, however, these educational requirements were not always met. Education, especially at the grammar (secondary) school level, was dependent upon private support and the payment of fees by pupils. Hence, school attendance was not mandatory and tended to favor the middle and upper classes, leaving lower-class children to rely upon their parents and the apprenticeship system for whatever education they might receive. As a result, only a few relatively well-to-do students went beyond an elementary level and even fewer to a university.

Despite these limitations, the New England schools were superior to those in the Middle Atlantic colonies and in the South. With private assistance, Southern and Middle Atlantic churches maintained some elementary schools which the poor could attend, but secondary education was entirely private and confined almost entirely to wealthier pupils. With all these limitations, Bremner (1970, I:74) maintains that colonial education in the 17th century was unmatched, reaching more children and providing them with a greater ability to read and write than a comparable number of children elsewhere.

Even more significant is the fact that the foundation was laid for the ultimate development of tax-supported public schools. An experiment in educational democracy was begun that was unparalleled in Europe. But, while the usual inclination has been to focus upon its presumed benefits, its significance in terms of its alteration of the nature of childhood and societal life, in general, often goes unnoticed. In almost unbelievable contrast to Europe in the Middle Ages, the stage was set for the ultimate confinement in the 20th century of children in youth ghettoes—the schools—for most of their formative years. More and more, the effects of the apprenticeship system and even those of the family itself would be eroded by the socialization functions of the school. The ultimate effects of the discovery of childhood had only just begun.

Effects of social stratification

In the context in which the modern concept of childhood developed, great changes were introduced into social relationships among the various strata of society—changes whose long-range effects may still be observed today. During the Middle Ages, there were only two principal groups in society—the nobility and the common people. When the Western world began to emerge from this period, however, trade and commerce with other parts of the world gradually increased. This trade was associated first with the commercial revolution of the 17th and 18th centuries and later with the Industrial Revolution of the 19th century. In response to both, a whole new middle stratum in society emerged—the entrepreneurs, the merchants, the traders, and the professionals with whom we are now so familiar. Eventually, many of these people became extremely powerful, replacing the aristocracy as the most influential segment of society. The old order was gradually phased out and a new one installed.

Most historians maintain that it was this segment of society, and not its working-class people, to whom the modern concept of childhood, the nuclear family, and the idea of schooling most appealed, at least originally. Businessmen, merchants, and professionals were inclined increasingly to shrink from the indiscriminate mixing of the generations and of the social classes that had probably been common in the Middle Ages. The privacy and special kind of identity provided by the nuclear family and the intellectual and moral skills that were derived from schooling were particularly suited to their special interests.

Various writers have tended to refer to this new segment of society as the "middle class." Though this term had some meaning in those days when it was useful to view the middle rank of society as intermediate between the nobility and the common people, it has become less useful today as a precise, descriptive term (Gould, 1964:426–428). Most people either describe themselves as "middle class" or use the word "upper class" to denote the powerful executives, the corporate officials, the politicians, or others who are now the most dominant stratum in society. Nonetheless, there is some utility in noting the effects on children of the emergence of merchants, businessmen, and professionals in earlier centuries.

Using the word "middle class" to describe them, Ariès (1962:414) traces their progressive separation in the 17th and 18th centuries from working-class people:

> There came a time when the middle class could no longer bear the pressure of the multitude or the contact of the lower class. It seceded: It withdrew from the vast polymorphous society to organize itself separately, in a homogeneous environment, among its families, in homes designed for privacy, in new districts kept free from all lower-class contamination. The juxtaposition of inequalities, hitherto something perfectly natural, became intolerable to it: The revulsion of the rich preceded the shame of the poor. The quest for privacy and the new desires for comfort which it aroused (for there is a close connection between comfort and privacy) emphasized even further the contrast between the material ways of life of the lower and middle classes. The old society concentrated the maximum number of ways of life into the minimum of space and accepted, if it did not impose, the bizarre juxtaposition of the most widely different classes.

> The new society, on the contrary, provided each way of life with a con-
> fined space in which it was understood that the dominant features should
> be respected, and that each person had to resemble a conventional model,
> an ideal type, and never depart from it under pain of excommunication.

Rather strong support for this interpretation may be found in Robert's (1971) recent social history of the lower working classes in England. Until World War I, he says, working-class people lived in a social environment that lay outside the mainstream of English society. Living according to their own provincial standards, they were left without much hope and without much contact with middle- and upper-class people. So separate were their worlds, in fact, that the guardians of public morality—the schools, churches, and courts—generally feared the poorer slum dwellers.

In a similar vein, Bremner (1970, I:343) and Platt (1969:passim) describe an American scene in which class, ethnic, and religious differences abounded. "What," asks Bremner, "did slave children, immigrant children in city slums, children of a doctor or minister, and the children of a proud aristocrat on a plantation, or those of a wealth New England merchant really have in common?" They had little in common; the American environment was one of great diversity. As in Europe, therefore, the significance of this diversity lay in the likelihood that children in different social worlds were being socialized in different ways. If the emerging concept of childhood was a possession largely of middle- and upper-class people, its influence on lower-class children would be lessened. Even more important, if the norms associated with that image were those of the rule makers of society, then it is likely that the children of the poor would be penalized. Without proper induction into the world of the successful, they could not compete on an equal footing. Worse still, they might be defined as deviant or unworthy to the extent that they departed from the expectations of teachers, employers, and community leaders. There is considerable evidence, in fact, that this is the kind of situation that developed.

Ariès (1966:272) reports that in 16th and 17th century Europe some private scholarships and special schools were set up for the poor. Soon, however, both were taken over by students of better means. In some cases, scholarships originally set aside for the poor were actually bought and sold for prices the poor could not afford. Losing such opportunities as these, most poor people could scarcely afford to place their children in lodgings and provide them with food.

Ariès (1962:413–415) also suggests that, for a much longer time than did the middle class, lower-class people retained their liking for crowds, for communal living, and for apprenticeship training. They preferred the old social order and its system of norms. Whether this preference was due to economic discrimination by the middle class or was voluntary is hard to say. Likely, both were important. In any event, a single school system in both France and England was eventually replaced by a dual system, one for the lower class and one for the "middle class." The lower-class school was of short duration, indeed, was called "primary" school, while the school for the middle class was called "secondary" education and extended for a much longer period.

Although to a lesser degree, early American schools also favored well-to-do over poorer children. But, in addition, Americans were confronted with ethnic, as well as class differences—differences that Europe did not face. At first, the predominant minority groups were the native Indians and the blacks, most of whom were slaves. But far more than discrimination by class, there was discrimination by race.

While dominant white groups in the colonies increasingly stressed the importance of education for their children, they did not do so for the minority groups. There were some religious groups, some individuals, and even some colonies who made an effort to see that both groups of children were educated, but these efforts produced few results (Bremner, 1970, I:72; 335–339).

Besides the Indians' understandable skepticism about the intentions and cultural ways of the white missionaries, they were constantly subjected to the manipulations of white traders, to massacres, and to the broken promises of the settlers. "With so many colonists regarding the Indians as the chief threat to their security and the Indians looking upon the colonists as hypocrites, it is little wonder that attempts to win converts and to educate them should fail" (Bremner, 1970, I:72).

Efforts to extend education to black children were equally dismal, although the opportunity to accomplish a great deal was undoubtedly greater. As with the Indians, colonists were more concerned with the religious conversion of blacks than with their learning in secular terms. Furthermore, the colonists openly confessed to a great deal of ambivalence, even on this score. On one hand, they felt obligated to carry the Christian message to the slaves, but, on the other, they were fearful that if the slaves were baptized they would consider themselves free.

The way this dilemma was resolved is captured in the remarks of a Virginia clergyman in 1724 (Bremner, 1970, I:98):

But as for the Children of Negroes and Indians, that are to live among Christians, undoubtedly they ought all to be baptized; since it is not out of the power of their masters to take care that they have a Christian education, learn their prayers and catechism, and go to church, and not accustom themselves to lie, swear, and steal, though such (as the poorer sort in England) be not taught to read and write; which as yet has been found to be dangerous upon several political accounts, especially self preservation.

In other words, both black and Indian children, like the poorer classes in Europe, ought to learn and adhere to the social rules that would make them willing to accept a subordinate position in society but not be armed with the kinds of educational skills that would make them politically or socially dangerous. As the new concept of childhood grew and spread, therefore, it was applied to all children in moral, but not educational, terms. While the children of dominant groups should receive both moral and secular education, those of subordinate groups should be content with the moral. The logic of this kind of thinking seemed to be that the two could be separated and result in a society without conflict. Such thinking, however, has not been supported by the events of history.

In the next chapter we will discover that the results of attitudes like these grew even more troublesome as ever-increasing numbers of different ethnic groups came to America in the 19th century—ethnic groups whose life-styles and images of childhood were different from those of the Anglo-Saxon middle and upper classes. While some groups were assimilated into the American culture more easily than others and while the class structure of the United States did not become so rigid as that in many European countries, the conflicts engendered by clashes over the appropriate image of childhood were numerous. Many contemporary theories of delinquency, in fact, as well as the actual operation of the juvenile justice system itself, are directly traceable to traditional beliefs about social class differences.

Sexual stratification

Another area of great interest today is how the modern concept of childhood may have affected the treatment of girls. Throughout Western history, girls were considered to be of considerably less value than boys, probably because the family line and family inheritances were traced through the males. Boys were the social security and pension plans of the preindustrial world. They were the best guarantees that parents could provide against the infirmities of sickness and old age. Hence, a failure to produce any sons, or a succession of girls, could destroy the best of well-laid plans (Gillis, 1974:11). After the discovery of childhood, girls were apparently spared some of the neglect and cruelty to which they had been subjected formerly, but this generally improved treatment did not eliminate the sexism of centuries past.

During the 17th century the belief still persisted that boys were not only preferable, but more healthy for the expectant mother. "A woman whose color was good and body temperature comfortably warm might expect a boy, while if she were carrying a girl she would be distinguished by 'a pale, heavy and swarthy countenance, a melancholique eye: She is wayward, fretful, and sad . . . her face is spotted with red' " (Illick, 1974:304). Furthermore, even if the mother survived the terrible effects of carrying a girl, her birth would not be especially welcome. After delivering her third girl, for example, Lady Frances Hatton wrote to her husband, saying, "I am sure you will love it though it be a Girle and I trust in God I may live to bring you boys" (Illick, 1974:304).

If aristocrats like Lord Hatton were not happy with girls, neither were peasants. French peasants, says Robertson (1974:409) were known to declare: "I have no children, monsieur, I havé only girls." And in Naples it was customary to hang out a black flag if a girl were born so that neighbors might be spared the terrible embarrassment of coming in to see her. People were still not crazy about girls. Hence, the treatment of girls under the new child-raising practices probably did not change as much for girls as it did for boys.

European schools, for example, were sexist; that is, they were off limits to females and remained off limits for a long time. Despite all the outcry over the necessity to improve the intellects as well as the morals of children, it was apparently felt that the needs of girls, as well as that of society, could be fulfilled without using the special ministrations of the school (Ariès, 1962:331–332). Most girls were already little women by the age of 10 or 12, devoting their time to family chores or to domestic service. Little of the education care and training expended on boys was expended on them.

One writer of the 17th century describes and criticizes the results (Ariès, 1962:332):

> How many masters and colleges there are!. . . this shows the high opinion people have of the education of boys. But the girls! It is considered perfectly permissible to abandon girls willy-nilly to the guidance of ignor-

ant or indiscreet mothers. . . . It is shameful but common to see women of wit and manners unable to pronounce what they read. . . . They are even more at fault in their spelling.

If virtual illiteracy was characteristic of "women of wit and manners" (of women of the upper classes) think what it was of women in poorer circumstances. Ariès (p. 334) maintains, however, that "girls of good family were no better educated than girls of the lower classes." Efforts designed to improve the skills and morals of boys through formal education were not extended to girls until much later. The thought that girls should receive much formal education, in fact, is largely a product of the 20th century. As with social class, therefore, differences in the status and socialization of girls has had lasting consequences.

Age stratification

A final element of social organization on which comment is vital is the extent to which the discovery of childhood resulted in an increasing tendency to stratify people by age; that is, to divide up the life cycle into major segments such as infancy, childhood, adolescence, adulthood, and old age and, then, to further subdivide among these by year of birth or grade in school. In antiquity and during the Middle Ages, such age-grading, especially where young people are concerned, seemed to be of relatively little importance. If a child survived infancy, that child was soon incorporated into a household where differences by age were not terribly important. "By the standards of today's biologically exacting vocabulary," says Gillis (1974:1), "the language of age in preindustrial Europe is hopelessly vague. Even as late as the 18th century, the French and German words *garcon* and *Knabe* referred to boys as young as six and as old as thirty or forty."

Children were entirely dependent upon their families only until about age six. Between that age and the time they were apprenticed out, they were working, contributing members of the family. By age 14 at the latest, they became semiindependent persons working either as servants, as apprentices living in the homes of their masters, or as students boarding away from home. They usually remained in that state until in their mid- or late twenties when they could afford to marry and start a household of their own. There was, then, a very short period of childhood followed by a long transitional period called "youth" and, finally, adulthood.

As the modern concept of childhood has grown, however, grading by age has extended further and further down the ladder of age. Nowadays, kindergarten children are kept apart from first graders, first graders apart from second graders, and so on and on—not only in school but elsewhere. We are terribly conscious of the ages of childhood, and our social institutions, our beliefs, and even our scientific theories reflect that consciousness. What is profoundly striking, however, is that such a consciousness is a function of only the last century or two.

Kett (1973:97), for example, notes that "the word 'adolescence' appeared only rarely outside of scientific literature prior to the 20th century." It was created in 1890 by G. Stanley Hall who wrote a two-volume work entitled *Adolescence*. In that work, he described "adolescence as a second birth, marked by a sudden rise of moral idealism, chivalry, and religious enthusiasm" (Kett, 1973:96). Yet, in the short space of less than a century, consider how extensively adolescence has been defined as the last stage of childhood and adolescents themselves relegated to a childlike status (Cf. Coleman, et al., 1972; Kett, 1973):

Following Hall's original work, a parade of books emerged describing adolescence as the "awkward age" and noting its relationship to problems of schooling and delinquency.

Adolescents have been largely eliminated from the job market.

The length of formal education has been stretched out to the late teens and early twenties.

Adolescents have been increasingly segregated from adults and expected to confine their primary relationships to their peers.

Adolescents are now a burden on the family rather than contributing economically to its welfare. Moreover, parents have become less and less capable of imparting specific work skills to their children, since the two no longer work together.

Our whole society, in other words, is organized to separate child from adult and to provide a host of ways for taking the presumed developmental stages of childhood into account. The invention of delinquency, the creation of the juvenile court, the drafting of child labor laws, legal requirements regulating the school-leaving age, pediatricians, child psychiatrists, and elementary and secondary school teachers are all a reflection of our modern construction of childhood.

What is fascinating about this construction is that while our modern norms suggest that we must stratify by age in order to take the needs of children into account, they do just the opposite where males and females are concerned. That is, modern norms suggest increasingly that in order to take the needs of females into account we must make them equal with males. We must eliminate all stratification by sex but not by age. Thus, we justify and support stratification in the instance of age but not in the instance of sex. The implications are profound and will appear again and again throughout our study.

Summary and conclusions

This chapter has analyzed the factors that contributed to the discovery of childhood in Western civilization. We have seen how during periods of great change in both the Old and New Worlds the members of society were increasingly stratified by age and how a new set of rules and social institutions gradually evolved for children. To insure their proper development, it was assumed that they must be stringently safeguarded, must receive a carefully structured education, and, only after long years of moral, physical, and intellectual quarantine, could they be allowed to join the adults.

Age-old tendencies—either to abandon, to ignore, or to exploit children—were replaced with a heightened, even fervent, moralistic concern over their welfare. Less and less were children permitted to join the adults at an early age. Rather, childhood became a transitional period in which the home and the school increased in importance: Family privacy and responsibility increased; community sociability across generational and class lines decreased; a new morality, especially for children, developed; and new forms of moral and intellectual training by family and school began to replace apprenticeship training and early adulthood.

The ideal image of childhood that evolved was probably a middle- and upper-class image. As these classes gradually replaced the aristocracy in power, the nuclear family rather than the communal household and the school rather than apprenticeship seemed particularly well-suited to their interests and aspirations. By contrast, members of lower class and minority groups were hindered from full participation in these new developments. Virtually nothing was done, for example, to educate black and Indian children in America. The concern of those in power was to insure that poor and minority people adhered to the behavioral requirements of the new morality, but they shied away from educating them. In a similar, but less obvious way, differences between the sexes persisted. While girls were undoubtedly affected by the altered child-raising practices of the family and by increased age-grading, they remained locked somewhat more strongly into traditional domestic roles.

The valuable lesson that all of this teaches is that social change, however desirable and significant it may seem, also brings unanticipated, and possibly negative, consequences. All societies are constantly evolving new ways of organizing themselves and of defining new rules for behavior. The results of this historical process for children have often been desirable: Infanticide is now rare; most babies are raised by their parents; swaddling has disappeared; and children are sent out as pupils rather than apprentices. But there may also be a darker side to the discovery of childhood. In seeking to moralize the lives of children, reformers looked at age-old behavior and discovered immorality; in seeking to foster conformity, they defined more of the acts of children (and adults) as deviant; and, in encouraging greater discipline and control, they narrowed the range of acceptable childhood conduct. Thus, while their discoveries resulted in vastly altered child-raising practices, they did not always represent a decrease in the exercise of arbitrary authority, only a shift in methods of control.

By grading people according to age, in fact, and by defining childhood as a special phase of the life cycle, the control of children may in some ways have become easier. Cast into age-graded categories, their behavior may have become more predictable and, thus, more managable. Whether the end product now represents a net gain over centuries past is difficult to say. There are no totally objective standards, no universal laws, by which one can decide such matters. Rather, one can only weigh a host of pros and cons.

The weighing of pros and cons will continue in the next chapter. After childhood was discovered and societal organization altered, still more changes occurred. But, rather than looking only at the ideal image of childhood, we will be examining its counterpart, delinquency—how delinquency was invented, why it was invented, and who its inventors were. After discovering childhood and attaching a special meaning to it, society was not only forced to indicate how the ideal child might be produced, but how the undesirable one might be prevented from developing, or controlled if he did. The invention of delinquency and the creation of a juvenile court to oversee it was but one of many new social institutions that emerged to provide for, and control, the lives of children.

References

Ariès, Phillippe
  1962 *Centuries of Childhood* (Trans. by Robert Baldick). New York: Alfred A. Knopf.

Bremner, Robert H. et al., (Eds.)
  1970 *Children and Youth in America: A Documentary History*. 2 vols. Cambridge: Harvard University Press.

Coleman, James S. et al.
  1972 *Youth: Transition to Adulthood*. Chicago: University of Chicago Press.

de Mause, Lloyd
  1974 *The History of Childhood*. New York: Psychohistory Press.

Demos, John
  1970 *A Little Commonwealth*. New York: Oxford University Press.

Farber, Bernard
  1972 *Guardians of Virtue: Salem Families in 1800*. New York: Basic Books.

Gillis, John R.
  1974 *Youth and History*. New York: Academic Press.

Goodman, Mary E.
  1970 *The Culture of Childhood: Child's-Eye Views of Society and Culture*. New York: Teachers College Press.

Gould, Julius
  1964 "Middle-class." Pp. 426–428 in Julius Gould and William L. Kolb (Eds.), *A Dictionary of the Social Sciences*. New York: Free Press.

Hobbes, Thomas
  1972 "The citizen." In T. S. K. Scott-Craig and Bernard Gert (Eds.), *Man and Citizen*. Gloucester, Mass.: Peter Smith Publisher Inc. (1st ed., 1642).

Illick, Joseph E.
  1974 "Child rearing in seventeenth century England and America." Pp. 303–350 in Lloyd de Mause (Ed.), *The History of Childhood*. New York: Psychohistory Press.

Kett, Joseph F.
  1971 "Adolescence and youth in nineteenth century America." Pp. 95–110 in Theodore K. Rabb and Robert I. Rotberg (Eds.), *The Family in History*. New York: Harper and Row.

Laslett, Peter
  1972 *Household and Family in Past Time*. Cambridge: Cambridge University Press.

Marvick, Elizabeth W.
   1974   "Nature versus nurture: patterns and trends in seventeenth century French child rearing." Pp. 259–302 in Lloyd de Mause (Ed.), *The History of Childhood*. New York: Psychohistory Press.

Platt, Anthony
   1969   *The Child Savers*. Chicago: Chicago University Press.

Plumb, J. H.
   1972   "The great change in children." *Intellectual Digest*, 2:82–84.

Roberts, Robert
   1971   *The Classic Slum: Salford Life in the First Quarter of the Century*. Manchester: Manchester University Press.

Robertson, Priscilla
   1974   "Home as a nest: middle-class childhood in nineteenth century Europe." Pp. 407–431 in Lloyd de Mause (Ed.), *The History of Childhood*. New York: Psychohistory Press.

Ross, James B.
   1974   "The middle-class child in urban Italy, fourteenth to early sixteenth century." Pp. 183–228 in Lloyd de Mause (Ed.), *The History of Childhood*. New York: Psychohistory Press.

Skolnick, Arlene
   1973   *The Intimate Environment: Exploring Marriage and the Family*. Boston: Little, Brown.

Tucker, M. J.
   1974   "The child as beginning and end: fifteenth and sixteenth century English childhood." Pp. 229–258 in Lloyd de Mause (Ed.), *The History of Childhood*. New York: Psychohistory Press.

4

THE INVENTION OF DELINQUENCY

Throughout the Middle Ages and as late as the 17th century, children participated in acts which, if committed today, could not only result in their being defined as delinquent but could require that their parents and other adults be charged with contributing to their delinquency. As soon as they could talk, most children learned and used obscene language and gestures; many engaged in sex at an early age, willingly or otherwise, they drank freely in taverns, if not at home; few of them ever went to school, and when they did, they wore sidearms, fomented brawls, and fought duels (Cf. Ariès, 1962; Sanders, 1970). In modern society, these same acts occur, but they are legally defined as undesirable, and authorities are charged with curbing them. How did this change come about? How should the modern response be interpreted?

Two major interpretations are possible: Either the undesirable behavior of children has increased over the centuries and become more dangerous, or significant modifications have been made in the way that behavior is defined. Likely, the latter is the more accurate interpretation. As the concept of childhood grew and expanded, the meanings attached to it were significantly altered. The acts of children which in previous centuries were not seen as particularly deviant now became unique problems. New norms and expectations developed as childhood became a special phase in the life cycle.

In this chapter, we will be tracing the development of those norms and expectations on the American scene. It was during the 19th century that most laws applicable only to children were actually written and a juvenile court created. But in order to understand these social inventions, it is necessary to begin our analysis in the 18th century. Only by clarifying the nature of their 18th century precedents is it possible to illustrate the remarkable societal changes that led to their development.

Eighteenth century childhood and organization

Although Puritan child-raising practices were by no means universal throughout the colonies, the moralist principles they espoused seem to have had great impact upon subsequent generations of 19th century reformers—the principles stressing obedience, submission to authority, hard work, modesty, and chastity.[1] Furthermore, the small towns in which the colonists lived were admirably suited to an implementation of these principles.

Few individuals or families in colonial times commanded the kinds of resources, tools, or labor that would free them from dependence upon their neighbors. Life was dominated by a subsistence existence in which cooperation was vital. "Common goals demanded community action" (Rothman, 1971:12). Most people were also Protestant and worshiped at the same church. In many parts of the country, particularly New England, there were few outsiders to intrude upon the daily routine of the average citizen. Frequent marriages turned many neighbors into relatives, and daily contacts with a limited number of people fostered a reliance upon strong, informal social control. In short, the environmental conditions of the time produced a kind of community interdependence and insularity that facilitated local community control, an emphasis upon individual responsibility, and a distrust of outside influence. There were exceptions, of course, especially toward the latter part of the 18th century. But, even then, change was relative. People still had to band together to build water lines, to protect themselves, or to care for the old, the sick, or the poor.

------

[1] The framework for this analysis relies heavily upon David J. Rothman's provocative work, *The Discovery of the Asylum* (1971). Attention is invited to this excellent volume for greater detail and for extended documentation of many of the points made here.

Family, church, and community

Life was dominated by a network of three major social institutions: family, church, and community. "Families were to raise their children to respect law and authority, the church was to oversee not only family discipline but adult behavior, and the members of the community were to supervise one another to detect and correct the first signs of deviancy" (Rothman, 1971:16). The values and beliefs surrounding this network provided whatever explanations or solutions that were needed to deal with the behavior of either children or adults.

The family was the guardian of the public as well as the private good. The functions it was expected to perform and the rules set forth for doing so were prescribed in the tracts and sermons of the day (Cf. Moody, 1715:17–19; Wadsworth, 1719:44–58). Parents should love their children and provide for them. "He that provides not for his own, especially those of his own house, hath denied the faith, and is worse than an infidel." (I Timothy 8) Conversely, as the following catechism indicates, children were expected to reciprocate with obedience and respect (Bremner, 1970, I:32):

> *Question:* What is the fifth commandment?
> *Answer:* Honor thy father and thy mother, that thy days may be long in the land which the Lord thy God giveth thee.
> *Question:* Who are here meant by father and mother?
> *Answer:* All our superiors, whether in family, school, church, and commonwealth.
> *Question:* What is the honor due to them?
> *Answer:* Reverence, obedience, and (when I am able) recompense.

Disobedience to authority could only lead to destruction. "Appetites and passions unrestricted become furious in youth; and ensure *dishonor, disease,* and an *untimely death*" (Cf. Rothman, 1971:17).

These admonitions for children, like most of the rules for adult conduct, revealed the strength of religious influence. The church tended not only to dominate family discipline and individual behavior, but to provide the core set of values around which community life was organized. The assumption prevailed that the existing social order was not accidental but divinely inspired. The church, as a consequence, set strict standards, stressed the need to observe them, and related obedience to eternal rewards and punishments. The person who came from a well-regulated family, worked hard, and attended church was obviously adhering to God's will. Even the legal codes of the time reflected the influence of religious belief.

Deviance and sin

The colonists were concerned about deviant behavior and adopted harsh methods for dealing with it. But they did not see it as a critical social problem in the sense that they blamed themselves or their communities for it, nor did they expect to eliminate it. Crime and evil, they believed, were inherent in people and, therefore, endemic to society (Rothman, 1971:115). To some later 19th century Americans this was a pessimistic and unenlightened view which they rejected. To the colonists, however, it made sense.

The reason lay in their religious explanation for deviance; they equated crime with sin. Hence, their criminal codes defined a wide range of behaviors as criminal—witchcraft, sexual misconduct, disrespect for parents, property crimes, blasphemy, or murder—and drew few distinctions between adults and children or between major and minor offenses. Any offense was a sure sign "that the offender was destined to be a public menace and a damned sinner" (Rothman, 1971:15–17).

At first blush, such thinking might appear to be contrary to the heavy emphasis colonists placed upon family life. If the seeds of crime and sin are present in everyone, why the heavy emphasis upon training children? The answer is that the colonists did not share the modern belief that people can be easily shaped into some desirable form. By nature, people are forever inclined to the temptations of the flesh. The purpose of training, therefore, is to secure the strict obedience of children to correct conduct, not to assume that evil impulses can ever be totally eliminated. Thus, the colonists were not bothered by any strong impulse to rehabilitate sinners once they had sinned. Rather, their transgressions demanded retribution. If offenders were allowed to escape, others would be implicated in their crimes, and God would be displeased.

The most common punishments were the fine and the whip, but wide use was made of such mechanisms of shame as the stocks, the pillory, and, occasionally, branding. Both the stocks and the pillory were located in a public place. The stocks held the offender sitting down, with his head and hands locked in the frame. The pillory held him standing up. In both, he was subject not only to physical pain and discomfort but to public scorn and ridicule. In some instances, he might also be whipped. In others, he might have his ears nailed to the pillory. Occasionally, criminals were driven through town in a cart and then whipped. Branding offenders with a "T" for thief, with a "B" for blasphemy, or with an "A" for adultery was also used. In all these instances, shame as well as pain was a source of control (Barnes, 1972:56–67).

Even capital punishment served a protective as well as retributive function. The criminal codes prescribed a long list of death-penalty offenses—arson, horse stealing, robbery, burglary, sodomy, murder, and many others. Sending offenders to the gallows for these crimes was a method of ridding the community of them forever. So was the practice of permanently banishing them from their home communities. And, since the colonists devoted little attention to reform, they built no prisons. Instead, the small jails found in most towns were used primarily to hold offenders awaiting trial or debtors who had yet to meet their obligations. The American invention of the prison was still to come (Rothman, 1971:48–53).

The child offender

What was the status of the child offender in this 18th century social system? How did he or she fare?

First of all, there was no distinct legal category called "juvenile delinquency." Americans still relied on the English common law which specified that children under the age of seven could not be guilty of a serious crime. Between the ages of eight and fourteen, they might be presumed innocent unless proved otherwise. Juries were expected to pay close attention to the child, and, if he was capable of discerning the nature of his sins, he could be convicted and even sentenced to death. Anyone over the age of fourteen, presumably, was judged as an adult, although some colonies made exceptions. In Pennsylvania, for example, only youths over the age of sixteen could receive such severe penalties for noncapital offenses as public whipping (Cf. Bremner, 1970, I:307–308; Platt, 1969:187–188).

Although the long list of forbidden criminal offenses applied to everyone, there were some that applied only to children: rebelliousness, disobedience, sledding on the sabbath, or playing ball on public streets. In some colonies, the penalty for rebelliousness against parents was death: "If a man have a stubborn or rebellious son of sufficient years of understanding, viz. 16, . . . such a son shall be put to death" (Cf.

Bremner, 1970, I:38). In other places, the prescribed punishment was whipping. In actual practice, however, courts and juries were often lenient towards the young. Children were often acquitted after a nominal trial or pardoned if found guilty. Some young children were severely punished or even put to death but the latest available evidence suggests that it may have been less common than originally thought (Cf. Platt, 1969:183 ff).

In many ways, elaborate legal machinery for children was unnecessary in the small-town colonial environment because the family, neighborhood, school, and apprenticeship system served so well as a tight-knit mechanism of social control. Thus, while town members may have shrunk from the punishment of children as criminals, they did not shrink from punishing them as subservient beings. Caning was a commonly accepted practice and was widely used. Moreover, if a family was unable to control or to educate its own children to the satisfaction of town officials, they had the power to remove those children from their own homes and to place them in others where they would receive a "decent" and "Christian" education (Cf. Rothman, 1971:14).

Treatment of poverty

Another matter relative to the understanding of 19th century delinquency has to do with the colonial conception of poverty. During that period, Americans came to view poverty, along with disordered families, as the roots of juvenile misconduct and crime. Eighteenth century Americans, by contrast, clearly separated the two. They did not believe, as Americans came later to believe, that being poor would almost automatically lead to illegal behavior. Rather, their religious beliefs provided them with a much different view of poverty (Rothman, 1971:7–14, chap. 2).

First, they accepted the long-standing Christian belief that the poor would always be with us. They did not lament their presence as evidence of a tragic breakdown in social organization but "serenely asserted that the presence of the poor was a God-given opportunity for men to do good" (Rothman, 1971:7). The presence of hungry children or poor widows, for example, was not evidence of God's lack of concern. Quite the contrary. Because of their presence, persons at all levels of society could be benefited. The poor would be given charity, and industrious stewards could do God's work by providing it.

Such pervasive beliefs led to a situation in which people did not fear and distrust the poor as they were to be feared later on. By providing spiritual sanction for earthly good works, the more common reaction to poverty was one of pity and sympathy. The one major exception was the idle ne'er-do-well who might be told to move on to some other town. But the sickly, the elderly, a widow with children, or a family down on its luck received help in one of two forms: "outdoor relief," wherein they received food and care in their own homes or "indoor relief" wherein they went to live or to board in the homes of others. As a result, poor adults did not live in constant dread of the poorhouse, and children, simply because they were destitute, did not face the prospect of being confined in a state institution. Such institutions, with rare exceptions, did not even exist. It was the duty of townspeople to see that children were cared for.

Treatment of minorities

Slave or free, child or adult, minority people were not an influential segment of community life during this period. This fact is striking in light of the size of the black population. In 1775, there were approximately 500,000 slaves in the colonies, or about one black in every five inhabitants (Bremner, 1970, I:316). There were a few free Negroes whose ranks were swelled somewhat during the War for Independence, but their impact upon the nature of organized community life was slight. This meant that while black children were expected to adhere to the legal rules of the white community they benefited little from any advantages it had to offer. Some slaves were taught to read and write, but the legal codes of the 1800s still suggested that slave children should be kept in utter ignorance and subservience as a means of protecting the security of whites (Bremner, 1970, I:317–318).

Northern states, one after another, began to take steps to free the slaves during the latter part of the 18th century, but a few slaves could still be found in those states on the eve of the Civil War. As a result, slave owners had almost complete legal authority. Short of willful murder, where the state might step in, an owner would do almost anything to a slave. Since the slave family did not exist in a legal sense, it was not protected by the hands of law. Eighteenth century owners could separate parents and children or keep them together as they wished. There were instances in which kindly owners or authorities would act to protect the needs of a mother and her children, but such practices were the result of informal, not official, practices.

Nineteenth century enlightenment

Colonial social organization did not survive for long into the 19th century. After the War of Independence, Americans were subjected to a series of changes which, on one hand, were intoxicating but which, on the other, altered irrevocably the tightly knit communities to which they were accustomed.

Changes in belief

Those Americans who framed the Declaration of Independence and the Constitution relied upon the philosophy of the Enlightenment for many of their ideas. Whereas the religious doctrine of the moralist and religious reformers of the past two centuries had suggested that people were inherently depraved and foreordained to a particular destiny, the philosophy of the Enlightenment was individualistic and stressed universal and unlimited human progress. Through the use of reason and by applying the principles of democracy, man could achieve unimagined heights. Optimism, not pessimism, was the cornerstone of Enlightenment thinking. Furthermore, newly won independence was itself evidence that the new philosophy worked. America's destiny, as well as that of the people in it, was of divine origin.

Just as they began to cast off the strictures of some of their former theological beliefs, Americans began to feel that some of their 18th century methods of social control were obsolete (Rothman, 1971:57–59). They reasoned that the legal codes of the mother country had stifled their better inclinations and had caused them to imitate the crude customs of the Old World (Bremner, 1972:104). They were inspired in this belief by such philosophers of the Enlightenment as Cesare Beccaria (1809), an Italian, who had proposed a series of reforms designed to make the treatment of law violators more rational and humane. The countries in which punishments had been the most severe, he argued, are also those in which the bloodiest deeds are committed. A more enlightened nation, by contrast, is one that reduces the severity, but increases the certainty, of punishment. Moderate punishments, equitably administered, will accomplish what severe punishments fail to accomplish. Indeed, such responses to lawbreaking as flogging or death only cause people to commit the very acts they are supposed to prevent. In order to escape vengeance for a first crime, the criminal is driven to new forms of violence and predation.

Such a message may have found fertile soil in the colonies because it seemed to square so well with the revolutionary experience. British legislation, like harsh punishments, had often seemed arbitrary and vengeful to Americans. They had been led to rebellion and had been successful at it. Harshly imposed controls on them had not worked. Hence, under the heady influence of their newfound freedoms, they significantly altered their responses to the lawbreaker. The death penalty for robbery, burglary, sodomy, or witchcraft was repealed; penalties for such acts as petty larceny were reduced; and such corporal punishments as burning the offender's hand, cutting off his ears, or nailing them to the pillory were done away with. In some states, legislation against whipping was also written, and the only crime left punishable by death was murder (Bremner, 1972:106–107). No longer, said a number of influential reformers, could Americans abide the use of barbarous punishments, particularly for children. Americans had a grand mission to fulfill, and one way they could do it was to uplift a formerly hopeless segment of mankind: the criminal class (Cf. Rothman, 1971:60–61).

Altered explanations for crime and sin

Ways by which the mission could be accomplished were suggested by the new explanations for deviant behavior that began to emerge in the late 18th and early 19th centuries. More and more, Americans began to reject the older colonial notions that crime and sin were synonymous, that lawbreaking was the result of inborn tendencies and the handiwork of the devil. Such theological conceptions were losing their currency. In their stead, the belief grew that deviancy could be traced back to early childhood. Almost always, there had been a breakdown in family discipline. Orphaned children or the children of drunks and licentious parents were those most likely to fall prey to temptation and vice. The typical road to crime was paved, first, by a lack of discipline and rudeness, then, drinking and intemperance, and, finally, lawbreaking itself. Criminals were those who were inadequately prepared early in life to take their places as respectable members of the community.

Another social evil—community corruption—was soon added to that of family disorganization (Rothman, 1971:57–59). Between 1790 and 1830, the population of the United States grew markedly, as did the size and density of several cities and states. Massachusetts doubled in numbers, Pennsylvania tripled, and New York increased fivefold. When

George Washington became President, most people lived in towns having less than 2,500 inhabitants. By the time Andrew Jackson was inaugurated in 1829, over 1 million people resided in towns larger than that. Some notion of the trends that were underway can be gleaned from the fact that in 1750 there were only about 1¼ million people in this country. By 1850, the figure had reached over 23 million—an incredible growth (U.S. Bureau of the Census, 1955). Simultaneously, as manufacturing and commerce continued to develop, the simple economic and social organization of the colonies was no longer adequate. Again, there was pressure to reconsider existing methods of social control.

The memories of small tightly knit towns were still fresh in the minds of many Americans so that they retained firm notions about the way a well-ordered community ought to appear. Thus, when they looked about them and saw growth, change, and instability, they concluded that these factors also promoted deviant behavior. Community disorder went hand in hand with the disorder of unstable families.

Such thinking demanded a major turnabout in thinking. Rather than preoccupation with the internal evils of the sinner, reformers now had to be concerned with the external forces that shaped him—a significant turnabout indeed, and it had paradoxical consequences for children. If, on one hand, deviant behavior was endemic to societal life and not to the human soul, then it could be rooted out or at least greatly reduced! If the criminal was no longer innately depraved, he could be redeemed! If there were young children in danger of becoming criminal, their misconduct could be prevented! The grounds for optimism were considerable.

On the other hand, the impact of such thinking could do little to alter the child-raising principles derived from the 18th century. Indeed, if families and communities, and not the devil, were at fault then even greater attention to childhood was required. Parents were warned of the awful consequences of an absence of discipline and admonished to take stern measures against any loss of family control. Likewise, the attention of community leaders were directed toward the sources of vice, evil, and societal corruption.

> Vicious propensities are imbibed at a very early age by children in the crowded population of a city. Parents, whose extreme poverty, casual calamity, or moral turpitude induces a neglect of their off-spring, expose them at once to be caught up by the profligate and knavish, to be made unsuspecting agents in the commission of offences, and to be trained into habits of idleness, cunning, and predatory vagrancy . . . . . Children, too,

accomplish petty thefts with ease, and with frequent impunity; they pass unnoticed by the busy or, if detected, are treated with indulgence. Success gradually emboldens; they become proud of their skill, form combinations among themselves, and grow ambitious to surpass each other in their daily contributions to the hoard of a common guide and pretended protector" (Committee of the Board of Managers of the Philadelphia House of Refuge, 1835:8–12. Cf. Sanders, 1970:363–364).

Rothman (1971:76) says that 19th century Americans were so sensitive to childhood, so concerned with matters moral that "they stripped away the years from adults and made everyone into a child."

Concern over the moral impact of change led to serious concerns over public safety. How was social order to be maintained? What were the best means for reducing the effects on children of poor family discipline and community instability?

The institution as panacea

In seeking some new forms of social organization, Americans took a step that was to leave an indelible imprint on the future treatment of both children and adults in trouble and to change irrevocably the search for community solutions to deviant behavior that had characterized the social order of colonial society. Out of the many methods that might have been tried to prevent crime and correct offenders, leading reformers chose *confinement*. They built prisons for adults and houses of refuge and orphan asylums for children. Asylums for abandoned children had been used in England and elsewhere in Europe for some time, but the idea was entirely new that places of confinement could be used effectively both to punish and correct criminals and to substitute for the family and community as the best method for raising neglected children. Not only was this idea a social invention of profound significance, but it was viewed as an extremely humane idea as well—an answer to the brutality of prior methods of control and punishment (Bremner, 1970, I:122).

Pennsylvania led the way in 1790 by converting the old Walnut Street Jail in Philadelphia to a state prison for criminals and in 1829 erected a huge and striking edifice called Eastern State Penitentiary. Through the mercies of incarceration rather than physical torment, stigma in the stocks, or death on the scaffold, the criminal would learn the errors of his ways. Reform, not brutality, would protect the community. Not to be outdone, New York erected the Newgate Prison in Greenwich Village in

1796 and built a rival to Pennsylvania's huge edifice around 1820 at Auburn. Other states soon followed suit (McKelvey, 1968:6–11).

The first houses of refuge, designed to separate children in trouble from hardened criminals, were built by private philanthropists in New York City in 1825, in Philadelphia in 1828, and by the Boston City Council in 1825. The fact that they first appeared in larger cities was no accident; the older colonial practice of placing unruly or neglected children in the home of a neighbor was more difficult in the impersonal metropolis. Indeed, houses of refuge were to become family substitutes, not only for the less serious juvenile, but for other children who were defined as a problem—the runaway, the disobedient or defiant child, or the vagrant who was in danger of falling prey to loose women, taverns, gambling halls, or theatres. Given what they considered to be laudatory goals, reformers were not bothered by any thought that they might be infringing on the rights or wishes of these children; that thought would not have occurred to them. "A good dose of institutionalization could only work to the child's benefit" (Rothman, 1971:209).

Orphan asylums appeared at about the same time. Again, the promise of incarceration seemed so great that officials cast a wide net for inmates. Besides abandoned and orphaned children, they accepted the children of women without husbands or even those whose parents were alive but poor. Such children, reformers reasoned, should not be penalized merely because they were the offspring of degenerates or paupers (Rothman, 1971:207). Either the house of refuge or the orphan's asylum was to become an instrument of the new social order whose purpose it was to produce the ideal child.

> . . . The whole community is deeply interested in its accomplishment. It has for its object, and promises to realize in its results, employment of the idle;—instruction of the ignorant;—reformation of the depraved;—relief of the wretched;—a general diffusion of good morals;—enlargement of virtuous society;—and the universal protection of property and life (Committee of the Board of Managers of the Philadelphia House of Refuge, 1835:8–12. Cf. Sanders, 1970:366).

In short, the progressive destruction of colonial social organization by new ideas, rapid immigration, the growth of cities, and a high degree of social mobility led to the belief that child-saving institutions could become society's superparents. If some families and communities were no longer fit places for children, then places of confinement could become effective surrogates. Older colonial practices continued to operate in many rural areas, and children in trouble were apprenticed directly to neighbor families. But the communities or states which had asylums or refuges were considered to be the progressive ones. The role of local families and neighborhoods in dealing with dependent or deviant children was progressively eroded and replaced by that of larger, more impersonal structures.

Failures of the superparent

The concept of *parens patriae,* derived from English tradition, suggests that the state may intervene to protect the rights of children and to assume the parental role should that prove necessary. In attempting to make a superparent out of child-saving institutions, Americans not only lent further legitimation to that concept but embodied it in obvious physical structures. There are two ways, as a result, that the construction of institutions can be interpreted. Since only a small minority of all children ever ended up in them, they could be seen solely as places designed by those in power to get rid of the misfits they did not like. On the other hand, they could be seen not merely as places of control but as evidence of concern over the welfare of children. Most historians lean toward the latter interpretation. The proper upbringing of children had become one of the foremost goals of American life.

Some European visitors, in fact, seemed to feel that Americans had created a new species of child. Alexis de Tocqueville (1945:192–197), for example, noted that, while American children were appropriately domesticated in their early years, they became increasingly independent in adolescence and young adulthood. He expressed some concern over this decrease in submissiveness to parental will but was impressed nonetheless. Almost certainly, however, de Tocqueville was alluding to the children of middle- and upper-class families whom he had visited. What about the children of poor and immigrant parents?

Given the ideal image of childhood that prevailed, it is clear that they were the ones most likely to be confined. More and more, 19th century Americans tended to do away with the colonial notion that poverty and crime were two different things and instead made destitution almost the inevitable precursor of lawbreaking. So popular did this notion become, in fact, that in the 1890s the Illinois Board of Public Charities warned that "every child allowed to grow up in ignorance and vice, and so to become a pauper or a criminal, is liable to become in turn the progenitor of criminals" (Cf. Platt, 1969:130). It had become almost impossible for reformers to see poverty and crime as two different things. The destitute child was but one short step from becoming the worst nightmare of all, a lawbreaker. Thus, the only way to save him was to remove him from the vice surrounding him and to place him under the control of one of society's superparents. American child savers not only felt justified in taking this action, but felt morally superior for doing so. It does not seem to have occurred to many of them that the assignment of a child to an institution was anything but fitting and proper. It was with considerable shock, therefore, when the superparent turned out to be a failure.

By 1850, criticisms of houses of refuge and asylums had begun to mount; by 1870, there was an overwhelming demand for change—a demand that placed rural-oriented, middle-class reformers on the horns of a dilemma. On one hand, rather than becoming model superparents, child-saving institutions had become prison-like warehouses for ever larger numbers of children from the margins of society. Rather than turning out ideal children, they were producing young things who marched, thought, and acted like automatons (Bremner, 1970, I:696–697; Rothman, 1971:258–260).

On the other hand, the need for child saving seemed to be greater than ever. All the things that reformers feared most were coming to pass. Besides the Civil War, the last half of the 19th century was marked by ever more immigrants, more urban growth, more mobility, and more social instability. Immigrant groups were seen as contributing disproportionately to this mess. As early as 1850, immigrant children constituted almost three quarters of the New York Refuge, over half of the Cincinnati Refuge and two thirds of the Philadelphia Refuge (Rothman, 1971:261–262). The parents of these children were often penniless when they arrived in the United States and thus found it necessary to remain in the big cities where they swelled the ranks of the unemployed and often contributed to high crime rates. Not only were native-born Americans concerned about this state of affairs, but were further alarmed by the new customs which some immigrant groups brought with them—different sexual habits, different marital patterns, and other ways of talking and behaving. Such customs were by definition deviant and further contributed to the belief that immigrants were an inferior lot and a threat to social order. The facts are that wherever people of different cultures come into contact, invidious distinctions almost inevitably are drawn. This certainly occurred in 19th century America.

New beliefs about poverty and crime

The tendency to depreciate immigrant, poor, and criminal groups was reinforced by the emergence of new scientific theories in the last half of the 19th century. Americans heard about Charles Darwin's notion that life is a competitive struggle for existence and that only the fittest survive. Applied to the societal realm, such ideas, in contrast to the optimism of the Enlightenment, were pessimistic and suggested that among men, as among the lower animals, nature selects the fittest and weeds out the unfit. Some people are biologically predetermined to succeed, others to fail. The implication was that destitution, poverty, and crime were the result of innate inferiority (Hofstader, 1959:31–50).

An Italian physician by the name of Cesare Lombroso lent further confirmation to such ideas in his study of criminals. He concluded that lawbreakers are born, not made. Some are measurable physical types who are throwbacks to a more primitive level of development; others, while not physically deformed, are mentally defective (Vold, 1958:28–32).

Such ideas appeared in the thinking of leading reformers. Enoch Wines, the most prominent reformer of the 1870s, described the criminal as being the consequence of three great "hindrances": "depravity," "physical degeneracy," and "bad environment" (Henderson, 1910:12, 19). Peter Caldwell, a reformatory superintendent, said that a typical delinquent is "cradled in infamy, imbibing with its earliest natural nourishment the germs of depraved appetite, and reared in the midst of people whose lives are an atrocious crime against natural and divine law and the rights of society" (Cf. Platt, 1969:52).

Fix the superparent

It was likely that such reasoning led a new generation of post-Civil War reformers to reaffirm the utility of the institution as a necessary parent substitute despite its initial failure. The task of saving children, if anything, had taken on more monumental proportions. "This whole mass of pestilent and pestiferous juvenility is already supported at your expense . . . They all have mouths to feed and bodies to be clothed . . . not only at the expense of your purses, but at the far more extravagant and alarming expense of your public and private morals (Report of Joint Special Committee, Hartford, 1863:2–7. Cf. Sanders, 1970:401). Hence, reformers reasoned that the fault with surrogate places of child raising lay in poor execution, not in concept; the methods, not the goals, had been bad. Furthermore, as the above comment indicates, the literature of the period reveals the persistent ambivalence of people toward potential or actual offenders, young or old.

In the famous Cincinnati Prison Congress of 1870, delegates framed a Declaration of Principles that was to incorporate a new philosophy, not only for children, but for adults as well. This new philosophy was less punitive than the one that prevailed when the first prisons and houses of refuge were built. An institution governed by force and fear, the Declaration stated, is an institution mismanaged. Punishment that degrades is a mistake. Degradation "destroys every better impulse and aspiration. It crushes the weak, irritates the strong, and indisposes all to submission and reform." Why not try the effects of reward upon the inmate? Cultivate his self-respect; educate him; provide him with honorable labor; and teach him self-control. These are the principles that should govern institutional life (Henderson, 1910:39–63). Yet, when these principles were translated into action, they did not result in remarkably different kinds of places.

Some new names for places of confinement were found— "reformatories" for young criminals and "industrial schools" for destitute or neglected children. New guidelines stressed the importance of locating both institutions in the country and reaffirmed the idea that they should emulate the character of a well-disciplined family. "Add to [them] the holy and softening influence of a quiet moral and Christian home and family, and we are complete" (Cf. Sanders, 1970:404). For the law violator, reformatories added the indeterminate sentence which allowed officials to keep a young person until they thought he should be released, a "marking" system for classifying offenders into different categories, and parole supervision after release (Brockway, 1910; Hart, 1910; Henderson, 1910:39–63). But when the country's model reformatory opened in Elmira, New York, its new director, Z. R. Brockway (1910), stressed that it should be run like a monarchy so that the offender's life could be stringently regulated and not be subject to the well-meaning, but misguided, interference of ministers and other outsiders. Likewise, reformers were prepared to keep dependent children for as long as it took to save them. Consider the following conclusions regarding what was needed for the giddy and restless teenage girl (Hart, 1910:72):

When she reaches the age of 14 or 15, she becomes restless, uneasy, discontented. She chafes under restraint, desires more liberty, wants to choose her own associations and recreations. She wants to go out at night. She craves pretty clothes and admiration. Perhaps she is the recipient of flattering and dangerous attentions from some young man. . . . The girl is not vicious, she does not want to do anything wrong, but she is in a critical and dangerous situation. She is giddy, headstrong, easily influenced. She needs to be kept safe for a few years or two, until she comes to herself, and in the meantime she ought to receive such training as will either enable her to support herself or will make her a more efficient housewife and mother. It is for this class of girls that [industrial] schools are now demanded.

Judgments such as this reveal the morality of influential Americans as the United States turned the corner into the 20th century. Because our morality is different, we often snicker at or condemn what appears to be their overweening self-righteousness. Yet, it we do so at the expense of understanding how they saw childhood and attempted to organize it, we exercise no better judgment than they did when they reacted negatively to the strange moral standards of immigrant groups. There were a few dissenters from the reformatory movement, of course, and most southern states did not bother with special institutions for juveniles (Bremner, 1970, 1:672; Platt, 1969:61–62). Otherwise, the new movement again swept the country. But, by 1900, it had come full circle just like the refuge movement before it. Institutions were still not a panacea.

From our privileged vantage point, it does not seem surprising that places of confinement should have failed as superparents. The added experience of the 20th century has indicated even more clearly that about the only function large institutions fulfill well is to immobilize dangerous offenders. Otherwise, they are poor devices for socializing people, young or old. But that is not the only lesson that can be learned from the 19th century experience. Another is associated with the efforts of Americans to develop effective forms of social control in a century of rapid ideological and social change. That was their major problem. Even if reformatories had been built on every street corner, it is unlikely that they could have done much to stabilize the effects of immigration, urban growth, ideological change, industrialization, and social mobility or to have served as a parent surrogate capable of producing the same kind of person as a nuclear family located in a small rural community. The means were totally inappropriate to the goals. The facts are, however, that we continue to face the same kinds of problems today. What we are still trying to find is a set of urban institutions that provide continuity, justice, and opportunity for the children of a pluralistic populace. It would be difficult to prove that we have done much better.

At any rate, the failure of the superparents was but one of many child-related problems that emerged during the 19th century. Consequently, by the end of that century, child savers were prepared to invest the problems of childhood with even greater rank and to give them an even more dramatic place in the whole of society. Perhaps the most striking way they did this was to create the juvenile court.

Creation of the juvenile court

The first juvenile court was established in Illinois in 1899. Pressures for its inauguration had been building up for years. But, when the step was finally taken, it marked a turning point that was no less significant than when the severity of punishment was reduced and the first institutions were created at the end of the 18th century. The juvenile court, in fact, was to become an even more powerful superparent, not only in concept but in actual practice. The following are some of the factors, along with the failure of institutions, that led to the development of a special court just for children.

The rights of children

Along with efforts to control closely and to mold children, the discovery of childhood was also characterized by efforts to limit their exploitation. The 19th century was marked by a continuation of these efforts although by present standards they were limited. Prior to the Civil War, several states had passed laws requiring that children attend school, that those under 12 be prohibited from employment, and that the work day of a child over 12 be limited to ten hours. Although such laws were supposed to provide some protection for the young, they proved largely unworkable. Employers ignored them; many children worked rather than attending school; and parents even joined in circumventing the law. Lower-class children, however, were the ones most likely to be exploited. While hard work was considered morally desirable by most people, it was the poorer classes who found the employment of children, to the exclusion of school, an economic necessity. The reality of circumstance in an entrepreneurial and capitalistic society kept tham at a disadvantage (Bremner, 1971, I:559).

As the country industrialized, child employment went up, not down. According to the census of 1870, one out of every eight children was employed, but by 1900 the figure had risen to one out of six. The greatest increases came in industry: One third of all workers in Southern mills, for example, were children, more than half of them between the ages of 10 and 13. Furthermore, over half of the children in industry were the children of immigrants. Such work, in short, fell heavily upon the poor, generating references to "cannibalism," "child slavery," and "slaughter of the innocents" by critics of child labor (Bremner, 1970, II:601–604).

Apparently, some middle-class consciences were pricked because a crusade against child labor gathered steam, led by lawyers, social workers, various charitable groups, and even some industrialists. By 1899, the same year the juvenile court was created, 28 states had passed laws regulating child labor. Significantly, this crusade seems to have been spawned by the same conditions that led to the creation of the juvenile court: (1) the fact that poor and immigrant children were the victims of existing laws and practices; (2) the existence of working conditions in factories that were similar to those found in reformatories; and (3) the growing belief that the prolongation and protection of childhood was essential to human progress. Even though by present standards the laws controlling child labor were minimal—applying only to manufacturing, not to agricultural and other forms of employment, and setting the minimum age of employment at 12 years—they seem to have been a part of the overall context of child reform in which the juvenile court was created.

Of perhaps even greater significance is the fact that a few court decisions began to appear in the late 1800s which attempted to set limits on the power of the state to assume the parental role. In light of current happenings, perhaps the most provocative decision was that of the *People* v. *Turner*, which was handed down in 1870 (Cf. Bremner, 1970, II:485–487). A boy by the name of Daniel O'Connell had been incarcerated in the Chicago Reform School under an Illinois law which specified that children under 16 found to be "vagrant . . . destitute of proper parental care or . . . growing up in mendicancy, ignorance, or vice" could be confined until they were reformed or reached the age of 21. Daniel's father sought to have him released.

Mr. Justice Thornton, writing the majority opinion, ordered Daniel discharged from custody. "The disability of minors," he wrote, "does not make slaves or criminals of them. . . . Even criminals cannot be imprisoned without due process of law. . . . Why should minors be imprisoned for misfortune? Destitution of proper parental care, ignorance, idleness, and vice are misfortunes, not crimes" (*People* v. *Turner*, 55 Ill. 280).

Court decisions in other states had opposite outcomes, permitting legal authorities to continue imprisoning children for truancy, vagrancy, and destitution so that the O'Connell decision did not represent legal thinking. Nonetheless, what was important was the growing number of cases questioning past practices and legal rules. Pressures were mounting to write laws and to establish procedures which spelled out more clearly the rights of children as persons in their own right.

The rights of juvenile criminals

In much the same vein, a number of court decisions and new laws helped to set limits on the treatment of children charged with crime (Cf. Bremner, 1970, II:485–501). In 1870, Boston began holding separate court hearings for juveniles under 16 as did New York in 1877. Massachusetts also passed a law in 1869 requiring that agents of the State Board of Charities should attend the trials of children to protect their interests and make recommendations to the judge (Caldwell, 1961:400). The history of the last part of the 19th century is also filled with protests over the continued confinement of children of all ages with presumably hardened criminals. "You cannot take a boy of tender years," said the warden of Joliet State Penitentiary, "and lock him up with thieves, drunkards, and half-crazy men of all classes and nationalities without teaching him lessons in crime" (Cf. Platt, 1969:132).

Most of the outcries came from the northern states, because in the South the reformatory movement with all its failures had never caught on. Children were still being tried as criminals and confined in unspeakably bad prisons. The result was the development of a racial double standard: White children were often pardoned while black ones were either imprisoned or leased out to railroads and other industries as cheap sources of labor. Reform schools in the South did not even start there until after 1900 (Cf. Bremner, 1970, II:443–448).

At any rate, these and other factors led to a more elaborate framework for approaching destitution and delinquency among children. The last charge apparently was led by women (Lathrop, 1925). In 1883, the

Chicago Women's Club engaged in an effort to improve jail conditions and the general treatment of criminals. But, when they began to visit local lockups, they were horrified to find that these places held a significant number of young children. Consequently, the focus of their efforts changed. After first trying to provide schooling and other amenities for confined children, they were ultimately led to a more radical step; namely, the creation of a special court and set of correctional procedures just for children. In 1895, the club had drafted a bill for a juvenile court but dropped it after their legal advisor questioned its constitutionality. This action was perceived by the women as a defeat, but, rather than resulting in failure, it caused a number of other influential people to join in support—clergymen, lawyers, judges, and prison wardens. Consequently, when the Illinois Conference of Charities met in 1898, its sole topic was children. After considering a number of issues, a new juvenile court act was drafted by the conference. The Chicago Bar Association then threw its support behind the act, and the Illinois legislature passed it.

Briefly, the new act contained the following provisions (Cf. Revised Statutes of the State of Illinois, 1899:225–259):

1. The act was to apply only to children under the age of 16.
2. Circuit and county courts were empowered to hold separate hearings for juveniles.
3. These courts were given power over dependent and neglected as well as delinquent children.
4. Any reputable person knowing of a delinquent or neglected child could file a petition with the court.
5. Upon the filing of a petition, the child's parent or guardian would be summoned to appear and to produce the child. Failing to do so, they could be held in contempt.
6. One or more "discreet" persons were to be appointed as unpaid probation officers to investigate the case, to represent the child, and to supervise the child, if directed by the court, before and after trial.
7. If a child was judged to be dependent or neglected, he or she could be committed to an accredited institution, public or private, or to some person of good moral character.
8. If a child were found delinquent, he or she would be left under the supervision of a probation officer in his or her own home, could be placed in another home, could be sent to a private institution, a county industrial school, or to a state reformatory.

9. Legal authorities were empowered to hold a child until age 21. Institutional authorities could parole the child before that time if the court agreed.
10. No child under 12 could be committed to an adult jail or police station. If a child was sentenced to an adult institution, he or she had to be kept in a separate building.
11. A board of six "reputable inhabitants" in each county were to be appointed to inspect all institutions receiving children at least once a year.

In short, this new Illinois law reaffirmed the traditional concept of *parens patriae* and for the first time located responsibility for official action in a special legal body. Prior to this time there had been no such centralization of authority. Furthermore, because the court was much broader in concept than the reformatory, it was to become a new and more powerful substitute parent. Indeed, the Illinois law was to be "literally construed to the end . . . that the care, custody, and discipline of a child shall approximate . . . that which should be given by its parents" (Revised Statutes of Illinois, 1899, Sec. 21). Because the court was empowered to take a child from an unfit home, it need not wait until he is "in jails, bridewells, and reformatories after he has become criminal in habits and tastes, but [can] seize upon the first conditions of neglect or delinquency" (Report of the Chicago Bar Association Committee, October 28, 1899. Cf. Platt, 1969:138–139).

The first juvenile court was hailed, almost universally, as a landmark in the treatment of children. Since its inception, in fact, it has become a dominant force in the lives of 20th century American children, especially those who do not fit the ideal image of childhood or those who have violated the criminal law. Within 25 years after the Illinois Court was created, juvenile courts were established in every state but two. Today, no state or territory is without one.

Summary and conclusions

The events of the 19th century and the creation of the juvenile court are significant in two ways: (1) in terms of their implications for the status of children; and (2) in terms of their implications for understanding the way society is organized to control and raise children.

Status of children

Despite the enthusiasm with which the juvenile court was greeted, it is obvious that its significance lay, not in the fact that it radically altered the prevailing status of children, but that it gave formal sanction to that status and provided a new set of legal institutions for dealing with it. For the first time, the place of children in society was unmistakably and officially defined as different from that of adults: The age parameters of childhood were set forth more carefully; the state's role in the care of children was clarified and strengthened; a special set of legal rules was written to define what constituted deviation from an ideal concept of childhood; a new judicial system was organized to implement and enforce these rules; and particular groups of persons and organizations were designated to assume the surrogate parental role for those children judged delinquent. Underlying all of these developments was a philosophy suggesting that because of their dependence children were to be given special care, not punishment, even those who had violated the criminal law. Thus, by defining childhood in this way, society also defined and invented delinquency.

Anthony Platt (1969; 1971; 1974), whose pioneering history of the first Illinois court is uniquely valuable, prefers to interpret these developments in Marxian terms. The primary goal of 19th century child saving, he says, was not the welfare of children but the maintenance of control by a group of middle- and upper-class child savers who had been co-opted into securing the existing political and economic order. "The child savers," he maintains, "were concerned not with championing the rights of the poor against exploitation by the ruling classes but rather integrating the poor into the established social order and protecting 'respectable' citizens from the 'dangerous classes' " (1971:ix).

There is much in late 19th century history to support Platt's view: the warehousing of poor and immigrant children in houses of refuge and reformatories; the exploitation of children in capitalist industries; or the tendency to equate poverty with vice. Such evidence notwithstanding, a Marxian interpretation probably does not do justice to the events of history. If there is anything to the notion that American behavior toward children was a reflection of cultural changes that had been going on in Western civilization for centuries, then some heed has to be paid to the total context of those changes, not just to the economic and the political. Though we now find ourselves at intellectual odds, if not morally repelled, by the beneficent presumptuousness of 19th century child savers, it is important to recognize that this presumptuousness arose out of a history of child infanticide, abandonment, sexual and economic exploitation, and general indifference. As recently as a century or two before, American colonists had been inclined to blame the innate depravity of the child for sin and to punish him or her severely. Now,

Americans were tending to externalize blame and to seek "treatment," not retribution. A few people were even beginning to think that children had rights—a far cry from the time when children were thought to exist in limbo in some formless state. Thus, while the new juvenile court was undoubtedly viewed as a new superparent primarily for poor and neglected as well as delinquent children, the economic and political factors that led to such a view were but two among a number of other institutional forces determining the status of children.

The organization of child raising

A second matter of importance has to do with the social function the juvenile court was expected to fulfill. In the 18th century, childhood was governed by a tightly knit constellation of three societal structures: home, church, and community. The primary goal of child-raising methods was to secure obedience to authority. Since crime and sin were viewed as synonymous, they were harshly punished. Poverty, on the other hand, was not equated with sin but was treated in other ways. Of special significance is the fact that the small communities of that period were organized to respond in a personal way, whether to the deviant child or to the destitute one who needed help. Personal and social responsibility were interrelated and a part of the total community fabric.

Under the impact of profound changes in the 19th century, all of this began to change. Cities and population grew, mobility increased, and the social control of small communities was dissipated. Simultaneously, it was assumed that deviant behavior was due more to bad families and to corrupt communities than to the influence of the devil. Crime was preventable and the offender redeemable. Partly as a result of these new beliefs and partly due to a loss in community cohesion, child-care institutions were invented to act as superparents and as community surrogates. They would substitute for tightly knit communities and produce the ideal child.

As community responsibility for destitute people declined and in the face of ever larger numbers of new immigrants, the population of child-care institutions became overloaded with the children of these people. The result was an increasing tendency to equate poverty and lawbreaking. A destitute child was almost as bad as a delinquent one and received much the same treatment. As a surrogate for the community, however, child-care institutions failed. They could not possibly have fulfilled all the responsibilities placed upon them.

In casting about for new methods of raising children who were poor, neglected, or delinquent, society created the juvenile court. While it might have chosen other alternatives, it did not. Hopefully, through a combination of legal and welfare activities, the juvenile court could become the new superparent. Thus, like the child-saving institutions before it, the court was given awesome responsibilities. For those children who fell through the institutional cracks of society, the juvenile court was to provide the answers. Since such faith was placed in it, the next chapter in the saga of child saving will be devoted to the growth and development of the court throughout the 20th century, particularly to the rules that defined its mandate.

References

Ariès, Philippe
    1962 *Centuries of Childhood* (Trans. by Robert Baldick). New York: Alfred A. Knopf.

Barnes, Harry Elmer
    1972 *The Story of Punishment* (2nd ed. rev.) Montclair, N.J.: Patterson-Smith.

Beccaria, Cesare
    1809 *Essay on Crime and Punishment* (American ed. trans by Stephen Gould). New York.

Bremner, Robert H. et al., (Eds.)
    1970 *Children and Youth in America: A Documentary History.* 2 vols. Cambridge: Harvard University Press.

Brockway, Z. R.
    1910 "The American reformatory prison system." Pp. 88–107 in Charles R. Henderson (Ed.), *Prison Reform and Criminal Law.* New York: Charities Publication Committee.

Caldwell, Robert G.
    1961 "The juvenile court: its development and some major problems." *Journal of Criminal Law, Criminology, and Police Science*, January–February, 51:493–511.

Hart, Hastings H.
    1910 *Preventive Treatment of Neglected Children.* New York: Russell Sage.

Henderson, Charles R. (Ed.)
    1910 *Prison Reform and Criminal Law.* New York: Charities Publication Committee.

Hofstader, Richard
  1959   *Social Darwinism in American Thought.* New York: G. Braziller.

Lathrop, Julia C.
  1925   "The background of the juvenile court in Illinois." Pp. 290–297, 320–330 in Julia Addams (Ed.), *The Child, the Clinic and the Court.* New York: New Republic.

McKelvey, Blake
  1968   *American Prisons.* Montclair, N.J.: Patterson-Smith.

Moody, Eleazar
  1715   "The school of good manners" Pp. 33–34 in Robert H. Bremner (Ed.), *Children and Youth in America.* Cambridge: Harvard University Press.

Platt, Anthony
  1969   *The Child Savers.* Chicago: Chicago University Press.

  1971   "Introduction to the reprint edition." *History of Child Saving in the United States,* National Conference of Charities and Conventions, Chicago, 1893. Montclair, N.J.: Patterson-Smith.

  1974   "The triumph of benevolence: the origins of the juvenile justice system in the United States." Pp. 356–389 in Richard Quinney (Ed.), *Criminal Justice in America.* Boston: Little, Brown.

Rothman, David J.
  1971   *The Discovery of the Asylum.* Boston: Little, Brown.

Sanders, Wiley B. (Ed.)
  1970   *Juvenile Offenders for a Thousand Years.* Chapel Hill: University of North Carolina Press.

Tocqueville, Alexis de
  1945   *Democracy in America* (Trans. by Henry Reeve). New York: Alfred A. Knopf (first published in 1835).

U.S. Bureau of the Census
  1955   *Current Population Reports, Population Estimates.* (Series P-25, No. 123).

Vold, George B.
  1958   *Theoretical Criminology.* New York: Oxford University Press.

Wadsworth, Benjamin
  1719   "The well-ordered family." Pp. 35–36 in Robert H. Bremner (Ed.), *Children and Youth in America.* Cambridge: Harvard University Press.

5

DELINQUENCY ACCORDING TO AMERICAN RULES

Our analysis of the history of childhood and the creation of the juvenile court indicates that if we are to understand delinquency we must recognize that it includes more than the illegal behavior of children. Acts that are frowned upon and punished at one point in history may escape with relatively little attention at another. Consequently, before we can make sense out of the behavior of children, we must know how society defines and governs that behavior. In this chapter, therefore, we will be concerned with *social rules* that have given delinquency its form and substance throughout most of the 20th century.

In order to assess fully the meaning of these rules, our review will concern itself with two things:

1. We will review the nature and function of social rules in general—the different kinds of rules that organize social interaction (of which laws are only one), what their purpose is, and how they operate in the maintenance of social order.

2. We will analyze the rules that defined delinquency as its invention spread throughout the country. We will seek to determine what it was that the various states sought to accomplish with children and how their efforts have been organized by the rules that were used.

The kinds of rules that characterized the first juvenile court experienced relatively little change during the first 60 years of this century. Our review, therefore, will be devoted largely to that period. Then, in a later chapter, we will analyze the striking series of rule changes that have occurred in recent years and are still ongoing. But, since they are the product of radical alterations in our explanations for delinquency and of recent disillusionment with the juvenile court, they will be better understood once these later parts of the book have been covered.

Nature and function of social rules

It has long been acknowledged that the one thing that most distinguishes human society from the social life of other animals is humankind's capacity to develop and transmit from generation to generation a vast array of social and technical arrangements called *culture*. Among the many elements of culture, social rules are of key importance. Speaking of that importance, Albert Cohen (1966:3) has noted that "If human beings are to do business with one another, there must be rules, and people must be able to assume that, by and large, these rules will be observed." Seen in these terms, we tend to think of a rule as being a formal written regulation that tells us what we should or should not, can or cannot, do in a given situation. We may think of the game of baseball and immediately agree that the rules forbid a batter from having more than three strikes or that the criminal law forbids one person from attacking another. Rules, as we usually think of them, possess three characteristics: They restrict us; they are assumed to provide the conditions for lawful conduct; and they set the boundaries beyond which behavior will not be tolerated.

The facts are, however, that besides restricting human interaction, rules also facilitate it. No matter what one may think of existing rules, one thing stands out: Organized human relationships depend upon them. Consider Cohen (1966:3) again:

> Whatever people want—food, clothing, shelter, sex, fame, contract bridge—they must get it by working with and through other people. They must take up positions in organized and complex social enterprises: families, clubs, schools, armies, political associations, ball teams. Each of these may be thought of as a way of fitting together the diverse actions of many people so that the work of the world gets done. . . . The first prerequisite to organized human activity is that there be *some* understandings, however arbitrary they may be.

The point is that life is organized in terms of various social games (Cohen, 1960). Each game operates according to a set of rules, some written, some unwritten. These rules specify a set of positions or roles—student, teacher, judge, delinquent, minister, or parishioner— and indicate what the player in each position is supposed to do in relation to the players in the other positions. If there is some social enterprise to which different individuals contribute in different ways, the participants see their contributions as hanging together and con- stituting an entity in its own right: a game of baseball, a course in sociology, a juvenile court hearing, a church service, or a prison racket. Rules also include criteria for evaluating the success of the total enter- prise or the contributions of the individual players. "In order to fit in," as Cohen (1960) puts it, "you have to know the rules; you have to 'have a program' so that you may know what position each man, including yourself, is playing; and you have to know how to keep score." You could not, for example, make sense out of the treatment of children in the Middle Ages, either as a participant or as an observer, unless you knew the rules that defined their treatment during that particular time.

In a very real sense, then, one's "self" is constituted of the positions one plays in various games. Other people are able to place us and have successful relations with us in terms of the positions we play and the positions they play. Our public reputation and self-respect depend upon how well we play our position and, if we are a part of a team game, how well our team as a whole does. If, on the other hand, we are like the proverbial man from Mars, we may have trouble playing vari- ous games. Not knowing the rules, we will have difficulty making much sense out of a third baseman charging toward the batter because he anticipates a bunt, a procter prowling up and down the aisles as stu- dents scribble frantically in their blue books, a priest genuflecting at the altar during mass, or an inmate who takes great pains to "bonaroo" his clothing. Only by knowing the rules of these games can we understand or be an effective part of them.

Because rules set the character of social games, it does not follow that there must be a blueprint for every action, nor that everyone needs to be satisfied with it. Every person and every social game—at home, school, business, or court—must tolerate a certain amount of ambiguity. Where there is dissatisfaction, there will be pressures for change because rules can be oppressive and can hinder rather than facilitate important human purposes. According to 20th century values, for example, some of the medieval rules governing the game of child raising were not desirable. Yet, with all this, there is some reason to stand in awe at the complex social games that are made possible by existing social rules. Whether we do or do not happen to approve of a particular rule or set of rules, there is no denying their centrality to organized human relationships.

Kinds of rules

Social games do not depend just upon formal written rules like laws. Legal regulations are but one kind of social rule. Rarely in our interaction with our families, friends, and associates, for example, do we have to take recourse to written orders or to police and referee in order to get along. We are able to live and work together because, in most cases, we willingly adhere to a host of unwritten rules—customary guides for behavior—that we have unthinkingly made a part of us as we grew and matured. There are informal, unwritten rules which suggest that one should not break into the front of a line of people waiting to check out their purchases at the grocery store, that one should be thoughtful and respectful toward one's mother, or that one should wipe one's greasy fingers on a napkin rather than on the tablecloth. Likewise, there are strongly held moral norms which set forth ways of doing and thinking which are considered essential to the welfare of society, such as not taking a human life or not having sexual intercourse with one's own child. We do not have to refer to the legal codes of the state to know that our society frowns upon these acts. Few of us, in fact, have ever actually read the laws that forbid them. Because of our socialization in this culture, we accept the legitimacy of such laws without much thought as to their specific content.

What all of this means is that there is a great deal of overlap between our informal customary rules and the formal rules that we have written into law. The term *social order* has been used, in fact, to describe in total all the kinds of rules—informal as well as formal—that serve to organize social relations whether they are actually a part of the law or not. Many premodern societies, in fact, have relied upon unwritten customs rather than laws for their sources of order. In modern society, however, there has been an increasing reliance upon formal laws to regulate behavior as older, more personal forms of social organization and the hold of custom have broken down. We have already seen, for instance, how 19th century Americans turned increasingly to the formal machinery of child-saving institutions, laws, and courts when the informal controls of the 18th century colonies began to deteriorate. A fundamental question that any society must face, therefore, is how best to define and organize rules for its young people. To what extent is there unity in the moral order so that any laws derived from it will receive widespread support? Are the members of a complex society like ours in agreement on what laws ought to govern juvenile conduct, or are the laws merely a reflection of those who have the power to write their particular morals into law? Such questions, as we will see, turn out to be highly important in considering the legal rules that define what delinquency is.

Enforcement of rules

A related matter has to do with the way rules are enforced. Rules have no meaning unless there is some way of insuring conformity to them, some way of rewarding the conformist and punishing or deterring the deviant. Ordinarily, punishments are applied to those who do not conform, and rewards are given to those who do. Every society possesses them.

Rewards and punishments, like rules, can be either formal or informal. A juvenile who steals, for example, can be punished formally by arrest and trial. But he can also be punished informally by friends and parents. His friends may say they no longer trust him and that they do not want to go around with him. His parents may "ground" him or refuse to let him use the car. Conversely, someone who observes the rules may receive both informal and formal rewards. The winner of the 100-yard dash in the Olympics not only receives the informal cheers of the crowd but a formal reward in the form of a gold medal. For lesser acts, a smile or an approving gesture from an important person can often be as rewarding as a letter of commendation.

The creation of the juvenile court, however, reflected a growing reliance upon formal methods of social control as a means of dealing with an increasingly complex and impersonal society. Yet, as we will see, this effort has been characterized by a great deal of ambivalence. On the one hand, there have always been those who would use the juvenile court as a means of last resort, only after all other alternatives have been exhausted. On the other hand, the juvenile court has often become a convenient place to refer children in the event of difficulty at home, in the neighborhood, or at school. As life in our urban centers has grown more detached and impersonal, many people have been quick to utilize the police and courts rather than struggling themselves to find ways for integrating problem youth into community and educational institutions.

To this must be added the fact that the classical concept of justice still carries a great deal of weight, particularly where criminal adolescents are concerned. Delinquency and punishment are inextricably linked in the minds of many people. To them, the best way to deal with deviants is to punish them. The young must learn that certain kinds of behavior will not be tolerated. Furthermore, a singular focus upon deviant children and how best to help them overlooks the possible social functions of punishment. What is done to public morale and to the maintenance of order if the deviant is not punished? What happens if it appears to other young people that the delinquent is kindly, rather than harshly, treated? Will morale suffer and will others be encouraged to deviate rather than to conform?

What all of this means, in short, is that the task of rule enforcement is not a simple one. Many questions arise for which there are no easy answers: What is the best way to enforce existing rules for children? Should those who deviate be punished, or are there other mechanisms that might be more effective? If legal machinery is desirable for the enforcement of some rules, such as those covering the commission of criminal acts, is such machinery also the most desirable for rules covering status offenses—drinking, truancy, or defying parents? Since the members of society are often torn over these issues, we should expect to find evidence of their ambivalence in the laws that have defined delinquency for much of this century.

Rules that define the official game of delinquency

The first juvenile court law, as we have seen, was written in Illinois in 1899. This law was broad and sweeping in character and gave the juvenile court jurisdiction over all children under the age of 16 who were in some kind of trouble. It provided for a special judge, a separate court room, and separate records, and it specified that court sessions were to be informal rather than formal, like a criminal trial. The actions of the court were not to be encumbered by official indictments, prosecutors, defense lawyers, a jury, and a sticky set of procedures. Rather, the processing of juveniles was to be like that which thoughtful parents might administer. Clearly, the official game of delinquency was to be played according to rules that were much different from those that governed the handling of adult criminals.

At the same time, there were some interesting paradoxes in the way this game was set up and operated. Its rules gave the juvenile court the power to deal, not just with young law violators, but with neglected, poor, and abused children as well. The reason, as the previous chapter indicated, was that 19th century child savers were not inclined to see much difference between the neglected child who was poor and un-supervised and the delinquent one who had actually violated the law. Since destitute children were but one short step from becoming law-breakers, there was little need to treat them differently. Furthermore, this kind of thinking has never died out but is a popular one today. In 1967, for example, the President's Commission on Law Enforcement and Administration of Justice (1967:56–57) stated that "Delinquents tend to come from backgrounds of social and economic deprivation. . . . It is inescapable that juvenile delinquency is directly related to conditions bred by poverty." Thus, while legal rules have charged the juvenile court with providing help rather than punishment, such rules have also been all-inclusive and indiscriminate with regard to whom the court clientele should be.

Delinquent children

The way these rules were supposed to apply to juvenile lawbreakers was stated in idealistic terms before the American Bar Association in 1909 by Julian W. Mack (1910:296–297) who was one of the first judges of the juvenile court in Chicago:

> Why isn't it just and proper to treat these juvenile offenders as we deal with the neglected children, as a wise and merciful father handles his own child whose errors are not discovered by the authorities? Why isn't it the duty of the State instead of asking merely whether a boy or a girl has committed the specific offense, to find out what he is, physically, mentally, morally, and then, if it learns that he is treading the path that leads to criminality, to take him in charge, not so much to punish as to reform, not to degrade but to uplift, not to crush but to develop, not to make him a criminal but a worthy citizen.

As Judge Mack's remarks indicate, those who invented the juvenile court saw themselves as decriminalizing the misconduct of children, not criminalizing it. They put an ideological stamp on the juvenile court that was to have lasting impact. First, delinquent behavior would be treated as something less than crime. Second, the court would inter-vene, not as a harsh and punitive monitor of evil conduct, but as a thoughtful, not unkindly, superparent. And, finally, the enforcement of rules would be characterized by help, not punishment; juveniles would be lent a hand rather than being forced into conformity. The purpose of the court was to discover a child's problems and then to correct them.

Other states were obviously charmed by these ideas because within 10 years 20 states and the District of Columbia had enacted similar juvenile court laws, and within 20 years all except 3 states had done so. Today, all states and territories and many foreign countries have similar laws (Caldwell, 1966:402–403). Though most of these laws were written in the first quarter of this century, little change has been introduced into them until very recently.

Of key significance is the way virtually every state defined delinquent behavior and the fact that most of them tended to follow the same general blueprint when they wrote their delinquency laws. Listed below is the South Dakota statue which is illustrative of that blueprint and which was not revised until 1968. It defined a delinquent as

> . . . any child who, while under the age of 18 years, violates any law of this state or any ordinance of any city or town of this state; who is incorrigible, or intractable by parents, guardian, or custodian; who knowingly associates with thieves, vicious, or immoral persons; who, without cause and without the consent of its parents, guardian, or custodian, absents itself from its home or place of abode; who is growing up in idleness or crime; who fails to attend school regularly without proper reason therefor, if of compulsory school age; who repeatedly plays truant from school; who does not regularly attend school and is not otherwise engaged in any regular occupation or employment but loiters and idles away its time; who knowingly frequents or visits a house of ill repute; who knowingly frequents or visits any policy shop or place where any gaming device is operated; who patronizes, visits, or frequents any saloon or dram shop where intoxicating liquors are sold; who patronizes or visits any public poolroom where the game of billiards or pool is being carried on for pay or hire; who frequents or patronizes any wineroom or dance hall run in connection with or adjacent to any house of ill fame or saloon; who visits, frequents, or patronizes, with one of the opposite sex, any restaurant or other place where liquors may be purchased at night after the hours of nine o'clock; who is found alone with one of the opposite sex in a private apartment or room of any restaurant, lodging house, hotel, or other place at nighttime or who goes to any secluded place or is found alone in such place with one of the opposite sex at nighttime with the evident purpose of concealing their acts; who wanders about the streets in the nighttime without being on any lawful business or lawful occupation, or habitually wanders about any railroad yards or tracks, or jumps or attempts to jump onto any moving train, or enters any car or engine without lawful authority; who writes or uses vile, obscene, vulgar, or indecent language, or

smokes cigarettes or uses tobacco in any form; who drinks intoxicating liquors on any street, in any public place, or about any school house, or at any place other than its own home; or who is guilty of indecent, immoral, or lascivious conduct (Cf. Rubin, 1974:1–2).

Few laws could be more all-inclusive and still be enforceable. The reason for this all-inclusiveness, however, was the endeavor by South Dakota legislators to anticipate almost any temptation to which a young person might be subjected and to insure that it would be covered. Yet, their efforts were not unique. Every state has labeled a variety of acts as delinquent which, if committed by an adult, would not be illegal. In 1959, Sussman (21–22) was able to count at least 34 such acts in different state laws. Many of them carefully listed these acts, as South Dakota did, while others merely used omnibus phrases such as "growing up in idleness and crime" or "in danger of leading an immoral life" to cover all of them. In either case, the net effect was the same. Officials were given great power to act against any behavior they considered disruptive or immoral on the presumption that it was harmful to children and might lead to crime.

Much can be learned about the intent of such laws by considering the kind of social game they proposed to set up for children. Earlier we noted that social games operate according to a set of rules and that these rules specify the social roles that different people are expected to play. Clearly, most state laws were intended not only to prohibit criminal conduct among children but to set forth and enforce a broad moral code for them. In the South Dakota law, for instance, only two or three lines were devoted to prohibiting the kinds of criminal acts for which adults can be charged; namely, those lines which state that a child should not violate "any law of this state or any ordinance of any city or town of this state." Otherwise, all of the remaining lines were devoted to describing *status offenses*—offenses that apply only to children.

This way of defining delinquent behavior indicates why it is, even now, that such behavior cannot be equated with criminal behavior. It covers much more ground than that. In virtually every case, state laws have represented an attempt to embody in formal language the modern concept of childhood. They have emphasized the dependent status of children and stressed the need to quarantine them from many activities in which adults are free to engage. It is true that these laws have concentrated on what children should *not* be, but, by turning them around, one can get a good picture of what legislators and other child savers have thought they should be. The list suggested by the South Dakota statute, for example, is amazingly like that drawn up in the child-raising manuals of the 18th and 19th centuries; namely, that the ideal child should be submissive to authority, obedient, hardworking, a good student, sober, chaste, circumspect in habit, language, and associates, and should otherwise avoid even the appearance of evil such as staying out late, wandering the streets, being alone with a person of the opposite sex, or playing in dangerous places like railroad yards. According to official rules, the child who avoids these acts and stays within the limits of his quarantine is playing the game of childhood appropriately. The one who commits them and violates his quarantine is delinquent.

This is not a very precise definition of delinquency and could include almost anyone, but it is the one that was intended. Advocates of the juvenile court simply did not set out to write a precise definition. Their goal, instead, was to legislate the morality of children so that the rules governing their conduct would be broader than the list covering adult behavior; otherwise, they could not insure that children would develop properly. And, because the announced goal of the court was help not punishment, they did not believe that well-meaning officials should be hampered by a host of legalistic regulations and practices. Rather, benevolence of attitude would triumph over any shortcomings in procedure (Platt, 1974).

The content of this benevolent ideology is well illustrated in the writings of early champions of the juvenile court. In 1910, Judge Harvey H. Baker (321) of the Boston Juvenile Court voiced the thinking of many of his contemporaries when he said that

> . . . the fundamental function of a juvenile court is to put each child who comes before it in a normal relation to society as promptly and as permanently as possible, and that while punishment is not by any means to be dispensed with, it is to be made subsidiary and subordinate to that function. . . . As far as practicable [children] shall be treated, not as criminals, but as children in need of aid, encouragement, and guidance. Proceedings against children . . . shall not be deemed to be criminal proceedings.

Dependent and neglected children

Attitudes toward, and the rules covering, dependent and neglected children were much the same. That such children were seen as being like delinquent ones is illustrated by the original Illinois statute (Cf. Bremner, 1971, II:507). "The words dependent and neglected child," it said,

shall mean any child who for any reason is destitute or homeless or abandoned; or dependent upon the public for support; or has not proper parental care or guardianship; or who habitually begs or receives alms; or who
is found living in any house of ill fame or with any vicious or disreputable
person; or whose home, by reason of neglect, cruelty, or depravity on the
part of its parents, guardian, or other person in whose care it may be, is an
unfit place for such a child; and any child under the age of eight years who
is found peddling or selling any article, or singing or playing any musical
instrument upon the street, or giving any public entertainment.

Besides noting that a dependent or neglected child might be homeless or destitute, this law described him or her in much the same way
that it and other laws also described the delinquent child. For example,
it noted that a "dependent" child is one who begs for alms, lives in a
house of ill fame, or lives with some vicious person. Yet, any difference
between this child and the "delinquent" one who frequents saloons,
loiters away his time, or stays out too late at night would seem to be
purely academic. For most of the century, there has been a tendency to
equate the two types of children probably because of the persistance of
the 19th century belief that poverty and neglect are inevitable precursors of criminal behavior. That is why, in attempting to understand
both the meaning of delinquency and the treatment of children, this
broad equation of types must be kept in mind.

At the same time, one must also keep in mind another important
reason why dependent and neglected children were brought under the
umbrella of the juvenile court. Until the 19th century, children were
treated as subservient subjects of parental and family government. They
had no separate legal status of their own. In 1874, for example, the
American Society for the Prevention of Cruelty to Animals was confronted with a case of cruelty to a little girl who had been beaten repeatedly and tormented by a foster mother. To the surprise of this society, it was found that the child had no protection under the law unless
someone took up her cause and until the guilt of her foster mother could
be estalished in an adult court (McCrea, 1910). Since no organization
existed for the prevention of cruelty to children, new state laws charged
the juvenile court with seeing that children who are hungry, forgotten,
and abused are given protection and care.

The need for such care was, and still is, obvious (Chase, 1976).
Recently, in Los Angeles, a three-year-old boy was beaten to death by
his father for wetting his pants. The child's five-year-old brother told
the police that his father "had hit and kicked his little brother and then

threw him into the commode head first" (*Los Angeles Times,* January 14, 1974). In another case, a steel worker was found guilty of manslaughter for beating a ten-month-old daughter to death. "Authorities said X-ray pictures showed that the dead baby's head looked like a broken eggshell" (*Los Angeles Times,* January 6, 1974). In such cases, where brutality and death are involved, parents may be tried in criminal courts, but, even then, the juvenile court is usually charged with determining whether such parents have the right to keep any other children they may have.

Likewise, in less spectacular cases of abuse or neglect, where parental crime is not involved, the juvenile court must decide whether parents are fit to keep their children. In some instances, the issues seem to be reasonably clear-cut. In 1974, for example, one couple was arrested after investigators found their five children, ages one to nine, living in a home where human excrement, rats, rotting food, and clothing were scattered throughout. None of the school-age children, moreover, had ever been sent to school (*Los Angeles Times,* February 2, 1974). Consequently, the court took the children from the parents and placed them in foster homes.

Few people have questioned the need for legal protection for children in cases like these. Where some serious questions have been raised, however, is over the fact that legal rules traditionally have not drawn very sharp distinctions between dependent or neglected and delinquent children. In 1914, Flexner and Baldwin (x–xi) argued forcefully that the juvenile court should not have jurisdiction over the children who are not lawbreakers:

> For many years [poverty] was regarded as a valid reason for judicial interference with the family status. It is a sad commentary that we should still be wrestling with this question in our courts. The presence of the dependent or destitute child in court, presenting family or home conditions remediable simply by relief measures, is an injustice to the court, and a worse injustice to the child and to the family.

But comments like this attracted little attention. Instead, views like those expressed by Judge Edward Schoen of the Newark, New Jersey, juvenile court in 1921 were the popular ones:

> The field of the juvenile court is the maladjusted child, whom the State is in duty bound to protect, correct, and develop; and the duty of this tribunal is to follow up the case by ascertaining all the facts and circumstances in the life of the child, to determine in what particulars that child has been deprived of essentials for a full moral and physical development.

> And if, as is common experience, it is found that certain essentials are lacking in the environment in which the child is being reared, the State, *in loco parentis,* acting through its instrumentality, the juvenile court, must provide the essentials of which the child has thus far been deprived.

Court practices have also been criticized from time to time because they have seemed contrary to our older classical concept of justice. If a person is not really criminal, he or she should not even be in court, let alone be confined in an institution with proven offenders. Yet, these criticisms have often missed the point: According to the fundamental premises upon which legal rules for children were drawn, the failure to distinguish between neglected and delinquent children is not bad. The juvenile court was set up to treat the needs of the young, whatever they may be, not to be particularly concerned with the acts that bring them to court. Whether young persons are continuously truant from school, refuse to obey their parents, are thieves, or are simply destitute and lacking supervision, they have serious problems and require the court's care. Thus, if every official is doing his or her job, labels do not matter. It is the quality of treatment that matters. Furthermore, if the juvenile court were not present to protect the legal rights of children, they would have none.

All of this has meant that for two thirds of this century the mystique of the juvenile court retained its hold. Most citizens apparently had positive feelings about it; school personnel, community officials, and beleagured parents supported the court's great powers because young troublemakers could be taken off their hands; lawyers remained ignorant of, and shied away from, court proceedings, and the constitutionality of juvenile court laws and practices were sustained almost universally by the decisions of various state appeal and supreme courts (Paulsen and Whitebread, 1974:4). There is little evidence that the benevolent ideology of the child-saving movement had anything but widespread support (Rosenheim, 1962). In recent years, however, dissatisfaction has mounted and important changes are underway. But we will leave those changes for discussion later on, since they are the product of very recent theoretical and cultural changes which we must review in later chapters before they will have much meaning.

Summary and conclusions

In summary, the juvenile court was based on the benevolent assumption that it could save all children in danger of slipping through the institutional and moral cracks of society, not just the serious lawbreakers. Because it has represented a formal attempt to enforce the modern concept of childhood, official rules have placed far more attention upon the capacity of the court to act as a surrogate parent than as a criminal court. But, since the status of children is broad and ambiguous, delinquency laws and court practices have likewise been ambiguous.

It was this ambiguity which at mid-century led one eminent lawyer-sociologist, Paul Tappan (1949:30), to suggest that "Delinquency has little specific behavioral content either in law or in fact." Because juvenile court philosophy has traditionally emphasized a child's background more than his conduct and because its procedures have not been systematized, about all that can be said is that "The juvenile delinquent is a person who has been adjudicated as such by a court of proper jurisdiction." (Tappan, 1949:30). Indeed, that definition still tends to hold. In 1974, the Office of Youth Development of the United States Department of Health, Education, and Welfare defined official delinquency as follows (1974(6):

> Juvenile delinquency cases are those referred for acts defined in the statutes of the State as the violation of a State law or municipal ordinance by children or youth of juvenile court age, or for conduct so seriously antisocial as to interfere with the rights of others or to menace the welfare of the delinquent himself, or of the community.

The Office of Youth Development also defines dependency and neglect as it has been defined throughout this chapter (1974:6):

> Dependency and neglect cases cover neglect or inadequate care on the part of parents or guardians; e.g., lack of adequate care or support resulting from death, absence, or physical or mental incapacity of the parents, abandonment or desertion, abuse or cruel treatment, and improper or inadequate condition in the home.

What all of this means in terms of making sense out of the official game of delinquency is that we should not expect to find precision in our past history where there has been none. Rather, imprecision was intended. Because both official rules and activities have been premised upon a sweeping and benevolent ideology, a person is correct in assuming that they have been intended to encompass any childhood behavior or condition thought to be a problem, not just a small segment of either.

The picture is now changing. As we trace the various theories of delinquency in Part Three of this book, we will find an increasing tendency to redefine what delinquent behavior is. Then, in Part Four, when we review the way society reacts to delinquency, we will also discover evidence of change. Hence, in the final chapters of the book, we will return to the subject of rules in order to bring ourselves totally up to date and to anticipate what the future might hold.

References

Baker, Harvey H.
   1910   "Procedure of the Boston juvenile court." Pp. 318–327 in Hastings H. Hart (Ed.), *Preventive Treatment of Neglected Children*. New York: Russell Sage.

Bremner, Robert H., et al. (Eds.)
   1970   *Children and Youth in America: A Documentary History* (Vol. II). Cambridge: Harvard University Press.

Caldwell, Robert G.
   1966   "The juvenile court: its development and some major problems." Pp. 399–423 in Rose Giallombardo (Ed.), *Juvenile Delinquency: A Book of Readings*. New York: John Wiley.

Chase, Naomi Feigelson
   1976   *A Child is Being Beaten*. New York: McGraw-Hill.

Cohen, Albert K.
   1960   "Delinquency as culturally patterned and group-supported behavior." Paper delivered at the Twelfth Annual Training Institute for Probation, Parole and Institutional Staff, San Francisco.
   1966   *Deviance and Control*. Englewood Cliffs, N.J.: Prentice Hall, Inc.

Flexner, Bernard and Baldwin, Roger N.
   1914   *Juvenile Courts and Probation*. New York: Century.

Mack, Julian
   1910   "The juvenile court as a legal institution." Pp. 293–317 in Hastings H. Hart (Ed.), *Preventive Treatment of Neglected Children*. New York: Russell Sage.

McCrea, Roswell C.
   1910   "Societies for the prevention of cruelty to children." Pp. 194–209 in Hastings H. Hart (Ed.), *Preventive Treatment of Neglected Children*. New York: Russell Sage.

Office of Youth Development
   1974   *Juvenile Court Statistics, 1973*. Washington, D.C.: Department of Health, Education, and Welfare.

Paulsen, Monrad G. and Whitebread, Charles H.
   1974   *Juvenile Law and Procedure*. Reno: National Council of Juvenile Court Judges.

Platt, Anthony
    1974   "The triumph of benevolence: the origins of the juvenile justice sys-
            tem in the United States." Pp. 356–389 in Richard Quinney (Ed.),
            Criminal Justice in America. Boston: Little, Brown.

President's Commission on Law Enforcement and Administration of Justice
    1967   *The Challenge of Crime in Free Society.* Washington, D.C.: U.S. Gov-
            ernment Printing Office.

Rosenheim, Margaret K. (Ed.)
    1962   *Justice for the Child: The Juvenile Court in Transition.* New York: Free
            Press.

Rubin, Ted
    1974   "Transferring responsibility for juvenile noncriminal misconduct
            from juvenile courts to nonauthoritarian community agencies."
            Phoenix: Arizona Conference on Delinquency Intervention (Mimeo).

Schoen, Edward
    1921   *Participant remarks. Proceedings of the Conference on Juvenile Court
            Standards.* U.S. Children's Bureau Publication, No. 97. Washington,
            D.C.: U.S. Government Printing Office.

Sussman, Frederick
    1959   *Law of Juvenile Delinquency.* New York: Oceana Publications.

Tappan, Paul
    1949   *Juvenile Delinquency.* New York: McGraw-Hill.

part two

EXTENT AND NATURE OF DELINQUENT BEHAVIOR

Introduction: How delinquent behavior is measured

At the very time when the first really serious questions were being raised about the sweeping powers of the juvenile court—i.e., during the late 1960s and early 1970s—concern over rising crime and delinquency rates reached a peak. For several years, evidence from official sources had indicated that both were on the rise. As a result, a significant segment of the populace responded positively to a body of rhetoric suggesting that the nation was in dire peril. As Bittner (1970:48) described it:

> A figure of speech that has recently gained a good deal of currency is the "war on crime." The intended import of the expression is quite clear. It is supposed to indicate that the community is seriously imperiled by forces bent on its destruction and calls for the mounting of efforts that have claims on all available resources to defeat the peril. The rhetorical shift from "crime control" to "war on crime" signifies the transition from a routine concern to a state of emergency. We no longer face losses of one kind or another from the depredation of criminals; we are in imminent danger of losing everything!

Beliefs in the imminence of peril were reinforced by the FBI's annual account of traditional crime. During the decade of the 1960s, crimes of violence (murder, forcible rape, robbery, and aggravated assault) per 100,000 population went up 104 percent, while crimes against property (burglary, larceny, and auto theft) went up 123 percent. Overall, the

113

total number of these seven offenses per 100,000 went up 120 percent (FBI., 1969:4). Furthermore, these official statistics implied that if a crime war were to be waged it would have to be directed against the nation's youth. According to the President's Commission on Law Enforcement and Administration of Justice (1967:44), more burglaries, larcenies, and auto thefts were being committed by young people ages 15 to 17 years than by any other group. Fifteen-year-olds were arrested most often, with 16-year-olds a close second. For crimes of violence, those from 18 to 20 were the most responsible, with the second largest group in the 21–24 age range.

Many juveniles were arrested, of course, for acts far less serious than those just mentioned. In 1966, it was estimated that between one and one-half million persons under 18 were arrested, with approximately half of them being referred to court for trial. Overall, the evidence indicated that delinquency was at a very low ebb before the onset of adolescence, rose sharply after its onset, hit its peak at around 16 or 17, and then declined sharply. Obviously, traditional forms of crime, as well as status offenses, were very much a youthful phenomenon.

Coupled with the campus protests and race riots of the 1960s, this frightening crime information evoked a vision of millions of Americans sitting crouched behind locked doors, fearful that if they ventured forth they would become victims of their own criminally disposed children. Will we, asked the National Commission on the Causes and Prevention of Violence (1969:xxv) have "to expect the establishment of the 'defensive city,' the modern counterpart of the fortified medieval city?" Will we "witness frequent and widespread crime, perhaps out of police control?" While such questions are noteworthy in their own right, they point to another issue that is even more central to our full understanding of delinquency; namely, that sentiments favoring a war on criminals are often opposed to sentiments inherent in the benevolent philosophy of the juvenile court. Our recent past, in other words, has been marked by contradictory trends.

On one hand, there has been a growing intellectual and legal resistance to the all-embracing character of juvenile court laws and practices. The benevolent assumptions upon which they are based have been questioned and efforts made to reduce their scope and power. Yet, on the other hand, mounting public fears over the rising crime and delinquency rates of the young suggest, to some people at least, that delinquents should be subjected to greater, not lesser, legal controls. Perhaps the idea of a strong juvenile court with a wide jurisdictional net is not so bad after all. Perhaps juvenile criminals should be treated like adult criminals. Whatever is done, society should get tougher, not more lenient.

Given these contradictory trends, it is obvious that we must pay attention to the extent of delinquent behavior at the present time, as well as to the past. Are great portions of America's children criminal violators? Are they becoming more delinquent? Are they a threat to the very foundations of society?

Such questions are not easily answered. Valid information on the amounts and trends of delinquent behavior have been difficult to obtain because much of it has gone officially undetected. Moreover, official police and court statistics have often been as much a reflection of what officials do as they have been of what delinquents do. In the recent past, however, important new sources of information have been developed and added to official accounts. In this part of the book, therefore, we will review these new sources of information as well as official accounts:

In *Chapter 6,* we will analyze official accounts of delinquent behavior derived from the records of the police and the juvenile courts.

In *Chapter 7,* we will utilize secret self-report accounts of delinquent behavior derived from young people themselves.

Then, in *Chapter 8,* we will utilize accounts from the victims of criminal acts in order to obtain yet a third estimate of the amount and character of crime.

As can be imagined, these three accounts differ markedly. But, by triangulating on delinquent behavior, we should be able to get a reasonably good fix upon it, just as the surveyor does when he attempts to locate a particular position by viewing it from different angles. Once this is done, we will be able to draw some relatively good conclusions about current trends in delinquent behavior, its extent, and its social location.

References

Bittner, Egon
  1970   *The Functions of the Police in Modern Society*. Publication No. 2059. Washington, D.C.: U.S. Government Printing Office.

Federal Bureau of Investigation
   1969   *Crime in the United States: Uniform Crime Reports—1968*. Washington,
          D.C.: U.S. Government Printing Office.

National Commission on the Causes and Prevention of Violence
   1969   *Crimes of Violence* (Vol. II). Washington, D.C.: U.S. Government
          Printing Office.

President's Commission on Law Enforcement and Administration of Justice
   1967   *The Challenge of Crime in a Free Society*. Washington, D.C.: U.S.
          Government Printing Office.

6

OFFICIAL ACCOUNTS OF
DELINQUENT BEHAVIOR

There are two major sources of official information on the extent of delinquent behavior. The first comes from juvenile court statistics. Beginning in 1940, the Children's Bureau of the Department of Health, Education, and Welfare (HEW) began publishing estimates of the number of delinquency, neglect, and dependency cases that were being handled by the nation's juvenile courts. Later, in the 1960s, that task was taken over by the Office of Youth Development, HEW. Now, it has been shifted to the National Institute of Juvenile Justice and Delinquency Prevention which is a part of the Law Enforcement Assistance Administration.[1]

Delinquency cases

The Office of Youth Development estimated that over 1 million (1,143,700) delinquency cases, excluding traffic offenses, were handled by juvenile courts in 1973. However, because some children appeared in court more than once, the actual number of individuals involved

---

[1] At this writing, the NIJJDP has not published statistics for years subsequent to 1973. Therefore, this analysis is based on the last report issued by the Office of Youth Development (1974).

(986,000) was less than the number of court cases. Since the total child population, ages 10 through 17 years, was approximately 33.4 million in that year, the 986,000 children who appeared in court was not proportionally large: only 3 percent of the total. Furthermore, less than half of those who were listed as court cases (46 percent) were actually tried in court; the remaining 54 percent were handled unofficially. Hence, such figures do not appear particularly alarming although it must be remembered that official reports only count how many court cases there are in a given year, not how many times children appear in court throughout their entire childhood.

In terms of the trends about which the country has been so worried, however, the latest information indicates that the number of court cases has continued to rise. Between 1960 and 1973, the number of court delinquency cases increased by 124 percent—from 510,000 in 1960 to 1.14 million in 1973. Meanwhile, the number of children in the country increased by only about one third. This long-term pattern, which is displayed in Figure 6–1, then, does lend some support to the concerns that have been expressed.

It is also significant that the number of girls involved in delinquency cases is becoming a larger proportion of the total. In 1960, only 19 percent of all cases handled by the courts were females. By 1973, the figure had reached 26 percent. Between 1965 and 1973, girls' delinquency cases increased by 110 percent, whereas boys' cases increased by half that amount, 52 percent. In both cases, this growth in court cases was far greater than was the comparable growth in both populations.

This kind of official information is important because it does suggest that the juvenile courts are dealing with an increasing number of cases and because policy decisions, court budgets, and staffs are based upon it. Yet, it is of limited, even questionable value, as an accurate indicator of the level and trends of youth crime. In the first place, the Office of Youth Development reports do not even provide information on the types of offenses for which delinquents are referred to court. Probably because of the historical tendency to lump both criminal and status offenders together, no distinctions between these two types are even drawn in the official court data.

Even more fundamental, the number of juvenile court cases reported from year to year reflect the changing practices and policies of the courts and the police as well as the illegal acts of the young. In two different studies of a large number of police departments, for example, the proportion of juveniles who were actually referred to the juvenile court after

FIGURE 6–1
Trend in juvenile court delinquency cases and child population 10–17 years of age, 1957–1973 (semilogarithmic scale)

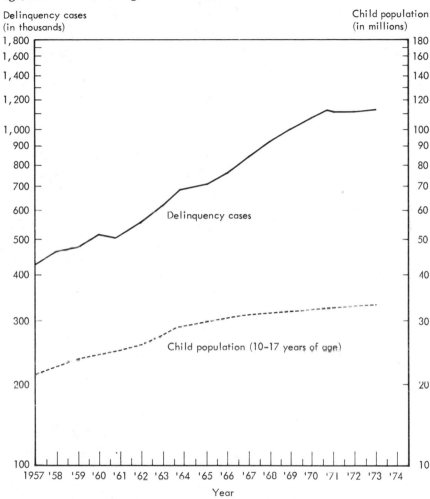

Source: Office of Youth Development, *Juvenile Court Statistics*, 1973:9.

having been apprehended for illegal acts varied from a low of only 18 percent in one department to a high of 98 percent in another, with the remaining departments lying somewhere in between (Goldman, 1969; Klein, 1970).

Such findings are confirmed by the *Uniform Crime Reports* compiled by the FBI which indicate that approximately half of all those juveniles who might become court cases after they are apprehended are actually handled entirely by the police and released (Compare FBI, 1967:110 with 1976:42). Yet, even this figure may underestimate the number of juveniles who are contacted by police since not all potential court cases are even brought to the police station where they might become a part of the official record. The reason is that the cop on the beat is also permitted to exercise some discretion in deciding whom he will bring in and, since most juveniles commit minor offenses, he often releases many. This conclusion is supported by Black and Reiss (1970:68) who found that only 15 percent of the encounters between police and juveniles actually result in arrest.

What this means is that the juvenile justice system acts like a large funnel, screening out significant numbers of individuals near the point of entry: First the police screen out large numbers of the children they apprehend, and then the courts repeat the process with the remainder. The actual number of children who are formally tried in court, therefore, is only a fraction of the total number who are apprehended. The presence of this heavy filtering process, moreover, makes it virtually impossible to determine what the relation is between the number of officially recorded court case and the actual rate at which children violate the law. A large, but unknown, number of delinquent acts never become a part of juvenile court statistics because officials are permitted to exercise a great amount of discretion in deciding who will become a part of them.

Dependency and neglect cases

Some of the same problems are inherent in trying to interpret the latest information on the number of dependency and neglect cases in the United States. The Office of Youth Development (1974) reported a total of 158,000 cases in 1973, an increase of 12 percent over 1972. Although the number of such cases is much smaller than the reported number of delinquency cases (1.1 million versus 158,000), this increase in dependency and neglect cases represents a sharp reversal of a general downward trend which began in 1967. Again, however, it is impossible to know with any precision what this increase means.

As with delinquency cases, no attempt was made to distinguish between cases of dependency and neglect in the federal reports, although technically they are much different things. In dependency cases, parents or guardians are presumably unable to care for their children through no fault of their own; while in neglect cases a deliberate failure, even cruelty or abuse, is implied. Furthermore, it is not possible to pinpoint the cause for the increase in reported cases or to know what the actual rates of dependency and neglect are. The increase may simply be due to greater attention being focused on children in need, or it may be due to a real increase in the numbers of these children. There is no way of knowing.

In short, while official information on the courts gives an estimate of the total number of cases being handled in the United States, it is not of much value in estimating the actual incidence of delinquent acts or of cases of dependency and neglect. If we are to glean more accurate information, therefore, we will have to turn to additional sources.

Official arrest rates

The second major source of *official* information on delinquent behavior is the *Uniform Crime Reports* issued yearly by the Federal Bureau of Investigation. The Uniform Crime Reporting Program was begun in 1930 and provides a national estimate of the criminal acts which come to the attention of the police. Today, several thousand law enforcement agencies, representing 93 percent of the total national population, voluntarily submit information to the *Uniform Crime Reports* (FBI, 1974:52). While, again, there are many reasons why it is not possible to know with scientific certainty what the accuracy of these reports is, they probably provide a more accurate official picture of the actual incidence of illegal acts than do court statistics. "Regardless of how rigorous the court . . . data are intended to be," said the National Commission on the Causes and Prevention of Violence (1969, II:14), "they are inherently less useful than police data in profiling the levels and trends of crime." Because the police have first official contact with any illegal event and because the juvenile justice system acts like a large filter, crimes reported to the police or arrests are more representative of the actual number of crimes committed than are cases tried in court.

The *Uniform Crime Reports* (1976:37) indicate that law enforcement agencies made an estimated 9.3 million arrests nationally during 1975, excluding traffic offenses.[2] As the arrest curve in Figure 6–2 indicates, the majority of these arrests involved young people. Prior to age 10, the

---

[2] Arrests, like court cases, do not measure the number of individuals involved in criminal acts since one person may be arrested several times during any given year. Mere arrest, moreover, does not measure conviction. Hence, while measuring police activity, these figures are an uncertain indicator of the actual amount of crime.

FIGURE 6–2
Arrest curve by age

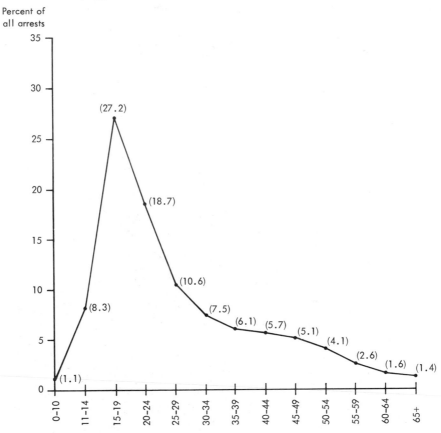

Source: FBI, *Uniform Crime Reports,* 1973:128–129.

arrest rate is low. Then it accelerates sharply until it reaches a peak for adolescents somewhere between ages 15 and 19, after which it decelerates rapidly and gradually wanes for people in the remaining phases of the life cycle. Arrest rates in 1975 were typically the same: 26 percent of all arrestees were under age 18; 42 percent under 21; and 57 percent under 25. More arrests were made of children ages 11–14 than were made of adults ages 30–34 (FBI, 1976:41).

Index crimes

More significant, perhaps, is the finding that juveniles under 18 years of age who constitute less than 20 percent of the population were arrested for 44 percent of the seven serious felonies that comprise the FBI's Crime Index Offenses (FBI, 1976:186):

1. *Criminal homicide.*   Willful murder and manslaughter by negligence.
2. *Forcible rape.*   Rape or attempted rape by force.
3. *Robbery.*   Stealing or attempted stealing by force.
4. *Aggravated assault.*   Assault with intent to kill or do severe bodily injury.
5. *Burglary.*   Breaking and entering to commit a felony or theft.
6. *Larceny-theft.*   Any theft involving force and violence except auto theft, forgery, and so on.
7. *Motor vehicle theft.*   Any theft or attempted theft of a motor vehicle.

Table 6–1 provides a detailed breakdown of the arrests for these offenses. It will be observed that juveniles are not as likely as adults to be arrested for such violent crimes as murder, rape, and aggravated assault, although they do account for 35 percent of all arrests for robbery. Thus, when arrests for violent crimes are combined, juveniles account for about one quarter of the total (23 percent).

Property crimes are another matter. Juveniles are arrested for 48 percent of all property crimes; 55 percent of the arrests for motor vehicle theft; 53 percent for burglary; and 46 percent for larceny. In short, the proportion of all arrests for Index crimes which are juvenile (44 percent) is more than double the proportion of all people who are juvenile (20 percent).

TABLE 6–1
Juvenile arrests for index crimes, 1975

Arrest offenses	All ages	Juveniles under 18	Males under 18	Females under 18
Total arrests				
Number	1,637,296	713,016	581,904	132,016
Percent	100	43.5	35.5	8.0
		Percent of all arrests		
Criminal homicide				
Murder and nonnegligent				
manslaughter	14,269	9.6	8.7	0.9
Manslaughter by negligence	2,481	11.7	9.8	1.9
Forcible rape	19,018	17.8	17.6	0.2
Robbery	116,421	35.0	32.4	2.6
Aggravated assault	170,483	18.1	15.2	2.9
Burglary—breaking or entering	382,500	52.7	50.0	2.7
Larceny—theft	827,743	45.8	32.5	13.3
Motor vehicle theft	104,381	54.5	50.5	4.0

Based on 5,974 agencies; 1975 estimated population, 145,719,972.
Source: FBI, *Uniform Crime Reports*, 1976:187.

It is the yearly publication of official figures like these which fuel public fear and which illustrate the tensions inherent in our traditional stance toward the young. Despite the notion inherent in the invention of the juvenile court that by attending to the moral, economic, and psychological needs of the young crime could be prevented, these figures suggest either that the assumption is false or that the juvenile court has not been very succcessful. Society swings from one ambivalent position to the other in attempting to choose between the interests of youthful criminals and the interests of those who are their victims.

Arrests for nonindex crimes

Besides the seven index offenses listed above, the *Uniform Crime Reports* furnish information on a long list of additional crimes extending all the way from arson to curfew violation. In Table 6–2, the nonindex offenses for which juveniles are arrested most commonly are shown. Juveniles account for all curfew violations and runnings away, since both are status offenses applicable only to children. Beyond these offenses, juvenile arrest rates for vandalism (65 percent), arson (54 percent), liquor law violations (41 percent), dealing in stolen property (33 percent), and violations of drug laws (24 percent) are high. While such violations are distinctively juvenile in the sense that they require little sophistication, others are distinctively adult. In 1975, for example, juveniles accounted for only 13 percent of the arrests for forgery and counterfeiting, 4 percent of the arrests for fraud, 10 percent of the arrests for embezzlement, and 5 percent of the arrests for prostitution and commercial vice.

There are other things about arrest statistics that also merit attention. One of the most pronounced has to do with the use of drugs. While society has been terribly concerned over heroin, marijuana, and pill use among young people, every official index indicates that this kind of drug use is far less serious than the use of the most common drug of all, alcohol. First, in terms of the overall magnitude of the problem, there were 919,324 arrests for drunkenness and 743,152 for drunken driving, as contrasted to only about 424,442 for all other drug violations. Second, evidence indicates that alcohol use is more of an adult than juvenile problem. Only 4 percent of those arrested for drunkeness in 1975 and 2 percent of those arrested for drunken driving were juveniles. Finally, alcohol use is more of a problem among juveniles than the use of other drugs. Forty-one percent of all those arrested for "liquor law violations"—drinking under age or buying liquor illegally—were juveniles. By contrast, only 24 percent of those arrested for use of all other drugs were juveniles.

By every official index, then, alcohol is our most serious drug problem. Yet, if one were to rely of popular accounts of it, one would not gain that impression. The reason, of course, is that alcohol use is far more acceptable socially than are other drugs, particularly among adults whose opinions count the most. Consequently, it is the way the use of drugs is defined, and not the actual incidence of use, that determines whether it will be defined as a problem. That is why an understanding of social rules, both formal and informal, is so important. It is the way social behavior is defined, not the actual nature of that behavior, that is most important.

Arrests of girls

The arrest of girls is of increasing interest because of the widespread effort to achieve greater equality for females and because girls have received very little attention in the delinquency literature. Two kinds of information, therefore, are useful: (1) information which contrasts the number of girl arrests with the number for boys; and (2) information which contrasts the number of arrests of girls under 18 with the number for females over 18. In some cases the information is striking, often more so than that for boys.

1. *Girls versus boys.* By referring again to Table 6–1, it can be seen that arrests of girls comprise only 8 percent of the total for the seven serious index offenses versus 36 percent for boys. Although the most common arrest for girls is for larceny (13 percent), that figure still lags far behind the rate for boys (33 percent) for the same offense. In short, arrests for serious traditional crimes are still predominantly male, typically young males, not females.

Table 6–2, showing nonindex crimes, also reaffirms the extent to which delinquency arrests are predominantly male. For only one offense—running away—were girls (57 percent) arrested more frequently than boys (43 percent), and this difference may have been due, at least in part, to the traditional double standard in which both society and the police are more concerned about unsupervised girls than they are about unsupervised boys. Otherwise, girls, like their adult sisters, are arrested less often than boys. Thus, in 1975, arrests of females of all ages constituted only about 16 percent of all arrests in the United States while 84 percent were male.

TABLE 6–2
Typical juvenile arrests for nonindex crimes 1975

	Total all ages	Percent of all arrests		
		Juveniles under 18	*Males under 18*	*Females under 18*
Curfew and loitering	99,100	100.0	80.2	19.8
Runaways	158,460	100.0	42.8	57.2
Vandalism	154,427	65.4	60.5	4.9
Arson	12,414	53.5	48.4	5.1
Liquor laws.....................	222,606	41.0	32.6	8.4
Stolen property				
buying, receiving, possessing....	87,269	32.8	30.1	2.7
Narcotic drug laws	425,442	24.3	20.3	4.0
Disorderly conduct	473,899	21.3	17.8	3.5
Sex offenses except rape and				
prostitution	44,479	21.2	18.9	2.3
Other assaults...................	302,472	20.3	16.0	4.3
All other offenses except traffic......	864,344	26.1	20.7	5.4

Based on 5,974 agencies; 1975 estimated population, 145,719,972.
Source: FBI, *Uniform Crime Reports*, 1976:187.

2. *Girls versus women.* When girls are compared with older women 18 and over, however, the picture changes considerably. The reason is that arrests of girls constitute a higher proportion of all female arrests (35 percent) than arrests of boys do of all male arrests (26 percent) (FBI, 1976:187). When only the serious index crimes are considered, as shown in Table 6–3, girls constitute an even higher proportion of the female total (41 percent). This figure, incidentally, is close to that of boys among all males (44 percent) for the same seven offenses. Like boys, moreover, girls rank high among all females on arrests for motor vehicle theft (58 percent), burglary (51 percent), larceny (42 percent) and robbery (37 percent). On a few nonindex offenses, they even constitute a higher proportion of all female arrests than do boys of all male arrests: liquor law violations (58 percent versus 38 percent), sex offenses excluding rape and prostitution (30 percent versus 20 percent), and narcotic drug violations (29 percent versus 24 percent). In short, arrests among females, like arrests among males, are very much a youthful phenomenon.

Arrest trends

The latest *Uniform Crime Reports,* like juvenile court statistics, suggest that the official delinquency rate is still continuing to rise. Indeed, the

TABLE 6–3

Arrest rates of girls and boys as proportions of all female and male index arrests, 1975

	Girls under 18		Boys under 18	
Arrest offense	Number arrested	Percent of all female arrests	Number arrested	Percent of all male arrests
Index offenses				
Criminal homocide				
Murder and nonnegligent manslaughter	138	6.2	1,235	10.2
Manslaughter by negligence	47	16.4	244	11.1
Forcible rape	49	26.0	3,345	17.8
Robbery	3,033	37.2	37,763	52.8
Aggravated assault	4,892	21.7	25,966	17.6
Burglary—breaking or entering	10,367	50.9	191,202	52.8
Larceny—theft (except auto)	109,298	41.5	269,415	47.7
Motor vehicle theft	4,192	58.3	52,734	54.3
Total	132,016	40.7	581,904	44.3

Based on 5,974 agencies; 1975 estimated population, 145,719,972.
Source: FBI, *Uniform Crime Reports*, 1976:187.

Office of Youth Development (1974:1) maintains that its juvenile court data and the police data gathered by the FBI are remarkably similar over time. Both sets of figures have climbed steadily since 1949, with the exception of some leveling trends in 1961 and in the early 1970s. With these two exceptions, the number of court cases increased by 124 percent between 1960 and 1973 while the total number of arrests of juveniles under 18 increased by 144 percent. The growth in both instances was considerably larger than the growth in the youth population (32 percent).

Another way of looking at some of the same issues is again to draw contrasts between different populations—juveniles versus adults and boys versus girls.

1. *Juvenile versus adult arrests.* When all types of crime are considered—from running away to using marijuana to committing murder—arrests of juveniles under 18 increased by 144 percent between 1960 and 1975, while the increase for adults was only 13 percent (FBI, 1976:182). From an official perspective, therefore, juveniles could be seen as constituting an increasingly criminal group. But in order to review that issue more decisively, one must consider the seriousness of the acts for which juveniles are arrested as well as the frequency.

FIGURE 6–3

Percent increases in index crimes, 1960–1975 juvenile versus adult*

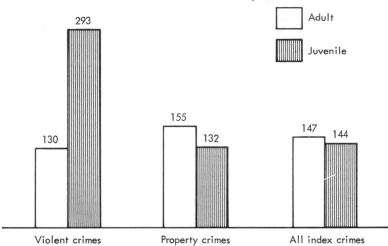

* Based on 2,726 agencies; 1975 estimated population, 96,428,998. Reconstructed from Tables 30–31, FBI, *Uniform Crime Reports,* 1976:182–183.

This can be done by examining increases in the arrest of juveniles for the seven index crimes on which the FBI gathers police data—homicide, rape, robbery, aggravated assault, burglary, larceny, and motor vehicle theft. Consider the findings which are displayed in Figure 6–3:

> Figure 6–3 shows that increases in arrest for both juveniles and adults have been considerable in the past decade and a half. When all index crimes are combined, for example, the increase for juveniles has been 144 percent while that for adults has been 147 percent. Significantly, however, arrests among juveniles for these serious crimes did not go up more than arrests among adults.
>
> Arrests for property crimes—burglary, larceny, and motor vehicle theft—actually increased less among juveniles than they did among adults. Though this increase is great in both cases and though juveniles still tend to commit more property crimes than adults, their tendency to do so since 1960 may not have increased quite so much as it has among adults,
>
> The same is not true, however, when violent crimes are considered—homicide, forcible rape, aggravated assault, and robbery. While arrests for these crimes among juveniles have increased by 293 percent, arrests among persons 18 and over have

increased by less than half that amount, 130 percent. These findings should not be interpreted to mean that juveniles commit more violent crimes than adults, since they do not as we saw earlier. Nonetheless, they do imply that violent crime among the young is increasing at a strikingly more rapid rate.

In order to be fully certain whether these figures represent real increases in the rate at which young people are arrested, one must consider changes in the youth population; it grew by about one third between 1960 and 1975. The basic question, therefore, is whether the rate of arrest per 100,000 juveniles actually increased or whether it was a function of population growth. The available evidence suggests that the increase was real, though diminished somewhat when rates are considered: The rate of arrest per 100,000 juveniles for property crimes grew by about 35 percent between 1960 and 1975, by approximately 123 percent for violent crimes, and by about 57 percent for all index offenses (Compare *U.S. Census Reports,* 1960–1970 with *Uniform Crime Reports,* 1960–1975).

A second issue has to do with the fact that official figures are affected by shifts within the youth population itself. For example, juveniles over 14 are arrested more frequently than those under 14. Therefore, when the large child population of the past few years moved into adolescence we should have expected increases in the volume of arrests. Indeed, that is what the findings of Chilton and Speilberger (1971) suggest may have occurred. After analyzing referrals to the Florida juvenile courts between 1958 and 1957, they concluded that about 70 percent of a large increase in court appearances was due to the passage of children into the adolescent years. As this portion of the youth population grew rapidly, so did the number of court referrals. Yet, even though such is likely to be reflected in the arrest figures cited above, there still remains considerable official evidence that juvenile arrest rates have been increasing and that when compared to adults juveniles may be becoming more violent.

2. *Girl versus boy crime.* The conclusion is strongly supported when increases in the arrest of girls is considered. Figure 6–4 indicates that:

Between 1960 and 1975, the number of arrests among girls for all index crimes increased by 425 percent as contrasted with an increase of 117 percent for boys.

The same was true of property crimes. Increases in the arrest of girls were over four times as large, 420 versus 104 percent.

Differences are not quite so large when violent crimes are considered. Arrests of girls, nevertheless, increased by almost twice as much, 504 versus 278 percent. There can be little doubt that the arrest rate of girls has gone up significantly.

FIGURE 6–4
Percent increases in index crimes, 1960–1975 boy versus girl*

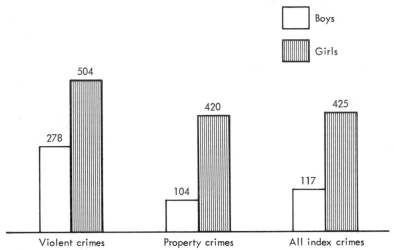

* Based on 2,726 agencies; 1975 estimated population, 16,428,998. Reconstructed from Tables 30–31, FBI, *Uniform Crime Reports,* 1976:182–183.

In later chapters, we will be seeking some explanation for large increases like these, but it is sufficient for now to suggest that this rise in girl arrests is partially a function of rapidly changing sex roles. Not only are the attitudes of females toward themselves changing, but society is changing its attitude toward females. Just as girls are becoming more assertive in overthrowing their traditional roles, so the police and courts are becoming less protective of them. The arrest rate of girls still has a long way to go to catch up with that of boys since in 1975 they constituted only about one fifth of all juvenile arrests. Nonetheless, if present trends continue, traditional differences will erode rapidly.

Delinquency in a cohort

All of the information presented thus far has reflected the number of court cases or arrests counted in single, separate years. This kind of information is limited because it says nothing about how many individuals were involved or how many times they might have been included as repeaters in the yearly figures. The *Uniform Crime Reports,* for example, count the number of arrests in any time period, not the number of children who were arrested. As a result, one cannot be certain whether official arrest figures indicate that crime is being committed by more and more minors or whether a few of them are committing more and more crime. Another way of determining the amount of official delinquency, therefore, is to follow a group or cohort of young people for the entire period of their childhood to determine how many delinquent acts are recorded for them. In this way, repeat, as contrasted with one-time, offenders can be detected and the total number of delinquent acts for each group accumulated.

The task of conducting this sort of study is difficult and is rarely accomplished, but it provides a much richer source of information. Three sociologists—Marvin Wolfgang, Robert Figlio, and Thorsten Sellin (1972)—recently conducted such a study. They obtained the names of an entire cohort of 9,945 boys born in 1945 who lived in Philadelphia from the time they were 10 until they were 18. These investigators then used official records to determine how much delinquency was recorded for these boys during the period between their 10th and 18th birthdays. Unfortunately, they collected no information on girls, but their findings on boys are valuable nonetheless.

Amount of delinquency

Thirty-five percent (3,475) of the 9,945 boys had at least one recorded police contact sometime during childhood, while 65 percent (6,470) had none (p. 54). Put in terms of delinquency rates, this means that for every 1,000 boys in this particular birth cohort, there were approximately 350 who became officially delinquent sometime during the period between their 10th and 18th birthdays. Translated into the broader kind of delinquency rate mentioned earlier, these findings suggest that for every 100,000 boys 35,000 become delinquent sometime during childhood.

Likewise, the findings corroborate the relation between age and delinquency mentioned earlier: Delinquency is at a relatively low level at age 10, increases steadily thereafter, reaches its apex at age 16, and, then, at age 17 begins to decline sharply (pp. 112–118). Interestingly, two specific status offenses—truancy and curfew violations—accounted for much of the reduction at age 17. After age 16 in Philadelphia, boys can legitimately leave school to work, and curfew restrictions no longer apply. Thus, merely because social definition changes, so does the delinquency rate. This fact notwithstanding, some other factors are obviously at work because the number of serious index offenses also declined at age 17. For some unexplained reasons, there was a sharp drop-off in all types of delinquency at that age.

Importance of chronic offenders

Perhaps the most significant finding of this cohort study has to do with the role of the delinquent repeater—the recidivist. It will be recalled that 3,475 boys (35 percent) became official delinquents. Forty-six percent (1,613) of these were one-time delinquents, while 54 percent (1,862) were repeaters or recidivists (p. 66). It was this group of recidivists who turned out to be the ones who contributed most heavily to the delinquency rate. While there were only 1,862 of them, they had 8,601 recorded offenses. The almost equal number of one-timers, meanwhile, had only 1,613 recorded offenses. Recidivists, moreover, committed most of the seven serious offenses used by the FBI for its crime index, while one-timers committed very few.

> In fact, recidivists committed over twice as many assaults alone (N = 726) as the total number of assaults, property offenses, and robberies committed by one-time offenders (N = 330). One-time offenders were responsible for only 10 robberies compared to recidivists, who committed 183. All told there were nearly 9 times as many index offenses committed by recidivists (2,935) as by one-time delinquents (330), with about the same proportion of property offenses. The assault-property-robbery rate of offenses for one-time offenders was 204.6 and for recidivists, 1,576.3 (p. 71).

In short, these career data suggest that the majority of police arrests may be occurring among a relatively small proportion of the total youth population, at least in Philadelphia. Although the 1,863 recidivists constituted less than one fifth of the 9,945 boys in the total cohort, they were responsible for the preponderant majority of all arrests, both serious and nonserious.

Even more striking was the outcome when among the recidivists the most chronic of all offenders were selected and studied—those who had five or more recorded offenses during their childhood. There were only 627 boys in this chronic offender group, a reassuring finding in one sense. Yet, in another sense, there was cause for alarm because this small number of boys was responsible for *over half* of all the offenses of the entire cohort. In other words, a group of boys who comprised only 6 percent of the total birth cohort and only 18 percent of all those who became delinquent were responsible for over 50 percent of all recorded violations.

There are data from an Oregon study of rural delinquents which indicate that these findings from Philadelphia may not be entirely unique (Center for Studies of Crime and Delinquency, 1974). One in four rural boys (versus 54 percent in Philadelphia) were recidivists; and, though the chronic offender group was smaller (11 versus 18 percent), they had committed one third of all the offenses.

Such findings again seem to suggest that the number of young people who become truly serious career offenders may only be a tiny proportion of all children. The majority of young people are either officially non-delinquent or are one-time offenders. Yet, because we have seen repeatedly that official statistics are a reflection of public sentiment and official practice as well as a reflection of juvenile misconduct, we must remain open to other possible interpretations. This need can be illustrated by referring again to history.

Impact of history

Recall that when we reviewed the discovery of childhood, the invention of delinquency, and the relation of these to race and social class, our findings went somewhat as follows:

Childhood as a unique and protected phase of the life cycle is a relatively recent creation in the history of Western civilization.

The ideal concept of childhood is a product largely of white middle-class values and experiences.

As the middle class gradually replaced the aristocracy in power and influence, new forms of family and educational life developed. The nuclear family and formal schooling have gradually replaced the communal household and the apprenticeship system for socializing the young.

As the ideal middle-class concept of childhood has grown and spread, it has become the social standard to which all children—middle- or lower-class, black or white—are expected to adhere and by which their behavior is judged.

For many generations, however, opportunities to develop and to maintain the nuclear family pattern, to share in educational programs, or to acquire economic resources have been restricted for black people, for American Indians, and, to a lesser degree, for other poor immigrant and lower-class whites. Hence, the children of minority and lower-class families have been hindered from full participation in the kinds of familial, educational, and economic activities that might have enhanced their abilities to acquire and to adhere to the ideal image of childhood.

Rooted in the profound changes of the 19th century, American beliefs have increasingly stressed the notion that the poverty, the disrupted families, and the ignorance of minority and lower-class groups are the likely, virtually inevitable, precursors of lawbreaking; all are part and parcel of the same thing. Reflecting the current strength and popularity of this point of view, the President's Commission on Law Enforcement and Administration of Justice stated, in 1967, that "Delinquents tend to come from backgrounds of social and economic deprivation. Their families tend to have lower than average incomes and social status. . . . It is inescapable that juvenile delinquency is directly related to conditions bred by poverty" (pp. 56–57).

Based on this view of delinquency, laws were written and the juvenile court was created to locate delinquents and, by protectively reforming them, to bring them into conformity with the ideal concept of childhood. In the interest of saving disadvantaged children, the agents of juvenile justice are not only expected to detect and suppress their crime but to compensate for their poverty, their family disruption, and their lack of education.

If there is some validity to this description of historical developments, we should expect their influence to be reflected in the offense statistics which were produced in the Philadelphia cohort study. If, on one hand, generations of minority and lower-class people have not shared the forms of family and educational life to which success in our culture is tied, we should expect the consequences of this lack of participation to appear in the behaviors of their children. These children will be more likely to experience difficulties in social adjustment, to achieve less successfully in school, and, in general, to behave in ways that are defined as deviant because they are contrary to the ideal concept of childhood. Not having been socialized in the same way as middle-class children, they will exhibit behaviors that are not only socially debilitating but which are contrary to law.

If, on the other hand, the agents of juvenile justice are geared to the enforcement of rules which, by definition, place the children of lower-class and minority groups in a vulnerable position, it is these children on whom they will be more likely to concentrate their attention. According to law as well as custom, it is their job not only to apprehend young criminals but to apprehend children who are not exhibiting behaviors consistent with the ideal concept of childhood. The records these officials collect, in short, will reflect not only delinquent behaviors of children but the concentration of officials upon that segment of the youth population that is believed to be the most delinquent. Other segments, even though they include law violators, will receive less attention.

Findings of the cohort study

The findings of the Philadelphia cohort study were highly consistent with the historical background just sketched and with the conclusions it suggests (Wolfgang, et al., 1972:65–129; 245–250):

Racial background was strongly related to official designation as delinquent. Twenty-nine percent of the 9,945 boys in the cohort were "nonwhite" (most of whom were black) and 71 percent were white. Yet, 50 percent of the nonwhites were classified as delinquent as contrasted with only 29 percent of the whites. The *Uniform Crime Reports* (1974:135), incidentally, also indicate that blacks are greatly overrepresented in the arrest statistics.

Socioeconomic status (SES) was related to delinquency but less strongly than race. Forty-six percent of the cohort was classified as lower SES of whom 45 percent were delinquent. Fifty-four percent were higher SES but only 27 percent were delinquent.

Race and SES were intertwined and overlapping; that is, nonwhite boys were more likely than whites to be lower SES. The double jeopardy in which this has placed them historically was reflected in the delinquency rates. Not only were nonwhite delinquents more likely to be lower SES, but to have experienced the disruption of a greater number of school and residential moves, to have achieved the lowest IQ scores and other measures of achievement, and to have completed the lowest average grade in school. All of these factors, not just their criminal acts, have not only limited their abilities to fulfill ideally the requirements of childhood, but have probably enhanced the likelihood that they would be defined as delinquent.

The impaired educational and economic status of nonwhites in American history has also taken its toll in terms of violent crimes committed by minority children. Fourteen homicides were recorded for this cohort of young people; yet, all were attributable to nonwhites. According to the index used by the investigators to measure the seriousness of delinquent offenses, these 14 homicides alone represented more social harm than all the acts of physical violence taken together committed by white boys. Further, although whites become slightly more violent as they grow older, violence among nonwhite boys increases considerably.

Finally, the study indicated that race was also associated with higher rates of recidivism. Although boys on the lower socioeconomic level, both white and nonwhite, were more likely than those of higher status to be chronic offenders, race was clearly the key factor. Nonwhites were more likely to be recidivists, and, of the recidivists, they were more likely to be found among the chronic offenders. They were, in fact, five times more likely than whites to be found among the small group of 627 boys mentioned earlier who were responsible for over half of all the offenses recorded by the entire cohort.

Summary and conclusions

This analysis of official delinquency raises two fundamentally important issues. The first has to do with the tensions inherent in society's preoccupation with children, on one hand, and their criminality on the other. Such tensions inevitably produce ambivalence—simultaneous feelings of attraction and repulsion. This chapter has helped to highlight the sources of that ambivalence.

After the discovery of childhood, society adopted an increasingly protective stance toward children. It proclaimed their innocence and instituted a host of legal as well as other institutional changes designed to oversee their social, psychological, and intellectual development. These events created a special status, not only for children in general, but for delinquent children as well. On one hand, they were protected from full accountability for their criminal acts and were viewed as persons in need of treatment and care rather than punishment. On the other hand, certain legal restrictions were placed upon them which did not apply to adults. They were required by law to be obedient to parents and other authorities, to attend school, and, in general, to adhere to a long list of other moral rules which applied only to them.

In recent years, there has been a growing tendency to question the wisdom of trying to circumscribe the lives of children with legal rules that do not apply to adults. While insisting that children should retain their protected position with respect to their responsibility for crime, there is a growing movement to free them from legal sanctioning for their status offenses. If successful, this movement would place children in a more privileged status. They would be freed somewhat from the requirements imposed upon them because of their subordinate position as children while, at the same time, they would retain some of the protections inherent in it. They would, in other words, be granted more privileges while being subjected to fewer forms of social control.

At the same time, society has been, and is now, confronted with the fact that children are often predatory. Although there is good reason to be cautious about the validity of official statistics, some confidence can probably be placed in this chapter's findings which show that:

1. Official crime is a youthful phenomenon. It reaches its apex at around age 16 and declines thereafter.

2. There has probably been a marked increase in juvenile crime over the past decade and a half. The most striking was the increase in violent crime. Murder, assault, and armed robbery which used to be most common among those in their late teens and early 20s may now be coming more common among those who legally are children.

3. Delinquency arrests are still predominantly male. Arrests among girls, however, are accelerating at a far more rapid rate than among boys. Furthermore, girls constitute a higher proportion of all female arrests than boys do among all males. The changing status of girls, as well as the changing status of children in general, is having its negative side effects.

The tensions inherent in these conflicting trends are obvious. Along with their desire to protect children, the members of society are bombarded with accounts of their criminality. This bombardment has its personal side as well. When asked what it most wants in terms of crime control, a harassed citizenry repeatedly reports that it would like to feel free from personal attack. People want to be able to ride subways and buses without fear of being mugged; they want to be reassured that, even within their own homes, they can be safe from burglary and assault. American society, in short, is confronted with a growing dilemma over the status and treatment of its children.

At issue is the fact that protection for the young and the suppression of their crime are partially inconsistent goals. Society cannot, at one and the same time, both protect criminal children and protect those who are their victims. These goals, at least in part, are contradictory. In assessing the implications of this official account of delinquency, therefore, this fundamental contradiction must be kept in mind. It is a contradiction that will appear again and again throughout our entire analysis of delinquency. As more information is gained on it, we will see that whichever way our society chooses to deal with delinquency it will have to select repeatedly between the interests of children and the interests of those who are their victims.

Chronic offenders and the dilemma over children

A closely related issue has to do with the ways in which society attempts to resolve its dilemma over children. Historically, we have seen that people have tended to believe that the most delinquent segment of the youth population is made up of children who are of minority extraction, are poor, uneducated, and from unstable families. Indeed, existing social customs and rules have viewed these conditions and lawbreaking as virtually synonymous.

Since the findings of the Philadelphia cohort study lent some credence to these traditional beliefs, they suggest that one way out of society's dilemma over children is to concentrate upon that tiny group of chronic offenders who were highlighted in the study. The evidence is compelling if taken at face value. Indeed, Wolfgang et al. (1972:87) concluded that of all the groups on which a delinquency reduction effort might be concentrated the one most likely to produce definitive results would be the nonwhite lower SES group. Since it was in this segment of the youth cohort that serious delinquency was most heavily concentrated, concerted efforts might not only reduce lawbreaking, in general, but drastically curtail the acts of violence and assault over which society has been so concerned. By suppressing a small minority of the child population, crime would be suppressed.

There are some important difficulties with this conclusion however. First, we can ill-afford to ignore the fact that while the chronic offender group was responsible for about half of all the official offenses the other half must still be accounted for. A considerable amount of official delinquency is still being committed by the nonchronic offender group.

Second, we must reserve judgment on the effectiveness of a crime reduction effort directed at the chronic group because official delinquency is a function not only of what young people do but how society in general, and the agents of juvenile justice in particular, define and react to them. At the very least, we must avoid the possibility that what we are observing is a self-fulfilling prophecy. Since the delinquency laws are predicated upon the belief that lawbreaking, race, and poverty are one and the same, it should come as little surprise to find that those most likely to be arrested are those who meet all these criteria, not just the criterion of law violation.

A final reason for reserving judgment has to do with the distinct possibility that official records represent the tip of the iceberg of juvenile misconduct. If the offenses that are counted by officials represent only a tiny fraction of this iceberg, they may present a distorted picture of it. Consequently, before we can reach any definitive conclusion, we require better information on the shape and size of that iceberg.

In search of that information, the next two chapters are devoted to an analysis of two kinds of additional data: (1) data derived from the self-reports of children on their own law violations rather than that from official records; and (2) data derived from the victims of crimes which indicate who they are, in what ways they have been victimized, and how often. By adding information from these two sources, we should be able to get a better fix on the extent of law-violating behavior and by whom it is committed.

References

Black, Donald J. and Reiss, Albert J., Jr.
　1970　"Police control of juveniles," *American Sociological Review*, February 35:63–77.

Center For Studies of Crime and Delinquency
　1974　Teenage delinquency in small town America. *NIMH Research Report*, 5. Washington, D.C.: U.S. Government Printing Office.

Chilton, Roland and Spielberger, Adele
  1971 "Is delinquency increasing? Age structure and the crime rate." *Social Forces*, March, *XLIX*:487–493.

Federal Bureau of Investigation
  1967 *Crime in the United States: Uniform Crime Reports—1966.* Washington, D.C.: U.S. Government Printing Office.

  1974 *Crime in the United States: Uniform Crime Reports, 1973.* Washington, D.C.: U.S. Government Printing Office.

  1976 *Crime in the United States: Uniform Crime Reports, 1975.* Washington, D.C.: U.S. Government Printing Office.

Goldman, Nathan
  1969 "The differential selection of juvenile offenders for court appearance." Pp. 264–290 in William Chambliss (Ed.), *Crime and the Legal Process.* New York: McGraw-Hill.

Klein, Malcolm W.
  1970 "Police processing of juvenile offenders: toward the development of juvenile system rates." Los Angeles County Sub-Regional Board, California Council of Criminal Justice, Part III.

National Commission on the Causes and Prevention of Violence
  1969 *Crimes of Violence* (Vol. II). Washington, D.C.: U.S. Government Printing Office.

Office of Youth Development
  1974 *Juvenile Court Statistics, 1973.* Washington, D.C.: Department of Health, Education, and Welfare.

President's Commission on Law Enforcement and Administration of Justice
  1967 *The Challenge of Crime in a Free Society.* Washington, D.C.: U.S. Government Printing Office.

Wolfgang, Marvin E., Figlio, Robert and Sellin, Thorsten
  1972 *Delinquency in a Birth Cohort.* Chicago: University of Chicago Press.

7

SELF-REPORTED DELINQUENT BEHAVIOR

Many people are uncomfortable, if not disbelieving, over official accounts of delinquent behavior. This discomfort is due not only to the finding that law violation is much higher for younger than for older people but that it is higher for the poor than for the rich, and higher for blacks than for whites. The probability that the police share in this judgment only adds to the discomfort. It is feared that because they relate crime more to the young, to the poor, and to blacks than to other groups they are more likely to round up these individuals, producing a disproportionate number of youthful, poor, and black offenders in arrest statistics.

In addition to the possibility that official accounts do result in a self-fulfilling prophecy, widespread discomfort is fueled by a number of technical flaws in official statistics:

1. *The "dark figure" of crime.* Official accounts of delinquency are like the tip of an iceberg. Since many delinquent acts go unobserved or unreported, we have had little knowledge until recently about the size and shape of the iceberg. The National Commission on the Causes and Prevention of Violence (1969:18) called this missing body of information the "dark figure" of crime—the gap between the amount of crime recorded by the police and the actual figure.

The reasons for this gap are numerous. First and foremost is the

141

capacity of most juveniles to keep their illegal acts secret—shoplifting, truancy, fornication, drinking, gambling, vandalism, joyriding, or even burglary. A second reason is closely related. The victims of some crimes are reluctant to have their victimization discovered—the victims of rape, seduction, or of hassling and assault by a juvenile gang from whom they fear reprisal. Likewise, the President's Crime Commission (1967a:18) found that victims often did not want to take the trouble to report having been victimized, that they had little confidence in the police to solve the crime, or that they simply did not know where and how to report. One flaw in the accuracy of official reports of delinquency, then, is the "dark figure" of crime.

2. *The village watchman.* A second flaw has to do with the fact that national statistics are collected on the local level, by people who may have a vested interest in seeing their reports turn out in a particular way. Nettler (1974:45) quotes Sir Josiah Stamp, an English economist, who put his finger directly on the problem. "The government," said Stamp, "are very keen on amassing statistics. They collect them, raise them to the nth power, take the cube root, and prepare wonderful diagrams. But you must never forget that every one of these figures comes in the first instance from the village watchman, who just puts down what he damn pleases."

The reason Stamp was concerned about the village watchman is because that watchman may want his findings to reflect favorably upon him—an understandable but potentially misleading desire. The recent comment of a high police department official illustrates the point extremely well.

> The unwritten law was that you were supposed to make things look good. You weren't supposed to report all the crime that actually took place in your precinct—and, if you did, it could be your neck. I know captains who actually lost their commands because they turned in honest crime reports (National Commission on the Causes and Prevention of Violence, 1969:18).

In this case, the police apparently wanted to underreport crime so that they could appear to be controlling it successfully. When such practices are discovered and corrected, however, they can have a distorting effect in the opposite direction—that is, they can make it appear as though a sudden increase in crime occurred. This very thing happened in Philadelphia (President's Crime Commission, 1967a:26).

In 1953, Philadelphia police reported an increase of 70 percent in index crimes over 1951—an increase which, when made public and taken at face value, could have had serious consequences. When this startling rise was reported, however, it was found to be due, not to an invasion of criminals or to delinquent children gone berserk, but to the discovery that crime had been underreported in the city for years. Consistent with the comments of the police captain quoted above, it was discovered that one precinct had actually handled over 5,000 more complaints than it had recorded.

The point is that a variety of city watchmen in the police, the courts, and in corrections often distort their reports, either through ignorance or for a variety of self-serving reasons. Their commitments to themselves and to their organizations are greater than their commitments to accurate knowledge. Like students cheating on a test or citizens misreporting their income to the IRS, other matters take precedence.

3. *Changing norms and expectations.* Changing norms for behavior and the social expectations that attend them also contribute to the technical difficulties in interpreting delinquency statistics—difficulties that often appear in an unexpected way. For example, one of the outcomes of political inequality traditionally has been the tendency for the police to ignore many but the most serious crimes in slum areas (Cf. President's Crime Commission, 1967b:26). The reason is that without political power poor and minority people were left to take care of their own problems. As a result, many common delinquent acts went unchecked and unreported. Unless poor and minority children committed crimes against more affluent members of society, relatively little attention was paid to them. As poor and minority people acquired some political clout, however, and as more attention was paid to them, demands were made that the police take a more active role in suppressing delinquency in the ghetto. The likely consequence, particularly in recent years, has been an increase in the number of reported delinquencies. Law-violating behavior that was customary heretofore—particularly status offenses, gang behavior, and petty crimes—now became a matter of public record. It is possible that without much increase in the actual incidence of delinquent behavior arrest and court records were inflated considerably.

Changing rules and expectations can alter crime records in other ways. In virtually every state, many forms of sexual conduct—fornication, adultery, prostitution, homosexuality, sodomy, and oral sex—have been against the law. In recent years we have experienced a so-called sexual revolution which has led to increasing demands that such laws be repealed. Nettler (1974:45–46) notes that after it was anticipated that the Wolfinden Committee would make similar recommendations in England the number of recorded homosexual offenses dropped by half over the space of a few years. Yet, the laws during that period were not actually changed. The reduction in official offenses was due to changes in police activity, not to legal changes or to changes in homosexual conduct.

What these examples illustrate is the fact that laws are selectively enforced, depending in part upon changing circumstance and social definition. Any adequate interpretation of the meaning of official statistics, therefore, requires some knowledge of them.

4. *Police professionalization.* Those who run the Uniform Crime Reporting System are not unaware of these problems. Both the President's Crime Commission (1967b:26) and the National Commission on Violence (1969:23) note that significant efforts have been made to correct and to professionalize police reporting practices. One thing that has been done, for example, is to include in the calculation of crime trends only those police agencies who have had comparable records and reporting practices over the years. Another is to improve the collection of data by the police and to standardize their methods of recording crimes.

Paradoxically, one of the reasons that care must be exercised in interpreting police findings is precisely because their recording practices have improved. As the number of statistical clerks has increased and as reporting systems have become better organized, known crimes are recorded more faithfully than ever before. Undoubtedly, some of the increase in reported crimes have been due to these improved methods, a fact that illustrates a sociological truism; namely, that as society becomes more aware of a problem and attempts to do something about it, the size of the problem seems to increase—the greater the awareness, the greater the problem.

By way of example, consider Table 7–1, taken from the President's Crime Commission Report (1967b:25). It shows that as one major city after another improved its record-keeping practices significant increases in crime were noted. Percentage increases in the various cities ranged from a low of 27 percent in one city to a high of 202 percent in another, all in the space of one or at most two years. Obviously, all of these increases were not due to local delinquency waves; they were due at least in part to changes in police reporting practices. Unfortunately, there is no way of knowing how sizeable that "part" is.

TABLE 7–1
Increases in index offenses following changes in record-keeping practices

Name of city	Years of increase	Amount of increase (index offenses)		Percent increase
		From	To	
Baltimore	1964–65	18,637	26,193	40.5
Buffalo	1961–63	4,779	9,305	94.7
Chicago	1959–60	56,570	97,253	71.9
Cleveland..........	1963–64	10,584	17,254	63.0
Indianapolis	1961–62	7,416	10,926	47.3
Kansas City........	1959–61*	4,344	13,121	202.0
Memphis	1963–64	8,781	11,533	31.3
Miami	1963–64	10,750	13,610	26.6
Nashville	1962–63	6,595	9,343	41.7
Shreveport........	1962–63	1,898	2,784	46.7
Syracuse	1963–64	3,365	4,527	34.5

* No report was published for Kansas City, Missouri, for 1960.
Source: President's Crime Commission, 1967b:25.

The basic issue

A great many other examples could be cited, but these are enough to highlight the basic issue. On one hand, it is clear that official records are less than ideal. The possibility is considerable that they are misleading. On the other hand, arguments against them are often ideological rather than factual. Like official records, therefore, they also deserve a healthy degree of skepticism. In contrast to the cynicism and ambivalence which many people now express, some well-known theorists have argued that these negative feelings are based on humanitarian inclinations than on facts.

Consider, for example, the argument that official records are biased against lower-class children. While granting that illegal behavior is by no means confined to lower-class children, Cohen (1955:42) maintains that its concentration among them is not an illusion. It is only our "egalitarian proclivities and sentimental humanitarianism," he suggests, "which cause us to think otherwise." Likewise, Cloward and Ohlin (1960:12) maintain that middle-class delinquency is "petty" in comparison with lower-class delinquency. They believe that the inclination to violate the law is more deeply ingrained in the lower-class youngster and that he possesses a greater potential for the development of a criminal career. Given the urgency of these contrasting points of view, therefore, alternative ways for measuring delinquent behavior have been sought. One of the more important has been self-reported delinquent behavior.

Self-reported law violation

In contrast to official methods of collecting data on delinquent behavior, a growing number of social scientists have gone to juveniles themselves to discover how many law violations they have committed and what led to them. They have done this by administering anonymous questionnaires, by interviewing youngsters, and by simply observing their behavior. Their findings help to answer a series of crucial questions.

   1. *How widespread is law violation among juveniles?* Virtually all self-report studies indicate that the amount of undetected law violation is enormous (Erickson and Empey, 1963; Gold, 1966 and 1970; Illinois Institute for Juvenile Research, 1972; Murphy, et al., 1946; Porterfield, 1946; Short and Nye, 1958; Wallerstein and Wyle, 1947; Williams and Gold, 1972). Almost every child by his or her own admission has broken the law at some time or another, sometimes repeatedly. This finding,

TABLE 7–2
Self-reported status offenses

Study	Percent admitting commission of offense					
	Truancy	Drinking	Defying parents	Forni-cation	Running away	Driving without license
Midwest						
Boys	54	68	22	39	13	81
Washington						
Boys	53	57	33	40	13	75
Utah						
Boys	66	52	40	—	22	72
Illinois						
Boys and girls..........	47	61	—	—	—	43
Michigan						
Boys	30	55	—	19	6	—
Girls	17	43	—	5*	6	—

—No information collected.
  * Validation information suggests that this figure would be a more accurate estimate if it were doubled (Gold, 1970:4).

moreover, is not limited to the United States but has been reported in other countries as well (Christie, et al., 1965; Elmhorn, 1965).

2. *What kinds of offenses are reported most commonly?* A series of tables follow which help to answer this question. They draw from self-report studies conducted in different parts of the country—from communities in a "midwestern" state, from Washington State, Utah, Michigan, and from a random statewide sample of adolescents in Illinois. Although the settings for these studies varied widely, though their data collection methods were not uniform, and though they covered a span of almost 20 years, they paint a fairly common picture.[1]

Status offenses. These studies indicate, first of all, that large proportions of the youth population admit to having committed a number of status offenses at least once. Table 7–2 shows that truancy and drinking would rank first with anywhere from half to two thirds of all adolescents having committed them. Defying parents and fornication would rank second, and running away last. Driving without a license would rank above all of these except that it applies to adults as well as children. Where information is recorded separately for girls (in the Michigan study), it shows that while they report less law violation their offense pattern is generally the same.

Crimes against property. In Table 7–3, self-reported crimes against property are shown. This table suggests that petty theft, shoplifting, and destroying property are about as common as drinking and truancy, involving considerable numbers of young people. Breaking and entering is also quite common. Sometimes it merely involves illegal entry into homes, public buildings, or businesses for the purpose of messing

---

[1] The self-report studies in question are:

Study	Locale(s)	Sample	Method	Investigators	Published
Midwest	Three communities: rural, rural-urban, suburban.	596	Questionnaire	Short and Nye	1958
Washington	Three communities: 10–40,000	2,350	Questionnaire	Short and Nye	1958
Utah	Community of 40,000	180	Interview	Erickson and Empey	1963
Illinois	Statewide	3,100	Questionnaire	Illinois Institute for Juvenile Research	1972
Michigan	Community of 200,000	522	Interview	Gold	1970

TABLE 7–3
Self-reported crimes against property

	Percent admitting commission of offense					
	Larceny				Breaking and entering	Auto theft or joyriding
Study	Less than $2	$2–$50	Shop-lifting	Destroying property		
Midwest						
Boys	63	17	—	61	—	11
Washington						
Boys	61	16	—	45	—	15
Utah						
Boys	92	22	—	66	32	2
Illinois						
Boys and girls..........	56*	16	50	31	13†	10
Michigan						
Boys	60‡	?	50	27	38	10
Girls	30‡	?	25	6	23	3

—No information collected.
* Petty theft.
† Burglary.
‡ Theft by stealth.

around; in others, illegal entry is made for the purpose of burglary. Auto theft, which among juveniles often involves taking a car to go joy riding, is the least common of these kinds of offenses and is reported by only about 10 percent of all respondents.

Crimes against persons.   Table 7–4 shows that, overall, self-reported crimes against persons are much less common among adolescents than are status offenses or property crimes. There are, however, two exceptions—fist fighting and, to a lesser degree, gang fighting. Fighting is an activity which has long been a part of adolescent life, and it apparently continues to be about as common as drinking, truancy, petty theft, and destroying property.

Deliberate assault on others for the purpose of doing them serious harm is another matter. According to most studies, it occurs less frequently, as does carrying a concealed weapon. Even less common is armed robbery, or "strongarming" someone, to obtain money or goods by force. Information on acts of this sort is limited, but where it is available it suggests that something near, or less than, one in ten adolescents is involved. Nonetheless, this proportion is still higher than that reported in official records. Furthermore, given the possibility that

TABLE 7–4
Self-reported crimes against persons

Study	Percent admitting commission of offense				
	Fist fighting	Gang fighting	Assault	Carry concealed weapon	Armed robbery or strong arming
Midwest					
Boys	87	24	16	—	6
Washington					
Boys	81	23	14	—	—
Utah					
Boys	52	—	—	—	0
Illinois					
Boys and girls	50	21	—	25	13
Michigan					
Boys . . . . , .	—	23	11	13	6
Girls	—	5	2	1	0

—No information collected.

young people are unwilling to be completely honest in reporting these kinds of felonies, these self-reports may underestimate the true figure.

Drug use. Information on drug use was not collected by all the studies on which this analysis is based. Therefore, it cannot be presented for all of them. It was collected, however, by the Institute for Juvenile Research in its recent statewide study of self-reported delinquency in Illinois (1972:25–28). Its findings are shown in Table 7–5.

Marijuana is by far the most commonly used drug with approximately one in four adolescents reporting having smoked it. Its use apparently increases with age: Only about 10 percent of all 14-year-olds report having smoked it, but among 18-year-olds the figure rises to about 50 percent. There are, however, no significant sex, racial, or re-

TABLE 7–5
Self-reported drug offenses (Illinois only)

Offense	Percent admitting offense
Used marijuana	22
Used psychedelics (e.g., mescaline, LSD)	8
Used downers (e.g., barbiturates)	8
Used uppers (e.g., speed)	7
Used inhalants	7
Sold drugs	5
Used heroin	3

gional differences among the Illinois respondents: Girls have smoked as often as boys, whites as often as blacks, and rural adolescents as often as those who live in cities like Chicago.

The use of other drugs—uppers, downers, inhalants and particularly heroin—seem to have been far below that of marijuana use. This fact notwithstanding, smoking marijuana is still much less common than drinking alcohol. Recall that in Table 7–2, it was shown that 61 percent of the Illinois adolescents reported having consumed alcohol—a figure that not only parallels figures reported in other states, but which is over twice as large as the number who smoke marijuana. The point is that alcohol is still our most popular drug. Besides the six out of ten who reported having used it, over half reported that they had been drunk at least once or twice.

3. *How large is the "dark figure" of crime? What proportion of all offenses reported by juveniles become a part of the official record?* Studies indicate that at least nine out of ten illegal acts either go undetected or unacted upon by anyone in authority (Erickson and Empey, 1963, Gold, 1966; Murphy, et al., 1946; Williams and Gold, 1972). This conclusion is based upon two kinds of information: (1) upon statements of young people on how often they have been caught, and (2) by checking official records to see how often the names of self-confessed offenders appear in them. For example, after having checked the official record against the self-reports of a national sample, Williams and Gold (1972:221) found that "Less than 1 percent of the chargable offenses committed in the three years prior to the interviews were recorded as official delinquency. . . . And when offenses do come to the attention of the police, they often result in warnings, 'station adjustments,' and a host of other police actions that fall short of delinquency records for teenagers."

These outcomes are particularly true with respect to so-called minor violations: traffic violations, petty theft, buying and drinking alcohol, destroying property, skipping school, and so on. There is some evidence, however, that the picture changes with respect to more serious violations—felonious theft, auto theft, breaking and entering, or armed robbery. Fewer of these offenses go undetected and unacted upon. Yet, even in these cases, eight out of ten violations go undetected, and nine out of ten do not result in court action (Erickson and Empey, 1963:465; Williams and Gold, 1972:221–222).

So striking are such findings that one is reminded of the statement made over 30 years ago by Murphy, et al. (1946) when they first encountered the large gap between actual lawbreaking and official delinquency. "Even a moderate increase in the amount of attention paid to [it] by law enforcement authorities," they said, "could create a semblance of a 'delinquency wave' without there being the slightest change in adolescent behavior." If all, or even a significant part of all, law violations became a part of the official record, the result would be unprecedented: A large majority of all adolescents would be official delinquents.

In light of current efforts to improve crime reporting by the police, such findings raise some important and provocative questions: To what degree might the youthful crime wave of the past 10 or 15 years be a function of better police records? To what extent are the frightening rises in official crime rates the result of tapping more successfully the high degree of juvenile lawbreaking that has always existed?

It is difficult to be conclusive about these questions, but there is some evidence. After comparing the results of two national surveys, Gold and Reimer (1974:13) found no overall increase in self-reported illegal behavior when information gathered in 1972 was compared with the same kind of information gathered in 1967. Rather than an increase in law violation, they found a change in both the nature of the offenses committed and who it was that committed them:

> Specifically, more of the '72 male respondents reported more frequent use of illicit drugs—mostly marijuana—than the 1967 respondents did and less larceny, threatened assault, trespassing, forcible and nonforcible entry, and gang fighting. The girls in '72 also reported greater use of drugs—mostly marijuana but including alcohol—than did girls in '67, while reporting less larceny, property destruction, and breaking and entering. But the decline of the latter kinds of offenses among girls in 1972 does not balance their greater use of drugs, so the girls in '72 reported more delinquent behavior overall.

In short, illegal behavior among boys may actually have declined, while among girls it may have risen due to their increased use of marijuana.

Since these unofficial findings conflict sharply with official reports indicating that youth crime is on the increase, they must be treated with caution. Nonetheless, Gold and Reimer (1974:29) maintain that some faith might be placed in them. They claim that their findings "approximate as closely as any available the real levels and nature of delinquent behavior in the years under consideration. And they simply do not testify to rapidly rising rates of juvenile delinquency." Perhaps improved record keeping is responsible for at least part of the increased crime noted in official reports.

4.   Do all young people report being equally delinquent or are some of them more delinquent that others?   This is an extremely important question. Until now we have seen that a large majority of young people are law violators. Illegal behavior is so common among them that it could be said to be a normal, not an abnormal, part of adolescent life. Hence, if actual behavior rather than legal rules were taken as the standard, it would be the nonviolator who would be out of step, not the violator. Does this mean, then, that all young people are equally deviant—that all have broken the law repeatedly, and that all have committed serious offenses?

The answer is "no." Without exception, every study of the subject suggests that law-violating behavior is not an either-or phenomenon—not something that one either does or does not do, like catching the chickenpox or the mumps—but that it is a more-or-less thing. Adolescent behavior, therefore, is best understood as lying along a continuum, not as divided into separate boxes, one called "delinquent" and the other called "nondelinquent" (Elmhorn, 1965; Erickson and Empey, 1963; Gold, 1970; Nettler, 1974; Short and Nye, 1958; Williams and Gold, 1972).

On one end of the continuum are the majority of young people, most of whom have committed a number of minor acts, although an occasional serious offense may be mixed in. Then, as one proceeds further along the continuum, one encounters fewer and fewer children who, at the same time, tend to be more and more delinquent. Not only do their illegal acts tend to increase in frequency but in seriousness. The further one goes along the line, the more this tends to be the case. Thus, at the extreme end of the continuum are a small minority of individuals who are both persistent and serious offenders. All young people are not equally delinquent.

5.   Who gets caught? Is being arrested entirely a chance thing? Are official records at all accurate in identifying those who by their own admission are the most delinquent?   There is some evidence that the possession of an official record is not entirely a chance thing—that those individuals who admit having been the most delinquent are somewhat more likely to have been arrested, to have appeared in court, and, particularly, to have been confined to a training school.

Consider arrest first. In their nationwide study, Williams and Gold (1972:219) found a small but nonetheless significant relationship between frequency of offense and likelihood of arrest. The greater the number of violations, the greater the chance of apprehension. To a lesser degree, seriousness of offense was also associated with getting caught. Crimes against persons, in particular, were those which increased the likelihood of arrest. Yet, despite these findings the evidence indicated that the odds are still greatly on the side of the lawbreaker. Even though the most frequent and serious violators are somewhat more likely to be arrested, the risks they take are small. The chances are far greater that they will avoid detection.

Once offenders are inserted into the juvenile justice system, however, the picture begins to change. For a first offense, especially if it is a petty or status offense, the risks are not so great that the offender will be sent to court since the police are inclined to counsel and release a large number of first timers. But, when some of these individuals begin to appear more than once in the police net, likelihood is increased that they will be sent to court. The evidence suggests, moreover, that the reason they reappear is because they have been more delinquent. Different studies have found a rather strong relationship ($r = 0.51$ and 0.66) between frequency of self-admitted law violation and appearance in court (Erickson and Empey, 1963:147; Erickson, 1972:394). Boys who admit having been highly delinquent are those most likely to be sent before a judge. Thus, the chances were much greater that the most serious delinquents would be sent to court, once arrested, than that they would be arrested in the first place.

Once in court, the same sort of process begins all over again. Most judges and probation officers, in seeking to treat rather than to punish children, are inclined like the police to be lenient with the individuals they see for the first time. If, therefore, these first timers have not committed a grievous offense and if they are not dependent and neglected, they are usually warned, perhaps treated informally, or placed on probation. Given the fact that the odds are all in their favor that they will not be arrested again, this kind of response seems to work for the majority. But, for a few individuals, partly because they continue to defy the gods of chance, another court appearance will follow. When that occurs, court officials tend again to react like the police; that is, they are inclined to respond negatively to the official repeater and to send him further on into the system. He is the one, therefore, who is most likely to end up in a training school. But is he the most delinquent, or is he just unlucky? Is he confined merely because of the chance factors associated with getting caught or because he is a more serious law violator?

The evidence of this issue is telling. Different self-report studies indicate that incarcerated delinquents or those who have a record of several court appearances are by their own admission individuals who fit on the most delinquent end of the adolescent continuum (Erickson and Empey, 1963; Short and Nye, 1958). Not only have they committed more offenses, most of which are unknown to authorities, but those offenses are of a more serious variety. The evidence regarding them, in fact, is very much like that presented in the cohort study by Wolfgang et al. (1972) which was discussed in the last chapter. Just as these investigators found that a small but chronic group of offenders were unusually delinquent so these self-report studies find that incarcerated offenders or those with repeated appearances in court are not only more delinquent than juveniles who have no official record, but more delinquent than official one-timers as well.

For example, the Erickson-Empey study (1963:462) showed that if non- and one-time offenders are combined—because their offense rates are more alike than different—and compared with the chronic repeater group the cumulative violations of the latter group exceed those of the former by thousands: theft (20,836 versus 2,851); violations of property (10,828 versus 1,450); violations of person (8,569 versus 457); and violations involving the purchase and drinking of alcohol (21,134 versus 564). In addition, far smaller proportions of non- and one-time offenders committed offenses of a more serious nature than did official repeaters or boys who were confined: theft of articles worth more than $50 (2 percent versus 50 percent); auto theft (2 percent versus 52 percent); forgery (0 percent versus 25 percent); and armed robbery (0 percent versus 9 percent).

A study of an entirely different population in Washington State by Short and Nye (1958:44) showed virtually the same thing; that is, far smaller proportions of nondelinquents when compared with incarcerated boys reported having committed various illegal acts: theft of articles worth more than $50 (5 percent versus 91 percent); auto theft (15 percent versus 75 percent); strong arming (6 percent versus 68 percent); and destroying property (45 percent versus 84 percent). Furthermore many of these large differences continue to appear when status rather than criminal offenses are considered: skipping school (53 percent versus 95 percent); running away (13 percent versus 68 percent); or buying and using alcohol (57 percent versus 90 percent).

What these findings suggest, in short, is that the juvenile justice system is like a coarse net that is dragged in a large ocean (Nettler, 1974:90). The chances are small that most fish will be caught, and, even when some are caught, they manage to escape or are released because they are too small. But, because a few fish are much more active than others and because they are bigger, they are caught more than once. Despite the large odds in their favor, their sheer size and activity repeatedly get them into trouble. Each time this occurs the chances that they will escape or be thrown back are lessened. At the very end, therefore, it tends only to be the biggest and most active fish who end up in the can. When they reach that point, they are a very select group, clearly different from most of the fish still in the ocean.

6. *Are most delinquent children members of the lower class?* Self-report evidence thus far has confirmed official evidence that law violation among children is considerable. What, therefore, is the evidence regarding the traditional belief that it is concentrated among the poorer segments of our society? Are lower-class children more delinquent than their middle- and upper-class peers?

Most studies of undetected delinquency seriously question this traditional belief. They suggest again and again that the relation between social class and law-violating behavior is either small or nonexistent (Akers, 1964; Dentler and Monroe, 1961; Empey and Erickson, 1966; Hirschi, 1969; Illinois Institute for Juvenile Research, 1972; Short and Nye, 1958; Williams and Gold, 1972; Voss, 1966). In a few studies, a relationship has been found, suggesting that lower-class children are more delinquent, but the relationship has been so small in most cases that it would serve as a poor means for separating law violators from nonviolators (Cf. Clark and Wenninger, 1965; Empey, 1967; Gold, 1966; Reiss and Rhodes, 1961). In others, there is a suggestion that middle- or upper-class children may be the more delinquent (Voss, 1966; Williams and Gold, 1972). But from a scientific standpoint, the best conclusion is that social class membership is not a good way to separate law violators from nonviolators. Children from the various classes are more alike than different.

Do such findings prove, then, that official records are biased? What about the recent statement by the President's Crime Commission (1967b:57) that "there is still no reason to doubt that delinquency and especially the most serious delinquency is committed disproportionately by slum and lower-class youth?" Have important policy makers, the police, and the public simply been wrong all these years? In some ways, the answer is "Yes." The assumption that lower-class children are more delinquent is not only a gross oversimplification of a highly complex issue, but it is unjust. Lower-class children are certainly not totally responsible for our high rates of law-violating behavior, or even more responsible than other children. Injustice, however, is not our only problem. Besides biased thinking, one reason we have tended to hold on to our 19th century beliefs about delinquency is because we have failed to distinguish clearly between official delinquency—that which official records measure—and *law-violating behavior*—that which self-report studies measure. These are not the same things.

Official delinquency reflects three things: (1) the behavior of children; (2) the social backgrounds and characteristics of these children; and (3) the responses of officials to both behavior and circumstance. *Law-violating behavior*, by contrast, involves only one of these—the delinquent act itself. A gross error is committed, therefore, when official accounts of delinquency are equated with law-violating behavior.

The reason, as we have seen, is that the laws require officials to respond to the conditions of deprivation to which lower-class law violators are the most vulnerable. In those circumstances where a middle-class law violator might be treated leniently because he or she has family resources, is in school, and conforms better to the ideal concept of childhood, the lower-class child might be arrested, made a formal ward of the juvenile court, and even removed from home because his social conditions do not conform to the ideal. Thus, it is often the case that lower-class children become a part of official statistics, not just because of deliberate and unthinking official prejudice, but because officials are expected to correct social conditions as well as criminal behavior. In any comparison of official delinquency and informal law-violating rates, therefore, this fact must be kept in mind. Since official delinquency rates reflect the peculiar nature of social rules and official practices as well as the behavior of children, interpretations which equate them with rates of law-violating behavior are seriously misleading.

At the same time, it should be recognized that social class position may still be of help in other ways in our struggles to understand law-violating behavior. There is some evidence, for example, that while differences between classes may not be quantitative, they may be qualitative. In their observations of middle-class "gangs" in Los Angeles, the Myerhoffs (1964) reported that the violations of these "gangs" were often more "mischievous" than violent. However, violence is not the only dimension of seriousness. Included in these "mischievous" acts was the frequent and regular theft of articles that were by no means small nor inexpensive: radios, phonographs, car accessories, television sets, all usually taken from employers or personal acquaintances.

Such findings received some support by Empey and Erickson (1966) and Williams and Gold (1972) in their efforts to enumerate offenses more systematically. They found that such violations as grand theft, forgery, stealing cars, breaking and entering, and even arson when they did occur, were more often committed by higher- than lower-status boys. In the Empey-Erickson study, these findings held true whether the self-reported data came from boys with no official record or from those who were incarcerated in a training school. The point is that our understanding of law-violating behavior might be enhanced by recognizing that the kinds of delinquent acts that different persons commit are often a function of the opportunities and life-styles available to them.

Another promising line of inquiry has been suggested by Clark and Wenninger (1962). They suggest that differences in both the quantity and quality of illegal behavior may be due more to the prevailing social pattern of an area than to the social class position of its individual residents. In those areas in which everyone tends to be more delinquent, these tendencies will be the determining factor. In a ghetto, in a mixed neighborhood, or in Beverly Hills, violation rates may vary, not along class lines, but according to prevailing expectations in the neighborhood. The greatest differences, therefore, may be between neighborhoods or school districts, not broad social classes. But, whatever is found in future studies, self-report findings suggest that lower-class children are not much more or less inclined to be law violators than others. It is only when official delinquency measures are used that this seems to be the case.

7. *Are the most delinquent children members of minority groups?* This question cannot be answered for all minority groups. Very little self-report study has been made of such important groups as Mexican Americans, Puerto Ricans, other Latin American groups, several Oriental groups, or even the many different Caucasian groups in American society (Cf. Voss, 1966, for an exception). Any conclusions, therefore, will have to be limited to contrasts between black and white Americans.

As a start, Hirschi (1969:43) found that 53 percent of the black and 26 percent of the white boys in Richmond, California—a city in the San Francisco Bay area—had official police records. These figures are strikingly similar to those reported by Wolfgang, et al. (1972) in Philadelphia; viz. 50 percent for blacks and 29 percent for whites. Thus, in opposite ends of the country, official records indicate that black boys are far more likely to be defined as delinquent. But when self-reported measures of "delinquency" are used, Hirschi (1969:75–76) finds that differences between blacks and whites are greatly reduced.

For example, 42 percent of the Negro and 35 percent of the white boys report having been picked up by the police; 49 percent of the Negro and 44 percent of the white boys report having committed one or more delinquent acts during the preceding year. By one [the official] measure, then, the difference between Negroes and whites is 24 percentage points, by another [the self-report] measure it is only 5 percentage points.

Hirschi's findings, it turns out, are not unique. While the chances are much greater that blacks will have police, court, and correctional records, differences are diminished considerably when self-report data are gathered. Several studies have indicated that the overall *frequency* of law violation may be slightly higher for blacks than for whites, but, if it is higher, it is not much higher (Gold, 1970; Hirschi, 1969; Institute for Juvenile Research, 1972; Williams and Gold, 1972).

There are, however, some important qualitative differences. Black children seem more inclined than white ones to commit *serious* offenses resulting in greater personal injury to others and perhaps in greater property loss. In its statewide study, the Illinois Institute for Juvenile Research (1972:23–24) found that "black adolescents are approximately twice as likely to report an act of violence as white adolescents." Whites, meanwhile, had a "distinct" edge over blacks in automobile violations—driving without a license, or recklessly joyriding, or stripping a car. Otherwise, the two races were generally alike in their self-reported offense rates.

Other studies also report that black boys are more likely to report having committed serious offenses. From its first nationwide sample in 1967, Williams and Gold (1972:217) found that "assaults, burglary and theft—in that order—account for the greater seriousness of the delinquent behavior of black compared to white boys." The same findings, moreover, reappeared in a second nationwide survey conducted in 1972 (Gold and Reimer, 1974:17). While there was some decline in the overall frequency of delinquent acts among both races in the intervening years, total seriousness declined only among whites. Assault among blacks was reported more frequently in 1972, while the threat of assault remained about the same. Differences in assault rates, in other words, continued to appear. These same differences, however, did not carry over to girls in the two surveys. Black girls were no more nor no less frequently or seriously delinquent than white girls.

When compared to official information, these self-report findings suggest two things. On one hand, they tend to support official accounts which suggest that the illegal acts of black children may be more serious than those committed by whites, particularly where crimes against persons are involved. There was no self-report study in which this finding did not appear or in which the two groups were equal. On the other hand, there was no instance in which the discrepancy between the two races in self-reported violations approached the discrepancy between them reported in official delinquency data. While official accounts indicate a large difference between blacks and whites, the difference uncovered by self-report studies is much smaller. How, then, does one account for these contrasting sets of findings?

The explanation is probably much the same as it was when social class differences were being considered. To be sure, apprehension for a serious offense is likely to increase the probability of arrest and trial. But beyond that, characteristics other than law-violating behavior will increase the likelihood that black children will be processed through the juvenile justice system. Because they are more likely to be lower class, as well as being of minority status, they are in a double bind. Almost inevitably, official delinquency rates for black children are made much higher. Even worse, the tendency to equate these rates with rates of law-violating behavior only adds to long-standing misconceptions about the relation of race to delinquency.

8.   *What do self-report studies show about girls?*   In the previous chapter we learned that official rates of delinquency among girls have traditionally been much lower than among boys but that female rates have been increasing at a more rapid rate in recent years. Self-report studies tend to support these conclusions, particularly the one suggesting that the gap between boys and girls is tending to close. In order to illustrate this point, we will review a series of studies beginning in 1961 and ending in 1972.

Reports from girls in 1961 suggested that they had been much less delinquent than boys, both in terms of frequency and seriousness (Gold, 1966). At the same time, they also tended to take issue with some long-standing assumptions about girls. Historically, such offenses as incorrigibility (hitting or resisting parents), running away, and fornication have come to be considered "girls' offenses" because they are the ones most frequently reported in official data. Gold (1966) found, however, that these acts accounted for only about 8 to 11 percent of all offenses reported. Considerably more common than these were drinking, shoplifting, truancy, theft, and illegal entry while property destruction, fighting, and even assault were about as common. These initial findings have since been confirmed by a series of subsequent studies.

Though girls usually report fewer delinquent acts than boys, the pattern of female delinquency parallels that for boys (Hindelang, 1971; Jensen and Eve, 1976; Williams and Gold, 1972; Wise, 1967). Clearly, then, prevailing notions about the illegal acts of girls have been misleading, particularly those which suggest that delinquency is the product of poverty or that girls' offenses are expressions of their femininity while other offenses are masculine offenses.

Not only do most self-report studies indicate that girls have been more delinquent than previously thought, but they suggest that their delinquent acts may be increasing. As a result of its statewide survey of adolescents in 1972, the Illinois Institute for Juvenile Research (1973) concluded that girls were reporting "a higher level of delinquent involvement than had ever been reported in the past." They were still somewhat less delinquent than boys, but historical differences were much less marked.

The investigators in this study were aware that their findings might be peculiar to Illinois but were disinclined to accept this view, not only because their findings for boys tended to confirm earlier self-report studies, but because the rate of violation for girls across a whole range of offenses was so pronounced. For example, they found that girls were just as inclined as boys to have cheated at school, been truant, gotten drunk, purchased liquor, or smoked marijuana. They were not as likely to have been involved in property violations or to have committed a long list of automobile offenses, but their rates were unexpectedly high. Girls, however, were still much less inclined to report having been involved in crimes of violence; boys were about twice as likely to admit offenses of this type. But, as reported earlier in the discussion on racial differences, there was some evidence that black girls in Illinois might have been more violent than white girls. "Gender and race distinctions," said the Illinois Institute Report (1973:23), "generate a range of incidence of violence which varies from a high of 81 percent involvement among black boys to a low of 36 percent among white girls." There did seem to be important differences along racial as well as sexual lines for such acts as gang fighting, using a weapon, and strongarming.

In their national survey conducted in the same year, Gold and Reimer (1974:15–17) achieved results that were both similar and dissimilar. On one hand, they found a rather significant increase of 22 percent in the number of delinquent acts reported by girls, something that was not observed among boys between 1967 and 1972. And, like the Illinois survey, they found these increases were related heavily to such things as drinking and drug use. "The frequency of drinking is nearly doubled, and per capita use of marijuana and drugs is nine times greater among females in '72 than in '67." On the other hand, there was not much increase in other offenses. Virtually all that observed was due to the increased inclination of girls to use drugs. Furthermore, this inclination was more pronounced among white than black girls. They were the ones whose use had increased the most. In terms of seriousness, however, black and white girls did not differ; neither group changed markedly from 1967 to 1972 (Gold and Reimer, 1974:17). The same was true when social class was taken into account; there were no pronounced differences (Gold and Reimer, 1974:19).

In summing up, then, these self-report studies suggest three things: (1) for some time, girls have probably committed a rather long list of illegal acts which historically have been viewed as "masculine" offenses; (2) they have not been as delinquent as boys, but their violation rate in recent years has increased at a considerably faster pace; and (3) there is a possibility that black girls may be more violent than white girls, but, at this stage, differences along racial lines may have been overdone.

9. *What are the limitations of self-report studies?* There are several possible limitations associated with self-report studies. The first has to do with the fact that few are representative of the population at large. Only two have retrieved information from a nationwide sample; the rest are local studies. Hence, care must be exercised in generalizing to all youth from the studies.

Self-report studies are not conducted on an annual basis so that it is impossible to measure delinquency trends like those measured by the *Uniform Crime Reports.* One cannot say for certain whether rates are going up or down or whether patterns of law violation are changing.

Self-report studies have gathered little information from adults. Hence, it is impossible to make comparisons between age groups as is done in the *Uniform Crime Reports.*

Self-report data are gathered by interview and questionnaire methods. It is not always possible, as a result, to be certain about the accuracy of those data, particularly as they apply to serious crimes. Some young people may not be willing to supply accurate information; sometimes they are not able to recall accurately the cases in which they violated the law; and they do not always understand what is being asked of them so that incorrect information is supplied.

Various investigators do not always gather information on a standardized list of delinquent acts. The lists of offenses about which they ask are not always the same. Consequently, comparability among studies is hindered.

In short, self-report studies, like other measures of delinquent behavior, have their limitations. Some of these limitations are no greater than those associated with other studies of human behavior. Nonetheless, they require that we exercise caution in assessing their meaning.

Summary and conclusions

Images of delinquency based solely on official records are probably misleading. Self-report studies suggest that many official assumptions about the extent, the nature, and the social location of juvenile lawbreaking are biased. But, if we are to benefit from this discovery, we must make certain that we interpret it correctly.

The reason is that bias comes in two forms. The first is ideological and can be equated with racism, bigotry, and discrimination. Self-report studies suggest that bias of this type is inherent in official measures, particularly where lower-class and black children are concerned. But that bias runs far deeper than personal bigotry on the parts of the police and other officials. Beginning in the 19th century, we built into our laws and legal institutions the belief that poverty plus minority status equals lawbreaking. Even well-meaning efforts to remedy the economic, educational, and other problems of the poor and black children led to their being recorded as official delinquents. It was inevitable, therefore, that they should have higher official delinquency rates.

At the same time, not all of the self-report findings fit equalitarian preconceptions. They show, for example, that, rather than discriminating against the young, official records may distort the extent of juvenile lawbreaking by grossly *under*estimating it. Large proportions of the youth population have committed a wide variety of delinquent acts, but few of them have official records. Whether offenders are black or white, lower- or middle-class, nine out of ten of their law violations either go undetected or unacted upon.

What is being illustrated is the fact that not all of the bias inherent in official records is ideological. Some of it is statistical. Statistical bias refers to the tendency for some estimate of delinquency (or any other phenomenon) to deviate from the true value. The reason that official and self-report measures depart so widely from each other is due to the fact that they are measuring different things. While self-report measures concern themselves solely with the illegal behavior of children, official measures are a reflection of official responses to children—which ones they catch or seek to help, whom they assign police records, and whom they process through the juvenile justice system. Consequently, these two measures introduce statistical bias by providing us with different estimates of "delinquency." Our problem occurs in deciding how to interpret them so as to eliminate as much bias as possible.

In order to do this, it is imperative that we choose the appropriate measure when attempting to answer questions about delinquency. If, on one hand, we wish to understand *law-violating behavior*—i.e., how many children violate the law and why they do it—then our best recourse is to self-report and similar measures. If, on the other hand, we wish to understand *official delinquency*—i.e., how the juvenile justice system operates and who is being processed by it—then our best recourse is to official measures. Above all, it must be remembered that *law-violating behavior* and *official delinquency* are not the same things. By keeping this difference in mind, we can do a better job of interpreting the self-report findings of this chapter.

The conclusions for which the evidence seems most solid are the following:

1. The extent of juvenile lawbreaking is far greater than the extent of official delinquency. Because official records better reflect what officials rather than what children do, they are not a good measure of the extent of law-violating behavior.

2. The chances that a law violator will be apprehended are all in his favor. Far more often than not, his law violations go undetected and unacted upon.

3. The traditional assumption that law-violating behavior is generated almost totally by conditions of poverty and race is incorrect. The relationship, if not nonexistent, is exaggerated. Black children appear somewhat more inclined to commit serious crimes, but young people from all races and classes violate the law.

4. Boys violate the law more often than girls, but the notion that girls commit only "girls' offenses" is misleading. Not only have they committed a variety of "boys' offenses," but their offense rate is increasing at a more rapid pace.

5. While most children are law violators, only a small minority violate the law with great frequency and seriousness—a conclusion which is supported by official findings.

6.   While the juvenile justice system is far from totally effective, it does seem to operate like a coarse net, catching and prosecuting some of the most serious and frequent law violators while letting some of the less serious escape. This conclusion, however, is tempered by the fact that the odds still seem to be all in favor of the violator.

7.   Self-report studies tend to question whether law-violating behavior is increasing at the rapid rate suggested by official measures. Both agree that it is increasing precipitously for girls, but self-report studies question whether this is true for boys. It could be that the increase observed by officials is due to better record keeping on their part. Perhaps they are tapping more successfully the high rates of law-violating behavior which self-report studies have always found to exist.

References

Akers, Ronald L.
>   1964   "Socio-economic status and delinquent behavior: a retest." *Journal of Research in Crime and Delinquency*, January, I:38–46.

Christie, Nils et al.
>   1965   "A study of self-reported crime." In K. O. Christiansen (Ed.) *Scandinavian Studies in Criminology* (Vol. II). London: Tavistock Publications.

Clark, John P. and Wenninger, Eugene P.
>   1962   "Socio-economic class and area as correlates of illegal behavior among juveniles." *American Sociological Review*, December, 27:826–834.

Cloward, Richard A. and Ohlin, Lloyd E.
>   1960   *Delinquency and Opportunity: A Theory of Delinquent Gangs*. New York: Free Press.

Cohen, Albert K.
>   1955   *Delinquent Boys: The Culture of the Gang*. New York: Free Press.

Dentler, Robert A. and Monroe, Lawrence J.
>   1961   "Social correlates of early adolescent theft." *American Sociological Review*, October, 26:733–743.

Elmhorn, K.
>   1965   "Study in self-reported delinquency among school children in Stokholm." In K. O. Christiansen (Ed.), *Scandinavian Studies in Criminology* (Vol. II). London: Tavistock Publications.

Empey, LaMar T.
> 1967 "Delinquency theory and recent research." *Journal of Research in Crime and Delinquency*, January, 4:28–42.

Empey, LaMar T. and Erickson, Maynard L.
> 1966 "Hidden delinquency and social status." *Social Forces*, June, 44:546–554.

Erickson, Maynard L.
> 1972 "The changing relationship between official and self-reported measures of delinquency: an exploratory predictive study.: *Journal of Criminal Law, Criminology, and Police Science*, September–October, 3:388–395.

Erickson, Maynard L. and Empey, LaMar T.
> 1963 "Court records, undetected delinquency, and decisionmaking." *The Journal of Criminal Law, Criminology, and Police Science*, December, 54:456–469.

Gold, Martin
> 1966 "Undetected delinquent behavior." *Journal of Research in Crime and Delinquency*, January, 3:27–46.

> 1970 *Delinquent Behavior in an American City*. Belmont, Ca.: Brooks/Cole Publishing.

Gold, Martin and Reimer, Donald J.
> 1974 "Changing patterns of delinquent behavior among Americans 13–16 years old: 1967–1972." *National Survey of Youth, Report No. 1*. University of Michigan Institute for Social Research (Mimeo).

Hindelang, Michael J.
> 1971 "Age, sex, and the versatility or delinquency involvements." *Social Problems*, Spring, 18:527–535.

Hirschi, Travis
> 1969 *Causes of Delinquency*. Berkeley: University of California Press.

Illinois Institute for Juvenile Research
> 1972 *Juvenile Delinquency in Illinois*. Chicago: Illinois Department of Mental Health.

Jensen, Gary and Eve, Raymond
> 1976 "Sex differences in delinquency." *Criminology*, February, 13:427–448.

Murphy, Fred J. et al.
> 1946 "The incidence of hidden delinquency." *American Journal of Orthopsychiatry*, October, 686–696.

Myerhoff, Howard L. and Myerhoff, Barbara G.
> 1964 "Field observations of middle-class 'gangs'." *Social Forces*, March, 42:328–336.

National Commission on the Causes and Prevention of Violence
      1969   "American criminal statistics: an explanation and appraisal." *Crimes of Violence* (Vol. II). Washington, D.C.: U.S. Government Printing Office.

Nettler, Gwynn
      1974   *Explaining Crime.* New York: McGraw-Hill.

Porterfield, Austin L.
      1946   *Youth in Trouble.* Fort Worth: Leo Potishman Foundation.

President's Commission on Law Enforcement and Administration of Justice.
      1967a *Task Force Report: Crime and Its Impact.* Washington, D.C.: U.S. Government Printing Office.

      1967b *The Challenge of Crime in a Free Society.* Washington, D.C.: U.S. Government Printing Office.

Reiss, Albert J., Jr. and Rhodes, Albert L.
      1961   "The distribution of juvenile delinquency in the social class structure." *American Sociological Review*, October, 26:720–732.

Short, James F., Jr. and Nye, F. Ivan
      1958   "Extent of unrecorded delinquency, tentative conclusions." *Journal of Criminal Law, Criminology, and Police Science*, November-December, 49:296–302.

Voss, Harwin L.
      1966   "Socio-economic status and reported delinquent behavior.: *Social Problems*, Winter, 13:314–324.

Wallerstein, James A. and Wyle, J. C.
      1947   "Our law-abiding law-breakers." *Federal Probation*, April, 25:107–112.

Williams, Jay R. and Gold, Martin
      1972   "From delinquent behavior to official delinquency." *Social Problems*, Fall, 20:209–229.

Wise, Nancy B.
      1967   "Juvenile delinquency among middle-class girls." Pp. 179–188 in Edmund W. Vaz (Ed.), *Middle-Class Juvenile Delinquency*. New York: Harper and Row.

Wolfgang, Marvin E. et al.
      1972   *Delinquency in a Birth Cohort.* Chicago: University of Chicago Press.

8

VICTIM ACCOUNTS OF
DELINQUENT BEHAVIOR

This is the third and final chapter on the extent and nature of delinquent behavior. It turns for its information to a series of surveys on criminal victimization in the United States. These surveys have an interesting history.

In July 1965, President Lyndon Johnson established a Commission on Law Enforcement and Administration of Justice and charged the commission with providing a more coherent picture of crime in American society and making recommendations as to what should be done about it (1967a:v). Almost immediately, knowledgeable staff and consultants expressed the conviction that information on the extent and nature of crime and delinquency required improvement. Their concerns stemmed from the well-known difficulties with police statistics that we have already discussed. Before sensible recommendations could be made, new information was required. Consequently, the decision was made to conduct a national survey of 10,000 representative American households to determine what experiences with crime their residents had had, whether they had reported those experiences to the police, and how those experiences had affected their lives.

The findings of the survey were striking. Like self-report studies, they indicated that there is far more crime than is ever reported officially. Rape, for example, appeared to be four times as frequent as police reports had indicated (Ennis, 1967:9). Likewise, many other crimes were underreported. The commission report noted that:

> Burglaries occur about three times more often than they are reported to police. Aggravated assaults and larcenies over $50 occur twice as often as they are reported. There are 50 percent more robberies than are reported. In some areas only one tenth of the total number of certain kinds of crimes are reported to the police. Seventy-four percent of the neighborhood commercial establishments surveyed do not report to police the thefts committed by their employees (President's Commission on Law Enforcement and Administration of Justice 1967a:*v*).

As a result of such findings, the commission expressed the fear that crime was eroding the quality of American life. This fear was fed by another commission study (1967a:*v*) which was conducted in high crime areas of two cities. It found that:

> 43 percent of the respondents say they stay off the streets at night because of their fear of crime.
>
> 35 percent say they do not speak to strangers any more because of their fear of crime.
>
> 21 percent say they use cars and cabs at night because of their fear of crime.
>
> 20 percent say they would like to move to another neighborhood because of their fear of crime.

Nationwide, the same fears were expressed. More than one third of all Americans, in fact, say they keep firearms in the house for protection against criminals. Almost that many keep watchdogs for the same reason.

The commission (1967a:*vi*) was also concerned over the fact that young people commit a disproportionate share of all crime. It warned that 15- and 16-year-olds not only have the highest arrest rate in the United States but that during the late 1960s the number of children was growing at a much faster rate than the total population. "The problem in the years ahead," it said, "is dramatically foretold by the fact that 23 percent of the population is 10 and under."

The significance of this fact, reported in 1967, should not be lost on us. This large population of young people was moving through its most crime prone years during the period on which this and foregoing accounts of delinquent behavior are based. This fact has undoubtedly contributed to the increasing numbers of official crimes that have been noted. Although official delinquency has increased more rapidly than the juvenile population has grown, the mere fact that there were more juveniles would also increase the total number of crimes.

It was for this and other reasons—most notably the questionable accuracy of police reports—that the crime commission (1967b:2) recommend that further victim surveys be conducted and made a part of the nation's regular data gathering procedures. Likewise, a more recent commission—the National Advisory Commission on Criminal Justice Standards and Goals (1973:32)—noted that it is unrealistic to expect any single measure of crime to be completely accurate. Therefore, victimization surveys might be useful in evaluating police crime statistics and vice versa.

Nature of victim surveys

After several years of preparation and pilot study, the first National Crime Survey under governmental auspices was conducted in 1973 by the U.S. Bureau of the Census in conjunction with the Law Enforcement Assistance Administration's newly created National Criminal Justice Information and Statistics Service (1975a:*iii–vii*). Information was gathered from a sample of approximately 125,000 people located in 60,000 households and 15,000 businesses in the entire nation. Current plans are to continue the National Crime Survey on a regular basis.

The specific crimes on which data were gathered are roughly equivalent to the index crimes measured by the *Uniform Crime Reports* of the FBI. So that the nature of criminal victimization could be better understood, however, these crimes were divided into three types.

1. *Crimes against persons.* These are crimes in which individuals are the victims— rape, robbery, assault, and personal larceny. In many instances, they involve personal confrontation and direct contact between the criminal and victim. However, in some kinds of personal larceny— pocket picking or the theft of money or property—force and confrontation do not always occur. Theft occurs without the victim knowing it.

2. *Crimes against households.* These are crimes in which dwelling units rather than individuals are the victims. They include three acts: burglary, household larceny, and motor vehicle theft. If the criminal should come into direct contact with one of the inhabitants of a household, however, the act is counted as a personal crime. For example, a burglary, begun as a crime against a household, becomes a personal robbery if the burglar is surprised by a member of the household and is forced to confront that person directly.

3. Crimes against commercial establishments. These are crimes against commercial establishments and involve only two illegal acts— burglary and robbery. In this instance, however, the robbery of an employee by a criminal is not counted as a personal crime. It still remains a commercial crime.

Limitations of victim surveys

Victim surveys have certain limitations. One of the most important for our purposes is that they deal only with one dimension of delinquent behavior; namely, criminal offenses rather than juvenile status offenses or with cases of cruelty and neglect to small children. Thus, we will gain no new information on these matters. However, this will not necessarily be an overwhelming loss.

In the chapter on the rules governing delinquent behavior, we saw signs that society is beginning to change the way it defines and constructs that behavior. There is a growing tendency to separate status and criminal offenses and to treat the former as less serious. Perhaps we will see the time when the problems of truancy, running away, disobedience, and similar acts are no longer handled by legal authorities. Already children with these kinds of problems are being routed to other agencies. Conversely, there is an increasing tendency for some states to lower the age of accountability for criminal behavior from age 18 to age 16. Sixteen and 17-year-olds are being tried in adult rather than juvenile courts. Given these trends, therefore, it is important to determine not only how many criminal offenses juveniles commit (which we have already done), but how often they are victimized.

Besides juvenile status offenses, the victim surveys also omit the collection of information on a long list of other crimes—on murder, for example, where victims cannot be interviewed or on kidnapping where victims are rare. Other types of crimes such as drunkenness, drug use, gambling, and prostitution, like juvenile status offenses, do not usually have immediate victims and thus are not measured. Finally, there is a third set of crimes that are difficult to document from the victim's standpoint—employee theft, shoplifting, income tax cheating, or even blackmail where the victim, as well as the blackmailer, has something to hide. The victimization surveys, therefore, do not collect data on illegal acts of these types.

Some of these omissions are serious in the sense that they tend to focus attention on youthful and lower-class crimes while ignoring the crimes of affluent, powerful, and older people—embezzlement, bribery, fraud, violation of antitrust laws, stock swindles, income tax evasion, and so on. While it is true that these are difficult to document in an interview—sometimes because the victim is unaware of them, because he may join in covering them up if his losses will be recovered, or because the "victim" is all of us—neither our knowledge of crime nor our social trust will be improved until something is done to measure them more effectively. In fact, the failure of the National Criminal Information Service (NCIS) to collect information on crimes like this is surprising in light of the fact that the victim survey conducted for the President's Crime Commission in 1967 did do so (Cf. Ennis, 1967). Too often, attention is focused on the extent of personal robbery or household burglary at the expense of knowing how extensive and what the social cost is of more sophisticated white-collar crimes.

A final set of limitations has to do with the survey method for collecting victim data. One question that is often asked is whether accurate estimates of crime can be obtained by interviewing only a sample of Americans rather than all of them. Why not interview everyone over age 12—over 160 million people? The answer is that this cannot be done because the expenses would outweigh the benefits; the yearly cost would be astronomical. Furthermore, it is unnecessary. By carefully selecting a representative sample of the entire population, it is possible to estimate what that population would have said had every one been interviewed. That is what the Censes Bureau and the Office of Criminal Justice Information did

They selected a representative sample of households and businesses and then interviewed about 125,000 people in them. Once having done so, they could generalize from that sample to the entire population, using scientific procedures to estimate the amount of sampling error in their results and informing the public as to its size. Because their sample was a large one, in fact, the error due to sampling was small (Cf. National Criminal Justice Information Service, 1975a:25–41). Collecting data by sample, then, is not an overriding problem providing it is carefully done.

The most serious problems, instead, are inherent in the actual process of interviewing people—overcoming language and communication barriers or being able to determine whether people tell the truth or whether they can accurately recall the events surrounding the crimes in which they were victimized. Sometimes memories or perceptions are unintentionally, if not deliberately, faulty. Those who conducted the survey attempted to deal with the problems of recall by asking people to describe only those events taking place within the last six months because they are the ones that can be recalled most accurately. But there is no way of knowing for certain the extent to which other kinds of distortions are present in the survey findings. After the survey has been run several times, some distortions will be located and eliminated, but others will always remain. Hence, we can never be satisfied that survey findings are totally accurate.

Benefits of victim surveys

With all their limitations, the expectation is that victim surveys will do much to improve our knowledge of crime and delinquency, not only because they avoid the filtering process through which the gathering of police and court statistics go, but because they will provide new kinds of information that have simply been unavailable heretofore:

Better information on the number of crime victims as contrasted to the number of crimes reported by the police.   Normally, the number of victims is greater than the number of crimes because more than one victim may be involved in the commission of any one of them. We will now have a better estimate of how many victims there are.

The risks of being victimized.   What are the chances of being robbed, assaulted, or having one's house or business broken into? When and where are these likely to occur? Over a period of time, year-by-year victim surveys can detect increases or decreases in these probabilities.

Variations in the risk of being victimized.   Who are the most likely victims of crimes—males or females, young people or old, blacks or whites, poor or the well-to-do? Does the risk of becoming a victim vary according to one's sex, age, or status in society? Do the victims of one type of crime differ from the victims of another?

Crime trends.   Although the victim survey has not yet been conducted over a long enough period of time, it will eventually provide us with a valuable assessment of crime trends; i.e., whether crime rates are going up or down.

Increased objectivity in crime reporting.   The victim survey will provide a most valuable addition to our measurement of crime. Along with official and self-report accounts, it will permit us to speak with a great deal more objectivity, not only with respect to crime rates and trends, but with respect to the nature and social location of crime. Many of our long-standing assumptions can be better tested thereby.

Annual victimization surveys, in short, have considerable potential. Their value is by no means exhausted by the few examples just cited. The information they provide, though limited in some respects, may not only throw new light on the nature and extent of delinquent behavior, but help to pinpoint both weaknesses and strengths in the way we explain and respond to that behavior.

Number of victims

Based upon its findings, the National Criminal Information Service (NCIS) estimated that there were approximately 37 million victims of successful or attempted crimes in 1973 (1975a:1). As may be seen in Table 8–1, about 55 percent of the victims were individuals, 41 percent were households, and 4 percent were businesses.

There are two things about these overall figures that are noteworthy. First, as Table 8–1 shows, the most common victimizations did not involve the direct use of threat or violence. The single most prevalent crime was personal larceny (40 percent)—such acts as stealing money, picking pockets, or property loss where force was not involved. The next

TABLE 8–1
Distribution of victimizations, by type of crime

Type of crime		Percent
All crimes		100.0
Crimes against persons		54.8
Rape	0.4	
Robbery	3.0	
Assault	11.2	
Personal larceny	40.3	
Crimes against households		40.8
Burglary	17.1	
Household larceny	20.2	
Motor vehicle theft	3.5	
Crimes against businesses		4.4
Burglary	3.7	
Robbery	0.7	

Source: National Criminal Justice Information Service, 1975a:1.

most common crime was household larceny (20 percent), an act of the same type. It refers to a theft or attempted theft from a home in which neither forcible nor unlawful entry is present. Apparently many household thieves are people who gain entry to a home through lawful means—service men, baby sitters, friends, or acquaintances.

Burglary, which ranked next (17 percent), does involve unlawful entry but not direct confrontation between victim and criminal. Thus, such violent crimes as assault (11 percent), robbery (3 percent), or rape (0.4 percent) rank relatively low in terms of overall frequency. Even though they are abhorrent crimes and terribly frightening to their victims, they are by no means the most common.

The second important finding is less consoling. If there were 37 million victims of crimes in 1973 as was estimated, that figure would be well over four times as large as the number of similar crimes (8.6 million) reported by the police for the same year (FBI, 1974:1). This large discrepancy must be discounted to some degree because of differences in the way police and victim data are collected. The police, for example, report only the number of criminal incidents that take place, while victim surveys record the number of victims. Since on some occasions there are multiple victims of a single crime, one would expect to find that there are more victims than crimes. Yet, even when this difference is taken into account, important discrepancies persist.

After counting only the number of crimes rather than how many victims there were, the NCIS (1974a:5) found that, for most crimes, the number of incidents reported by victims in the first half of 1973 still exceeded the number reported by the police by large amounts: rape, three times; robbery, three times; aggravated assault, three times; burglary, three times; larceny, six times; and auto theft, one time. Overall, the victim reported incidents for these six crimes were still four times larger than those reported by police. Thus, victim reports, like self-reports from law violators, lend support to the notion that official police accounts grossly underestimate the actual number of criminal incidents.

The risk of being a victim

Since the risks of becoming a victim of crime are probably greater than police records indicate, it is useful to examine those risks in two ways: (1) to examine what the chances are in general of being the personal victim of crime or of having one's home or business victimized;

and (2) to examine variations in the risk of being victimized depending upon one's social class position, sex, race, or age. In this section, we will be concerned with risks in general. Some review of them is important because of prevailing beliefs that crime rates are increasing and that the "average" person is in danger.

The average citizen does fear random violence, committed by a complete stranger, because it is the most frightening of all crimes. There is really no way to predict or to guard against it. Newspaper accounts like the following, therefore, are far more important in constructing our social image of the dangers we face than any number of statistical accounts put out by the federal government.

THREE TEENAGERS HELD IN SLAYING OF MAN, WOMAN FOR $13 LOOT

Three teenaged boys were held by Inglewood police Wednesday after a violent night in which a housewife was beaten and shot to death for $3 and a man was killed for $10. Each of the victims had been shot in the eye.

The first murder victim was . . . apparently dragged from her car in her driveway . . . about 8 P.M. Tuesday after taking her husband to night school.

Neighbors heard her screams and called police. She had been beaten around the head and shot through the eye. Her car and purse containing $3 were gone.

An hour later . . . near Dodger stadium residents heard shots. A short time after that, the body of an unidentified Latin man was found by strollers. Police said this victim, too had been shot through one eye. They said $10 was believed taken from him (*Los Angeles Times*, May 9, 1974).

Personal victimizations

Even though the findings of statistical studies can never be so dramatic as newspaper accounts, they can help to put it into a larger perspective. Table 8–2 is constructed for that purpose. It contrasts the rates of various personal crimes reported by victims in the National Crime Survey with those reported by the police in the *Uniform Crime Reports.*

The table illustrates once again the disparity between police and citizen reported crimes. According to the police, there were about four victims of violent crimes per 1,000 people in 1973. By contrast, the victim survey puts the rate at about 34 per 1,000, a rate that is over eight times as great. For personal larceny (theft without forcible or unlawful

TABLE 8–2
Victim and police reported rates for crimes against persons, 1973

Type of crime	Victim survey*	Uniform Crime Report*
Crimes of violence	33.9	4.1
Murder	—	0.1
Rape	1.0	0.2
Robbery	6.9	1.8
With injury 2.4		
Without injury 4.6		
Aggravated assault	10.4	4.9
Simple assault	15.6	—
Personal larceny	93.4	20.5
Larceny with contact	3.2	
Larceny without contact	90.3	

* Rates and subrates may not add to total because of rounding.
—Not reported.
Rate calculations: Survey: Rate per 1,000 population, age 12 and over. UCR: Rate per 1,000 population, all ages.
Sources: National Criminal Justice Information Service, 1975a:12 and FBI, *Uniform Crime Report*, 1973:1.

entry), the differences were also large, 21 versus 93 per 1,000. Added to media accounts, such finding could be interpreted as suggesting that the risks of being victimized are overwhelming. But there is another side to the issue.

If the 1973 survey is used to assess the chances that the "average" person would be victimized sometime during that year, it puts a somewhat different light on the subject. Table 8–2 shows that the chances were only about 3 percent that a person age 12 or older would be a victim of a violent crime. Almost 97 times out of 100, the odds were against it. Furthermore, the crime that contributed most heavily to the overall violence rate was assault. The chances were between 2 and 3 in 100 that a person would be attacked. Yet, even then, the most common assault was simple assault which did not involve the use of a weapon or result in serious injury.

By contrast, the more serious crimes—rape, robbery, and murder—were much less likely to occur. In 1973, the chances that a person would be the victim of one of these crimes were: about 1 in 1000 that a woman would be raped; about 7 in 1000 that a person would be robbed; about 2 in 1000 that a person would be injured during a robbery; and about 1 in 10,000 that a person would be murdered (according to the *Uniform Crime Reports*, which on this issue are thought to be accurate.)

What these findings suggest, in short, is that the risks for an "average" person in any given year are not overwhelming. One is inclined to be relieved, therefore, upon learning that the overall probability of being murdered in 1973 was only about 1 in 10,000.

Household victimizations

The chances that one's household will be victimized are as great, or are greater, than the chances that one will be victimized personally. This fact has not always been common knowledge because the *Uniform Crime Reports* base their rates for such household crimes as burglary on the total number of people in the United States. By contrast, the NCIS (1975a) based its victim rates on the number of households in the country, not on the number of people. As a result, some important things were discovered.

In 1973, the chances that one's home would be victimized in one of the three household crimes—burglary, larceny, and motor vehicle theft—were as follows (NCIS, 1975a:19):

Burglary: about 9 chances in 100.
Larceny (theft without forcible or unlawful entry): about 11 chances in 100.
Motor vehicle theft: about 2 chances in 100.

These rates, at least for burglary and larceny are relatively high—about 1 in 10 in a single year.

Commercial victimizations

Perhaps even more striking is the rate at which commercial establishments are reportedly victimized. Again basing its rates on the number of commercial establishments rather than the total population, the NCIS (1975a:23) found that the chances a business would be burglarized in 1973 were about 20 in a 100—a rate that was at least twice as high as that for burglary against households. Similarly, the chances that one's business would be robbed (about 4 in 100) were about five times as high as the chances that one would be robbed personally. This was particularly true of retail establishments as contrasted to service or other kinds of business; they were particularly vulnerable.

In short, if one were to assume that all people in the United States are equally vulnerable to crime, there are certain points that could be made about the risks involved. In any given year, the chances that the "average" person will be victimized are relatively small. If that person is victimized, moreover, it is much more likely that she or he will have money or property stolen than that she or he will be assaulted, raped, or robbed by force. The notion that most crimes are characterized by direct, violent contact between victim and criminal is inaccurate. Furthermore, the chances that one's household or business will be victimized are even greater.

Special vulnerability to crime

The foregoing conclusions about the "average" person are useful, but they are only partially accurate. The reason is that all people are not equally vulnerable to crime; criminal acts are not randomly distributed. Rather, some people are more likely to be victimized than others based upon their age, sex, race, or where they live. Hence, in order to be fully informed, it is necessary to see how these factors affect the risks of being victimized. They will greatly alter the odds just described for the "average" person.

Age

Because of our concern with the young, it is significant that age is highly related to the chances of becoming a victim of crime (NCIS, 1974a:15). As may be seen in Figure 8–1, the people most likely to suffer from personal crimes—rape, robbery, assault, and larceny—are the young. After adolescence or young adulthood, the risks of victimization decrease steadily, with each age group reporting a lower rate than its predecessor.

What is striking about Figure 8–1 is that it so closely parallels the overall rate at which juveniles are arrested for crime. Just as the high crime producing years are during adolescence, so the victim survey shows that adolescents, ages 12–19, are the most likely to be victimized. Fully 24 out of every 100 reported having been victimized personally in 1973. Furthermore, the rate for 12- to 15-year-olds is almost identical with that for 16- to 19-year-olds and is somewhat higher than for young adults ages 20 to 24. By contrast, the rates reported by middle-aged and elderly people are only a fraction of those reported by the young. For people ages 50 to 64, for example, the chances are only about 6 in 100

FIGURE 8–1

Victimization rates for personal crimes by age of victim, 1973

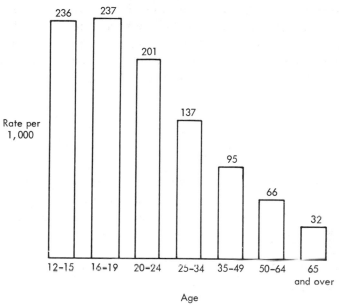

Source: National Criminal Justice Information Service, 1975a.15.

that they will be victimized. After age 65, risks decline even further to only about 3 per 100—a rate that is almost eight times lower than that for adolescents, 12 to 19 years of age.

There are also some striking findings when we consider the types of crimes for which juveniles are victimized. In both police statistics and self-report studies, we saw that young people are far more likely to commit property crimes—burglary, larceny, and auto theft—than they are to commit violent crimes—murder, rape, robbery, and assault. As may be seen in Table 8–3, the victim survey parallels these findings. Larceny among the young is the most common of all personal crimes, with the two youngest groups having the highest victim rates while each older group has a successively lower rate. But the victim survey findings do not parallel police and self-report accounts where violent crimes are concerned. Younger, not older, people are the ones most likely to be victimized in cases of rape, robbery, and assault (Table 8–3). Up to about age 25, there are relatively few differences among age groups, but, after that age, rates drop off sharply and continue to drop.

Clearly, it is younger, not older, people who run the greatest risks of being victimized in violent as well as property crimes.

The same pronounced pattern is also characteristic of crimes against households (NCIS, 1975a:20). As with personal crimes, the risks of victimization decrease steadily with age. On the one extreme, almost *half* (467 per 1,000) of the households headed by teenagers in the 12- to 19-year age range reported having been victimized in 1973. Losses to burglary (219 per 1,000) and household larceny (209 per 1,000) are about equal, with motor vehicle theft a distant third (39 per 1,000). On the other extreme, the overall victimization for people 65 and over is only 109 per 1,000. Such findings suggest that, if any segment of our society is close to living in a predatory jungle, it is the young, many of whom are legally children. Not only may they be more likely to commit crime, but they are more likely to suffer its consequences.

Sex

Special vulnerability to crime does not end with age; sex is also important. Its effects can be demonstrated in two ways. First, the general effects of sex can be considered. Who run the greater risks of being victimized—males or females? Second, the effects of sex and age can be combined to determine how they interact to alter the chances of victimization. Are young females more likely to be victimized than older males or older females? Who run the greater risks?

In general terms, Table 8–3, suggests that males are more vulnerable to personal crimes than are females. The only exception is an obvious one—rape. Otherwise, when overall rates are compared or when males and females of the same age are contrasted, the chances that a male will be victimized, particularly in a violent crime, are much greater. Not only are they more vulnerable to assault and robbery, but three out of four murder victims are male (FBI, 1974:6). Women, by contrast, run far fewer risks.

Consider an illustration of this general conclusion. Table 8–3 shows that the overall victimization rate for 16- to 19-year-old boys is 286 per 1,000, while for girls of the same age it is 189. Clearly, boys are the more vulnerable. Yet, when one combines the effects of sex and age, the picture begins to change. Our general conclusion must be qualified.

This is indicated by the fact that the chances men will be victimized more than women declines steadily after age 25. Although differences between the sexes remain statistically significant as people grow older,

TABLE 8–3

Victimization rates, crimes against persons, for 1973, by sex and age of victim (rate per 1,000 population age 12 and over)

Sex and age	Total crimes against persons	Rape	Robbery		Assault		Larceny
			With injury	Without injury	Aggravated	Simple	
Both sexes	127.3	1.0	2.4	4.5	10.4	15.6	93.4
Male	151.9	0.1*	3.4	7.0	15.7	20.0	105.7
12–15	267.0	0.4*	5.0	14.7	22.2	37.5	187.1
16–19	285.7	0.0	5.0	10.3	38.7	38.5	193.2
20–24	246.7	0.1*	5.8	11.8	33.1	37.1	158.8
25–34	161.0	0.1*	2.1	6.2	17.3	22.2	113.1
35–49	104.3	0.0	3.0	4.1	8.9	10.8	77.5
50–64	67.8	0.0	3.0	3.3	3.9	7.6	50.0
65 and over	40.3	0.0	1.9	4.3	1.4	3.6	29.1
Female	105.0	1.8	1.4	2.3	5.5	11.6	82.3
12–15	203.9	1.8	0.9*	3.1	9.6	24.3	164.2
16–19	189.4	5.3	2.3	2.7	10.7	23.2	145.2
20–24	159.1	5.4	2.2	3.0	10.9	21.2	116.4
25–34	113.8	2.3	1.9	2.5	6.2	12.7	88.2
35–49	86.8	0.5*	0.9	1.9	4.8	8.6	70.2
50–64	54.4	0.3*	1.0	1.7	1.5	4.0	46.0
65 and over	25.6	0.3*	1.5	2.4	1.0	1.6	18.8

Note: Detail may not add to total shown because of rounding.
* Estimate, based on about ten or fewer sample cases, is statistically unreliable.
Source. National Criminal Justice Information Service, 1975a:15–16.

they are of decreasing magnitude. Thus, by ages 50–64, the difference has diminished to 68 per 1,000 for men versus 54 for women. Contrast these relatively low rates with those shown above for teenagers: 286 for boys and 189 for girls. Obviously, the risks that older men and women run are not only much lower than those for adolescent boys but for adolescent girls as well.

What all of this means is that males run greater risks than females only when age is held constant; that is, only when males and females of the same age are compared. When they are not, the general conclusion that men are more vulnerable than women tends to break down. For example, adolescent girls, 16–19, have higher victimization rates, not only over much older males, but over those as young as ages 25–34. Their respective rates are 189 per 1,000 versus 161 (Table 8–3). Furthermore, the older men become, the more the discrepancy between them and young girls becomes.

As a result, two conclusions are warranted by these findings: (1)

when age is held generally constant, males have higher victimization rates than females, but (2) when the effects of age and sex are combined, young people, whether male or female, tend to have higher rates than middle-aged or older people. In fact, the victim survey findings indicate that if we were to rank different groups according to their vulnerability to crime, taking both sex and age into account, they would rank as follows:

1.   Young males.
2.   Young females.
3.   Adult males.
4.   Adult females.

Such findings seem contrary to popular belief. While there seems to be a widespread awareness of the disproportionate contribution of the young to the commission of crime, the idea is not so commonplace that the young are the most likely to be victimized. Instead, a more common belief is that it is older people who run the greatest risks—the defenseless old lady whose purse is snatched by young hoods or the reputable citizen who is robbed by a crazed addict or is terrorized on a city bus by a teenage gang. These findings strongly suggest otherwise.

Almost six out of ten *unarmed* robbers are juveniles, most of whom rob other juveniles (Mulvihill, et al. 1969:207–215). A child is backed up against the wall in the school lavatory and is robbed of his lunch money. In rare instances, such robberies may involve large amounts of money from terrorized victims:

> Four [17-year-old] students . . . faced criminal charges Thursday for allegedly extorting $1,686 from a 14-year old pupil. . . .
> The young victim told officials the "terrorizing" began after he accidentally stepped on the shoes of one of the suspects.
> Demands were made for "damages," police said, first in amounts of $3 to $10 and later increasing to $50 and $100.
> "This kid said he got the money to pay them by draining his bar mitzvah account," the police investigator said.
> The victim went to [the police] last week after he was allegedly taken to a rest room, threatened with a knife and told to give the four $1,000 by February 14.
> When he said he did not have that kind of money, the suspects reportedly punched him and threatened to kill his parents. . . . (*Los Angeles Times*, February 4, 1977).

Finally, some juvenile crimes have deadly consequences. Many killings, for example, particularly in our larger cities, are gang-related or at least are a function of the kinds of subcultural environments in which poorer people live. In one bizarre case, three boyfriends of the same teenage girl were shot to death in a period of four months (*Los Angeles Times,* November 22, 1974). The chances that such a sequence of events could occur without the girl and her boyfriends being tied to a unique, but unusually deadly, social network are small. In another case, the members of a rival gang tortured, and ultimately killed, a 16-year-old boy by tying him to the underside of a car and dragging him to death (*Los Angeles Times,* November 3, 1974). Even though such cases are statistically rare, they are much more a part of everyday life in some of the neglected areas of our central cities than in some of the more affluent.

Race

A third factor that is related to the chances of being victimized is race. Table 8–4 shows that if one looks only at overall victimization rates,

TABLE 8–4
Victimization rates, crimes against persons, for 1973, by sex of victim (rate per 1,000 population age 12 and over)

Sex	Total crimes against persons	Rape	Robbery		Assault		Larceny
			With injury	Without injury	Aggravated	Simple	
Both sexes*	127.3	1.0	2.4	4.5	10.4	15.6	93.4
White	127.2	0.9	2.1	3.9	9.5	16.0	94.8
Black	131.9	1.7	4.9	9.5	18.1	12.7	85.0
Male*	151.9	0.1†	3.4	7.0	15.7	20.0	105.7
White	151.5	0.1†	2.9	6.0	14.8	21.0	106.6
Black	161.0	0.1†	7.6	15.2	27.7	11.7	101.6
Female*	105.0	1.8	1.4	2.3	5.5	11.6	82.3
White	104.9	1.7	1.3	2.0	4.7	11.4	83.9
Black	107.8	3.1	2.6	4.8	12.5	13.5	71.3

Note: Detail may not add to total because of rounding.
* Includes "other races" not shown separately.
† Estimate, based on about ten or fewer sample cases, is statistically unreliable.
Source: National Criminal Justice Information Service, 1975a:14.

vulnerability to personal crimes seems to be about equal for blacks and whites—132 per 1,000 for blacks versus 127 for whites. However, within these overall rates are some highly important differences.

While whites are somewhat more likely to report having been victimized for personal larceny and simple assault where weapons and injury are not involved, blacks are much more likely to have suffered from violent crimes. Indeed, the rates at which blacks are victimized for rape, robbery, and aggravated assault are from two to three times greater than for whites. Furthermore, the *Uniform Crimes Reports* (FBI, 1974:6) indicate that the murder rate among blacks is staggeringly high when compared to that for whites. Although blacks constitute only about 11 percent of the total population, approximately 52 percent of all murder victims nationwide are black. In some places, the rate may be even higher. Between 1965 and 1970, for example, over 7 out of every 10 homicide victims in Chicago were black (Block and Zimring, 1973:3).

Again, the persons who suffer most from these high victimization rates are, in this instance, black males. Ranking considerably below them are white males, followed closely by black females. Black women, in fact, are almost as likely as white men to be victims. This fact is striking in light of the general tendency for female rates to be well below those of males. It underscores the excessive vulnerability of black people to crime. White women, meanwhile, rank last; their victimization rates are by far the lowest of all.

The first report of the 1973 victim survey did not contrast the victim rates of black and white children (NCIS, 1975a). The findings of the National Violence Commission, however, indicated that black children are many times more likely to be victimized violently than are white ones (Mulvihill, et al., 1969:91–94, 181–184). Even when one takes into account the propensity of white America to expect higher rates among minority children, the differences are at once both numbing and alarming.

More recent findings on the victims of murder suggest the same thing. Historically, the victims of murder, in contrast to the victims of other types of crime, have tended to be young and middle-aged adults (Mulvihill, et al., 1969:210). In Chicago, however, Block and Zimring (1973:5) found that the most dramatic single increase in murder victimization rates between 1965 and 1970 was among young, black males, ages 15–24. The rates went from 54 per 100,000 in 1965 to 193 in 1970—an increase of 350 percent. This increase was accompanied by a similar increase in the number of young, black males in the same age range who committed murder—from 108 per 100,000 in 1965 to 298 in 1970. Hence, by 1970, the most vulnerable group to murder were black youth, 15–24.

The ghettoes to which American society has confined its black citizens have become places of dismay and terror to many of its young. In his classic work, *Manchild in the Promised Land*, Claude Brown

(1965:126–128), supposedly a hardened delinquent by the age of 13 or 14, describes what was expected of him in Harlem, and how heartsick he was over those expectations:

> I was growing up now, and people were going to expect things from me. I would soon be expected to kill a nigger if he mistreated me, like Rock, Bubba Williams, and Dewdrop had.
>
> Everybody knew these cats were killers. Nobody messed with them. If anybody messed with them or their family or friends, they had to kill them. I knew now that I had to keep up with these cats; if I didn't, I would lose my respect in the neighborhood.
>
> It made life seem so hard. Sometimes I just wanted to give it up.
>
> The bad nigger thing really had me going. I remember Johnny saying that the only thing in life a bad nigger was scared of was living too long. This just meant that if you were going to be respected in Harlem you had to be a bad nigger; and if you were going to be a bad nigger, you had to be ready to die. I wasn't ready to do any of that stuff. But I had to. I had to act crazy.
>
> Sometimes I used to get headaches thinking about it. I used to get sick. I couldn't get up. And sometimes I'd just jump out of bed and run out and say, "C'mon, man, let's go steal somethin'!" I'd get Turk, I'd get Tito, I'd get anybody who was around. I'd say, "C'mon, man, let's go pull a score." It seemed like the only way I could get away.

Then, to a white correctional counselor who had befriended him, Brown made a fatalistic remark that this author has heard other ghetto boys make: "I don't think I'm gonna stay on the street, Papanek, not for much longer. I don't think I'll see Christmas on the streets." Why plan for the future? There is no future.

It is not just from personal crimes and violence that black people suffer the most. They also suffer the highest victimization rates in crimes against households (NCIS, 1975a:21). The overall rates for blacks is 269 per 1,000 households versus 216 for whites. Again, however, it is for the more serious crimes that blacks suffer the most. For burglary, the rate for blacks is 136 versus 88 whites, while for motor vehicle theft, it is 24 versus 18. Only in cases of household theft are rates identical—110 per 1,000 for each group. Added to what we have already seen, therefore, membership in the black race, along with being young and male, greatly increases vulnerability to victimization. If the rates at which they were victimized in 1973 were projected over a lifetime, the results would be shocking.

Income

A fourth factor that affects vulnerability to crime is income. When total personal crimes are examined from the standpoint of annual family income, the NCIS survey (1975a:6 and 18) indicates that people on the highest income levels have the highest overall victimization rates; they appear to be the most vulnerable. But, as when race was examined, these overall rates mask some important differences.

When a distinction is made between personal crimes of violence and personal larceny, the data show that families with the lowest incomes are those who are the most vulnerable to violent crimes. The rates of victimization for families with incomes less than $3,000 are from 2 to 3 times greater than the rates of those with incomes of $15,000 and over— rape, 2 versus 0.7 per 1,000; robbery with injury, 5 versus 2; aggravated assault, 17 versus 7. Conversely, the higher a family's income, the more likely it is to suffer from personal larceny (NCIS, 1975a:18). In short, poverty is associated with greater violence while affluence is associated with greater theft.

Survey findings also show that race interacts with income in ways that are important. On the one hand, the general pattern just described is characteristic of blacks as well as whites when comparisons are made *within* races; that is, poor people, whether black or white, have the highest rates of violent victimizations when compared to their more affluent brothers and sisters. Conversely, the greater the income, the greater the larceny.

On the other hand, comparisons *across* races reveal that blacks, no matter what their income, are more likely than similar whites to suffer from all types of crime—from violence as well as from larceny. Whether poor or well-to-do, blacks experience more crime than similarly situated whites.

Essentially the same relationships characterize household victimizations. When income levels *within* races are considered, families in the lower-income brackets have higher burglary rates but lower larceny and motor vehicle rates (NCIS, 1975a:8 and 22). That such is the case is not very surprising. Not only are poorer households less likely to have cash and property lying about to be stolen, but they are even less likely to have an automobile. But, as with personal crimes, comparisons *across* races reveal that black households on all income levels tend to suffer more from crime than do white households on the same levels. Whether poor or well-to-do, they are much more heavily victimized by burglary than their white counterparts, and the rate of motor theft among affluent blacks is approximately twice that of affluent whites. Only on household larceny are victimization rates approximately equal (NCIS, 1975a:22).

Despite the obvious influence of income, one additional fact is noteworthy. The NCIS (1975a:6) reports that income, by itself, does not provide the sharp and consistent differences in victimization rates that such variables as age, sex, and race provide. While victimization decreases steadily with age, for example, it does not do so as consistently where income is involved. Instead, differences are clear-cut only between the most poor and the most affluent. On income levels between these two extremes, differences are much less apparent. The implication is that it is not poverty alone that must be considered in trying to understand criminal behavior and its consequences, but the way poverty interacts with other important variables.

Community

The final factor associated with vulnerability to crime is community—the place where one lives. Official accounts by the police have long tended to confirm the 19th century American belief that the city is where the greatest amount of crime is spawned. Official crime rates are highest in city centers, lower in suburban areas, and lower still in rural areas. In 1973, for example, police reported victimization rates per 1,000 people were as follows (FBI, 1974:2):

	Cities over 25,000	Suburban	Rural
Violent crimes	10.0	2.5	1.5
Property crimes	55.8	33.1	13.2

While the final results on this issue for the 1973 NCIS victim survey have not been reported at this writing, the study conducted by the President's Crime Commission in 1967 lent strong support to police accounts (Ennis, 1967:23–30).

Table 8–5 displays the findings. Generally, they show that as one moves from the central city to the suburbs and out into smaller towns and rural areas, victimization rates decline. This trend is particularly pronounced for rural areas where, except for burglary, victimization rates are far lower than rates in city centers and suburbs. When the rates for all crimes are combined, in fact, the risks of victimization for violent crimes are about twice as small as for property crimes (Ennis, 1967:30).

TABLE 8–5
Victimization rates by urbanization (rate per 1,000 population)

Type of crime	Central city	Suburban	Rural
Rape	0.8	0.4	0.08
Robbery	2.1	1.0	0.00
Aggravated assault	2.9	2.9	1.1
Larceny ($50+)	7.0	8.1	3.5
Burglary	13.4	8.4	7.3
Vehicle theft	2.4	2.8	0.7

Source: Ennis, 1967:24.

However, for such property crimes as larceny and motor vehicle theft, and perhaps even for aggravated assault, rates in the suburbs may not differ much from those in the city center. For these crimes, suburban as well as city rates are higher than rural rates.

Such findings not only tend to support modern fears about crime in the streets, but lend credence to traditional beliefs that the city is the primary source of corruption and evil. Coupled with prior findings, they also lend substance to the assumption that age, race, and poverty are also tied in with the deplorable conditions in the cities that lead to high crime rates. Given this seeming confirmation of long-standing beliefs, therefore, our final task will be that of summarizing and assessing the meaning of these findings.

Summary and conclusions

A careful assessment requires that we concern ourselves with two issues: (1) with the findings of this chapter and (2) with how well these findings fit with official and self-reported accounts of delinquent behavior. As promised earlier, our goal was to use all three accounts as a method of obtaining as accurate a picture as possible of the extent and social location of delinquent behavior and whether or not it seems to be increasing.

Conclusions about victimization

1. Extent of crime. The information provided by the new victimization surveys is not likely to quiet American fears over the extent of crime. This chapter has revealed that:

The number of victim reported crimes is far in excess of the number reported by the police.

Should present rates continue, however, the chances that the "average" person will be victimized in any given year, particularly in a violent crime, are not great.

The chances that one will be victimized personally are higher than previously reported by the police, and the chances that one's household or commercial establishment will be victimized are higher still.

2. *Social location of crime.* Despite the likelihood that these findings will be viewed with alarm, the victim studies did not conform to the notion that it is older people or members of the white, middle, and upper classes who are the most vulnerable to crime. Instead, vulnerability is concentrated much more heavily elsewhere:

Young people are more vulnerable than older people.

Males are more vulnerable than females.

Blacks are more vulnerable than whites.

Poor people are more vulnerable than the affluent, at least to violent crimes.

City dwellers are more vulnerable than country dwellers.

The prototype of the most likely victim, particularly of violent crime, is the young, black male who lives in an urban ghetto. The young, poor, white male is not far behind, followed closely by the young, poor, black female.

There is irony in such findings, particularly where children are concerned. Despite the notion that we take special steps to nurture and protect them, they are far more likely than mature adults to be the victims of crime. Furthermore, the findings show that those sections of our population that are the most disadvantaged economically and culturally are also those who suffer most from violent crimes.

3. *Trends in crime.* The victim surveys have not yet been conducted over a long enough period of years to draw any firm conclusions about increases in crime. Recently, however, the NCIS (1976) published findings which compare 1973 with 1974 rates of victimization. Briefly, the findings were these:

During 1974, an estimated 39,694,000 victimizations of persons, households, and businesses were recorded, an increase of 7.5 percent over the 36,925,000 measured in 1973.

Crimes of theft involving no contact between victim and thief accounted for 90 percent of the increase. Most of the losses were to private persons and households where something was stolen without a confrontation between the victim and the offender.

Violent crimes in 1974—robbery, rape, and assault—did not increase over 1973.

Taken as a whole, it is likely that the victim surveys will do little to allay public fears of crime even though they do help to highlight misconceptions regarding who it is that is most likely to be victimized. Indeed, there is every possibility that the yearly conduct of such surveys will result in even greater attention being paid to delinquent behavior as a social problem. The reason is that we have done more in recent years to locate, to count, and to analyze such behavior than at any time in our history. Hence, whether delinquency rates have actually gone up or down, it is virtually inevitable that higher rates will be recorded. Given this possibility the extent to which these findings are congruent with official and self-report accounts assumes all the more importance.

Congruence of official, self-report, and victim accounts

Before drawing conclusions about the congruence of all three accounts of delinquent behavior, it is important that we recall and keep in mind the difference between *official delinquency* and *law-violating behavior*. Official delinquency is a product of the acts and characteristics of offenders coupled with the responses of officials to those acts and characteristics. Law-violating behavior, by contrast, involves only the delinquent act itself. An individual can become a law violator by committing an illegal act, but an official delinquent is not created until the act is detected, until official action is taken, and until the act is recorded. Thus, although the two measures of delinquent behavior are overlapping, they are not the same thing.

1.   *Extent of delinquent behavior.*   There are compelling reasons to conclude that there are far more law violators than there are official delinquents. Self-report and victim studies are unanimous in suggesting that police and court accounts of delinquency grossly underestimate the actual amount of law violation. And while it is difficult to be absolutely precise about the size of this underestimation, it is possible to derive an approximation. Beginning with all juvenile law violations as a base of 100 percent, official accounts, combined with self-reports, suggest the following:

According to juveniles, at least 90 percent of all their illegal acts go undetected. Representatives of the juvenile justice system, principally the police, detect 10 percent at most.

Studies of the police indicate that of that 10 percent only a small proportion result in arrest. What that proportion is we do not know, but it is probably very small.

The *Uniform Crime Reports* indicate that of those acts that do result in the arrest or detection of the offender about half are handled entirely by the police and are not referred to court for trial. This means that, at most, only 5 percent of all the acts remain in the system after detection. Likely, the figure is lower than that. One national self-report survey found that less than 1 percent of all chargeable offenses were recorded as official delinquency.

Whatever the figure, court statistics indicate that this small number is reduced even further after police processing. They show that of those cases referred to the court by the police less than half are actually tried. The remainder are handled unofficially. Some of these "unofficial" cases may appear in court statistics, but, at most, something less than 2.5 percent of all acts actually result in trial.

What all of this means is that the juvenile justice system is a course net indeed. Even though the foregoing estimates may include considerable error, the general conclusion remains the same. Not only do self-report studies indicate that the agents of juvenile justice remain unaware of most law violations, but victim surveys suggest the same thing. They also indicate that police and court records underestimate by severalfold the actual number of criminal acts committed by juveniles.

2. *Social location of delinquent behavior.* Despite differences in the way they get at delinquent behavior, arrest and victim studies provide some impressive, and perhaps surprising, similarities in their social location of those kinds of delinquent acts that are criminal:

Official police records show that arrest rates are higher for the young than for the old, higher for males than for females, higher for blacks than for whites, higher for low-income than for high-income persons, and higher in the city than in the country.

Victimization studies, though they look at crime from a totally different perspective, paint an identical picture: Young people are more vulnerable to crime than older people; males are more vulnerable than females; blacks are more vulnerable than white; poor people are more vulnerable than affluent people; and city dwellers are more vulnerable than country dwellers.

In short, though arrest reports represent those who are caught and victim reports represent those who are preyed upon, they seem to be drawing from a common universe of behavior. Thus, despite their differences over the size of that universe, both methods are in general agreement regarding the social location of crime.

The picture painted by self-report studies is somewhat different. These studies support the idea that illegal behavior is disproportionately concentrated among the young and that males are more delinquent than females. But they tend to question whether differences in crime concentration between low- and high-income persons and between blacks and whites are as great as arrest and victim studies indicate. Differences along these dimensions were uncovered in the self-report studies, but they were less strong, particularly with respect to differences along socioeconomic lines.

It must be remembered, however, that the self-report studies did not retrieve information from adults and that they dealt more with property than with violent crimes. And it was precisely along these dimensions that some of the greatest discrepancies between blacks and whites and between low- and high-income persons occurred. Young adults are more inclined than juveniles to commit violent crimes, and both black and low-income people are more likely to be their victims. Furthermore, the few self-report studies that examined racial differences did find that black boys tend to commit more serious crimes than white boys. It is highly possible, therefore, that if these dimensions were more thoroughly explored in self-report studies they would result in a picture not unlike that sketched by police and victimization studies. The congruence between the arrest and victim supplied information is so consistent that one can ill-afford to ignore the picture it paints.

3. Trends in delinquent behavior. We are largely dependent upon measures of official delinquency for conclusions as to whether law-violating behavior is increasing, since victim and self-report data have not been systematically collected over an extended period of time. To the extent that official records represent law-violating behavior, they suggest the following:

Illegal acts are on the increase. The rates at which children are arrested and tried have gone up steadily for the past decade and a half.

Official delinquency among girls has been increasing at a much faster
pace than among boys.

Official violence among children has been increasing at a much more
rapid rate than among adults.

Some of these increases could be due to recent efforts to professionalize and to improve record keeping, but how much they have
contributed to higher official rates is difficult to say. Thus, if official
records are taken at face value, they indicate that delinquent behavior is
increasing. For certain, the juvenile justice system is processing
juveniles at a rate that exceeds the growth in the youth population.

A few self-report studies present conflicted findings on this issue. Two
national studies did not record an increase in law violations among boys
between 1967 and 1972 and showed only a modest increase for girls. A
recent statewide study in Illinois, however, concluded that delinquent
behavior is increasing because it uncovered rates of law violation that
were higher than other localized studies had shown previously. But
such findings are almost beside the point. Conflicted or not, self-report,
along with official findings, easily lead to the conclusion that law-
violating behavior is increasing.

The reason is that the mere collection of self-report information has
helped to create the impression that illegal acts are on the increase.
Because the actual extent of juvenile law violation was unknown until
self-report data were collected, the finding that it is much higher than
officials previously indicated has helped to construct an image of delinquent behavior that could be viewed as ominous. So extensive have
self-report studies shown it to be that if all, or even a significant portion
of all, illegal acts became a part of the official record the result would be
unprecedented. Even though adolescent behavior, as such, might have
changed little, official delinquency rates would jump to alarming proportions overnight.

This is not to suggest that present levels of juvenile crime are acceptable and that they should be ignored. Indeed, there are grounds for
feeling that all is not well. To begin with, it is significant that there are
relatively few differences in the amounts and types of crime committed
by juveniles ages 15 to 17 and those committed by young adults 18–25.
The fact that violence seems to be increasing among younger age groups
only underscores this conclusion. The point is that age 18, as the magic
dividing line between childhood and adulthood, does not have much
meaning when looking either at victimization or crime. Indeed, were it

not for our present construction of childhood, our responses to adolescent offenders might be altered considerably.

Secondly, the extent to which children prey upon other children, particularly in some areas of our central cities, is a serious matter, even if adults are not their victims.

Finally, it should be recalled that during the last decade and a half crimes of violence seem to have gone up faster among juveniles than among any other age group. By almost every index, this seems to be the case. Thus, the quality of life, particularly for juveniles, has been, and may always have been, deeply affected.

References

Block, Richard and Zimring, Franklin E.
    1973 "Homicide in Chicago, 1965–1970." *Journal of Research in Crime and Delinquency*, January, 10:1–12.

Brown, Claude
    1965 *Manchild in the Promised Land*. New York: Signet Books.

Ennis, Philip H.
    1967 *Criminal Victimization in the United States: A Report of a National Survey*. University of Chicago: National Opinion Research Center.

Federal Bureau of Investigation
    1974 *Uniform Crime Reports for the United States, 1973*. Washington, D.C.: U.S. Government Printing Office.

Mulvihill, Donald J., Tumin, Melvin M. and Curtis, Lynn A.
    1969 *Crimes of Violence: A Staff Report Submitted to the National Commission on the Causes and Prevention of Violence* (Vol. 11). Washington, D.C.: U.S. Government Printing Office.

National Advisory Commission on Criminal Justice Standards and Goals
    1973 "Victimization surveying: its history, uses, and limitations." *Report on the Criminal Justice System*. Washington, D.C.: U.S. Government Printing Office.

National Criminal Justice Information and Statistics Service
    1974a "Typical crime victim is young, poor, and black." *LEAA Newsletter*, December, 4:1 and 5.

    1974b *Crimes and Victims: A Report on the Dayton-San Jose Pilot Survey of Victimization*. Washington, D.C.: U.S. Government Printing Office.

1975a *Criminal Victimization in the United States: 1973.* Advance Report, May, 1. Washington, D.C.: Law Enforcement Assistance Administration.

1975b *Criminal Victimization Surveys in the Nation's Five Largest Cities.* Washington D.C.: U.S. Government Printing Office.

1976 *Criminal Victimization in the United States: A Comparison of 1973 and 1974 Findings.* Washington, D.C.: Law Enforcement Assistance Administration.

President's Commission on Law Enforcement and Administration of Justice
1967a *The Challenge of Crime in a Free Society.* Washington, D.C.: U.S. Government Printing Office.

1967b *Task Force Report: Crime and Its Impact—An Assessment.* Washington, D.C.: U.S. Government Printing Office.

part three

EXPLANATIONS OF DELINQUENT BEHAVIOR

Introduction: Theories as constructions of reality

The nature of delinquency theory is like the nature of childhood. It has changed a great deal. In the past 200 years, ways of explaining delinquent behavior have ranged all the way from those which locate its causes entirely within the individual to those which locate its causes entirely within the organization of society. The assumptions about human nature upon which these theories are based are equally diverse. Some suggest that children are born inherently primitive and savage while others suggest they are inherently good. Hence, in an effort to make sense out of views so diverse as these, it is essential that we set up a framework for assessing their implications, both for the way we construct delinquency and for the way we try to control it.

Classical theory

By way of setting the stage, consider again the "theories" of deviant behavior that preceded the emergence of science. It will be recalled that early American colonists tended to equate crime with sin. People who got into trouble were possessed by the devil and cursed by God. Any transgressions, therefore, demanded stern punishments. It will also be recalled that this way of viewing and treating crime began to change as a result of Enlightenment philosophy—the 18th century philosophy stressing the universality of human progress and the importance of human reason. Indeed, Enlightenment philosophy was partly responsible for what we now call the *Classical School of Criminology* (Cf. Radzinowicz, 1966; Taylor, et al., 1973).

This school attacked the systems of criminal justice in all Western countries for their arbitrary, cruel, and oppressive practices. Its goal was to reduce the severity of punishment and to achieve equal justice for everyone, noble or commoner. But basic to the pursuit of this goal were new and fundamental assumptions about human nature and social order—assumptions that were naturalistic rather than supernaturalistic in character. Classical reformers believed strongly in human reason and the perfectibility of social institutions. They assumed that humans are rational beings who calculate the pleasures and pains associated with different courses of action and freely choose that one which will maximize their personal advantage over social cost. But, because they are rational beings, humans are also inclined to be law-abiding if an enlightened system of justice is designed to control them.

It was these features of human nature that led to the classical conception of crime control. Classical theorists assumed that the members of society agree generally as to the desirability of protecting private property and personal welfare. Common people recognize that individuals are responsible for their actions and that excuses for committing crime are unacceptable. Hence, they freely enter into a social contract with the state to refrain from crime and to preserve the peace.

But how shall self-seeking individuals be deterred from preying on others? Classical criminologists believed that a humane and equitable system of justice would provide the means. Since humans are rational beings by nature, harsh and animal-like punishments—whipping, branding, drawing and quartering, or putting people in the stocks—are inappropriate for many criminal acts. Instead, four basic forms of control will suffice: (1) laws that are clear and simple; (2) methods of determining guilt that carefully protect the rights of the accused; (3) punishments that are graded according to the seriousness of criminal acts; and (4) responses by the criminal justice system that are swift and unavoidable. In short, all that is necessary to control crime is to convince rational people that they will suffer somewhat more pain than pleasure from committing an illegal act (Cf. Beccaria, 1963).

Obviously, classical theory postulated a simplistic view of both human nature and social order. It ignored all personal, social, and cultural differences and suggested that only three factors—the human capacity to reason, individual responsibility for one's own acts, and the proper imposition of punishments—are all that are necessary to control crime. Yet, the theory had lasting impact, appealing strongly to the interests of the middle class as it threw off the last vestiges of feudalism. Indeed, many remnants of classical thinking remain locked in our legal system today. Our laws still distinguish among different kinds of crime—petty theft, burglary, robbery, or aggravated assault—and allocate punishments accordingly. Furthermore, the classical argument that punishment deters crime still retains a great deal of vigor and may now be experiencing a resurgence (Cf. Martinson, 1974; Wilson, 1975).

Scientific theory

The emphasis of the classical school upon human kind's rationality and free will gradually declined during the 19th century. As more understanding of the complexities of human nature and social order was gained, there was an increasing tendency to concentrate upon forces external to the individual in trying to explain his behavior. A trend was started which has grown only stronger over the years suggesting that human nature is the product of forces over which the person has relatively little control. With this trend, therefore, a new school of criminology was spawned called the *Positive School*.

Though this school was no less a product of Enlightenment philosophy than was the classical school and no less convinced that human reason and human progress go hand-in-hand, its approach to the understanding and control of crime was markedly different. Briefly, that approach can be characterized by a stress upon four major ideas.

Empirical documentation. The positive school is based upon the philosophical assumption that in the social as well as the physical sciences logical arguments are not enough. Despite the plausibility of any theory, it may be false. Therefore, it should be subjected to test by carefully designed research and the gathering of factual data. For example, one could not accept classical notions about people and punishment without proof. Instead, through the measurement and quantification of social phenomenona, such ideas should be carefully examined. If they are not consistent with the universal laws that govern human behavior, others should be sought. Once discovered, they would be more likely to point the way to a humane society and the elimination of misery and evil.

A doctrine of determinism. A corollary of the stress upon empirical verification in the positive school is the doctrine of determinism. This doctrine suggests that any phenomenon—human nature, for example—is determined by prior causes. It does not just happen. Delinquent behavior, for instance, is probably not simply the product of momentary exercise of rational free will. Rather, there are universal laws or forces that determine the course of natural or human affairs and the forms that human nature takes.

The doctrine of determinism was highly compatible with the child-saving movement of the 19th and 20th centuries, both tending to grow out of common historical trends. The belief that children are innocent and fragile, that they must be quarantined from adult vices, and that they must be carefully trained is deterministic in character. Like positivistic science, therefore, it seriously questioned the classical belief that human behavior is rational and suggested, instead, that it is determined by forces over which children have little control and about which they may not even be aware. How can children who are poverty-stricken, poorly socialized, or mentally retarded be deterred from delinquent behavior if they are the product of forces over which they have no control and if they have not been taught to comprehend the difference between right and wrong? The only hope for controlling their antisocial behavior is to discover its causes. By themselves, neither good intentions nor punishment will accomplish this task. Instead, rational policies of control require a scientific understanding of the causes of delinquent conduct and of appropriate methods for treating them. Contrary to classical philosophy, therefore, positivistic philosophy suggests that societal reaction should be fitted to the particular ills of the offender rather than to the seriousness of the act he committed.

Value neutrality. Though it is their task to discover the causes of delinquent behavior and possible cures, scientists should remain neutral with respect to societal values. Criminology is a discipline whose boundaries are determined by the interests and laws of the society in which they live. Thus, while politicians, the citizenry, and the agents of juvenile justice must be concerned with implementing policies that are consistent with prevailing values, scientists should be concerned exclusively with trying to understand how delinquent behavior occurs within the context of existing rules and what effects alternative control policies might have on it. Scientists may become involved with social policy, but their role is that of helping others to understand the implications of various courses of action, not with suggesting which values are preferable. This is not to say that in their role as ordinary citizens scientists may not espouse certain values. But, in their role as scientists, they should confine themselves to statements of fact based on objective evidence.

Knowledge building.   This stance with respect to values has a direct effect on the uses to which scientific theory is supposed to be put. While scientific theories have been many and varied during the past century, the ideal positivistic view suggests that any one of them should not be used, particularly by scientists, to control human behavior until it has been confirmed by evidence. Instead, it is supposed to be nothing more than an unbiased and dispassionate statement whose sole purpose is to help organize disparate facts about behavior and to make sense out of them. Prior to its confirmation, it should be of use to science only because it provides direction for the accumulation of knowledge. Until its claims are proven by evidence, it should not be equated with truth and used to affect the lives of people.

Positivistic philosophy, in short, became a powerful, new belief system in Western civilization suggesting (1) that there is order in the universe, (2) that knowledge is superior to ignorance, (3) that cause-and-effect relationships exist and (4) that, in order to document these relationships, the gathering of empirical facts is necessary. At the same time, this philosophy suggested that the greatest good will be accomplished if scientists remain *neutral* with respect to societal values, *objective* in their search for truth, *skeptical* about the nature of their findings, and *humble* in the assertions they make.

Given these constraints on science, positivistic philosophy suggests that the scientific community has a limited role to play in society. While it may contribute to societal welfare by accumulating knowledge, the uses to which that knowledge is put ultimately should be decided by others. It is the members of society, and not scientists, who should decide how the findings of science shall be used.

Radical theory

In recent years, a whole new school of criminology—the *Radical School*—has emerged. Its philosophy, however, is sharply at odds with that of either the classical or positive schools. But, since the positive school has been preeminent throughout the 20th century, the main concern of radical theorists is with discrediting that school and with asserting a new approach for explaining and dealing with delinquency (Chambliss and Mankoff, 1976; Platt, 1974; Quinney, 1970; 1974; Taylor, et al., 1975).

To begin with, radical theorists are quick to point out that because they are human the work of scientists is inevitably affected by the particular values they hold. This is particularly true with respect to their theories of delinquency. They do not grow like plants in a hothouse, untouched by the outside environment. Instead, like any other element of culture, theories are social constructions which are as likely to reflect traditional beliefs and prejudices as to add new dimensions to them; that is, they not only affect the course of social thought, but are affected by it. For that reason, some theories of human or delinquent behavior tell us as much about our changing values and culture as about behavior—as much about past and emerging beliefs as about human action. Scientific theories, therefore, are not detached and neutral with respect to prevailing values, but are much affected by them.

Given this state of affairs, radical theorists assert that scientific positivists have been the unreflective handmaidens of existing power groups because of their stress upon value neutrality. This is particularly true with regard to their tendency to use existing laws as the yardstick by which to determine who is delinquent and who is not. Such a practice leads to injustice because the social order is characterized by value conflict, not consensus. Current laws do not reflect a general agreement among the entire populace as to what existing morality should be. Instead, they reflect only the values of a ruling elite who seek to use existing rules for their own ends, above all as a means of maintaining political and economic power over such powerless groups as the poor, ethnic minorities, and women. Rather than being morally neutral, therefore, scientists are unthinking perpetrators of the status quo.

The cornerstone of the positivistic philosophy since its inception has been based upon the belief that the application of scientific study to human affairs would lead to a better world. Rational procedures and the accumulation of evidence would point the way to the elimination of human predation and to the improvement of all. Radical theorists argue that this faith not only reflects a particular set of questionable values, but that it is naive with respect to the way the world actually operates. The groups who dominate society do not seek justice and equality.

Their values and rules are not designed to improve the lives of those who constitute the underclasses of society. Instead, they seek only to preserve favored positions they occupy. By clinging to a positivistic philosophy, therefore, scientists not only fail to support ways for eliminating real criminogenic conditions like poverty, racism, and sexism, but, because of their misguided emphasis upon value neutrality, they give tacit approval to those who would perpetuate them.

This stance by radical criminologists has led to the espousal of a new ideology possessed of several unique features. Radicals argue that criminologists should adopt a value position opposing the status quo rather than acting as though they are neutral with respect to it. They assume that children are born inherently good and that if they become bad it is because society made them that way. They believe that the social order is characterized by conflict and diversity, not consensus. They suggest that the struggle for justice is a struggle between those who have and those who have not. In short, it is late capitalist society that is criminogenic, not the unlucky people who happen to be caught up in the toils of the criminal and juvenile justice systems.

Given these arguments, radicals are not deterred by the possibility that existing knowledge may be incapable of suggesting ways to reconstruct our social institutions in such a way that crime is forever eliminated. Instead, it is their position that the inherent goodness of humankind, combined with the inexorable processes of history, will lead ultimately to a socialist utopia in which all people will be equal and in which all crime will disappear. Hence, scientists should not be neutral with respect to existing values but should be at the forefront in producing change.

Implications

This contrasting set of philosophical arguments makes one conclusion all too clear: The historical search for a full understanding of delinquency has been characterized by a mixed, not pure, bag of values and standards. It is obvious that delinquency theorists, even those in the positivistic tradition, are not entirely unaffected by cultural bias and a particular moral position. Indeed, long before radical criminology came along, William Graham Sumner, (1907:521–522), one of the pioneers of American sociology, once commented that "It is vain to imagine that a scientific man' can divest himself or prejudice or previous opinion and put himself in an attitude of neutral independence toward the mores. He might as well try to get out of gravity or the presence of the atmosphere.''

Like everyone else, scientists are influenced by the time, the values, and the culture in which they live. Even though the game of science *does* subject them to sterner demands for detachment and objectivity than do most other social games, they are inevitably affected by nonscientific demands and interests. Consequently, in our review of various theories, we should be prepared to examine them, not merely in terms of their intellectual content and the actual evidence that bears upon them, but in terms of the value assumptions upon which they are built and the ways in which they contribute to society's changing construction of delinquency. Indeed, if one were to draw a simple diagram of the place of delinquency theories in our cultural life, it might look something like the accompanying diagram:

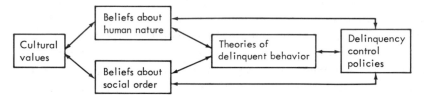

The diagram indicates that cultural values lead to certain assumptions about human nature and social order. These, in turn, contribute both to the construction of theories of delinquent behavior and to policies designed to control it. But the relationship is not all in one direction. While theories of delinquent behavior are affected by prevailing values and beliefs, they also tend to alter these beliefs in return. In fact, it is often difficult to tell whether changes in belief reflect new theories or whether new theories are merely revisions of old beliefs. Since in many cases both things happen, theories not only play an important role in the scientific game of accumulating knowledge, but play a central role in constructing new social values and ways of responding to delinquent conduct. Moreover, it is not always the scientific quality of any theory that will determine the uses to which it is put. Rather, its capacity to capture and to give expression to emerging cultural trends may determine its fate. How well it conforms to emerging beliefs and to delinquency control policies may determine its popularity every bit as much, if not more, than the actual evidence that can be brought to bear upon it.

Classification of theories

Given this state of affairs, two things will be done to assist us in sorting out the many theories that exist and to draw some overall conclusions about them. First, they will be classified into major types, extending all the way from the deterministic theories of the late 19th century, which tended to locate the sources of delinquent behavior in the inherent characteristics of defective children, to the most recent theories which are no less deterministic but which describe society as being entirely at fault. The historical progression of these ideas across the societal stage and the changes they have wrought in our construction of delinquency will be described.

Secondly, the examination of each of these bodies of theory will be organized to answer a series of fundamental questions:

1. What are the beliefs about human nature and social order upon which it is constructed? What values does it reflect and what pictures of children and society does it portray?
2. What is its underlying logic and basic content, the kinds of factors upon which it concentrates in trying to explain delinquent conduct?
3. What are its implications for social policy, and how has it actually affected policy?
4. How well does it stand up to logical and empirical scrutiny?

Once these steps have been taken, we will be in a position to draw some conclusions about the overall contribution of scientific and scholarly communities to our social construction of delinquency and to policies designed to prevent and to control it.

References

Beccaria, Cesare
    1963 *On Crimes and Punishments* (Trans. by Henry Paolucci). Indianapolis: Bobbs-Merrill.

Chambliss, William J. and Mankoff, Milton (Eds.)
    1976 *Whose Laws? What Order?* New York: John Wiley.

Martinson, Robert
    1974 "What works?—questions and answers about prison reform." *The Public Interest*, Spring, 35:22–54.

Platt, Anthony
  1974   "The triumph of benevolence: the origins of the juvenile justice system in the United States. Pp. 356–389 in Richard Quinney (Ed.),
          Criminal Justice in America. Boston: Little, Brown.

Quinney, Richard (Ed.)
  1974   *Criminal Justice in America.* Boston: Little, Brown.

Radzinowicz, Leon
  1966   *Ideology and Crime.* New York: Columbia University Press.

Sumner, William
  1907   *Folkways,* New York: Ginn.

Taylor, Ian et al.
  1973   *The New Criminology.* New York: Harper and Row.

Taylor, Ian et al. (Eds.)
  1975   *Critical Criminology.* Boston: Routledge and Kegan Paul.

Wilson, James Q.
  1975   *Thinking about Crime.* New York: Basic Books.

9

CONTROL THEORY

In this chapter we will analyze a body of theories called "control" theories. They are given this name because of their emphasis upon the idea that delinquent or conformist behavior is a function of the ability of the child to control his antisocial impulses. They start from the assumption that children require training if they are to behave socially. Delinquent behavior will result either if a child lacks the ability for effective training or because he has been trained badly.

During the past 100 years, control theories have been of three major types—biological, psychodynamic, and psychosocial. Although these types reflect the complexity of scientific theorizing, they have obvious roots in 19th century traditions suggesting that depraved or uncaring parents are responsible for difficult and antisocial youth. The way these theories construct delinquency is to suggest that the biological and psychological characteristics which children receive from their parents are the characteristics that will determine whether they remain trouble-free or delinquent.

Biological control theory

Biological theories are the oldest of the scientific control theories. More than any other, they are "kinds-of-people" theories. The children who commit delinquent acts are presumed to have inherited anatomical or genetic weaknesses from their parents. They are persons who are inherently disposed to deviant behavior and for whom inner controls are naturally deficient. These kinds of explanations probably owe their beginnings to the widespread growth of evolutionary theory and research in the late 19th and early 20th centuries. The giant among all biological theorists, of course, was Charles Darwin. But evolutionary theories of delinquency and crime were expounded by others.

Physical degeneracy

Among the first of the biological criminologists was Cesare Lombroso, an Italian physician. In 1876, Lombroso published a pamphlet, which later grew to a three-volume work, in which he theorized that offenders are "atavistic" types; that is, they are people who have reverted to an earlier, more primitive stage of evolutionary development (Wolfgang, 1961). The essence of Lombroso's theory can be captured in the following propositions (Sutherland and Cressey, 1974:53):

1. Law violators are a distinct physical type at birth.
2. Law violators possess physical features, or stigmata, characteristic of an earlier form of evolutionary development—imbalanced regions of the brain; an asymmetrical face and cranium; an abnormal nose; fleshy, protruding lips; excessively long arms; abundant wrinkles; abnormal sex organs; insensitivity to pain; and other physical anomalies.
3. People who possess at least five of these physical characteristics lack adequate personal controls and are predisposed to crime.

Lombroso also argued that crime rates are lower for females than for males because females are less intelligent. Although they are naturally revengeful, jealous, and lacking in moral sense, these defects are usually neutralized by an inherited sense of piety, maternity, and sexual coldness. Thus, it is only when females possess the usual physical stigmata that they become criminal like men (Simon, 1975:7).

Lombroso based his conclusions upon his measurements of the inhabitants of Italian prisons, but he never really tested his theory by making a careful, scientific comparison of criminals and noncriminals. Nonetheless, his thinking dominated much of European and American criminology for over a third of a century. It was not until 1913, when a study was published by Charles Goring, an English physician, that his popularity began to wane. After comparing several thousand criminals and noncriminals, Goring concluded that there is no such thing as a physical criminal type (1913:19). But, until his work was published, Lombroso's theory rode the crest of naturalistic thinking.

It was picked up by Dr. Hamilton Wey, a physician at Elmira Reformatory for young offenders in New York. Like Lombroso, he maintained that law violators have distinctive features: they have big ears; the heads of thieves are small; the heads of murderers are large; and there are crafty offenders who have yellow irises which give them a snakelike appearance (Cf. Vold, 1958:58). Even more important, Arthur McDonald, an employee of the U.S. Department of Education, appealed to Congress in 1908 for funds to establish a laboratory for the physical study of delinquents. He was particularly concerned with their height and weight; hair and skin color; nationality; size of hands, ears, and mouth; thickness of lips; sensitivity to heat and pain; and whether, as a result of parental death or drunkenness, they had been subjected to "hereditary taint" or to the "stigmata of degeneration." "There is little hope of making the world better," McDonald told Congress, "if we do not seek the causes of social evils at their beginnings" (Cf. Bremner, 1971, II:562–563).

Poor heredity

It is significant that McDonald should suggest that "hereditary taint," as well as the "stigmata of degeneration," should be taken into account in studying delinquents. What his concern reflected was an awareness of another variation in biological thinking that had been proceeding in parallel with Lombroso's for several years; namely, the possibility that it is poor heredity rather than physical degeneracy that leads to delinquent behavior.

Charles Goring, the English scholar, also lent his prestige to this point of view. Even though his study of English convicts had convinced him that there is no such thing as a physical criminal type, he concluded that the tendency to be delinquent is inherited and that environment plays little part in producing it (1913:369). Defective intelligence, due to poor heredity, is the cause of delinquent behavior.

This concern with feeblemindedness was given greatly increased respectability by the growth of experimental psychology in the late 19th century and by its attempt to measure intelligence scientifically. After several years of investigation, Alfred Binet and Theodore Simon, two

French scholars, published a scale in 1905 for measuring intelligence. Then, in 1908, they published a revised scale based upon two ideas: (1) that childhood is characterized by developmental stages and, (2) that "mental age" can be measured by taking these developmental stages into account (Vold, 1958:79–81). The concept of "mental age" suggests that intelligence should grow with age and should peak at about age 16—ideas that are now widely accepted. Thus, it should be possible not only to measure what average or normal intelligence is for children of different ages, but to determine, as well, which ones are feebleminded. Those whose IQs fall below the norm for their age are mentally defective.

It should come as no surprise that intelligence testing was soon applied to delinquent populations. In 1914, Henry Goddard, an American psychologist, published the results of several studies, each purporting to show that significant numbers of law violators were feebleminded. Based upon them, Goddard concluded that at least 25 percent, and perhaps as many as 70 percent, of all delinquents are defective (Compare Goddard, 1911:563 with Goddard, 1914:569). Hence, in the heyday of biological thinking, the implication was that degenerate parents, far more than society at large, were responsible for producing problem children—children who were incapable of learning right from wrong. But this belief suffered a near fatal blow when, during World War I, intelligence tests were used to determine the fitness of draftees to serve in the Armed Forces.

In testing convicted offenders, Goddard had concluded that anyone whose mental age was 12 or under should be considered feebleminded. It was this standard, therefore, that was applied to thousands of young men entering military service. But, after having tested them, officials were astounded to find that about one third would have to be considered feebleminded if Goddard's standard were retained (Zeleny, 1933). To his credit, Goddard agreed with others that such a conclusion would be absurd. A large proportion of all young men were not feebleminded. Furthermore, when the test scores of delinquents and draftees were compared, the data indicated that these two groups were more alike than different; in fact, only about 5 percent of all offenders could be considered feebleminded. Thus, the prevailing standard not only proved incorrect for draftees, but for delinquents as well.

Intelligence testing continued as a device for classifying offenders for several more years after these discoveries, but that use was short-lived. In 1931, Edwin H. Sutherland, perhaps the most eminent of all American criminologists during the mid-20th century, wrote an essay debunking "mental testers"—an essay that has represented the standard response of most criminologists since that time (Sutherland, 1931). Even though intelligence tests have improved markedly since World War I, sociologists, in particular, have objected to their use with offenders on two grounds.

First, they object to the idea that intelligence tests can measure innate ability. "So-called intelligence tests measure only 'test intelligence' not innate intelligence" (Clinard, 1968:170). Furthermore, "test intelligence" is a product of culture, not heredity. "So-called intelligence tests tend to measure the degree to which the individual has assimilated and internalized middle-class values rather than intelligence" (Haskell and Yablonsky, 1971:71).

The second objection is to the Lombrosian idea that it is something defective within the individual that produces delinquent behavior. Sociologists are inclined to argue that such behavior, like conformist behavior, is a product of learning. Motivations to violate the law are socially produced and are a characteristic part of normal life. The idea that delinquent behavior is predominantly a product of idiots who are unable to understand the difference between right and wrong is nonsense.

Biological control theory: 20th century vintage

The fate of intelligence testing was symptomatic of a general tendency to discard physical and hereditary explanations for delinquent behavior as society moved ever further into the 20th century. Then, in the 1930s, Earnest A. Hooton (1931; 1939), a Harvard anthropologist, published a series of volumes which quickly put both physical inferiority and poor heredity back on the agenda of scientific discussion.

After measuring 13,000 inmates in jails and reformatories, and comparing them with 3,203 noncriminals—college students, firemen, policemen, and patients in regular and mental hospitals—Hooton again concluded that offenders are physically and mentally inferior. His long list of findings can be distilled into three major propositions (1939, I:229; 301–308):

1. Criminals are physically inferior to noncriminals.
2. Physical inferiority is associated with mental inferiority.
3. The basic cause of both types of inferiority is poor heredity.

Like Lombroso, Hooton also asserted that offenders are characterized by physical stigmata—low foreheads, long thin necks, sloping shoulders, compressed faces, narrow jaws, speckled eyes, and small protruding ears. He also asserted that different types of criminals have different physiques: tall, heavy men are killers and commit forgery and fraud; tall, thin men also murder but are inclined to be robbers; rapists are squat, heavy persons; undersized men are thieves; and men of mediocre physique have no specialty because their delinquent acts are like their physical makeup—characterless (1931:376–378).

As it had not done in the 19th century, the publication of this type of theory stirred up a great deal of controversy. By now, the social sciences had grown in stature, and their emphasis upon cultural and environmental, as contrasted to biological, factors had assumed increased importance. Unfavorable and critical reviews were made by sociologists in particular, the most telling of which was Hooton's use of poor scientific procedures and circular reasoning (Cf. Vold, 1958:63; Sutherland and Cressey, 1974:119). First, he used conviction for a crime as a method of separating criminals from noncriminals. Then he measured the criminal group and concluded they were inferior. Having done that, he turned around and used their inferiority to account for their criminality. From a scientific standpoint, this procedure is unacceptable. There must be independent evidence that physical characteristics are proof of inferiority before their relationship to delinquent behavior can be demonstrated. Indeed, by what criterion can it be said that a low forehead, a long neck, or small ears are evidence of organic inferiority? The desirability of one set of physical characteristics over another is more often a product of cultural definition than of some universal biological standard.

So convincing were these and other criticisms that few investigators felt it necessary actually to test Hooton's conclusions with further research. Only a small number pursued the biological quest. One was William Sheldon, who, like Hooton, argued that body type and mental type go together and that both are inherited (1949:352). But his scheme for classifying individuals was markedly different.

After comparing the physical measurements of 200 boys in a private institution with those of 200 college boys, he reported that the body types of these samples fell into three major categories: (1) *endomorphs* who are fat and round; (2) *mesomorphs* who are large-boned and muscular; and (3) *ectomorphs* who are lean and delicate (Sheldon, 1949:14–30). While rarely pure in form, Sheldon argued that these body types are genetically determined and that each produces a different personality and temperament. *Mesomorphs* are aggressive, insensitive, quick to translate impulse into action, and are inherently deficient in internal controls. By contrast, *endomorphs* are easygoing, sociable, and comfort-loving, while *ectomorphs* are introverted, sensitive, and nervous. Hence, *mesomorphs* are most likely to be delinquent.

In a study that was far more defensible than Sheldon's, the Gluecks (1956) reported findings that supported Sheldon, as did Cortes and Gatti (1972). But such findings have not been widely accepted. Indeed, the derisive comments of S.L. Washburn (1951:563), a physical anthropologist, sum up the feelings of most criminologists today. Suggesting that Sheldon's work had now brought us full circle from the days of phrenology, he described it as a "new phrenology in which the bumps of the buttocks take the place of the bumps on the skull."

Policy legacy of biological theories

Most people would now agree with Washburn, but, in their day, biological theories had considerable impact on social policy. As the first scientific representatives of the positivistic philosophy, they seriously questioned the classical emphasis upon free will and the use of punishment. How could a physical degenerate or a mental defective be deterred from illegal behavior if he were the product of genetic forces over which he had no control? The only hope for controlling his behavior was to neutralize its causes.

This could be done in two ways. The first was for the state to remove defective children from their degenerate parents and to care for them itself. Consider the suggestions for public policy made by a University of Kansas sociologist in 1897:

> It is seen at once that families of this class . . . are the most difficult to deal with, because they have no place in social life, and it is difficult to make a place for them. . . . The principle of social evolution is to make the strong stronger that the purposes of social life may be conserved, but to do this the weak must be cared for or they will eventually destroy or counteract the efforts of the strong. We need social sanitation, which is the ultimate aim of the study of social pathology (Blackmar, 1897:499–500).

Though this call for "social sanitation" was a stern one, it still retained a humane flavor, suggesting that defectives should be cared for rather than eliminated. These sentiments were also echoed by Henry

Goddard (1911:564). The defective delinquent, he commented, should not be turned loose on the streets, but neither should he be locked up in a jail or in prison. Rather, "He must be cared for . . . in a place we care for irresponsibles." Goddard also believed that delinquency could be prevented by using the Binet +test in the public schools to pick out defectives at an early age. "When we have learned to discriminate and recognize the ability of each child and place upon him such burdens and responsibilities only as he is able to bear, then we shall have largely solved the problem of delinquency." In short, the first scientific theories helped to perpetuate the 19th century belief that state intervention and institutional confinement were the best methods for dealing with delinquents and for protecting society. Rather than grading punishments to fit the misdeeds of children, controls should be graded to fit their levels of presumed incompetence.

A second, and perhaps more questionable, method was suggested for preventing delinquent behavior. This could be accomplished by the proper application of eugenics. Eugenics is a "science" concerned with improving the quality of the race by controlled breeding. Its basic rationale was well stated by Hooton. Since offenders are organically inferior, he said, "It follows that the elimination of crime can be effected only by the extirpation of the physically and morally unfit; or by their complete segregation in a socially aseptic environment" (1939, I:309). Likewise, Sheldon (1949:872) suggested that since delinquency "is mainly in the germ plasm" the only hope for control is selective breeding by which harmful constitutional types can be weeded out.

Actually, a eugenics movement designed to realize these objectives had begun several years before Hooton and Sheldon stated these opinions. Though this movement was by no means universally supported, it gained some importance in the first two decades of this century. It was concerned not merely with weeding out the "mental defectives" and "physical degenerates," but with avoiding the pollution of the race by people who masturbated excessively or overindulged in the sex act (Shannon, 1916:160). In pursuit of these objectives, 31 states passed laws between 1907 and 1937 permitting the sterilization of the feeble-minded, the mentally ill, and epileptics. As late as 1973, 21 states still retained such laws (McCaghy, 1976:20). Moreover, the people who are eligible for sterilization are often described in terms with which Lombroso and Hooton would have been at home: "hereditary criminals," "degenerates," and "moral degenerates" (Kittre, 1973:314). Estimates are that as many as 70,000 people have been sterilized as a result of the eugenics movement (McCaghy, 1976:21).

In short, this way of trying to prevent delinquent and other undesirable behavior is a sobering illustration of the extent to which scientific theories can be applied to the control of human conduct without much proof that they are accurate. Between the first appearance of biological theories in the late 19th century and the time they were disavowed by scientists in the 1920s and 1930s, they gained considerable lay support and were translated into social policy, policy which is still in effect in some states.

Scientific legacy of biological theories

We have already seen that criminologists have been inclined to reject biological theories on three grounds. The first is theoretical. Only if delinquent behavior were rare could biological defects take a prominent role in explaining it. Yet, as our analysis of self-reported delinquent behavior indicated, virtually every young person is delinquent at one time or another. Hence, it follows that since all are not defective other factors must play a prominent role.

The second reason for rejection has to do with the lack of supporting evidence for biological theories. They have been rejected because the research designed to test them has been so shoddy (Sutherland, 1951; Cohen, 1966:53). It simply does not warrant support for the claims made by the theories.

A third reason that has not been discussed is ideological. In their review of recent biological studies, Shah and Roth (1974) argue that modern criminologists, most of whom are social scientists, have overreacted to biological theories in their efforts to discredit the more extreme ones. Indeed, biologists, as well as social scientists, have engaged in a fruitless and nonscientific argument over the effects of "nature" versus "nurture."

Two comments illustrate the nonscientific character of the argument. An eminent anthropoligist argues that "from the standpoint of human behavior . . . all evidence points to an utter insignificance of biological factors as compared with culture in any consideration of behavior variations" (White, 1949). By contrast, an eminent biologist asserts that, "The materials of heredity contained in the chromosomes are the solid stuff which ultimately determines the course of history" (Darlington, 1953). But, from a strictly scientific view, say Shah and Roth (1974:104–105), a "nature" versus "nurture" dichotomy is "untenable, incorrect, and meaningless. The subject has to be discussed in terms of the continuous and complex interactions between an organism and its environment and the relative contributions of both sets of variables in determining the behavior of the organism."

This comment illustrates an important fact. The construction of delinquency theory as it relates to current knowledge in the natural as well as social sciences has simply not kept pace with existing research. For example, few geneticists today believe that genes, by themselves, determine behavior. Rather, genes only help to determine a person's potential. But how that potential develops is dependent upon environment. Furthermore, the way in which biological and environmental factors interact may be directly relevant to the overrepresentation in the juvenile justice system of minority and poor children.

A series of recent studies have shown that minority and poor children run much greater risks of biological impairment due to poor environment than do other children (Shah and Roth, 1974:126–129). The rate of mental retardation is far higher among the children of poor parents because their mothers have no prenatal care during pregnancy. Furthermore, this lack of prenatal care also leads to an excessive number of premature births. Premature births, in turn, further increase the likelihood of physical and mental impairment. The reason is that the first few months of life are crucial to growth and maturation: The cells of the brain are continuing to develop and to divide, and other key developments are taking place. What happens during this period, therefore, can either help to repair or to make worse the long process of development that began in the mother. Yet, it is among poor children that the risks of malnourishment, neglect, and child battering during formative years are most likely to occur. Some clue as to the extent of the problem is indicated by the fact that infant deaths during the first year of life are much higher for nonwhites than for whites: about 40 per 1,000 versus 22 per 1,000 in 1965.

Shah and Roth (1974:129) take pains to point out that a direct link between biological impairment and criminal acts has yet to be established. Still, it is impossible to ignore the fact that those poor and minority segments of the populace which suffer most from prenatal, postnatal, and environmental problems are the very ones among whom official delinquency and victimization rates are the highest. Since these groups are one and the same, the existence of a possible relationship cannot be ignored, particularly where status offenses and official cases of child neglect are involved.

A preliminary report by Britain's National Child Development Study lends some support to this conclusion. The growth and maturation of every child born during a seven-day period in 1958 in England, Scotland, and Wales have been followed and measured for 15 years. The study found that disadvantaged children, on the average, were three years behind ordinary children in school; that they were notably smaller and more likely to suffer physical defects; and that one out of 11 of them had had contact with the juvenile justice system as contrasted with only one in 300 of the ordinary children. (*Time*, 1973:88).

In this same vein, different investigators continue to point out that intelligence tests which have improved markedly since the days of Goddard tend to reveal a persistent, though relatively small, difference in IQ between delinquents and nondelinquents (Gordon, 1976; Hirschi and Hindelang, 1977). Whether in this country or elsewhere, delinquents—official and self-reported—tend to score somewhat lower than do nondelinquents.

In noting these findings, Hirschi and Hindelang do not argue that all delinquents are feebleminded. Rather, their point is that lowered intellectual capacity, whatever its source, may play an indirect role in contributing to official delinquency. For example, the lack of educational achievement among delinquents has been well documented (Empey and Lubeck, 1971:49–84; Hirschi, 1969; McCord, 1968:86; Short and Strodtbeck, 1965). Thus, while IQ may not be associated directly with delinquency, it may contribute to the kinds of educational and other problems that lead some persons to violate the law or to be defined as status offenders.

From a positivistic point of view, what all of this means is that "it would be incorrect to draw the conclusion that the case for biology has been refuted or that further research along this line would be fruitless" (Cohen, 1966:53). The most objective conclusion would be that no final conclusions can be drawn. At the same time, the interactions among biological and environmental factors are so complex and the nature of delinquent behavior is so varied that we must be modest in our expectations. While some linkages between biology and the various expressions of delinquent behavior may exist, they will not be anything like the direct and powerful ones postulated by older biological control theories.

Psychodynamic control theory

Following the gradual decline of biological theories in the first third of this century, the next group of control theories to gain widespread popularity were psychodynamic in nature. These are theories which locate the sources of delinquent behavior in the psychological development of the individual rather than in his genetic makeup. Much of the credit for their development goes to Sigmund Freud (1856–1939), a Viennese psychiatrist. Though his ideas have since been modified in many ways, they remain strikingly important as the cornerstone upon which many later theories have been built.

Freud was far less concerned with explaining how delinquent behavior is produced than with explaining how children can be made good. The reasons for this concern become obvious when one considers the main elements of his theory:

1. *Human nature is inherently antisocial.* Unlike the biologists who believed that only delinquents are born bad or defective, Freud theorized that *every* child possesses a set of primitive and antisocial instincts which he called the *id* (Freud, 1963:14). "The primitive, savage, and evil impulses of mankind," Freud wrote, "have not vanished in any individual, but continue their existence, although in a repressed state." Children are not gentle, friendly creatures who simply defend themselves if attacked. They possess a measure of aggression that will cause them to exploit their neighbor "to use him sexually without his consent, to seize his possessions, to humiliate him, to cause him pain, and to torture and to kill him" (Hughes, 1961:143). In short, all of us, not just delinquents, are born with ample capacity to be bad.

2. *Good behavior requires effective socialization.* Given this pessimistic view of human nature, Freud believed that the capacity of the individual to renunciate the antisocial instincts of the id can come about only through socialization—the process by which internal controls are cultivated within children by their parents. In order to describe how this process takes effect, Freud posited the existence of two other elements within the mind and personality besides the id.

The first is called the *ego*. It is the conscious manager and organizer of the personality (Cohen, 1966:57). Its main purpose is the preservation of the individual which is accomplished by its acting as an intermediary between the instinctual drives of the id and the external world. On one hand, the ego seeks to gain control over the id by deciding when it shall be allowed to pursue instinctual gratifications, when it shall be suppressed, and when gratifications will be postponed until a more propitious time. On the other hand, the ego also seeks to manipulate the external world to the individual's advantage (Freud, 1963:15).

The remaining psychic element is the *superego*. In layman's terms, it is the child's conscience, reflecting the moral rules cultivated in him by his parents. To the degree that the superego develops, it becomes the internal mechanism which acts in place of the external world to control impulses, to correct wrongdoing, and to threaten punishment for delinquent acts. Along with the ego, it is the means by which basic instincts are directed and controlled (Freud, 1963:121).

3. *The life-long features of the personality are registered in infancy.* Freud theorized that by the age of five all of the essential features of a child's adult personality will have been determined. Whether the antisocial and aggressive instincts of the id are to become dominant or whether the ego and superego are to be effective in controlling them are the product of parental socialization during the first few years of life (Cf. Aichorn, 1936).

This socialization occurs in a series of developmental stages (Cf. Freud, 1963, Abraham, 1927, Abrahamsen, 1960, Freud, 1965). The first is called the *oral* stage because the mouth is the principal source of gratification to the newborn infant—sucking, swallowing, gurgling, and kissing. If he is fondled, is fed on time, and is weaned at the right time, the child will feel loved and will develop properly. But, if he is not, he will experience a sense of deprivation and frustration the rest of his life.

The second stage is the *anal* stage, which lasts from about ages one to three. During this stage, two things happen. First, the infant begins to gain erotic satisfaction from the evacuation of urine and bowels rather than from oral activities. Second, the superego begins to receive particular attention because of the importance of toilet training. If children are trained improperly, difficulties will result. Rigid training—too much emphasis upon superego controls—can either produce a person who is stubborn and sadistic or one who is totally subdued and passive. Indifferent training, on the other hand, will result in a child who is sloppy, careless, and dirty. Only if training is just right will the child be freed from an anal fixation later in life.

The third stage is the *phallic* stage. It lasts from about the third to the sixth years. Whereas the child previously sought pleasure from mouth and anus, it now switches to the genitals. Masturbation, voyeurism, and sex play are common. More important, the male child unconsciously develops intense incestuous cravings for his mother (the Oedipus complex) and begins to hate his father who stands in his way. The reverse is true for the female, except that her problem is compounded. According to Freud, the girl envies those who have a penis, desires to possess one, and so turns to the adult figure who has one—her father (the Electra complex). She now experiences sexual attraction for him and perceives her mother as a rival. But, since both she and her brother still require love from both parents, their incestuous cravings soon arouse intense guilt feelings, the result of a developing superego. If both children are socialized properly, therefore, they can overcome their negative feelings and can learn to identify with the parent of the same sex. But, if not, emotional illness or delinquent behavior may result. For example, the boy who never gets over his hate for his rival father will grow up to hate all authority. Later in life, delinquent acts will be committed which reflect spite for this parent and an immature fixation at the phallic stage.

Freud postulated the existence of two additional stages of development—the *latency* and *genital* stages—but they are seen as less crucial than the first three. Hence, the implications are clear: the future behavior of any individual is not the result of personal choice, cultural differences, or changing social conditions. Rather, it is the product of parental training imposed upon the antisocial instincts of the infant.

Sources of delinquent behavior

Because Freud believed that delinquent tendencies are inherent in everyone, he devoted little attention to the many ways they might be manifested. His followers, however, have outlined at least five ways by which ineffective socialization might allow them to slip through (Feldman, 1969).

1. *Delinquent behavior is neurotic behavior.* The delinquent suffers from a compulsive need for punishment because he feels intolerably guilty over some unconscious, but socially unacceptable, drive, such as a boy's incestuous craving for sex with his mother. Though his superego tells him that such a craving is wrong, his ego is not sufficiently strong to suppress it totally. Hence, he may commit any one of a number of delinquent acts—theft, robbery, or even rape—so he can be caught and punished. Punishment will help to expiate his overwhelming sense of guilt.

2. *Delinquent behavior is the result of a defective superego.* Some delinquents are poorly socialized. Failing to identify with the appropriate parent, they do not develop internal controls over the id. Lacking a superego and any sense of guilt over their acts, they easily submit to antisocial instincts.

3. Delinquent behavior is the result of a gap in superego training.
Closely related is the notion that delinquent behavior can occur in a
child who has been properly socialized in the sense that she identifies
with the appropriate parent. But, because that parent has failed to teach
her appropriate values and expectations, she becomes delinquent. She
is not fully oriented as to what is expected of her.

*4. Delinquent behavior represents a search for compensatory
gratifications.* The child who was deprived at some early stage of
development still seeks the gratifications which he missed. For example, an adolescent may become an alcoholic in order to satisfy an oral
craving, or he may be sadistic and cruel because of bad toilet training
during the anal stage. His behavior is symbolic of deeply hidden needs
that were unsatisfied in infancy.

5. Delinquent behavior (in girls) is the result of penis envy. Much of
the delinquent behavior among girls is due to instinctive penis envy
and a sense of castration. It is due to a "masculinity complex." The
well-socialized girl compensates for her lack of a penis by submitting to
a man and becoming a mother. The deviant one, however, defies society
and pursues masculine roles. Such girls are "immature," "incomplete,"
and in a state of "arrested development" (Simon, 1975:5).

In short, the Freudian view of humankind is a highly deterministic
one, suggesting delinquent behavior is always much more than it appears to be. It can never be understood as the simple product of
momentary circumstance or fleeting impulse. Rather, it is always symbolic behavior that has been determined by personal motives that lie
deep within the individual—motives that were implanted in infancy
and which continue to defy easy detection. The only hope for understanding and correcting them, therefore, is some kind of psychotherapy
that first uncovers the source of unconscious, forbidden desires and then
brings them to conscious awareness so they can be examined and subjected to the controls of ego and superego.

Social impact of Freudian theory

The impact of Freudian theory on our social construction of delinquency has been profound, probably because it captured and gave expression to a host of ideas about childhood and human development
which, until Freud came along, had not been well articulated. On the
one hand, many of his ideas were by no means radical. For example, his

notions about human nature departed little from age-old religious traditions which suggested that children are inherently inclined to evil. Freud merely stated in secular and psychological terms what the Puritans had said long before in religious terms: "Children become good, not by birth, but by education." Furthermore, he reaffirmed the validity of traditional sex roles by suggesting, like the biologists, that such roles are instinctive and not due to culture. His view of appropriate behavior for girls, for instance, could scarcely have been more conservative.

On the other hand, Freud's preoccupation with childhood and his tremendous emphasis upon the importance of parental child-raising practices reflected a set of middle-class concerns that had been emerging for centuries. Not only was the formulation of his theory coincident with the disappearance of apprenticeship as a method of raising children, but a growing urban populace found itself increasingly cut off from extended family ties and isolated in emotionally packed small family units. Never before had parents and children been thrown so completely on their own resources, nor in such an all-consuming way (Laslett, 1973). Hence, Freud's theory contributed to a modern school of thought which suggests that the life-long characteristics of the human personality are determined almost exclusively by a combination of organic nature and the relation of a child to its parents. It had tremendous impact because it both reflected social trends and seemed to provide a highly sophisticated scheme for making sense out of them, particularly of indicating to the white-middle class the terrible consequences of poor child-raising practices.

This is not to suggest that Freud's complex ideas were published in the *Reader's Digest* and read by everyone. Rather, they gradually filtered into public awareness and, more important, into the organization of societal life via intellectual, academic, and professional circles. Later theoretical variations on the Freudian theme are too numerous to list in detail, but certain ones have found repeated expression:

> The first few years of life are critical. If an infant does not secure satisfying relationships with affectionate, nurturant parents, the damage will be irreversible (Abrahamsen, 1960; Cohen, 1966:54). The child lingers on as a selfish infant, failing to develop as a self-sufficient responsible person.

> The ego and superego, if not the id, remain key concepts in most psychodynamic theories. When both are weak, the child is unable to subordinate antisocial impulses, to defer gratifications, and to

adhere to rational and moral courses of action (Redl and Wineman, 1951).

Moral maturity is attained when the child has successfully moved through a series of developmental stages and is no longer fixated at infantile levels (Piaget, 1932; Kohlberg, 1964). According to one theory, there are seven stages of interpersonal maturity, but most delinquents remain fixed between the second and fourth stages. Almost half of them are neurotics whose emotional disturbance is characterized by feelings of guilt and inadequacy (Warren, 1969).

Early childhood experiences produce in every individual a deeply ingrained and enduring personality. It is this personality which spells the difference between troublemakers and well-adjusted children. Troublemakers possess personality traits that predispose them to antisocial conduct (Healy and Bronner, 1936; Abrahamsen, 1960; Glueck and Glueck, 1950).

In short, most psychodynamic theories tend to remain in the Freudian tradition, sharing with it "the idea that the wellsprings of behavior, and especially deviant behavior, are largely irrational, obscure energies relatively inaccessible to observation and conscious control by the actor" (Cohen, 1966:54). They have helped to perpetuate a deterministic tradition that has tended to grow stronger, not weaker, over time.

Policy legacy of psychodynamic theories

Far more than biological theories, psychodynamic ideas found a rich seedbed in the philosophy of the juvenile court. The notion that delinquent behavior is not a deliberate defiance of social norms but is an unconscious response to a combination of antisocial instincts and to poor parental practices helped greatly to legitimize the ideology of the court. Delinquents are sick, not wicked. Their acts are not the disease that must be cured, only symptoms of it.

Translated into public policy, these ideas strongly supported the belief that judges should not sentence delinquents according to the crimes they had committed but should prescribe sentences based upon diagnosis of their ills by psychological experts. Once this was done, treatment could then be carried out throughout the whole correctional process. Such treatment, moreover, would require the use of professional counseling, psychotherapy, and medical care, as well as the more traditional academic and vocational training.

This need for psychological treatment, in turn, contributed to a growing professionalism among those who worked with delinquents. Specialists rather than well-intentioned lay persons were required—psychiatrists, clinical psychologists, and social workers. Schools of social work, which had traced their origins to 19th century muckrakers and settlement workers, ironically, now began to take on a new identity. Much more than previously, their prestige was associated with their capacity to turn out students with a psychodynamic orientation. Not only did these changes lead to an emphasis upon psychological cures for known delinquents, but it led to the creation of a child-guidance movement designed to neutralize the presence of "latent delinquency" in young children. The assumption was that since "predelinquent traits" can be identified at a very early age professional treatment should begin then.

> If children were intelligently examined and treated during the course of their school attendance, it would be no difficult matter to predict which ones, upon graduation, would be likely to continue to have emotional difficulties resulting in deviant behavior. The most seriously disordered children could be treated and trained in special clinics (Banay, 1948:186).

During the 1950s, numerous influential groups—the United States Children's Bureau, the World Health Organization, and the United States Senate—made similar recommendations (Hakeem, 1957:488–489). And, for over ten years, the New York City Youth Board ran a prevention program for first graders who had been identified as "predelinquents" (Craig and Glick, 1963). Though such efforts stirred up much controversy (Cf. Toby, 1965), considerable enthusiasm was exhibited over the idea that the potential carriers of delinquency disease might be identified early and an antitoxin successfully administered.

On the other side of the coin, treatment programs based on a psychodynamic model are very expensive because of the assumption that therapy may require years of effort by a highly skilled staff. Hence, many jurisdictions have not been able to afford them. Nonetheless, the treatment model suggested by psychodynamic theory has remained the standard to which most courts and correctional agencies have aspired until very recently. As professional ideology, if not a vehicle, for the proper treatment of children, therefore, few bodies of theory have enjoyed the widespread popularity that psychodynamic theories have enjoyed.

Scientific legacy of psychodynamic theories

Despite their widespread social impact, most psychodynamic theories have not received much empirical support. The major reason is that they are not readily amenable to scientific test. For example, Alexander and Healy (1935:67) concluded that repeated thefts by a delinquent were due to guilt feelings from excessive dependency upon his mother, accompanied by a desire to compensate for this dependency by being delinquent. Only through this symbolic substitute could the boy prove his manhood and get some relief from his inner torments. But how can one ever demonstrate that such an explanation is valid, especially if the boy's dependency developed in infancy and is repressed and hidden in his unconscious? There is virtually no way that a causal connection between this subjective internal state and delinquent behavior can be established. Indeed, there is always the danger that any such connection is a construction that exists only in the mind of the clinical observer, not in the mind of the offender.

Some investigators have used retrospective case studies as a method of overcoming those problems. After obtaining the life histories of delinquents, analyzing their dreams, or putting them under hypnosis, an attempt is made to explain their behavior (Cf. Alexander and Healy, 1935; Lindner, 1944). Most such studies, however, have had a fatal flaw.

The flaw is produced by the kind of reasoning that is associated with clinical, after-the-fact methods of investigation. It goes something like this:

1. Delinquent behavior is the product of psychological abnormality.
2. Joe is a delinquent.
3. Therefore, Joe is psychologically abnormal.

The problem with this kind of reasoning is that it is circular. For example, until Joe becomes delinquent, he is not defined as abnormal. But, once he has gotten into trouble, this abnormality is used to explain his behavior (Wootton, 1959:250). Yet, the only empirical evidence that he is abnormal is the delinquency that his abnormality is supposed to explain.

A far more defensible attempt to test psychodynamic theories has come about through the use of personality tests—tests designed to measure the various traits that different persons are assumed to possess (McCord, 1968). In contrast to the case study method, personality tests have permitted psychologists to seek independent proof that some people are abnormal and then to see whether this abnormality is linked to delinquent behavior.

Alas! The results have not been encouraging. Schuessler and Cressey (1950) reviewed 113 studies conducted prior to 1950 and concluded that they did not demonstrate a direct link between delinquency and specific personality traits. Many of the studies were of doubtful quality, and others presented contradictory findings. A second review of the same type covered 97 studies completed between 1950 and 1965 (Waldo and Dinitz, 1967). Its authors found that the quality of investigation had improved but that the results were still inconclusive. There was precious little evidence that personality abnormality and delinquent behavior are strongly related.

One of the better studies of this relationship illustrates why results have not been encouraging. Hathaway et al. (1960), selected nearly 2,000 ninth graders who were first tested with the Minnesota Multiphasic Personality Inventory (MMPI) to determine their personality configurations. Then, the investigators checked both public and private records two years later to determine how many of the students had become official delinquents. If differences in personality were related to official delinquency, they should appear in this follow-up. Though some differences were uncovered, Hathaway, et al. (1960:439) expressed disappointment over the results. Personality measures, they said, "are much less powerful and apply to fewer cases . . . than would be expected if one reads the literature on the subject. . . . Surely we cannot say that these data put us very far ahead either in understanding or prediction."

There are several things that may have contributed to these inconclusive findings. In the first place, it is a gross oversimplification simply to equate psychological abnormality and delinquent behavior: A child is disturbed so he or she commits a delinquent act. By their own accounts, most young people have been delinquent, but it is unlikely that all are abnormal.

Secondly, any relationship between abnormality and delinquent behavior is probably a limited one. Hathaway, et al. (1960:434) found, for example, that while "psychopathy," "schizophrenia," and "hypomania" were associated with higher rates of delinquent behavior, such traits as "introversion," "depression," and "masculinity-femininity" were associated with *lower* rates. In short, abnormality is not a unidimensional phenomenon that is universally associated with delinquent behavior. Sometimes, in fact, it may be associated with excessive or compulsive conformity, not delinquency.

Finally, there are theoretical problems associated with the concept of personality. Its use as a predictor of behavior rests upon the assumption that it is an enduring characteristic that will affect the individual in much the same way throughout life. It suggests, for example, that a child who possesses a delinquency prone personality will possess the same personality as an adult. Yet, as we have seen, delinquent acts among people tend to peak at about age 16 and to decline thereafter. Few young people become adult criminals. Why is this? If psychodynamic theory were correct, it suggests that the pattern should be just the opposite. The fact that it is not indicates that it possesses some serious limitation. There are grounds for suspecting that a person's behavior, and thus the psychological motivations that give rise to it, are likely to change markedly throughout life.

Despite these limitations, it would be less than wise to dismiss all psychological factors as irrelevant. In the first place, the failure to find a consistent relationship between personality and delinquency may be due, in part, to weaknesses in the body of research on the subject. As was noted earlier, many of the investigations in this area have been poorly conducted. Hence, until research methods are improved, conclusions must remain tentative.

Secondly, numerous studies indicate that children who grow up in brutal homes, in hospitals, orphanages, or concentration camps where warmth and nurturing are lacking are more likely to suffer mental and social damage (Cf. Nettler, 1974:237–238). Some of them become abnormally aggressive and do not exhibit any sense of guilt over outrageous behavior (Redl and Wineman, 1951). A lack of nurturing, however, does not always result in antisocial behavior. Sometimes it produces children who are so overly controlled and so submissive that they appear to have no ego at all. Thus, while the relationship between the psychodynamic factors and delinquency is not always consistent, there is no denying their importance nor the need to learn more about them.

Finally, so long as one is concerned with the questions, "Why is she delinquent?" or "Why did he do it?", one must deal with matters of psychological motivation. Indeed, as Cohen (1966:65) points out, "Sociologists . . . are no less interested in internal motivation than are psychologists, but they are interested in it from a special point of view." What they want to know is how the culture at large or how membership in a particular social class, ethnic group, peer group, or phase in the life cycle are likely to affect a person's psychological state. Just as forces within the family can shape one's way of viewing and responding to the world, so forces outside of it can also do so. Seymour Halleck (1971), a psychiatrist, has noted this fact and has suggested that those who are concerned with the relationship between personality and delinquency must take this larger body of forces into account.

But this is getting ahead of our story. All of the control theories we have examined thus far have not attributed delinquent motives to class, ethnic, or subcultural differences but to hereditary or psychodynamic forces that are closely linked to the offender's genetic or family background. In the remaining section of the chapter, we will be examining a psychosocial version of control theory which does much the same thing but which also relates much more closely to traditional, commonsense constructions of childhood and delinquency.

Psychosocial control theory

In order to set the stage for our examination, we need to review a bit of history. It will be recalled that during the 19th century Americans became convinced that of all the causes of juvenile misconduct the most important was broken or depraved families. That is why the child-saving institutions were invented—to get the children of disrupted families off the street and into a moral environment.

In her analysis of the impact of this traditional view upon 20th century criminologists, Wilkinson (1974) documents the following major points. From about 1900 until 1932, the relationship between broken homes and delinquency was widely accepted in the scientific community. Most investigators were rural-born migrants to the city who were convinced that divorce and desertion were serious threats to social stability, since the family was the foundation of society. Hence, though their investigations were often characterized by serious inadequacies, they were convinced that their findings were accurate. It is now clear, however, that this conviction was affected as much by prevailing cultural beliefs as by evidence (Wilkinson, 1974:726–732).

Then, from about 1933 until 1950, a new generation of criminologists, most of whom were sociologists, rejected the broken home explanation (1) because prior investigations lacked scientific rigor, and (2) because of the rural biases of early sociologists. But, instead of improving the methods of investigation on the family, they rejected its importance altogether. More of the new generation were urban dwellers who saw less danger in divorce and social change. Furthermore, there was a growing aversion to family research because of its link to psychodynamic explanations of delinquency. Once again, therefore, the course of scientific investigation was affected by nonscientific values and disciplinary provincialism.

Finally, during the 1950s and 1960s, renewed interest in the family was shown by a few investigators. Though their findings did indicate a relationship between disrupted families and delinquency, it was neglected again by most criminologists (Monahan, 1957; Nye, 1958; Wilkinson, 1974). The reason for this neglect lay in a growing inclination to view delinquency as a kind of normal social functioning, due more to membership in the lower class and in delinquent peer groups than in disrupted families (Rodman and Grams, 1967:208). As Bordua put it in 1962 (p. 249), "the discussion of delinquency in recent sociological theory . . . seems to be distinguished more by a desire to avoid 'pyschologizing' than by a·desire to understand delinquency." If a boy is humiliated by his teacher, said Bordua (1962:250), then that is social class and is admissible as a legitimate concern of the sociologist, but, if he is humiliated by his father, that is child psychology and inadmissible.

It was out of this context that the most recent and systematic expression of psychosocial control theory grew. In 1969, Travis Hirschi, a sociologist, not only reasserted the importance of many 19th century beliefs about the family, but related them as well to traditional beliefs about the importance of schooling. His work was noteworthy both because of his resurrection of these ideas and because he did something his predecessors had failed to do: He stated his theory in systematic and testable terms. But, before taking that step, he also linked his theory to earlier versions of control theory.

Hirschi (1969:31–34) observes that it has now become fashionable to disdain the assumptions made by philosophers like Hobbes, by religionists like the Puritans, or by theorists like Freud that human nature is inherently antisocial. Most moderns prefer to believe that people are inherently moral at birth or, at worst, that they are born with the potential to be either good or bad. Hirschi rejects both points of view, however, and asserts that control theory remains what it has always been—a theory which suggests that it is not criminals and delinquents alone who are animals "but that we are all animals, and thus all naturally capable of committing criminal acts" (1969:31). If we strip away the veneer of civilization, we will find that all people are subject to animal impulse.

If that is true, then there is nothing to be explained when the question is asked: "Why did they do it?" Since human nature is inherently antisocial, all children would commit delinquent acts if they dared. Hence, the central question which control theory is designed to answer is: "Why don't they do it?" (Hirschi, 1969:34). "Why do most children stay out of serious trouble?" "What is it that prevents them from becoming habitual and lifelong criminals?"

The social bond

Hirschi (p. 16) answers these questions by suggesting that it is an individual's *bond* to society that makes the difference (Cf. Reckless, 1961, for a similar statement). He cites the French sociologist, Emile Durkheim (1951:209) to illustrate what he means. "The more weakened the groups to which the individual belongs," said Durkheim, "the less he depends on them, the more he consequently depends only on himself and recognizes no other rules of conduct than what are founded on his private interests." In short, we are moral beings to the extent that we have internalized the norms of society and have become sensitive to the needs of others. Indeed, sensitivity to others *is* the social bond. By contrast,

> To violate a norm is . . . to act contrary to the wishes and expectations of other people. If a person does not care about the wishes and expectations of other people—that is, if he is insensitive to the opinion of others—then he is to that extent not bound by the norms. He is free to deviate (Hirschi, 1969:18).

This way of defining the bond to society requires that one make certain assumptions about the social order. Indeed, like other control theorists, Hirschi is disinclined to see value conflicts in society as being responsible for an individual's insensitivity to the wishes of others. Instead, he assumes that the members of society are tied together by a common value system; people share a common definition of good and bad (pp. 18:23).

This is a crucial assumption. If morality were not self-evident—that is, if the delinquent were faced with conflicting rules for behavior—one could not charge him with failing to respect the wishes of others. Unknowingly, he might be adhering faithfully to a set of expectations which, though they ran counter to convention, were those that he was taught to respect. But this is not what control theory suggests. Instead, it assumes that the social order can be taken for granted. Delinquent behavior cannot be interpreted as a response to social inequality, to conflicting subcultural rules, or to the imposition of one group's values upon another's. Rather, since morality is self-evident, it is the delinquent who defies convention and threatens social stability. His behavior is due to natural human impulses which remain unconstrained by a strong and lasting bond to the norms of a united society.

Elements of the bond

Hirschi theorizes that the *social bond* is made up of four major elements. Far more than Freudian concepts, these are the elements which bear directly on the traditional concept of childhood and which would have made sense to 19th century reformers as well as to lay persons today. Furthermore, Hirschi defines them in such a way that they can be tested, thus avoiding the weaknesses of Freudian theory.

The first element is *attachment*. It refers to the ties of affection and respect between children and such key persons as parents, teachers, and friends. A strong bond with all three will be a major deterrent to delinquency. Attachment to parents, however, is the most important, since it is by parents that children are first socialized. Furthermore, it is not whether families are broken by divorce or desertion that is of greatest importance, but what the nature of the bond is between children and one or both parents. If children are strongly attached to their parents, they are much more likely to internalize the norms of society and to develop feelings of respect for persons in authority, like teachers, or for equals, like friends. But, if they are alienated from their parents, they will likely be alienated from others. They will not learn or have a feeling for moral rules, nor will they develop an adequate conscience (Hirschi, 1969:86).

In a sense, Hirschi's *attachment* is analogous to Freud's "superego." But it locates "the 'conscience' in the bond to others rather than making it a part of the personality" (p. 19). Thus, the extent to which a person is attached to others can be measured independent of one's delinquent behavior—something that was not possible with Freud's superego.

The second element of the bond is *commitment*. This is a rational component similar to Freud's "ego," but it also has roots in long-standing traditions. It has to do with the extent to which children are committed to the ideal requirements of childhood—getting an education, postponing participation in adult activities like drinking and smoking, or dedicating themselves to long-term goals. If children commit themselves to these activities, they will develop a stake in conformity and will be disinclined to engage in delinquent behavior. To do so would be to endanger their futures (p. 21). And, though commitment refers to an internalized set of expectations, it too is amenable to measurement.

The third element is *involvement.* This is the equivalent of the traditional belief that "idle hands are the devil's workshop." It is a concept that has particular relevance for adolescents, since they are in that phase of the life cycle when they are neither under total parental domination nor are they totally free to behave as adults. Instead, they are in a semilimbo where expectations are not as clear-cut as they might be. Hence, large amounts of unstructured time may decrease the effectiveness of the social bond and increase the likelihood of delinquent behavior. By contrast, adolescents who are busy doing conventional things—duties around the home, studying, or engaging in sports—do not have time to be delinquent (pp. 21–23).

The fourth element is *belief.* Some persons simply do not have an attitude of respect for the law. They feel no moral obligation to conform to it. This is not to say that such persons do not know that they are breaking the law or that they are doing wrong. It is just that their consciences are not offended by deviant behavior. Thus, the less a juvenile believes in the morality of law, the greater the likelihood he will be delinquent (pp. 25–26).

Social legacy of psychosocial theory

The ideas in Hirschi's version of control theory are not new, but the way it combines them is unique as well as orderly. On one hand, Hirschi agrees with those theorists and philosophers who have suggested that the impulse or motivation to be delinquent does not need explaining, since we are all naturally capable of committing criminal acts. On the other hand, his attention to social relationships beyond the first few years of life not only extends the scope of control theory, but captures traditional perspectives strikingly well. Whether most people would agree that all children are inherently antisocial is debatable, but the parallel between Hirschi's theory of social control and that expressed by W. I. Thomas in 1923 is obvious:

> As soon as the child has free motion and begins to pull, tear, pry, meddle, and prowl, the parents begin to define the situation through speech and other signs and pressures: "Be quiet," "Sit up straight," "Blow your

nose," "Wash your face," "Mind your mother," "Be kind to your sister," etc. This is the real significance of Wordsworth's phrase, "Shades of the prison house begin to close upon the growing child." His wishes and activities begin to be inhibited, and gradually by definitions within the family, by playmates, in school, in the Sunday School, in the community, through reading, by formal instruction, by informal signs of approval and disapproval, the growing member learns the code of his society (Thomas, 1923:43–44).

Many contemporary Americans would be inclined to support this version of control theory (Nettler, 1974:247). In 1975, for example, Betty Ford, wife of the President of the United States, candidly admitted in a television interview that her teenage children might have experimented with pot-smoking and that her daughter might have engaged in pre-marital sex (*Los Angeles Times,* October 7, 1975). The public outcry was considerable; the First Lady had rubbed a raw nerve. Many people took her remarks to mean that she and the President had abandoned the tried and true morals of the American past. Traditional beliefs about appropriate roles for children retain considerable vigor.

These same beliefs are also evident in the way officials continue to respond to delinquents. While psychodynamic theory has been a legitimizing professional ideology for workers in the juvenile court, they are practical people who must work with factors that can be manipulated *now.* Psychodynamic theory does not provide easy access to such factors. While workers are hard put to know how to undo the effects of unconscious drives and early fixations, they can readily see the need to respond to the factors defined as important by Hirschi: to *reattach* delinquents to parents and school; to get them to *commit* themselves to the demands of childhood; to *involve* them in a heavy routine of conventional activities; and, above all, to have them acquire *beliefs* in the morality of law. Consequently, it seems clear that while Freudian theory added many complex elaborations to traditional beliefs about child raising Hirschi's theory does a remarkable job of capturing the essence of those beliefs without undue elaboration and of reflecting what it is that officials actually do with delinquents. A most important question, therefore, is whether there is evidence to support it, particularly since Freudian theory is so difficult to test.

Examination of psychosocial theory

Hirschi not only conducted a comprehensive examination of his own theory, but avoided some of the pitfalls into which earlier researchers had fallen. He selected a representative sample of over 4,000 junior and senior high school students—black and white, lower-, middle- and upper-class—ranging in age from 13 to 18. From this sample, he obtained three types of information: (1) independent measures of the four elements of the social bond; (2) measures of self-reported delinquent behavior, including several types of monetary theft, auto theft, vandalism, and assault (no status offenses were included); and (3) measures of official delinquency. By obtaining self-reported data, he could avoid the problems associated with official records and could provide a more definitive test of his theory. Apparently girls were excluded from the analysis, however, because relatively few had official records. Hence, the findings cover only boys—2,336 of them.

1.   *Distribution of delinquent behavior.*   Since control theory assumes that all segments of society share the same values, it is not a class or racially based theory. Therefore, the first question addressed by Hirschi was whether delinquent behavior is distributed across the class structure rather than concentrated in the lower class as many competing theories suggest.

Using self-reported data, Hirschi (pp. 66–74) found what most other investigators have found: Social class is not a good predictor of delinquent behavior. Furthermore, there was surprisingly little disagreement among students from different social classes on whether the law should be obeyed or whether a person has the right to take advantage of others. The great majority believed in the importance of adhering to law (p. 215). In short, such findings lent some support to the assumption that delinquency is not just a lower-class phenomenon and that the social order is characterized by agreement on basic values.

2.   *Attachment.*   Hirschi measured the attachment of his respondents to parents, school, and friends. With regard to parents, he found that the more a boy identifies with his parents and respects their expectations for him, the lower his chances of delinquent behavior (p. 94). The same findings have been reported by others (Empey and Lubeck, 1971, passim; Hindelang, 1973:475). These relationships, however, were by no means perfect; that is, some boys who report good relations with their parents are delinquent, and vice versa. Nonetheless, the probabilities of delinquent behavior are greater if relations between parents and children are detached and disharmonious.

Second, and perhaps more significant, Hirschi and others have discovered that these relationships extend across racial and class lines: "Regardless of the class or racial status of the parent, the closer the boy's ties to him, the less likely he is to commit delinquent acts" (p. 97; Dinitz, et al.; 1962). Therefore, says Hirschi, "We may infer that those lower-class boys committing delinquent acts are not finding support for their actions from their parents or from their 'class culture' " (p. 97).

In assessing attachment to school, Hirschi alludes to the significant place that education has come to occupy in the lives of children. Insofar as this "eminently conventional institution" is able to command their attachment, he says, "they are . . . presumably able to move from childhood to adulthood with a minimum of delinquent acts" (p. 110). As with the family, therefore, the bond to the school will be determined by the extent to which children retain favorable feelings for it. However, Hirschi suggests that intellectual capacity will have a great deal to do with whether children like school or not. If they have the capacity to do well, the chances are much greater that they will become attached to the school. But, if they are intellectually impaired, this condition will contribute to a lack of attachment. In order to illustrate what he means, Hirschi suggests that the following causal chain is likely to produce a lack of attachment, followed by delinquent behavior (p. 132):

Academic impairment	$\rightarrow$	Poor school performance	$\rightarrow$	Dislike of school	$\rightarrow$	Rejection of authority	$\rightarrow$	Delinquent behavior

Most of Hirschi's findings appear to lend some support to the validity of this chain:

Impairment: The lower a boy's score on numerous achievement tests, the more likely he is to have been delinquent and to have been picked up by the police (pp. 113–115).

Performance: The lower a boy's grades, the more likely he is to have been delinquent (pp. 117–118).

Liking for school: The less a boy likes school, the more likely he is to be delinquent (pp. 120–121).

Rejection of school authority: The less a boy cares about what his teachers think of him and the more inclined he is to reject school authority, the more likely he is to be delinquent (pp. 123–124).

Numerous other studies have reported similar findings—that delinquents may be less competent than nondelinquents (Dinitz, et al., 1962; Toby and Toby, 1962:27; Reiss and Rhodes, 1961:723; Short and Strodtbeck, 1965:237–238); that delinquents do less well in school (Cohen, 1955:117 ff; Polk, 1967; Empey and Lubeck, 1971:96–97); or that delinquents are more likely to reject school authority (Stinchcombe, 1964; Hindelang, 1973:478). The real question, therefore, is not whether some of these relationships exist but how one interprets them.

As we saw earlier, delinquency theorists, since the days of the mental testers, have been increasingly inclined to reject the notion that intellectual impairment plays a role in contributing to delinquency, however indirect that role may be. Although most acknowledge the central role of the school they tend to theorize that it is the life-style and the disadvantaged position of the lower-class student in this middle-class institution that produces delinquent behavior, not any impaired capacity on his part (Cf. Cohen, 1955; Miller, 1958; Cloward and Ohlin, 1960). Control theorists, by contrast, continue to call attention to the latter, especially since lowered intellectual capacity, followed by a dislike of school, often cuts across class and racial lines and characterizes middle- and upper- as well as lower-class students. Thus, this is an issue that should be kept in mind when later theories are considered.

Affinity with friends is the final dimension of *attachment*. As we have seen, control theory suggests that young people who do not like and respect their parents and teachers will be more likely to be delinquent. But it also suggests that these same individuals are not likely to develop respect for their friends either. The reason is that they have never developed feelings of compassion and responsibility for anyone. Thus, while they may join together in groups or gangs, their relations will not be characterized by warmth and respect.

Hirschi's findings lent support to this view (pp. 145–152). Those boys who are least attached to, and least respectful of, their friends were most likely to have committed delinquent acts. This was not always true, but, overall, the findings lent considerable support to those investigators who suggest that relations among delinquents may be characterized more by brittleness and threat than by solidarity and warmth (Yablonsky, 1963:196; Matza, 1964:53–55; Short and Strodtbeck, 1965:221–234; Klein and Crawford, 1967). In fact, Hirschi concludes (p. 159) that "The idea that delinquents have . . . warm, intimate relations with each other is a myth." Because they have not learned to respect the wishes of adults, they do not respect the wishes of peers.

By contrast, another group of investigators have argued that their friends become a sort of substitute society for delinquents, providing the satisfactions that nondelinquents find through conventional groups (Thrasher, 1963:41–46; Cohen, 1955; Cloward and Ohlin, 1960). Because they are outside conventional society, they are more dependent upon their friends than are nondelinquents and, thus, are more attached to them. Some studies have also lent some support to this view (Empey and Lubeck, 1968; Hindelang, 1973:479). Hence, what we have are competing theories and evidence without resolution. This is another fact, therefore, that should be filed for future reference when we consider the role of friends more thoroughly later on.

3.   *Commitment.*   As the second element of the social bond, *commitment* assumes that the motivation to adhere to the ideal concept of childhood and to strive for conventional goals is a built-in constraint on delinquent behavior. The individual has a stake in conformity which he feels will be jeopardized by deviant conduct. For example, Hirschi theorizes that those children who engage in such "adult" activities as smoking, drinking, dating, and driving at an early age are more likely to commit delinquent acts. By claiming the right to do these things, they deny their status as children, express contempt for the expectations of parents and teachers, and free themselves from the norms governing childhood. Again, Hirschi produces some evidence in favor of his hypothesis (pp. 166–169). Boys who smoked, drank, dated frequently, and paid excessive attention to cars were more likely to have committed delinquent acts. Furthermore, these activities were cumulative in effect: The more a boy is involved in them, the greater his involvement in delinquency (Hindelang, 1973:481).

So much for the deviant side of the coin. What about the other side, the conformist side? What effect does commitment to an education and to a career have? Like other investigators (Briar and Piliavin, 1965; Toby, 1957; Hindelang, 1973), Hirschi found that better grades, higher educational aspirations, and long-range ambitions are associated with lower rates of delinquency (pp. 171–179). Whether among black or white boys, the stronger the adherence to the ideal concept of childhood, the lower the commission of criminal acts.

4.   *Involvement.*   The findings on involvement closely paralleled those on commitment. Those boys who spent an inordinate amount of time riding around in cars or who reported that they were bored were considerably more delinquent (pp. 193–194). By contrast, those who devoted a lot of time to homework and other school activities were not only less inclined to feel bored but to be less delinquent (Cf. Hindelang, 1973:483). This was true not only of low achievers in school, but high achievers as well. In short, involvement, like commitment, helped to deter delinquent behavior.

5.   *Belief.*   Hirschi's data on belief reflect on two basic assumptions of control theory: (1) that attachment to parents produces the belief that one should respect both the law and persons in authority; and (2) that

people from all social strata share the same basic beliefs. With regard to the first, boys who were poorly attached to parents and school were those who had the least respect for the law and for the police. These same boys, moreover, were the ones most likely to be delinquent (pp. 200–203). Although there were exceptions, such tendencies have been reported by others (Dinitz et al., 1962; Hindelang, 1973.

The findings with respect to agreement on basic values were more conclusive. There was surprisingly little disagreement among students from different social classes on what people ought to do: whether they should obey the law, whether one has the right to take advantage of others, or even whether it is uncontrolled fate rather than personal competence that determines a person's destiny (pp. 215–220).

Similar findings have been reported by others. Rather than having different values, adolescents from all social strata tend to share so-called middle-class values—the desire to get ahead, the importance of education, or the acquisition of a high status occupation (Empey, 1956; Gordon, et al., 1963; Kobrin, 1951). Gang, lower-class and middle-class boys, Negro and white, say Short and Strodtbeck (1965:271), "evaluate images representing salient features of the middle-class style of life equally high." Consistent with this finding, therefore, Hirschi found that it was not class position that led to differences in values, but the strength of the social bond; the weaker it was, the less likely an individual was to believe in conventional values.

Once again, these findings are significant, not only in terms of possible support for control theory, but in terms of the theories we will be considering next. In contrast to control theory, they suggest that it is a child's class membership, his place in the social structure, not his family or school ties, that determine his basic beliefs. Indeed, because society is divided into different social strata, contrasting beliefs will be far more important in understanding delinquent behavior than will the strength of the social bond.

In summary, Hirschi's version of control theory has stood the test of empirical investigation better than any other version. The findings would seem to warrant putting traditional constructions of delinquency back on the agenda of scientific discussion. But, for reasons mentioned earlier, there are still resistances to doing so, some ideological, some scientific. His findings raised a series of questions on which there are strong differences of opinion: whether it is intellectual impairment or the disadvantage of class position that contributes to poor school performance; how strongly delinquents are tied to their friends; or whether society is characterized by competing or similar standards and values. Furthermore, Hirschi's theory fares better because of the remarkable consistency of his findings than because of the strengths or predictive power of his results. While the various elements of the bond are more or less related to delinquent behavior, they still account for only about 25 percent of the variation between delinquents and nondelinquents. What this means is that many of the factors contributing to delinquent behavior remain unexplained. Thus, the need to consider the causes suggested by competing theories remains important.

Summary and conclusions

Control theories have contributed to our social construction of delinquency in unique ways. That contribution can be summarized by reference to the basic questions that will be asked about all theories:

1. *What assumptions do control theories make about human nature and social order?* Biological theories assume that delinquents and nondelinquents are different kinds of people at birth. Delinquents possess genetic traits or depraved tendencies which predispose them to antisocial behavior. Nondelinquents, however, are inherently good people, predisposed to good conduct.

Psychodynamic and psychosocial theories, by contrast, assume that *all* children are animals at birth—impulsive, self-centered, and lacking the ability to control themselves in socially approved ways. Their tendency to be antisocial "is as original as sin" (Rieff, 1959:274).

Given these views of human nature, all control theories tend to take the social order for granted; that is, to assume that its various elements reflect a high degree of consensus, that morality is self-evident, and that it is the delinquent individual on whom attention must be focused, since the social order does not create problems that might contribute to the commission of delinquent acts.

2. *What is the underlying logic and content of control theories?* Since all control theories assume that the tendency to be delinquent is inherited, they are less concerned with why children become delinquent than with discovering why it is that some refrain from it. Psychodynamic and psychosocial theories provide the best answers, suggesting that it is the way children are socialized. If they are properly trained to control their impulses and to respect the wishes of others, conformist behavior will result. But, while psychodynamic theories stress the need to under-

stand obscure, unconscious motives hidden deeply within the child's personality, psychosocial theory locates the forces that constrain his conduct in the elements of the social bond. The explanatory framework of these theories can be combined and diagrammed simply as in Figure 9–1.

FIGURE 9–1

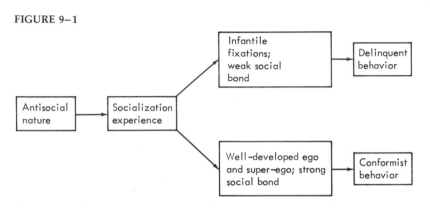

3.   *What are the implications of control theories for social policy, and what impact have they had?*   Biological theories imply the need to forbid defective people from reproducing and to incapacitate those already with us. They have contributed to a eugenics movement designed to accomplish this purpose.

Psychodynamic theories imply the singular importance of early child-raising practices. If those fail, predelinquent or delinquent children should be diagnosed and placed in special clinics for long-term treatment. As a professional ideology for the juvenile court, this doctrine has probably been the most influential of all theoretical doctrines.

Psychosocial theory relates more directly to the ideal concept of childhood, stressing the importance of the school and respect for authority as well as the family. Though less influential as a professional ideology, its appeal to commonsense traditions has been strongly reflected in what court and correctional people actually do in working with delinquents.

4.   *How well do control theories stand up to logical and empirical scrutiny?*   The fact that control theories have been heavily applied to the conduct of social policy is striking when contrasted with their lack of acceptance among positivistic criminologists. This is particularly true of biological and psychodynamic theories. Biological theories have not

been well received (1) because, as originally stated, they were logically inadequate and lacked empirical support; and (2) because of ideological bickering between social and biological scientists over the role of "nature" versus "nurture." As a result, current theories of delinquency have failed to reflect a growing body of knowledge which documents profoundly complex relations among biological and environmental factors.

Many of the same conclusions apply to psychodynamic theories: (1) most of them are impossible to falsify; (2) the assumption that life-long behavior patterns are set within the confines of the family in early infancy is overly simplistic; and (3) the tendency to equate personality abnormality with delinquent behavior has not been confirmed by empirical evidence. Yet, psychological motivation can scarcely be ignored. What has been lacking in the psychodynamic approach, therefore, are postulates which link motivation to social and cultural factors, as well as to those which are familial.

Psychosocial control theory dealt with these matters more completely and conformed better to the ideals of positivistic science: (1) it is amenable to test; (2) it pays more attention to the status and role of children in American culture; and (3) some evidence has been garnered in support of it. With all that, the assumptions that psychosocial (and other control theories) make about human nature and social order are open to other interpretations; many questions remain unanswered about the role of subcultural and peer group influences outside the family and school; and the overall effects of social change require consideration. In the chapters that follow, these issues become the center of focus in lieu of the kinds with which control theories are concerned.

References

Abraham, Karl
    1927 *Selected Papers on Psychoanalysis*. London: Hogarth.

Abrahamsen, David
    1960 *The Psychology of Crime*. New York: Columbia University Press.

Aichorn, August
    1936 *Wayward Youth*. New York: Viking Press.

Alexander, Franz, and Healy, William
    1935 *Roots of Crime*. New York: Alfred A. Knopf.

Banay, Ralph S.
   1948   *Youth in Despair.* New York: Coward-McGann.

Blackmar, F. W.
   1897   "The smoky pilgrims." *American Journal of Sociology,* June, II:490–500.

Bordua, David J.
   1962   "Some comments on theories of group delinquency." *Sociological Inquiry,* Spring, 33:245–260.

Bremner, Robert H. et al. (Eds.)
   1971   *Children and Youth in America: A Documentary History* (Vol. II). Cambridge: Harvard University Press.

Briar, Scott and Piliavin, Irving
   1965   "Delinquency, situational inducement and commitment to conformity." *Social Problems,* Summer, 8:35–45.

Clinard, Marshall B.
   1968   *Sociology of Deviant Behavior.* New York: Holt, Rinehart and Winston.

Cloward, Richard A., and Ohlin, Lloyd E.
   1960   *Delinquency and Opportunity: A Theory of Delinquent Gangs.* New York: Free Press.

Cohen, Albert J.
   1955   *Delinquent Boys: The Culture of the Gang.* New York: Free Press.

   1966   *Deviance and Control.* Englewood Cliffs, N.J.: Prentice Hall.

Cortes, J. B. and Gatti, F. M.
   1972   *Delinquency and Crime: A Biopsychosocial Approach.* New York: Seminar Press.

Craig, Maude M. and Glick, Selma J.
   1963   "Ten years of experience with the Glueck prediction table." *Crime and Delinquency,* July, 9:249–261.

Darlington, D. C.
   1953   *The Facts of Life.* London: Allen and Unwin.

Dinitz, Simon et al.
   1962   "Delinquency vulnerability: a cross group and longitudinal analysis." *American Sociological Review,* August, 27:515–517.

Durkheim, Emile
   1951   *Suicide* (Trans. by John A. Spaulding and George Simpson). New York: Free Press.

Empey, LaMar T.
   1956   "Social class and occupational aspiration." *American Sociological Review,* December, 21:703–709.

Empey, LaMar T. and Lubeck, Steven G.
  1968 "Conformity and deviance in the situation of company." *American Sociological Review*, October, *33*:761–774.

  1971 *Explaining Delinquency.* Lexington: D. C. Heath.

Feldman, David
  1969 "Psychoanalysis and crime." Pp. 433–442 in Donald R. Cressey and David A. Ward (Eds.), *Delinquency, Crime and Social Process.* New York: Harper and Row.

Freud, Anna
  1965 *Normality and Pathology in Childhood: Assessments of Development.* New York: International Universities Press.

Freud, Sigmund
  1963 *An Outline of Psychoanalysis.* New York: Norton.

Glueck, Sheldon and Glueck, Eleanor T.
  1956 "Early detection of future delinquents." *Journal of Criminal Law, Criminology, and Police Science,* 1956, *47*:169–181.

Goddard, Henry H.
  1911 "The treatment of the mental defective who is also delinquent." Pp. 563–564 in Robert II. Bremner et al. (Eds.), *Children and Youth in America: A Documentary History* (Vol. II). Cambridge: Harvard University Press.

  1914 *Feeblemindedness: Its Causes and Consequences.* New York: Macmillan.

Gordon, Robert A.
  1976 "Prevalence: the rare datum in delinquency measurement and its implications for the theory of delinquency." Pp. 201–284 in Malcolm W. Klein (Ed.), *The Juvenile Justice System.* Beverly Hills, Ca.: Sage Publications.

Gordon, Robert A. et al.
  1963 "Values and gang delinquency." *American Journal of Sociology,* Summer, *LXVIX*:109–128.

Goring, Charles
  1913 *The English Convict.* London: His Majesty's Stationery Office.

Hakeem, Michael
  1957 "A critique of the psychiatric approach to the prevention of juvenile delinquency." *Social Problems,* Winter, *5*:194–205.

Halleck, Seymour
  1971 *Psychiatry and the Dilemmas of Crime.* Berkeley: University of California Press.

Haskell, Martin R. and Yablonsky, Lewis
  1971 *Crime and Delinquency.* New York: Rand McNally.

Hathaway, Starke R., Monachesi, Elio D. and Young, Laurence A.
    1960 "Delinquency rates and personality." *Journal of Criminal Law, Criminology and Police Science*, February, L:433–440.

Healy, William and Bronner, Augusta F.
    1936 *New Light on Delinquency and Its Treatment*. New Haven: Yale University Press.

Hindelang, Michael J.
    1973 "Causes of delinquency: a partial replication." *Social Problems*, Spring, 21:471–487.

Hirschi, Travis
    1969 *Causes of Delinquency*. Berkeley: University of California Press.

Hirschi, Travis and Hindelang, Michael J.
    1977 "Intelligence and delinquency: a revisionist review." *American Sociological Review*, August, 42:571–587.

Hooton, Ernest A.
    1931 *Crime and the Man*. Cambridge: Harvard University Press.

    1939 *The American Criminal: An Anthropoligical Study* (Vol. I). Cambridge: Harvard University Press.

Hughes, H. Stuart
    1961 *Consciousness and Society: The Reorientation of European Social Thought 1890–1930*. New York: Vintage Books.

Kittre, Nicholas N.
    1973 *The Right to Be Different: Deviance and Enforced Therapy*. Baltimore: Penguin Books.

Klein, Malcolm W. and Crawford, Lois Y.
    1967 "Groups, gangs and cohesiveness." *Journal of Research in Crime and Delinquency*, January, 4:63–75.

Kobrin, Solomon
    1951 "The conflict of values in delinquency areas." *American Sociological Review*, October, 16:653–661.

Kohlberg, Lawrence
    1964 "Development of moral character and moral ideology." Pp. 383–431 in Martin Hoffman and Lois Hoffman (Eds.), *Review of Child Development Research* (Vol. I). New York: Russell Sage Foundation.

Laslett, Barbara
    1973 "The family as a public and private institution: an historical perspective." *Journal of Marriage and the Family*, August, 35:480–492.

Lindner, Robert M.
    1944 *Rebel without Cause*. New York: Grune and Stratton.

Matza, David
    1964 *Delinquency and Drift*. New York: John Wiley.

McCaghy, Charles H.
   1976   *Deviant Behavior.* New York: Macmillan.

McCord, William
   1968   "Delinquency: psychological aspects." Pp. 86–93, vol. 4 in David L.
          Sills (Ed.), *International Encyclopedia of the Social Sciences.* New York:
          Macmillan and Free Press.

Miller, Walter
   1958   "Lower class culture as a generating milieu of gang delinquency."
          Journal of Social Issues, 15:5–19.

Monahan, Thomas P.
   1957   "Family status and the delinquent child: a reappraisal and some new
          findings." *Social Forces,* March, 35:250–258.

Nettler, Gwynn
   1974   *Explaining Crime.* New York: McGraw-Hill.

Nye, F. Ivan
   1958   *Family Relationships and Delinquent Behavior.* New York: John Wiley.

Piaget, J.
   1932   *The Moral Judgment of the Child.* London: Routledge and Kegan Paul.

Polk, Kenneth
   1967   "Urban social areas and delinquency." *Social Problems,* Winter,
          14:320–325.

Reckless, Walter C.
   1961   "A new theory of delinquency and crime." *Federal Probation,* De-
          cember, 25:42–46.

Redl, Fritz and Wineman, David
   1951   *Children Who Hate.* New York: Free Press.

Reiss, Albert J., Jr. and Rhodes, Albert L.
   1961   "The distribution of juvenile delinquency in the social class struc-
          ture." *American Sociological Review,* October, 26:720–732.

Rieff, P.
   1959   *Freud: The Mind of the Moralist.* New York: Viking Press.

Rodman, Hyman and Grams, Paul
   1967   "Juvenile delinquency in the family." Pp. 188–221 in President's
          Commission on Law Enforcement and Administration of Justice,
          Juvenile Delinquency and Youth Crime. Washington, D.C.: U.S. Gov-
          ernment Printing Office.

Schuessler, Karl F. and Cressey, Donald R.
   1950   "Personality characteristics of criminals." *American Journal of Sociol-
          ogy,* March, 55:476–484.

Shah, Saleem A. and Roth, Loren H.
   1974   "Biological and psychophysiological factors in criminality." Pp.

101–173 in Daniel Glaser (Ed.), *Handbook of Criminology*. Chicago: Rand McNally.

Shannon, T. W.
1916   *Eugenics*. Marietta, Oh.: S. A. Mullikin.

Sheldon, William H.
1949   *Varieties of Delinquent Youth*. New York: Harper.

Short, James F., Jr. and Strodtbeck, Fred L.
1965   *Group Process and Gang Delinquency*. Chicago: University of Chicago Press.

Simon, Rita James
1975   *The Contemporary Woman and Crime*. Washington, D.C.: U.S. Government Printing Office.

Stinchcombe, Arthur L.
1964   *Rebellion in High School*. Chicago: Quadrangle Books.

Sutherland, Edwin H.
1931   "Mental deficiency and crime." Pp. 357–375 in Kimball Young (Ed.), *Social Attitudes*. New York: Holt, Rinehart and Winston.

1951   "Critique of Sheldon's varieties of delinquent youth." *American Sociological Review*, February, 16:10–14.

Sutherland, Edwin H. and Cressey, Donald R.
1974   *Crimonology* (9th ed.). Philadelphia: J. B. Lippincott.

Thomas, W. I.
1923   *The Unadjusted Girl*. Boston: Little, Brown.

Thrasher, Frederic M.
1963   *The Gang* (Abridged ed.). Chicago: University of Chicago Press.

Time Magazine
1973   "Born to fail." *Time Magazine*, November 12, 102:88.

Toby, Jackson
1957   "Social disorganization and stake in conformity." *Journal of Criminal Law, Criminology and Police Science*, 48:12–17.

Toby, Jackson
1965   "An evaluation of early identification and intensive treatment program for predelinquents." *Social Problems*, Fall, 13:160–175.

Toby, Jackson and Toby, Marcia L.
1962   "Low school status as a predisposing factor in subcultural delinquency." New Brunswick: Rutgers University (Mimeo).

Vold, George B.
1958   *Theoretical Criminology*. New York: Oxford University Press.

Waldo, Gordon P. and Dinitz, Simon
1967 "Personality attributes of the criminal: an analysis of research studies, 1950–1965." *Journal of Research in Crime and Delinquency,* July, 4:185–201.

Warren, Marguerite Q.
1969 "The case for differential treatment of delinquents." *The Annals,* January, 381:47–59.

Washburn, S. L.
1951 "Review of W. H. Sheldon, varieties of delinquent youth." *American Anthropologist,* December, 53:561–563.

White, L.
1949 *The Science of Culture.* New York: Grove Press.

Wilkinson, Karen
1974 "The broken family and juvenile delinquency: scientific explanation or ideology?" *Social Problems,* June, 21:726–739.

Wolfgang, Marvin E.
1961 "Pioneers in criminology: Cesare Lombroso (1835–1909)." *Journal of Criminal Law, Criminology, and Police Science,* November-December, 52:361–391.

Wootton, Barbara
1959 *Social Science and Social Pathology.* New York: Macmillan.

Yablonski, Lewis
1963 *The Violent Gang.* New York: Macmillan.

Zeleny, L. D.
1933 "Feeblemindedness and criminal conduct." *American Journal of Sociology,* January, 38:564–576.

10

CULTURAL DEVIANCE THEORY

In this chapter, we will be dealing with a body of theory called *cultural deviance theory*. This type of theory is noteworthy because of its sharp contrast with control theory. Control theory suggests that since the impulse to be delinquent is present in everyone delinquent acts are made possible by the *absence* of effective beliefs forbidding them. By contrast, cultural deviance theory rejects the notion that delinquent impulses are universal and suggests that delinquent acts are caused by learned beliefs that may *require* them. Delinquent behavior is an expression of conformity to cultural values and expectations that run counter to those of the larger society. The delinquent is a social individual who is behaving in accordance with the values and norms of his particular group.

Origins

The origins of cultural deviance theory can be traced to the pioneering work of two Chicago sociologists, Clifford R. Shaw and Henry D. McKay. When Shaw and McKay began their work in the 1920s, they were confronted with a confusing welter of explanations for delinquency. On one hand, religiously oriented social reformers were preoccupied with the waves of foreign-born immigrants and rural native-born Americans who ended up as industrial workers in our burgeoning cities. High rates of urban delinquency, poverty, and vice led the reformers to bemoan the corruption of the cities and to see them as major sources of trouble. Their commonsense explanations suggested that the moral standards of rural civilization were being destroyed and that children were being led into debauchery and sin. On the other hand, prevailing scientific theories reflected the thinking of biological and psychological determinists. The delinquent was innately inferior, psychologically abnormal, or both. As a result, the social construction of delinquency that emerged was an interesting combination of these two bodies of lay and scientific thought. Attempts to explain delinquency were simultaneously religious, moralistic, biological, and psychological. The impersonal city was described as a place where many vices first appealed to the baser instincts of biological and psychological misfits and then failed to provide an upright and religious climate by which to control them.

Shaw and McKay took exception to this point of view. But rather than trying to advance an alternative explanation without facts upon which to build it, their first goal was to establish the factual character of delinquency in the city. They began a series of studies designed to answer two fundamental questions:

1. *How are official delinquents distributed geographically in the city?* Shaw and McKay gathered information on all official delinquents in Chicago who had police records, court hearings, and correctional commitments during various periods between 1900 and 1940—over 60,000 cases in all (Shaw et al., 1929; Shaw and McKay, 1942). In order to determine how these thousands of cases were distributed geographically, Shaw and McKay plotted the address of each of them on city maps. What they found, over and over again, was that official delinquents were highly concentrated in particular areas of the city: adjacent to the central business district, around the railroads and stockyards, and in the industrial and steel districts. They lived in the most dilapidated, least desirable portions of the metropolis.

The extent of this concentration is illustrated in Figure 10–1. It is a radial map which breaks Chicago into a series of concentric zones. Near the center of the city, the rate of official delinquency per 100 boys was 24.5. By contrast, it declined to a rate of 3.5 in the outer areas. Not only were male delinquents concentrated near the core of the city, but their rate declined progressively the further one moved from this core.

Such findings were not confined to boys. Shaw et al. (1929:158) found that female delinquents were also concentrated in deteriorated areas

FIGURE 10–1
Rate of delinquents based upon the 8,056 male juvenile delinquents, by mile zones surrounding the loop

ZONE MAP V

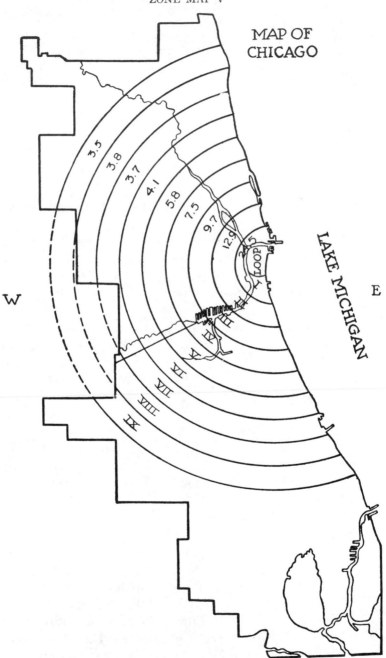

adjacent to the center of the city and to industrial districts. And, like boys, the delinquency rate for girls, though much lower, declined from city center to periphery.

These initial findings were not destined to remain unique. Between the mid-1920s and 1940, Shaw and McKay studied the distribution of delinquents from almost every conceivable angle: They plotted the locations of truants, juveniles with police records, juveniles committed to correctional schools, or juveniles who became recidivists (repeat offenders); and they plotted the locations of delinquents, male and female, in Philadelphia, Boston, Cincinnati, Cleveland, and Richmond. Finally, after Shaw's death, McKay continued to update delinquency data in Chicago for additional time periods up to 1966 (Shaw and McKay, 1929; 1931; 1942; 1969). Yet, for three quarters of a century and in different locations, the findings remained the same: Official delinquents were concentrated in the overcrowded and deteriorated areas of the city. Of crucial importance, therefore, became the second question they sought to answer.

2. *What are the social conditions associated with high delinquency areas?* Shaw and McKay found that certain clear-cut social conditions are associated with high delinquency areas:

Physical deterioration and population loss. As the city expands outward, commercial and industrial enterprises continue to invade areas formerly used for residential purposes. As a result, living conditions, from which a decreasing population flees as soon as it can, grow progressively worse.

Economic segregation. The low rents in old, dilapidated buildings and deteriorated neighborhoods attract the population with the lowest income (Shaw and McKay, 1969:147–149). Sometimes the straits for children can be desperate. In his extraordinary autobiography, Claude Brown (1965:34) describes an event that happened in Harlem when he was a child of six or seven. He had gone to the home of his friend Bucky and found Bucky choking his younger sister Debbie. Meanwhile, Bucky's older sister Dixie was hitting Bucky over the head with a broom trying to free Debbie. All three were crying. When finally the fight stopped, Brown saw what it was over. "The three of them had been fighting over one egg, and the egg was broken in the scuffle." There was nothing else in the house to eat.

Racial and ethnic segregation. Delinquency areas have a high percentage of foreign-born and minority populations who come to

American cities seeking the promised land (Shaw and McKay, 1931:79):

> I want to talk about the first Northern urban generation of Negroes. I want to talk about the experiences of a misplaced generation, of a misplaced people in an extremely complex, confused society . . . .
>
> The characters are sons and daughters of former Southern sharecroppers. These were the poorest people of the South, who poured into New York City during the decade following the Great Depression. These migrants were told that unlimited opportunities for prosperity existed in New York and that there was no "color problem" there. They were told that Negroes lived in houses with bathrooms, electricity, running water, and indoor toilets. To them, this was the "promised land." . . .
>
> One no longer had to wait to get to heaven to lay his burden down; burdens could be laid down in New York (Brown, 1965:vii).

Black people were not the first to seek salvation in American cities. In the 1880s, the central city in Chicago was occupied largely by German, Irish, and English immigrants. These groups gradually gave way to Scandinavian, Polish, Italian, and Jewish immigrants around the turn of the century. Only after the 1920s did the large migration of Southern blacks begin. In each case, the newest immigrants were the poorest and helped to push the earlier inhabitants into more stable working-class areas (Shaw, et al., 1929:17–18).

In the process, the central city became an incredible mixture of people and cultures. "In my naborhood," said one delinquent, "there were jews, polocks and irish, mostly foreigners and a poor class of people that could hardly read or write but had a flock of kids" (Shaw, 1931:19). Today, the cast of characters has changed, but the play remains the same. Earlier groups of white migrants—foreign- or native-born—have been gradually replaced by more recent groups: rural blacks, Latins, Mexicans, or Puerto Ricans.

High incidence of social ills. In the areas in which delinquency rates are the highest, the rates of other problems are also highest: truancy, infant mortality, mental disease, tuberculosis, and adult crime. In every instance, these problems vary together; that is, they are highest near the center of the city and become progressively lower as one moves toward the periphery (Shaw and McKay, 1969:105–106).

In summary, Shaw and McKay conclusively demonstrated that official delinquency rates vary widely and consistently across the city and that high delinquency areas are characterized by the highest incidence of poverty, segregation, and disease. How, then, could such findings be used to explain delinquency?

The Shaw-McKay Theory

Before trying to answer that question, Shaw and McKay had to deal with a provocative and highly significant finding. On the one hand, their studies tended to support 19th century beliefs that delinquency is associated with the "corruption" of American cities. Yet, on the other, they did not support the belief that delinquency is due to the moral depravity of particular ethnic and racial groups (Shaw and McKay, 1969:153–154). They rejected this conclusion because they discovered that the population composition of high delinquency areas had changed again and again as successive, but highly different, groups had moved through them. Yet, the delinquency rates remained the same. Changes in race and nationality did not alter them. Moreover, as each successive ethnic group moved outward into more desirable areas, its delinquency rate declined. Thus, Shaw and McKay concluded that delinquency rates—high or low—are associated more with the kinds of neighborhoods in which people live than with their racial or ethnic backgrounds. Hence, they theorized that the explanation for delinquency lies in the kind of community life that deteriorated neighborhoods produce, not in the kinds of people who live in them. The following postulates capture the essense of that explanation.

1. *The deteriorated areas of the city produce social disorganization.* Shaw and McKay argued that there is an almost total absense of a sense of community in slum areas. They agreed with Frederic Thrasher, another pioneer investigator, that the cultural standards of different immigrant and racial groups not only conflicted with each other, but that these groups were beset with a host of additional ills: "inadequate family life, poverty, deteriorating neighborhoods; ineffective religion, education, and recreation" (Thrasher, 1927:339). These problems, moreover, were compounded by the constant threat of invasion by business and industry and by high levels of population mobility which only make conditions worse. In short, slum conditions produce socially disorganized neighborhoods (Shaw et al., 1929:204–205; 1969:171–172).

2. *Socially disorganized neighborhoods lead to a lack of social control over children.* "The absence of common community ideals and standards prevents cooperative social action . . . to . . . suppress delin-

quency" (Shaw and McKay, 1931:102). Children who grow up in disorganized neighborhoods have little access to the cultural heritage of the larger society (Shaw, 1931:15). Under such conditions, parents are relatively helpless to control or to help their children, though they often try.

> Mama soon realized that hiding my clothes would not keep me in the house. The next thing she tried was threatening to send me away until I was 21. This was only frightening to me at the moment of hearing it. Ever so often, either Dad or Mama would sit down and have a heart-to-heart talk with me. These talks were very moving. I always promised to mend my bad ways. I was always sincere and usually kept the promise for about a week. During these weeks, I went to school every day and kept my stealing at a minimum. By the beginning of the second week, I had reverted back to my wicked ways, and Mama would have to start praying all over again (Brown, 1965:21).

In brief, then, demoralized slum parents are unable either to provide direction for their children or to control their delinquent tendencies.

3. *Loss of social control encourages the development of street gangs.* Shaw and McKay (1969:173) found that approximately eight out of ten delinquent boys had committed their offenses in groups. Hence, they concluded that "membership in such groups is an important contributing factor in delinquency, since it is found that very often the boy's contact with the delinquent group marks the beginning of his career in delinquency and that his initial delinquencies are very often identical with the traditions and practices of his group" (1931:256).

> So I grew old enough to go out on the street. The life in the streets became fascinating and enticing. I had two close companions that I looked up to with childish admiration and awe. One was William, my stepbrother. The other was Tony, a dear friend of my stepbrother William. They were close friends, four years older than me and well versed in the art of stealing (Shaw, 1966:50).

But where did William and Tony learn to steal? Where do delinquent traditions come from? Does each small group of boys develop its own? The answer is "No." Delinquent traditions have a broader base of support in slum communities.

4. *Delinquent traditions are transmitted from one generation of gang boys to the next.*

> The heavy concentration of delinquents in certain areas means . . . that boys living in these areas are in contact . . . with groups which sanction such behavior and exert pressure upon their members to conform to group

standards. . . . . This means that delinquent boys in these areas have contact not only with other delinquents who are their contemporaries, but also with older offenders, who in turn had contact with delinquents preceding them, and so on, back to the earliest history of the neighborhood. This contact means that the traditions of delinquency can be and are transmitted down through successive generations of boys in much the same way that language and other social forms are transmitted (Shaw and McKay, 1931:256).

What this suggests, then, is that a child's immediate play group becomes a vehicle for perpetuating delinquent traditions and for forcing adherence to them, but such traditions are actually learned from older groups and individuals.

> Whenever the boys got together they talked about robbing and made more plans for stealing. I hardly knew any boys who did not go robbing. The little fellows went in for petty stealing, breaking into freight cars, and stealing junk. The older guys did big jobs like stick-ups, burglary, and stealing autos. The little fellows admired the "big shots" and longed for the day when they could get into the big racket. Fellows who had "done time" were big shots and looked up to and gave the little fellows tips on how to get by and pull off big jobs (Shaw, 1966:54).

Although Shaw and McKay wrote mostly about boys, their life history documents imply that girls were also caught up in delinquent gangs and traditions:

> Tony had two sisters who always played with us and went on our stealing adventures. They could steal as good as any boy. Also they had sex relations openly with all the boys in the neighborhood. I remember how the boys boasted that they had had sex relations with each of them. All the boys talked about it and the girls didn't care; they seemed to be proud of it and expect it. The funny thing about it was that Tony knew all about his sisters and their behavior and only made merry of it (Shaw, 1966:50).

According to this postulate, then, conventional values have relatively little salience for slum children because of the demoralization of their parents and the lack of consensus in the neighborhood. Instead, unsupervised play groups and delinquent traditions fill the void.

5. *Delinquent traditions produce high delinquency rates.* In the disorganized vacuum of the central city, delinquent traditions are the culmination of a long series of delinquency-generating community conditions: Deteriorated areas produce social disorganization; social disorganization leads to a loss of control over children; loss of control

encourages the existence of street gangs; street gangs perpetuate delinquent traditions; delinquent traditions produce high delinquency rates. In short, delinquents are portrayed as inherently sociable people whose response to parental indifference and neighborhood demoralization is the development of alternative forms of organization whose norms happen to be delinquent according to the standards of the larger society (Kobrin, 1971:124).

Implications and impact on policy

The implications of this kind of theory are profound. If delinquency cannot be attributed to some racial or biological defect in children or to the moral shortcomings of their parents, there are grounds for a heavy load of social embarrassment (Kobrin, 1971:123). Despite a societal concept of childhood favoring the idea that all children should be quarantined from vice and corruption, carefully nurtured, and diligently educated, a large portion of them have been relegated to despicable living conditions because of ethnic and class segregation. Perhaps because of this embarrassment, the work of Shaw and McKay has had marked impact on the policy recommendations for delinquency prevention made by two major national commissions: The National (Wickersham) Commission on Law Observance and Enforcement (1931), and the President's Commission on Law Enforcement and Administration of Justice (1967).

"It is inescapable," said the President's Commission (1967:57), "that juvenile delinquency is directly related to conditions bred by poverty." It suggested, therefore, that the most promising method for dealing with delinquency would be to ameliorate the conditions that "drive" people to commit it: Strengthen the ability of lower-class families to guide and control their children, reduce unemployment, improve housing, enrichen slum schools, combat racial and economic segregation, put more personnel on the streets to work with gangs, and establish youth service bureaus in slum areas (pp. 58–77). "The commission doubts that even a vastly improved criminal justice system can substantially reduce crime if society fails to make it possible for each of its citizens to feel a personal stake in it—in the good life it can provide" (p. 58).

In some ways, these recommendations reflect the efforts of Shaw, himself, to prevent delinquency. But Shaw did not see slum dwellers and new immigrants as victims of injustice and oppression, nor did he assume that these ethnically disparate, largely rural, people could be easily assimilated into a complex urban civilization. Rather, he saw them as people who needed help in developing a sense of community and in finding ways to adjust more effectively to a totally different culture. Delinquency and other social ills might be prevented if parents and neighborhoods could learn to control their own children and could provide them with educational and other resources, so that as they grew up they would be better adapted to urban industrial life than their parents. Hence, in the 1930s Shaw fathered the Chicago Area Project which sought to realize three goals: (1) to induce the residents of slum areas to take up the cause of prevention; (2) to assist them in gaining greater influence over their children by organizing local programs and resources for them; and (3) to foster cooperative action among local residents, the schools, the police, and the courts.

Shaw was a charismatic leader who threw himself into the Chicago Project for more than a quarter of a century. Solomon Kobrin (1959:584–586), a later colleague of Shaw and McKay's, concludes that the results of the project vindicated Shaw's untiring efforts. Not only was he highly respected among different generations of various ethnic groups, but the Chicago Area Project is still in operation. Not only has it been applied in Chicago over the years, but special legislation was passed in Illinois and a Juvenile Delinquency Prevention Commission created, so that the model developed by Shaw could be utilized and applied throughout the state. In no other locale has such a feat been duplicated, combining both theoretical and applied work over such a long period of time.

In light of this outcome, it is significant that today's theorists, about whom we will be reading in later chapters, would argue that Shaw's efforts represented nothing more than the application of a Band-Aid when radical surgery was required. Since the most fundamental tenet of the Shaw-McKay theory is that it is the poverty, overcrowding, and misery of modern capitalist society which, first, spawn disorganization and, then, delinquency, the Chicago Area Project did nothing more than address symptoms, not basic causes. Hence, what is required are radical economic and political changes, not efforts to help the poor victims of society to adjust more effectively to unacceptable conditions.

The magnitude of the effort that would be required is indicated by the fact that the sweeping recommendations of the two Presidential commissions may have had even less effect than Shaw's efforts. Our largest cities are now closer to bankruptcy than before; their urban cores continue to deteriorate; unemployment rates among ghetto dwellers remain staggeringly high; racial and economic segregation persist; and delinquent gangs are omnipresent. Thus, it could be argued that the most fundamental implications of the Shaw-McKay theory have never been successfully implemented.

Scientific implications

The scientific legacy left by Shaw and McKay is of two kinds. The first is their set of empirical findings. They have never been excelled, and little subsequent research has altered the picture they presented (Short, 1972).

The second is their theory. It could be interpreted in two ways. In one sense, it could be described as a sociological control theory (in contrast to the psychological control theories we reviewed in the last chapter).[1] That is, Shaw and McKay could be interpreted as stressing the disorganized character of impersonal modern cities and the need to foster more effective means of raising and controlling the children in them. But, rather than seeking to alter the internal states of these children, one by one, the task would be that of understanding and developing more effective social institutions by which to socialize them—modern counterparts of the families, churches, and communities which were so effective in the small rural towns of 18th century America. Indeed, the fact that Shaw and McKay worked so hard to foster the Chicago Area Project suggests that it was this interpretation of their theory that they preferred. To them, delinquent traditions among lower-class youth seem to have been analogous to Freud's unrestrained, but potentially evil, tendencies in individuals, only in collective form. But, in this case, effective socialization would require the concerted efforts of all social institutions, not just the family.

This interpretation, however, is not the one that most modern theorists have placed upon the theory. For many years, the concept of social disorganization was a popular one, but, in recent decades, it has declined in popularity. Instead, contemporary theorists have picked up and expanded upon the role played by delinquent gangs in fostering delinquent traditions and a culture of deviance. When seen in this light, as Kobrin (1971:117) points out, the theory becomes totally deterministic and evokes an image of delinquency that has an all-or-none charac-

---

[1] I am indebted to James F. Short, Jr., for bringing this interpretation to my attention.

ter. The influence of the gang in the slum areas exceeds the influence of the family, the school, and other conventional groups, "requiring and demanding that its members follow its norms and take on its attitudes" (Clark, 1972:2). Even more striking, it implies that virtually all lower-class children will become young criminals, wed only to the traditions of their peers.

This way of constructing delinquency has had immeasurable impact during the past quarter of a century. On one hand, it has reinforced long-standing beliefs that the primary threat to social order comes from lower-class groups and ethnic minorities. Indeed, the idea has been accepted as an established fact by many people, lay and scientific. On the other hand, when Shaw and McKay began their work, the scientific tendency was to view the delinquent as a different kind of person— genetically inferior, mentally retarded, or psychologically abnormal. By contrast, their theory suggested that delinquent responses are the only ones feasible by inherently social children, given the circumstances to which they must adapt. Although Shaw and McKay never used the word "culture" to describe the ties that bind lower-class children, their emphasis upon gang "traditions" has since been a major source of many subsequent theories, all stressing the idea that delinquency is the product of unique cultures or subcultures. A major question, therefore, is whether this construction of delinquency is an accurate one. Consider some questions that have been raised about it:

1. *Social disorganization in deteriorated areas.* Shaw and McKay attributed the development of delinquent traditions to the disintegration of community controls in blighted areas. Yet, they offered no direct evidence that the residents of higher-income areas in the city engage in collective problem solving any more effectively than do residents in low-income areas (Kobrin, 1971:128–129). Furthermore, they did not provide direct evidence that the population in outlying areas is any less heterogeneous than in the central city. Hence, their assumption that inner city areas are more disorganized than other areas was not supported by compelling evidence, though such may be the case.

Because of this possibility, it became fashionable among sociologists to suggest that what we should look for in high delinquency areas is differential social organization, not social disorganization (Cohen, et al., 1956:21; Kobrin, et al., 1967; Whyte, 1943). While our overall society is often divided by competing subcultural norms, slum communities are not necessarily jungles, continuing high rates of crime, victimization, and lowered life expectancy notwithstanding. Instead, there is an awareness of community in slum areas and a concern among individuals about their reputations in that community. "The organization which exists may indeed not be adequate for the effective control of delinquency and for the solution of other social problems, but the qualities and defects of organization are not to be confused with the absence of organization" (Cohen, 1955:33).

2. *Delinquency as a lower-class phenomenon.* Shaw and McKay documented the existence of heavy concentrations of *official* delinquents in slum areas. Yet, their own findings do not support the all-or-none concentration of their theory on lower-class children. The reason is that their data *do not* show that official delinquency disappears outside of deteriorated areas. Instead, they show that official rates *decline* in a decreasing gradient from the central city outward (See Figure 10–1). Although the rates in deteriorated areas are the highest, they are also present in middle-class and suburban areas.

Even more questionable was their construction of a theory based exclusively on *official* measures of delinquency. On one hand, repeated studies have confirmed the Shaw and McKay finding that lower-class children are overrepresented in official statistics (See Chapter 6). It is an accurate finding. On the other hand, *official* data are not accurate measures of *law-violating behavior*. Yet, Shaw and McKay treated them as if they were because their theory is concerned primarily with explaining why slum children *violate the law*, not how official rates are created. Yet, as we have already learned, official data not only represent the way children behave, but the way society in general, and legal agents in particular, respond to the children of different classes and colors. Furthermore, studies of self-reported delinquency suggest that the relation between social class and law-violating behavior may not be nearly so strong as the relation between social class and official delinquency (compare Chapters 6 and 7). For these reasons, it is now clear that Shaw and McKay's theory possesses two additional limitations: (1) it is not a complete explanation of *official delinquency* because the defining role of officials is not included in it; and (2) it is not a complete explanation of *law-violating behavior* because it is built on official data.

3. *The group nature of delinquency.* This finding has remained considerably more stable than the one suggesting that law-violating behavior is predominantly lower class. Repeated studies have confirmed it (Erickson, 1973; Erickson and Empey, 1965; Eynon and Reckless, 1961; Glueck and Glueck, 1950; Hindelang, 1971; Short, 1957). Consequently,

an important issue is not so much whether delinquent acts are committed in groups, but how one interprets the finding.

Shaw and McKay suggest that delinquent norms become widespread in lower-class areas because of the high prevalence of unsupervised play groups. Yet, Kobrin (1971:130) found that "approximately half the boys of a high delinquency rate area did not participate at all in its juvenile street life." Because some children are unsupervised, all need not be. Many lower-class parents supervise their children rather carefully, and a life of crime is not the only adjustment open to them.

There are also some problems with assuming that young children have the capacity to develop the sense of group purpose necessary to maintain delinquent traditions in the face of a disapproving society (Kobrin, 1971:130). Whereas Shaw and McKay suggest that deteriorated areas are so demoralizing to lower-class adults that they cannot maintain a sense of community, they reach the rather startling conclusion that lower-class children are able to do so. They can establish a community when adults cannot.

This point of view, whether intended or not, started a trend in which lower-class gangs are portrayed as possessing strong *esprit de corps*, a free and easy life, and members whose commitments to the purposes of the gang exceed their commitments to any other purpose (cf. Thrasher, 1927). Yet, a number of recent investigations have questioned this nostalgic view of lower-class gangs.

Klein and Crawford (1967:63) argue that such groups are not close knit-and internally strong. Where it not for the external pressures of police and other officials or the threats of rival groups, delinquent gangs would have little to unify them. By themselves, gangs do not develop the kind of group goals and instrumental activities which are indicative of much organization. Similarly, Short and Strodtbeck (1965:233) report that they "find the capacity of lower-class gangs to elaborate and enforce norms of reciprocity is very much below what might be required to sustain the group if alternative forms of gratification were available." They found that gang boys were characterized by a long list of "social disabilities": unsuccessful school adjustment, limited social and technical skills, a lower capacity for self-assertion, lower intelligence scores, and a tendency to hold other gang members in low esteem (p. 331). Interaction within the gang seemed to be characterized by an omnipresent tone of aggression rather than by close personal ties. In short, there is real question regarding the extent to which adolescent street groups have developed widely shared and mutually supported norms, to say nothing of a life-style that could qualify as a unique and independent culture.

What is missing in most discussions of this issue, however, is a sense of history, a sense of the extent to which lower-class culture, in general, has either remained different from middle-class culture or has modified it in response to modern urban life. Some of the descriptions of lower-class youth by Shaw (1931; 1936; 1966), and by his contemporary, Frederick Thrasher (1927), are quite consistent with descriptions of lower-class groups in earlier centuries (Cf. Gillis, 1974). In the crowded, teeming streets of the slum, children are attracted by innumerable exciting opportunities for fun and adventure. They swipe fruit, tip over garbage cans, stay out all night, and roll drunks. To be sure, they are unsupervised by middle-class standards, but does this mean that their behavior is entirely inconsistent with lower-class traditions? According to Shaw and McKay and Thrasher, it is.

They imply that the standards of lower-class adults may have become more middle-class during the 20th century, even though those same adults are ineffective in enforcing their beliefs. That is why, as youth groups develop and solidify, they are increasingly at odds with parental expectations. But this interpretation may be incorrect. It could be that lower-class children are not at odds with their parents. It could be that their behavior is consistent with norms shared by all lower-class people. Indeed, there are those who argue that such is the case and that lower-class communities, today at least, are not the way Shaw and McKay describe them.

Delinquency as a product of integrated lower-class culture

In 1958, Walter Miller, an anthropologist, gave voice to a theory which suggests that delinquency is the product of a united, not a divided, lower-class culture. The picture that he painted is as follows:

1.   *The slums are organized by a distinctive lower-class culture.*   According to Miller (1958), delinquent groups are neither the product of disorganized communities nor are they isolated from adult influence. Adults and children in lower-class communities share a common set of values. In response to the processes of economic and social segregation in American society, "there is emerging a relatively homogeneous and

stabilized native American lower-class culture" (Miller, 1959:225). It is the result of many years of immigration and internal migration to which several ethnic populations have contributed. This culture now represents a common adaption of *unsuccessful* whites and blacks to the American system.

2.   *Lower-class culture emphasizes membership in one-sex peer groups.* A key to understanding this culture is the way it organizes family life and relations between the sexes. Family life is dominated by the female. Men do not usually play a consistent and predictable role in it, nor do they provide it with reliable economic support. After generations of failure, conventional work and family roles no longer attract them. Instead, new values have emerged which tend to separate males and females into different groups. Except for transitory relations between the sexes, males and females lead relatively separate lives. As a result, the lower-class family does not possess the close, intimate ties found in the middle-class family. Not only does responsibility for raising children fall to the mother, but they may be the offspring of different men.

This means that children spend the first few years of life under the domination of women, during which time they receive mixed messages about the male role. They learn from their mothers that men are rogues: simultaneously despicable and desirable, luring but hateful, irresponsible but very attractive on Saturday night. This message poses some problems for girls but is particularly difficult for boys. They are faced with a problem of sexual identity. A mother does not want her boy to grow up like his father but anticipates that he will.

This problem is resolved during adolescence. While girls continue to identify with their mothers, boys take up membership in male street gangs, a natural outcome of the lower-class emphasis upon one-sex peer groups. These gangs are simultaneously a haven for escaping female domination and for learning how to be a man. Indeed, Miller suggests that gang members are probably the most able young members of the community. Why, then, do they tend to get into trouble? What motivates them?

3.   *One sex-peer groups are organized by a unique set of "focal concerns."*   The answer lies in the unique "focal concerns" of lower-class culture: trouble, smartness, toughness, fate, and autonomy. "Adult status [for males] is defined less in terms of the assumption of 'adult' responsibilities than in terms of certain symbols of adult status—a car, ready cash, and, in particular, a perceived 'freedom' to drink, smoke,

and gamble as one wishes, and to come and go without external restrictions" (Miller, 1958:17).

The lower-class street group is merely an adolescent expression of these adult focal concerns. Whereas a major dimension for evaluating a man's status in middle-class culture is achievement in education and work, criteria in the lower class suggest that hard work and deferred gratification are for suckers. Consequently, young members of street gangs gain a sense of belonging and acquire status by demonstrating physical prowess, by committing delinquent acts which demonstrate their ability to live by their wits, by resistance to authority and by freedom from the drudgery of a daily job. Thus, while lower-class people, young and old, are aware of middle-class norms, they do not value them. They may express verbal support for them, but they do so to escape getting into trouble with the police not because they are committed to middle-class standards (Miller, 1958:8).

4. *Adherence to lower-class "focal concerns" produces delinquency.* What this suggests, then, is that the better the members of lower-class gangs conform to the values and beliefs of their culture, the more likely they are to be defined as officially delinquent. They are delinquent merely because of their faithful conformity to lower-class values which by middle-class standards are deviant.

Compared with Shaw and McKay's theory, then, Miller's cultural deviance theory has two distinctive features. On one hand, it is like that of Shaw and McKay's in that it suggests that delinquency is predominantly a lower-class group phenomenon and it indicates that deviant behavior is due to cultural values and beliefs which require it. On the other hand, it departs widely from Shaw and McKay's formulation in the location of delinquent traditions. Whereas Shaw and McKay suggest that they are the sole possession of unsupervised gangs and playgroups, Miller indicates that they belong to the entire lower-class community. Delinquent behavior is an expression of a distinctive culture in which effective socialization by adults results in deviant values which everyone shares.

Perhaps even more important, Miller "alerts us to a possible historical development that has received relatively little attention—the emergence of something like a stable American lower class" (Bordua, 1961:131). This possibility seems to have been overlooked by Shaw and McKay and by later investigators. Indeed, it was not until 1976 that Bayard Rustin, a long-time black civil rights activist advanced an argument similar to Miller's (*Los Angeles Times*, August 11, 1976). "The future advancement of blacks and other poor in this country," said Rustin, "has very little to do with the color of their skin." A few years ago that was not true, but the problem of poverty and its assorted ills like delinquency have become a class, not a race, problem. Whereas 19th and early 20th century immigrants could find work and make advancements, poor and uneducated people today can no longer do so because society no longer has any use for muscle power. Automation and technology have rendered it obsolete. The result has been the creation of a class of "economic untouchables" made up of blacks, browns, and whites.

Rustin's description of the family and social life of these "untouchables" is much like that of Miller's:

> Many of the "economic untouchables" come from families where the parents don't work. The "untouchables" themselves never had a job, and unless something is done there will not be jobs for their children. Many have not had an alarm clock in the house. Meals are not eaten with the family. When anyone is hungry, he just goes to the refrigerator by himself . . . .
>
> These are some of the consequences of being in a situation where you make no contribution to your own economic existence. It is not just true of blacks but of all below the poverty line.

In short, both Miller and Rustin suggest that a permanent underclass has developed in the United States that has given up on the American Dream. American society, contrary to its equalitarian principles, has become permanently stratified and has witnessed the development of a lower class with an increasingly distinctive culture of its own.

As we will see in the next chapter, there are theorists who take strong exception to this conclusion, arguing that the tradition of wanting to get ahead is shared by all Americans. Middle-class values stressing the importance of education, hard work, and deferred gratification have filtered down to members of the lower class and are highly motivating to them. It strains the imagination to believe that lower-class youth are so deeply immersed in lower-class culture that their contacts with the school, with the mass media, and with other middle-class dominated institutions have had no effect on them. Furthermore, Miller "also forgets that none of the lower status groups in the society, with the possible exception of lower status Negroes, has any history of his female-based household, at least not in the extreme form he describes"

(Bordua, 1961:130–131). Such households are under continuous pressure from welfare workers and other officials to conform to the pattern of middle-class families.

Miller's position, of course, is that lower-class families successfully resist these pressures. That is why lower-class adolescents become delinquent. They get into trouble because they remain faithful to cultural standards which they learn from their parents. This position, however, has been disputed by control theorists who point to some research findings to back up their argument. Regardless of class background, they find that the closer juveniles are to their parents, the less likely they are to commit delinquent acts (Dinitz, et al., 1962; Hindelang, 1973:475; Hirschi, 1969:97). Furthermore, Hirschi (pp. 215–220) has found that there is little disagreement among adolescents from different social classes on what people ought to do: whether they should obey the law, whether it is right to con others, or whether it is fate rather than personal competence that determines a person's destiny. Hence, Hirschi (p. 97) concludes "that those lower-class boys committing delinquent acts are not finding support for their actions from their parents or from their 'class culture.' "

Such findings notwithstanding, much of the delinquency literature throughout this century continues to stress the idea that society is divided into competing class cultures and that these cultures are intimately linked to the commission of delinquent acts. This is true not only of theories of lower- but of middle-class delinquency. They paint a picture that is strikingly at odds with the theories of lower-class delinquency we have just reviewed. It is as though American youth on different class levels live in totally different cultural worlds and that to understand their delinquency we must understand those worlds.

Middle-class subculture theory

Cultural theories of middle-class delinquency grow out of two traditions in social science. The first is a concern with adolescence in general. It is seen as an ill-defined period in the life cycle in which peer relationships take on unusual significance. Because adolescents are segregated from the adult world, a youth subculture is created that is hedonistic and irresponsible (Coleman, 1961; Davis, 1944; Glaser, 1971; Parsons, 1942). The second tradition grows out of a direct concern with delinquency. Shortly after midcentury, the first of the self-report studies and some official data suggested that middle-class delinquency might be increasing. These findings led to scattered efforts to explain the deviant acts of more affluent youth (Bloch and Niederhoffer, 1958; England, 1960; Bohlke, 1961; Scott and Vaz, 1963).[2]

Though these two bodies of theory had different origins and though the first was ostensibly concerned with all adolescents, they are remarkably alike. The reason is that they are constructed from the world view of the middle class, the world view that most social scientists hold. So consistent are their theories with the middle-class concept of childhood and with the historical values surrounding that concept that it is clear that they apply far more to middle-class than to lower-class youth—to youth whose families are intact, who are attending school, and who are preparing for college and a white-collar job. Furthermore, both groups of theorists are not inclined to see middle-class delinquency as particularly serious. Rather, they tend to describe the values of middle-class delinquents as being a parody of the worst features of adult values. Thus, as Kvaraceus and Miller (1959:234) put it, middle-class delinquency appears less as a "social problem" than as a "home problem." The main theme of this way of constructing delinquency is captured in the following postulates:

1.   *The social status of middle-class adolescents is ill-defined.*   Reflecting historical changes in the status of children, most theorists point out that adolescents do not possess a clear-cut and responsible position in society. The groundwork for this state of affairs

> . . . was laid a century and more ago when youngsters were gradually removed from functional roles in the economy through restrictive apprenticeship codes, protective labor legislation, the compulsory education movement, and the withdrawal of children from agricultural activities attendant upon urbanization. However diverse the forces were which led to this removal from productive roles, the result was that for probably the first time a major society deactivated a large and energetic segment of its

---

[2] Parenthetically, a noteworthy feature of these bodies of theory is their failure to distinguish between "middle" and "upper" class youth as they do between those who are "middle" and "lower" class. The reasons are twofold: The first has to do with the meaning of the term "middle" class. It is used uncritically and usually includes all youth whose family backgrounds are white collar but whose incomes range from modest to affluent. Thus, the children of school teachers and small businessmen are lumped together with those whose parents are highly prestigeful professionals and corporate executives. Secondly, almost no theoretical attention has been paid to the "upper"-class children of wealthy people, revealing once again the bias of existing theory toward the lower class. As a result, such children are either ignored in existing theories or are included in formulations of "middle" class subculture theory.

population without clearly redefining the status and function of that segment (England, 1960:536–537).

As a result, "the adolescent finds an absence of definitely recognized, consistent patterns of authority. . . . [He] is subjected to a confusing array of competing authorities" (Davis, 1944:13). Adolescents are barred from productive labor but are expected to be hardworking; they attend school to develop their intellects, but they are not expected to challenge the opinions of parents and teachers; they are sexually mature and encouraged to be socially skilled but are supposed to refrain from adult vices; they are expected to be civic-minded but cannot hold public office or serve on juries; they are often separated from the direct supervision of parents and are granted considerable freedom, yet they lack the kinds of ties to other adults by which privilege and freedom can be prevented from deteriorating into license (England, 1960:537). As they attempt to deal with these ambiguous directives, therefore, "Boys and girls . . . often find it difficult to tell when and how 'adult' behavior is expected" (Williams, 1952:71).

This problem has worsened in recent years because middle-class parents have been enjoined to pay greater heed to new theories of child development which question the wisdom of premature responsibility for children and which recommend that they be allowed to develop at a slower, less pressured pace (Scott and Vaz, 1963:210–213). Concomitantly, opportunities for ambitious youngsters to become proprietors by opening their own small businesses have also declined. Instead, more and more young people have been corralled into large corporations and industries. As a result, the work skills required of middle-class youth have also changed. "We used to look primarily for brilliance," said one corporation president at midcentury. "Now . . . we don't care if you're a Phi Beta Kappa or a Tau Beta Phi. We want a well-rounded person who can handle well-rounded people" (quoted by Whyte, 1956:150).

These changes have produced a situation in which the standards of right and wrong for young people are less certain. About all that can be said is that some admixture of technical skill and social competence will produce satisfaction and success. As a result, both parents and school have gradually become more permissive and have placed more stress on personality development and peer adjustment than upon strict adherence to carefully defined rules.

2. *An ill-defined social status separates adolescents from the adult world.* To make matters more complicated, the ill-defined adolescent

period has been growing longer (Flacks, 1971; Keniston, 1972), and this extension has further diminished the contact of young people with the adult world (Coleman, 1961; Berger, 1971). As recently as 1950, many students did not even finish high school (Glaser, 1971:34). Rather, at about age 16 or 17, they moved into an adult role because jobs were still available to them. But since that time, increasing numbers have been confined to society's youth ghetto—the school. In the 1960s for the first time, a majority of high school graduates entered college. Indeed, many more students have extended their studies into graduate school. As a result, the modal upper limit of adolescence has increased from around age 16 or 17 a few years ago to around 21 or 22 now. Hence, more than ever before, young people are separated from adult work roles and civic responsibilities.

3. *Social separation produces middle-class youth subculture.* Virtually all theorists argue that the separation of adolescents from adult responsibility produces new customs and values. However, they tend to disagree over the extent to which these new standards are at odds with those of middle-class adults. One group suggests that the difference is dramatic. "A fundamental law of sociology and anthropology," says Glaser (1971:35), "is that social separation results in cultural differentiation. The more adolescents interact exclusively with each other, the more their customs and values become different from those of other age groups." A youth culture develops which is inward-looking, which fosters a psychic attachment among the young to others their own age, which rejects adult standards and presses for autonomy, which develops an unusual regard for the underdog, and which seeks to foster change (Colemen, et al., 1972:116–125). "The so-called youth subculture . . . sharply cuts off adolescent experience from that of the child and from that of adult" (Green, 1952:95). Eventually, it becomes intolerant for young people to be different from their peers (Parsons, 1950). "So extreme is the gap [between the generations] that parents and their adolescent children literally represent [different] subcultures" (Williams, 1952:73). Yet, the development of a unique culture by youth "is their natural response to the somewhat unnatural position in which they find themselves in society" (Coleman, et al., 1972:125).

A second group of theorists take a much softer position, suggesting that any youth subculture is likely to reflect a great many adult expectations and teachings. For example, middle-class parents want their children to be skilled socially because their success, both as adolescents and as adults, depends upon it (Berger, 1963). Hence, for parents as well as for adolescents, successful involvement with the youth crowd becomes a moral imperative (Scott and Vaz, 1963:211; Whyte, 1956:434). Not only do parents exhibit great concern over the popularity of their children, but the school becomes the central agency for facilitating it. Indeed, says Cohen (1957:205), "Status in the school is increasingly defined in terms of the standards and values of adolescent peer groups, and the role of the adult becomes to create a benign atmosphere in which every child can integrate happily with some group." In other words, parents help to facilitate youth relations rather than feeling totally alienated from them.

4. *Middle-class youth subculture produces delinquent behavior.* Despite differences over the uniqueness of adolescent subculture, most theorists suggest (1) that it helps to produce an adolescent world of hedonism and irresponsibility, and (2) that the more involved adolescents are in it, the more likely they are to be delinquent. At the same time, most of them argue that the delinquent acts it encourages are not likely to be very serious because they evolve from legitimate activities that are sanctioned and supported by adults as well as by peers: dating, parties, athletics, extracurricular activities, owning an automobile, and being up on the latest fads (England, 1960; Scott and Vaz, 1963). The only reason these activities lead to delinquent behavior is because the youth subculture is peopled by immature and inexperienced persons:

> Delinquent motivations among middle-class teenagers arise from [an] adaptive process in which the teenage world, peopled by immature and inexperienced persons, extracts from the adult world those values having strong hedonistic possibilities, with the result that the values of the teenage culture consist merely of distorted and caricatured fragments from the adult culture (England, 1960:539).

Thus, the dominant forms of middle-class delinquent conduct are joy riding, drinking, using pot, staying out late, gambling, or engaging in sex—acts that are scarcely unknown to middle-class adults in their hedonistic moments.

Occasionally, parties or athletic contests, combined with drinking or drugs, result in destructive acts such as letting the air out of tires, pitched battles, breaking street lights, ripping antennae off cars, or vandalizing the school. But, while these activities are tolerated by the standards of middle-class youth subculture, such acts as assault, armed robbery, or burglary stand outside its boundaries. In fact, say Kvaraceus and Miller (1959:241), when serious delinquency is committed by a middle-class adolescent, it probably represents "pathological" rather than group-supported behavior. Hence, most prevailing theories construct an image of middle-class delinquency that is nonserious, one that is comprised of status offenses and misdemeanors, not of dangerous felonies. At the same time, such theories are like other cultural deviance theories because they suggest that delinquent behavior is motivated by shared beliefs which make it the desirable thing to do.

Implications for social policy

The social implications of this kind of theory are readily apparent and apply as much to lower-class as to middle-class adolescents. Society can reduce delinquency by taking one or both of two steps: (1) it can cease defining such acts as drinking, smoking pot, premarital sex, joy riding, staying out late, or sluffing school as delinquent offenses; and (2) it can seek to reduce the social separation of adolescent and adult worlds by giving adolescents a greater stake in conformity (Toby, 1957). In some ways, both steps have been recommended and are being tried.

1. *"Decriminalizing" status offenses.* For almost two decades, a growing number of influential organizations and people have recommended that juvenile status offenses should be "decriminalized" (Empey, 1973). In part, these recommendations imply the emergence of a new middle-class morality. Morris and Hawkins (1970:2) express its policy implications:

> We must strip off the moralistic excrescences on our [juvenile] justice system so that it may concentrate on the essential. The prime function of the criminal law is to protect our persons and our property; these purposes are now engulfed in a mass of other distracting, inefficiently performed legislative duties. When the criminal law invades the spheres of private morality and social welfare, it exceeds its proper limits at the cost of neglecting its primary task. . . . Man has an inalienable right to go to hell in his own fashion, provided he does not directly injure the person or property of another on the way.

This new philosophy is based upon the assumption that individual morality has become situational and peer related rather than sacred and universal, as it was in the 19th century. Hence, while various states have not yet eliminated status offenses from the jurisdiction of the juvenile court, they are moving in that direction. It is merely a matter of time. This process is being speeded up by increases in the legal rights of children: The Supreme Court has granted the right of abortion to teenage girls without parental consent—a revolutionary step in light of our traditional concept of childhood; school attendance laws are being relaxed; and the age for drinking has been lowered in many states. These rights are simply an extension of rights that have already been granted to youth who are slightly older. Not long ago, colleges and universities were expected to guard the morals of students in their parents' absence. Now, they are no longer charged with that responsibility. Dorms have been sexually integrated, and other changes of this type have taken place. The idea is that there should be less official interference in the private moral conduct of young people.

At the same time, society may be hoping that these changes will produce some kind of sociological magic. On one hand, they imply a greater tolerance for a number of acts that have long been common among adolescents—skipping school, incorrigibility, engaging in sex, or drinking. A legal response has done little to prevent them. On the other hand, a refusal to police these acts does not mean that some of their more serious consequences will go away—being poorly educated, running away from home, having an unwanted pregnancy, or becoming an adolescent alcoholic. Changing their definition will not eliminate these problems. Furthermore, the decriminalization of status offenses will do little to reduce the gap between adolescent and adult worlds. If, as existing theory suggests, adolescents are alienated because they lack a meaningful role in society, then changes now underway will do little to solve that problem. For example, allowing teenagers to leave school at age 16 will not assure that they can find employment if jobs do not exist (and they do not). It is likely, therefore, that the status of out-of-school youth will remain ambiguous. Indeed, the possibility that "desirable" reforms can have unanticipated, negative consequences leads us to the second implication of this body of theory.

2. *Providing adolescents with a stake in conformity.* If delinquent subculture is due to the separation of adolescents from responsible middle-class adults, then the following remedies are implied: (a) eliminate the ambiguity and lack of purpose inherent in the adolescent status; (b) close the generation gap; and (c) provide adolescents with socially desirable adult roles—a productive place in the economy, civic responsibilities, and the power of decision making. Theoretically, if these steps were taken, the functions served by the youth culture would no longer exist. Because they are inherently social, adolescents will develop a sense of competence and belonging. Generational conflict will be eliminated, and youth will exhibit a firm attachment to the aims,

values, and norms of a unified adult-youth culture (Polk and Kobrin, 1972).

In recent years, society has taken some hesitant steps in this direction: The voting age has been lowered to age 18; work-study programs, combining both schooling and work, have been tried; and more young people are becoming active in the political process. Yet, when all is said and done, these steps are far short of those necessary to integrate adolescent and adult roles.

In the first place, it is difficult to imagine either that adolescent misconduct or the belief by adults that adolescents are inherently disposed to deviant behavior will be eliminated by these attempts to neutralize the presumed effects of a middle-class youth culture. "Delinquency"—the making and enforcing of rules as well as the behavior they proscribe—will continue, at least if history is any criterion. We have already seen that in the 18th and 19th centuries relations between the generations were far more integrated than they are today. Work roles for adolescents were plentiful, and their labor was much in demand. Yet, youth deviance and complaints about it were widespread. Furthermore, many of the people who now seek to undo the effects of child labor laws and other protective devices for children are the same ones who loudly decry the apprenticeship system of earlier times and the employment of children in factories. They fail to see that children cannot be both protected and equal at the same time.

Industrial technology in this century has compounded the problem. Not only has adolescent labor become superfluous in our technically sophisticated and affluent society, but our economy is unable to employ all of its adults. This problem will have to be solved before policy makers, labor unions, and other powerful groups will become serious about more work opportunities for teenagers. Furthermore, the most desirable jobs still require levels of literacy and training that only schooling can provide. Indeed, artificially devised and demeaning roles for teenagers might only increase their sense of separation. Finally, many questions have been raised in the scientific literature regarding middle-class subculture theory and its implications for policy.

Scientific questions

There are several important questions that can be raised about theories of middle-class delinquency. The first has to do with their deterministic character. The original statements of this kind of theory suggested that it would be the exceptional adolescent indeed who was not programmed to follow the hedonistic dictates of the adolescent subculture. To be sure, there is some disagreement between the generations, but recent evidence suggests that it may have been overdone. At the very least, there is considerable "selective continuity" between young and old (Bengston, et al., 1974; Kandel and Lesser, 1972). While adults and youth may differ on some issues—child-raising practices or authority relationships—they agree considerably on others—educational goals, occupational aspirations, or even religious affiliations (Elkin and Westley, 1955; Hill, 1970). It would be difficult, for example, to convince adolescents who are planning middle-class careers in medicine, law, classical music, or science that the older values of delayed gratification, hard work and self-discipline always defer to adolescent group norms. The point is that while class related variations in beliefs and practices surely exist they are neither uniformly hedonistic and irresponsible nor do they obtain conformity from everyone. There are many exceptions.

A second question is closely related. Middle-class subculture theory asserts that the more involved adolescents are with their peers, the more likely they are to be delinquent. As indicated earlier in the chapter, there is indirect support for this hypothesis because repeated studies have found delinquency to be a group phenomenon. But there are more subtle issues to be considered. Why do middle-class adolescents commit delinquent acts in groups? Is it because they are strongly attached to each other, because they are so concerned with acceptance that they will do whatever the group demands, or for some other reason?

The evidence on these questions is mixed. On one hand, Hirschi (1969) found that admiration and respect for peers acted as a barrier to delinquent behavior: the greater the attachment, the less the delinquency. Hindelang (1973), by contrast, found just the opposite: Attachment to peers is more likely to lead to delinquency.

In their attempt to resolve this issue, Jensen and Erickson (1976) could find strong support for neither position. It was not clear whether group violations were due to strong feelings of attachment among friends or whether it was merely a situational act committed by people who merely went along with the group. Matza (1964:27–30) maintains that it is the latter. The majority of delinquents are "drifters" who are committed neither to conventional nor to delinquent values. If so, this is another case in which the deterministic character of delinquent subculture is called into question. It may not be so all-consuming in its scope and power as theory suggests.

Finally, there is the assertion that middle-class adolescents do not ordinarily commit serious delinquent acts, that virtually all of their offenses are status offenses. Such an assertion is not supported by the facts. It is true that recent victimization studies have tended to support official accounts of crime suggesting that the highest rates of serious crime are located among the poorest segments of society (Chapter 8). But our review of self-report studies also indicated that this relationship has been exaggerated and that middle-class adolescents commonly commit some serious property, if not personal, crimes (Chapter 7). Hence, while middle-class theorists have been partially right, they have overemphasized class differences. Furthermore, in assuming that most middle-class offenders are status offenders, they have failed to account theoretically for the criminal offenders among middle-class youth.

Summary and conclusions

In opposition to control theories, cultural deviance theories have constructed an entirely different image of the delinquent:

1. *Assumptions about human nature and social order.*   Cultural deviance theories assume that human nature is inherently social. No less than conventional behavior, delinquent behavior is an expression of a universal tendency to behave in accordance with the values and beliefs of one's own culture. But, while human nature is essentially good, the social order is conflicted because competing cultures are found in it. There is no overriding standard of good and bad. Moral values range from those that are strictly conventional to those that are unconventional and delinquent.

2. *The underlying logic and content of cultural deviance theories.*   Cultural deviance theories represent an ideological, as well as theoretical, reaction to biological and psychodynamic theories. Yet, some of them are no less deterministic. Delinquents are socialized in cultural settings which justify, make attractive, and, eventually, require delinquent behavior. Such behavior is as "normal" and as "moral" to the members of delinquent cultures as law-abiding behavior is to the members of conventional cultures. However, the various versions of cultural deviance theory differ in indicating the source of delinquent traditions.

Lower-class theory is comprised of two versions. The Shaw-McKay version indicates that delinquent culture is produced in disorganized slum communities by unsupervised playgroups and adolescent gangs. The only coherent traditions perpetuated from one generation to the next in these communities are delinquent and criminal traditions (see accompanying diagram):

Slum	Social	Loss of	Street	Delinquent	Delinquent
areas →	disorganization →	adult control	→ gangs →	youth culture	→ behavior

By contrast, the Walter Miller version suggests that American society has become progressively stratified and has witnessed the development of a lower class with an increasingly distinctive culture of its own. Adolescent misconduct, therefore, is merely a reflection of widely shared lower-class values (see accompanying diagram):

Slum	Lower	One-sex	Unique	Delinquent
area →	class culture	→ peer groups	→ focal concerns	→ behavior

Middle-class theory suggests that delinquency is a subcultural variation of middle-class culture. This kind of delinquency is not very serious and is merely a distorted caricature of adult values and standards (see accompanying diagram):

Ill-defined	Separation	Middle-class	Delinquent
adolescent →	of	→ youth	→ behavior
status	generations	subculture	

3. *Policy implications.* The Shaw-McKay version of lower-class theory implies the need for radical economic and social changes: full employment, improved housing, enriched schools, elimination of economic and ethnic segregation, and more effective control by family and neighborhood over children—in short, a full assimilation of lower-class people into the middle-class way of life.

Miller's version implies even more. Either society must accept and tolerate a unique, but seemingly deviant, culture among lower-class people, or it must seek ways for reasserting the importance of the American Dream among them. If they no longer value the things that middle-class people value, then they not only require realistic opportunities, but a change in the lower-class values that no longer define middle-class goals as worth pursuing. A mass conversion is implied.

Middle-class theory suggests two possible remedies for the delinquency of privileged youth: the acceptance of a new morality in which juvenile status acts are no longer defined as delinquent offenses and means by which adolescents can be given a greater stake in conformity—closer ties with adults and a greater involvement in socially desirable and productive roles.

4. *Logical and empirical adequacy.* Certain of the facts upon which some or all cultural deviance theories are constructed have continued to receive empirical support: (1) that law-violating behavior occurs most frequently among adolescents; (2) that *official* delinquency is concentrated in the most overcrowded, deteriorated areas of the city; (3) that delinquent behavior tends to be committed in groups; and (4) that there is some discontinuity between the generations. Unless one takes the position that all these conditions are due to inherently antisocial or pathological tendencies among large numbers of youngsters, then one must pay attention to the possible existence of cultural values and standards that are deviant. Yet, important questions can be raised about the excessive determinism of cultural deviance theories and the utopian solutions they imply.

Some part of delinquent behavior is due to the ambiguous or class status of adolescents in American society. It is often an expression of either status and of an attempt to establish oneself in a social context in which peers play an important role. But it is a gross oversimplification, except in Miller's case, to suggest that the single most important source of direction and acceptance for adolescents lower or middle-class—is that afforded by peers. Young people are not programmed like a computer to conform only to delinquent peer standards. Conventional adults and institutions also perform a socializing role. Indeed, even the most delinquent of adolescents behave conventionally most of the time.

The point is that American culture is a complex and pluralistic culture in which people are confronted with alternative guides for behavior, some conventional, some deviant. And, while certain individuals or groups may be influenced more by one than by the other, both determine behavior to a considerable degree. Hence, what is needed from cultural deviance theories is some specification of the conditions under which some individuals or groups resist temptation and remain wedded to conventional alternatives, while others accept it and join in the commission of delinquent acts. Control processes exerted by interested adults, as well as pressures by peers to be delinquent, operate in any setting, and reasonable theories should acknowledge the presence of both (Cf. Rivera and Short, 1967). At the present time, however, cultural deviance theories make little provision for this possibility. Individual or group choice is ignored.

In attempting to deal with these issues and yet to reflect the social character of delinquency, theories have tended to go in two major directions. The first continues to develop the traditional theme that delinquency is predominantly a lower-class group phenomenon. But, rather than suggesting that law violation arises in cultural isolation from middle-class values, it suggests that delinquent acts result from the very attractiveness and pursuit of those values. This is called strain theory and will be discussed in the next chapter. The second kind of theory—symbolic interactionist theory—also continues to suggest that delinquency is largely a group phenomenon but discards the notion that it is the function of any particular class culture. It can occur on any class level in response to learning and reinforcement in small groups. This theory will be discussed in Chapter 12.

References

Bengston, Vern L. et al.
   1974   "Time, aging, and the continuity of social structure: themes and issues in generational analysis." *Journal of Social Issues* (No. 2), 20:1–30.

Berger, Bennett M.
   1963   "Adolescence and beyond." *Social Problems,* Spring, 10:394–408.

   1971   *Looking for America: Essays on Youth, and Suburbia and Other American Obsessions.* Englewood Cliffs, N.J.: Prentice Hall.

Bloch, Herbert A. and Niederhoffer, Arthur
   1958   *The Gang: A Study in Adolescent Behavior.* New York: Philosophical Library.

Bohlke, Robert H.
   1961   "Social mobility, stratification inconsistency and middle-class delinquency." *Social Problems,* Spring, 8:351–363.

Bordua, David J.
   1961   "Delinquent subcultures: sociological interpretations of gang delinquency." *The Annals of the American Academy of Political and Social Science,* November, 338:119–136.

Brown, Claude
   1965   *Manchild in the Promised Land.* New York: New American Library.

Clark, Robert E.
  1972 *Reference Group Theory and Delinquency.* New York: Behavioral Publications.
Cloward, Richard A. and Ohlin, Lloyd E.
  1960 *Delinquency and Opportunity: A Theory of Delinquent Gangs.* New York: Free Press.
Cohen, Albert K.
  1955 *Delinquent Boys: The Culture of the Gang.* New York: Free Press.
  1957 "Middle-class delinquency and the social structure." Pp. 203–207 in Edmund W. Vaz (Ed.), *Middle-Class Juvenile Delinquency.* New York: Harper and Row.
Cohen, Albert K., Alfred Lindesmith and Karl Schuessler
  1956 *The Sutherland Papers.* Bloomington: Indiana University Press.
Coleman, James S.
  1961 *The Adolescent Society.* New York: Free Press.
Coleman, James S., et al.
  1972 *Youth: Transition to Adulthood.* Chicago: University of Chicago Press.
Davis, Kingsley
  1944 "Adolescence and the social structure." *Annals of the American Academy of Political and Social Sciences,* November, 236:1–16.
Dinitz, Simon, Scarpitti, Frank R. and Reckless, Walter C.
  1962 "Delinquency vulnerability: a cross group and longitudinal analysis." *American Sociological Review,* August, 27:515–517.
Elkin, Frederick and Westley, William A.
  1955 "The myth of adolescent culture." *American Sociological Review,* December, 20:680–684.
Empey, LaMar T.
  1973 "Juvenile justice reform: diversion, due process and deinstitutionalization." Pp. 13–48 in Lloyd E. Ohlin (Ed.), *Prisoners in America.* Englewood Cliffs, N.J.: Prentice Hall.
England, Ralph W.
  1960 "A theory of middle-class juvenile delinquency." *The Journal of Criminal Law, Criminology, and Police Science,* April, 50:535–540.
Erickson, Maynard L.
  1973 "Group violations and official delinquency." *Criminology,* August, 11:127–160.
Erickson, Maynard L. and Empey, LaMar T.
  1965 "Class position, peers, and delinquency." *Sociology and Social Research,* April, 49:268–282.

Eynon, Thomas G. and Reckless, Walter C.
  1961 "Companionship at delinquency onset." *British Journal of Criminology*, October, 2:162–170.

Flacks, Richard
  1971 *Youth and Social Change.* New York: Markham.

Gillis, John R.
  1974 *Youth and History.* New York: Academic Press.

Glaser, Daniel
  1971 *Social Deviance.* Chicago: Markham.

Glueck, Sheldon and Glueck, Eleanor
  1950 *Unraveling Juvenile Delinquency.* Cambridge: Harvard University Press.

Green, Arnold
  1952 *Sociology.* New York: McGraw-Hill.

Hill, Reuben
  1970 *Family Development in Three Generations.* Cambridge: Schenkman.

Hindelang, Michael J.
  1971 "The social versus solitary nature of delinquent involvements." *British Journal of Criminology*, August, 11:127–160.

  1973 "Causes of delinquency: a partial replication and extension." *Social Problems*, Spring, 21:471–487.

Hirschi, Travis
  1969 *Causes of Delinquency.* Berkeley: University of California Press.

Jensen, Gary F. and Erickson, Maynard L.
  1976 "Peer commitment and delinquent conduct: new tests of old hypotheses." Tucson: University of Arizona. (Unpublished).

Kandel, Denise B. and Lesser, Gerald S.
  1972 *Youth in Two Worlds.* San Francisco: Jossey-Bass.

Keniston, Kenneth
  1972 "Youth: a 'new' stage of life." In Thomas J. Cottle (Ed.), *The Prospect of Youth.* Boston: Little, Brown.

Klein, Malcolm W. and Crawford, Lois Y.
  1967 "Groups, gangs and cohesiveness." *Journal of Research in Crime and Delinquency*, January, 4:63–75.

Kobrin, Solomon
  1959 "The Chicago Area Project—a 25-year assessment." *The Annals of the American Academy of Political and Social Science*, March, 322:20–29.

Kobrin, Solomon
  1971 "The formal logical properties of the Shaw-McKay delinquency theory." Pp. 101–132 in Harwin L. Voss and David M. Petersen

(Eds.), *Ecology, Crime and Delinquency.* New York: Appleton-Century-Crofts.

Kobrin, Solomon, Puntil, Joseph and Peluso, Emil
   1967   "Criteria of status among street corner groups." *Journal of Research in Crime and Delinquency,* January, 4:98–118.

Kvaraceus, William and Miller, Walter B.
   1959   "Norm-violating behavior in middle-class culture." Pp. 233–241 in Edmund W. Vaz (Ed.), *Middle-Class Juvenile Delinquency.* New York: Harper and Row.

Matza, David
   1964   *Delinquency and Drift.* New York: John Wiley.

Miller, Walter B.
   1958   "Lower-class culture as a generating milieu of gang delinquency." *Journal of Social Issues,* Summer, 14:5–19.

   1959   "Implications of urban lower-class culture for social work." *The Social Service Review,* September, 33:219–236.

Morris, Norval and Hawkins, Gordon
   1970   *The Honest Politician's Guide to Crime Control.* Chicago: University of Chicago Press.

National Commission on Law Observance and Enforcement
   1931   *Social Factors in Juvenile Delinquency* (No. 13, Vol. 2). Washington, D.C.: U.S. Government Printing Office.

Parsons, Talcott
   1942   "Age and sex in the social structure of the United States." *American Sociological Review,* October, 7:604–616.

   1950   "Psychoanalysis and the social structure." *Psychoanalytic Quarterly,* 19:371–384.

Polk, Kenneth and Kobrin, Solomon
   1972   *Delinquency Prevention through Youth Development.* Washington, D.C.: U.S. Government Printing Office.

President's Commission on Law Enforcement and Administration of Justice.
   1967   *The Challenge of Crime in a Free Society.* Washington, D.C.: U.S. Government Printing Office.

Rivera, Ramon J. and Short, James F., Jr.
   1967   "Significant adults, caretakers, and structures of opportunity: an exploratory study." *Journal of Research in Crime and Delinquency,* January, 4:76–97.

Scott, Joseph W. and Vaz, Edmund W.
   1963   "A perspective on middle-class delinquency." Pp. 207–222 in Edmund W. Vaz (Ed.), *Middle-Class Juvenile Delinquency.* New York: Harper and Row.

Shaw, Clifford R.
　1931　*The Natural History of a Delinquent Career.* Chicago: University of Chicago Press.

　1936　*Brothers in Crime.* Chicago: University of Chicago Press.

　1966　*The Jack-Roller: A Delinquent Boy's Own Story.* Chicago: University of Chicago Press.

Shaw, Clifford R. and McKay, Henry D.
　1931　*Social Factors in Juvenile Delinquency.* Report of the National Commission on Law Observance and Enforcement (Wichersham Commission) (No. 13, Vol. 2). Washington, D.C.: U.S. Government Printing Office.

　1942　*Juvenile Delinquency and Urban Areas.* Chicago: University of Chicago Press.

　1969　*Juvenile Delinquency and Urban Areas* (Rev. ed.). Chicago: University of Chicago Press.

Shaw, Clifford R. et al.
　1929　*Delinquency Areas.* Chicago: University of Chicago Press.

Short, James F., Jr.
　1957　"Differential association and delinquency.: *Social Problems,* January, 4:233–239.

　1972　"Introduction to the revised edition." Pp. xxv–liv in Clifford R. Shaw and Henry D. McKay, *Juvenile Delinquency and Urban Areas.* Chicago: University of Chicago Press.

Short, James F., Jr. and Strodtbeck, Fred L.
　1965　*Group Process and Gang Delinquency.* Chicago: University of Chicago Press.

Thrasher, Frederick M.
　1927　*The Gang.* Chicago: University of Chicago Press.

Toby, Jackson
　1957　"Social disorganization and a stake in conformity." *Journal of Criminal Law, Criminology, and Police Science,* May-June, 48:12–17.

Whyte, William F.
　1943　*Street Corner Society.* Chicago: University of Chicago Press.

Whyte, William H., Jr.
　1956　*The Organization Man.* New York: Simon and Schuster.

Williams, Robin
　1952　*American Society.* New York: Alfred A. Knopf.

11

STRAIN THEORY

Strain theory possesses some features in common with cultural deviance theory. It assumes that human nature is inherently social: Young people feel morally obligated to conform to social rules and are sensitive to the expectations of others. It also sees delinquent behavior as an expression of conformity to subcultural values and standards. When young people violate the law, their behavior represents an effort to adjust collectively to problems which society has created.

At the same time, strain theory departs in significant ways from cultural deviance theory. Rather than suggesting that delinquent behavior is spread throughout the class structure or across the sexes, it suggests that it is primarily the product of lower-class boys. Rather than suggesting that each of the social classes possesses its own distinctive set of goals, it suggests that Americans are alike and want the same things. Rather than suggesting that lower-class adolescents are without justification for their delinquent acts, it suggests that their behavior is due to anger and frustration over a lack of opportunity. In short, strain theory suggests that the social order is characterized by value consensus: Lower- as well as middle-class children share in the American Dream and want to achieve it. The delinquent, moreover, is a normal youth with normal expectations. His problems stem from the fact that conventional opportunities are blocked. Hence, pressures to be delinquent are generated by legitimate desires, not immature fixations or pathological motives.

Historical origins

This way of constructing delinquent behavior can be traced to Robert Merton, an eminent American sociologist. In a series of statements, beginning in 1938, Merton first discounted Freudian explanations of deviant behavior and then formulated an alternative view (1938; 1957; 1968):

> Until recently . . . one could speak of a marked tendency in psychological and sociological theory to attribute the faulty operation of social structure to failures of social control over man's imperious biological drives. . . . In the beginning, there are man's biological impulses which seek full expression. And then there is the social order, essentially an apparatus for the management of impulses, for the social processing of tensions, [and] for the "renunciation of instinctual gratifications," in the words of Freud. Nonconformity . . . is thus assumed to be anchored in original nature. . . . And by implication, conformity is the result of a utilitarian calculus or of unreasoned conditioning (1968:185).

Such a view, said Merton, is faulty (Cf. 1968:185–248). Humankind is not, by nature, inherently deviant. Deviant impulses are socially induced. In American society, for example, a great emphasis is put upon monetary success and the achievement of high social status. Yet, at the same time, society does not provide all of its citizens with equal opportunity for success. For the lower-class people, in particular, "culturally induced" goals cannot be realized; they lack the means. As a result, they are faced with a cruel dilemma: Either they must give up the pursuit of that which everyone values and thus appear to be morally inferior, or they must seek out illegal means and, again, run the risk of censure. But, should they choose the latter course, it will be the product, not of an inherently evil nature, but of the discrepancy between culturally valued goals and socially available means. "A cardinal American virtue, 'ambition,' promotes a cardinal American vice, 'deviant behavior' " (1957:146).

Two different versions of this general view have been applied specifically to juveniles, the first by Albert K. Cohen in 1955 and the second by Richard A. Cloward and Lloyd E. Ohlin in 1960. So provocative were their statements, ideologically as well as scientifically, that throughout the 1960s and into the 1970s they had considerable impact upon policy makers as well as criminologists. Each version is set forth below.

Cohen: Status frustration and delinquency

Cohen's introduction to his theory (1955) reveals the extent to which, by the middle of this century, cultural explanations of delinquency had gained widespread acceptance, at least among sociologists. His theory, he says, is designed to explain two sets of "known facts": (1) the existence and content of delinquent subculture; and (2) the concentration of this subculture among the male working-class segments of American society. To him at least, both of these "facts" were not arguable. The prevalence of delinquent traditions was widely accepted, and the prevailing opinion was that female delinquency was not serious. "Authorities are agreed," said Cohen, "that female delinquency, although it may appear euphemistically in the records as 'ungovernability' or 'running away' is mostly sex delinquency. Stealing, 'other property offenses,' 'orneriness' and 'hell-raising' . . . are primarily practices of the male" (p. 45).

It was upon this foundation, then, that Cohen advanced the following propositions to explain delinquent subculture and the functions it serves for lower-class boys.

1. *Lower-class Americans embrace the middle class success ethic.* Cohen rejects the notion that a distinctive culture has been perpetuated or has developed among lower-class Americans. The middle-class values which have played such an important part is shaping the American character and our concept of childhood have now established a foothold in the lower class. Its members watch television, go to the movies, listen to the radio, and attend middle-class dominated schools. Thus, over time, they have come more and more under the spell of a set of norms which stress ambition, resourcefulness, achievement, respect for property, and, above all, the desire for material success. The American Dream has become a possession of the lower class.

This acceptance of the American Dream has been encouraged by the democratic belief that every child should be free to compete with every other, regardless of background. "The cards are not dealt and the hands all played . . . before the child appears on the scene" (p. 85). Each child should be judged as an individual, and it should be his achievement that determines his future status, not the social position into which he is born. However, since every individual should be encouraged to compete, there can only be one standard for measuring success: *the middle-class measuring rod*—the ability to get ahead. Hence, no less than middle-class children, each lower-class boy should be expected to compete for success with all comers.

   2. *The socialization of lower-class children hinders their capacity to compete.* Unfortunately, the desire to share in the American Dream does not mean that all children have an equal ability to compete. Lower-class parents, for example, do not have the economic resources and social power that middle-class parents have to assist their children—money, clothes, a home in the right neighborhood, or the capacity to intercede effectively with the school or influential employers. Even more important, lower- and middle-class parents socialize their children in different ways. Middle-class parents are rational, deliberate, and demanding. They leave little to chance, stressing self-discipline and close adherence to the age-graded demands of childhood. They abhor physical violence and prefer reason and diplomatic maneuver. They surround their children with books and toys that are selected for their educational value. They budget their time and fill their days with participation in the Boys Scouts, Junior Achievement, music or tennis lessons. Finally, they teach their children that love and acceptance by parents and teachers are earned by disciplined effort and achievement. Neither comes automatically. Rather, the child must show that he deserves them. By comparison, lower-class parents are easygoing and permissive. Their children receive less training in self-discipline and are granted greater latitude with respect to the use of their time. They have much less contact with books and highly structured recreational and educational activities. Instead, they are thrown far earlier into the company of their peers where they are freer to play in the streets or to get into trouble. Fighting as a method of settling problems is more acceptable, and the love of parents is less dependent upon achievement, respect for authority, and self-discipline. In short, lower-class children are handicapped in terms of their ability to compete because they are still socialized in ways that reflect the lower-class traditions of centuries past—communal living, earlier induction into adult activities, and immediate rather than deferred gratification.

   3. *Decreased ability to compete produces strain.* The one place in which the children of all social levels come together to compete for

status is the school. The school is a mirror reflection of the larger society: Its goals are avowedly democratic, and it idealizes the development of each child's potential. Yet, throughout history, the school has been a middle-class institution that is designed to foster and to reward middle-class character, skills, and manners. Hence, because the lower-class child lacks these skills and manners, it is he who is found most wanting.

Like everyone else he wants status and acceptance, but the techniques he has learned for acquiring it are not those of the middle class: his boisterous behavior destroys the order and routine of the classroom; he does not read well; he has little experience in being studious, docile, and obedient; and he lacks interest in intellectual matters. In short, he is placed in an arena in which he must compete for status against all others but for which his prior training is inadequate. More than others, there-fore, he is programmed to fail. Classroom failures are disproportion-ately drawn from the lower class.

The same pattern of failure is encountered in other middle-class in-stitutions. Even the settlement houses of the slums or other recreational centers are sponsored and run by middle-class people. Such people often feel a special regard for the "rough," "dirty" boys of the slum who do little else but hang around the street corner. But, as Cohen points out, "it is common to hear that remedial programs are very successful and do a lot of good but don't seem to get the children who need them the most" (pp. 116–117). There are some good reasons why this hap-pens. In order to maintain some degree of control and in order to run "wholesome" and "constructive" activities, staff members are drawn to the occasionally polite, personable, mannerly child, not the one who is continually disruptive and boisterous. Like teachers, these people find it almost impossible to sponsor and to reward "desirable" (middle-class) behavior if they do not punish its opposite (lower-class behavior). Hence, many lower-class boys experience failure, rejection, and punishment wherever they turn. Any desire they may have to adapt successfully is hindered by their incapacity to exhibit appropriate middle-class behavior.

The result is that lower-class children tend to find themselves at the bottom of the status ladder in most of the official youth institutions in society, not only among adults but among their peers. They do not participate in the extracurricular activities of the school and are ex-cluded from the cliques that help to provide prominence in the larger adolescent world. Even more important, this loss of social status is accompanied by a growing sense of personal failure. If lower-class boys did not share middle-class values, their failure might not bother them. But, having adopted the middle-class measuring rod for judging themselves, they share the view that they are failures. Falling short of their own expectations, their sense of self-worth is lowered, and they experience a growing sense of ambivalence toward prized middle-class goals. Hence, as Cohen puts it, they face a serious problem of adjustment and are in the market for a solution. How shall their sense of strain be resolved?

4.   Increased strain produces identification with the delinquent subculture.   Cohen argues that most people adjust to strain by joining with others to seek a solution. Only the rare individual becomes mentally unstable by remaining totally alone. Hence, he suggests the availability of three possible solutions. The first is likely the most common. Many lower-class boys deal with their sense of frustration and failure by accepting their lower-class status, disengaging themselves psychologically from competition and withdrawing into a sheltering community of like-minded peers—the "corner boy" society of the lower class. By so doing, they avoid rupturing their ties with parents and neighbors and of incurring intense hostility from middle-class persons. They may have a few minor scrapes with the law, but, in the main, they will acquire a limited education, a job, and a family and will eventually become stable members of working-class society. To the degree that they still aspire to the American Dream, they will be saddled with a chronic load of frustration, but at least they will have the satisfaction of living in a world with which they are familiar and in which they are not continually confronted with failure.

The second alternative is the "college boy" alternative. It involves the relatively few boys who rupture their ties with the corner boy society and who accept the challenge of the middle-class status system. This solution entails considerable sacrifice on their parts, requiring the acquisition of unfamiliar linguistic, academic, and social skills. But, by hard work and deferred gratification, they can be among the few lower-class boys who go on to college and who play the game of life according to middle-class rules.

The third alternative involves those boys who turn to the standards of the delinquent subculture for a solution. According to Cohen, the delinquent subculture is *nonutilitarian*, *malicious*, and *negativistic*. Ordinarily, he says, people steal things because they can use them, can buy something with them, or can wear them. But the delinquent acts of lower-class boys usually do not appear to have a useful purpose. Instead, they steal things "for the hell of it"—clothes they cannot wear food they do not eat, or articles they do not use. They delight in terrorizing "good" kids or older people. They vandalize, even destroy, their own schools. They dump garbage on their neighbors' doorsteps, deface public buildings, or defecate on their teacher's desk.

Such behavior makes no sense to middle-class people, but it is precisely for this reason that it makes sense to rejected lower-class delinquents. "The hallmark of the delinquent subculture is the explicit and wholesale repudiation of middle-class standards and the adoption of their very antithesis" (p. 129). Its appeal lies in the fact it does not temporize with middle-class values. An ordinary lower-class boy skips school because it is dull and unrewarding, but a member of the delinquent subculture does so because "good" boys are not supposed to play truant. A corner boy steals some hubcaps to dress up his car, but a member of the deliquent subculture merely destroys them because he disdains the middle-class love of property. In short, the delinquent subculture is appealing because it rejects everything valued by the middle-class and because it compensates for the humiliation that middle-class institutions cause lower-class boys. In these ways it serves important functions because it helps delinquents to deal psychologically with the shame and degradation they have experienced in middle-class settings.

Cohen implies that delinquents are boys who, perhaps more than the majority, continue to prize middle-class goals. Thus, the only way they can handle their anxiety is to deny middle-class values completely. Their behavior is a collective expression of reaction-formation: an "exaggerated," "disproportionate," "abnormal" reaction against repressed desires that continue to press for attention. Only by "irrational," "malicious," "unaccountable" hostility to these middle-class desires can delinquents remain free of their seductive blandishments.

Cohen says that membership in the delinquent subculture is not the only road to delinquency, but, given the problems that lower-class boys face and the group support that it provides, it is the most likely road. Lone individuals by themselves could not handle the personal and social tensions inherent in rejecting the moral imperatives of society. But the delinquent subculture compensates for these problems: It provides the support of like-minded peers, it grants status for noncomformity to middle-class standards, and it sets the successful delinquent on a higher pedestal than the ordinary corner boy or the upward-bound college boy.

In short, it becomes a sort of substitute society for the delinquent, providing an alternative for the middle-class dominated society in which he has not been successful.

5.   *Identification with the delinquent subculture produces delinquent behavior.*   Since the hallmark of the delinquent subculture is the wholesale repudiation of middle-class standards, the delinquent behavior of its members will reflect this spirit. Delinquent boys are resistant to the efforts of home, school, or community to regulate their behavior. They are impulsive and impatient, seeking out "fun" without regard to long-run gains or costs. Their delinquent acts are not well planned nor highly specialized. They may steal anything from tomatoes to cars; they may disobey parents and defy teachers; they may vandalize graveyards, public buildings, or churches; or they may attack their conventional peers or outsiders who invade their turf. In short, the delinquent subculture is a contraculture; that is, a way of life opposed to everything conventional. As an alternative means of avoiding failure, achieving recognition, and acquiring status, it rewards almost any behavior that attacks the morality of the middle class.

Cohen says that the circumstances which lead some boys to choose a delinquent adjustment while others choose a corner boy or college boy adjustment are obscure. Nonetheless, when the delinquent adjustment is chosen, boys respond in a collective, but irrational and malicious, way to the society that has humiliated them and denied them status. It is this humiliation, then, which provides the motive for delinquent behavior, while the delinquent subculture provides the means for translating that motive into action and for granting status to those who act on it.

Cloward and Ohlin: Delinquency and opportunity

Cloward and Ohlin's version of strain theory (1960) possesses some of the same features as Cohen's. Like Cohen, they assume that delinquent subcultures and gangs "are typically found among adolescent males in lower-class areas of large urban centers" (p. 1). Hence, their goal is to explain how these subcultures arise and persist. They also start from the premise that virtue promotes vice; i.e., that the desire to get ahead promotes delinquent behavior. But, beyond these similarities, their theory possesses some distinctive features of its own. Cohen's delinquents are irrational and malicious, the opposite of everything middle class. Cloward and Ohlin's, by contrast, are often rational and utilitarian. When legitimate channels for success are closed to them, they simply turn to illegitimate ones if at all possible. Consider the propositions that carry this theme:

1. *The success ethic is a prized possession of all Americans.*   Cohen suggests that middle-class values have only established a recent and somewhat tenuous foothold in the lower class. Cloward and Ohlin go much further. To them, the success ethic in our democratic society is so widely shared that it scarcely deserves to be called "middle class." America has been the Promised Land to all its people; everyone wants to get ahead. In fact, lower-class people feel a relatively greater need to be upwardly mobile than persons already higher in the social structure. Because their problems are greater, the pressures to escape them are impelling.

2. *Opportunities for success are not equally distributed throughout the class structure.*   No less than Cohen, Cloward and Ohlin indicate that education is an indispensable tool for upward mobility. They also suggest that the early socialization of lower-class children may inhibit their capacity to do well in school. But, to them, this is not the most serious problem. Educational achievement is not just a matter of favorable attitudes or the ability of the child to sit still in school and to put off immediate needs. The more serious problems are "structural"—a result of a class system in American society. Many lower-class families simply cannot afford to keep their children in school, particularly beyond high school. This is the major reason so many lower-class children drop out, not because they devalue education, but because they and their parents cannot afford it. If and when lower-class children scale down their educational expectations, therefore, it is not because they want to—they know full well that education is vitally important. It is because they must. For them, opportunities to climb upward are blocked.

3. *Blocked opportunities produce strain.*   A serious condition of strain is produced when a society submits some of its people to confusing, conflicted, and impossible demands. When it stresses the importance of achieving certain goals but denies the legitimate means by which to realize those goals, discontent can be expected. "The disparity between what lower-class youth are led to want and what is actually available to them is the source of a major problem of adjustment. . . . Faced with limitations on legitimate avenues of access to conventional goals and unable to revise their aspirations downward, they experience intense frustrations" (p. 86). However, unlike Cohen's, Cloward and Ohlin's boys do not see themselves as failures. It is the system that is the failure.

Consequently, the strain they feel is not due to a lowered sense of self-esteem but to a sense of injustice.

4. *Strain produces delinquent subcultures.*   When people feel that existing norms are unjust, they are likely to withdraw support from them and to search for alternatives. Indeed, Cohen suggested that when delinquents do this they not only reject the norms governing access to major goals they reject the goals themselves. That is why, according to Cohen, delinquent subculture is so malicious and negativistic; it rejects *everything* middle class.

Cloward and Ohlin advance a much different thesis. As they see it, the American Dream rarely loses its hold on lower-class boys. Hence, when they are frustrated by limited access to legitimate means, they merely turn to ones that are illegitimate. They do not give up easily. Yet, even in this endeavor, they often fail. Whether their dream ever comes true will depend upon the way their slum communities are organized.

Some slum neighborhoods provide opportunities for success through criminal means. There are close ties between adults and children, and the adults transmit traditions that are criminal and career oriented. In other words, a *criminal* subculture exists which provides illegitimate, if not legitimate, means for success. Thus, while middle-class youngsters are learning to be bankers, lawyers, or businessmen, some in the lower class may be learning how to be professional burglars, how to run the numbers racket, how to be a bookie or a professional fence. Furthermore, they learn the importance of building strong political ties and of hiring the best lawyers, so they can avoid prosecution and conviction. Thus, in neighborhoods where criminal subcultures are found, delinquent behavior is rational and utilitarian, not the opposite as Cohen suggested. Indeed, where adults and youngsters are linked in criminal activities, the wild, untrammeled delinquent gang is frowned upon because it interferes with "business" by bringing the attention of the police to the neighborhood.

The closest thing to Cohen's subculture, according to Cloward and Ohlin, occurs in totally disorganized neighborhoods like those described by Shaw and McKay. In these neighborhoods, young people can find neither legitimate *nor* illegitimate means. They are deprived of both kinds of opportunity. To be sure, there are criminals in these neighborhoods, but they tend to be the unorganized, petty, poorly paid members of the criminal world, not the sophisticated, well-organized members found in neighborhoods where a criminal subculture exists. The result, for juveniles, is a *conflict* subculture characterized by malicious and violent activities that symbolize protest against the meaninglessness of the social experience. This is where one will find the aggressive fighting gangs that people so often associate with lower-class delinquency. Actually, however, their behavior is a way of calling attention to the futility of a life in which opportunity is lacking.

Disorganized neighborhoods also produce a third delinquent subculture—a *retreatist* subculture. This is made up of juveniles who give up on the struggle for success and who turn to drugs. They are double failures, individuals who have not been a success in the use either of legitimate or illegitimate means. But, rather than blaming society, they blame themselves, retreat from the struggle, and seek solace in escape. It is a mistake, however, to view drug users as total isolates. Even in drug use, where "kicks" become the purpose for existence, one needs other people: to learn how to use drugs, to gain access to a steady supply, and to obtain group support for denying the validity of conventional behavior. In other words, drug use, no less than other forms of delinquent behavior, is subcultural behavior.

In summary, all three modes of adaption—*criminal*, *conflict*, and *retreatist*—are symbolic of blocked opportunities, not the repudiation of fundamental societal goals. In each case, illegitimate activity and subcultural standards develop as alternative means for the satisfactions which all people seek.

5. *Delinquent subcultures produce delinquent behavior.* Cloward and Ohlin have suggested that delinquent subcultures are specialized. For that reason, they imply that we should guard against the tendency to see all delinquent behavior as representing responses to subcultural requirements. For example, drinking, truancy, destroying property, petty theft, or disorderly conduct are all delinquent acts. Yet, say Cloward and Ohlin, "we would not necessarily describe as delinquent a group that tolerated or practiced these behaviors *unless they were the central activities around which the group was organized*" (p. 7. Emphasis added).

This is the key distinguishing factor: Delinquent subcultures must have a relatively narrow focus before they can be considered subcultures. For example, the members of a *criminal* subculture are rational and commit delinquent acts for material gain and social status. To them, the fighting of conflict gangs or the drug use of retreatist groups might not even be tolerated. By contrast, the members of a retreatist subculture are preoccupied only with the next fix and the means by which it can be obtained. Using delinquent means to get ahead is of little concern to them. Hence, "a *delinquent subculture is one in which certain forms of delinquent activity are essential requirements for the performance of the dominant roles supported by the subculture"* (p. 7).

This emphasis is a crucial one because it is at odds with other subcultural theories. According to Cloward and Ohlin's definition, the delinquent acts of middle-class groups could not be considered to be expressive of delinquent subculture unless they were the central concerns of these groups. If their major concerns are with school, dating, and going to college, then their delinquent behavior is incidental to other concerns and does not deserve to be called subcultural delinquency. Likewise, even Cohen's definition of lower-class delinquent subculture would be too broad for Cloward and Ohlin. To them, delinquent subcultures and the acts they endorse are relatively narrow and specialized. This is why the only really serious delinquency arises in the lower class, since it is only in lower-class communities that tightly knit, narrowly focused subcultures exist.

Implications and impact on social policy

The idea that delinquency is a failure of American society was enough to assure the fame of strain theory.[1] But, as luck would have it, the Cloward-Ohlin version in particular was destined to become a rationale for some of society's most ambitious attempts at social engineering. The reason is that it is a prime example of a case in which a new theory gives expression to long-standing and widely shared beliefs. It is quintessentially American; it is a better reflection of American culture than apple pie.

> A half century of international sociology had produced a set of propositions not far from Father Flanagan's assertion that "There is no such thing as a bad boy." Cloward and Ohlin argued that delinquents were resorting to desperately deviant and dangerous measures in order to *conform* to the routine goals of the larger society. If that society wished them to conform not only in their objectives but in their means for achieving them, it had only to provide the *opportunity* to do so. Opportunity was the master concept. *And what else was America all about?* (Moynihan, 1969:51. (Emphasis added in last sentence).

---

[1] This discussion of implications is drawn from three major sources: Daniel P. Moynihan (1969), Peter Marris and Martin Rein (1973), and James F. Short, Jr. (1975).

The processes by which earlier generations of immigrants were assimilated into the mainstream of American life had now broken down, and the remedy must lie in the reopening of opportunity.

Cloward and Ohlin did not stand aloof from the implications of their theory. Instead, they set about seeing its principles translated into programs for lower-class boys. While writing their book on delinquency, they worked with the Henry Street Settlement on the lower east side in New York to draw up a large action research program which would utilize its ideas. To be called Mobilization for Youth, this program was outlined in a 617-page volume entitled *A Proposal for the Prevention and Control of Delinquency by Expanding Opportunities*. Among other things, Mobilization for Youth was designed to accomplish the following objectives:

> *To improve education:* Improve teacher training and curriculum, provide preschool programs for young children, and improve other educational service.
>
> *To create work opportunities:* An Urban Youth Services Corps, a Youth Jobs Center, and better vocational training.
>
> *To organize the lower-class community:* Take steps to reach and organize unaffiliated persons, organize neighborhood councils, and establish the Lower East Side Neighborhood Association.
>
> *To provide specialized services to adolescent groups:* A detached worker program for gangs, an Adventure Corps, and a Coffee Shop Hangout.
>
> *To provide specialized services to individuals and their families:* Organize Neighborhood Service Centers that would provide counseling, assistance to families, and other services of this type.

This ambitious endeavor was not conceived solely as a service program. It was to be a social experiment, carefully conceived and systematically evaluated. Indeed, says Moynihan (1969:51), the proposal "is one of the more remarkable documents in the history of efforts to bring about 'scientific' social change: lucid, informed, precise, scholarly, and, above all, candid."

A major problem with the proposal, however, was its price tag, several million dollars. But the early 1960s was a time of opportunity for scholars as well as for delinquents. A new President, John Kennedy, had just been elected. His campaign slogan had been "The New Frontier.'' Change was in the wind and new ideas were being sought. And, since Cloward and Ohlin's ideas were better formulated than most, they soon came to the attention of the new administration.

The Kennedy family had a long-standing interest in the problems of youth. Soon after the President was inaugurated, therefore, efforts were made to develop a new federal initiative against delinquency. A high-powered committee entitled the President's Committee on Juvenile Delinquency and Youth Crime was created by executive order on May 11, 1961. Its chairman was Robert Kennedy, the President's brother and the new Attorney General. Other committee members included Abraham Ribicoff, the Secretary of Health, Education, and Welfare and Arthur Goldberg, the Secretary of Labor. David Hackett, a friend and close associate of Robert Kennedy's, was named as executive director for the committee.

Hackett sought to inform himself on the latest thinking about delinquency and was introduced to strain theory and the philosophy of Mobilization for Youth by officers of the Ford Foundation, for whom both Cloward and Ohlin were consultants. Their innovative and stimulating ideas, along with those of Albert Cohen, appealed to the spirit of the New Frontier, and Hackett was soon persuaded that opportunities for lower-class youth was what the President's Committee should be pushing. Hence, he invited Ohlin to help him develop the federal program.

Accepting Ohlin's notion that delinquency reduction required large-scale effort, the President's Committee stressed the need to bring all possible resources to bear upon the delinquency problem. Therefore, one of its first efforts was to promote the coordination of the several departments and agencies of the federal government relating to delinquency. Hopefully, they would cooperate with each other and encourage the same process on state, local, and private levels. New delinquency legislation was also written and passed. The preamble to this legislation bore the unmistakable stamp of strain theory:

> Delinquency and youth offenses occur disproportionately among school dropouts, unemployed youth faced with limited opportunities and with employment barriers, and youth in deprived family situations. . . . Prevention and control of such delinquency and youth offenses require intensive and coordinated efforts on the part of private and governmental interests (Cf. Marris and Rein, 1973:22).

The new legislation authorized the expenditure of $10 million a year for three years. The key concepts in the disbursement of this money were "opportunity," "coordination," and "community action." Communities throughout the nation were invited to submit proposals, but they had to indicate how they would mount an interdisciplinary, broadly based attack on delinquency in which the goal was institutional, not personality, change. The federal government would provide planning and seed money, but communities had to commit local resources and to indicate how those resources would be reallocated in a more effective manner. Furthermore, they had to involve members of the target population—poor people themselves—in the planning process, and they had to use research to evaluate their efforts.

Because Mobilization for Youth had served as the blueprint for the entire effort, it only made sense that it should be among the first programs funded. Indeed, "a singular consortium consisting of the Ford Foundation, the city of New York, and the federal government was put together to provide a three-year $12.5 million grant. In round terms, Ford put up 15 percent, the city of New York 30 percent, and the rest came from Washington" (Moynihan, 1969:58). This was the New Frontier at its best. Hence, the launching of Mobilization for Youth was accomplished with great fanfare.

> The program was launched in a sunny ceremony in the White House garden on May 31, 1962. . . . The Democratic Party, the Chief Executive of the nation, and the mayor of its largest city were sponsoring the project. "New York's program," the President declared, "is the best in the country at this time and is the furthest along." He thanked the members of Congress who had worked on this problem of juvenile delinquency, which, he added, "is really perhaps not the most descriptive phrase; it's really a question of young people and their opportunity" (Moynihan, 1969:58–59).

The War on Poverty

Mobilization for Youth and the President's committee had scarcely gotten under way when opportunity theory became the rationale for social intervention on even a grander scale. A nationwide War on Poverty was declared. In October 1963, the President's Council of Economic Advisers asked David Hackett to submit a proposal for a series of community programs, something like Mobilization for Youth, which would cost $500 million in the first year of operation. Just one month after that, President Kennedy was assassinated in Dallas. The nationwide shock and mourning that followed might have spelled the end of the War on

Poverty, but the new President, Lyndon Johnson, decided to go ahead with it.

Significantly, most of the senior staff members who had worked on the President's committee now became leaders in the War on Poverty. They simply took many of the ideas originally outlined in the Mobilization for Youth proposal and transferred them to the new agency. The staff also retained the notion of "scientific" planning and urged that local communities be permitted to prepare carefully for the new "experiment." The War on Poverty would be fought in stages as communities gained knowledge and experience. But President Johnson wanted an all-out attack mounted immediately, and his order was carried out (Piven and Cloward, 1971).

Space precludes a detailed analysis of what happened to the War on Poverty and its precursors, Mobilization for Youth and the President's committee. Suffice it to say that from 1965 to 1970 billions were spent in an endeavor to assimilate the poor into the opportunity structure of American society and, thereby, to reduce delinquency and its attendant problems. What, then, were the results?

Those who have chronicled the history of this effort have concluded that, at best, it had mixed results and, at worst, it was a failure.

Even before the poverty program got underway in 1964, Mobilization for Youth was described by the *New York Daily News* as an organization that was infested with "Commies and Commie sympathizers." Some of its staff members were also accused of misappropriating funds (Moynihan, 1969: chap. 6). Actually, these accusations were levied more because MFY had become involved in a political struggle with city hall than because there was much substance to them. Hence, some important forces rallied to the defense of MFY and calm was restored. Nonetheless, the damage was done. "The logic of scientific problem solving collapsed in piecemeal pragmatism" (Marris and Rein, 1973:214). Despite its auspicious launching, MFY slowly sank in a sea of conflict.

The President's Committee also withered away. From the beginning, it encountered resistance from established old-line departments in the federal bureaucracy. Then, influential members of Congress made it clear that the mandate of the President's committee was to reduce delinquency, not to reform urban society or to try out sociological theories on American youth. Finally, interest in the Committee simply shriveled as interest was transferred to the grander strategy of the War on Poverty.

The War on Poverty, meanwhile, initiated numerous new programs, among them Head Start, the Job Corps, Vista, and Neighborhood Legal Services, but the heart of its effort was the Community Action Program. Modeled after MFY, it was designed to establish in every local community an organization in which the poor would join with members of the Establishment in planning and operating the poverty program. It was this feature of the federal effort that encountered the greatest difficulty. Its goal to bring about profound changes in the opportunity structure was never realized.

Several reasons for this failure have been cited. Moynihan (1969) argues that CAP did much harm to the true interests of the poor because it was based on an unproven theory, because it was poorly conceived and poorly run, and, most of all, because it resulted in a dogma about the evils of powerlessness and a strategy of stirring up trouble. Both in MFY and in the CAP, the poor were enjoined to engage in rent strikes, to organize social protests, and to attack the political and welfare establishments. The obvious goal was to let political leaders know that the poor were an increasingly organized constituency to which they would have to respond with jobs, better housing, improved education, and more social services. Apparently, the organized protests had the reverse effect. Both Congress and local politicians withdrew support from MFY and the War on Poverty. As a result, says Moynihan (p. 193), "an immense opportunity to institute more or less permanent social changes—a fixed full employment program [and] a measure of income maintenance—was lost while energies were expended in ways that very probably hastened the end of the brief period when such options were open." In other words, Moynihan suggests, the wrong tactics were used. Efforts should have been concentrated on using practical political means to provide economic resources for the poor rather than trying to force them by outright attack.

In some ways, Marris and Rein (1973) agree. They point out that neither sociologists nor the poor have political constituencies. Moreover, "When intellectuals take over policy, they lack the professional politicians' sense of the constituency for reform and are likely to attempt the impossible. They not only spoil the opportunity for practical interventions, but raise expectations [among the poor] which cannot be met" (p. 244). At the same time, say Marris and Rein (pp. 244–246), there is real question regarding the extent to which there was ever full political support, even among the Kennedys, for the kinds of radical social changes that the philosophy of strain theory implied. One does not easily alter the basic structure of society—economically, politically, and socially—without incurring great opposition.

With all this, there was some useful fallout from the War on Poverty. Perhaps the most significant was the formation and training of a strong cadre of minority leadership in the CAP program. Far more than ever before, blacks, Mexican Americans and Puerto Ricans took up places in the structure of American political life and have since organized their constituencies into more potent political forces. Thus, "If [their] rights can be secured and applied at every level of government to a more open process of arbitrating the allocation of resources, then the experiment of community action may be vindicated after all" (Marris and Rein, 1973:296). Furthermore, preschool programs initiated by MFY and Head Start have become more or less permanent fixtures in our educational system, as have Neighborhood Legal Services for the poor. Both of these activities are central to any effort to achieve equality of opportunity and, therefore, may contribute to the goals that the War on Poverty sought.

To those of a more radical persuasion, such results are far too little and come far too late. Indeed, as we will see in Chapter 14 on radical theory, some writers believe that the philosophy of MFY and the War on Poverty was far too conservative, little more than a sop to the oppressed masses. Such programs were destined to fail because they did not really mount an attack on American capitalism and the class structure it perpetuates. These are at the root of all our troubles, and delinquency will never be eliminated until they are eliminated. Indeed, the real criminals are not those who protest oppression but the capitalist exploiters who perpetuate it.

Scientific adequacy of strain theory

Given the questionable success of MFY and the War on Poverty, an examination of the scientific adequacy of strain theory becomes all the more important. The reason has to do with the deterministic picture it paints of lower-class youth. While the boys in Shaw and McKay's groups had a great deal of fun running the streets, dumping over garbage cans, and stealing from the neighborhood grocery, those described by Cohen and by Cloward and Ohlin "are driven by grim economic and psychic necessity into rebellion" (Bordua, 1961:136). Delinquency is no fun for them. They are virtually forced to use desperate measures, either to overcome a gnawing sense of inadequacy or to open up new avenues to success. But is this construction of what delinquent boys are like an accurate one?

The answer to that question requires attention, first, to the fundamental assumption upon which strain theory is built—namely, that serious delinquency is largely restricted to the lower class—and, then, to the complex series of events that are supposed to produce delinquent behavior: internalization of the American Dream, failure or dropout in school, a sense of strain, and, finally, the discovery of a solution in one or more delinquent subcultures.

The class foundation.   One of the most serious limitations of strain theory may be the "factual" foundation upon which it is built. Not only have repeated self-report studies tended to question the idea that delinquent behavior is restricted to lower-class boys, but, as will be seen below, such things as failure in school or even attachment to parents may be far more predictive of illegal behavior than is class membership. Hence, if one of the basic "facts" which strain theory purports to explain is not factual, then its basic accuracy is called into question.

The American Dream.   There is considerable evidence that the American Dream is widely shared. Existing studies lend greater support to the argument of strain theorists that lower-class children internalize conventional values than to the Miller (1958) argument that middle and lower-class values are separate and distinct (Empey, 1956; Gold, 1963, Gordon, et al., 1963; Gould, 1941, Kobrin, 1951).

School failure and blocked opportunities.   Research findings confirm the notion that school performance is highly related to delinquency. Study after study indicates that those boys who do the worst in school are the most likely to be delinquent (Elliot, 1966; Empey and Lubeck, 1971; Hirschi, 1969; Polk and Halferty, 1966; Polk and Schafer, 1972). Indeed, Elliot (1966) found that delinquency rates are higher while boys remain in school than after they drop out, suggesting that status problems associated with the school may contribute to higher violation rates. But such studies do not support the idea that this problem is largely a lower-class problem, as strain theory suggests. Rather, they indicate that it is a problem that cuts across the social classes. It is failure in school that is associated most strongly with delinquent behavior, not the class position from which a child starts.

Since this is the case, there must be factors other than class position alone which lead to school failure. For example, Bordua (1961:134) points out that a blockage of opportunity for some gang members is the product of their own delinquent acts, of their own tendency to reduce their chances by progressively destroying their relationships in the school. What strain theorists failed to mention is the possibility that participation in gang delinquency may lead to poor performance in school rather than the reverse. Boys who use the school as a battleground or who "use school property as arts and crafts material do not meet the criteria for advancement" (Bordua, 1961:134).

Control theorists like Hirschi (1969) also stress poor family relations or lack of basic intellectual ability to perform academic tasks as reasons for failure in school (Chapter 9). And though strain theorists tend to disavow this point of view, research findings provide greater support for it than for strain theory. Numerous studies have indicated that delinquents may be somewhat less competent than nondelinquents and that they are more likely to reject school authority (Dinitz, et al., 1962; Hindelang, 1973:478; Reiss and Rhodes, 1961:723; Short and Strodtbeck, 1965:237–238; Stinchcombe, 1964; Toby and Toby, 1962:27). Other investigations also indicate that the better a boy gets along with his parents and the more he respects their expectations for him, the lower his chances are of delinquent behavior (Empey and Lubeck, 1971, passim; Hindelang, 1973:475; Hirschi, 1969:94). Indeed, like failure in school, attachment to parents is far more predictive of law-violating behavior than is class membership (Aultman and Welford, 1976; Empey and Lubeck, 1971; Hindelang, 1973; Hirschi, 1969). Hence, while strain theory was accurate in highlighting the school as a source of difficulty, it was not accurate in suggesting that this difficulty is one that is restricted to lower-class boys or that the sole reason for their failure is a lower-class life-style or a lack of economic resources.

Sense of strain. There is some evidence that failure in school results in frustration and a lowered sense of self-esteem (Empey and Lubeck, 1971:chap. 5; Quicker, 1974). However, there is not much sign that delinquent behavior is due to the frustration of long-range ambitions held by highly motivated boys. Indeed, Hirschi (1969:182–183) found that high rates of aspiration are associated with low rates of delinquent behavior, a relationship that is just the opposite of that predicted by Cloward and Ohlin. Hence, he concluded that "frustrated occupational ambition cannot be an important cause of delinquency."

Such findings are not particularly surprising. Cloward and Ohlin, in particular, painted a picture of lower-class boys that is exceedingly utilitarian and goal oriented. They have no childhood. By the age of adolescence, they have already sized up the class structure and the job market and have recognized that the door to opportunity has been slammed. Clearly, this picture is overdrawn. Occupational planning, particularly for boys whose fathers may not work steadily, is often vague and uncertain. Like most adolescents, they are far more concerned with school, friends, members of the opposite sex, and having fun than with an occupational career. Thus, while loss of status and self-esteem in school may be associated with delinquency, there is little evidence that such is true of occupational frustrations. Moreover, there is serious doubt as to whether these problems are restricted largely to lower-class boys.

Delinquent subculture. There are three issues which must be considered with respect to delinquent subculture: (1) whether lower-class boys identify with one another to the degree that delinquent subculture is made possible; (2) whether delinquent subculture serves an important function by providing a solution to the psychological problems which boys face; and (3) whether delinquent subculture(s) are of the type which Cohen and Cloward and Ohlin describe.

With regard to the first, we have already seen that delinquent behavior tends to be a group phenomenon (Chapter 10). There is something about group processes which makes deviant behavior easier to justify and to carry out. There is also some evidence that habitual delinquents are more amenable to group influence than are other adolescents (Erickson and Empey, 1965; Empey and Lubeck, 1968). In short, the stability and persistence of delinquency as a group phenomenon is a persuasive indicator that delinquent subcultures actually exist (Erickson and Jensen, 1976; Hindelang, 1973). In drawing our attention to this possibility, therefore, strain theorists have made a valuable contribution. Yet, if subcultures do exist, there are two problems unaccounted for in strain theory.

The first is the fact that neither Cohen nor Cloward and Ohlin included any indication why in response to strain some boys choose to identify with delinquent subculture while others select a conventional adjustment. Instead, they were concerned only with accounting for the content and nature of delinquent subculture. Yet, some answer to this crucial question is needed. It is entirely possible that some of the variables stressed by control theory—attachment, commitment, belief, and involvement—play an important role in making the difference.

The second problem has to do with the puzzling lack of evidence that delinquent subculture does much to compensate for the serious problems of adjustment which lower-class boys are supposed to possess. Strain theory implies that delinquent groups become a substitute society of lower-class boys, easing the pains produced by frustration and a loss of self-esteem. But repeated studies indicate that gang members, like inmates in prison, are held together, not by feelings of loyalty and solidarity, but by forces much less attractive. Delinquent groups possess a structure all right, but that structure is not one that provides understanding and warmth as well as status. Gang members tend to hold each other in low esteem (Hirschi, 1969:159; Short and Strodtbeck, 1965:chaps. 10 and 12). Their relationships are characterized by aggression and insult and by a constant need to protect status and to assert masculinity (Matza, 1964:33; Miller, 1958). The highly stylized, even threatening, kind of interaction that is found in them is not of the type that is ordinarily associated with internally strong and emotionally satisfying groups (Yablonsky, 1959). Instead, what emerges is a picture which suggests that delinquent groups may stay together simply because they have no other alternative or because they have more to lose than to-gain by any breach in their ranks. While they may appear to the outsider to be dogmatic, rigid, and unyielding in their loyalty to each other, the sources of this loyalty are not internal but external. Remove the threat of rival gangs and of the authorities, and you remove the ties that bind (Klein and Crawford, 1967).

Since this empirical picture is so different from the one painted by strain theory, there is serious question as to whether delinquent groups serve the psychological needs of rejected lower-class boys. If such groups are their only sources of understanding and respect, they face a lamentable life indeed. What is more, if delinquent groups are not cohesive and internally gratifying, it is questionable whether they provide the personal motivation or the organizational skills necessary to promote and maintain a deviant subculture which is in total opposition to prevailing values. Indeed, rather than indicating that the members of delinquent gangs are led eventually to reject such values, several studies indicate just the opposite.

Cohen, it will be recalled, argued that in response to humiliation and a loss of status delinquent boys repudiate middle-class values completely. The only way they can handle their sense of failure and frustration is to react against them. The same would also be true, perhaps, of Cloward and Ohlin's conflict and retreatist gangs. Yet, that is not what studies find.

The members of delinquent gangs do not seem to be alienated from the goals of the larger society (Gold, 1963; Gordon, et al., 1963). "Even the gang ethic," say Short and Strodtbeck (1965:271), "is not one of 'reaction-formation' *against* widely shared conceptions of the 'good' life." Gang, lower-class, and middle-class boys, black and white, evaluate "images representing salient features of the middle-class style of life equally high" (Short and Strodtbeck, 1965:59). There is little evidence, in short, that lower-class delinquent boys eventually become alienated from conventional goals. Indeed, if they continue to view these goals as desirable, the motive for delinquency is not the repudiation of everything middle class, as Cohen suggested. Other motives must be at work, some of which are shared by middle-class boys, since they also tend to commit delinquent acts in groups (Empey and Lubeck, 1968; Erickson, 1973).

Finally, there is need to know whether delinquent subcultures of the type described by strain theories actually exist. Cohen suggested the presence of a "parent" delinquent subculture characterized by malicious and negativistic behavior, a subculture in which delinquents are not specialized. Cloward and Ohlin, by contrast, theorized that delinquent subcultures are specialized, falling into three types: criminal, conflict, and retreatist. Before a delinquent subculture can be said to exist, they say, it has to be organized around a specific activity.

Studies of this issue provide some support for the Cohen version but little for the Cloward and Ohlin version (Short and Strodtbeck, 1965:13). In the first place, even the most delinquent groups of boys spend most of their time in nondelinquent activities (Short, 1963:xlvii). Even in so-called violent gangs, few boys actually become involved in acts of assault (Miller, 1965). Finally, when delinquent behavior does occur, it does not tend to follow any particular pattern. Delinquent boys drink, steal, damage property, smoke pot, or even experiment with heroin and pills, but rarely do they limit themselves to any single one of these activities (Erickson and Empey, 1963; Gold, 1966; Illinois Institute for Juvenile Research, 1972). Thus, while there is little support for the idea that delinquent subcultures are autonomous and highly specialized, there is some support for the notion of a ubiquitous "parent" subculture which encourages a "garden variety" of delinquent acts (Cohen and Short, 1958). About the only time that highly organized criminal gangs appear is when they are linked to the criminal rackets of adults, and these links are relatively rare (Kobrin et al., 1967; Spergel, 1961).

At the same time, it would be unwise to assume that all delinquent acts are malicious and without any useful purpose. If one understands the nature of street life, then some acts take on a utilitarian character, at least from the view points of their perpetrators.

> If a group of boys lives days or even weeks away from home, then the theft of food or of things which are sold to buy food is hardly nonutilitarian. If such a group steals from freight cars, peddles the merchandise to neighbors for movie money, . . . this can hardly be considered nonutilitarian. . . .
>
> Such youngsters may, of course, spend the two dollars gained from selling stolen goods entirely on doughnuts and gorge themselves and throw much of the food away. [But] this largely indicates that they are children, not that they are nonutilitarian (Bordua, 1961:121–122).

Indeed, the finding that most delinquent behavior is of a garden variety is consistent with the idea that delinquent subculture is characterized more by childish, than by narrowly focused, values and standards. It must be remembered, after all, that delinquent groups are peopled by young and inexperienced adolescents. Since that is the case, the construction of delinquency suggested by strain theory may be overly elaborate and deterministic.

Summary and conclusions

Strain theory is a historical derivation of cultural deviance theory. It represents an attempt to explain certain phenomena which by mid-20th century were accepted as "facts": that delinquency is predominantly a lower-class phenomenon, that it occurs in groups, and that it represents the existence of delinquent subculture.

1. Assumptions about human nature and social order. Strain theory is like cultural deviance theory in that it assumes that human nature is inherently social. The delinquent is a moral animal who prefers to follow conventional rules, given reasonable opportunity to do so. Unlike cultural deviance theory, however, strain theory paints a more complicated picture of the social order.

Cultural deviance theory also implies that the social order is characterized by conflict because there is no overriding standard of good and bad. Since society is divided into different cultural groups, there is no consensus on appropriate rules for behavior. Strain theory, by contrast, implies that there is a moral consensus, particularly on basic values and goals. Everyone hails these as desirable and recognizes appropriate ways for achieving them. Ironically, however, this very consensus promotes conflict and deviance because some persons cannot achieve success by obeying cultural rules. Frustrated by a loss of status or a lack of opportunity, delinquents introduce strife into society, either by an emotional, but collective, repudiation of prized goals or by the substitution of illegitimate means for acquiring them. Yet, the impression is pervasive throughout strain theory that there would be no conflict and no deviance if only society were organized differently. Were there no structural impediments to self-esteem and material success, the inherently social natures of all people would cause them to be law-abiding.

2. *The underlying logic and content of strain theory.* Strain theory suggests that lower- as well as middle-class children share in the American Dream. If they become delinquent, therefore, it is because they are subjected to intense pressure. This pressure occurs when they experience failure in middle-class institutions or are frustrated because opportunities for achievement are blocked. In desperation, they turn for solutions to like-minded peers. Delinquent subculture(s) and behavior are the result. The two expressions of this kind of theory are shown in Figure 11–1.

FIGURE 11–1

Cohen

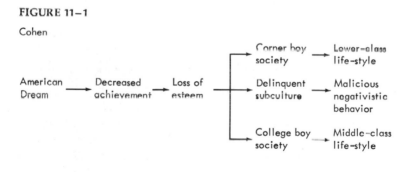

Cloward and Ohlin

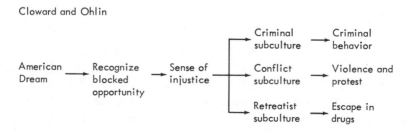

3. *Policy implications.* Strain theory implies that there is no such thing as a bad boy. If delinquency occurs, it is because of the failure of the social order. Hence, that order must be changed.

This construction of delinquency resulted in some of the most deliberate and comprehensive efforts yet tried to address such "root causes" of deviant behavior as poverty, inadequate education, economic segregation, and powerless lower-class communities. For the most part, these efforts encountered opposition and were not successful.

4. *Logical and empirical adequacy.* Strain theorists have made highly valuable contributions to the delinquency literature by focusing exclusively upon lower-class boys and by suggesting that delinquent subculture(s) may be the consequence of the problems they face. It was Cohen, in fact, who first used the term "delinquent subculture" to refer to the delinquent traditions that Shaw and McKay first wrote about. And it was Cloward and Ohlin who first alerted us to the possibility that different kinds of subcultures may be linked to the opportunity structures of different kinds of communities. Their stress upon these matters highlights the likelihood that lower-class boys have a more difficult transition from childhood to adulthood than middle-class boys. But do they handle that transition in the way that strain theory suggests? Are many of them virtually driven to membership in delinquent subculture(s)?

The elements of strain theory that have measured up best to empirical scrutiny are those which suggest that lower-class boys want what other boys want, that failure in such middle-class institutions as the school may provoke serious problems, and that delinquent behavior is a group, possibly a subcultural, phenomenon. By contrast, the elements about which there is the greatest question are those which indicate that serious delinquent behavior is restricted to the lower class, that it is a boy's position in the class structure rather than his relation to his parents or even his basic abilities which are likely to produce problems in school, that delinquent behavior represents a repudiation of societal values, and that delinquent subculture is capable of solving serious problems of adjustment.

Such findings suggest that strain theorists may have attempted to account for too much. In their construction of delinquency, they seemed to forget that delinquents are young and immature people and that such people have childhoods, grow up in families, and differ in their basic abilities and interests. Rather than reflecting an attempt to redress some of society's most serious inequities, therefore, their group behavior may represent little more than an unfettered, irresponsible, and sometimes predatory pursuit of childish desires. To be sure, the deprivations, disillusionments, and the frustrations of being lower class contribute heavily to their problems. But Cohen's humiliated, irrationalistic, angry boys, or Cloward and Ohlin's hard-driving, rationalistic criminals, or their double failured retreatists seem to be overdone. As Bordua (1961:136) puts it, "It seems peculiar that modern analysts have stopped assuming that 'evil' can be fun and see gang delinquency as arising only when boys are driven away from 'good.' "

References

Aultman, Madeline and Charles F. Wellford
  1976 "Evaluations of major sociological theories of delinquency." Paper presented at the Annual Meetings of the American Society of Criminology. Tucson, November, 1976.

Bordua, David J.
  1961 "Delinquent subcultures: sociological interpretations of gang delinquency." *Annals of the American Academy of Political and Social Science*, November, 338:119–136.

Cloward, Richard A. and Ohlin, Lloyd E.
  1960 *Delinquency and Opportunity: A Theory of Delinquent Gangs.* New York: Free Press.

Cohen, Albert K.
  1955 *Delinquent Boys: The Culture of the Gang.* New York: Free Press.

Cohen, Albert K. and Short, James F., Jr.
  1958 "Research in delinquent subcultures." *Journal of Social Issues*, Summer, 14:20–36.

Dinitz, Simon et al.
  1962 "Delinquency vulnerability: a cross group and longitudinal analysis." *American Sociological Reveiw*, August, 27:515–517.

Elliot, Delbert S.
  1966 "Delinquency, school attendance and dropout." *Social Problems*, Winter, 13:306–318.

Empey, LaMar T.
  1956 "Social class and occupational aspiration: a comparison of absolute and relative measurement." *American Sociological Review*, December, 21:703–709.

Empey, LaMar T. and Lubeck, Steven G.

　1968　"Conformity and deviance in the 'situation of company.'" *American Sociological Review*, October, *33*:760–774.

　1971　*Explaining Delinquency*. Lexington: D.C. Health.

Erickson, Maynard L.

　1973　"Group violations, socioeconomic status and official delinquency." *Social Forces*, September, *52*:41–52.

Erickson, Maynard L. and Empey, LaMar T.

　1963　"Court records, undetected delinquency, and decision making." *Journal of Criminal Law, Criminology , and Police Science*, December, *54*:456–469.

　1965　"Class position, peers and delinquency." *Sociology and Social Research*, April, *49*:268–282.

Erickson, Maynard L. and Jensen, Gary F.

　1976　"Delinquency is still group behavior!" Department of Sociology, University of Arizona. (Unpublished).

Gold, Martin

　1966　"Undetected delinquent behavior." *Journal of Research in Crime and Delinquency*, January, *3*:27–46.

　1963　*Status Forces in Delinquent Boys*. Ann Arbor: Institute for Social Research, University of Michigan.

Gordon, Robert A. et al.

　1963　"Values and gang delinquency." *American Journal of Sociology*, September, *LXVIX*:109–128.

Gould, R.

　1941　"Some sociological determinants of goal striving." *Journal of Social Psychology*, May, *13*:461–473.

Hindelang, Michael J.

　1973　"Causes of delinquency: a partial relication and extension." *Social Problems*, Spring, *20*:471–487.

Hirschi, Travis

　1969　*Causes of Delinquency*. Berkeley: University of California Press.

Illinois Institute for Junvenile Research

　1972　*Juvenile Delinquency in Illinois*. Chicago: Illinois Department of Mental Health.

Klein, Malcolm W. and Crawford, Lois Y.

　1967　"Groups, gangs and cohesiveness." *Journal of Research in Crime and Delinquency*, January, *1*:63–75.

Kobrin, Solomon

　1951　"The conflict of values in delinquency areas." *American Sociological Review*, October, *16*:653–661.

Kobrin, Solomon, Puntil, Joseph and Peluso, Emil
   1967 "Criteria of status among street corner groups." *Journal of Research in Crime and Delinquency*, January, 4:98–118.

Marris, Peter and Rein, Martin
   1973 *Dilemmas of Social Reform* (2nd ed.). Chicago: Aldine.

Matza, David
   1964 *Delinquency and Drift*. New York: John Wiley.

Merton, Robert K.
   1938 "Social structure and anomie." *American Sociological Review*, 3:672–682.

   1957 *Social Theory and Social Structure* (2nd ed.). New York: Free Press.

   1968 *Social Theory and Social Structure* (Enlarged ed.). New York: Free Press.

Miller, Walter B.
   1958 "Lower-class culture as a generating milieu of gang delinquency." *Journal of Social Issues*, Summer, 14:51–119.

   1965 "Violent crimes in city gangs." *Annals of the American Academy of Political and Social Science*, March, 342:105–115.

Moynihan, Daniel P.
   1969 *Maximum Feasible Misunderstanding: Community Action in the War on Poverty*. New York: Free Press.

Piven, F. F. and Cloward, Richard A.
   1971 *Regulating the Poor*. New York: Pantheon Press.

Polk, Kenneth and Halferty, David S.
   1966 "Adolescence, commitment and delinquency." *Journal of Research in Crime and Delinquency*, July, 4:82–96.

Polk, Kenneth and Schafer, Walter E. (Eds.)
   1972 *School and Delinquency*. Englewood Cliffs, N.J.: Prentice Hall.

Quicker, John C.
   1974 "The effect of goal discrepancy on delinquency." *Social Problems*, October, 22:76–86.

Reiss, Albert J., Jr., and Rhodes, Albert L.
   1961 "The distribution of juvenile delinquency in the social class structure." *American Sociological Review*, October, 26:720–732.

Short, James F., Jr.
   1963 "Introduction to abridged edition." Frederick M. Thrasher, *The Gang*. Chicago: University of Chicago Press.

Short, James F., Jr.
   1975 "The natural history of an applied theory: differentail opportunity and mobilization for youth." Pp. 193–210 in N.J. Demerath, III, et al. (Eds.), *Social Policy and Sociology*. New York: Academic Press.

Short, James F., Jr. and Strodtbeck, Fred L.

  1965   *Group Process and Gang Delinquency.* Chicago: University of Chicago Press.

Spergel, Irving

  1961   "An exploratory research in delinquent subculture." *Social Service Review*, March, 35:33–47.

Stinchcombe, Arthur L.

  1964   *Rebellion in High School.* Chicago: Quadrangle Books.

Toby, Jackson, and Toby, Marcia L.

  1962   "Low school status as a predisposing factor in subcultural delinquency." New Brunswick: Rutgers University. (Mimeo).

Yablonsky, Lewis

  1959   "The delinquent gang as a near-group." *Social Problems*, Fall, 7:108–117.

12

SYMBOLIC INTERACTIONIST THEORY

Symbolic interactionist theory grows out of the larger field of social psychology which is shared both by sociologists and psychologists. This fact gives us some clue as to its character. Like other theorists, symbolic interactionists believe that parental training is important and that broad cultural standards affect behavior. But they do not believe that children are cast into a permanent mold by either set of forces. Instead, they theorize that human behavior reflects a changing concept of self. Initially, children acquire a view of themselves based upon their relations with their parents. Over time, however, these views change, acquiring new forms as the children interact with new groups and learn new definitions for behavior. Because of this unique perspective, therefore, symbolic interactionist theory has ways for locating the motive for delinquency and for defining human nature and social order that are different from other theories.

These differences can be illustrated by recalling the major premises of other theories. While control theory suggests that the motive for delinquent behavior lies in a human nature that tends to be antisocial, cultural deviance and strain theories assume just the opposite; namely, that human nature is social and that the motive for delinquent behavior lies in the organization of society and the cultural adaptations which people make to that organization. In opposition to both of these perspectives, symbolic interactionists view human nature and social order as opposite sides of the same coin. Neither is permanent; both are plastic and subject to change. On one hand, individuals are constantly being modified, taking on the expectations and points of view of the people with whom they interact in intimate small groups. On the other hand, these same individuals contribute to the process of change, helping to shape the groups of which they are a part. Thus, it is out of this ongoing process of interaction that the motive for delinquent behavior arises, not out of permanent antisocial impulses or broad cultural imperatives that require it. Furthermore, since any individual participates in intimate groups in several different settings, the roles he or she plays will often by inconsistent and conflicting. For example, a high school girl who is known as a pot-smoking, makeout artist among her friends would not exhibit the same kind of "self" at home. The self conception and rationalizations that make such a role acceptable in one group of intimates would not be acceptable in another.

This is a significant point of view because it not only implies a human nature that is malleable, but suggests that the social order is conflicted; that is, that society is not organized by a monolithic set of conventional values on which there is universal consensus. Rather, all people are exposed to deviant as well as to conformist traditions. Both are a part of culture, and people are aware of them. Whether or not they are delinquent, therefore, will depend upon the kinds of groups in which they participate on an intimate basis. If one or more is a delinquent group, it may provide the individual with all the justifications he or she needs for violating the law. If none is delinquent, conformist traditions will be supported. In short, symbolic interactionist theory assumes three things: (1) that human nature is plastic and changing; (2) that the social order presents deviant as well as conformist guides for behavior; and (3) that the motive for delinquency resides in the rationalizations and techniques supplied by intimate, personal groups.

Origins

Delinquency was first constructed in this way by Edwin H. Sutherland in 1939. But, as a broader theory of human behavior, symbolic interactionism owes its origins to others. The first was Charles H. Cooley (1902), a sociologist who first penned his ideas at the turn of the century. As Cooley observed his own children, he concluded that they began to develop a self-image very early in life. It was his opinion, however, that this image is not something with which the child is born. Rather, it is the product of involvement and communication with others. It emerges, first, as the result of interaction within the family and, then, is further developed in play groups, the school, and other social settings.

In the first years of life, the voices, facial expressions, and moods of parents are largely indistinguishable from other phenomena surrounding infants. Gradually, however, young children begin to attach special significance to other people and to perceive themselves as being different. They also become aware that others are judging them, responding positively to certain behaviors and negatively to others. They begin to realize that these responses are patterned and that their conduct and appearance are evaluated in terms of predictable standards. Over time, therefore, children learn to make increasingly significant judgments about themselves and the reactions of others to them. A *self-image* emerges that is primarily the product of group involvement and communication. Without group involvement, in fact, the human self might never develop.

In order to illustrate the importance of interpersonal interaction, Cooley used an interesting metaphor. He likened the responses of others to our selves as a mirror. Just as we can look in the mirror and be pleased or displeased with what we see, so we can judge ourselves in terms of the way people respond to us. We develop what Cooley called the *looking glass self*. We imagine how others perceive our appearance, our clothes, our manners, and our behaviors and evaluate ourselves accordingly. If the reflection is a favorable one, we are pleased, but, if it is an unfavorable one, we are mortified and attempt to change our image. This image, in other words, is a social product, the result of the responses of others to us.

This way of describing the emergence of the self represented a radical departure from the biological and psychodynamic theories that prevailed during Cooley's life. It suggested that human nature is the product of social interaction, not something that is due to biological endowment or to fixed, but unconscious, psychological drives. To Cooley, it was the imagination of oneself which a person develops in response to the social mirror that constitutes the essence of human nature. Furthermore, the process by which the looking glass self is developed does not end in childhood. As the person moves through successive stages in the life cycle—from childhood, to adolescence, to adulthood, and, then, to old age—the social mirror reflects an ever-changing image. According to this perspective, then, human nature is not a fixed attribute, social or antisocial, but is something that is capable of reflecting many faces.

The symbolic element

It fell to another theorist, George Herbert Mead (1934), to expand upon the symbolic element in symbolic interactionism. Mead stressed the importance of symbols as the basis for human interaction and communication. A symbol is a word or a gesture that is a shorthand way of representing something else like an idea, a person, or a thing. Some symbols are amazingly complex. Take the word "culture." Though it is now familiar to the average lay person, this single symbol is used to represent the total way of life of a people—their beliefs, knowledge, values, technology, tastes, and prejudices. We take for granted the idea that the contrasting life-styles of Eskimos, Turks, or Chinese are due in large part to their indoctrination into contrasting "cultures."

The significant thing about such complex symbols is that only humans, among all the animals, are capable of using them to construct reality. Once a symbol has become conventional in a given group, each person using it can experience the same general meaning from it. Even more important, a person can respond to a symbol in much the same way as one does to the thing or idea it represents. Once having learned what a "cow" is, one does not have to see it again when the symbol is used. The three-letter word will do.

Mead was concerned with symbols because, collectively, they become language, and language is essential to the process of communication by which human nature is developed. Other animals can communicate on a primitive level, but only through the use of language can people acquire a concept of self, engage in systematic thought, or deal in complex and abstract ideas. The point is that language becomes the means by which the world view of children is constructed. The way symbols are tied together and the visions they conjure up are crucial in determining not only how they see other things and people, but how they see themselves.

Like Cooley, Mead also believed that the self is not a fixed entity but is something that is subject to change. At the same time, he was somewhat unclear on just how plastic the human self is. According to one interpretation Mead saw the self as a process and not as a structure; that is, it is something that is constantly being shaped and reshaped, something that is never cast into a permanent mold as some other theories might suggest (Cf. Blumer, 1969:62). According to a second interpretation, however, Mead considered the self to be both a process *and* a structure; it is not something that is totally plastic. Rather, it is the result of the accumulation of one's experiences as well as of the result of recent social interactions. While the self does change some over time, therefore, it also develops a structure of attitudes and perspectives that are relatively permanent and which do move with the individual from group to group (Mead, 1974:158–174).

This is not an idle issue because of its importance in trying to understand human behavior. If we are inclined to believe that people are totally plastic, then we can determine what they might do only by looking at their immediate situation, who is present, and how the interaction of the moment results in a particular outcome. Little could be gained by assuming that an individual's behavior will be relatively constant from situation to situation or that it can be predicted in advance.

If, by contrast, we believe that people are both a structure *and* a process, attempts to understand their behavior would have to be concerned with that which is relatively permanent in their makeups as well as with the outcomes of their interactions with others. Both would help to determine how they behave.

As will be seen later, the validity and implications of symbolic theory are affected by the way this issue is resolved. For now, however, the thing to be remembered is that this body of theory, much more than others, stresses the importance of seeing the human being as an active organism which, on the one hand, is subject to modification by social interaction but which, on the other, contributes to change in the self conceptions of others. In other words, the social relations and self conceptions of a particular group of people will reflect a continuous process of change in which new ideas and courses of action emerge which may not have existed before they came together.

The theory of differential association

When Edwin H. Sutherland applied these ideas to crime and delinquency, his theory was a direct reflection of the thinking of theorists like Cooley and Mead. He considered their points of view to be far superior to the views of biological and psychodynamic control theorists against whom he was a powerful and persuasive anatagonist. His theory consists of nine propositions which have remained unchanged since the fourth edition of his *Principles of Criminology* which was published in 1947, three years before his death. However, later statements by Donald R. Cressey, Sutherland's student and coauthor, have helped to clarify the propositions. As stated by both authors, therefore, they are as follows (Cf. Sutherland and Cressey, 1955:77–80):

1.   *Criminal behavior is learned.*   People are not inherently antisocial, nor do they possess permanent personlaity traits that predispose them to delinquent behavior. Rather, if they violate the law, it is because they have learned to do so.

2.   *Criminal behavior is learned in interaction with other persons in a process of communication.* "What . . . we should study if we are going to establish a theory for explaining criminal conduct is, in a word, *words*" (Cressey, 1965:90). It is not enough to say that delinquent acts are made possible by the absence of effective constraints over human nature, as control theory suggests. People require positive motives or justifications for deviant behavior. These are supplied by symbols, by language. Gestures and nonverbal communication contribute to the process but are much less important. It is the symbolic learning of deviant values, attitudes, norms, and techniques that leads a person to commit delinquent acts.

3.   *The principal part of the learning of criminal behavior occurs within intimate personal groups.* "The person (personality) is not separable from the social relationships in which [the individual] lives. . . . Criminal behavior is, like other behaviors, attitudes, beliefs, and values which a person exhibits, the *property of groups*, not of individuals" (Cressey, 1965:90). Consequently, such impersonal sources of learning as movies, television, and newspapers are relatively unimportant. While they might provide the individual with some delinquent ideas, these ideas are not likely to be carried out unless they receive the sanction and support of an intimate group of associates.

4.   *When criminal behavior is learned, the learning includes (a) techniques of committing the crime, which are sometimes very complicated, sometimes very simple; (b) the specific direction of motives, drives, rationalizations, and attitudes.* People do not become mechanics, school teachers, or quarterbacks until they learn the necessary techniques. The same is true of delinquents. It takes training to hot-wire a car, to become a successful shoplifter, or even to smoke marijuana properly. Even more important, the commission of illegal acts requires the development of appropriate motives, attitudes, and rationalizations. These are derived from group definitions which make delinquent behavior ac-

ceptable: "Everybody cheats. Why shouldn't we?" "What your parents don't know won't hurt them." "Stealing from a crooked company like this is no crime." "Those guys had it coming to them." Without rationalizations like these, delinquent behavior is not likely to occur. "It is the presence or absence of a specific learned verbal label in a specific situation which determines the criminality or noncriminality of a particular person" (Cressey, 1952:44).

5. *The specific direction of motives and drives is learned from definitions of the legal codes as favorable or unfavorable.*   Sutherland (1956:20–21) called his theory a "theory of differential association." He did this, he said, because the social order is characterized by cultural conflict. Reactions to the criminal law are not uniform in any modern society. Instead, people associate in groups which put them in contact with two kinds of culture, one kind whose norms favor adherence to law and the other which encourages law violation. This is "differential association." Individuals are confronted with mixed definitions for behavior, some conformist, some deviant. Whether they become delinquent, therefore, will depend on what they learn from the particular groups they encounter, and how those groups define the legal codes. If they define them favorably, the person will be motivated to be law-abiding. If they define them unfavorably, delinquent motives will be supplied.

6. *A person becomes delinquent because of an excess of definitions favorable to violation of law over definitions unfavorable to violation of law.*   This is the proposition that sets forth the crucial condition for delinquent behavior to occur. If persons become delinquent, it is because their contacts with delinquent patterns exceed their contacts with ones that are nondelinquent. Some individuals, in fact, are almost completely isolated from antidelinquent groups and definitions. Hence, delinquent behavior on their parts is a virtual certainty since there is nothing to counter the delinquent self concepts, values, and norms which their groups perpetuate.

7. *Differential associations may vary in frequency, duration, priority, and intensity.*   These four elements explain the nature and effects of association in different groups. Sutherland did not explain them well, but, presumably, "frequency" refers to how often a person associates with delinquent groups, while "duration" refers to the length of the associations. Hence, the greater the frequency and/or the duration of delinquent associations, the more likely delinquent conduct will follow. "Priority", meanwhile, has to do with the time in life when delinquent associations begin—the earlier they develop, the more likely they will

persist. Finally, "intensity" has to do "with such things as the prestige of the source of a criminal or anticriminal pattern and with emotional reactions related to the associations" (Sutherland and Cressey, 1955:78). If a delinquent group has high prestige and is emotionally satisfying to its members, the more likely its members are to be delinquent.

8. *The process of learning criminal behavior by association with criminal and anticriminal patterns involves all the mecahnisms that are involved in any other learning.* Sutherland considered the meaning of this proposition to be self-evident; namely, that the same mechanisms that are involved in learning nondelinquent behavior—reward, punishment, imitation, coercion, or search for self-acceptance—are involved in learning delinquent behavior.

9. *While criminal behavior is an expression of general needs and values, it is not explained by those general needs and values since noncriminal behavior is an expression of the same needs and values.* In striking contrast to strain theorists, Sutherland argued that the pursuit of money, success, and prestige does not help to explain delinquent behavior. He put it this way:

> Thieves generally steal in order to secure money, but likewise honest laborers work in order to secure money. The attempts by many scholars to explain criminal behavior by general drives and values, such as the happiness principle, striving for social status, the money motive, or frustration, have been and must continue to be futile since they explain lawful behavior as completely as they explain criminal behavior (Sutherland and Cressey, 1955:79).

In short, delinquent behavior cannot be explained by reference to the drive for status, money, or success since these also explain conformity. Rather, it is differential association and the learning of delinquent motives and rationalizations in small, intimate groups that make the difference.

Implications and impact on policy

Sutherland's way of constructing delinquency is more optimistic than most of the theories we have discussed thus far. In contrast to control theories, for example, it suggests that people may be easily affected by others. They are not cast into psychological or biological molds that are relatively impervious to outside influence. Instead, they should be changeable because they are so subject to the opinions and values of others. If one wants to reduce delinquency, moreover, one does not have to change an entire society, as strain or cultural deviance theories suggest. Rather, the chief task is that of paying attention to the small groups in which children associate and insuring that prosocial values are constantly taught and reinforced.

Despite these implications, Sutherland said relatively little about them, leaving their discussion to Cressey. He has expanded upon them in considerable detail (1954; 1955; 1965). He suggests that if delinquent behavior is the result of deviant motives, values, and rationalizations acquired in intimate groups then intimate groups should be used to change that behavior. Indeed, one of the most significant implications of interactionist theory is its suggestion that the practice of keeping delinquents separate from nondelinquents in detention centers and correctional institutions may do more to encourage delinquent behavoir than to discourage it. When they are isolated from law-abiding juveniles and locked up only with each other, the strength of delinquent norms, rationalizations, and identities can only increase.

Interactionist theory, in other words, lends strength to the common-sense assumption that separate institutions for delinquents can only become schools of crime. If we want delinquents to become like nondelinquents, the two groups should be reintegrated, not kept apart. It is people who view themselves as deviant from whom delinquents should be separated; they require associates who are confirmed law abiders. Were the two groups mixed, the goal would be to have nondelinquents substitute words which define delinquent conduct as undesirable, illegal, and immoral for the deviant symbols which delinquents use to justify and make illegal behavior acceptable. Offenders must learn that a delinquent self-image is *bad* and that criminal conduct is *wrong*.

Despite the theoretical attractiveness of mixing a few delinquents in a strongly conventional group, Cressey seems to prefer a second alternative—that of trying to change delinquents by altering the symbolic structure and beliefs of their present prodelinquent groups. He seems to feel that efforts to reintegrate delinquents with nondelinquents would be impractical. Community leaders and conventional parents would not stand for it; they would fear that good children would be corrupted by bad ones, rather than the reverse. But there is an additional reason why Cressey takes this position.

He also argues that delinquents and criminals should be more effective as change agents than are people who have never been serious offenders, particularly such professional reformers as social workers, group therapists, or probation and parole officers. Delinquents have better rapport with each other, they trust each other more, and they have a greater sense of belonging to the same group.

Even more important, any delinquent who attempts to change someone else is more likely to be changed himself than he is to change the other person. Cressey (1955:119) calls this "retroflexive reformation." If a delinquent is serious in his attempts to reform others, he must automatically accept the common purpose of the reformation process, identify himself closely with others engaged in it, and grant prestige to those who succeed in it. In so doing, he becomes a genuine member of the reformation group and, in the process, is alienated from his previous prodelinquent group. A good example of a setting in which this is presumed to occur is in Alcoholics Anonymous. That organization depends upon alcoholics, not outsiders, to "cure" other alcoholics.

These principles, says Cressey, have not been applied on any wide scale in correctional organizations because of their adherence to other theories of delinquency: (1) to classical deterrence theory which suggests that punishment will reform offenders and deter others; and (2) to psychodynamic theory which stresses individualized treatment and the need to alter unconscious drives, pathological fixations, and psychological frustrations. Even when group therapy has been used, group leaders have been concerned more with changing the psychological makeup of the individual than with changing the values, standards, and rationalizations of the group with which he identifies. The two are quite different things. In traditional group therapy, the goal is to give offenders insight into the unconscious forces that are presumed to be at the roots of their separate disorders. Attention is focused upon psychodynamics and upon treating the individual in the group rather than through it. By contrast, Cressey's principles suggest that the group, itself, should become both the target and the medium of change. The assumption is that, once the group becomes antidelinquent, individual change will follow.

Although these ideas have not been widely applied in public agencies, they have been used in small, private, or experimental programs. Perhaps the best known is Synanon, a program for drug addicts run by drug addicts (Yablonsky, 1965). Synanon was founded in 1958 by a member of Alcoholics Anonymous. Under his direction, a few addicts began living together voluntarily in an abandoned store. Since that time, the organization has expanded to several different cities and now owns its own residential property and several different businesses which its members run.

Synanon is an ideal example of Cressey's suggestion that offenders should be isolated from people who view themselves as delinquents and surrounded by those who view themselves as antidelinquent. Addicts are free to join Synanon only if they are willing to adhere to a stringent set of group demands: to give up drugs, to have their hair cut off, to give up all their money, to take up permanent residence at Synanon, and to sever all former ties that might prevent the Synanon group from assimilating them entirely. All personal desires must be subverted to the antidelinquent, antidrug group.

The following excerpt from an admission interview illustrates the kinds of language used at Synanon to stress the stupidity of drug addition and to introduce a sense of guilt over it (Cf. Volkman and Cressey, 1963:132):

> We ask him things like "What do you want from us?" "Don't you think you're an idiot or insane?" "Doesn't it sound insane for you to be running around the alleys stealing money from others so's you can go and stick something up your arm?" . . . We tell him, "We don't need you." "You need *us*." And if we figure he's only halfway with us, we'll chop off his hair.

Synanon first helps addicts to kick their habits and then requires that they participate in regular group meetings as well as to perform other tasks when they are able. They may remain at Synanon so long as they stay away from crime, drugs, and alcohol. Indeed, Synanon is unrelenting in its implementation of the principle that no other goal in life is so important as becoming a noncriminal, nonaddict.

Other examples of experimental programs which have applied Cressey's principles of symbolic interactionism are Highfields (McCorkle, Elias, and Bixby, 1958), the Provo Experiment (Empey and Erickson, 1972), and the Silverlake Experiment (Empey and Lubeck, 1971b). All of these programs, however, were for convicted delinquents, not for volunteer addicts. And, though they were like Synanon in their attempts to develop an antidelinquent group culture, they were different in other ways. First, delinquents did not join them voluntarily. Instead, they were assigned by the juvenile court. Secondly, these programs were started and run by conventional adults who, though they gave considerably more power to the delinquent group to make decisions and to enforce norms than do conventional programs, were still officially responsible for what went on. Thirdly, these experiments could not use some of the coercive techniques that Synanon used such as requiring delinquents to cut off their hair, demanding money from them, or requiring that they give up all former associates. Even then, one of the programs—the Provo Experiment—was accused of using "Communist brain-washing techniques" because of the methods it did use (Empey and Rabow, 1962; Cf. Gordon, 1962). Finally, unlike Synanon where addicts might take up lifelong residence, the goal of these programs was to get delinquents back home, in school, or on the job as soon as possible. Indeed, in the Provo Experiment, delinquents continued to live at home and came to the program only during the day. With all these differences, however, there was evidence of support for some of Cressey's ideas.

One of these ideas, as expressed by a delinquent himself, was that offenders may be better change agents than official reformers (Empey and Erickson, 1972:58–61):

Boys: Boys know more about themselves than grownups do. The first couple months [in this program] don't do any good. Then you find out that the meetin' knows you better than you know yourself. They can tell when you're lyin'. They can tell you things about yourself an' find out what your problems are. . . I jus' don't like to listen to adults lecturing. . . it is boring as hell. All the help I got, I got from other guys in the meetin'—nine other guys instead of one stupid adult talkin' to you. I felt they done the same things I done, an' know exactly how I feel, an' why I do them things.

Another plausible generalization from Cressey's approach is that a delinquent group which makes use of the principle of symbolic interactionism might be more successful in producing change than traditional punishment:

Boy: I mentioned that being locked up won't help a guy out of trouble. Understanding why you got there might, but the jail itself won't. You have to get the understanding, an' that comes in group meetings.

Adult: Looking back, did the boys in your group do anything that helped you?

Boy: They helped me most when they put me in jail for not showin' up. When I got out, I said I wanted to get drunk that night an' the meeting talked to me about it.

Adult: How did that help?

Boy: Well, for one thing, I didn't go out an' get drunk. They talked to me quite a bit. They pointed out to me I was playing a tough role, an' that going on a blast now was the same ol' thing with me.

Adult: So what happened?

Boy: I can't say I was a goodie-goodie right off, but one thing that stuck with me was when they showed me that how I was acting was the way I was talking and treating my mother and my girl. I was being a hard-ass. I thought a lot of my girl an' I saw I was only makin' things worse, not better, Her ol' man don't like me anyhow, an' gettin' drunk wouldn't help (Empey and Erickson, 1972:57).

Besides impressionistic comments like these, systematic research has also indicated that a group-oriented program may produce a greater sense of commitment to correctional goals than do traditional programs. The members of such programs are less likely to be split into competing adult and delinquent groups and are more likely to reinforce antidelinquent values and points of view (Shichor and Empey, 1974). Yet, despite such findings, there is also evidence that the principles of symbolic interactionism are something less than a panacea.

Some limitations. Programs which develop a strong and demanding antidelinquent group are unable to hold onto many potential members. At Synanon, 72 percent of 263 persons who joined that organization during a three-year period dropped out after a short stay. Fifty-nine percent of the dropouts left with one month, 90 percent within three months (Volkman and Cressey, 1963:142). In the Silverlake Experiment, the same phenomenon was observed among delinquents, though it was not so marked (Empey and Lubeck, 1971b:chap. 10). Located in the open community, this program had 37 percent of its members run away, most of them during the first month or two of residence. As a result the findings suggest that delinquents are not so malleable as symbolic interactionist theory suggests. Many persist in old patterns of behavior and do not readily accept prosocial values from their peers.

Likewise, group-centered programs may not be strikingly more successful in inducing criminals and delinquents to refrain permanently from new offenses. At Synanon, only about 29 percent of the addicts who joined the organization remained free from drugs for any appreciable length of time. However, the longer they stayed there, the higher their success rate became—after staying one month, 48 percent remained drug free; after three months, 66 percent; and after seven months, 88 percent (Volkman and Cressey, 1963:142). The evidence seems to indicate that if a person is successful in actually becoming a member of an anticriminal, antidrug group the probability is increased that he or she will remain prosocial. The problem, however, is that in the early days of Synanon at least approximately 7 out of 10 members did not stay long enough to become committed to the program.

Among delinquents in the Silverlake and Provo Experiments, longrun success rates were much higher (Empey and Lubeck, 1971b: chap. 12; Empey and Erickson, 1972: chaps. 9–10). Approximately 60 percent had no recorded arrests after being released for one year, and around 80 percent had no more than one arrest. Furthermore, their commission of serious offenses declined markedly following group involvement. Yet, when the delinquents in all these experiments were compared with control groups of delinquents assigned to regular probation or traditional places of incarceration, their postprogram success rates were not markedly higher. The only time they remained significantly less delinquent was when they were still in the experimental program and still members of the antidelinquent group (Empey and Erickson, 1972: chap. 5). Once removed from it, their behavior was much like that of delinquents who had never had contact with it.

Policy implications. Such findings raise some serious questions about the relevance of symbolic interaction theory for public policy. Early in the chapter, it was noted that according to interactionist theory the human self can be viewed in two ways: (1) as nothing more than a process that undergoes constant modification, or (2) as both a structure and a process in which the self retains considerable continuity. The research findings described above do not totally resolve the issue.

On the one hand, many of the members of Synanon and of the Provo and the Silverlake Experiments resisted involvement in prosocial groups. They were not easily changed; they seemed to possess self-concepts that were rather structured and resistant to change. On the other hand, those who did become participating members in these programs were not much more inclined than nongroup members to remain faithful to group standards once they left the program's influence. This finding, therefore, could be said to confirm the plasticity of human nature. What success Synanon has had, for example, seems to be based on the necessity for addicts to remain in the program all of their lives if they are to remain free from drugs. They can never plan on leaving it because, once they do, they are easily converted back to drug use.

Given this set of inconsistent findings, one policy alternative would be to organize more programs like Synanon. Offenders would choose to live voluntarily in their own miniature communities, totally isolated from the rest of society. But such an alternative, particularly for children and adolescents, is not likely to receive public endorsement. Not only is it reminiscent of the ideas that led to the asylums of the 19th century, but it is contrary to the democratic values that govern our concept of childhood. Furthermore, it is not likely that anything approaching a majority of offenders, if given a choice, would choose this alternative.

A second alternative would be to reconsider the way Sutherland's theory has been implemented, particularly Cressey's suggestion that offenders are the best change agents. It will be recalled that the theory could just as well be interpreted as suggesting that offenders should be totally separated from other offenders and integrated into prosocial groups instead. What if delinquents were placed on an individual basis into conventional groups in schools, neighborhoods, and places of recreation rather than in correctional programs with other offenders? Two possible outcomes are suggested.

First, nondelinquent groups might be confronted with the need for some kind of change on their parts. Cressey's reading of the principles of symbolic interactionism overlooks this need. If the individual and the group are two sides of the same coin, then group as well as individual change is implied. Rather than being a source of stigma for delinquents, conventional groups are required which will accept them as equals and work with them on that basis. Secondly, delinquents might not only encounter an excess of definitions unfavorable to violation of law in normal group settings, but they would have a greater chance to participate in activities that might help to reinforce those definitions. The evidence seems clear that words, attitudes, and rationalizations alone will not do the trick. This would be particularly true for those delinquents, described by control and strain theories, who lack social skills, who are behind in their educational development, or who lack access to the means for success. These factors require attention as well.

There has been a growing attempt in recent years to address some of these problems by locating correctional programs in the open community. Yet, officials still remain more concerned with changing offenders than with changing the networks of adolescent relations on local neighborhoods, schools, and clubs so that delinquents might be integrated more effectively with nondelinquents. Consequently, if the implications of symbolic interaction theory are to be assessed more thoroughly, public policies are needed which would cease separating official delinquents from conventional adolescents and help to reduce the sea of social distance which still separates these two groups.

Scientific legacy

There are two ways to view the scientific legacy of Sutherland's theory of differential association: (1) the extent to which it meets scientific criteria for a good theory and is supported by evidence; and (2) its impact on the scientific construction of delinquency.

Scientific adequacy

According to Sutherland, the theory of differential association was designed to explain why an individual becomes delinquent.[1] If it is to accomplish that task, however, it must possess a set of propositions that enable one to predict delinquent behavior under a clearly specified set of conditions, and it must be readily amenable to scientific test. Most criminologists agree that Sutherland's theory does not meet these criteria.

It does not provide a clear statement on the process by which an individual becomes delinquent. While it stresses the existence of competing norms in the community and suggests that a person learns to be delinquent through excessive contact with delinquent patterns, it does not provide a set of deductive statements indicating how this comes about: how membership in delinquent groups occurs, how delinquent behavior is learned and reinforced, or at what point definitions favorable to violation of law override defintions unfavorable to it and lead to actual delinquent behavior. The propositions, as presently stated, simply do not permit one to predict this sequential series of events. As a result, Cressey (1969:420) suggests that Sutherland's propositions should be "viewed as a set of directives about the kinds of things that ought to be included in a theory of criminality, rather than as an actual statement of theory." They are a valuable starting point for the development of precise theory, but by themselves they do not yet accomplish that task.

The theory of differential association does not lend itself to rigorous scientific test (Cf. Short, 1960). For example, how does one determine when a person has been subjected to an "excess of definitions" favorable to violation of law? Can it be shown that this "excess" actually precedes delinquent behavior or that all people define an "excess" in the same way? In the same vein, Sutherland said that "differential associations vary in frequency, duration, priority, and intensity." Yet, he neither defined these terms carefully nor did he indicate how, when combined in some way, their relationship to delinquent conduct could be measured. Indeed, he noted that a "formula" by which this could be accomplished would be extremely difficult to develop (Sutherland and Cressey, 1955:79). He was right. No one has been able to construct one.

---

[1] A host of investigators have raised questions about the theory of differential association. For a comprehensive review of their questions and of a critique of them by a proponent of the theory, see Donald R. Cressey (1969). The following analysis is indebted to that review.

Drawing upon the broader field of symbolic interactionism, the theory of differential association suggests that beliefs, attitudes, and rationalizations provide the motive for delinquent behavior. Yet, an increasing number of studies find that beliefs and attitudes are poor predictors of actual human conduct (Deutscher, 1973). Words do not always lead to action. As a result, there is reason to suspect that verbal symbols and attitudes alone do not constitute the only reasons for law-violating acts. If people often behave in ways that are contrary to their expressed attitudes and values, then other factors—a lack of stake in conformity, sense of strain, or, in the case of heroin users, physical addiction—may also be important.

In the same vein, the theory of differential association provides little help in explaining the delinquent conduct of the lone individual who invents and carries out an illegal act by himself or who, in a fit of rage, attacks a loved one. There are many instances in which delinquent acts cannot be traced to a former group of associates who endorse and teach this kind of behavior.

The theory of differential association suggests that the motives for delinquent behavior are solely the product of membership in delinquent groups. Virtually every other theory, by contrast, suggests that motives, at least in part, are due to other factors: Control theory emphasized the absence of a stake in conformity; cultural deviance theories stress class position and the way society is organized; and strain theory concentrates on blockage of opportunity. In each instance, some condition in the life of the individual is thought to motivate *both* delinquent behavior *and* membership in delinquent groups as a method of solving some problem of adjustment.

These theoretical differences are most apparent when one contrasts control and differential association theories. Most control theorists argue that membership in delinquent groups occurs only *after* an individual becomes delinquent, not before (Glueck and Glueck, 1950:163–164; Hirschi, 1969:135–138). In other words, it is only following their involvement in delinquency that delinquents, like birds of a feather, flock together. According to this view then, their "flocking" is a by-product of their delinquent behavior, not the primary cause of it. Delinquents take up with other delinquents because they have already lost their stakes in conformity and because they have already become detached from parents and conventional friends and have no where else to turn for support and confirmation. As a basic cause of delinquent behavior, therefore, peer relations are of secondary importance.

Which explanation is correct, the one suggested by Sutherland or the one suggested by control theorists? Existing evidence suggests that neither is entirely accurate (Hirschi, 1969:152–160; Empey and Lubeck, 1971a:Chap. 9; Jensen, 1972). Both the lack of a stake in conformity and group associations make independent contributions to the commission of delinquent acts; that is, a child's lack of attachment to family and school can lead to delinquent behavior as well as to membership in a delinquent group. Either, or both, may contribute. Hence, even if there is some support for Sutherland's theory in this finding, it certainly does not constitute a full affirmation of it. Factors other than group associations are sources of delinquent behavior.

In summary, then, a number of serious questions have been raised about the scientific adequacy of Sutherland's theory and about symbolic interactionism in general. Like most other explanations of human conduct, both are extremely difficult to verify or to disprove, and both leave many questions unanswered.

Scientific construction of delinquency

Despite the scientific inadequacies of Sutherland's theory, its new and stimulating way of constructing delinquency gave it immense popularity. For an entire generation of sociologically oriented criminologists, his statement, like Darwin's theory of evolution among biologists, became the orienting schema around which new theories were organized. Cohen (1955) and Cloward and Ohlin (1960) drew upon it in constructing their strain theories, particularly the idea that delinquent behavior reflects group norms and support. Indeed, Cloward and Ohlin expressed their indebtedness to Sutherland by dedicating their book to him (along with Robert Merton who had suggested that the disjunction between societal goals and means is likely to produce deviant behavior).

Other criminologists have attempted to reformulate Sutherland's theory to account for some of the criticisms made of it (Cf. De Fleur and Quinney, 1966). Daniel Glaser (1956:440–441) argues that its organizing principle should be "differential identification" rather than "differential association." In essence, his point of view suggests that *"a person pursues criminal behavior to the extent that he identifies himself with real or imaginary persons from whose perspective his criminal behavior seems acceptable"* (p. 440). In other words, Glaser suggests that people often identify with persons or groups with whom they have had little intimate contact. Actual group associations are not necessary. They might identify with a deviant TV hero or a group of peers, though they have had close associations with neither. Although this emphasis upon "identification" is much different than Sutherland's emphasis on "association," it is more consistent with a body of theory which suggests that the roles we play are often dictated by our "reference" groups rather than by the many less important groups in which we hold membership. Only those to which we look for normative direction are those that influence our behavior.

In quite a different way, Burgess and Akers (1966) reformulated Sutherland's theory to make it more consistent with recent developments in psychological learning theory. They attempted to account for research findings which suggest that neither symbolic interaction nor Glaser's differéntial identification are enough by themselves to reinforce delinquent behavior. Other kinds of rewards and punishments must also be present—money, a personal sense of accomplishment, or excitement. Nonetheless, their final set of propositions are like Sutherland's in the sense that they provide a set of orgainizing principles for enlarging the scope of differential association theory rather than a deductive set of statements which would allow one to predict delinquent behavior.

Finally, several theorists have amplified three of Sutherland's basic ideas and have added some new dimensions to them; (1) the idea that the social order is characterized by cultural conflict; (2) the idea that delinquent behavior is an emergent phenomenon; and (3) the idea that verbal symbols provide both the motive and justification for delinquent behavior.

Culture conflict.   Sykes and Matza (1957; 1961) argue that there is a subculture of delinquency in American society but that this subculture is not something that is possessed only by adolescent groups. American culture, they believe, is not a simple puritanism exemplified by middle-class norms. Instead, it is a complex and pluralistic culture in which, among other subcultural traditions, there are "subterranean," deviant traditions. These traditions do not represent ignorance of the law nor even general negation of it. Rather, they have a complex relationship to law that is symbiotic rather than oppositional; that is, they do not represent a separate set of beliefs which distinguish delinquents from other youth or youth from adults. Instead, they are that part of the overall culture which consists of the personal, more deviant, and less publicized version of existing standards for behavior. The two sets of traditions—conventional and deviant—are held simultaneously by almost everyone, and, while certain groups may be influenced more by one than the other, both determine behavior to a considerable degree.

Daniel Bell's (1953) analysis of crime as an American way of life is probably a good illustration of Sykes and Matza's point. Bell notes that Americans are characterized by an "extremism" in morality, yet they also have an "extraordinary" talent for compromise in politics and a "brawling" econmic and social history. These contradictory features form the basis for an intimate and symbiotic relationship between crime and politics, crime and economic growth, and crime and social change, not an oppositional relationship. The tradition of wanting to get ahead by cheating in school or by using any means to succeed in business or politics is no less an ethic than wanting to observe the law.

Illegal acts have been a major means by which a variety of people have achieved the American success ideal and have obtained respectability. Sykes and Matza suggest, therefore, that deviant traditions contribute more than we realize to the behavior of younger as well as older people. Rather than a delinquent subculture being uniquely the property of adolescents, it may have its roots in the broader culture. Everyone is aware of deviant traditions, as Sutherland suggested, and resort to them when it seems expedient to do so.

Emergent quality of delinquent behavior

Though stressing the idea that delinquent acts are a product of social interaction, David Matza (1964) places far less emphasis than did Sutherland on the constraining influences of group relations. He considers the theory of differential association (as well as all other theories in the positivistic tradition) to be too deterministic and calls attention to the uncertain status of adolescents in out society. Given their ambiguous social position, it should not be too surprising that they commit delinquent acts. Law violators may be a little bit out of the ordinary but not by much. Hence, in order to understand their behavior, it is necessary to recognize that they exist in a condition of "drift":

> The image of the delinquent I wish to convey is one of drift; an actor neither compelled nor committed to deeds nor freely choosing them; neither different in any simple or fundamental sense from the law-abiding, nor the same; conforming to certain traditions in American life while partially unreceptive to other more conventional traditions. . . .

> Drift stands midway between freedom and control. . . . The delin-
> quent *transiently* exists in a limbo between convention and crime, re-
> sponding in turn to the demands of each, flirting now with one, now
> with the other, but postponing commitment, evading decision. Thus, he
> drifts between criminal and conventional action (p. 28).

The line of analysis suggested by Matza is consistent with symbolic
interactionism because it asserts that human behavior emerges out of a
continuous process of interaction. But the process suggested by Matza
is far more fluid and open than the one suggested by Sutherland. In
the first place, adolescents have a modicum of choice in deciding
whether to violate the law. In the second place, that choice will be
determined not by some prior set of cause, but by an intermix of factors
present in the situation where a choice is made—who is present, what
the risks are, and so on. According to this view, then, nobody *has* to
be delinquent. If an adolescent does break the law, it will depend upon
a process that is dictated more by immediate circumstance than by conditions that are predetermined by personality, social position, or membership in an intimate group.

Justifications for delinquent behavior. One set of factors that is likely to
affect the choice that is made in the immediate situation is the set of
verbal justifications for delinquent acts so strongly emphasized by symbolic interactionists. Sykes and Matza (1957) argue that by using verbal
symbols and shared rationalizations delinquents are able to make use of
subterranean traditions as a method of "neutralizing" the commission
of delinquent acts. According to Hartung (1965:62–83) these rationalizations make up a "vocabulary of motives" for misconduct. They
not only protect delinquents from self-blame, but precede their deviant
behavior and make it possible. Consider some examples:

Denial of responsibility. Delinquents, no less than conventional
people, are aware of the deterministic character of many theories of
delinquency. Therefore, they use these theories to deny personal responsibility for their delinquent acts. Some humorous but telling verses
from the Broadway musical, *West Side Story*[2], provide an illustration of
this way of neutralizing delinquent conduct.

> Dear, kindly Sergeant Krupke, you gotta understand. It's just our bring-
> ing upke that gets us otta hand. Our mothers all are junkies, our fathers all
> are drunks. Golly, Moses, naturally we're punks. Gee, Officer Krupke,

---

[2] Book by Arthur Laurents. Music by Leonard Bernstein. Lyrics by Stephen Sondheim.
Directed and choreographed by Jerome Robbins.

we're very upset. We never had the love that every child outta get. We ain't no delinquents, we're just misundertood. Deep down inside us there is good. There is good. There is good. There is untapped good.

Yes, Officer Krupke, you're really a slob. This boy don't need a doctor, just a good, honest job. Society played him a terrible trick and, sociologically, he is sick. . . . We are sick. . . . We are sick, sick, sick. . . . We are sociologically sick.

Gee, Officer Krupke, we're down on our knees. 'Cause no one likes a fellow with a social disease. Gee, Officer Krupke, what are we to do? Gee, Officer Krupke, Krup you.

Denial of injury.   Delinquent acts are often defined in popular discourse as harmless "mischief" or as youthful "pranks." Utilizing these popular conceptions, therefore, delinquents often deny that their illegal behavior is injurious. Instead, their grafitti on public buildings is an expression of ethnic identity; bodily injury to a fraternity pledge is youthful hazing; or gang fighting is a private quarrel. "Boys will be boys."

Denial of victim   Moral indignation over a crime may be neutralized by transforming the victim into someone who deserves injury: physical assault on a homosexual, wrecking a schoolroom as revenge on an unfair teacher; theft from a "crooked" store owner; or taking the law into one's own hands in order to punish a "criminal" that the police cannot touch.

Condemning the condemners   Not uncommonly, people who violate the law shift attention from the wrongfulness of their own acts by attacking those who are charged with upholding the law: The police are corrupt; judges take bribes; conventional persons are hypocrites. Such techniques are a means of deflecting moral condemnation and of making others the focus of disapproval.

Appeal to higher loyalties.   Delinquents, like most members of society, are often confronted with a choice between two sets of expectations: those of the larger society and those of close friends or associates. Frequently, they justify violating society's laws by arguing that their loyalty to associates takes precedence over other loyalties: "Never squeal on a friend." "Don't turn on your brother." In a recent dispute over salary raises, off-duty New York policemen mauled a commanding officer who was attempting to guard the home of a police commissioner and prevented on-duty policemen from protecting citizens from bands of marauding youth at Yankee Stadium. The reason: "We've had 3,000 officers laid off in the financial crisis," said an official of the policeman's union. "It's time to draw the line" (*Los Angeles Times*, September 30, 1976). Obviously, appeals to higher loyalties as a method of neutralizing delinquent conduct are so widespread that they can scarcely be said to be the sole property of habitual lawbreakers.

In summary, there are two things about these techniques of neutralization which merit special mention. First, they do not represent a complete rejection of conventional norms. Rather, they are subterranean traditions which come into play as a method of lessening the effectiveness of prosocial norms in circumstances which uncommitted children consider special. They do not intend that rules should be replaced, only that they should not apply in their case. Thus, "[techniques of neutralization] are 'definitions of the situation' [which] represent tangential or glancing blows at the dominant normative system rather than a creation of an opposing ideology" (Sykes and Matza, 1957:69). They are part of a subterranean tradition which interacts constantly with conventional tradition.

Secondly, in order to grasp the significance of the way conventional norms are neutralized by subterranean definitions, we must be aware of verbal symbols, of competing cultural standards, and the kinds of rhetoric which one can often hear in supposedly law-abiding as well as delinquent groups. Habitual lawbreakers are not the only ones who resort to neutralizing statements like the following:

> "It's fuck your buddy week, 52 weeks of the year."
>
> "Do unto others as they would do unto you, only do it first."
>
> "If I don't cop (steal) it . . . somebody else will.
>
> "You know, man, everybody's got their little game." (Schwendinger and Schwendinger, 1967:98).

In a condition of adolescent drift, it is these verbal constructions of the situation that are likely to produce delinquent conduct, not the lasting and relatively permanent causes suggested by other, more deterministic theories.

Short and Strodtbeck have provided some empirical support for these ideas as well as expanding their domain (Cf. chaps. 8; 9; 11). They point out that even among the members of lower-class urban gangs there is considerable verbal support for conventional values: "fidelity in marriage, small families, hard work and thrift, and keeping one's son in school" (p. 250). Yet, these same gang members are often school dropouts, job failures, fathers of illegitimate children for whom they assume no responsibility, and are participants in serious delinquent acts. Why?

Short and Strodtbeck (p. 263) conclude that their behaviors "are not satisfactorily explained by . . . deviance in values or neurotic or irrational tendencies" nor by short-run hedonism. Rather, situational elements play a key part: A serious threat to the status of a gang leader which can be avoided only by his willingness to engage in a successful, albeit delinquent, act; advantages from a delinquent act which can be realized without entailing much risk of detection; or perceived threats from outside groups which might require an aggressive response. In most instances, therefore, delinquent acts occurred in situations where the range of choice is narrowed and focused. But, contrary to the notion that gang members always feel compelled to engage in them, some remain aloof, as Matza theorizes, while others choose the delinquent alternative. Furthermore, it is relatively easy for boys to rationalize either choice by drawing upon readily accessible techniques of neutralization.

Summary and conclusions

Symbolic interactionist theory was instrumental in establishing a new tradition in our social construction of delinquency. It suggested that delinquent behavior is the product of learning and communication in small intimate groups, not something that is determined by biological endowment, by unconscious psychological drives, by poverty, or by small societies of deviants who have their own unique way of life.

1. Assumptions about human nature and social order. Symbolic interactionists assume that human nature is the product of social interaction rather than something with which people are born. The mind and the self develop in response to the processes of communication among small groups of intimate associates. Furthermore, the human self is not a permanent attribute but is something that is undergoing constant change as the person moves through the life cycle or moves from one group to another.

In a sense, the social order is seen as the reverse side of the same coin. Like human nature, it is not a fixed and monolithic set of values characterized by a high degree of consensus. Rather, all members of society are confronted with contrasting and emergent definitions for behavior, some deviant, some conformist. Along with conventional traditions, therefore, there are subterranean traditions to which people may resort depending upon circumstance and the way any situation is defined by significant others.

2. *The underlying logic and content of symbolic interactionist theory.* Sutherland's theory of differential association is the most completely developed criminological version of symbolic interactionism. While it does not provide an adequate description of the process by which an individual becomes delinquent, it does imply something akin to the following sequence.

All young people are confronted with conflicting standards for behavior. Whether or not they become delinquent, however, will depend upon the groups with which they associate. If, by chance, they happen to establish intimate contacts with a group of delinquent companions, they will encounter an excess of definitions favorable to the violation of law, will learn techniques for committing crime, and will acquire the necessary motives and rationalizations by which delinquent behavior is made possible. This sequence might be diagrammed as in figure 12–1.

FIGURE 12–1

Matza suggests, however, that this process will provide a greater degree of choice for the individual and will be more fluid and open than Sutherland suggested.

3. *Policy implications.* Since people are easily subject to change, the theory of differential association implies that delinquent behavior can be unlearned by the same process it is learned. Delinquents should be surrounded by associates who define illegal behavior as immoral and conventional behavior as desirable. Deliberate attempts by public agencies to apply these ideas have not been extensive but when used by private, experimental programs, they have achieved only partial success. Experiments like those at Synanon, Provo, and Silverlake raise questions about the plasticity of the human self and suggest that reinforcements other than words are necessary to sustain conventional behavior.

4. *Logical and empirical adequacy.* Sutherland's theory possesses many inadequacies: it does not provide a clear statement of the process by which a person becomes delinquent; it is very difficult to translate it into propositions that are testable; it fails to account for crimes in which intimate associates and shared definitions are lacking; and it probably overdoes the extent to which rationalizations, by themselves, provide the necessary motive for delinquent behavior. The available evidence suggests that some of the factors stressed by other theories also play an important role in producing delinquent behavior. With all these inadequacies, the theory has had immense impact on the construction of other theories, directing our attention to the possibility that society is characterized by cultural conflict, that delinquent acts are highly situational, and that verbal defintions do help to neutralize delinquent conduct and make it possible.

References

Bell, Daniel
>   1953   "Crime as an American way of life." *Antioch Review*, Summer, *XII*:131–153.

Blumer, Herbert
>   1969   "Sociological implications of the thought of George Herbert Mead." Pp. 62–65 in Blumer (Ed.), *Symbolic Interactionism*. Englewood Cliffs, N.J.: Prentice Hall.

Burgess, Robert L. and Akers, Ronald L.
>   1966   "Differential association-reinforcement theory of criminal behavior." *Social Problems*, Fall, *14*:128–147.

Cloward, Richard A. and Ohlin, Lloyd E.
>   1960   *Delinquency and Opportunity: A Theory of Delinquent Gangs*. New York: Free Press.

Cohen, Albert K.
>   1955   *Delinquent Boys: The Culture of the Gang*. New York: Free Press.

Cooley, Charles H.
>   1902   *Human Nature and the Social Order*. New York: Schocken Books, 1964.

Cressey, Donald R.
>   1952   "Application and verification of the differential association theory." *Journal of Criminal Law, Criminology, and Police Science*, May–June, *LXIII*:43–52.
>   1954   "Contradictory theories in correctional group therapy programs." *Federal Probation*, June, *XVIII*:20–26.

1955   "Changing criminals: the application of the theory of differential association." *American Journal of Sociology*, September, *LXI*:116–120.

1965   "Theoretical foundations for using criminals in the rehabilitation of criminals." *Key Issues*, January, 2:87–101.

1969   "Epidemiology and individual conduct." Pp. 557–577 in Donald R. Cressey and David A. Ward, *Delinquency, Crime and Social Process*. New York: Harper and Row.

DeFleur, Melvin, and Quinney, Richard

1966   "A reformulation of Sutherland's differential association verification." *Journal of Research in Crime and Delinquency*, January, 3:1–11.

Deutscher, Irwin

1973   *What We Say/What We Do: Sentiments and Acts*. Chicago: Scott, Foresman.

Empey, LaMar T. and Erickson, Maynard L.

1972   *The Provo Experiment: Evaluating Community Control of Delinquency*. Lexington: D.C. Heath.

Empey, LaMar T. and Lubeck, Steven G.

1971a   *Explaining Delinquency*. Lexington: D. C. Heath.

1971b   *The Silverlake Experiment: Testing Delinquency Theory and Community Intervention*. Chicago: Aldine.

Empey, LaMar T. and Rabow, Jerome

1962   "Reply to Whitney H. Gordon." *American Sociological Review*, April, 27:256–258.

Glaser, Daniel

1956   "Criminality theories and behavioral images." *American Journal of Sociology*, March, 61:433–444.

Glueck, Sheldon and Glueck, Eleanor

1950   *Unraveling Juvenile Delinquency*. Cambridge: Harvard University Press.

Gordon, Whitney H.

1962   "Communist rectification programs and delinquency rehabilitation programs: a parallel?" *American Sociological Review*, April, 27:256.

Hartung, Frank

1965   *Crime, Law and Society*. Detroit: Wayne State University Press.

Hirschi, Travis

1969   *Causes of Delinquency*. Berkeley: University of California Press.

Jensen, Gary F.

1972   "Parents, peers, and delinquent action: a test of the differential association perspective." *American Journal of Sociology*, November, 72:562–575.

Matza, David
1964   *Delinquency and Drift.* New York: John Wiley.

Matza, David and Sykes, Gresham M.
1961   "Juvenile delinquency and subterranean values." *American Sociological Review*, October, 26:712–719.

McCorkle, Lloyd W., Elias, Albert and Bixby, F. Lovell
1958   *The Highfields Story.* New York: Holt, Rinehart and Winston.

Mead, George H.
1974   *Mind, Self and Society.* Chicago: University of Chicago Press, 1934.

Schwendinger, Herman and Schwendinger, Julia
1967   "Delinquent stereotypes of probable victims." Pp. 92–105 in Malcolm W. Klein (Ed.), *Juvenile Gangs in Context.* Englewood Cliffs, N.J.: Prentice-Hall.

Shichor, David and Empey, LaMar T.
1974   "A typological analysis of correctional organizations." *Sociology and Social Research*, April, 58:318–334.

Short, James F., Jr.
1960   "Differential association as a hypothesis: problems of empirical testing." *Social Problems*, Summer, 8:14–25.

Sutherland, Edwin H.
1956   "Development of a theory." Pp. 20–31 in Albert K. Cohen et al. (Eds), *The Sutherland Papers.* Bloomington: Indiana University Press.

Sutherland, Edwin H. and Cressey, Donald R.
1955   *Principles of Criminology* (5th ed.). Philadelphia: J.B. Lippincott.

Sykes, Gresham M. and Matza, David
1957   "Techniques of neutralization: a theory of delinquency." *American Sociological Review*, December, 22:664–670.

Volkman, Rita and Cressey, Donald R.
1963   "Differential association and the rehabilitation of drug addicts." *American Journal of Sociology*, September, LXIX:129–142.

Yablonsky, Lewis
1965   *The Tunnel Back: Synanon.* New York: Macmillan.

13

LABELING THEORY

The theories of delinquency we have examined thus far have been concerned primarily with one central issue: that is, with whether the factors that distinguish law violators from conventional people can be identified. The causes for delinquent behavior have been sought in the inherent characteristics of individuals, in the way communities are organized, or in the groups with which delinquents associate. In recent years, however, there has been a marked shift away from this central concern. Rather than devoting primary attention to the presumed causes of delinquent behavior, a new group of theorists—labeling theorists—have become preoccupied with societal reactions to it.

Most labeling theorists are symbolic interactionists. Their assumptions about human nature and social order, therefore, are generally the same, but with a special twist. Like symbolic interactionists, labeling theorists assume that human nature is relatively plastic and subject to change. Yet, they are far more concerned with the stigmatizing effects of arrest and trial on delinquents than with the processes of interaction that produce their illegal behavior in the first place. The reason is that labeling theorists are inclined to believe that delinquents are relatively normal people. Hence, if they persist in delinquent behavior and become serious offenders, this will be due less to evil tendencies on their parts than to the negative effects of police, judges, and correctional authorities upon them.

The assumptions of labeling theorists about social order reflect this same bias. Although they acknowledge that society is characterized by cultural conflict, they suggest that this conflict is usually resolved in favor of people in positions of power and influence. Thus, the definition and imposition of social rules will reflect their interests, not those of less powerful groups.

If these assumptions about human nature and social order are combined, they suggest that delinquent characteristics are not an inherent property of individuals, but, rather, a property that is conferred upon them by others—by legal officials and by those who have the power to legislate their own brand of morality. Hence, children become delinquent, not because of their behavior or because they are predisposed to do so, but because they are labeled by someone in a position of power.

Dramatization of evil

Frank Tannenbaum (1938) was probably the first person to set forth some of the principles of labeling theory in explicit terms. Tannenbaum argued that the final steps in the making of a serious delinquent occurs, not when some child violates the law, but when he or she becomes enmeshed in the juvenile justice system. An official step taken that only makes an insignificant problem into a serious one.

Many children break windows, push over garbage cans, skip school, shoplift, and annoy people. From their childish perspective, however, these acts are defined as "play, adventure, excitement, interest, mischief, fun" (p. 17). But the community has a different definition of them. They are seen as a nuisance, as an evil, as delinquency. Hence, they often result in chastisement, court action, and punishment. Should these acts continue, and should this difference in the definition of the situation persist, two things will happen. First, the attitude of the community will harden. Soon, its tendency to define specific acts as evil will be transformed into a tendency to define mischievous children as evil. "The individual who used to do bad and mischievous things [will] now become a bad and unredeemable human being" (p. 17). Secondly, the community's view of the child will leave a lasting and destructive impact on him. He will soon come to feel that he is different from other children. "The young delinquent becomes bad because he is defined as bad and because he is not believed if he is good" (p. 17). In short, he will have acquired a new and delinquent self-image which will have been produced by the negative reactions of the community to him.

Tannenbaum called this process the "dramatization of evil," a process that sets up a self-fulfilling prophecy which tends to evoke and make worse the very behavior that was complained about in the first place. As he put it, "The process of making the criminal . . . is a process of tagging, identifying, segregating, describing, emphasizing, making conscious and self-conscious; it becomes a way of stimulating, suggesting, emphasizing, and evoking the very traits that are complained of. . . . The person becomes the thing he is described as being" (p. 19).

The relatives of mischievous children, the police, the juvenile court, and correctional officials are often enthusiastic and well-intentioned in their efforts to reform them, but their very enthusiasm defeats their objective. "The harder they work to reform the evil, the greater the evil grows in their hands" (pp. 19–20). Left alone, mischievous children will not become serious delinquents or adult criminals. But, so long as they are defined as bad and thereby isolated from conventional groups and activities, their only recourse is to join other children like themselves—children who have also been defined as evil.

It is when this occurs that really serious problems begin to emerge. Delinquent gangs tend to develop which provide the only source of security for labeled children. Even worse, these gangs begin to generate their own delinquent norms—norms which now seriously overemphasize the conflict between gangs and the community. In other words, a whole new game is set up in which "innocent maladjustment" is escalated into criminal behavior and in which the delinquent gang becomes the child's major reference group. Therefore, said Tannenbaum, the only way out is through a refusal to dramatize evil in the first place. "The less said about it the better" (p. 20). It is the community's action in labeling children as evil and then making them self-conscious of that label that is the major source of delinquent gangs and serious crime, not something that is inherent in the children themselves.

Primary and secondary deviation

In 1951, some 13 years after Tannenbaum made his pioneering analysis, Edwin M. Lemert, a professor at the University of California, added some new concepts to labeling theory. First of all, said Lemert

(1951:75–76), it is necessary to distinguish between two kinds of deviant behavior: *primary* deviance and *secondary* deviance.

Primary deviance

Something which Tannenbaum failed to mention is the fact that many delinquent acts go undetected. This is *primary* deviance— deviance that is not identified and punished by anyone in authority. Such deviance is common, as self-report studies indicate, and can be due to any number of "original" causes. In fact, says Lemert, there are an "embarrassingly" large number of theories designed to explain these "original" causes—control theories, cultural deviance theories, strain theories, and others which we have already discussed. Although most of these theories possess elements of truth and thus are important from a scientific standpoint, they are relatively unimportant in terms of actually understanding how official delinquents are created.

The reason is that until primary deviance is detected there are no delinquents. Hence, its impact on children will be minimal, and they will not develop a deviant identity. Rather, they will be inclined, as most people are, to use techniques of neutralization to disavow the implications of their deviant acts and to continue defining themselves as good. Since their reputations have not been destroyed by labeling, they will tend to retain a conformist self-concept and to avoid many of the negative consequences of being defined as evil persons.

If, on the other hand, their primary deviance is discovered, then the results may be like those described by Tannenbaum. The evil will be dramatized and the status of the offenders transformed. For example, labeled delinquents must not only deal with the stigma associated with their delinquent status, but they must respond to a host of new clues regarding what is expected of them. The reactions of parents, teachers, and friends, as well as legal authorities, will tend to affirm their delinquent status. Hence, to the extent that labeled children are sensitive to the expectations of others, their behavior may mirror not their normal, conventional roles, but a deviant one. Even their clothes, their speech, or their mannerisms may be altered, reflecting the characteristics of a delinquent status.

Lemert (1971:13) also suggests that once people are labeled they are expected to adhere to an additional set of official rules that apply only to them. But, rather than helping to reduce their problems, these new requirements only increase them. When status offenders are placed on probation, for example, they are often forbidden to live with "unfit" parents, to associate with their old friends, or they may be expected to reverse suddenly their patterns of failure at school. Any failure to adhere to these special rules will, in itself, constitute a new act of deviance. In some states, in fact, such a failure can result in a status offender being redefined as a "criminal" offender. Hence, in attempting to "treat" delinquents, the juvenile justice system can actually escalate the number of rules whereby their future behavior may be termed delinquent—rules that do not apply to nondelinquents.

Secondary deviance

This increase in rules, coupled with the tendency for delinquents to begin behaving in accordance with the expectations of their deviant status, may result in what Lemert defines as *secondary deviance*. This kind of deviance evolves out of the adaptions that the labeled person makes to the problems created by official and conformist reactions to his primary deviance. "When a person begins to employ his deviant behavior as a role based upon it as a means of defense, attack, or adjustment to the overt and covert problems created by the consequent societal reactions to him, his deviation is secondary" (1951:76). Thus, even though unique personal or situational factors—"original" causes—contribute to a child's *primary* acts of deviance, the reactions of society to them are likely to escalate the chances that more serious *secondary* forms of deviance will be forthcoming. According to Lemert, these are the most important and "effective" causes of serious delinquent behavior. Just as Tannenbaum had suggested, "the person becomes the thing he is described as being."

Lemert (1951:77) does not suggest that secondary deviance will follow hard upon the heels of any single, even punitive, reaction to an individual. Rather, as Tannebaum indicated, it is the product of a rather long process—primary deviance, social penalties, further deviance, and more penalties until eventually the individual accepts his deviant status and becomes a full-fledged delinquent. Inherent in the arguments of both men, then, are three basic ideas:

> 1.   Some kind of deviant behavior—i.e., *primary* deviance—must occur as a means of initiating the labeling process. Even though neither theorist thought that primary deviance by itself would cause a child to become a serious offender, neither would deny that official reactions do arise in response to actual misconduct.

2.   Both men implied the existence of community norms against acts of primary as well as secondary deviance. Though they argue that overreaction on the parts of parents, teachers, and legal authorities inevitably makes the problem worse, they would not question the idea that these people do share a set of rules that define certain acts as deviant.

3.   It is clear that both men are symbolic interactionists. They view the creation of the official delinquent as the end product of a sequence of interactions between a child and various authority figures, a sequence that might be diagrammed as in Figure 13–1.

FIGURE 13–1

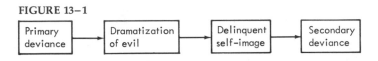

Only after several instances in which acts of primary deviance result in official reaction and labeling does the child eventually become the thing he is described as being. It is not until he begins to mirror the social image of himself as a delinquent that he adopts a delinquent identity and engages in acts of secondary deviance.

The social creation of delinquency

The 1960s were characterized by a wave of excitement over this new way of constructing delinquency. No longer could society and its reactions to delinquent behavior be taken for granted. All of the frustrations associated with 100 years of trying to explain delinquency now took on new light. In concentrating upon the inherent characteristics of offenders, positivistic science had been searching in the wrong place. It is society's reaction to the deviant, more than the deviant himself, that creates the problem. Rather than inherited or learned predispositions to be evil, it is the dramatization of evil which transforms children into delinquents. Were it not for society's reactions to their deviant acts, entangling them in a web of rigidity and self-fulfilling prophecy, there would be few serious offenders.

As symbolic interactionists, Tannenbaum and Lemert had described the child as someone whose own behavior contributed to the process by which eventually he is labeled as delinquent. Some later theorists acknowledged this point of view. Howard Becker (1963:14), for example, said that "whether a given act is deviant or not depends in part on the nature of the act (that is, whether or not it violates some rule) and in part on what other people do about it." But, as increased attention was paid to this exciting conception of the problem, newer versions of it began to concentrate less on the role of mischievous children and their acts of primary deviance and more on society's role in making delinquents out of them. As Schur (1971:19) describes it, labeling theory began to exhibit a high degree of ambivalence. On one hand, early versions described the delinquent as a person who had a hand in shaping his own fate by the commission of a deviant act. On the other hand, later versions described him as being at the mercy of those who react to him. More and more, he was treated as a passive social object, helplessly transported without much input on his part to the process by which he was labeled. In other words, the emphases of the symbolic interactionists upon the dynamics of the social process were downgraded in favor of a structural approach in which the organization of society became the center of attention. A new kind of determinism was asserted in which the issue was less that of explaining why children violate the law than that of indicating why it is that society selectively transforms some of them into "outsiders." This new determinism stressed the importance of paying attention to three activities in society: the nature and construction of social rules, the selective enforcement of rules, and the social functions of deviance.

Social rules and moral crusaders

In a most significant series of statements, Howard S. Becker (1963:9) argued that it is not just the way the agents of control react to a person that determines whether he or she will be defined as deviant. The process of creating the deviant occurs even earlier. It is rooted in the inclinations of all groups, particularly of "moral crusaders" to create rules.

> . . . *social groups create deviance by making the rules whose infractions constitute deviance* and by applying these rules to particular people and labeling them as outsiders. From this point of view, deviance is *not* a quality of the act a person commits, but rather a consequence of the application by others of rules and sanctions to the "offender." The deviant is one to whom that label has successfully been applied; deviant behavior is the behavior that people so label.

There are several things about Becker's statement that require clarification. In one sense, there is little in it that is entirely new. Criminologists have long known that rules are of great importance because definitions of crime and delinquency vary considerably from society to society and because they are under constant change even within the same society. As Becker suggests, deviance is behavior that people so label; indeed it cannot occur until there are rules by which the behavior can be defined either as good or evil. In the absence of rules, behavior is neither; it is simply behavior. For example, a prehistoric man who took food from a weaker person did not really become a "thief" until the group of which he was a part decided that "theft" was bad. Until a group consciousness evolved and until there were shared expectations, there were no thieves, or burglars, or cheaters. Likewise, there was little chance that a 13th century child could be defined as a truant. Until schools were created centuries later and until education was defined as important, truancy did not exist. In short, it is not merely reactions to behavior that must be considered in understanding why people are labeled as deviant, but the rules that serve to organize and direct official attention to certain behaviors while neglecting others. Unless they are understood, the creation of deviants will not be understood.

But Becker (1963:147–163) was not interested merely in calling attention to an important and well-recognized fact. Instead, his concern was with directing attention to people in modern society whom he called "moral entrepreneurs"—people who become crusading reformers. They are the ones most likely to seek the new rules by which new forms of deviance are created. They are disturbed by some evil, and they will not be content until it is corrected. Typically, they believe their mission is a holy one. "They are . . . fervent and righteous, even self-righteous" (p. 148).

Moral crusaders, however, are not always just busybodies. Often, they are like the ecologists of today or the child-savers of past centuries who, in seeking to correct a set of problems, exhibit humanitarian concerns. They want new rules by which to address difficulties they consider important. Nonetheless, said Becker, moral crusades are typically dominated by people in positions of influence and power—people on the upper levels of society who want to change those beneath them. As a result, it is their vision of good and bad that is usually imposed upon society.

In their zeal, moral crusaders often fail to anticipate the consequences of doing good. For example, in order to correct some evil, it is not enough merely to pass a new set of rules. Rules must also be enforced, and this often requires the creation of a whole new set of agencies and officials. The crusade must be locked into the institutional fabric of society. Thus, a drive that starts out to convince the world of the moral necessity of a new set of rules eventually becomes a bureaucracy devoted to their enforcement.

This can have all sorts of ramifications. Those people charged with enforcing the new rules are often less concerned with their content than with the fact that they are on the books. People are arrested, convicted, and punished because the rules say that they should be. Furthermore, it is in the self-interest of the rule enforcers to see that the rules are perpetuated. After all, rules now provide them with a job, a profession, a reason for being. Rule enforcers must justify their existence, therefore, by convincing others of the importance of the rules and by seeing that they are carefully safeguarded.

Sometimes the cure is worse than the disease. In seeking to reduce sex crimes, laws have been passed which permit the indefinite confinement of "sexual psychopaths" even though psychiatrists do not know for sure what a "sexual psychopath" is. In seeking to prevent the reproduction of delinquent children, a eugenics movement was started and laws passed which permitted authorities to sterilize "hereditary criminals" and "moral degenerates." This was done despite the absence of scientific proof that crime is inherited or is the result of "moral depravity." In seeking to keep "giddy," "headstrong," and "restless" teenage girls away from temptation, some of them have been charged with status offenses and kept "safe" for a year or two in state-run industrial schools. It has been deemed more important that these girls should be institutionalized than that they should run the risk of violating the moral rules associated with childhood.

In short, deviance is a far larger enterprise than the commission of a particular act. Before any behavior can be viewed as deviant, there must be moral crusaders to call attention to something about it that is undesirable and to see that the necessary things are done to make rules that outlaw it. Once the rules are created, moreover, a new group of officials and agencies must be organized to enforce them—officials who have a vested interest in seeing that the rules are perpetuated. Only after all this is done are the necessary conditions set for creating deviants.

Selective enforcement of rules

Despite the intent of moral crusaders to establish rules that will be universally enforced, Becker (1963:156–161) suggests that, in fact, they are selectively applied. Not everyone who is caught is actually labeled. Instead, the actual labeling of a person depends upon many things that are extraneous to his behavior: who the person is, of what class or race he is a member, whether he shows proper respect to officials, or whether a given rule is high or low on the list of an agency's list of rules to be enforced. The point is that rule enforcers have a great deal of discretion in deciding whom to label, if only because it is absolutely impossible for them to process all rule breakers. Hence, if they cannot tackle all violators at once, they must temporize with evil by selectively choosing whom to label.

Writing during the same period, other labeling theorists agreed with Becker. Universal definitions of good and bad, John I. Kitsuse (1964) argued, exist only in theory, not in fact. In a complex society like ours, it is virtually impossible to establish a set of moral rules that will be universally supported, moral crusaders notwithstanding. Consequently, "the socially significant differentiation of deviants from the nondeviant population is increasingly contingent upon circumstances of situation, place, social, and personal biography, and the bureaucratically organized activities of agencies of control" (p. 101). It is clear that factors other than actual behavior are of crucial importance in determining who will finally be labeled as deviant.

Reflecting these same ideas, Kai T. Erikson (1964:11) argued that the most crucial factor is the "social audience."

> Deviance is not a property *inherent* in certain forms of behavior; it is a property *conferred upon* these forms by the audiences which directly or indirectly witness them. The critical variable in the study of deviance, then, is the social audience rather than the individual actor, since it is the audience which eventually determines whether or not any episode of behavior or any class of episodes is labeled deviant.

Even the most deviant of persons, Erikson noted, engages in delinquent acts only a fraction of the time. When the community decides to bring sanctions against him, therefore, "it is responding to a few deviant details in a vast array of entirely acceptable conduct. Thus it happens that a moment of deviation may become the measure of a person's position in society" (p. 11). Hence, the most pressing question for which an answer is needed is how it is that a community decides what forms of conduct should be singled out for attention.

The social functions of deviance

In seeking an answer to this question, Erikson did not concern himself with the characteristics of the deviant, as criminologists had done historically, but with the characteristics of society. Drawing upon the ideas of Durkheim (1952) and Mead (1918), he said that "it is gradually becoming more evident . . . that deviant behavior can play an important role in keeping the social order intact" (p. 12). Deviance serves important social functions.

Any social system requires boundaries. Some of these are geographical, but others are normative. In order to do business with one another, there must be rules, and people must have some assurance that those rules will be obeyed. Yet, the only material found in the system for marking its boundaries are the deviant behaviors of its members. In contrast to acts of conformity, deviant acts help to establish the outside limits of the kinds of behavior that can be tolerated. Should they become too extreme, the system will deteriorate. Therefore, said Erikson (p. 14), "Each time the group censures some act of deviation, . . . it sharpens the authority of the violated norm and declares again where the boundaries of the group are located."

> As a trespasser against the group norms, [the deviant] represents those forces which lie outside the group's boundaries: He informs us what evil looks like, what shapes the devil can assume. And, in doing so, he shows us the difference between the inside of the group and the outside. It may well be that without this ongoing drama at the outer edges of group space, the community would have no inner sense of identity and cohesion, no sense of the contrasts which set it off as a special place in the larger world.
>
> Thus deviance cannot be dismissed simply as behavior which *disrupts* stability in society, but may itself be, in controlled quantities, an important condition for *preserving* stability (p. 15).

According to Erikson, then, the selective labeling of persons by the agencies of control can be viewed as boundary-maintaining activities. But, if such is the case, some delicate, possible frightening, questions are raised: Is it possible that society is organized to use labeled persons as a resource? Since the police, courts, and correctional agencies cannot catch everyone, is it possible that they selectively label some persons because they feel it is necessary to mark society's boundaries and to deter others?

Though final answers are not available, Erikson (p. 15) suggests that "the institutions devised by society for discouraging deviant behavior are often so poorly equipped for that task that we might well ask why this is considered their 'real' function at all." Victimization and self-report studies indicate that only a small fraction of all delinquents and criminals are apprehended. Yet, those who are caught are ushered into a deviant status by a dramatic ceremony—the court trial, a ritual that is clearly visible to everyone. Once that is completed, many deviants are then warehoused in institutions where, instead of being separated from deviant influences, they are tightly segregated into groups where the chance to learn more criminal behavior is the greatest. Furthermore, once having paid their debt to society, they are retired from their deviant status with virtually no public notice. Nothing equivalent to the court trial is used as a rite-of-passage out of that status. Instead, our agencies of control set up traffic patterns which concentrate on moving persons into a deviant status, not back out of it. So far as the public is concerned, therefore, these people are permanently labeled. Hence, it could be that instead of acting efficiently to suppress deviance the major function of the agencies of control is to dramatize the badness of the relative few they do process. By maintaining these people in an undesirable position, society can use them as permanent sign posts, indicating to others what the outer limits of society are. If that is the case, the labeled person is a resource and is of greater worth to society as a deviant than as a nondeviant.

Summary

In the course of its development then, labeling theory tended to shift from a process to a structural orientation (Finestone, 1976:208–211). If a child is lucky enough to aviod being labeled as delinquent, he is viewed, at least in part, as being the master of his own fate. But, should that unfortunate circumstance befall him, his fate is totally determined by others. Due to the rule-making crusades of moral entrepreneurs, the selective enforcement of rules by officials, and social functions performed by dramatizing his evil, his individual autonomy is lost, and he is permanently stigmatized. Though he remains a valuable resource for marking the boundaries of society, he has been lastingly transformed from a normal to a deviant person.

The delinquency generating sequence suggested by this line of thought might be diagrammed as in Figure 13–2. In this scheme, the primary deviance of the individual as a contributor to the labeling process is relatively unimportant. Rather, it is the use of the individual as a symbol of evil that is of the greatest significance. He is a pawn in the need of society to maintain order.

FIGURE 13–2

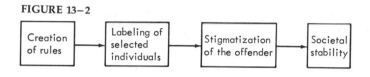

Implications and impact on policy

The uses to which labeling theory have been put in the construction of policies for dealing with juveniles are a better reflection of its earlier than its later versions. Writing for the President's Commission on Law Enforcement and Administration of Justice in 1967, Lemert (p. 96) stated their implications in classic terms:

> The aims of preventing delinquency and the expectations of definitively treating a profusion of child and parental problems have laid an impossible burden upon the juvenile court, and they may be seriously considered to have no proper part in its philosophy. *If there is a defensible philosophy for the juvenile court, it is one of judicious nonintervention.* It is properly an agency of last resort for children, holding to a doctrine analogous to that of appeal courts which require that all other remedies be exhausted before a case will be considered. (Emphasis added)

Although Lemert's philosophy has by no means been fully implemented, it has been reflected in a significant number of recent changes, some of which began occurring even before Lemert penned his statement. These changes can best be summarized under a series of three D's: *decriminalization, diversion* and *due process.*

Decriminalization

Since the early 1960s, a growing number of influential organizations and people have recommended that juvenile status offenses and cases involving dependency and neglect should be "decriminalized" and "destigmatized." It is probably no accident that these recommendations were coincidental with the growth of labeling theory. Both seem to reflect significant changes in cultural beliefs, each tending to influence the other. Labeling theory reflected a changing morality and vice versa.

It will be recalled that in his discussion of social rules Becker suggested that moral crusades are likely to produce regulations and agencies of enforcement whose cures may be worse than the disease they were designed to remedy. Other persons have suggested that such may be true of the juvenile court. Roscoe Pound (1964), an eminent legal scholar, expressed grave reservations over the extent to which the court has exercised jurisdiction over the health, education, and morals of children, to say nothing of its attempts to use elaborate legal means to control truancy, curfew violation, running away, smoking, and drinking. "When these matters are committed to courts," agrees Lemert (1971), "they necessarily delegate the work of enforcement to administrative agents, such as probation officers, whose capacity to achieve these ends is questionable." How can a probation officer or a policeman insure proper morals for a child or an adequate education?

In response to these kinds of criticisms, recommendations have been made suggesting that the large jurisdictional net of the juvenile court should be narrowed. The rules should be changed so that some forms of juvenile conduct can be decriminalized. At the very least, the President's Crime Commission (1967:85) recommended, "serious consideration should be given to complete elimination of the court's power over children for noncriminal conduct."

In his role as a consultant to the President's commission, Lemert (1967:97) sounded much like Becker in suggesting that children need protection from moral crusaders:

> It has become equally or more important to protect children from unanticipated and unwanted consequences of organized movements, programs, and services in their behalf than from the unorganized, adventitious "evils" which gave birth to the juvenile court. . . . The forms of delinquency have changed as the nature of society has changed.

Lemert (1967:97) also agrees with theorists of middle-class delinquency (Chapter 10) who suggest that changing moral values require a reduction in the mandate of the court.

> The basic life process today is one of adaption to exigencies and pressures; individual morality has become functional rather than sacred or ethical in the older sense. To recognize this at the level of legislative and judicial policy is difficult because social action in America always has been heavily laden with moral purpose. However, if the juvenile court is to become effective, its function must be reduced to enforcement of the ethical minimum of youth conduct necessary to maintain social life in a high energy, pluralistic society.

Despite this growing body of recommendations, the various states have not yet seen fit to eliminate status offenses entirely from their regulations, choosing instead to draw distinctions between them and criminal offenses and to treat the two types of offenders differently. Nonetheless, a social movement is underway which seems likely to lead eventually to a greater reduction in the mandate of the juvenile court. Meanwhile, until that is accomplished legislatively, other changes are occurring which tend to realize the same purpose in other ways.

Diversion

One of these ways is "diversion"—turning juveniles aside from entry into the juvenile justice system. Many people have accepted Tannenbaum's notion that the dramatization of evil only makes the evil worse, not better. Indeed, if his recommendations were followed, nothing would be done about the offenses of any but the most serious offenders. "The less said about them the better." Some recent theorists agree. Edwin M. Schur (1973), for example, enjoins us to *"leave kids alone wherever possible"* (p. 155). We should develop a policy of "radical nonintervention" which would "accommodate society to the widest possible diversity of behavior and attitudes, rather than forcing as many individuals as possible to 'adjust' to supposedly common societal standards" (p. 154).

Social movements, however, proceed at a more deliberate pace. Hence, policymakers have not chosen to leave kids entirely alone. Instead, they have taken a more modest course based upon the traditional assumption that delinquent offenses, even if petty, are symptomatic of personal problems which might lead to more serious acts if left unattended. What should be done, therefore, is to limit the penetration of youth into the juvenile justice system but, at the same time, to see that their difficulties are addressed by other agencies.

In 1967, the President's Crime Commission (pp. 82–84) suggested several ways by which this might be accomplished. There should be juvenile specialists at every police department whose function it is to decide promptly which juveniles might be referred elsewhere rather than to court. Community agencies should be available to them to provide immediate counseling, tutorial, occupational, or recreational services. Even better, every community or large neighborhood should have a Youth Service Bureau which could provide all of these services in one setting for all children, delinquent or nondelinquent. Not only the police, but families, schools, and other agencies could refer children to them.

Based upon suggestions like these, diversion has now become a national fad (cf. Carter and Klein, 1976; Klein, et al., 1976). Hundreds, if not thousands, of agencies have set up "diversionary" programs, encouraged first by the Office of Youth Development in the Department of Health, Education, and Welfare and later by the Office of Juvenile Justice and Delinquency Prevention, a part of the Law Enforcement Assistance Administration. The latter agency, in fact, recently committed over $8 million to a national program of diversion projects (1976). Diversion, in short, has become a part of the national movement designed, presumably, to eliminate the negative effects of labeling by limiting the legal processing of children.

Due process

Yet a third part of the movement is an emphasis upon "due process." Not only have juvenile court rules been criticized for legal overkill, but the failure of the court itself to protect the constitutional rights of children has also been criticized. Throughout most of this century, children have been tried in informal hearings, in the absence of defense counsel, in the absence of sworn testimony, and through the use of hearsay evidence. Not only would such procedures be totally unacceptable in adult court, but they could not be used as the basis for imposing severe sanctions on guilty persons—placing them in a foster home, assigning them to probation, or locking them in an institution.

According to the original concept of the juvenile court, these procedures were acceptable because the ostensible goal of the court was to treat children, not to punish them. Hence, it was assumed that constitutional protections need not apply to children, since their trials were civil, not criminal, proceedings. But, partly due to the impact of labeling theory, this view of the court began to change during the 1960s. In 1961, the jurisdiction of the juvenile court in California was narrowed: The police lost some of their power to detain juveniles; judges could no longer run court hearings informally, and attorneys were introduced into court to defend juveniles. In the late 1960s, and early 1970s, the Supreme Court of the United States also rendered a series of decisions designed to limit the traditional powers of the juvenile court. In the first of these, the *Kent* case (383 U.S. 541, 1966), the Supreme Court expressed an opinion that might have come directly from the pen of a labeling theorist. "There is evidence," said the Court, "that the child receives the worse of two possible worlds: that he gets neither the protections accorded to adults nor the solicitous care and regenerative treatment postulated for children."

Later decisions then went on to define in much narrower terms the way that the juvenile court should operate. But, since these decisions will be thoroughly discussed in Chapter 16, suffice it to say for now that labeling theory had an ever-widening effect. Its principles and ideas have been incorporated into public policy, not only in terms of the way the juvenile court operates, but in leading to the development of alternatives to the juvenile court. These, too, will be discussed in later chapters and their capacities for lasting "reform" evaluated.

Scientific legacy

Labeling theory made a significant turn in scientific theorizing because of its stress upon a point to which science had not paid much attention; namely, that official delinquency is far more than the deviant behavior of children. Societal reactions, perhaps more than delinquent behavior, should become the object of study.

The scientific implications of this new way of focusing on delinquency were nothing less than profound. Labeling theory challenged the deterministic views of positivistic science by questioning the idea that there are universal laws by which delinquency can be explained. There is no cosmic glue, it suggested, by which the world is held together; there is no objective reality beyond some person's or group's conception of it. Rather, delinquency is a social construction that is relative both to time and place. Groups create delinquency, in fact, by setting forth the rules that define it and by selectively applying those rules to certain persons. At best, therefore, we can only hope to understand how our own society operates since it is impossible to derive theories that locate causes for delinquent behavior which are both inherent within the individual and which transcend both time and culture.

Since the first flurry of excitement over this new conception of delinquency, there has been a general retreat from some of its more extreme implications. This retreat has stressed the need to put three of its ideas into a more modest perspective: the role of moral crusaders in creating social rules, labeling theory's own special brand of determinism, and the importance of reconciling labeling theory with other scientific theories.

Rules and moral crusaders

In their concern with moral crusaders, labeling theorists tended to imply that virtually all rules are a reflection of some elite group's own special brand of morality and that these rules inevitably work to the disadvantage of other less powerful groups. Among children, for example, such acts as truancy, premarital intercourse, drinking, or talking back to parents were defined as evil by 19th century child-savers and legally sanctioned. Yet, today, acts of this type are often better understood in terms of the evolution of the *ideal* middle-class concept of childhood than in terms of what children actually do. They are so common that it is difficult to separate deviants from conformists. But what about the rules that prohibit serious predatory crimes such as murder, unprovoked assault, robbery, or rape? Should they be viewed in the same way as those covering status offenses?

Wellford (1975:335) maintains that "all societies have found it functional to control certain kinds of behavior" and that this fact seriously questions the statement that no act is intrinsically criminal today. Even though labeling theorists were correct in suggesting that today's criminal acts did not constitute crimes until they were defined as such by some ancestral group, their predatory character has long since led virtually every civilization to establish laws prohibiting many of them. Were this not the case, there would be no norms by which labeling theorists could allude to "secret" deviance or distinguish, as Lemert does, between primary (unsanctioned) and secondary (sanctioned) deviance. Some acts, in other words, can be readily identified by allusion to widely shared norms, particularly in any one society. Studies of American society, for example, indicate that, whether black or white, middle or lower class, educated or uneducated, most people today are inclined to rate certain kinds of predatory acts as serious and in need of condemnation (Chilton and DeAmicis, 1975; Rossi, et al., 1974). Hence, in considering the nature and function of social rules, there is need to recognize that they are of various types and that not all of them can be attributed to the unique standards of some elite group of moral crusaders.

Nettler (1974:210) cites another fallacy that is likely to be associated with the labeling position. He alludes to Becker's famous statement '(1963:9) that *"social groups create deviance by making the rules whose infraction constitutes deviance."* "Some readers," says Nettler,

> will translate statements like this as saying that "social groups create crime by making the laws whose infraction constitutes crime." This translation is slippery: It slides between the truth that social groups create the *definitions* of "crime" and the falsehood that the *injuries* condemned by these definitions would disappear (or would not have been "created") if the definition had not been formulated. To the layman, it sounds as though the labeling theorist believed that people would not wish to defend themselves against burglary or murder if they had not learned a rule defining these acts as crimes. It sounds, also, as though the labeling theorist believed that there would be less "burglary" if we did not use that term. The nonprofessional consumer of criminological explanations recognizes this for the semantic trick that it is—the trick of saying, "If a crime is a breach of a rule, you won't have the crime if you don't have the rule." The ordinary reaction to this semantic sleight of hand is to say, "A mugging by any other name hurts just as much."

In short, certain kinds of injurious acts have existed for a long time. It is not too surprising, therefore, that rules prohibiting them should have arisen and that those rules enjoy wide support.

Determinism of labeling theory

Along the same vein, labeling theorists urge us to discover what the processes are by which a person is labeled as deviant. Carried to their logical extreme, their statements suggest that labeling is a necessary and sufficient explanation for the creation of delinquents (Mankoff, 1971).

> One sometimes gets the impression from reading this literature that
> people go about minding their own business, and then—"wham"—bad
> society comes along with a stigmatized label. Then, forced into the role of
> deviant, the individual has little choice but to be deviant. This is an
> exaggeration, of course, but such an image can be gained easily from an
> overemphasis on the impact of labelling. However, it is exactly this image,
> toned down and made reasonable, which is the central contribution of the
> labelling school to the sociology of deviance (Akers, 1967:46).

Carried to its logical extreme, the "wham" conception of delinquent
behavior could be badly misleading. What if labeling became the sole
concern of the scientific community? What if no attention were paid to
the causes of robbery or assault? What if it was assumed that children do
not begin to commit serious acts of delinquency until they are labeled?

Lemert (1972:16) suggests that such an approach would simply substitute one form of determinism for another.

> What began as some tentative and loosely linked ideas about deviance
> and societal reaction in my writings subsequently were replaced by the
> theoretical statement of Becker that social groups create deviance and that
> deviant behavior is that which is so labeled. This position got further
> elucidation in Erikson's functionalist derived assertion that the social au-
> dience is the critical factor in deviance study. In retrospect these must be
> regarded as conceptual extrusions largely responsible for the indiscrimi-
> nate application of "labeling theory" to a diversity of research and writing
> on deviance. Unfortunately, the impression of crude sociological deter-
> minism left by the Becker and Erikson statements has been amplified by
> the tendency of many deviance studies to be preoccupied with the work of
> official agencies of social control, accenting the arbitrariness of official
> action, stereotyped decision making in bureaucratic contexts, bias in the
> administration of law, and the general preemptive nature of society's
> control over deviants.

Later versions of labeling theory, in other words, have become as
deterministic as many of the earlier theories which they seek to
supplant. Yet, since serious acts of primary deviance are common despite the way apprehended offenders are labeled, persons concerned
with protecting the citizenry, along with social scientists, must be concerned with the causes of their behavior as well as with societal reactions to it.

Given its preoccupation with societal reaction, labeling theory
provides little direction for learning more about these problems. Gibbs
(1966:12), for example, has expressed concern over the inability of label-

ing theory to explain why the incidence of primary deviation may differ from one population to another. "(A)re we to conclude," he asks, "that the incidence of a given act is in fact a constant in all populations and that the only difference is in the quality of reactions to the act?" Obviously, the answer is "no." Adolescents, for instance, are more likely than any other group to commit property crimes. Why? Labeling theory is incapable of providing a satisfactory answer. Carried to its logical extreme, it suggests that the only difference between adolescent and adult populations is the way the agents of control react to them, not in the way they behave. Such a conclusion is absurd (Gove, 1970; Wellford, 1975).

Labeling theory is also deterministic in another way. It suggests that delinquents are simply unfortunate children who lack the power to challenge the arbitrary rules and processes by which they are labeled. It denies the possibility that the label "delinquent" is ever earned or that children differ from one another (Nettler, 1974:207). Such a denial is both misleading and inaccurate. Children do differ from one another, as we have seen, and the factors that contribute to these differences also contribute to the commission of delinquent acts. Thus, by denying their existence, labeling theory denies the importance of trying to understand individual variation and blocks efforts to do something about it.

Finally, the concept of secondary deviance suggests that only after a person's delinquent behavior has been labeled and dramatized is he or she likely to become a career deviant. Were it not for the label, the individual would retain a conformist identity. Again, this is a deterministic oversimplification. Everyone does not respond uniformly to punishment and stigma. Upon being labeled, some young people feel so threatened that they refrain from further delinquent acts. They have such a stake in conformity—a loving family, a career, their entire future—that they choose not to endanger it by additional deviant behavior.

Conversely, there are some self-help groups—Alcoholic's Anonymous, Synanon, or Weight Watcher's Anonymous—which maintain that they cannot be successful with alcoholics, drug addicts, and fat people until these people are willing to identify themselves as deviant. Ironically, these organizations have shown that until their clients are willing to acknowledge that they have a problem, little can be done to help them. In this instance, therefore, social and personal labeling becomes a device for getting people to deal with their problems, not act as if they did not exist.

What all of this means, in short, is that labeling theory has contributed to an increasing emphasis upon the arbitrary nature of social control at the expense of careful investigation into the enormous complexities of law-violating behavior, human interaction, and the constraints that are inevitable if society is to remain a functioning unit. Further, as Manning (1973:123) point out,

> A political and moral tone suffuses the work of labeling theorists which tends to cast us "good guys" in defense of politically weak groups against the "bad guys" lurking behind badges and guns, sinisterly wielding the establishment's power. . . . [T]he central drift has been toward the vulgarization and politicization of ideas, a failure to develop conceptual precision and to construct detailed analyses of the conditions (historical, cultural, social, social-psychological, biological) under which a given tenet of labeling theory might hold.

Reconciling labeling and other theories

Such criticisms have not been lost upon labeling theorists and the rest of the scientific community. In the first place, numerous observers have pointed out that the labeling perspective does not contain some of the elements of a sound substantive theory—a careful delineation and definition of concepts and a logically developed and integrated set of propositions (Gibbs, 1966; Goode, 1975; Schrag, 1974; Schur, 1971). Indeed, the most eminent labeling theorists maintain that they have been misinterpreted, that their statements were never intended as a full explanation of deviance. Hence, they do not warrant being called "theories" in any rigorous sense (Becker, 1974; Lemert, 1972; Rains and Kitsuse, 1973).

Becker (1974:4–5) also maintains that labeling theorists never intended to suggest that only after a person has been labeled does that person begin to do deviant things. Such a notion, he indicates, is ridiculous.

> . . . [T]he act of labelling, as carried out by moral entrepreneurs, while important, cannot possibly be conceived as the sole explanation of what alleged deviants actually do. It would be foolish to propose that stick-up men stick people up simply because someone has labelled them stick-up men or that everything a homosexual does results from someone having called him a homosexual.

There are reasons that people do these things quite apart from the way others react to them. Hence, the causes of delinquent behavior, no less than reactions to it, must be studied.

Given this need, both Lemert and Becker propose doing away with one-sided approaches and substituting an interactional model for studying delinquency. While we "can't go home again" to the old style positivistic criminology, Lemert says (1974:466–467), neither can we place total reliance upon the study of social reactions to deviance. Becker (1974:6) agrees. He recommends that the term "labelling theory" be discarded and a new term adopted: "interactionist theory." In its simplest form, interactionist theory would be concerned with all the actors involved in any episode of deviance: rule creators, rule breakers and rule enforcers. All three, not just one or the other, would be treated as raw material for scientific analysis (Gibbs and Erickson, 1975; Rains, 1975; Scheff, 1974).

The significance of these conclusions is considerable. On one hand, they represent a retreat from the more extreme versions of labeling theory, suggesting that we must be concerned with explaining and controlling law-violating behavior as well as reactions to it. On the other hand, this retreat is somewhat ironic in light of the widespread popularity of labeling theory. Like the rare Broadway musical, it has become an instant success. Lay people hum its familiar lines, and policymakers have faithfully revised their roles in light of it. Despite its many limitations as a comprehensive and well-articulated set of statements, therefore, labeling theory has had remarkable impact on cultural beliefs and practices.

Summary and conclusions

Labeling theory has challenged the preoccupation of positivistic criminology with the presumed causes of delinquent behavior and has directed our attention to another part of the mosaic of which delinquency is comprised; namely, the roles of rule makers and rule enforcers. It has made an exceedingly valuable contribution, markedly extending the range of behavioral phenomena with which both scientific and policy-making communities must be concerned.

1. *Assumptions about human nature and social order.* Given their recent reaffirmation of the interactionist position, labeling theorists tend to assume that human nature is plastic and subject to change. By humanizing the delinquent and normalizing his actions, they are inclined to believe that most children will be good if they are not pushed into adopting a delinquent self-image by the negative reactions of others to them. The assumptions of labeling theorists about social order

reflect the same bias. Although society is characterized by conflicting definitions for behavior, it is the tendency of rule makers and rule enforcers to dramatize this conflict that exacerbates the delinquency problem and makes it worse.

   2. Underlying content and logic of labeling theory.   Early proponents of the labeling school stressed the notion that delinquents become bad because of the unnecessary dramatization of their primary acts of deviance. If this drama is repeated several times, offending children are likely to adopt a delinquent self-image and to engage in acts of secondary deviance. The process of interaction implied by these theorists can be diagrammed as in Figure 13–3:

FIGURE 13–3

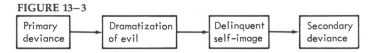

By contrast, more recent members of the labeling school have tended to treat the delinquent as a passive social object, helplessly transported from a normal to a delinquent status by society's legal apparatus; moral crusaders create unnecessary and arbitrary rules; rule enforcers selectively impose these rules; and the unlucky labelee is stigmatized and used as a symbol for maintaining social stability and marking society's boundaries. Hence, the steps implied by this later version are different from the first (see Figure 13–4).

FIGURE 13–4

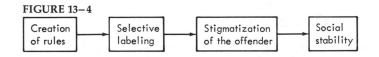

   3. Policy implications.   The more modest implication of these two bodies of theory is to use the juvenile court as an agency of last resort for only the most serious of offenders. The more radical implication is to do absolutely nothing. Refuse to dramatize evil.

   Society has tended to implement the first implication. Consistent with the statements of labeling theory, some blatantly arbitrary and obviously discriminatory practices in the operation of the juvenile court have been documented. Consequently, three "reforms" are being pursued: (1) decriminalization—narrowing the jurisdiction of the juvenile court, particularly over status offenders; (2) diversion—turning juveniles away from the juvenile justice system and into other social agencies for help; and (3) due process—requiring the juvenile court to become a court by insuring that alleged delinquents are provided with the constitutional protections afforded adults.

Though these "reforms" are revolutionary in character, there is reason to remain skeptical about them. What proof is there, for example, that other social agencies are less likely to stigmatize diverted children than is the juvenile court? Since this is what the juvenile court set out to do in the first place, only the passage of time will tell whether our fervent "reforms" are more humane and helpful than were those of the 19th century child-savers.

4. *Logical and empirical adequacy.* Labeling theory performed a valuable service by reminding positivistic criminologists that official delinquency involves rule making and societal reaction to deviant acts as well as the behavior of children. Yet, in its more extreme versions, it is possessed of several deficiencies: It ignores the fact that not all social rules are attributable to the unique standards of some elite group but that many are widely shared and direct our attention to acts that produce innocent victims as well as official delinquents; in suggesting that social reactions are sufficient to explain delinquency, it became as deterministic, and as one sided, as have many theories before it; and it fails to acknowledge the possibility that social reaction does not always produce a deviant identity in labeled persons but may be a deterrent to more deviance on their parts.

Given these limitations, recent statements by labeling theorists have suggested that we should return to an interactional frame of reference in scientific study. While we cannot rely on the older models of positivistic criminology, neither can we adopt a one-sided approach stressing only social reaction. Instead, all the actors in the drama of creating delinquency must be studied: rule makers, rule breakers, and rule enforcers.

References

Akers, Ronald L.

    1967   "Problems in the sociology of deviance: social definitions and behavior." *Social Forces*, 46:455–465.

Becker, Howard S.

    1963   *Outsiders: Studies in the Sociology of Deviance.* New York: Free Press.

    1974   "Labelling theory reconsidered." Pp. 3–32 in Sheldon Messinger et al. (Eds.), *The Aldine Crime and Justice Annual.* Chicago: Aldine.

Carter, Robert M. and Klein, Malcolm W.
  1976   *Back on the Street: The Diversion of Juvenile Offenders.* Englewood
          Cliffs, N.J.: Prentice Hall.

Chilton, Roland and DeAmicis, Jan
  1975   "Overcriminalization and the measurement of consensus." *Sociology
          and Social Research*, July, 59:318–329.

Durkheim, Emile
  1952   *The Division of Labor in Society* (Translated by George Simpson). New
          York: Free Press.

Erikson, Kai T.
  1964   "Notes on the sociology of deviance." Pp. 9–22 in Howard S. Becker
          (Ed.), *The Other Side: Perspectives on Deviance.* New York: Free Press.

Finestone, Harold
  1976   *Victims of Change: Juvenile Delinquents in American Society.* Westport:
          Greenwood Press.

Gibbs, Jack P.
  1966   "Conceptions of deviant behavior: the old and the new." *Pacific
          Sociological Review*, Spring, 9:9–14.

Gibbs, Jack P. and Erickson, Maynard L.
  1975   "Major developments in the sociological study of deviance." *Annual
          Review of Sociology*, 1:21–42.

Goode, Erich
  1975   "On behalf of labeling theory." *Social Problems.* June, 22:570–583.

Gove, Walter
  1970   "Societal reaction as an explanation of mental illness: an evaluation."
          American Sociological Review, October, 35:873–884.

Kitsuse, John I.
  1964   "Societal reaction to deviant behavior: problems of theory and
          method." Pp. 87–102 in Howard S. Becker (Ed.), *The Other Side:
          Perspectives on Deviance.* New York: Free Press.

Klein, Malcolm W. et al.
  1976   "The explosion in police diversion programs." Pp. 101–120 in Mal-
          colm W. Klein (Ed.), *The Juvenile Justice System.* Beverly Hills, Calif.:
          Sage Publications.

Lemert, Edwin M.
  1951   *Social Pathology.* New York: McGraw-Hill.

  1967   "The juvenile court—quest and realities." Pp. 91–106 in the Presi-
          dent's Commission on Law Enforcement and Administration of Jus-
          tice, *Task Force Report: Juvenile Delinquency and Youth Crime.* Wash-
          ington, D.C.: U.S. Government Printing Office.

1970 *Legal Action and Social Change.* Chicago: Aldine.

1971 *Instead of Court: Diversion in Juvenile Justice.* Public Health Service Publication No. 2127. Washington, D.C.: U.S. Government Printing Office.

1972 *Human Deviance, Social Problems and Social Control* (2nd ed.). Englewood Cliffs: Prentice Hall.

1974 "Beyond Mead: the societal reaction to deviance." *Social Problems,* April, *21*:457–468.

Mankoff, Milton
  1971 "Societal reaction and career deviance: a critical analysis." *Sociological Quarterly,* May, *12*:204–218.

Manning, Peter
  1973 "Survey essay on deviance." *Contemporary Sociology,* March, *2*:123–128.

Mead, George H.
  1918 "The psychology of punitive justice." *American Journal of Sociology, 23*:577–602.

Nettler, Gwynn
  1974 *Explaining Crime.* New York: McGraw-Hill.

Office of Juvenile Justice and Delinquency Prevention
  1976 *Diversion of Youth from the Juvenile Justice System.* Washington, D.C.: Law Enforcement Assistance Administration.

Pound, Roscoe
  1964 "The juvenile court and the law." *Crime and Delinquency, 10*:490–504.

President's Commission on Law Enforcement and Administration of Justice
  1967 *The Challenge of Crime in a Free Society.* Washington, D.C.: U.S. Government Printing Office.

Rains, Prudence
  1975 "Imputations of deviance: a retrospective essay on the labeling perspective." *Social Problems,* October, *23*:1–11.

Rains, Prudence and Kitsuse, John I.
  1973 "Comments on the labeling approach to deviance." Unpublished manuscript.

Rossi, Peter H. et al.
  1974 "The seriousness of crimes: normative structure and individual differences." *American Sociological Review,* April, *39*:224–237.

Scheff, Thomas J.
  1974 "The labelling theory of mental illness." *American Sociological Review,* June, *39*:444–452.

Schrag, Clarence
   1974   "Theoretical foundations for a social science of corrections." Pp. 705–743 in Daniel Glaser (Ed.), *Handbook in Criminology*. Chicago: Rand McNally.

Schur, Edwin M.
   1971   *Labeling Deviant Behavior*. New York: Harper and Row.

   1973   *Radical Nonintervention: Rethinking the Delinquency Problem*. Englewood Cliffs, N.J.: Prentice Hall.

Supreme Court of the United States
   1966   *Kent v. United States*. 383 U.S. 541:555:6.

   1967   *In re Gault*. Pp. 57–76 in President's Commission on Law Enforcement and Administration of Justice. *Task Force Report: Juvenile Delinquency and Youth Crime*. Washington, D.C.: U.S. Government Printing Office.

Tannenbaum, Frank
   1938   *Crime and the Community*. New York: Columbia University Press.

Wellford, Charles
   1975   "Labelling theory and criminology: an assessment." *Social Problems*, February, 3:332–345.

14

RADICAL THEORY

Radical theory is the last of the bodies of theory with which we will be concerned. It has been of particular importance in recent years because it represents the culmination of a line of social thought which has progressively led away from the notion that delinquent tendencies are inherent in individuals toward the notion that they are inherent in the political and economic organization of society.

According to radical theory, delinquency is the product of a perpetual class struggle in which the ruling segments of capitalist society (1) define what delinquent behavior is, based on their particular self-interest, (2) create the social conditions which make delinquents out of the children of working-class people, and, then, (3) devise legal machinery by which to maintain control over these children. The rules and practices that govern delinquency, therefore, and the criminogenic conditions that produce it are the product of the inequities and injustices of a capitalist social order.

Given this view of the sources of delinquency, radical theorists strongly imply that human nature is inherently good. While children may be possessed of some selfish tendencies, they become really bad only if society defines or makes them that way. Hence, if they were liberated from the evils of the class struggle, the cooperative instincts of the young would become dominant, and a humane, crime-free society would emerge.

Origins

Radical beliefs of this type are not really new. Why then did they experience a revival in the last third of the 20th century? In part, the answer lies in the broad historical trends of preceding centuries, but, more important, they are the product of a series of crises that arose in the 1960s and 1970s: The continuing presence of racism in American society resulted in nationwide protests and urban riots; an increasingly unpopular war in Vietnam divided the nation and led to an alarming loss of faith in American leaders; the Watergate affair revealed an attempt by the President of the United States and his closest advisors to subvert fundamental democratic institutions and processes; and the investigations of other highly placed politicians and businessmen uncovered repeated instances of bribery and corruption.

When events like these were coupled with a growing sense of dismay over the decay of American cities, over rising crime and delinquency rates, over the persistence of sexual inequality, over the worldwide destruction of the environment, over an escalating arms race, and over the seeming inability of the average citizen to do anything about these matters, faith in traditional values and the American system was gravely weakened. The nation experienced a crisis of legitimacy (Schaar, 1974).

This crisis not only undermined the principles and sources of authority upon which order and obedience are based but contributed to widespread social despair. Pessimistic critics, many of them students, renounced their faith in the American system of justice, the capitalist division of labor, and the world of technology. They also made universities and academics the target of attack:

> Time is short; we cannot wait years for research to give us impregnable theses. America's academia fiddles while the fires are burning. Where are the studies of the new corporate power, of the Defense Department, of the military-industrial complex, of the new bureaucracies, of Vietnam? American academics are prisoners of liberal democratic ideology. Even as the chains rust, they do not move. A new current of reason and passion is arising in America—outside of its conventional institutions. The current of reason must flow faster to create an image of reality and hope for the future, for a ruling class in despair will soon reach for some other kind of ideology, and all that is left for the American establishment is "patriotism," that is fascism (quoted by Bendix, 1970:831).

In such a climate, it is not surprising that a new way of viewing American justice should emerge. Responding to their feelings of despair, a new generation of criminologists began to search for political and legal alternatives. Radical theory is the result. It expresses dismay over the past, places blame on capitalist rulers for having created crime and injustice, and provides a different course of action for the future. In constructing this new view of delinquency and justice, however, radical theorists did not create an entirely new body of theory. Rather, along with labeling theory, they borrowed heavily from two other bodies of theory: conflict theory and Marxian theory.

Conflict theory

Because of their belief that society is characterized by injustice and class conflict, radical theorists argue that greater attention should be paid to the nature of existing laws and whom they serve. They point out that it was not until early in this century that much attention was paid to these matters. At that time, however, a number of legal scholars were responsible for the development of a legal philosophy known as *sociological jurisprudence*. In order to understand the law, they argued, one must examine its relationship to the social order; that is, study its history in relation to the culture in which it develops and determine in what ways the law reflects the underlying values and morals of its people.

The social nature of law

Sociological jurisprudence emphasizes the idea that the law is not merely a set of formal rules, immutable and unchangeable, but is a dynamic body of norms heavily influenced by the society of which it is a part (Pound, 1942). Not only does it reflect the society in which it is embedded, but it also influences that society. As Quinney (1974:6) puts it, the law is "both a social product and a social force." Like other cultural elements, it not only reflects the main course of a civilization and its people, but, in a sense, takes on a life of its own. It helps to shape the course of that civilization as well as to be shaped by it.

A second point emphasized by sociological jurisprudence is the idea that the law is a form of social engineering which will ultimately improve the social order. Roscoe Pound, who was perhaps its foremost proponent, believed that the law regulates social behavior and establishes the kind of social organization that will eventually, perhaps inevitably, improve society. As he put it (1922:98–99):

> I am content to see in legal history the record of a continually wider recognizing and satisfying of human wants or desires through social control; a more embracing and more effective securing of social interests; a continually more complete and effective elimination of waste and precluding of friction in human enjoyment of the goods of existence—in short, a continually more efficacious social engineering.

Finally, sociological jurisprudence emphasized the idea that the law is an instrument for reconciling the many competing and different interests in society. It is a means of protecting the needs of little people against the wishes of the powerful, of seeing that justice is done for the lawbreaker, and of mediating between the conflicting demands of different interests groups (Fuller, 1971; Selznick, 1968). The law, in short, represents an attempt to accomplish the greatest good for the greatest number.

There are few scholars today who would take issue with the view that the law does have its roots deep in our cultural history or that it is a force that strongly shapes the future. But radical criminologists sharply disagree with the notion that the law necessarily improves society or that it equitably serves the interests of all. Such a view, they suggest, is the consequence of a consensual view of social order, of an assumption that there is general agreement among the members of society on basic goals and the laws that should govern the pursuit of those goals.

This view, radicals argue, is a mythical contruction of reality designed to preserve order in an unjust society. Society is not organized by a widespread consensus, but by the exercise of undisguised power by a small ruling class (Quinney, 1974:*v*). "[T]hose who control the means of production also control the production of values in the society" (Chambliss, 1976:3). As a consequence, legal scholars have developed their view of the nature and purpose of law upon a misguided, potentially sinister conception of the way social order is maintained. Perhaps even worse, the same is also true of most social scientists. From Lombroso to Sutherland, from Freud to Cloward and Ohlin, they have developed theories of delinquency which not only provide a misleading description of its causes, but which furnish the ruling class with an ideology for maintaining its own self-serving brand of social control (Quinney, 1974:3–4). In order to understand how this came about, say radical criminologists, it is necessary to contrast the consensual conception of social order within which scientific positivists have conducted their analyses of delinquency with the conflict framework within which radical theorists have conducted theirs.

The consensus framework

The consensus framework grows out of a long tradition in science which has stressed the importance of trying to understand any phenomenon in its entirety, whether it is the human body, the solar system, or society (Cf. Merton, 1968: chap. II). For example, how do all parts of society contribute to its ongoing operation? Which of its parts and functions are necessary for it to survive? If some basic part is destroyed, how does society adapt? By attempting to answer such questions, scientists have sought to identify the key structural elements of any social system and to indicate how they function in order to keep it operating.

Advocates of the consensus model have assumed that while all the parts of society are never fully integrated they do tend toward a condition of stability and equilibrium (Van den Berghe, 1963:695–697). While total stability is never fully achieved, it is toward stability that society moves. If change occurs, it is more likely to occur in gradual fashion rather than in a revolutionary or violent way. But, above all, the thing that makes societal integration and stability possible is the general agreement of its citizens on basic values and beliefs. In its most ideal from, therefore, the consensus model suggests that

> (1) society is a relatively persistent stable structure, (2) it is well integrated, (3) every element [in it] has a function, and (4) [it possesses] a functioning social structure . . . based on a consensus of values (Quinney, 1970:9 from Dahrendorf, 1959:161–163).

According to this model, then, there would be little disagreement as to whom the delinquent is. By definition, a delinquent is anyone who rejects the community's basic values, violates the law, and threatens the stability of the whole. As the French sociologist, Emile Durkheim (1949:73), put it, "the only common characteristic of crimes is that they consist . . . in acts *universally disapproved of* by members of each society" (emphasis added). People seek to control delinquency because they are uniformly against it. Furthermore, since the consensus model assumes that moral values are widely shared in society, it implies that anyone who becomes delinquent is a person who has somehow become different from law-abiding people—a person who suffers from some psychological abnormality, is undersocialized, or has learned subcultural standards for behavior which run counter to those of the larger community. In some way, he is different. In seeking to control delinquency, therefore, efforts must be directed to determining the causes for delinquent behavior and to finding ways by which those causes can be remedied or prevented.

The conflict framework

In sharp contrast to this point of view, radical criminologists argue that the analysis of social order should be cast within the framework of a conflict model. Like the consensus framework, this model has a long and respected history in scientific study (Cf. Dahrendorf, 1959). But, unlike the consensus model, it attributes much less influence to shared traditions and mutual agreement as the sources of order. Instead, it stresses the importance of social change and the exercise of power by a limited few. It assumes that:

> "(1) at every point society is subject to change, (2) it displays at every point dissension and conflict, (3) every element contributes to change, and (4) it is based on the coercion of some of its members by others" (Quinney, 1970:9).

According to this point of view, then, society is held together, not by an overriding consensus on basic values and rules, but by force and constraint. Although certain values predominate, they do so more by the fact that they are enforced by dominant power groups than by the members of society as a whole (Chambliss, 1973; Dahrendorf, 1958; Turk, 1969). Hence, conflict theorists believe that while different ethnic groups or social classes may have their own unique values and customs social order throughout society is maintained through the exercise of power by a ruling class. Acts are defined as delinquent because, and only because, it is in the interest of the ruling group to so define them.

Since this is the case, the causes for delinquency are not to be understood by trying to explain the behavior of the delinquent. That is a fruitless task. Delinquency is merely a label that is attached to the youth whose behavior is contrary to the interests and morality of the ruling class. If we wish to understand it, therefore, we must concentrate upon the distribution of power in society and upon the processes by which laws are written and labels attached to some people but not others.

Marxian Theory

The interest of radical criminologists in the history of class conflicts and social order also springs from a second theoretical source: Marxian theory. Karl Marx was a German philosopher (1818–1883) whose writings reflect the economic and social ferment that accompanied the growth of Western industrial capitalism in the early and middle 19th century. Like radicals today, Marx was a conflict theorist who adopted a dialectical theory of human progress; that is, he viewed history as a reflection of a perpetual struggle between the economic classes.

Marx obtained the seeds for his dialectical theory from Georg Friedrich Hegel, another German philosopher (1770–1831). Along with others, Hegel had been bothered by the fact that philosophers had never been able to develop an explanatory system for the world because it was constantly changing (Taylor, 1967:8). In order to deal with this apparent fact, he constructed a dialectical theory of change.

Webster's dictionary defines the term "dialectic" as the "practice of weighing and reconciling . . . contradictory arguments for the purpose of arriving at truth, especially through discussion and debate." Hegel suggested that whenever some basic idea prevails in society—the "thesis" he called it—that idea is eventually challenged by an opposing idea—the "antithesis." A conflict between the two ideas usually ensues, but rarely does a clearcut victory for either side occur. Rather, a new "synthesis" of the two ideas emerges. In time, this new synthesis is accepted and becomes the prevailing thesis. But, true to the march of history, the new thesis is challenged in turn by a new antithesis. Once again a new synthesis emerges, and thus mankind rolls forward and upward. This was Hegel's way of accounting for human progress and social change.

While he made use of Hegel's idea, Marx suggested that change is due, not to the conflict of contrasting ideas, but to the conflict of competing economic systems. History is a succession of economic arrangements in which the weak must forever struggle against exploitation by the powerful. The inevitable consequence of this struggle, however, is a succession of ever-improving economic orders. Time after time, the powerful in each of them is eventually overthrown by angry workers who rise up against their oppressors and install a more just order. Marx's theory, therefore, became a theory of "dialectical materialism." Human progress, he suggested, is due to the rise and fall of contrasting economic systems rather than to the rise and fall of contrasting ideas.

Nature of economic history

Forcing history into this mold, Marx argued that humankind has gone through three major economic and social epochs: ancient slave society, the feudal society of the Middle Ages, and capitalism (Meyer,

1968). Each has represented a step forward in the inevitable progress of humanity, but each has also included the seeds of its own destruction. Capitalism, for example, represents the peak of social development thus far. It has overthrown the stagnating influence of feudalism, provided more material goods, and instituted constitutional government. But capitalism—today's prevailing economic thesis—also possesses weaknesses that will lead to a new synthesis.

The ruling class under capitalism—the bourgeosie—has made the accumulation of wealth and property its goal rather than continuing to pursue fundamental human rights or using its wealth to eliminate human misery and chaos. The result has been to force larger and larger masses of people—the proletariat—into a dehumanizing position in society. Although people are inherently social and inclined to pursue freedom, these virtues have been distorted and imprisoned by capitalist economic arrangements. Workers have been converted into a commodity whose labor, talents, and personalities are for sale on the free market. Like any other element of production, these precious qualities are bought and sold. Human dignity and the worth of the individual have been sacrificed to the prevailing interests of the bourgeosie in accumulating wealth (Taylor et al. 1973:219–220).

Although this development has acted to dehumanize the masses, it has served one valuable purpose: It has helped to create the conditions that will lead to a liberated civilization. "Society as a whole is more and more splitting into two great hostile camps, . . . bourgeosie and pro-letariat" (Marx and Engels, 1955:10). Eventually, this split will lead to a new and final synthesis—an epoch of socialism, a dictatorship by the proletariat—in which all vestiges of capitalism will be liquidated, the class struggle will cease, and the historical dialectic will come to an end.

"In place of the old bourgeois society, with its classes and class antagonism, we shall have an association in which the free development of each is the condition for the free development of all" (Marx and Engels, 1955:32). The proletariat will become the liberators of society, rising above all narrow interests and ideologies to liberate humankind from the curses of property and class. The Millennium will have been reached.

Propositions of radical thoery

Radical theory is a direct reflection of these historical antecedents. The following propositions by Richard Quinney (1974:24) represents a contemporary expression of them:

1. *"American society is based on an advanced capitalist economy."* The term *capitalism* is generally used to refer to an economic system in which "the greater proportion of economic life, particularly ownership of an investment in production goods, is carried on under private (i.e., non-governmental) auspices through the process of economic competition and the avowed incentive of profit." (Cole, 1964:70). Those who favor such a system argue that if left free from governmental interference capitalism maximizes production and results in the most equitable distribution of scarce resources.

Radical theorists maintain, however, that capitalism denotes a system in which the private owners of the means of production extract a profit by paying laborers less than the full value of their labor, thus exploiting them. This is particularly true in an advanced capitalist economy like ours where control has passed into hands of fewer and fewer financiers, bankers, and corporate investors who, though they are divorced from the day-to-day management of industrial enterprises, extract huge profits from them.

2. *"The state is organized to serve the interests of the dominant economic class, the capitalist ruling class."* The people who dominate the huge corporations and financial institutions are those who constitute the ruling class in American society. It is "that class which owns and controls the means of production and which is able, by virtue of the economic power thus conferred upon it, to use the state as its instrument for the domination of society" (Miliband, 1969:23).

3. *"Criminal law is an instrument of the state and ruling class to maintain and perpetuate the existing social and economic order."* Law is "the ultimate means by which the state secures the interests of the ruling class. Laws institutionalize and legitimize the existing property relations" (Quinney, 1974:23). Even our delinquency laws are designed to accomplish this purpose. They were written by a group of elitist child-savers who

> . . . were concerned not with championing the rights of the poor against exploitation by the ruling classes but rather with integrating the poor into the established social order and protecting "respectable" citizens from the "dangerous classes." Given this perspective, it is not surprising that the child-savers sought curbs on immigration, staunchly defended the unequal distribution of wealth, and discussed ways of imposing birth control on the lower classes. The child-savers regarded the children of the urban poor with a mixture of paternalism and contempt (Platt, 1971:*ix*).

Their only concern was with keeping such children under control, thus securing their selfish economic interests.

4. *"Crime control in capitalist society is accomplished through a variety of institutions and agencies established and administered by a governmental elite, representing ruling class interests, for the purpose of establishing domestic order."* In simple undeveloped societies, the modern state with its governing elite of armed policemen, judges, prison wardens, and other officials was unknown. Rather, order was maintained by democratic means in a communal social system. But, with the rise of capitalism, new methods of control were required. The emergence of a new ruling class required that the state by invented "as a means for coercing the rest of the population into economic and political submission" (Engels, 1942).

> It is through the legal system, then, that the state explicitly and forcefully protects the interests of the capitalist ruling class. Crime control becomes the coercive means of checking threats to the existing social and economic arrangements. The state defines its welfare in terms of the general well-being of the capitalist economy (Quinney, 1974:23–24).

5. *"The contradictions of advanced capitalism—the disjunction between existence and essence—require that the subordinate classes remain oppressed by whatever means necessary, especially through the coercion and violence of the legal system."* Capitalist society dehumanizes and alienates people. It does this because of the contradictions inherent in it (Cf. Edwards, et al., 1974:430–434):

> Though it has created a wealth of consumer goods, it has failed to provide for "creative and socially useful work, meaningful community, and liberating education for individual development" (Edwards, et al., 1974:431).
>
> It has been predicated on the pursuit of profit by creating obsolescent consumer goods and military waste, a pursuit that undermines the legitimacy of the irrational system that produced it.
>
> It makes promises it cannot deliver. There is no hope, for example, that it will provide the means by which women, the poor, racial minorities, and the members of the Third World can be liberated.
>
> It draws an ever larger share of the world's population into alienating wage and salary work, thereby creating an enormous expansion of exploited people.
>
> By fostering education and worldwide communication so that its enterprises can be manned, it has created a sophisticated proletariat who grow increasingly dissatisfied with the present division of labor and unequal distribution of power. In short, capital-

ism has created a great gulf between humankind's present existence and its true essence.

Given this state of affairs, it is clear why the legal system must resort to whatever means necessary to maintain control over the exploited and dehumanized classes (Chambliss, 1976:6).

A. The criminal law is obviously not the product of custom and consensus but "is a set of rules laid down by the state in the interests of the ruling class. . . ."

B. "[S]ome criminal behavior is no more than the 'rightful' behavior of persons exploited by extant economic relations—what makes their behavior criminal is the coercive power of the state to enforce the will of the ruling class."

C. "[C]riminal behavior results either from the struggle between classes wherein individuals of the subservient classes express their alienation from established social relations or from competition for control of the means of production."

Even the juvenile justice system was designed to advance the interests of the capitalist system and to insure an excess labor supply.

The juvenile court system was part of a general movement directed towards developing a specialized labor market and industrial discipline under corporate capitalism by creating new programs of adjudication and control for "delinquent," "dependent," and "neglected" youth. This in turn was related to augmenting the family and enforcing compulsory education in order to guarantee the proper reproduction of the labor force (Platt, 1974:377).

Delinquents, in other words, are idle, obscene, dirty children who are not only in danger of producing crime but of producing more children like themselves. Hence, it has been necessary to find legal means to discipline them or they would be unprepared to man the alienating system of capitalist work.

6. *"Only with the collapse of capitalist society and the creation of a new society, based on socialist principles, will there be a solution to the crime problem."* Since capitalist rulers define any behavior as criminal that threatens the capitalist system, crime and delinquency can never be eliminated until that system is destroyed. The only alternative to it is a socialist system of government that places the ownership and control of the means of production into the hands of the community as a whole. "When there is no longer the need for one class to dominate another,

where there is no longer the need for a legal system to secure the interests of a capital ruling class, then there will no longer be the need for crime" (Quinney, 1974:25). Once humankind is liberated from the curses of property and class, as Marx suggested, a crime-free truly equalitarian society will emerge.

Policy implications

One cannot think in traditional terms when considering the implications of radical theory. It clearly denies the possibility that anything can be done to lessen the delinquency problem by working within the framework of capitalist society or merely tampering with its system of juvenile justice. Nothing short of a complete alternation of both will do. Unlike Marx, however, radical criminologists have not issued a call to arms (Cf. Marx and Engels, 1967:120–121). Instead, their prescriptions for reform are marked by two characteristics: (1) by an indictment of academic criminologists for their commitment to positivistic values which are said only to sustain capitalist values, and (2) by the suggestion that these criminologists should join in the task of developing a self-conscious and self-educated political movement designed to promote revolution. Whether or not this revolution will require armed rebellion or will simply have to await the inexorable processes of history is not entirely clear.

Indictment of academic positivists

The following statements illustrate from the radical perspective what the most serious failings of academic criminologists have been:

1. *Reinforcement of capitalist values.*   Capitalism is a criminogenic system; that is, it perpetuates values which are themselves criminal and which lead to imperialistic war, racism, sexism, and poverty (Schwendinger and Schwendinger, 1975). These are the real crimes. But, because they do nothing about them, criminologists "systematically ignore moral questions about the legal order, devoting attention instead to supporting the existing order" (Quinney, 1974:13). What they should be doing is redefining crime so that criminologists become the guardians of human rights rather than the defenders of a bankrupt and inhumane system (Schwendinger and Schwendinger, 1975).

2. Criminologists are technocratic servants of capitalism. Criminologists have provided the "brain trust" and the "technical skills" for the operation of oppressive legal and penal institutions. Their devotion to the rehabilitative ideal has so dominated their thinking that "officially constituted agencies of the criminal law have not been subjected to serious criticism and research" (Platt, 1974:356). Instead, "criminologists today are furnishing the information and knowledge necessary for the manipulation and control of those who threaten the social system (Quinney, 1974:15).

3. Proponents of liberal reform. This is not to say that traditional criminologists have failed to advocate reform. They have been critical of "inefficiency," "mismanagement," "corruption," and "brutality." They have urged reform in several ways: "reform of criminals, reform of the criminal justice, and even reform of society" (Platt, 1974:357). But, in believing that such "technocratic solutions" as enlightened managers, diagnostic centers, public defenders, probation officers, or youth service bureaus would provide the necessary answers, their efforts have always been marked by a singular failure: They "are invariably formulated within the framework of corporate capitalism and designed to shape new adjustments to existing political and economic conditions" (Platt, 1974:357).

4. Absence of passion. The emphasis of positivistic criminologists upon value neutrality and the need for evidence has caused them to be a cynical and passionless lot who are more concerned with trivia than with the central issues of our age (Platt, 1974:359). Even worse, their trivial findings are not the product of a concerned group of people seeking after truth, but of a self-serving group whose major concern is with maintaining the favor of the dominant ruling elite. "In the name of developing knowledge about crime, most criminologists support current institutions at the expense of human freedoms and social revolution" (Quinney, 1974:13).

Prescriptions for revolution

Since from the radical perspective criminologists have been the cynical servants of capitalism, what should they do now? How might delinquency be eliminated?

> Our task as students of crime is to consider the alternatives to the capitalist legal order . . . at this advanced stage of capitalist development, law is a

little more than a repressive instrument of manipulation and control. We must make others aware of the current meaning of crime and justice in America. The objective is to move beyond the existing order. And this means ultimately that we are engaged in socialist revolution (Quinney, 1974:25).

What are the steps by which this revolution can become a reality?

1. *Understand the contradictions of capitalist society.* We must become better aware of the dialectical nature of history and of the contradictions inherent in capitalism that were outlined earlier. The mere existence of these contradictions, however, is not enough nor are individual rebellions, strikes, or campus protests. "The capitalist class is a privileged and exploiting class, and it is not about to give up its special place without resistance. It will . . . mystify discontent, offer sham concessions, co-opt leaders and causes, . . . and suppress movement organizations" (Edwards, et al., 1974:432). Thus, a second developmental step is required.

2. *Create class consciousness.* "Fundamental social change will occur only if a self-conscious class emerges and engages in organized political struggle." This class "must articulate and struggle for a vision of a liberated society, in which all social relations are transformed and all hierarchical divisions of labor are abolished" (Edwards, et al., 1974:432). But what is the vision for which people should struggle? What are the goals of a liberated socialist society? How will it be organized?

The liberated society

The goals of the liberated society are clearly stated: the end of all class and status differences, nonalienating work, cooperation and the use of production to meet human needs. A society would be created in which group differences and individual rights would be guaranteed. Human greed and the historical tendency for people to disagree over religious, political, economic, or cultural differences would disappear; all racism, sexism, poverty, and crime would be eliminated (Edwards, et al., 1974:433–434). Though the history of civilization up to now has been characterized by value conflict and clashing interests, order in the liberated society would apparently be maintained by an enlightened consensus.

Despite these impressive goals, the organization of the liberated society is not clearly stated by radical theorists. They do suggest that private ownership of capital would be abolished and the wealth redistributed;

that all governmental bureaucracies and other social hierarchies would be destroyed; that monolithic criminal law would be eliminated and replaced with local community laws (if such are necessary); and that people would become self-governing and self-managing (Edwards, et al., 1974:433–434; Quinney, 1972).

But, if all people are to be made equal and self-managing, without any differences in wealth or status and without the need for any governmental or industrial bureaucracies, an institutional redesign of the greatest magnitude is implied. Presumably the Constitution of the United States, its Bill of Rights, its system of government, and its legal, economic, and educational institutions would either have to be drastically changed or eliminated. Hence, the need for a socialist blueprint of some kind is strongly implied, particularly since we are talking about the total alteration of an exceedingly complex, ethnically heterogeneous highly technological society of over 200 million people. Indeed, in taking issue with value-neutral stance of positivistic criminologists, Chambliss (1976:3) says that "The ultimate test of a theory's utility is not its logical structure or its 'fit' with empirical data, but its ability to create workable recipes for changing the existing set of social conditions (both material conditions and the superstructure derived therefrom)." Astonishingly, however, radicals have either failed to provide "workable recipes" thus far or have disavowed the need to be specific. To do so, Edwards et al. (1974:433) suggest, would be to appear excessively "utopian."

> We cannot present a blueprint or an exact specification of how a socialist "utopia" would work; nor should we attempt to do so, since constructing imaginary utopias bears little relation to the actual task of building a decent society. Any *real* alternatives to capitalism will be historically linked to the forces and movements generated by the contradictions of capitalist society itself. *New institutions which liberate rather than oppress can only be created by real people confronting concrete problems in their lives and developing new means to overcome oppression.* The political movements arising from capitalism's contradictions therefore constitute the only means for society to move from its present condition to a new and more decent form, and only out of these movements will human as well as practical new institutions be generated (Emphasis added).

In other words, radical doctrine should be accepted on faith. Having experienced a generation of social despair over the contradictions of capitalism, other Americans should join radicals in pursuing the radical vision of tomorrow, even if it is somewhat clouded.

Implications

The implications of this philosophy are great. It helps us to focus on economic factors which other theories overlook or underplay. Cultural deviance theory, for example, stresses the ambiguous position of youth in American society: They are neither child nor adult; they do not have a responsible and productive role to play in society; left in a structural vacuum, their delinquent acts may be due to the development of deviant norms among them. Radical theory, however, helps to explain why these conditions have occurred. Capitalism and the Industrial Revolution have created an affluent machine-intensive society in which less and less human power is needed. Many young people, particularly the poor, are on a transmission belt that goes nowhere. There are no permanent jobs for them, even as adults.

At the same time, radical theory enriches our sense of human possibility. Since the search for justice is based on hope, the impressive values of radical theory to those who despair are values possessed of widespread appeal. Indeed, radical theory is representative of a larger social movement among intellectual and social scientists which not only challenges the emphasis of the positivistic philosophy upon scholarly detachment, but sees our salvation in overthrowing capitalism. In its mildest form, this movement suggests that social scientists should be changing the world while investigating it (Taylor, et al., 1–75, 1973). Unless they are strongly committed to change, scientists will often be unguided and insensitive to the uses to which their findings may be put (Gouldner, 1970). In its more extreme form, this philosophy indicates that we already know what the solution is—it lies in a liberated socialist society. Since the dialectical processes of history are inevitable, science should be engaged in documenting its march toward socialism, thus speeding up the process (Edwards, et al., 1974).

Such strong assertions raise crucial questions, especially since radical theory is imbalanced toward the importance of making people conscious of capitalism's contradictions at the expense of providing clearly articulated guidelines for positive actions. Radicals urge us to move forward without any blueprint. But can we do so unless someone addresses a number of crucial questions: Will the effort be made in the perfect society to limit human wants and, therefore, to gain satisfactions through shared austerity? Or will human wants be allowed to multiply as they have under capitalism? How will the insatiable appetites of the human animal be managed so that exploitation does not occur? Will the enormous bureaucracy necessary to run a modern socialist state be any more than its capitalist counterpart?

It is not entirely satisfying for radicals to suggest that answers should be left to "real" people who face "concrete" problems. This is not a novel idea even under capitalism. Since the days of Andrew Jackson, many Americans have shared the belief that social salvation lies not in the minds of intellectuals, but in the good sense of the common man. Yet, even in his day, Marx complained about the unwillingness of "common" people to revolt (Taylor, 1967:19). They had begun to acquire property, their own homes, and other possessions. Since such is far more true today, there is a question as to whether workers would be willing to revolt, especially without a clearer knowledge of the society they should be pursuing and how it will be run.

Actually, the inability of radicals to provide a blueprint is likely due to a complex problem that is not really new, a problem that has long been familiar to common people as well as to intellectuals; namely, that it is far easier to list impressive goals than it is to provide concrete and workable means for achieving them. *Webster's Dictionary*, for example, defines *socialism* as "any of various economic and political theories advocating collective or governmental ownership and administration of the means of production and distribution of goods." The *Oxford English Dictionary*, meanwhile, defines it as "a theory or policy that aims at or advocates the ownership or control of the means of production—capital, land, property, etc.—by the community as a whole and their administration in the interests of all."

These definitions illustrate the ambiguous meaning of the term socialism. Furthermore, its implementation in various countries has been characterized by even greater ambiguity (Cf. Hunt, 1964:670–672).

In many countries, socialism has resulted in *State Capitalism* rather than ownership and control by the community.

Many countries view themselves as *socialist* without taking over *all* the means of production.

It is often difficult to distinguish the difference between *capitalism* and *socialism* when it comes to the practical matter of deciding what programs shall actually be implemented.

There has often been a great difference between saying that workers will control the means of production and finding practical and equitable means for doing this in complex modern societies.

The definition of *socialism*, itself, is not a constant. It, too, changes in response to wider social and cultural change.

And crime and delinquency, to say nothing of all other social ills, have not been eliminated in countries that call themselves *socialist*.

In light of these ambiguities, we are left only with slogans and catchwords—"exploitation" and "oppression" versus "liberation" and "equality"—if no guidelines are provided by radicals for organizing *their* socialist society. Moreover, if one is particularly concerned with delinquency, how can it be said that these slogans are any less overworked and any more helpful than the catchwords of the 19th century child-savers—"industrial slavery" and "slaughter of the innocents" versus "loving treatment" and "personal care?"

In many ways, both the radical and child-saving movements represent well-intentioned efforts, growing out of different periods in our history to address real problems. But, just as we have observed a gross slippage between the slogans of the child-saving movement and what it has actually accomplished, so there are grounds for remaining skeptical about the panaceas suggested by radicals. Both movements have been characterized by an unusual amount of rhetoric and religious fervor. For that reason, there is merit in further consideration of the intellectual content of radical theory as it relates specifically to delinquency.

Intellectual legacy of radical theory

There are three major issues that merit careful scrutiny: the stress of radical theory upon the importance of demystifying law and legal practice; its suggestion that delinquency is best understood as an artifact of the capitalist system of production; and its logical adequacy, both with respect to its construction of delinquency and the solution that it proposes.

Demystification of law and legal practice

Like labeling theory, radical theory has performed an extremely valuable service in directing our attention to the sources and effects of existing law. Indeed, this book borrows heavily from some of the insights of labeling and of radical theories. We have seen that delinquency was legally invented in the 19th century as a result of historical changes that had been taking place for centuries. We have also seen how that invention has gone through a significant number of changes during the 20th century. Our analysis, in other words, has helped to "demystify" this important segment of our cultural history. It clearly indicates that delinquency is not a universal concept, timeless and unchanging throughout the ages.

By the same token, radical theory, particularly as stated by Marx, has had profound impact on our understanding of political and economic history. Except perhaps for Freud, no writer in recent centuries has enjoyed the attention that Marx has received. For colonized people in particular—the leaders of revolution in Russia and China or the members of the Third World today—the writings of Marx have provided a gospel of hope and a rallying cry for change.

Finally, radical theory has stimulated greater study of the impact of political and economic factors on the construction and implementation of law. The results, however, have been mixed. On one hand, some support has been found for the contention that laws are often written as a means of controlling the labor force and of insuring the position of powerful groups (Chambliss, 1973; 1976; Nelson, 1974). There is evidence as well that affluent people are less likely to be convicted of the crimes with which they are charged because of their social position and because they can afford better legal talent. On the other hand, several investigators have found that once they are convicted higher status offenders are not likely to be favorably treated. The punishments they receive are no less severe than those received by lower status offenders (Chiricos and Waldo, 1975; Terry, 1967; Thornberry, 1973).

It would also be a mistake to take at face value the radical contention that the scientific study of delinquency has but one purpose: the legitimation of the existing social order. One of the greatest achievements of social science is that it has played a leading role in altering the mythical view that any one legal or social system is inevitably superior; anthropologists have helped to demolish the conceit of Western peoples that their values and institutions are always preeminent; the findings of social scientists were instrumental in the 1954 Supreme Court decision which led to the desegregation of the public schools; sociologists and psychologists helped to discount the notion that delinquency is solely the result of biological or genetic weaknesses by documenting the influence of cultural and structural factors; and, for much of this century, criminologists have been calling attention to the unequal protection of white-collar and other powerful criminals. In short, the process of demystifying law and legal practice is not a new one and is not due just to the resurgence of radical theory.

What, then, is the specific contribution of radical theory? Its contribution lies in reasserting the value of the conflict perspective for extending the boundaries of knowledge.

It holds out the promise of a better understanding of law and justice, informed by a greater sense of history. It directs our attention to persistent discrimination or to collusion between governmental and ruling class interests—matters to which criminologists have not paid enough attention. It correctly notes the persistence of exploitation, sexism, and racism. And it reminds us, as the 19th century child-savers needed reminding, that delinquency is not merely an expression of pathological individuals or depraved immigrant groups colliding with an always equitable and just legal system. Rather, that system and its underlying values must be taken into account and its contribution to creation of delinquents assessed. It is this lesson, therefore, that may constitute the greatest contribution of radical theory.

Delinquency in capitalist society

The contribution of radical theory to the explanation of delinquency is much less certain. Radical theorists assert that little is to be gained by trying to understand the causes of delinquent behavior. Instead, delinquency is nothing more than an artifact of the capitalist system of production. Like labeling theory, therefore, radical theory suggests that capitalist rulers create delinquents by making the rules whereby infractions constitute delinquent behavior.

The evidence supporting this point of view thus far has been derived primarily from the historical analysis of conditions leading to the creation of the juvenile court in the 19th century (Cf. Platt, 1971; 1974). It will be recalled that from the time this country was settled up through the 19th century child labor was much in demand. White children were gathered up on the streets of Europe and sent to the colonies as indentured servants while black children were submitted to a worse fate—slavery. Meanwhile, the colonists themselves were enjoined to have many children and to train them to be good producers. Then, in the 19th century, work for children was extended to the mines and factories of capitalist enterprises. During these periods, the idle hands of little people were indeed viewed as the devil's workshop. But, if one looks at history in broader perspective, it does not always support the radical position. Capitalists have exploited children alright, but they certainly did not originate the idea.

We learned in Chapters 2 and 3 that the practice of putting children to work, and training them for that work via the apprenticeship system, was a product of the Middle Ages, not of capitalism. Long before the Industrial Revolution, children were expected to take their place alongside adults in performing useful work roles. If they did not, they were in violation of long-standing custom. Hence, to say that capitalism is responsible for the notion that idle children are bad children is to distort history.

Radical historians also tend in ignore, or to oversimplify, the creation of the modern concept of childhood and its contribution to the invention of delinquency. As early as the 16th and 17th centuries, increasingly influential groups decried the traditional treatment of children and demanded that they be protected from adult pursuits and vices. That is why, in the 19th century, laws were passed which required children to attend school, not merely to train them for capitalist jobs, but because it was considered the moral thing to do. Reflecting the long-term trends of history, there was a rising concern over the fact that more and more young people had nothing to do. Attempts were made to fill their leisure hours with schooling and other educational activities (Katz, 1975). These trends, of course, were aided by the labor-saving technology provided by capitalism, but capitalism was scarcely responsible for many changes that were religious, familial, and social in origin as well as political and economic.

Poorer children are overrepresented in our courts and correctional institutions, clearly attesting to the importance of economic factors. Yet, studies of self-reported delinquency not only reveal that law violation is widespread throughout the class structure, but the judges are more likely to detain and to punish middle-class and female status offenders than they are to punish lower-class and male status offenders (Cf. Chapter 16). Poverty and unemployment are said to be the primary roots of juvenile crime. Yet, research studies show that delinquency increases, not in times when unemployment rates are the highest, but in times of prosperity. The loosened controls that are associated with increasing affluence and opportunity may be somewhat more important than poverty per se (Bogen, 1944; Glaser and Rice, 1959). Radical theorists suggest that capitalism exploits the labor of the lower classes. Yet, youth culture theorists lament the lack of work roles for the young, particularly for those who are the most poor (Cf. Chapters 10 and 11). In short, the social and cultural roots of delinquency are enormously complex and are not likely to be satisfactorily explained by theories which concentrate on only a selected few of those roots.

The explanation of juvenile crime

A major problem in coming to grips with radical theory is its sweeping character and its lack of concern with specific, but highly important, issues. For example, in suggesting that capitalist rulers create delinquents by passing discriminatory rules, radical theory falls prey to some of the same weaknesses we observed in labeling theory. The idea that gang killings or street muggings would not exist if the rules had not been passed simply will not do. A killing or a mugging by any other name still hurts just as much. By over generalizing, therefore, radical theory does not pay adequate heed to such matters. Furthermore, since lower-class people are more likely than capitalist rulers to be the victims of assaults and robberies, they are no less likely to want them prohibited.

Radical theory is also something akin to strain theory in its suggestion that crime is due to the demoralization and lack of opportunity produced by capitalist society. Yet, it does little to indicate how the processes of demoralization lead to delinquent acts or why some demoralized juveniles are delinquent and others are not. The motivation to be delinquent is either assumed or considered unimportant.

In his brief concerns with these matters, Karl Marx clearly suggested that criminals are not to be confused with ordinary working-class people. Somehow, they and their motivations are different:

1. *Marx's view of criminals.*   Marx maintained that criminals are members of the *lumpenproletariat*, not members of the proletariat or the bourgeosie. The *lumpenproletariat*, he said, are a "dangerous class, " a "social scum," a "passively rotting mass thrown off by the lower layers of society" (Marx and Engels, 1967:92). Such people cannot be relied upon for anything constructive. They are "a parasitic class living off productive labor by theft, extortion, and beggary, or by providing 'services' such as prostitution and gambling" (Hirst, 1975:216). In short, Marx used the same derogatory terms to describe criminals that the most vitriolic of the 19th century child-savers used to describe delinquents. They are a "dangerous class" not to be confused with the responsible workers of society.

2. The motive for crime.   In using such derogatory terms, Marx clearly implied that the *lumpenproletariat* are somehow different from solid working-class people or even the bourgeoisie. Perhaps their crimes are due to demoralization. But, if that is the case, he did nothing to explain why they become demoralized "scum" while others resist demoralization and remain moral (Taylor, et al., 1973:218). The same is true of radicals today. They either ignore individual differences and motivations or consider them irrelevant.

3. The crimes of advantaged youth.   Radicals also tend to ignore the crimes of advantaged youth. Why are the self-reported illegal acts of bourgeois juveniles so great? Why do they vandalize property, steal autos, commit rape, defraud the phone company, or rip property off for the hell of it? Why do some of them grow up to white-collar criminals?

Some radicals argue, of course, that capitalist society demoralizes everyone, not just members of the *lumpenproletariat* (Roszak, 1969; Teodori, 1969). But, even if that is the case, radical theory still fails to indicate why some privileged juveniles, but not others, are motivated to commit crime.

4. Class versus age as explanation.   Since radicals contend that modern society is dominated by class conflict and the "dangerous class" are members of the *lumpenproletariat*, then class membership should be a good predictor of crime. But, as we have seen, class is related much less strongly to crime than is age. Radical theory does virtually nothing to explain this fact. Why do the highest crime-producing years occur during adolescence and young adulthood? Why is it that progressive urbanization and industrialization in virtually every society is associated with higher rates of crime among the young? Why do delinquency rates go up in times of prosperity rather than in times of depression? Since crime is more closely related to the age than to the class structure of society, greater attention to this matter might add exceedingly valuable information to our store of knowledge.

In short, radical theory is like labeling theory in the sense that it deals more with social rules and reactions to crime than with its causes. But, while labeling theorists have now returned to an interactionist position so that rule breakers as well as rule makers and rule enforcers might be studied, radical theorists apparently reject the need to do. Why is this? The answer seems to lie in the insistence of radical theorists on explaining not only delinquency, but all of history in political and economic terms. Other cultural forces or the inclinations and motivations of individuals are relatively unimportant. It is political and economic oppression which determine the course of events. Hence, if capitalism were destroyed and a socialist society constructed, we would not need to worry about motives for delinquent conduct or differences by class and age. They would disappear. But how sound is this argument? In our final comment, we will consider the logical adequacy of radical theory, both with respect to its construction of delinquency and the solution it proposes.

Logical adequacy

Radical theory possesses some logical deficiencies which make it virtually impossible to confirm or to falsify. The most serious of these deficiencies is its circularity. That is, repression is inferred from capitalist society while capitalist society is explained by repression. Values which produce sexism, racism, poverty, and crime are, at one and the same time, both the cause and the consequence of capitalism. This kind of reasoning is like that associated with the Freudian theory in which mental abnormality is inferred from delinquent behavior while delinquent behavior is explained by mental abnormality.

Similarly, in relying upon the dialectical conflict theory of social order, radical theory maintains that history has been characterized by a succession of economic orders in which the law inevitably reflects the interests of the powerful.

> The problem with this position is that it can never specify the conditions under which law would not be simply an instrument of a currently powerful interest. Thus, it can never specify the conditions under which there is the optimum chance for guaranteeing individual liberties and freedom for people who are not affiliated to the powerful interest groups of the day (Taylor, et al., 1973:266).

Perhaps this is why radical theorists experience so much difficulty in providing a blueprint for the liberated society. Their theory provides few directions for doing so. China and Cuba are often cited as socialist societies in which the streets are safe from delinquents and criminals. But the same is also true of countries like Norway, Finland, or Sweden which are capitalist welfare states. Furthermore, a country like China is scarcely democratic. Thus, since adequate models are lacking, we are asked not to compare our system of government with some real society, but with a mythical one—the truly liberated society.

The results are ironic. While urging us to demystify the past, radicals mystify the future. On one hand, they accept the Marxian notion that the history of civilization has always been characterized by value conflict and rule by the powerful. Yet, on the other, they indicate that conflict and crime will cease in the liberated society, and order will be maintained by enlightened consensus. Otherwise, how will human greed or disagreements over religious, political, and economic differences be eliminated? How will people reach the stage where, at one and the same time, they are willing to guarantee individual and group differences and yet view themselves as equals? Obviously, if this is to come about, relations in the liberated society must be explained by something other than a conflict theory of social order. Yet, radical theorists do not deal with this contradiction nor indicate how it will be resolved.

Given these logical inconsistencies, one can resort to one of two alternatives in deciding how to interpret radical theory. The first is to ignore its inconsistencies and to accept radical theory as a doctrine that is not to be confused with theories in the positivistic tradition. This is an attractive alternative because people have always aspired to create a civilized utopia in which intolerance, exploitation, and crime no longer exist. Once the repressive rules of modern society are eliminated, love, brotherhood, and freedom will prevail.

The second alternative is to search for other theoretical frameworks of which radical theory might be a part. Not only might cultural deviance, strain, and interactionist theories be combined fruitfully with radical theory in explaining the creation of official delinquents, but several theorists have suggested that neither a conflict nor a consensus model by itself is adequate for explaining the origins and maintenance of order. Both have something to offer (Dahrendorf, 1959; Hills, 1971; Hopkins, 1975). Many of our laws, for example, do seem to reflect a high degree of consensus—laws which prohibit murder, assault, fraud, robbery, or rape. The interests of most people, not just the powerful, are served by them. Other laws by contrast are expressions of special interests—laws against marijuana, gambling, vagrancy, or opportunities for women and minority groups. More attention could be devoted to the historical origins of both types of laws as well as to the way they operate in modern society.

A problem with this alternative, however, is that it would not lend itself to the optimistic outlook inherent in radical theory. Radicals are correct in suggesting that criminologists are skeptical about the notion that delinquency and other forms of deviant behavior can ever be eliminated. They argue, instead, that we must be leery of utopian schemes because crime, like disease, is a normal aspect of human life (Durkheim, 1938:chap. 3). It is virtually impossible to conceive of a society in which all passion, all innovation, all inclinations to deviate would be so effectively managed that deviant behavior would be nonexistent or that its elimination would even be desirable. To accomplish this, one would have to purchase harmony at the cost of creating a totalitarian state. Hence, the idea that either crime or disease can be ultimately vanquished is said to involve "a particularly trivial kind of utopian dreaming. Out of control, malfunction and crime could possibly overcome life, but control could never succeed in more than keeping them to a level appropriate to the prevailing form of human life" (Bittner, 1970:49).

Paradoxically, some scholars make this argument not just because they assume that people remain unalterably bad, but because their standards of morality are constantly changing. Consider Durkeim's (1938:68) well-known allegory:

> Imagine a society of saints, a perfect cloister of exemplary individuals. Crimes, properly so called, will there be unknown; but faults which appear venial to the layman will create the same scandal that the ordinary offense does in ordinary consciousness. If, then, this society has the power to judge and punish, it will treat them as such.

What Durkeim meant was that,

> if all those acts we know as crime were extinguished, small differences in behaviour that have no moral significance [at present] would take on new and larger meaning [in the future]. Small improprieties and breaches of manners and good taste would become crimes of a lesser degree, and so on. In short, there *cannot* be a society of saints because a process of social redefinition operates continuously to insure that all the positions on the scale from wickedness to virtue will always be filled and that some will always be holier than others (Cohen, 1973:5).

In other words, there is a law in social relations which suggests that the solution to a current set of problems inevitably produces its own set of new problems. We mortals seem to have a chronic tendency to redefine misery, injustice, delinquency, or poverty in such a way that regardless of what we do about them they are always with us (Cohen, 1973:5). There can be little doubt, for example, that actual rates of malnutrition, infant mortality, and disease during the Middle Ages were higher than they are today. But we are no less concerned about them.

Indeed, radical theory, itself, suggests that we are more concerned, since capitalism represents an improvement in morality over feudalism, and socialism will be an improvement over capitalism. Our standards are getting better. But, if this is the case, why will morality stop improving in socialist society if it does not do so among saints in heaven? Even if life is improved according to today's standards, it will be marked by serious problems according to tomorrow's standards. Thus, while it is difficult to take issue with the impressive values and the humane society which radicals pursue, serious questions can be raised about their particular construction of delinquency and the solution they propose.

Summary and conclusions

Radical theory cannot be viewed as theories in the positivistic tradition are viewed. Instead, it is built upon an entirely different set of philosophical principles.

The cornerstone of the positivistic philosophy is based upon the enlightenment notion that the application of scientific study to human affairs would lead to a better world. Although knowledge can be gained only by patience, skepticism, and considerable tolerance for uncertainty, scholarly investigation will contribute ultimately to humankind's long search for a more just and humane society.

Radical theorists argue that this faith not only reflects a particular set of questionable values, but that it is naive with respect to the way the world operates. By clinging to a positivistic philosophy, scientists not only fail to eliminate oppression and injustice, but give tacit approval to those who would perpetuate them. Radical theorists, as a consequence, suggest that criminologists should be guided by values which oppose the status quo. Since delinquency is the product of capitalist oppression, criminologists should be engaged in documenting this oppression, making people aware of it and joining in socialist revolution.

In brief, then, the radical school of criminology stresses research and action toward predetermined socialist goals while the positive school stresses tentativity and scholarly detachment in the pursuit of goals that are not always predetermined. Since ultimate truth is not known, scientists must keep an open mind in pursuit of it. More than theories in the positivistic tradition, therefore, radical theory is doctrinal in character; that is, it expresses beliefs that are laid down as true and beyond serious dispute. What, then, are these beliefs?

1.   Assumptions about human nature and social order.   Radical theory assumes that human nature is good. Were people not enslaved by the historical struggle between the classes, their humane inclinations would produce an elightened and liberated civilization. The social order by contrast is characterized by conflict and coercion. It is maintained through the oppression of the masses by society's rulers.

2.   Underlying content and logic of radical theory.   The history of civilization has been characterized by a succession of economic arrangements in which the powerful have always exploited the weak. The period of advanced capitalism in which we now live is the latest in this series of arrangements. A modern society like America, its laws, and its legal system are organized to serve the capitalist ruling class. Delinquency, therefore, is any behavior that threatens the vested interests of this class.

3.   Policy implications.   Delinquency cannot be eliminated by working within the framework of a capitalist society or by attempting to reform its system of juvenile justice. The only solution lies in the creation of class consciousness, the overthrow of capitalism, and the creation of a socialist society.

4.   Logical and empirical adequacy.   Radical theorists have extended the boundaries of knowledge in several important ways: by questioning the limitations of positivistic philosophy, by their analysis of social conflict and its role in maintaining social order, by their stress upon a better understanding of law and legal practice, and by their attention to the persistence of sexism, racism, and exploitation in modern society.

At the same time, radical theory itself is marked by serious contradictions and omissions:

It presents a circular argument that is virtually impervious to confirmation or falsification.

By insisting that social order has always been characterized by conflict, it cannot specify the conditions under which law would not be an instrument of some powerful group. Yet, it concludes that socialist society will be characterized by cooperation, brotherhood, and equality.

In relying solely upon the notion that delinquency and crime are an artifact of political and economic oppression, it tends to deny that the delinquent label is ever earned by an offender or that his personal motivation, however induced, is important in explaining his acts.

Radicals hold that crime will disappear in the liberated society, but they also maintain that capitalists are criminals. How will these enemies of socialism be treated? Will they not be defined as criminals?

It denies the possibility that cultural forces other than those which are political and economic were instrumental in the creation of childhood and the invention of delinquency.

In concentrating upon class conflict, it ignores the fact that age is usually more closely related to the commission of delinquent acts than is the class structure.

Given these problems, several questions might be raised. The first has to do with the nature of the radical philosophy itself. Radicals are correct in suggesting that traditional criminologists have tended to confine their research to the context provided by existing values and laws and that this practice sometimes gives tacit approval to injustice. But what about the radical approach to research? What if investigators insisted on conducting research in which only their values provided the context for analysis? Would this not be like the anthropologist who goes to a foreign country and, without trying to understand the values which give rise to behavior there, judges that society as inferior because it does not conform to his values?

In some ways, that is what radical theorists have done. Like Marx, they have been more intent on using research to justify conclusions they have already reached than to weigh carefully both the pros and cons of their argument. This approach to research is an old one, but it is closer to the kinds used by lawyers and debaters than it is to the kind used by scientists. The object of science is not to win a debate or a legal case, but to weigh evidence on both sides of the question.

It must be pointed out, however, that positivists have not been free of this problem. For a century now, the changing construction of delinquency has sometimes been as much the result of new values and beliefs as it has been the result of confirmed scientific evidence. Earlier groups of social scientists did not reject biological explanations, Freudian theory, or the mental testing movement for scientific reasons only. Their objections instead were often as value-laden and political as the radical movement today. Hence, the differences between radicals and positivists are not absolute but are a matter of degree. While positivists remain relatively more skeptical about the ultimate truth of their theories and their proposals for reform, their personal values are apparent in their work nonetheless.

For these reasons, the ultimate test of the radical school of criminology will remain much the same as it has for the positivist school. Its acceptance as a philosophy and as a method for studying and responding to delinquency will depend, in part, on its doctrinal character and, in part, on the evidence that can be found to support it. Thus far, the doctrine is much stronger than the evidence.

References

Bendix, Reinhard
    1970   "Sociology and the distrust of reason." *American Sociological Review*, October, *35*:831–843.

Bittner, Egon
    1970   *The Functions of the Police in Modern Society*. Washington, D.C.: U.S. Government Printing Office.

Bogen, David
    1944   "Juvenile delinquency and economic trends." *American Sociological Review*, April, *9*:178–185.

Chambliss, William J.
    1973   *Functional and Conflict Theories of Crime*. New York: MSS Modular Publications.

    1976   "Functional and conflict theories of crime: the heritage of Emile Durkheim and Karl Marx." Pp. 1–30 in William J. Chambliss and Milton Mankoff (Eds.), *Whose Law? What Order?* New York: John Wiley.

Chiricos, Theodore G. and Waldo, Gordon P.
    1975   "Socioeconomic status and criminal sentencing: an empirical assessment of a conflict proposition." *American Sociological Review*, December, *40*:753–772.

Cohen, Albert K.
    1973   *The Elasticity of Evil: Changes in the Social Definition of Deviance*. Oxford University Penal Research Unit, Occasional Paper No. 7.

Cole, G. D. H.
    1964   "Capitalism." Pp. 70–72 in Julius Gould and William L. Kolb (Eds.), *A Dictionary of the Social Sciences*. New York: Free Press.

Dahrendorf, Rolf
    1958   "Out of utopia: toward a reorientation of sociological analysis." *American Journal of Sociology*, September, *67*:115–127.

1959 *Class and Class Conflict in Industrial Society*. Palo Alto: Stanford University Press.

Durkheim, Emile
1938 *The Rules of Sociological Method (1895)*. Chicago: University of Chicago Press.
1949 *The Division of Labor in Society*. New York: Free Press.

Edwards, Richard C., Reich, Michael and Weisskopf, Thomas E.
1974 "Toward a Socialist Alternative." Pp. 429–434 in Richard Quinney (Ed.), *Criminal Justice in America*. Boston: Little, Brown.

Engels, Friedrich
1942 *The Origins of the Family, Private Property and the State*. New York: International Publishers.

Fuller, Lon L.
1971 "Human interaction and the law." Pp. 171–217 in Robert P. Wolff (Ed.), *The Rule of Law*. New York: Simon and Schuster.

Gibbs, Jack P.
1966 "Crime, unemployment and status integration." *British Journal of Criminology*, January, 24:49–58.

Glaser, Daniel and Rice, Kent
1959 "Crime, age and employment." *American Sociological Review*, October, 24:679–686.

Gouldner, Alvin W.
1970 *The Coming Crisis of Western Sociology*. New York: Basic Books.

Hills, S. L.
1971 *Crime, Power, and Morality*. Scranton: Chandler.

Hirst, Paul Q.
1975 "Marx and Engels on law, crime and morality." Pp. 203–232 in Ian Taylor, Paul Walton, and Jock Young (Eds.), *Critical Criminology*. Boston: Routledge and Kegan Paul.

Hopkins, Andrew
1975 "On the sociology of criminal law." *Social Problems*, June, 22:608–619.

Hunt, R. N. Carew
1964 "Socialism." Pp. 670–672 in Julius Gould and William L. Kolb (Eds.), *A Dictionary of the Social Sciences*. New York: Free Press.

Katz, Michael B.
1975 *The People of Hamilton, Canada West: Family and Class in a Mid-Nineteenth Century City*. Cambridge: Harvard University Press.

Marx, Karl
1973 *Selected Writings in Sociology and Social Philosophy*. T. B. Bottomore and Maximilien Rubel (Eds.). London: Watts.

Marx, Karl and Engels, Friedrich
   1955   *The Communist Manifesto (1848).* S. H. Beer (Ed.). New York:
          Appleton-Century-Crofts.
   1967   *The Communist Manifesto.* Baltimore: Penguin Books.
Merton, Robert K.
   1968   *Social Theory and Social Structure* (3rd ed.). New York: Free Press.
Miliband, Ralph
   1969   *The State in Capitalist Society.* New York: Basic Books.
Meyer, Alfred G.
   1968   "Marxism." Pp. 40–44 in David Sills (Ed.), *International Encyclopedia
          of the Social Sciences* (Vol. 10). New York: Macmillan.
Nelson, William E.
   1974   "Emerging notions of modern criminal law in the Revolutionary era:
          an historical perspective." Pp. 100–126 in Richard Quinney (Ed.),
          Criminal Justice in America. Boston: Little, Brown.
Platt, Anthony M.
   1971   "Introduction to the reprint edition." Pp. v–xvi in *National Confer-
          ence of Charities and Correction, History of Child Saving in the United
          States.* Montclair, N.J.: Patterson-Smith.
   1974   "The triumph of benevolence: the origins of the juvenile justice sys-
          tem in the United States." Pp. 356–389 in Richard Quinney (Ed.),
          Criminal Justice in America. Boston: Little, Brown.
Pound, Roscoe
   1922   *An Introduction to the Philosophy of Law.* New Haven: Yale University
          Press.
   1942   *Social Control through Law.* New Haven: Yale University Press.
Quinney, Richard
   1970   *The Social Reality of Crime.* Boston: Little, Brown.
   1972   "The ideology of law: notes for a radical alternative to legal repres-
          sion." *Issues in Criminology,* Winter, 7:1–35.
   1974   *Criminal Justice in America.* Boston: Little, Brown.
Rozak, Theodore
   1969   *The Making of a Counter Culture.* Garden City: Anchor Books.
Schaar, John H.
   1974   "Legitimacy in the modern state." Pp. 62–92 in Richard Quinney
          (Ed.), *Criminal Justice in America.* Boston: Little, Brown.
Schwendinger, Herman and Schwendinger, Julia
   1975   "Defenders of order or guardians of human rights?" Pp. 113–138 in
          Ian Taylor et al. (Eds.), *Critical Criminology.* Boston: Routledge and
          Kegan Paul.

Selznick, Philip
  1968   "The sociology of law." Pp. 50–59 in David L. Sills (Ed.), *International Encyclopedia of the Social Sciences* (Vol. 9). New York: Macmillan.

Taylor, A. J. P.
  1967   "Introduction." Pp. 7–47 in Karl Marx and Friedrich Engels, *The Communist Manifesto.* Baltimore: Penguin Books.

Taylor, Ian, Walton, Paul and Young, Jock
  1973   *The New Criminology.* New York: Harper and Row.

Teodori, Massimo
  1969   *The New Left: A Documentary History.* New York: Bobbs-Merrill.

Terry, R. M.
  1967   "Discrimination in the handling of juvenile offenders by social control agencies." *Journal of Research in Crime and Delinquency*, 4:218–230.

Thornberry, T. P.
  1973   "Race, socioeconomic status and sentencing in the juvenile justice system." *The Journal of Criminal Law and Criminology*, March, 64:90–98.

Turk, Austin T.
  1969   *Criminality and the Legal Order.* Chicago: Rand McNally.

Van den Berghe, Pierre L.
  1963   "Dialectic and functionalism: toward a synthesis. *American Sociological Review*, October, 28:695–705.

part four

SOCIETY'S REACTION TO DELINQUENT BEHAVIOR

Introduction: Juvenile justice and the impending revolution

In this section of the book, we move to an analysis of another part of the delinquency picture, the part that is constructed by policemen, judges, correctional authorities, and a new generation of reformers. The roles played by these important actors have been profoundly affected by the various theories of delinquency we have just reviewed, particularly by their suggestion that delinquent tendencies are inherent in the way society is organized rather than in the pathological and immoral tendencies of individual children. But the impact of these theories has, by no means, superseded our traditional concept of childhood and the other historical forces that led to the invention and growth of the juvenile court. They still remain highly important. In support of this notion, consider the following.

The invention of the juvenile court by the state of Illinois in 1899 was hailed almost universally as a triumph of benevolent progressivism over the forces of reaction and ignorance (Aichorn, 1964; Chute, 1949; Mead, 1918; Platt, 1971). By 1920, all states except three had enacted juvenile court laws, although it was not unitl almost mid-century that Wyoming became the last state to join the movement. Meanwhile, it became a success in many other countries as well (Caldwell, 1961:496).

The rehabilitative philosophy of the juvenile court not only spread geographically, but its jurisdiction over adults, as well as juveniles, was greatly extended (Caldwell, 1961:496–497). The tendency in most states was to raise the upper limit of childhood from 16 to 18, and even to 21 in a few states. The definition of delinquency was broadened to include cases of illegitimacy and mental or physical defectiveness. Adults could be brought into court charged with contributing to the delinquency of a minor. Some cities created family or domestic relations courts designed to deal with family problems of any kind: dependency and neglect, illegitimacy, adoption, nonsupport by a father, or crimes committed by one family member against another. Other cities set up special courts which combined juvenile with criminal court procedures for older youth up to age 21. States such as California and Minnesota created special youth authorities whose purpose was to diagnose ills and to provide unique correctional procedures for youth, many of whom were over 21. The notion of presentence investigation, diagnosis, and treatment found its way into adult courts and became accepted parts of procedure there. For the first half of this century, in short, the philosophy of the juvenile court movement enjoyed ever-widening acceptance.

Rehabilitative ideology

The beliefs and assumptions that sustained this movement are best understood as an ideology—as a kind of visionary theorizing about children and the best way to nurture and to protect them. The strength of this ideology was derived primarily from the assumptions inherent in the modern concept of childhood:

    a.   Children are qualitatively different from adults—innocent, fragile, and uncalculating—and are entitled to special care.

    b.   Children are more malleable than adults and, thus, are more susceptible to helpful intervention.

    c.   Problems during childhood leave a lasting imprint. The earlier the intervention, therefore, the greater the chances for rehabilitation.

The emerging status of social science during the first half of this century also reinforced the juvenile court movement. But the theories of delinquency that were most supportive of it were primarily those of a control variety, particularly psychobiological theories that concentrated on the defects of the individual. Hence, in addition to suggesting that delinquent behavior is due to causes over which the child has little control, they also suggested that the primary problem is defective intelligence, uncaring parents, and a poor home environment. The only way to deal justly with delinquents, therefore, was to adapt legal responses to their moral, hereditary, and emotional problems. Little thought was given to societal defects, to differential opportunities, or to the pluralistic nature of American culture.

According to the rehabilitative ideology, then, officials could not react uniformly to different children for the same delinquent act because each offender was unique and because each one's behavior required special diagnosis and treatment. Furthermore, differential responses to children were the only rational way to protect society. Unless the factors that caused individuals to violate the law were isolated and removed, legal processing and punishment would do no good. Short of killing off all delinquents or of incarcerating them permanently, the only way the citizenry could be protected in the long run was to cure delinquents of their tendencies to violate the law. If this was not done, they would eventually be released only to prey upon innocent victims once again.

Since, in theory, the original purpose of the juvenile court was not to convict children of crimes but to protect, aid, and guide them, it was not viewed as unconstitutional if it denied them certain rights that were guaranteed to adults. If disturbed and ignorant children were properly treated, they could be saved and made into healthy and law-abiding adults. Indeed, rather than taking issue with this ideology, important higher court decisions served only to sustain it.

> To save a child from becoming a criminal, or from continuing in a career of crime, to end in maturer years in public punishment and disgrace, the legislatures surely may provide for the salvation of such a child, if its parents or guardians be unable or unwilling to do so, by bringing it into one of the courts of the state without any process at all, for the purpose of subjecting it to the state's guardianship and protection. . . . The act simply provides how children who ought to be saved may reach the court to be saved (*Commonwealth* v. *Fisher*, 1905).

Although this judicial statement was made in 1905, the ideology upon which it was based had changed little by 1962. In that year, Orman Ketcham (1962:25), judge of the juvenile court in Washington, D.C., observed that "The juvenile in America may [still] be brought within the protective power of the juvenile court without the operation of legal safeguards customarily offered to a person accused of law violation."

Explaining further, Caldwell (1961:497) added that "The balance between rights, on the one hand, and duties and responsibilities, on the other, which every court must seek to maintain, has been upset as the juvenile court has been pushed more and more into the role of a social work agency."

Almost to the present day, then, the view of the juvenile court as a rehabilitative instrument has not only provided the agents of juvenile justice with a broad mandate but with awesome responsibilities. On the one hand, it has suggested that problem children should be treated in a much more thoughtful and humane way than adult offenders. Retribution, in particular, should be avoided; the care, custody, and discipline provided for delinquents should approximate that of loving parents. On the other hand, officials should not wait until children become criminal in taste and habit before they act. Rather, they should respond at the first sign of parental neglect or of departure on the part of any child from accepted moral and legal standards, even if stern and arbitrary methods were required. It mattered little whether children were dependent and neglected, status offenders, or young criminals. Using the same methods, all were to be saved.

So pervasive was this benevolent ideology that little thought was given to the possibility that its theoretical premises might be faulty or that interventions by the court might be more harmful than helpful. As a consequence, the development of sociological theories of delinquency had relatively little impact on court philosophy and practice until after 1960. It was not unitl 1961, for example, that strain theory became the rationale for the President's Committee on Juvenile Delinquency and Youth Crime and for the creation of Mobilization of Youth. But, since these programs were concerned more with changing communities than with judging or correcting known delinquents, they had little impact on the practices of judges and correctional people. As yet, these key officials had paid relatively little attention to the suggestion that society itself might be criminogenic or that the procedures they used in identifying, tagging, and segregating delinquents might serve as much to dramatize, and to reinforce, evil as to suppress it.

The impending revolution

In recent years, profound changes have begun to appear. The juvenile justice system is now in a state of ferment: Its rehabilitative ideology is being challenged; its effectiveness is being questioned; and its basic procedures are being altered. This section of the book is devoted to analysis of the factors that have contributed to this ferment. By analyzing the history and functions of all segments of the juvenile justice system, we will trace the effects of the rehabilitative ideology upon them and determine what has happened in the past 20 years to being about important changes:

> *Chapter 15* will be concerned with the police: their historical development in this country, their perception of the rehabilitative ideology and its impact upon them, and, how, in response to a highly conflicted set of social expectations, they actually process juveniles.

> *Chapter 16* will conduct the same sort of analysis of the juvenile court: the historical spread of its benevolent ideology, the way the courts have actually dealt with juveniles, and the events and ideologies of recent years which have seriously tarnished the image of the court and led to cries for reform.

> *Chapter 17* will be concerned with the history of society's efforts to reform delinquents, all the way from the time when they were whipped, disfigured, or banished from the country to the present when they are placed in complex programs of diagnosis and treatment. Although the prevailing approach since the invention of the juvenile court has stressed rehabilitation, feelings regarding its success have turned from optimism to dismay. Serious questions have been raised about the capacity of probation officers, training schools, and halfway houses to correct delinquents. Nothing seems to work!

> *Chapter 18* will be devoted to the new social inventions that are now being constructed in response to the belief that the juvenile court and rehabilitation have not worked. Indeed, we are at a turning point in history when a revolution in juvenile justice is taking place. Hence, that revolution will be described and an assessment made of it.

> Finally, *Chapter 19* is a concluding chapter that attempts to draw together the various elements of delinquency—beliefs about childhood, rules, behavior, explanations, and social reactions—and to make sense out of them. Our social construction of delinquency is now undergoing radical change, but this change is due, not merely to the failures of the juvenile justice system, but to changes in the

concept of childhood, to alterations in family life, and to profound demographic changes in the age structure of society. We will peer into a misty crystal ball in an attempt to determine what the future might hold for young people, delinquent and otherwise.

References

Aichorn, August
    1964   "The juvenile court: is it a solution? Pp. 55–79 in *Delinquency and Child Guidance: Selected Papers.* New York: International Universities Press.

Caldwell, Robert G.
    1961   "The juvenile court: its development and some major problems." *Journal of Criminal Law, Criminology, and Police Science,* January-February, *51*:493–507.

Chute, Charles L.
    1949   "Fifty years of the juvenile court." Pp. 1–10 in *National Probation and Parole Association Yearbook.* New York: National Probation and Parole Assn.

Commonwealth v. *Fisher*
    1905   213 Pa. 48, 62 Atl. 1. 198.

Ketcham, Orman W.
    1962   "The unfulfilled promise of the American juvenile court." Pp. 22–43 in Margaret K. Rosenheim (Ed.), *Justice for the Child.* New York: Free Press.

Mead, George H.
    1918   "The psychology of punitive justice." *American Journal of Sociology,* March, *23*:577–602.

Platt, Anthony
    1971   "Introduction to the reprint edition." Pp. v–xvi in *History of Child Saving in the United States.* Montclair, N.J.: Patterson-Smith.

15

POLICING JUVENILES: FIGHTING CRIME VERSUS SOCIAL WORK

The police are the most visible symbol of the juvenile justice system to the community because they are the port-of-entry to the system. Whenever a crime, a family fight, or some other disturbance occurs, it is the police to whom most citizens turn. Hence, most of the juveniles entering the juvenile court are referred by the police.

In order to understand how the police have played this crucial role, one must be aware, not just of the rehabilitative ideal for juveniles, but of the history and organization of police work, of prevailing public perceptions of the police, and of the way the police see themselves. Taken together, these have served to create a view of the delinquency problem which is unique to the police and which determines how they respond to juveniles.

History of police work

What may be surprising to the average person is that large, organized police forces, as we know them, have not been in existence for much longer than the juvenile court.[1] Like the juvenile court, in fact, they

---

[1] Except where indicated, this brief history is drawn from the Task Force report: *The Police*. President's Commission on Law Enforcement and Administration of Justice (1967a:3–7).

seem to have arisen in response to the growth of large cities, technology, and industrialization. As the informal controls of rural civilization gradually broke down, society turned increasingly to more impersonal secondary kinds of control—juvenile institutions and the juvenile court as well as the police.

The origin of the police forces in this country can be traced to earlier developments in Western European countries, particularly England. France and some other European countries had professional police forces of a sort as early as the 17th century. England, however, did not begin to create such a force until the 19th century. This delay was due, in part, to the changing nature of English life and, in part, to the fear of police oppression. "During the period of absolute monarchy the police came to represent the underground aspects of tyranny and political repression, and they were despised and feared even by those who ostensibly benefited from their services" (Bittner, 1970:6–7). Thus, in lieu of a large police force, England had long used the "mutual pledge" system for apprehending criminals. Local citizens were encouraged to maintain law and order, and every person was responsible for his or her own actions and for those of neighbors. Hence, when a crime was committed, each citizen was expected to raise the "hue and cry," to collect his or her neighbors, and to go in pursuit of the criminal. If people failed in this task, they could be fined.

These efforts were coordinated by a local constable, or sheriff, who performed three functions: organizing citizens into groups of ten families to enforce the laws; supervising the "watch and ward"—a group of people who were expected to protect property against fire, to guard city gates, and to arrest criminals between sunset and daybreak; and inquiring into offenses, serving summonses, taking charge of prisoners, and otherwise assisting the local justices who were responsible for judging cases in each county. So long as England was a rural country, this system was viewed as adequate. But, with the advent of the Industrial Revolution, accompanied by the migration of thousands of people to factory towns, it was no longer sufficient. Anonymity increased, neighborhood networks were broken up, and the people were no longer willing or capable of enforcing the law. In the second quarter of the 19th century, therefore, professional police forces began to develop.

American police

The same pattern characterized the development of the police in this country. American colonists in the 17th and 18th centuries brought the "mutual pledge," the "watch and ward," and the constable systems with them and installed them in the small colonial towns about which we read earlier. These were sufficient to supplement the informal controls of family, church, and community. But, as some of these towns began to expand in the late 18th and early 19th centuries, informal methods could no longer cope with increasing disorder.

> New York City was alleged to be the most crime ridden city in the world, with Philadelphia, Baltimore and Cincinnati not far behind. . . . Gangs of youthful rowdies in the larger cities . . . threatened to destroy the American reputation for respect for the law. . . . Before their boisterous demonstrations the crude police forces of the day were often helpless (Cole, 1934:154–155).

Then as now, the most crime-ridden communities were the large urban centers, not the small towns.

In response to this state of affairs, different cities, led by New York, Boston, and Philadelphia, created police forces in the 1830s and 1840s. By the 1870s, all major cities had full-time police forces. But they proved to be less than a panacea: Police officers were drawn from the least educated segments of society, were ill-trained, and were poorly paid. Worse still, police forces often became instruments of political corruption when elected officials used them for personal gain and political advantage:

> Rotation in office enjoyed so much popular favor that police posts of both high and low degree were constantly changing hands, with political fixers determining the price and conditions of each change. . . . The whole police question simply churned about in the public mind and eventually became identified with the corruption and degradation of the city politics and local governments of the period (Smith, 1960:105–106).

The police, in short, became objects of disrespect. Ancient fears were often confirmed.

These feelings were also encouraged by the fierce independence and mobility of settlers on the American frontier. The development of police forces in the small towns and mining communities of the West was much later in coming than it was in the larger eastern cities. The same was true in the rural South. In both places, modern police forces did not begin to develop on any scale until the turn of the century. Until then, it was the local constable or sheriff, along with the citizenry, who were responsible for maintaining law and order.

The real expansion of police forces and interest in them came after World War I. By that time, most state legislatures had created state police forces because local departments could not, or would not, enforce laws beyond their own jurisdictions. Then, in 1924, J. Edgar Hoover organized the Federal Bureau of Investigation to deal with federal crimes. Finally, in 1931, the first National Commission on Law Observance and Enforcement (pp. 5–7) called for the reform of a growing number of police problems: The average police chief, it suggested, was too subject to political manipulation and control; there was a lack of competent, honest patrolmen; little effort was being made to educate, train, and discipline officers; and the police lacked the necessary equipment, skill, and personnel to enforce the flood of new laws produced by an increasingly complex, industrial society.

In recent decades, some progress has been made in correcting earlier problems, much of it since 1967 when, in response to a second Presidential commission (the President's Commission on Law Enforcement and Administration of Justice), federal legislation was passed and large sums of money were expended in an effort to improve police training, to improve record-keeping systems, and to add to crime control techniques. Today, as a result, there are approximately 40,000 police agencies in the United States: 50 on the federal level, 200 on the state level; and 39,750 dispersed throughout counties, cities, towns, and hamlets. By far, the most significant of these, insofar as the policing of juveniles is concerned, are the thousands of municipal police departments.

Public perceptions of the police

Given the long-standing distrust and spotty history of the police, experts allude repeatedly to the public's ambivalence about them (Cf. Bittner, 1970; Niederhoffer and Blumberg, 1973; Wilson, 1968a). Ben Whittaker, a lawyer who studied the English police system, described this ambivalence as follows (Cf. Morris and Hawkins, 1970:89):

> The public use the police as a scapegoat for its neurotic attitude toward crime. Janus-like we have always turned two faces toward a policeman. We employ him to administer the law, and yet ask him to waive it. We resent him when he enforces the law in our own case, yet demand his dismissal when he does not elsewhere. We offer him bribes, yet denounce his corruption. We expect him to be a member of society, yet not to share its values. We admire violence, even against society itself, but condemn force by the police in our behalf. We tell the police that they are entitled to

information from the public, yet we ostracize informers. We ask for crime
to be eradicated, but only by use of "sporting" [i.e., constitutional]
methods.

Whittaker's description is valuable because it indicates that police
behavior, good or bad, usually mirrors public attitudes. To be sure,
mixed feelings are inevitable as a result of the storm-trooper image that
the police often project. Dressed in jodhpurs and boots, wearing a hel-
met and dark glasses, with a pistol and club strapped to their belts, their
approach creates a tinge of panic in even the most innocent of citizens.
But for many citizens who are themselves law-violating hypocrites, the
suspicion cannot be allayed that the police are likewise less than law-
abiding and hypocritical. The notion lingers "that those who do battle
against evil cannot themselves live up fully to the ideals they presumably defend (Bittner, 1970:7).

Sometimes these suspicions are confirmed. In one recent case, for
example, criminal charges were levied against five policeman for alleged sexual misconduct with 16- and 17-year-old girls who were members of a police-sponsored Explorer Scout Program. Unconfirmed reports were that the police had seduced the girls on out-of-town camping
trips or had established sexual liaisons with them in private (Los Angeles
Times, October 8, 1976). As can be imagined, public indignation over
the matter was considerable. Though the police are certainly not the only
citizens—young or old—who engage in premarital or extramarital affairs or who read Playboy, Playgirl, Penthouse, or Oui, they are judged by
standards that are applied only to such guardians of public morality as
ministers or teachers. As Whittaker says, we have always turned two
faces toward policemen: distrusting them, on one hand, but expecting
exemplary behavior from them, on the other.

This Janus-like attitude is only made worse by the conflicting roles
that the police are expected to play: the tough crime fighter when dealing with human predators and the thoughtful social worker when responding to the cries of citizens for help.

The crime fighter

In a rather remarkable document, a group of policemen recently
penned an article in which they analyzed the public, media-created
image of the main protagonists in the war on crime: the criminal versus

the crime fighter (Carter, et al., 1971). First, they noted the fact that criminals are often far more famous than are the police who fight them. Stretching over the past four decades, many famous criminals could be listed (p. 80):

> John Dillinger, "Baby Face" Nelson, "Pretty Boy" Floyd, "Machine Gun" Kelly, [Bonnie and Clyde], "Willie the Actor" Sutton, the Boston Strangler, nurse killer Richard Speck, Charles Whitman of University of Texas notoriety, Charles Manson and his family, Lindbergh Kidnapper Bruno Hauptmann, Alcatraz "Birdman" Robert Stroud, Caryl Chessman, Hickok and Smith of *In Cold Blood* infamy, San Francisco's Zodiac killer, farmhand killer Juan Corona, . . . Charles Starkweather and a host of Mafia-type hoodlums including "Scarface Al" Capone, "Lucky" Luciano, Frank Costello, Albert Anastasia, Joseph "Bananas" Bonnano, and Vito Genovese.

One could also add some recent names, which have also become famous: Patricia Hearst, former Attorney General, John Mitchell, and former White House advisors, H. R. Haldeman and John D. Erlichman. "The list," as the policemen noted, "is seemingly endless" (p. 80).

But who remembers real-life crime fighters? Who are they? At best, people can name only a few: J. Edgar Hoover (who, today, is as notorious as he is famous), Elliott Ness of *Untouchables* fame, and perhaps O. W. Wilson, August Vollmer, and William Parker. Even though the latter were chiefs-of-police, they are not well known outside of law enforcement circles. Instead, most policemen are known to people by a series of stereotypes: the dumb Irish cop, the flatfoot, the dick, the gumshoe, the fuzz, or the pig. "Sad, but true, the 'good guys' are not very good" (Carter, et al., 1971:80).

This is ironic in light of the fact that the crime problem has usually been portrayed in American folklore as black and white, as the "good guys" versus the "bad guys." But, if regular policemen are distrusted and unknown, who are the "good guys?"

The "good guys" are not ordinary policemen; they are fictional, SUPERcrime fighters: Dick Tracy, Bruce Wayne, the Batman, Peter Gunn, Bulldog Drummond, Superman, the Saint, the Lone Ranger, Joe Mannix, Frank Cannon, the FBI in Peace and War, Barnaby Jones, the Mod Squad, Chief Ironside, Baretta, Wonder Woman, Kojak, the Six Million Dollar Man and the Bionic Woman, Steve McGarrett, Banacek, Starsky and Hutch, and even Mighty Mouse, Johnny Quest, and Chester Rabbit (Carter, et al., 1971:81–86). Since ordinary policemen are incapable of fighting the War on Crime, SUPERcrime fighters have been created to fill the void. Moreover, there are certain themes running through America's crime-fighting mentality which suggest that unusual characteristics and techniques are required of SUPERcrime fighters (Carter, et al., 1971:82–88):

The successful crime fighter is no mere mortal. He or she is possessed of exceptional intuition, intelligence, toughness (and even bionic limbs like the Six Million Dollar Man) which make him or her indestructible and all powerful.

Crime is best stamped out by gimmicks, hardware, and the products of science. Dick Tracy has a two-way wrist radio; Batman's belt is loaded with scientific devices; James Bond's Aston-Martin has a bullet-proof shield, machine guns, an ejection seat, and a device for spewing oil on the road in front of evil pursuers; and Steve McGarrett has computers that can spill out the most detailed of information on crooks anywhere in the world.

The SUPERcrime fighters always triumph over evil; the bad guys are always caught; crime does not pay.

Violence is inevitably present in crime and its control. Most comic strip and TV shows portray heroes and villains who are involved in an almost endless orgy of violence. Even Mighty Mouse dispatches cat villains by punching them in the nose, to say nothing of the brawls in which James Bond, Baretta, Starsky and Hutch, or Boy Wonder become engaged.

It is usually necessary for SUPERcrime fighters to operate outside the law in order to control crime. As Chester Gould, the creator of Dick Tracy, noted:

The trend of the times seemed to be exactly right for a straight shoot-'em down detective. We had a crime situation . . . that was beyond coping with legally—or what we would call legally today. So I brought out this boy Tracy and had him go out and get his man at the point of a gun, and, if necessary, shoot him down (*Orange County Register,* January 17, 1971)

It is not surprising, therefore, that most SUPERcrime fighters burglarize places in order to collect evidence, use illegal wiretaps, obtain confessions through threats or brutality, or engage in a long list of other activities that are contrary to law.

Given this stereotyped construction of the way crime is successfully fought, ordinary policemen are losers. The image of the successful crime fighter cannot possibly fit a law-abiding policeman who is constrained by constitutional provisions protecting the rights of the individual. As a New York precinct captain recently stated, "A [policeman] out to violate people's rights will have to answer for his actions . . . In real life, a Clint Eastwood character . . . wouldn't last two weeks" (*Los Angeles Times*, March 23, 1977). Furthermore, the popular image of what it is that policemen do has little resemblance to the actual nature of their work.

The social worker

Studies of police behavior reveal that at most 20 to 30 percent of all calls from citizens involve crimes of some sort, even in those areas where crime rates are the highest (Cumming, et al., 1973:186; Reiss, 1971:15). The tour of duty for the average policeman, in fact, does not even include the arrest of a single person (Reiss, 1971:15). Unlike Baretta or Kojak, most policemen never fire a shot from their weapons during a total career of 25 or 30 years, nor do they engage in wild conflicts involving karate chops and judo holds with bullets zinging through the air (Carter, et al., 1971:86). How, then, *do* policemen spend most of their time?

They spend much of it doing "social work" or, as Cumming, et al. (1973) describe it, playing "philosopher, guide, and friend." After monitoring hundreds of calls from citizens to the police, these investigators found that about half of them were requests for some sort of assistance in difficult personal and interpersonal situations (pp. 189–190):

> "A man, reported by his ex-wife as dangerous and perhaps mentally ill, is found asleep." But, since the ex-wife was in the man's home, the police asked her to please leave.
>
> "A car accident severely injures a woman, and the police supervise her removal to a hospital."
>
> A woman calls because neighborhood children are bullying a small boy who wears glasses. After doing a little shouting and getting shouted at in return, the police watch the problem wither away and leave.
>
> "A woman complains that her husband doesn't bring home enough money to feed the kids." The police advise her to go to children's court.

"A slightly drunk man is an unwelcome visitor in his ex-wife's home. Police send him home in a cab."

In short, the closest the media have come to portraying this consuming side of police work is in Adam 12, a TV show which, like police work, is often filled with tedium. Jim Reed and Pete Malloy "spend endless hours on patrol . . ., eat chili and hamburgers . . ., rescue cats from trees and break up family disturbances" (Carter, et al., 1971:88).

For the poor, in particular, the police must often play this kind of amateur social work role—calming unruly children, feeding information into a troubled situation, or acting as counselors in interpersonal conflicts. Other resources, other problem-solving networks, are simply unavailable to them. "All citizens can count on emergency help from the police when there is sudden illness at night, but only a certain kind of citizen takes his marital troubles to them" (Cumming, et al., 1973:192).

It might be anticipated that efforts to deal with problems like these could balance out some of the negative public perceptions of the police, but the evidence is by no means clear that it does.

> Most citizens express attitudes that are highly inconsistent with the actual demands that they place on the police. Instead, they want them to be SUPERcrime fighters, not social workers. Eight out of ten say they want policemen to be "tougher than they are now in dealing with crime and lawlessness" (Hindelang, 1975:11).
>
> While approximately six out of ten Americans hold generally favorable views of the police, significant proportions of them do not, particularly poor and minority people (Ennis, 1967:52 58; Hindelang, 1975:10). For at least half of the latter group, the police are viewed as intruders who are too often unfair, racist, and brutal in ghetto neighborhoods (Ennis, 1966:66–67; Skolnick, 1973).
>
> Large proportions of all crime victims or witnesses to crimes do not report them to the police (Hindelang, et al., 1976:338–339). This failure is due, not just to the feeling that the police will be of little help, but because many people do not want to become involved in the dirty, time-consuming work of the police: identifying offenders, going to court, or testifying as witnesses.

Given this state of affairs, how do the police respond to the public view that their work is "tainted" and that people are highly ambivalent about them?

Police views of police work

The police seem to view themselves in two ways: as *social outcasts* and as *crime fighters.*

Social outcasts

The police share the public view that theirs is a "tainted" occupation. They see themselves as pariahs, as outcasts.

> [The policeman] regards the public as his enemy, feels his occupation to be in conflict with the community, and regards himself to be a pariah. The experience and the feeling give rise to a collective emphasis on secrecy, an attempt to coerce respect from the public, and a belief that almost any means are legitimate in completing an important arrest (Westley, 1975:35).

The police, as a result, are highly sensitive to criticism and are impatient with high-flown academic definitions of their work. Consider the response of a Los Angeles police sergeant to one such definition by a well-known academician, Egon Bittner (1970:46):

Bittner: The role of the police is best understood as a mechanism for the distribution of nonnegotiably coercive force employed in accordance with the dictates of an intuitive grasp of situational exigencies.

Sergeant: What the fuck does that mean? (Carter, 1976:121).

Some definitions that the police do understand and which Carter (1976:131) says characterize their feelings about their work are *frustration, anger, anxiety, alienation,* and *hostility:*

> People don't like cops. Now, maybe some cops did some stupid things, but most of us are trying to do good. . . . You wonder why we stick together; you almost have to. . . . Nobody understands; noncops can't understand it. Maybe we don't understand it ourselves. Next time you're in a bar, tell the dude next to you that you're a cop. Watch him come apart. Or try to make it with some broad and tell her you're a cop. Shit. Nothing. People want you around and they don't want you around. They love you, they hate you. They need you, they don't need you. God, if the role is fuzzy, it's probably because no one really knows what they want from police (Carter, 1976:122–123).[2]

---

[2] This and excerpts on pp. 419–420 from "The police view of the justice system" by Robert M. Carter is reprinted from *The Juvenile Justice System,* vol. 5, Sage Criminal Justice System Annuals, Malcolm W. Klein (Ed.), 1976. By permission of the author and of the publisher, Sage Publications, Inc., Beverly Hills/London.

Crime fighters

Despite their feelings of frustration and anger, the police also share the popular view that they should be crime fighters, not social workers. As a Philadelphia police inspector put it, "once a police officer becomes a social worker, he isn't any good anymore as a policeman" (Ennis, 1966:139). Speaking explicitly of work with juveniles, a second officer expressed precisely the same point of view:

> The juvenile bureau is not always in step with [the rest of the police]. A lot of guys with a lot of time in the Department don't believe in all this prevention activity, except what is crime related. . . . They'll tell you they didn't join the Department to become a social worker. They want to work patrol or detective bureau, out on the streets. And that is the majority of the people in the Department (Carter, 1976:130).

It is for reasons like these that eight out of ten calls for assistance are regarded by the police as a waste of time (Reiss, 1971:73). Even though citizens consider their own family disputes and neighborhood disturbances as requiring police attention, the police tend to resent them. "You ought to talk to Sergeant _____ . . . . He'll tell you straight out that prevention isn't our job: Parents ought to be doing more, the schools ought to get rid of the fuckups, and people ought to go to church" (Carter, 1976:130).

The police, in short, see themselves as the last "guardians of the morals of the community" (Carter, 1976:131). Since ordinary citizens are themselves so often ambivalent and hypocritical about crime, the first job of the police is to fight it. "They are the 'thin blue line' against the forces of evil" (Carter, 1976:131).

Police attitudes toward juvenile work

Since the police regard themselves primarily as crime fighters, it is not difficult to imagine how they view the rehabilitative concept of justice for juveniles and the criminology professors who push it:

> Nothing personal, but most professors don't know what they are talking about. They sit on the campus putting out all this good shit about rehabilitation and causes of crime. Most of them haven't ever been on the street; and if you want to know what's happening, you have to be on the street. They haven't seen these assholes after the sun goes down, laughing and scratching, shucking and jiving. Instead of them telling us about

crime, we ought to be telling them. If they would spend a couple of days with us, they might find out what's happening. No, they don't want to do that; it might upset all their theories. I've heard some of those theories in school. Bullshit! What has toilet training got to do with anything? Nothing. They ought to be teaching stuff we can use, not all that sociology and social work. Like they say in the army: they don't know shit from shinola. It's a shuck (Carter, 1976:123).

To many, if not most, policemen, rehabilitative justice is a gross distortion of reality. It forces them to play a social work role with large groups of neglected children and status offenders who would be better cared for by parents, schools, and churches. And it interferes with their job of fighting serious crime among young "hoodlums" and "pukes":

I don't want to sound like a hardass, but we have some really bad young hoodlums on the streets in L.A. These aren't the nickel and dime kid shoplifters; they are hardcore. Some of them have dozens of arrests, but they're still out there ripping off people. Some of them have killed people, but they are still out there. These pukes are into juvenile hall and out twenty minutes later; seriously, some of these hoodlums are back on the street before I finish the paperwork. If you are going to correct kids they have to get their hands whacked the first time they put them in the cookie jar, not six months later. Juvenile justice is slow. Jesus, the rights these kids have got. They have more rights than I have. . . . I'm not talking about the Mickey Mouse cases; I mean the hoodlums (Carter, 1976:124).

It is clear, then, that most policemen regard work with status offenders as "shit work" and that they would like to see a tougher, more retributive system of justice prevail. Faced, as they see it, with serious juvenile crime on one hand and with a soft-headed rehabilitative system on the other, their reactions are a reflection of the fuzzy and frustrating role into which society places them. Indeed, as one officer suggests, the juvenile justice system on the streets does not include any kindly judges or probation officers; it includes only two, often lonely, men in a squad car:

When you turn a corner, drive into an alley, or respond to a 211 IP or 459 silent, you don't know what's going to happen. It might be a psycho, a street junkie, some kid on speed, or even some dude who wants to waste a cop. Might not be anything. You don't know. But let me tell you what the justice system is then. It is me and my partner. We have a car, a radio, a backup unit, two .38s, one shotgun in the rack. That is the justice system on the street. To make it complete, you add one criminal (Carter, 1976:123).

The police, in short, have little patience with the child-saving ideology and purposes of the juvenile court. Serious offenders are the proper concerns of the police, but saving neglected children and truants ought to be left to parents, ministers, teachers, and welfare workers. Yet, they know full well that the law reads otherwise and that they are expected to perform a social work as well as crime fighting role. Hence, it is important to determine how they actually go about reconciling their own views with the legal mandate they are expected to fulfill.

How police process juveniles

The methods the police use in processing juveniles can be determined by seeking answers to a series of important questions:

1. How do the police respond to widespread law violation by juveniles? In Chapter 7, we learned that the amount of undetected law violation among juveniles is enormous. Almost every child breaks the law, sometimes repeatedly and sometimes seriously. Are the police at all aware of this state of affairs?

The evidence seems to indicate that they are but that they do not regard much juvenile lawbreaking as particularly serious and, therefore, do not take formal action against it. Thus, even though few state laws provide specific directions for doing so, the police have been allowed to exercise a tremendous amount of discretion in deciding which of the many children that come to their attention shall be arrested (Levine, 1973:558). For example, Bordua (1967) found that patrolmen in Detroit had contacts with juveniles nine times more frequently than they made arrests. Of well over 100,000 "encounters" or "interviews," only 5,282 resulted in actual arrest. Findings of the same sort were reported by Terry (1967) in Racine, Wisconsin. Of 9,023 offenses known to the police, only 755 were referred to the probation department and only 246 actually resulted in a court hearing. Such figures vary from department to department, but, overall, they suggest that the police are inclined to avoid arresting many juveniles who might otherwise be sent to court for disposition there (Black and Reiss, 1967; Goldman, 1963; Klein, 1970; Williams and Gold, 1972).

2. How many juveniles are actually arrested each year? In terms of their part of the total population, the proportion of juveniles actually arrested each year is not great. In 1975, for example, there were approximately 33.3 million juveniles in the United States between the ages of

10 and 17 (National Center for Juvenile Justice, 1977:3). By contrast, there were only about 1.7 million juvenile arrests (FBI, 1976:177). If each arrest represented one juvenile, the percentage of those arrested would be only 5.1 percent. But, since one person can be arrested more than one time, it is likely that the proportion of all juveniles who were arrested was smaller than the 5.1 percent.

At the same time, the proportion of adolescents who are arrested sometime between their 10th and 18th birthdays is considerably larger than the proportion arrested in any single year. In their study of a birth cohort in Philadelphia, for example, Wolfgang et al. (1972:54) found that 35 percent of the 9,945 boys in the cohort had at least one official police contact sometime between the age of 10 and 18. But, since a "contact" may not always lead to an arrest, and, since almost half of the boys had only one police contact, it is likely that the formal arrest rate was lower. This study did indicate, however, that about 17.5 percent of the total cohort were recidivists, juveniles with two or more police contacts.

3. *For what kinds of offenses are juveniles arrested most often?* Juvenile court laws in all states grant the police an unqualified right to arrest any juvenile who has violated the criminal law, as they would arrest any adult. But, in addition, they have also been empowered to take a child into custody in situations that would not justify the arrest of an adult—a disobedient, runaway, or truant child or a child who is dependent, neglected, or abused (Levine, 1973:556–557). This latter practice has come under recent criticism, and the suggestion has been made that the legal process in such cases should begin with a summons to parents, not with the apprehension of the child. But, for the most part, the right of the state to intervene, as it has done traditionally, has not been greatly altered.

Since the police have been charged with apprehending juveniles for both criminal and juvenile offenses, official statistics are revealing. In 1975, juveniles under the age of 18 were arrested for 48 percent of all serious property crimes—burglary, larceny, and motor vehicle theft— and 23.1 percent of all violent crimes—homicide, rape, robbery, and aggravated assault (FBI, 1976:188). Yet, though juveniles account for more than their share of serious arrests, these are but a small part of the total. They are arrested far more frequently for "petty larceny, fighting, disorderly conduct, liquor related offenses, and conduct not in violation of the criminal law such as curfew violation, truancy, incorrigibility, or running away from home" (President's Commission on Law Enforcement and Administration of Justice, 1967b:56).

This is revealed in Table 15–1. It is a record of the rates of juve-

TABLE 15–1

Juvenile arrests: specific rates for 1960, 1965, and 1970 (in rates per 100,000 youth ages 10–17 and percent distribution for each year)

Arrest category	Rates per 100,000 youth, ages 10–17			Percent distribution		
	1960*	1965*	1970†	1960	1965	1970
Specific crime offenses	3,232	3,636	4,214	37.4	35.8	33.9
Drugs only	59	87	1,189	0.7	0.9	9.6
Delinquent tendencies	5,340	6,421	7,014	61.9	63.3	56.5
Total arrest rates	8,631	10,144	12,417	100.0	100.0	100.0
(Number of arrests)........	(182,715)	(277,649)	(382,935)			

* Numbers arrested and computed rates for 1960 and 1965 can be found in *Crime and Delinquency in California,* 1960 (Sacramento: Bureau of Criminal Statistics, 1969), Table I–2, p. 10, and Table I–14, p. 44.

† Numbers arrested used in rate computations can be found in *Crime and Arrests: Reference Tables, 1970* (Sacramento: Bureau of Criminal Statistics, 1970), Table VI, p. 61; population figure used in computations can be found in *Juvenile Probation and Detention: Reference Tables, 1970* (Sacramento: Bureau of Criminal Statistics, 1970), Table 1, p. 5.

This table is reproduced by permission of the author, Paul Lerman, and the Kenyon Public Affairs Forum, Kenyon College (Cf. Lerman, 1978).

nile arrest in California between 1960 and 1970 (Lerman, 1978:6).

The table shows two things. First, it shows that only slightly more than one third of all juvenile arrests were for criminal offenses. By contrast, almost two thirds were for "delinquent tendencies"—truancy, incorrigibility, malicious mischief, drinking, disturbing the peace, glue sniffing, and other status offenses—and for using drugs (mainly marijuana). Secondly, it shows that while rates of arrest increased between 1960 and 1970—from 8,631 per 100,000 in 1960 to 12,417 in 1970—this change was due more to increases in arrest for "delinquent tendencies" and for drug use than for specific personal and property crimes. There can be little doubt as a result that the traditional concern of American society with the moral behavior of young people still retains considerable vigor. Indeed, Table 15–1 shows that while the rate of arrests for "delinquent tendencies" went up between 1960 and 1970 the proportion of all arrests for specific criminal offenses decreased slightly over the period, from 37.4 percent in 1960 to 33.9 percent in 1970.

4. *What do the police do with the juveniles whom they do arrest?* Theoretically, legal rules should apply equally to all juveniles. Once a child is arrested, he or she should be processed uniformly through the system. But that is not what happens. Again, the police are inclined to make use of a number of dispositional alternatives: (1) to take the child to the stationhouse and there to release him to the custody of his parents; (2) to refer the child to the juvenile bureau of the police

department (if it has one) and to leave further decisions to the officers who work there; (3) to refer the child to some community welfare agency; or (4) to refer the child directly to the juvenile court. The police in some jurisdictions have also had the right to place a child in detention while in others that decision is made by probation officers acting as an arm of the juvenile court.

On the average, the police handle about half of all arrests entirely within their own departments or juvenile bureaus (FBI, 1976:177; California Bureau of Criminal Statistics, 1968:215). This procedure is often known as "counsel and release." The juvenile's parents are summoned to the stationhouse, and, if they seem interested and willing, both they and the child are warned about the evils of bad conduct and urged to take steps to see that it does not happen again. The practice, however, seems to be used more often for petty and status, than for serious criminal, offenders. In a single year in California, for example, less than one third of all criminal violators were counseled and released. By contrast, 55 percent of the minor violators and 57 percent of the status offenders were counseled without referral to court (California Bureau of Criminal Statistics, 1968:208). At the present time, the police are being urged to refer more of their minor offenders to private and public welfare agencies for treatment but, historically, the number has not been large. In 1974, for example, the proportion so referred was only 2.5 percent nationwide (FBI, 1975:177).

5.   *What about the questioning of juveniles? Are they warned of their rights and protected against self-incrimination?* According to the provisions of the Fifth Amendment of the Constitution, any person charged with a crime should be protected from self-incrimination; that is, he or she is not required to answer questions which might result in prosecution and conviction. For most of this century, however, children have not enjoyed the protection of this amendment. Since the presumed purposes of the juvenile justice system were treatment, not punishment, ordinary protections were not guaranteed, and the practices of the police and courts were not subjected to the scrutiny of the higher courts.

Subsequent to several landmark Supreme Court decisions, however, police and court practices have begun to change (*Kent v. United States*, 1966; *In re Gault*, 1967; *Miranda v. Arizona*, 1966). The police are supposed to advise juveniles that they need not answer any questions; that anything they say may be used against them; that they have the right to have an attorney present during any discussion with the police; and that, if they cannot afford an attorney, one will be provided. Even further, the Supreme Court has noted that juveniles may not fully appreciate a warning of rights or what it means if they waive them. Because they are immature and incapable of resisting a threatening or persuasive adult, mere warning is not enough. Instead, the child's parents should be notified of any proposed interrogation and should be present when one occurs (Levine, 1973:559).

Such requirements, however, are relatively new and are probably not practiced universally. Official rules and practices are still in a state of transition, and, until that transition is completed, older traditions will prevail, particularly in those communities where the police do not have specially trained juvenile officers, where juvenile judges are part-time practitioners, and where informality, rather than formality, remains the rule.

6. *What criteria contribute to police decision making?*   Our findings thus far raise some perplexing questions. We have seen that the police are more inclined to avoid arresting juveniles than to arrest them, that they are not always inclined to insure juveniles the protection of their constitutional rights, but that they counsel and release half of those whom they do arrest. Even more perplexing, we have also seen that about two thirds of all juveniles who are arrested and many of those who are referred to juvenile court are charged with petty and status offenses. How can one reconcile such seemingly contradictory findings? Are there no criteria by which to make sense of police behavior? The answer is that there are criteria, other than those which are strictly legal, which influence police decision making:

a. *Offense seriousness.*   We have already seen that offense seriousness is a key factor in determining the course of police response. Such acts as murder, rape, robbery, aggravated assault, grand larceny, arson, or auto theft almost always result in arrest and referral to court while many less serious offenses do not, (Black and Reiss, 1970; Goldman, 1963; Piliavin and Briar, 1964; Terry, 1967).

b. *Citizen complainants.*   Most potential arrest situations are the result of complaints from citizens, not the result of police patrol (Black and Reiss, 1970; Terry, 1967). It is they who initiate many of the contacts. And when they do, police decisions may well hinge on whether the complainant is present and what his or her wishes are. "In not one instance," reported Black and Reiss (1970:71), "did the police arrest a juvenile when the complainant lobbied for lenience." But, if the citizen demanded action, it was taken (Emerson, 1969:42). As a result, it is clear that the sensitivity of the police to the presence of a citizen plays a key role in what happens to juveniles. A child who might be warned and released in one setting might be arrested and processed in another.

c.   Departmental policy.   Police practices vary widely from community to community, depending not upon differences in law, but upon differences in departmental policy. In his study of four Pennsylvania communities, for example, Goldman (1969) found that the proportion of juvenile arrests referred to court varied from a low of 9 percent in one community to a high of 71 percent in another. Klein (1970) found much the same thing in his study of 46 police departments in southern California. In one department, virtually all juveniles were counseled and released while in another 4 out of 5 were referred to court.

Many times, these widely varying policies reflect the sentiments of the community in which the departments are located. In other instances, however, they are associated with internal departmental policies and structures. In one highly professionalized department, Wilson (1968b) found that the police were highly impersonal with juveniles, went strictly by the book, arrested many of them, and released very few. In another city, by contrast, he found a much less professionalized department in which officers were permitted a wide latitude of personal choice. Many of the officers came from the neighborhoods in which they worked, dealt with juveniles in a highly personal manner, and viewed the arrest of one of them as a Mickey Mouse low status arrest.

Such findings once again illustrate the important principle that "justice" is not a monolithic concept that operates uniformly throughout the land. Instead, it is a concept that takes on widely different meaning, depending not only upon the policies of various departments, but upon varying community sentiments, the kinds of offenses juveniles commit, and upon other criteria such as the sex or social status of an offender.

d.   Sex of the offender.   Theoretically, legal rules are supposed to apply equally to girls and to boys. Actually, their application tends to reflect a double standard of justice. This double standard has had some striking and paradoxical consequences. Since for centuries the sex roles of males and females have been different, the police have not reacted to their offenses in similar ways. On one hand, our analysis of self-reported delinquent behavior revealed that though girls usually report fewer delinquent acts than boys the kinds of offenses they commit are not strikingly different (see Chapter 7). Like boys, they commonly drink, shoplift, skip school, destroy property, commit theft, and even burglarize. Indeed, these kinds of offenses, not "female" offenses such as fornication, running away from home, and incorrigibility, are the most common. Yet, because criminal offenses have traditionally been defined as "masculine" offenses, girls are much less likely to be arrested and referred to court for them. Instead, they tend to receive chivalrous treatment from the police (Armstrong, 1977; Chesney-Lind, 1977). In Honolulu, for example, Chesney-Lind (1977:124) found that "only 6.1 percent of the girls arrested for the most serious offenses and 12.7 percent of the girls arrested for less serious adult offenses were referred to court, compared with 33.7 percent of those arrested for juvenile [status] offenses."

On the other hand, the response of the police to "female" offenses has tended to be just the opposite. Girls are far more likely to be taken into custody if they violate traditional expectations for girls: run away from home, fail to obey ·their parents, or are sexually promiscuous (Chesney-Lind, 1974; 1977; Perlman, 1970). In their nationwide sample, for example, Sarri and Vinter (1975:47) found that 75 percent of the girls in the juvenile justice system were charged with status, not criminal, offenses. This high percentage is not due entirely to police action, since parents often bring their ungovernable and promiscuous girls to the attention of officials. Nonetheless, when the police are brought into such cases, their responses are likely to reflect the views of complaining parents; namely, that girls should be modest and chaste and should be protected from unladylike behavior.

This kind of thinking is reflected in the latest figures released by the Children's Bureau (1967) comparing the numbers of boys and girls who are officially charged with committing status offenses. While girls made up only about one third of those arrested for such offenses, they comprised about half of those referred to juvenile court for them. By contrast, only about 20 percent of the boys charged with status offenses were referred to court. Clearly, then, our society has tended to perpetuate traditional sex roles which require girls to be obedient and chaste while looking aside if boys "sow their wild oats" (Chesney-Lind, 1977:129). This traditional perspective is changing, but it has had, and continues to have, considerable impact on police decision making.

d. Race and socioeconomic status. The race and socioeconomic status of a juvenile are additional criteria that undoubtedly affect police decision-making. A basic problem, however, is that of deciding whether the use of such criteria is due to a kind of bigotry that is unique to the police or is a reflection of influences that are far more pervasive in our society. Throughout our history, minority children have been overrepresented in arrest statistics and in our courts and correctional institutions. Numerous social scientists, as a result, have concluded that they are the scapegoats of frustrated policemen (Clinard, 1963:440–451; Glaser, 1960:12; Lemert, 1951:311). Furthermore, many ghetto dwellers would agree with this conclusion. To them, the police are the most obvious symbols of white oppression:

> Their very presence is an insult, and it would be, even if they spent their entire day feeding gum drops to children. They represent the force of the white world, and that world's criminal profit and ease, to keep the black man corralled up here, in his place. The badge, the gun in the holster, and the swinging club, make vivid what will happen should his rebellion become overt (Baldwin, 1962:65–66).

Aside from the fact that the policeman is a symbol of oppression, Wilson (1968a:40–41) believes that unusual attention to young ghetto dwellers by the police is justified.

> The patrolman believes with considerable justification that teenagers, Negroes, and lower income persons commit a disproportionate share of all reported crimes. . . . Patrolmen believe that they would be derelict in their duty if they did not treat such persons with suspicion, routinely question them on the street, and detain them for longer questioning if a crime has occurred in the area.

It should come as no surprise, then, that youthful ghetto dwellers and the police often view themselves as mortal enemies. Anyone familiar with the war mentality that characterizes their relationships knows that minor incidents can easily be escalated into major battles. Each group fears and distrusts the other, and it does little good to know that in earlier times the same kinds of relationships existed between white police and white gang members. But, because our ghettos are now populated largely by browns and blacks, battles can be interpreted as race wars and the police charged with instigating much of the combat.

Likewise, it provides little solace to know that studies do not always confirm the notion that the police are biased against minority and lower-class juveniles. On one hand, one group of investigators has concluded that this is the case. After controlling for offense seriousness and prior record, they found that the police are more inclined to arrest minority and low-income juveniles, particularly black boys (Ferdinand and Luchterland, 1970; Goldman, 1963; Thornberry, 1973). Piliavin and Briar (1964) concluded, for example, that boys whose race, group affiliations, grooming, and language suggest to the police that they are "tough" guys are more likely to be arrested. These characteristics, perhaps more than any offense they might have committed, are those that determine police response.

On the other hand, a second group of investigators has failed to find much evidence of bias (Black, 1970; Eaton and Polk, 1961; Hohenstein, 1969; Shannon, 1963; Terry, 1967; Weiner and Willie, 1971). However, most of them point out that one can reach this conclusion only by taking many complex factors into account: (1) that arrest rates vary widely from one community to another; (2) that the highest rates of arrest occur in minority and low socioeconomic areas; and (3) that police actions are strongly related to the offense histories of offenders and to the seriousness of the acts they commit. But, when one sorts through all of these factors, one finds that race and social status are not the major determinants of arrest. Rather, higher rates of arrest in low-income areas are due to the fact that the juveniles in them are more likely to be recidivists and more likely to commit serious offenses. Furthermore, it will be recalled from our analysis of self-reported delinquency that the juveniles who are arrested most often are persons who, by their own admissions, are the most frequent and serious law violators (Chapter 7). Even though minority and low-status juveniles are overrepresented in our courts and institutions, therefore, it may be that they are the most delinquent.

But, since this and the first set of findings are contradictory, we are faced with a dilemma in knowing how to interpret them. Gibbons (1976:43) resolves the dilemma, however, by concluding that one cannot generalize about police bias. Rather, "what these divergent findings reflect is real differences among communities and police departments." Just as other practices vary from department to department, so practices with respect to poor and minority youth also vary. Although this conclusion may be accurate, it unfortunately does not begin to exhaust the complexities of the issue.

Throughout our history, American beliefs have stressed the notion that the poverty, the disrupted families, and the ignorance of minority and poor people are the inevitable precursors of child neglect and juvenile lawbreaking; all are part and parcel of the same thing. As a consequence, laws were written, and the juvenile court was created to locate dependent and neglected, as well as law-violating, children, and to bring them into conformity with the ideal concept of childhood.

Given this construction of the nature and causes of delinquency, it should not be surprising that minority and lower-class children have become the special targets of the police and of the other agents of juvenile justice. Not only are these children more likely to be members of one-parent families, to be malnourished and otherwise deprived, but the police have been conditioned to expect higher rates of delinquency among them. As a result, we may be confronted with a self-fulfilling prophecy: The very problems the police (and other citizens) have been conditioned to expect actually occur.

If generations of minority and poor people have not shared the economic, familial, and educational advantages to which success in our culture is tied, we should expect the consequences to be evident among their children. Indeed, they are: infant death rates are much higher among poor and minority children, they run much greater risks of biological impairment due to environmental deprivation, and they are victimized in serious crimes far more often than are affluent children (Cf. Shah and Roth, 1974:126–129; Chapter 8 herein). This disastrous circle is finally completed when these children experience difficulties in social adjustment, achieve less successfully in school, and turn to street gangs for alternative sources of satisfaction and protection. Not having been socialized according to the dictates of the ideal concept of childhood and lacking a stake in conventional society, they exhibit behaviors that are not only socially debilitating to themselves, but which are contrary to law.

If there is merit in this interpretation, it is clear that the tendency of the police to find and to report higher rates of law-violating behavior, child abuse, and neglect among poor and minority children is not just the product of bigotry that is peculiar to them. Rather, it is a function of conditions that are real but for which the police are not solely responsible. Instead, the police are merely the front-line troops of conventional society who are expected to mop up ghetto communities after a long war of attrition in which racism and social segregation have taken a heavy toll. Though they often try to play diplomat, social worker, and child saver, as well as crime fighter, their status in these communities is like that of naive draftees in an occupied country:

> It is hard . . . to blame the policeman, blank, good-natured, thoughtless, and insuperably innocent, for being such a perfect representative of the people he serves. He, too, believes in good intentions and is astounded and offended when [his good intentions] are not taken for the deed. He has never, himself, done anything for which to be hated, which of us has? And yet he is facing daily and nightly, the people who would gladly see him dead, and he knows it. There is no way for him not to know it: There are few things under heaven more unnerving than the silent accumulating

contempt and hatred of a people. He moves through Harlem, therefore, like an occupying soldier in a bitterly hostile country; which is precisely what, and where he is, and is the reason he walks in twos and threes (Baldwin, 1962:66–67).

It is no wonder, then, that the policeman often feels like a pariah. Not only is he distrusted by the affluent members of society, but he is hated by the members of ghetto communities for symbolizing and failing to resolve a host of profound problems which he alone did not create. Indeed, this conclusion sums up very well the main message of this chapter.

The actions of the police and the criteria they use in processing offenders are a striking reflection of our cultural history and the kind of society it has produced. The ambivalent attitude of the police toward work with all juveniles, their differential treatment of boys and girls, and their behavior in ghetto communities are the result, not merely of views which they alone hold, but of the way delinquency is defined and constructed in our society. If we are to understand how and why they behave as they do, therefore, we must look not merely at them, but at the role into which they have been cast by the society which they serve. For the last century, that role has become increasingly important as the social control functions of the family, age-integrated places of work, and the community have declined. So long as there are no new social inventions to reverse this trend, the role of the police will continue to increase in importance and will likely become more, not less, controversial.

Summary and conclusions

Throughout history, the police have been viewed with a great deal of public ambivalence: distrusted and feared on one hand, but expected to play social worker as well as crime fighter on the other. Police views of themselves reflect this Janus-like attitude. They view their chosen profession as "tainted" and themselves as outcasts, particularly in ghetto communities where they are viewed as hated symbols of social oppression. Hence, while much of their time is spent rendering assistance to adults or processing neglected children, they receive relatively little credit for this side of their work.

This conflicted situation is reflected directly in the way the police handle and process juveniles:

1.   *The police exercise a tremendous amount of discretion in deciding whom to arrest and to refer to juvenile court.*   This discretion produces a filtering process that is portrayed graphically in Figure 15–1. While, at best, this figure is an estimate of the actual number of juveniles who

FIGURE 15–1
The police filtering process

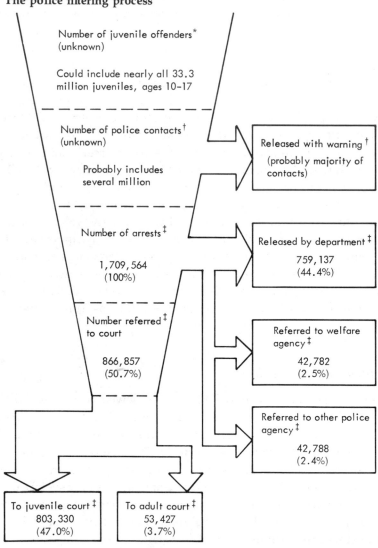

Number of juvenile offenders[*]
(unknown)

Could include nearly all 33.3 million juveniles, ages 10–17

Number of police contacts[†]
(unknown)

Probably includes several million

Released with warning [†]
(probably majority of contacts)

Number of arrests[‡]

1,709,564
(100%)

Released by department [‡]
759,137
(44.4%)

Number referred[‡]
to court

866,857
(50.7%)

Referred to welfare agency[‡]
42,782
(2.5%)

Referred to other police agency[‡]
42,788
(2.4%)

To juvenile court[‡]
803,330
(47.0%)

To adult court[‡]
53,427
(3.7%)

[*] See Chapter 7 on self-reported delinquency.
[†] See Chapter 7 and the way the police process juveniles in this chapter.
[‡] See FBI, *Uniform Crime Reports,* 1974:177.

violate the law and what the police do with them, it does reflect what we have learned in this and previous chapters. (The official information shown in the figure is for the year 1974, but it does not differ significantly from other recent years. Furthermore, this particular year was chosen because it will be related in the next chapter to the latest available information on what the courts do with juveniles once they are filtered through by the police).

Briefly, the evidence summarized in Figure 15–1 is this:

Most juveniles, ages 10–17, report violating the law. The actual number of offenders probably numbers several millions each year, if not all juveniles.

The police have contacts with many of these law violators. Although the exact number is not known, they could legally arrest many of them. Yet, they release the majority with a warning.

The number of juveniles who are actually arrested is only a fraction of all those who have contacts with the police. In 1974, it was 1.7 million.

Of those arrested, only about 50 percent are actually referred to court (about 867,000 in 1974). Most of the remainder are counseled and released.

2.　This police-filtering process is not a random one. Instead, it is affected by several criteria that help to determine who will be arrested and for what reason:

Although the police arrest virtually all juveniles whom they suspect of committing highly serious crimes, the majority of those whom they do arrest are still status offenders. The police resent playing social worker but their actions reveal considerable support for society's concern with enforcing traditional moral rules for children.

The police are highly sensitive to public attitudes, arresting or releasing offenders according to the wishes of citizen complainants.

The police apply a double standard in making decisions about girls and boys. They are less inclined to process girls for criminal offenses than they are boys. The reverse is true where status offenses are involved.

The actions of the police help to produce higher rates of arrest and court referral among low-status and minority youth. These rates may be due partially to greater criminality on their parts, but they are also a reflection of the expectation that the police will respond to the greater incidence of dependency and neglect in these populations as well as to their law-violating behavior.

3.   *The police are pragmatic labeling theorists.*   Within the constraints of the criteria they use, the police are far more likely to avoid taking official action than they are to take it. They seem to share the belief of academic labeling theorists that the process of tagging, segregating, and stigmatizing many youngsters may make the cure worse than the disease. This is particularly true where girls are involved in criminal offenses or where a juvenile comes from a "good" family, is in school, and displays appropriate respect for authority.

4.   *Many, if not the most, important decisions made by the agents of juvenile justice are made by the police—on the streets and in the stationhouses—not by judges or probation officers in their chambers.*   Given the discretion exercised by the police, their actions could be said to be clearly contrary to the original child-saving philosophy of the juvenile court; namely, that *all* children with problems should be uniformly referred to court, not just the ones whom police choose to refer. It should be a wise, deliberative judge with his or her supporting cast of experts who should decide whether intervention is required, not the ordinary street cop.

The actions of the police, however, reflect the ambivalent attitudes of the larger society and the practical problems of day-to-day police work. Indeed, if the police were to follow the letter of the law, the courts would be inundated with "offenders," and the rise in official delinquency rates would be unprecedented (without the slightest change in juvenile behavior). Whether right or wrong, therefore, the police probably play the most crucial role in determining the nature and character of juvenile justice. Although academicians, policy makers, lawyers, and citizens engage in endless philosophical debate over the form that juvenile justice should take, the fact that society has chosen to turn ever more of its social control functions over to the police means that it is they, and not others, who make most of the practical decisions.

References

Armstrong, Gail
    1977   "Females under the law—'protected' but unequal." *Crime and Delinquency*, April, 23:109–120.

Baldwin, James
 1962   *Nobody Knows My Name*. New York: Dell Publications.

Bittner, Egon
 1970   *The Functions of the Police in Modern Society*. National Institute of
        Mental Health. Publication No. 2059. Washington, D.C.: U.S. Gov-
        ernment Printing Office.

Black, Donald J.
 1970   "Production of crime rates." *American Sociological Review*, August,
        35:733–748.

Black, Donald J. and Reiss, Albert J., Jr.
 1967   "Patterns of behavior in police and citizen transactions." Section I of
        Studies of Crime and Law Enforcement in Major Metropolitan Areas (Vol.
        II). Washington, D.C.: U.S. Government Printing Office.

 1970   "Police control of juveniles." *American Sociological Review*, February,
        35:63–77.

Bordua, David J.
 1967   "Recent trends: deviant behavior and social controls." *Annals of the
        American Academy of Political and Social Science*, January,
        CCCLIX:149–163.

California Bureau of Criminal Statistics
 1968   *Crime and Delinquency in California, 1967*. Sacramento: Department of
        Justice.

Carter, Robert M.
 1976   "The police view of the justice system." Pp. 121–132 in Malcolm W.
        Klein (Ed.), *The Juvenile Justice System*. Beverly Hills, Ca.: Sage
        Publications.

Carter, Robert M. et al.
 1971   "SUPERcop and SUPERcriminal: the media portrait of crime." *Daily
        Variety*, 38th Anniversary Issue, October, 153:80–88.

Chesney-Lind, Meda
 1974   "Juvenile delinquency: the sexualization of female crime." *Psychol-
        ogy Today*, July, VIII:43–46.

 1977   "Judicial paternalism and the female status offender." *Crime and De-
        linquency*, April, 23:121–130.

Children's Bureau
 1967   *Statistics on Public Institutions for Delinquent Children*. Washington,
        D.C.: Department of Health Education and Welfare.

Clinard, Marshall B.
 1963   *Sociology of Deviant Behavior* (Rev. ed.). New York: Holt, Rinehart
        and Winston.

Cole, Arthur C.
  1934 "The irrepressible conflict, 1859–1865." Pp. 154–155 in Arthur M.
        Schlesinger, Sr., and Dixon R. Fox (Eds.), *A History of American Life*
        (Vol. VIII). New York: Macmillan.

Cumming, Elain, Cumming, Ian and Edell, Laura
  1973 "Policeman as philosopher, guide and friend." Pp. 184–192 in Ar-
        thur Niederhoffer and Abraham S. Blumberg (Eds.), *The Ambivalent
        Force: Perspectives on the Police*. San Francisco: Rinehart Press.

Eaton, Joseph W. and Polk, Kenneth
  1961 *Measuring Delinquency*. Pittsburgh: University of Pittsburgh Press.

Emerson, Robert M.
  1969 *Judging Delinquents: Context and Process in Juvenile Court*. Chicago:
        Aldine.

Ennis, Philip H.
  1966 *The Police and the Community* (Vol. 2.). Washington, D.C.: U.S. Gov-
        ernment Printing Office.

  1967 *Criminal Victimization in the United States: A Report of a National Sur-
        vey*. Washington, D.C.: U.S. Government Printing Office.

Federal Bureau of Investigation
  1975 *Crime in the United States: Uniform Crime Reports, 1974*. Washington,
        D.C.: U.S. Government Printing Office.

  1976 *Crime in the United States: Uniform Crime Reports—1975*. Washington
        D.C.: U.S. Government Printing Office.

Ferdinand, Theodore N. and Luchterland, Elmer G.
  1970 "Inner-city youths, the police, the juvenile court, and justice." *Social
        Problems*, Spring, 17:510–527.

Gibbons, Don C.
  1976 *Delinquent Behavior* (2nd ed.). Englewood Cliffs, N.J.: Prentice Hall.

Glaser, Daniel
  1960 As quoted in Richard A. Cloward and Lloyd E. Ohlin, *Delinquency
        and Opportunity*. New York: Free Press.

Goldman, Nathan
  1963 *The Differential Selection of Juvenile Offenders for Court Appearance*.
        New York: National Council on Crime and Delinquency.

  1969 "The differential selection of juvenile offenders for court appear-
        ance." Pp. 264–290 in William Chambliss (Ed.), *Crime and the Legal
        Process*. New York: McGraw-Hill.

Hindelang, Michael J.
  1975 *Public Opinion Regarding Crime, Criminal Justice, and Related Topics*.
        Washington, D.C.: U.S. Government Printing Office.

Hindeling, Michael, et al.
   1976   *Source Book of Criminal Justice Statistics—1975.* Washington, D.C.:
          U.S. Government Printing Office.

Hohenstein, William F.
   1969   "Factors influencing the police disposition of juvenile offenders." Pp.
          138–149 in Thorsten Sellin and Marvin E. Wolfgang (Eds.), *Delin-*
          quency: Selected Studies. New York: John Wiley.

In re Gault
   1967   387 U.S. 1.

Kent v. *United States*
   1966   383 U.S. 541.

Klein, Malcolm W.
   1970   "Police processing of juvenile offenders: toward the development of
          juvenile system rates." Los Angeles County Sub-Regional Board,
          California Council on Juvenile Justice, Part III.

Lemert, Edwin M.
   1951   *Social Pathology.* New York: McGraw-Hill.

Lenroot, Katharine
   1949   "The juvenile court today.: *Federal Probation,* September, *10*:9–15.

Lerman, Paul
   1978   "Order offenses and juvenile delinquency." In LaMar T. Empey
          (Ed.), *Juvenile Justice: The Progressive Legacy and Current Reforms.*
          Charlottesville: University of Virginia Press.

Levine, Martin
   1973   "The current status of juvenile law." Pp. 547–606 in Gary B. Adams
          et al. (Eds.), *Juvenile Justice Management.* Springfield, Ill.: Charles C.
          Thomas.

Miranda v. *Arizona*
   1966   384 U.S. 436.

Morris, Norval and Hawkins, Gordon
   1970   *The Honest Politician's Guide to Crime Control.* Chicago: University of
          Chicago Press.

National Center for Juvenile Justice
   1977   *Juvenile Court Statistics, 1974.* Pittsburgh: National Center for
          Juvenile Justice.

National Commission on Law Observance and Enforcement
   1931   *Report on the Police.* Washington, D.C.: U.S. Government Printing
          Office.

Niederhoffer, Arthur and Blumberg, Abraham S. (eds.)
   1973   *The Ambivalent Force: Perspectives on the Police.* San Francisco,
          Rinehart Press.

Perlman, I. Richard
   1970   "Antisocial behavior of the minor in the United States. Pp. 35–43 in
          Harwin L. Voss (Ed.), *Society, Delinquency and Delinquent Behavior.*
          Boston: Little, Brown.

Piliavin, Irving and Briar, Scott
   1964   "Police encounters with juveniles." *American Journal of Sociology,*
          September, *70*:206–214.

President's Commission on Law Enforcement and Administration of Justice
   1967a *Task Force Report: The Police.* Washington, D.C.: U.S. Government
          Printing Office.

   1967b *The Challenge of Crime in a Free Society.* Washington D.C.: U.S.
          Government Printing Office.

Reiss, Albert J., Jr.
   1971   *The Public and the Police.* New Haven: Yale University Press.

Sarri, Rosemary C. and Vinter, Robert D.
   1975   "Juvenile justice and injustice." *Resolution,* Winter, *18*:43–51.

Shah, Saleem A. and Roth, Loren H.
   1974   "Biological and psychopsyiological factors in criminality." Pp. 101–
          173 in Daniel Glaser (Ed.), *Handbook of Criminology.* Chicago: Rand
          McNally.

Shannon, Lyle W.
   1963   "Types and patterns of delinquency referral in a middle-sized city."
          British Journal of Criminology, July, *10*:206–214.

Smith, Bruce, Sr.
   1960   *Police Systems in the United States* (2nd ed.). New York: Harper and
          Bros.

Skolnick, Jerome H.
   1973   "The police and the urban ghetto." Pp. 223–238 in Arthur Niederhof-
          fer and Abraham S. Blumberg (Eds.), *The Ambivalent Force: Perspec-
          tives on the Police.* San Francisco: Rinehart Press.

Terry, Robert M.
   1967   "Discrimination in the handling of juvenile offenders by social-
          control agencies." *Journal of Research in Crime and Delinquency,* July,
          4:218–230.

Thornberry, Terence P.
   1973   "Race, socioeconomic status and sentencing in the juvenile justice
          system." *Journal of Criminal Law and Criminology,* March, *64*:90–98.

Weiner, Norman L. and Willie, Charles V.
   1971   "Decisions by juvenile officers." *American Journal of Sociology,* Sep-
          tember, *76*:199–210.

Westley, William A.
   1975   "Violence and the police." *American Journal of Sociology*, July, *LIX*:34–41.

Williams, Jay R. and Gold, Martin
   1972   "From delinquent behavior to official delinquency." *Social Problems*, Fall, 20:209–228.

Wilson, James Q.
   1968a   *Varieties of Police Behavior: The Management of Law and Order in Eight Communities*. Cambridge: Harvard University Press.

   1968b   "The police and the delinquent in two cities." Pp. 9–30 in Stanton Wheeler (Ed.), *Controlling Delinquents*. New York: John Wiley.

Wolfgang, Marvin E., Figlio, Robert and Sellin, Thorsten
   1972   *Delinquent in a Birth Cohort*. Chicago: University of Chicago Press.

16

JUVENILE COURT: THE TARNISHED SUPERPARENT

A former judge of the Denver Juvenile Court, Judge Ted Rubin (1976a:66), has described the juvenile court as follows:

> This court is a far more complex instrument than outsiders imagine. It is law, and it is social work; it is control, and it is help; it is the good parent and, also, the stern parent; it is both formal and informal. It is concerned not only with the delinquent, but also with the battered child, the runaway, and many others. . . . The juvenile court has been all things to all people.

What Judge Rubin's remarks reflect is the fact that the historical and ideological trends which led to the invention of the juvenile court in 1899 have carried forth with great vigor into this century. So vigorous have they been, in fact, that it was not until a decade ago that they first came under serious attack.

Impact of historical trends

It will be recalled that both the modern concept of childhood and the juvenile court were the outgrowth of trends covering centuries of change in both Europe and America. By the 19th century, the progressive notion had gained widespread acceptance that children, because

440

they are fragile and guileless, require special protection and care. They should be raised and loved by their own parents, not apprenticed to others. They should be encouraged to attend school so that they can learn moral principles as well as how to read and write. They should be permitted to develop at a leisurely pace rather than taking their place alongside adults at an early age. And they should be protected from the evil blandishments of city streets, immoral associates, and places of vice and corruption.

At the same time, such beliefs meant inevitably that the social status and influence of children would be subordinate to that of adults. They could not be both protected and equal. Persons who are supposedly guileless and immature cannot enjoy equal rights with those who know what is best for them and who are supposed to safeguard and to discipline them. Thus, throughout much of the 19th century, children were committed to houses of refuge, asylums, and industrial schools, not merely to preserve order and to protect society, but because such commitments were seen as being in the best interests of the child. To be sure, such commitments proved to be less than a panacea, but their failure simply led reformers to redouble their efforts. These efforts, moreover, were spurred by other signs that ideals for children were not being realized. Indeed, the very factors with which 19th century child-savers were most concerned and which led them to invent the juvenile court sound very familiar today.

Decriminalizing children

One of the reasons the juvenile court was invented was to decriminalize the misconduct of children, whether that misconduct was criminal or merely disobedient and unruly. Such children, said Judge Julian W. Mack of Chicago (1910:293), were generally "huddled together" with older criminals in the station houses, jails, and workhouses of America.

> What was the result of it all? Instead of the state training its bad boys so as to make of them decent citizens, it permitted them to become the outlaws and outcasts of society; it *criminalized* them by the methods that it used in dealing with them. It did not aim to find out what the accused's history was, what his heredity, his environments, his associations; it did not ask how he had come to do the particular act which brought him before the court; it put but one question, "Has he committed this crime?" It did not inquire, "What is the best thing to do for this lad?" (Mack, 1910:293; Italics added).

Judge Mack's lament reflected the fact that the actual treatment of children throughout the 19th century had not caught up with the belief that they were qualitatively different from adults and should be so treated. Instead, "children tried for committing crimes were routinely processed primarily by lower municipal courts, which presumably did not adhere to the most libertarian conceptions of due process and adversary rights" (Schultz, 1974:248). At the discretion of their parents and guardians, as well as the police and courts, children were also committed to industrial and reform schools for being "destitute of proper parental care, or growing up in mendicancy, ignorance, idleness, or vice" (Platt, 1969:103). Many were also committed to adult jails and to prisons for the blanket charge of "disorderly conduct," which might cover anything from assault with a deadly weapon to building bonfires in the street or playing on the railroad tracks (Lathrop, 1916:2). In order to correct such problems and to avoid making outlaws out of children, the juvenile court would destigmatize them by calling them "delinquents" rather than "criminals," and it would devise a set of remedies that were better suited to their particular needs.

Preventing crime by neglected children

Nineteenth century Americans also grew increasingly concerned with the poverty and neglect of children. Following the Civil War, dissatisfaction over the failure of houses of refuge and asylums to solve these problems reached a peak. Yet, the need for child-saving was greater than ever. Not only had the labor-saving technology of the Industrial Revolution begun to dissipate the need for child labor—leaving increasing numbers of children in idleness—but wave after wave of penniless immigrants added their offspring to the problem. These new Americans usually settled in the burgeoning cities; they did not know the law; in desperate need, they sometimes became criminal; their strange customs were viewed with alarm; and they were so busy earning a living that they could not supervise their children adequately. Caught between the customs of their parents, meanwhile, and those of American society, immigrant children used the streets for their playground and often became involved in the delinquent acts and rowdy gangs over which people became increasingly alarmed. Another goal of the juvenile court, therefore, was to intercede with the poor and neglected children who were treading the path to criminality.

Backing up the schools

For two centuries, schooling had been increasing in importance as a device for socializing children. But, after 1850, it took on even more importance. Between 1852 and 1918, all states passed compulsory school attendance laws (Hoffman, 1974:51). Schools, it was now held, should serve not only the children of the elect but should become a device for inducting poor and immigrant children into the American way of life. But the task of insuring that children would learn was more easily hoped for than accomplished. In 1898, the Educational Commission of Chicago complained that the schools could not control many children (Harpur, 1899:161):

> The Compulsory Attendance Act has for its purposes the reformation of these vicious children. They cannot be received or continued in the regularly organized schools; they were admitted into these schools; they were encouraged to do right; they were reproved; they were punished for misconduct; they have been suspended from further attendance in their classes; their parents cannot or will not control them; teachers and committees fail to correct their evil tendencies and vicious conduct. What shall be done with them?

The answer was that they should be disciplined by the juvenile court. It would rescue them from dissolute parents and see that they were trained for productive work.

> The welfare of the city demands that such children be put under restraint. . . . We should rightfully have the power to arrest all the little beggars, loafers, and vagabonds that infest our city, take them from the streets, and place them in schools where they are compelled to receive education and learn moral principles. (Harpur, 1899:163–164).

Treating disturbed children

Finally, the growth of science at the turn of the century only added to the apparent need for some kind of remedy. Since crime in the streets and bad conduct in the school were presumed to be due to causes over which children had no control, perhaps even due to defective genes as well as to bad environment, each misbehaving child required personal attention. Reflecting these ideas, William Healy, an influential psychiatrist who directed the psychopathic institute of the first Chicago juvenile court, argued that only by a detailed analysis of each offender could suitable remedies be found (Cf. Rothman, 1978). Poverty, alone, does not cause bad behavior, he concluded. Rather, it is due to "bad habits of mind" and "mental imagery of low order," both of which are the consequences of some combination of defective interests, depraved parents, poverty, and bad companions.

Indeed, when studying an urban juvenile court in 1969, Emerson (p. 249) noted the persistence of psychodynamic theory in the court. "Illegal behavior," he observed "is held to be 'pathological' and to reflect psychological conflicts which the psychiatrist can identify." His quotation from the guidelines of the court's psychiatric clinic illustrates this belief (p. 250):

> The commission of an offense must, by its antisocial nature, indicate some breakdown, overpowering, or remission of that facility which human beings have, or are expected to have, to maintain their status as law-abiding citizens. In a sense, then, an offense may be seen as symptomatic of an inner conflict which the ego is not able to effectively deal with.

Belief in such a doctrine has continued to suggest that the only solution to delinquency is to proceed, case by case, to discover what the causative factors are in each child. Fortunately, so the opinion ran, the juvenile court could be the screening mechanism by which this could be accomplished and remedies found.

In summary, then, the needs to be served and the remedies for meeting them were clear. The juvenile court would be endowed with all the discretion and power it needed to save America's children. In so doing, there was little need to draw sharp distinctions between 7-year-olds and 16-year-olds or between criminal children and those who were poor, neglected, or failing in school. As Judge Julian W. Mack (1910:297) of Chicago proudly proclaimed: It is the duty of the state not to ask merely whether a boy or a girl has committed a specific offense, but "to find out what he is physically, mentally, and morally and then, if it learns that he is treading the path that leads to criminality, to take him in charge, not so much to punish as to reform, not to degrade but to uplift, not to crush but to develop, not to make him a criminal but a worthy citizen."

The ideal juvenile court

In pursuit of this noble objective, the procedures of the juvenile court have generally been divided into three major steps: *intake*, *adjudication* and *disposition.* By reviewing each of them, we can determine how, according to proponents, each child is supposed to have been treated by the court.

Intake

Intake is the process during which a juvenile referral is received by the court and a series of important decisions made: whether to release or to hold the child in detention while his case is being investigated, whether to file a petition for a formal court hearing, whether to dismiss the case entirely, or whether to refer the child to some other agency or court.

One of the major innovations of the juvenile court was the appointment of probation officers to conduct this screening process, as well as to supervise juveniles following court action. Indeed, early judges were eloquent in their praise of this invention. "The ideal probation officer," said Judge Baker (1910:326), "should have all the consecration of the devoted clergyman, all the power to interest and direct of the efficient teacher, and all the discernment of the skillful physician." Likewise, Richard Tuthill, who, along with Julian Mack, was one of the first judges in Chicago, called probation "the cord upon which all the pearls of the juvenile court are strung. . . . Without it, the juvenile court could not exist" (Rothman, 1978).

The intake inquiry conducted by the probation officer was designed to fulfill two major functions. The first was diagnostic. He was charged with obtaining detailed information on the background, character, and needs of the child, information that would enable the judge to look beyond his offense to his condition. As a result, the probation officer was given unfettered authority to obtain case history data from the police, parents, teachers, neighbors, welfare workers, and any other relevant persons. He was also expected to seek information from court appointed experts—psychologists, physicians, and social workers. Depending upon the probation officer's findings, he or she might dismiss the case, authorize a full court hearing, or dispose of it by informal methods, such as the "counsel and release" procedures used by the police. As Judge Baker of Boston described it (1910:322), the role of the probation officer was like that of the medical technician who gathers the necessary information for making a diagnosis and recommending a cure.

The second major function of the probation officer prior to a court hearing was that of deciding whether the juvenile should be held in detention. This was a key function because one of the major goals of juvenile court legislation was to get juveniles out of adult jails and into special "homes" for children. This need was all the more important because four out of five states have not extended the right of bail to the young. Therefore, it fell to the probation officer to decide which children should be retained in custody. If, in his judgment, parents or guardians were unfit to supervise their children or if the children were viewed as a serious threat to themselves or to the community, they were to be detained. Otherwise, they could be released pending court action.

Adjudication

For those juveniles for whom the intake procedures results in a court hearing, *adjudication* refers to the legal process conducted by the judge, with the probation officer assisting. The judge is to determine whether the allegations in the petition are sustained and whether the child is defined as delinquent or dependent and neglected.

Since, in theory, the juvenile court was charged with exploring the mental and social condition of a child, every state moved to relax the style of the adjudicatory proceedings. Judges were supposed to be selected on the basis of their special qualifications—their knowledge of child psychology and social problems perhaps more than their legal training. Thus, though they were not technically empowered to banish lawyers from their courts, that, in effect, was what happened. This was done on the grounds that the hearing of a case should be like that which thoughtful parents might administer. Hence, judges were not inclined to keep to accepted rules of evidence designed for adult proceedings nor to restrict admissions of guilt by youthful defendants. As Judge Orr of Minnesota put it, "the laws of evidence are sometimes forgotton or overlooked" (Rothman, 1978).

In 1910, the Russell Sage Foundation fostered the publication of a volume entitled, *Preventive Treatment of Neglected Children.* Included in it were articles by leading reformers, among them an article by Judge Baker of Boston. The following is his description of the way he, and presumably any enlightened judge, should run his court:

> [T]he judge excludes all newspaper reporters and all other persons having only a general interest in the proceedings. The sheltered location of the room, the absence of decoration, the dispensing with attendants, and the exclusion of outsiders give the simplicity which is necessary to gain the

undivided attention of the child and give the quiet which is indispensable for hearing clearly what the child says and speaking to him in the calmest tone.

When the judge is ready to hear a case, the probation officer brings in the child from the waiting room. The child does not stand in front of the desk, because that would prevent the judge from seeing the whole of him, and the way a child stands and even the condition of his shoes are often useful aids to a proper diagnosis of the case. The child stands at the end of the platform, where the judge can see him from top to toe, and the judge sits near the end, so he is close to the child and can reassure him if necessary by a friendly hand on the shoulder. The platform is just high enough to bring the average child's eye about on a level with the eye of the judge (Baker, 1910:319).

While these general procedures should prevail, boys and girls were treated somewhat differently. Judge Baker wanted to see a boy alone at first to spare him the embarrassment and the fear "which he often feels in speaking the truth in the presence of the parents" (p. 319). The judge's objective, if possible, was to get the boy to admit his guilt. "The child is told . . . that in this court there is only one thing worse than stealing (or whatever the child is supposed to have done) and that is not telling the truth afterward" (p. 320). If the boy continued to deny his guilt, Judge Baker, like a good father, continued to reason with him, pointing out why such a denial was harmful. Lying to protect oneself, one's friends, or one's parents only made things worse, not better. Indeed, all these pains were taken to get an admission of guilt because it would enhance the effectiveness of treatment. After the boy had unburdened himself to an understanding judge, he would be more ready to accept the helpful intervention of the court.

It is significant that this set of beliefs and practices has been neither exceptional nor isolated throughout this century. In 1962, Judge Paul W. Alexander (p. 88), a former president of the National Council of Juvenile Court Judges, agreed with Judge Baker in virtually the same terms, though their careers were half a century apart.

To help the child change his attitude, a confession is a primary prerequisite. Without it the court is aiding the child to build his future on a foundation of falsehood and deceit, instead of on the rock of truth and honesty. [A]nything that may tend to discourage a child from making a clean breast of it, that may tend to encourage him to try to escape the consequences of his actions by denial or other means, must retard, and possibly defeat, the court's efforts to correct the child.

If the child persisted in denying his guilt, parents and police, and sometimes defense counsel, could be brought in, and the case would be heard in a more formal way. But to both judges this was not the most desirable procedure. As Judge Alexander (1962:89) put it, "the question is almost never "Did he or didn't he?" but rather "What is the best way to change his wrong attitude and correct his unlawful behavior?" Or as Judge Baker (1910:322) indicated, a confession of guilt would enable him to say to parents, police, and aggrieved parties: "John says it is true that he took Mrs. Doe's money, and I adjudge him delinquent, and he has the right to appeal."

By contrast, Judge Baker was more chivalrous with girls (p. 325). He warned that every step should be taken to protect their reputations and, by implication, that of the judge. From the time of arrest, therefore, a girl should be turned over to an "accredited" woman. Furthermore, "when [the girl] comes into the judge's chamber she is attended by a woman. . . . The judge never talks with girls alone as he does with boys." With the chaperone present, however, he could go on to conduct his informal, fatherly hearing.

But whether the offender was male or female, the first concern of a judge was not with establishing guilt or innocence, but with using the court hearing to begin reforming the delinquent. The general reasoning seemed to be that if children were in enough trouble to be in court they probably needed help whether they were technically guilty of some criminal act or not.

Disposition

Disposition refers to the process by which a judge decides what shall be done with a juvenile—whether he shall be released, separated from his parents, placed on probation and required to meet certain standards of conduct, or committed to a correctional facility for treatment. In criminal trials the disposition hearing is separated from the adjudicatory process so that decisions regarding the guilt or innocence of a person will not be confused with those having to do with sentencing and disposition. But, since the inventors of the juvenile court were concerned less with the guilt of a child than with his condition, the two hearings were often intermixed. Consider Judge Baker again (p. 322):

> Of course the court does not confine its attention to just the particular offense which brought the child to its notice. For example, a boy who comes to court for some such trifle as failing to wear his badge when

selling papers may be held on probation for months because of difficulties at school; and a boy who comes in for playing ball in the street may (after the court has caused more serious charges to be preferred against him) be committed to a reform school because he is found to have habits of loafing, stealing, or gambling which cannot be corrected outside.

The differences between this and the procedures carried on in adult courts are obvious. An adult cannot be brought to court on one offense and found guilty of another. Not only is he defended by a lawyer and protected against self-incrimination, but he could not be incarcerated upon the initial charge of playing ball in the street. Furthermore, the decision as to what will be done with an adult once his case has been adjudicated is made in a separate disposition hearing. A few juvenile courts have followed that procedure, but most have not (President's Commission, 1967c:5). Instead, as Judge Baker (p. 322) described it, the procedure should follow that of the medical clinic:

> The judge and the probation officer consider together, like a physician and his junior, whether the outbreak . . . was largely accidental, or whether it is habitual or likely to be so, whether it is due chiefly to some inherent physical or moral defect of the child, or whether some feature of his environment is an important factor; and then they address themselves to the question of how permanently to prevent a recurrence.

If the child was thought to suffer from feeblemindedness, bad adenoids, or poor eyesight, he would be sent to a specialist, but, if the environment seemed to be at fault, "a change is secured through the parents by making them realize that the child will be taken from them if they do not make the change." (Baker, 1910:322).

The indeterminate sentence

Another striking feature of the juvenile court has been its use of the indeterminate sentence. In order to secure the best possible long-term care for children, most states have empowered the court to maintain supervision over them until the age of 21. In the event of some trifling matter, such as throwing stones in the street, a child might be given a light punishment, such as copying the laws governing the proper use of public thoroughfares. Once this was done, the probation officer or the judge could check his work, "just as a physician might do in the case of a burn or a bruise" (Baker, 1910:323). If the "burn" had healed, the patient could be released. But, if the offense was serious and likely to lead to a bad breakdown, the child "was seen by the judge at frequent intervals, monthly, weekly, or sometimes daily, just as with the patient and the physician in case of tuberculosis or typhoid." A "disease" such as this might take a long time to cure.

Judge Baker (1910:323) noted that the only place the medical analogy was not quite appropriate for the juvenile court was its voluntary character. "The patient attends the dispensary of his own volition," he said, "but the offender is compelled to court and obeys the orders of the officials on pain of the loss of his liberty for disregarding them." Whatever had to be done to secure a child's compliance would be done, even if it meant reform school.

Public acceptance

Early reactions to the juvenile court and its rehabilitative ideology were overwhelmingly favorable; opposition was weak and divided. Some municipal judges objected to their loss of jurisdiction over juveniles, and a few police departments expressed fears that probation would return many serious offenders to the streets. A leading scholar, Roscoe Pound, also warned in 1913 that "the powers of the court of star chamber were a bagtelle compared with those of American juvenile courts. . . . If these courts chose to act arbitrarily and oppressively they could cause a revolution quite as easily as did the former" (Rothman, 1978). Yet, when he addressed the annual meeting of the National Council of Juvenile Court Judges in 1950, Pound described the juvenile court as "the greatest forward step in Anglo-American jurisprudence since the Magna Charta!" (National Probation and Parole Association, 1957:127).

As a result of this kind of acceptance, the philosophy and procedures just described were those that dominated the operation of the juvenile court until well after mid-century. As Judge Orman Ketcham of the District of Columbia put it in 1962 (p. 26), "the first two decades of the juvenile court movement produced a wealth of philosophical comment so sound in conception and so modern in tone that it has scarcely been modified or improved upon since that time." In short, the concern of most authorities was not with protecting children from possible arbitrary procedures but with finding ways by which they could be made more effective. The juvenile court was not an agency that needed to be fettered.

Court processing today

Today's reformers strongly oppose the image of the juvenile court as a benevolent parent. Before discussing their position, however, it is wise to obtain a general picture of the way juveniles have been processed through the three major steps of the juvenile court in recent years. Though change is underway, many older patterns still prevail.

Intake

The results of intake procedures can best be understood in terms of the following major topics:

1. *Number of delinquency cases referred to court.* As may be seen in Table 16–1, the rate at which juveniles have been referred to court has

TABLE 16–1
Estimated number and rate of delinquency cases disposed by juvenile courts, United States, 1958–1974

Year	Estimated delinquency cases*	Child population 10–17 (in thousands)†	Rate per thousand‡	Percent increase in rate
1958	470,000	23,443	20.0	3
1962	555,000	26,989	20.6	20
1966	745,000	30,124	24.7	31
1970	1,052,000	32,614	32.3	16
1974	1,252,700	33,365	37.5	
Total percent increase in rate				87.5

* Data for 1958–1968 estimated from the national sample of juvenile courts. This sample represents 60 percent of the population of the United States.
† U.S. Bureau of Census, *Current Population Report*, 1974.
‡ Based on the number of delinquency cases per 1,000 U.S. child population, 10–17 years of age.
Source: National Center for Juvenile Justice, *Juvenile Court Statistics*, 1974. Pittsburgh: National Council of Juvenile Court Judges, 1977:14.

been going up steadily since 1958. In that year, approximately 470,000 juveniles, ages 10–17, were received at intake at a rate of about 20 children per 1,000. By 1974, the overall number had increased to about 1,252,700 and the rate to 37.5 per thousand. Clearly, then, the number of juveniles referred to court has increased far faster than the growth in the youth population. Indeed, the rate of referrals per thousand increased by 87.5 percent between 1958 and 1974.

It is probably significant that the largest increase occurred between 1966 and 1970 (31 percent). Those were the years during which civil rights protests, campus riots, and resistance to the Vietnam War were at their highest. Apparently these events had some impact on the juvenile population and the way officials responded to them. It is also of interest that between 1958 and 1974 the majority of cases came from urban areas—between 62 and 69 percent; less than a third came from semiurban areas; and only about 1 in 10 from rural areas. (National Center for Juvenile Justice, 1977:10).

2. *Number of dependency and neglect cases.*   In sharp contrast to the number of delinquency cases, in 1974 only about one tenth as many juveniles (151,300) were referred to court for dependency and neglect. This meant that in contrast to the rate of 37.5 delinquency cases per 1,000 in 1974 the rate of dependency and neglect cases was only 2.2. This rate, moreover, has remained strikingly constant since 1958, rarely fluctuating much below or above the 2.0 figure (NCFJJ, 1977:14). While it seems unlikely that this number of cases in a child population of over 33.3 million reflects the true incidence of dependency and neglect, one thing is certain: The juvenile courts of the country for the past 20 years have been preoccupied far more with delinquency than with dependency and neglect. Hence, we will devote most of our attention to this matter.

3. *Distribution of delinquency cases by sex.*   Table 16–2 documents the rising number of female cases being referred to juvenile court. Between 1958 and 1966, there was little change; only about one fifth of all cases were female. Between 1966 and 1974, however, the proportion of female

TABLE 16–2
Estimated number and percent distribution of delinquency cases disposed by juvenile courts, by sex, United States, 1958–1974

	Boys		*Girls*	
Year	*Number*	*Percent*	*Number*	*Percent*
1958	383,000	81	87,000	19
1962	450,000	81	104,500	19
1966	593,000	80	152,000	20
1970	799,500	76	252,000	24
1974	927,000	74	325,700	26

Source: National Center for Juvenile Justice, *Juvenile Court Statistics*, 1974. Pittsburgh: National Council of Juvenile Court Judges, 1977:14.

cases rose from 20 to 26 percent, an increase of almost a third in the space of a decade. This growth, moreover, was relatively constant across urban, semiurban and rural courts; that is, about one fourth of all cases have been female in recent years (NCFJJ, 1977:10).

4. *Sources of court referrals.* In the previous chapter we learned that in 1974 the police reported referring 866,857 juveniles to court. This is about 70 percent of the 1.25 million cases that the juvenile courts reported receiving that year. A similar figure, 73 percent, was reported by a research team at the University of Michigan as a result of their survey of several hundred juvenile courts (Cf. Sarri and Hasenfeld, 1976). The remaining referrals are made by parents and relatives (9.7 percent), the schools (7.7 percent), social service agencies (4.4 percent), and by a variety of other community sources and court jurisdictions (5.1 percent) (Hasenfeld, 1976:4).

What these figures suggest, then, is that the juvenile court is still serving one of its original purposes; namely, as a backup institution designed to help the community enforce the moral rules governing childhood (Emerson, 1969:269). Parents, schools, and welfare agencies make referrals when their authority is seriously challenged or when they are sufficiently concerned about the insubordination and misconduct of troublesome youth.

5. *Reasons for court referral.* The reasons for which juveniles are referred to court further substantiates the point just made. Based on additional findings of the Michigan research group, Table 16–3 reveals

TABLE 16–3
Reasons for court referral

Offense	*Percent of total*
Offenses against persons	7.3
Offenses against property	36.2
Drug offenses	7.3
Status offenses	37.2
All others	12.0

Source: Hasenfeld, 1976:68.

that the greater part of court referrals are for status (37.2 percent) and property (36.2 percent) offenses. While the latter are clearly alleged cases of criminal conduct, the former are not. Indeed, about six out of ten status offenses involved runaways, incorrigibles, and curfew violators.

When status offenses are added to drug violations, moreover, they constitute almost half of all court referrals (Hasenfeld, 1976:68).

6.   *Use of detention.*   Estimates of the number of juveniles who are held in detention during some, or all, of the intake process vary considerably. As a result of their analysis of limited numbers of juvenile courts, Cohen (1975a) and Pawlack (1977) estimate that about one quarter of all juveniles are held in detention awaiting a court hearing. Based on the 1.25 million court referrals in 1974, this would mean that something over 300,000 delinquency cases were detained. Other studies, however, indicate that this figure may be a gross underestimation of the actual number. A national survey, in 1965, for example, revealed that approximately two thirds of all apprehended juveniles are detained for an average of 12 days each (President's Commission, 1967c:121). If this proportion prevailed in 1974, the number of detained juveniles would have been about 827,000. Indeed, one investigator has estimated that the annual figure may go as high as 1 million (Sarri, 1974a).

Whatever the exact figure, policemen and probation officers, often at the insistence of parents and other citizens, are equally, if not more, inclined to detain status as criminal offenders, both male and female (Cohen, 1975a; Pawlack, 1977; Sarri, 1974a; Sumner, 1971). Equally significant is the fact that in about 93 percent of the nation's counties, serving 50 percent of the youth population, there are no juvenile detention facilities (National Council on Crime and Delinquency, 1967:122). Juveniles in these counties, therefore, must often be detained in adult jails, police lockups, and drunk tanks. Not only do they number in the hundreds of thousands, but they also include large populations of status offenders (Goldfarb, 1976; Sarri, 1974a). But, since the excessive use of jails and detention centers for juveniles is so inconsistent with the original goals of the juvenile court, almost a century after its invention, it has been severely criticized and will be discussed in greater detail later in the chapter.

7.   *Disposition of cases at intake.*   National juvenile court statistics since 1958 have shown consistently that about half of all court referrals have been handled unofficially by intake personnel; that is, they have not been subjected to a formal court hearing (NCFJJ, 1977:14). Other studies which have scrutinized court practices more closely indicate that the unofficial rate may be considerably higher (Blumstein and Stafford, 1974; California Youth Authority, 1974; Sarri and Hasenfeld, 1976). In its study of several hundred juvenile courts, for example, the Michigan

research group reported that approximately 58 percent of all juveniles were handled unofficially (Hasenfeld, 1976:70).

> The most typical pattern is either to dismiss the case or to counsel, warn, and release the youth. Only a small fraction . . . are put on informal probation (16 percent) or referred to other social service agencies. In other words, most courts seem to cope with the inflow of juvenile cases through very minimal intervention which may, at most, produce a court record, but no significant action by court staff (Hasenfeld, 1976:69).

What is striking about these procedures, however, is the fact that they do not always take the form of handling status offenders informally and criminal offenders formally. Indeed, the Michigan study found that status offenders are as likely to be tried officially as are property offenders and that together they comprise more than seven out of ten court hearings. Only juveniles charged with crimes against persons were more likely to receive a court hearing. These findings are displayed in Table 16–4 (Creekmore, 1976:127).

TABLE 16–4
Actions at intake by type of offense charged
(in percentages)

		Action taken	
Type of offense	*Dismiss*	*Informal handling*	*Formal handling*
Status	26	36	38
Misdemeanor	33	34	33
Property	39	34	35
Person	16	32	51

Source: Creekmore, 1976:127.

Such findings reflect in a striking way the persistence of the benevolent assumption that the moral and social condition of the child is more important that the act he or she commits. When intake personnel encounter children who are out of parental control, who are persistently truant from school, or who are habitual runaways, they often feel that formal action is required. While this behavior may offend our classical beliefs about justice—i.e., that everyone should be treated alike, based not upon personal need but upon the offense committed—it is entirely consistent with the individualized, rehabilitative concept of justice which the juvenile court has traditionally held.

Adjudication

Before considering the adjudication process, two things should be kept in mind: (1) that only about 40 to 50 percent of all court referrals are actually subjected to a formal adjudicatory hearing; and (2) that since the late 1960s the juvenile court has come under increasing attack for failing to afford juveniles the same constitutional protections that adults are afforded in criminal trials: a clear statement of charges, the employment of defense counsel, and the use of due process procedures. If these attacks have been successful, therefore, they should be evident in the recent conduct of adjudicatory hearings.

The national study by the Michigan group, however, reveals a mixed picture. On the one hand, virtually all courts now give written notice to defendants on the specific charges made against them; no new ones can be sprung on them in court as Judge Baker was used to doing. Likewise, seven out of ten judges indicate that they try to explain charges in simple as well as legal language. They also agree that juveniles have a right to legal counsel and that one will be appointed if necessary (Sosin and Sarri, 1976:195).

On the other hand, the actual participation of prosecutors and defense attorneys in formal proceedings still remains small. For example, juveniles have the theoretical right to have a hearing with legal counsel present if detention is contemplated for them. Few lawyers, however, are present in such hearings; many times they are not even held; and, in those states where they are held, they average less than three minutes (Sarri, 1974b:7).

The same picture prevails in the adjudication of a case. While the judges in a study of 234 courts said that prosecutors had a moderate influence, in 6 out of 10 cases in deciding whether a petition should be filed against someone, they had little to do with formal proceedings in court (Creekmore, 1976:139). The same was true of defense attorneys. Only about half of the judges reported that attorneys always confront prosecution witnesses; only 20 percent call their own witnesses; and few make legal motions for dismissal of cases (Sosin and Sarri, 1976:196). As a result, prosecutors in 25 percent of the courts and defense attorneys in 33 percent were reported by judges to have no influence whatsoever (Creekmore, 1976:138–139).

The type of offense with which a child was charged, however, did make a difference. Juveniles charged with serious crimes—assault, burglary, or robbery—were almost always defended in formal proceedings. Children charged with status offenses, by contrast, were rarely defended, despite the fact that these are the most ambiguous kinds of charges and the most difficult to prove (Sosin and Sarri, 1976:196).

A further problem had to do with the fact that, even in serious cases, lawyers did not take an active role in formal proceedings, as they would in criminal court.

> For the most part, attorneys tended to prefer to plea bargain with the judge on small points rather than on the adjudication decision itself. For example, some lawyers would have their clients admit guilt on three of six counts if the other three would be dropped. Judges often agreed to this arrangement, and for good reasons: once a child is adjudicated delinquent, three rather than six counts makes no legal difference, as legally the judge need not fit the disposition to the number of charges (Sosin and Sarri, 1976:196).

Since it has only been in recent years that attorneys have participated in juvenile proceedings, they seemed both to be unsure of themselves and to share the traditional view that children should not be permitted to escape censure, even if their guilt could not be proven in court. Sanford Fox (1970:161) describes the feeling:

> Lawyers generally tend to share the view that misbehaving children ought not to be permitted to believe that they can get away with breaking society's rules. To the extent that a vigorous demand for legal rights would produce an acquittal on delinquency charges, there develops a conflict between this shared belief and the professional role as children's advocate.

With all that, there were signs of change. In those courts where attorneys were active, the social and moral condition of the juvenile was less at issue in the adjudication hearing than in courts where they were not active. Attorneys and parents also had more access to the files and records of the court (Creekmore, 1976:143). Judges in these courts were also less inclined to believe that such status offenses as truancy and promiscuity should be the business of the juvenile court (Creekmore, 1976:144).

What all of this suggests, in short, is that procedures in the adjudicatory process have begun to change and to appear less like those described by Judges Baker and Mack. Nonetheless, it is only in a minority of courts where attorneys and due process procedures are uniformly present. As more courts begin to adhere to this model, however, it seems likely that less attention will be paid to the moral condition of the child and more to the evidence in support of the charge. It is likely, moreover, that resistance will grow to the formal trials of status offenders, not only because they are not charged with crimes, but because status offenses are not only noncriminal but are more difficult to prove.

Disposition

According to the latest thinking, more due process procedures should appear in the dispositional hearing where decisions are made as to what shall be done with juveniles. As yet, however, the majority of such hearings remain informal. As in earlier times, the judge and probation officer are the "clinical team" who make the diagnoses and decide on a treatment (Creekmore, 1976:147–9).

Before considering the results of their deliberations, it should be recalled that something less than half of all referrals remain for disposition following the adjudicatory hearing. In the Michigan survey, for example, almost 6 out of 10 were handled informally. Thus, only 42 percent remained for dispositional decisions. Of this group, therefore, 12 percent of the cases were dismissed without a finding of guilt; 22 percent were put on probation; 7 percent were committed to a correctional institution; and 1 percent were waived to adult court (Hasenfeld, 1976:70). Though these proportions vary from court to court, the same general pattern prevails. Most adjudicated cases are put on probation; relatively few are confined (Cf. Blumstein and Stafford, 1974; California Youth Authority, 1974; Cohen, 1975b; Hasenfeld, 1976).

Minority and status offenders. As with the way the police process juveniles, the evidence is mixed as to whether these dispositional decisions discriminate against poor and minority juveniles. Some investigators believe that this is the case; minority youth—Spanish-speaking as well as black—are more likely to be incarcerated and less likely to be put on probation (Arnold, 1971; Lemert and Rosburg, 1948). Other investigators, by contrast, maintain that intake, adjudicatory, and dispositional decisions are more a function of prior record and seriousness of offense than of outright bias (Cohen, 1975b; Eaton and Polk, 1961; Terry, 1967).

Again, however, the issue does not lend itself to simple conclusions and easy generalizations. First, decisions vary from place to place, revealing wide differences in dispositional patterns (Cohen, 1975b). Secondly, the evidence suggests that, along with prior record and seriousness of offense, social disadvantage, psychiatric disturbance, and family neglect also play key roles. Juveniles who appear to require removal from their homes for these reasons are often sentenced to correctional facilities (Axelrad, 1952; Scarpitti and Stephenson, 1971). Finally, the dispositional decision may rest more on prior intake and detention decisions than on other factors. Cohen (1975b), for example, found that children who had been detained and had had formal petitions filed against them were the most likely to be committed to a training school, even though the reasons for these actions varied widely from court to court. While, in one court, severity of offense and prior record might be the most crucial variables, the deciding factors in another might be idleness, referral by a community agency, and coming from a broken home. Thus, the conduct of juvenile justice does not follow a uniform pattern; rather, it seems to be more a function of variations from community to community and the way the courts reflect the norms and pressures of those communities (Cohen, 1975b; Emerson, 1969).

Other striking features of court processing. Although we have been preoccupied with the effects of race and social class on court decision making, they may not be the most crucial factors requiring attention today. Two other features are at least as salient.

The first has to do with the confinement of juveniles in detention centers and jails prior to court action, not their commitment to a training school following it. It will be recalled that hundreds of thousands of juveniles are so detained each year. By contrast, those who are placed on formal probation or are committed to a training school constitute a much smaller number. For example, in 1971, 494,286 juveniles were detained (Sarri, 1974a:17). Yet, a one-day census of all the nation's training schools, ranches, forestry camps, farms, halfway houses, and group homes in the same year revealed that only 48,050 juveniles were confined in them—a figure that was less than 10 percent of the number who had been detained (Law Enforcement Assistance Administration, 1974:7).

What all of this indicates, in short, is that it is the informal decision making at the intake stage of the court process, not the more formal procedures at the adjudicatory and dispositional stages, that results in the confinement of most juveniles, even if only for short periods of time. This is an important issue because it is another indication of the belief that short periods of detention may be a useful corrective device, as well as insuring that juveniles will appear in court. Yet, the fact that detainees are only alleged, not convicted, delinquents raises some serious questions about the legitimacy of such procedures, particularly since they rarely involve the presence of defense attorneys and formal proceedings.

A second striking feature has to do with status offenders. Except for juveniles convicted of serious personal crimes, status offenders have been as likely to be sentenced to training schools as criminal property offenders. Thus, anywhere from one quarter to one third of all juveniles in state correctional facilities have been of this type (Lerman, 1978). Furthermore, status offenders who are considered incorrigible or sexually promiscuous, if they are girls, tend to be institutionalized for longer periods of time (Gibbons and Griswold, 1957; Lerman, 1978). By contrast, serious criminal offenders constitute only about 11 to 16 percent of the total population in correctional facilities—about 6,000 in all (Mann, 1976:10). (This does not mean that serious offenders receive partial treatment—only that they are a small part of the whole). As much as anything else, therefore, the wide use of detention and the confinement of status offenders has led to cries for reform and demands for change.

The tarnished superparent

Despite the persistence of older patterns in the juvenile court today, its reputation as an all-wise superparent had become badly tarnished by the late 1960s. It had become like an overpainted, frumpish dowager in whose company only a few former friends wanted to be seen. Today, as a result, a new generation of reformers is searching frantically for some foster parents to replace her. But, besides some of the more obvious problems we have already witnessed, there are additional reasons that the reputation of this once virtuous mother has become sullied.

Rising crime rates

One contributing factor has been the rise in official crime rates among the young about which we read in earlier chapters. We are of the opinion, said the President's Commission on Law Enforcement and Administration of Justice (1967b:56), "that juvenile delinquency has increased significantly in recent years." "One in every nine youths—one in every six male youth—will be referred to juvenile court . . . before his 18th birthday" (p. 55). But the belief that juvenile crime rates had risen was only the tip of the iceberg.

During the turbulant years of the 1960s, civil rights protests, urban riots, campus rebellions, and opposition to the Vietnam War gave the appearance of a nation gone berserk, particularly its youth:

> American youth in increasing numbers have withstood tear gas and mace, billy clubs and bullets, insults and assaults, jail and prison in order to lie-down in front of troop trains, sit-in at a university administration building, love-in in public parks, wade-in at nonintegrated beaches, and lie-in within our legislative buildings. . . . They have also challenged socially oriented norms with "mod" dress and hair styles, language, rock music, and psychedelic colors, forms, and patterns. [The nation] has watched the development of the hippy and yippy, the youthful drug culture, black, yellow, brown, and red power advocates, and organizations such as the Third World Liberation Front, the Peace and Freedom Party, and Black Studies Departments on the campus. We have been exposed to violence, vandalism, assault, destruction, looting, disruption, and chaos on our streets. (Carter and Gitchoff, 1970:52).

It is obvious that this disruption and chaos could scarcely be blamed entirely on the juvenile court, nor were many protesters juveniles. But reactions to chaos, like chaos itself, are rarely rational. Hence, the court could not escape unscathed. On the one hand, many ordinary Americans began to agree with the police that the court was incapable of preventing crime and controlling rebellious youth. Its progressive rehabilitative philosophy, like progressivism in general, had contributed not to order, but to anarchy. In 1968 as a result, Richard Nixon promised if elected President to wage a "war on crime," even if many of the nation's young were numbered among the enemy. And the National Commission on the Causes and Prevention of Violence (1969:xxv) asked rhetorically whether we were about to "witness widespread crime, perhaps out of police control." The feeling was that the country no longer faced losses of one kind or another from young people; it was in danger of losing everything! The only solution, therefore, was to return to a more *retributive* concept of justice, favoring punishment and deterrence rather than rehabilitation.

The vast net of the juvenile court

A second source for disillusionment has come from two quite different sources: from classical, libertarian conceptions of fair play and from the new and growing influence of labeling theory. Meeting in London in 1960, the Second United Nations Congress on the Prevention of Crime and the Treatment of Offenders recommended "that the meaning of the term juvenile delinquency should be restricted as far as possible to violations of the criminal law" (United Nations, 1961:61). If this recommendation were followed to the letter, status offenses by children— such things as running away, defying parents, or being truant—would no longer be defined as "delinquent"; the only delinquents would be those who violated the criminal law.

In 1967, the President's Commission on Law Enforcement and Administration of Justice (1967b:25) made essentially the same recommendation. In leading up to that recommendation, it first lamented the vague and ambiguous laws that gave the juvenile court the right to act:

> The [legal] provisions on which intervention . . . is based are typically vague and all-encompassing: growing up in idleness and crime, engaging in immoral conduct, in danger of leading an immoral life. They establish the judge as arbiter not only of the behavior, but the morals of every child (and to a certain extent the parents of every child) appearing before him. The situation is ripe for overreaching, for imposition of the judge's own code of youthful conduct. . . . One need not expound on the traditional American virtues of individuality and free expression to point out the wrong-headedness of so using the juvenile court.

The Crime Commission (1967b:27) then recommended that "Any act that is considered a crime when committed by an adult should continue to be, when charged against a juvenile, the business of the juvenile court." But it added: "Serious consideration, at the least, should be given to complete elimination of the court's power over children for noncriminal conduct." Such things as staying out late, smoking, or running away should not be grounds for the use of coercive court power.

Lack of due process

A third source of change, like the second, revealed the imprint of classical thinking. For the first time in the history in 1966, the basic philosophy and practices of the juvenile court were reviewed by the U.S. Supreme Court. In a now celebrated case, the *Kent* case (383 U.S. 541, 1966), the Supreme Court disavowed the idea that juvenile judges should ignore constitutional protections for juveniles in favor of paying attention only to their personal and moral problems:

While there can be no doubt of the original laudable purpose of the juvenile courts, studies and critiiques in recent years raise serious questions as to whether actual performance measures well enough against theoretical purpose to make tolerable the immunity of the process from the constitutional guarantees applicable to adults. . . . *There is evidence, in fact, that there may be grounds for concern that the child receives the worse of two possible worlds: that he gets neither the protections accorded to adults nor the solicitous care and regenerative treatment postulated for children* (Emphasis added).

In a second landmark case, the *Gault* case (387 U.S. 1), the Supreme Court held in 1967 that the code and practices of the state of Arizona deprived children of procedural safeguards guaranteed by the Fourteenth Amendment. Gerald Gault was a 15-year-old boy charged with making an obscene phone call to a neighbor. As a result of the juvenile court process, Gerald was incarcerated in a state institution where, according to law, he could have been held until the age of 21. By contrast, the maximum punishment he could have received, had he been an 18-year-old adult, would have been a fine of from $5 to $50 or imprisonment in jail for not more than two months.

Although the severity of this penalty is questionable by itself, it was but one of a long list of dubious court practices which the Supreme Court noted in reversing the original decision: Gerald was arrested and held in detention without notification of his parents. A petition outlining the charges was not served on his parents prior to trial; in fact, the petition made no reference to any factual basis for taking court action. It recited only that "said minor is under the age of 18 years and in need of the protection of this Honorable Court [and that] said minor is a delinquent minor."

Although the police and court action that led to the incarceration of Gerald was based on a verbal complaint by his neighbor, a woman, that complainant never appeared in court to give sworn testimony. In fact, no one was sworn in at the hearing, nor were any transcripts or recordings kept, nor was Gerald represented by counsel. Gerald was alleged to have confessed to making the call, but his "confession" was never reduced to writing, was obtained out of the presence of his parents, without legal counsel, and without any advice of his right to remain silent. In short, due process, so carefully pursued in adult criminal proceedings, was totally disregarded.

Expressing his opinion of the case, Mr. Justice Fortas wrote as follows:

Under our constitution, the condition of being a boy does not justify a kangaroo court. The traditional ideas of Juvenile Court procedure, indeed, contemplated that time would be available and care would be used to establish precisely what the juvenile did and why he did it—was it a prank of adolescence or a brutal act threatening serious consequences to himself or society unless corrected? Under traditional notions, one would assume that in a case like that of Gerald Gault, where the juvenile appears to have a home, a working mother and father, and an older brother, the Juvenile Judge would have made a careful inquiry and judgment as to the possibility that the boy could be disciplined and dealt with at home, despite his previous transgressions. . . . The essential difference between Gerald's case and a normal criminal case is that safeguards available to adults were discarded in Gerald's case. The summary procedure as well as the long commitment was possible because Gerald was 15 years of age instead of over 18. (*In re Gault*:28–29).

The Supreme Court also suggested that the failure to exercise adequate safeguards is a general one that characterizes many jurisdictions, not just Gerald's court in Arizona. "Juvenile court history," said the Supreme Court, "has again demonstrated that unbridled discretion, however benevolently motivated, is frequently a poor substitute for principle and procedure." Most of the justices concluded that "due process of law is the primary and indispensable foundation of individual freedom."

The Supreme Court reaffirmed many of these ideas in 1970 in the *Winship* case (397 U.S. 358). Again, it broke new ground by noting that proof of guilt beyond a reasonable doubt is required in juvenile as well as in adult cases. "The same considerations," wrote Mr. Justice Brennan, "that demand extreme caution in fact-finding to protect the innocent adult apply as well to the innocent child" (*In re Winship*:365). Along with *Kent* and *Gault*, then, *Winship* set forth two important guidelines for the juvenile court: (1) procedures that insure fairness cannot be discarded merely because the juvenile court purports to be benevolent and rehabilitative; and (2) guarantees of due process need not interfere with the rehabilitative and other traditional goals of the juvenile court (Paulsen and Whitebread, 1974:20).

Reactions of juvenile court judges. The National Council of Juvenile Court Judges tended to respond negatively to these guidelines. Meeting in national conference shortly after the *Gault* decision in 1967, they adopted a resolution stating that the Supreme Court decisions had "left unresolved more questions than they had resolved" (Rubin, 1976b:136). The message of the Supreme Court was far from clear.

On one hand, the Court had said that the informal practices of the juvenile court were no longer acceptable. Juveniles must be accorded most of the constitutional protections afforded adults. On the other hand, the Supreme Court had also said that the juvenile court should not become like the criminal court. "The observance of due process standards, intelligently and not ruthlessly administered, will not compel the States to abandon or displace any of the substantive benefits of the juvenile process. . . . Nothing will require that the conception of the kindly judge be replaced by its opposite" (*In re Gault,* 1967:21).

How, the National Council of Juvenile Court Judges seemed to be asking, can two seemingly contradictory procedures operate at one and the same time? Can judges remain impartial with respect to proving the acts that juveniles commit and yet appear to be partial and fatherly throughout the court hearing? Can prosecutors and defense attorneys argue the merits of a case without resorting to the outrageous game-playing that sometimes characterized their adversary procedures in adult courts? Even worse, will not adversary procedures destroy the informality of the juvenile court and contribute to the belief among children that they can escape censure for delinquent acts?

Although such questions have never been satisfactorily answered, there is a growing consensus that the juvenile court must become a court, not a social agency. More prosecutors and defense attorneys must be employed in juvenile court, and judges must pay more attention to matters of due process. For the first time in modern history, the decisions of the highest court in the land seemed to be saying that the right of the state to act in lieu of parents, no matter how benevolently motivated, must be curbed; judges do not always know what is best for children. Instead, like grown-ups, children cannot be deprived of liberty without guarantees of constitutional rights.

Detention

A third source of change came from a growing awareness of the failure of the juvenile court to realize some of its most fundamental goals. One of these was to get children out of adult jails, pending their court hearings, and to find homelike detention facilities for them. Indeed, most states wrote statutes early in the century, directing that children should be released to their parents pending trial, unless they had to be restrained from running away or might be a danger to themselves or others. Evidence reveals, however, that this dream has never been realized:

Age. Studies indicate that children under 12 are less likely to be detained than are adolescents. Nonetheless, 3 percent of the nation's detention centers in 1971 were holding children under 6 years of age; 9 percent were holding children from 6 to 8; and 43 percent of all detainees were holding children from 9 to 11 (Law Enforcement Assistance Administration, 1974:12–13). In one jurisdiction, 33 percent of all detainees were children under age 12 (Cohen, 1975a:20). In some communities, there are no other places to put children who are neglected or abused, but the thought is repugnant to many people nevertheless. To make matters worse, these same children are often housed with adolescents charged with crimes (LEAA, 1974:12–13). As in the institutions of the 19th century, therefore, all types of children are still "huddled together" in places of confinement.

Type of offense.   Generally, juveniles with prior records are more likely to be detained than are neglected children or first time offenders (Cohen, 1975a; Pawlack, 1977). This generalization, however, should not be interpreted to mean that only those juveniles who commit crimes are numbered among the repeater group. Many of them are status offenders who are idle, who come from disrupted homes, or who are charged with drug or alcohol use. Furthermore, they are more likely to be detained than those with specific criminal offenses (Cohen, 1975a; Pawlack, 1977; Sarri, 1974; Sumner, 1971). In California, for example, Lerman (1978) found that while the detention of juveniles charged with specific crimes declined from 49 percent in 1960 to 35 percent in 1970 the detention of juveniles charged with status offenses stayed constant— about 50 percent. Since many "repeaters" are status offenders, they find themselves numbered in this latter group.

The same kinds of findings appear when seriousness of offense is taken into account. "In light of this variable," says Cohen (1975a:30), "it is somewhat surprising that severity of offense appears to play a rather negligible part in [the detention] decision." Again, court officials are as inclined to detain status offenders as to detain those who are criminal, often because they are referred to court by parents, teachers, or welfare workers (Cohen, 1975a:39–42):

> [T]ruant officers appeal to the court to use its authority and its threatened sanctions to get truants to attend school; school officials to discipline and

control in-school "behavior problems"; the Child Welfare Department to augment caseworker and group home control over troublesome youths; and parents to support efforts to deal with their recalcitrant children. (Emerson, 1969:270).

Sex. The use of detention for girls, in particular, seems to reflect the sensitivity of the court to the requests of these influential people. It is they, as much as the police, who refer girls to the court, often for traditional "female" offenses—running away and sexual promiscuity. As a result, a double standard of justice immediately comes into play. "Females who commit juvenile code offenses," says Pawlack (1977:6), "regardless of race and prior court contacts, have a larger percentage of detention than males who commit such offenses." Indeed, some observers have suggested that 75 percent of all females charged with status offenses are detained, as contrasted with only 25 percent of the male status offenders (Chesney-Lind, 1977:124; Sarri, 1974a:18).

Such findings raise some interesting questions about the so-called sexual revolution and the new freedoms presumably enjoyed by females. Not only are girls detained for moral reasons more often than boys, but the treatment they receive in detention indicates that the "revolution" is far from complete. Chesney-Lind (1977:124) notes, for example, that all girls brought before the courts in New York and Philadelphia are given vaginal smears to test for venereal disease, even if the charges against them are nonsexual. Similarly, Wakin (1975:45) reported that in one detention center all girls were required to undergo a pelvic examination to determine if they were pregnant. Describing the same sort of a situation in Philadelphia, an official noted that girls do not have a choice in the matter:

> "We do put a girl on the table in the stirrups and we do have a smear. . . . We do have a swab. You go in and get a smear." When asked whether a girl who refused to undergo this pelvic exam would be placed in "medical lock-up"—a polite term for solitary confinement—he responded, "Yes, we may have to." (Chesney-Lind, 1977:125).

It is impossible to say how widespread such practices are. But, in general, they reflect the rather common assumption that if a girl comes to the attention of authorities she must be sexually promiscuous. By contrast, tests for venereal disease among boys are almost unheard of. Thus, it is the application of a legal double standard which contributes to higher rates of confinement among girls for status offenses, as well as to the degrading experiences to which some are subjected.

Race and social class. Despite the traditional equation of poverty with crime in this country, the evidence is by no means clear that minority and poor youth suffer higher rates of detention than white middle-class youth. Most studies do indicate that minority and lower-income juveniles experience somewhat higher rates of detention, but differences between them and others is surprisingly small (Cohen, 1975a; Pawlack, 1977; Sarri, 1974a; Sumner, 1971).

Two factors seem to be at work. On one hand, as we have seen, minority and poor youth experience higher rates of arrest and victimization for criminal offenses than do their more affluent peers. This may explain why slightly higher proportions of them are detained. On the other hand, research indicates that officials are highly inclined to discriminate against white middle-class youth for the commission of status offenses, particularly white females. It is these groups which have the highest rates of confinement for these kinds of offenses (Cohen, 1975; Pawlack, 1977). Thus, as Cohen (1975a:43) puts it, "these findings do necessitate qualifying the widespread accusation of racial and class discrimination in all phases of juvenile processing." While the results of a few studies cannot be taken to represent court practices nationwide, they are contrary to expectation.

What they may reflect, in fact, is a kind of reverse discrimination. The persistent tendency for officials to act paternalistically toward higher-status youth by confining them could mean that they are more concerned about their morality than about the morality of lower-status youth. If so, that may help to explain why the detention rates of both groups are almost equal. To many people today, as well as to earlier generations, detention is defined as a desirable, not undesirable, gesture for those they consider worth saving.

Juveniles in jail

Earlier in the chapter, it was pointed out that detention centers are not uniformly available to all juveniles. Four out of five are located in urban areas, and, while they serve about 50 percent of the youth population, they are found in only about 7 percent of the nation's counties (NCCD, 1967:122). What happens, then, to juveniles in the remaining 93 percent of the counties?

The answer is that many of them are still being detained in adult jails. This is due to a discrepancy between ideology and practice that dates back to the first juvenile court in Illinois. After passing the new court legislation, the legislature in that state refused to vote one penny to construct detention facilities (Schultz, 1974:245). Other states did likewise. Most of them continued to put children in jail. It was not until after World War II that more communities began to build special detention homes (NCCD, 1967:120). Even so, most communities do not have one, and those that do, ironically, still continue to put juveniles in jail (Pawlack, 1977).

Jail population. During the 1960s the National Council on Crime and Delinquency (1961:xxi; 1967:121) estimated that about 100,000 juveniles were being jailed annually. In some jurisdictions, children were placed in adult penal institutions, if local jails were lacking. For example, "As of mid-1969, Goochland County, Virginia . . . held all its pretrial detainees at a maximum security cellblock within the Virginia State Farm, an institution for adult convicts ranging from vagrants to murderers" (Goldfarb, 1976:310). Testifying before a Congressional Committee, an attorney described one of the consequences:

> [A] 15-year-old, Bobby Lee Taylor, awaiting trial at Goochland, was held in this maximum security block and was teargassed twice while he was locked in his cell. Both teargassing attacks on him by a guard were made because he was calling to the guard for medical assistance for another prisoner. On one occasion it was to assist a prisoner who was deaf and dumb and appeared to be in physical agony (Cf. Goldfarb, 1976:310).

A national census in 1970 continued to document the use of jails for juveniles. On a single day that year, March 15th, 7,800 juveniles were counted in 4,037 city and county jails (LEAA, 1971:10). Not included in this census, however, were juveniles held in police lockups, in drunk tanks, or in state operated jails. Furthermore, the number of juveniles detained in jails on an annual basis would be considerably higher. Several state surveys, for example, indicate that if the number of juveniles held in jail each year were added up the total would be large: in Illinois in 1969 there were 10,250 (Mattick and Sweet, 1969); in Minnesota, in both 1970 and 1972, approximately 6,000 (Minnesota Department of Corrections, 1970–72); in Wisconsin in 1972, 9,924 (Wisconsin Division of Family Services, 1974). Because these are "progressive" states and because there were only four states which did not have juveniles in jail in the 1970 census, one investigator has estimated that as many as 500,000 juveniles are being jailed each year across the country (Sarri, 1974a:5). Since that estimate is much higher than the one made by the National Council on Crime and Delinquency in the 1960s, it must be treated with caution. But, whether it is completely accurate or not, it is clear that the child-saving ideal of keeping children out of jail has never come close to fruition.

Reasons for jailing. The available information suggests that the reasons juveniles are jailed are strikingly like the reasons they are detained in juvenile facilities. In 1960, for example, a one-day census by the Children's Bureau found 33 children under 5 in jail; 13 were ages 5 to 9; about 550 were ages 10 to 14; and more than 12,000 were between 15 and 19 years (Low, 1965:6).

In the 1970s, it has been found that about two thirds of the juveniles in jail are awaiting trial (LEAA, 1974). Likewise, almost half of them are status offenders, the majority of whom are not segregated in separate quarters from adult criminals (Sarri, 1974:7–9; Children's Defense Fund, 1976:20). Some judges, in fact, have reported that "they chose jails for juveniles to 'teach them a lesson'" (Sarri, 1974:10). Others are abused or neglected children who are held in "protective custody." "One child was in jail because her father was suspected of raping her. Since the incest could not be proven, the adult was not held. The child, however, was put in jail for protective custody" (Children's Defense Fund, 1976:21).

Though it is bad enough for status offenders or a child who has just been raped to be put in jail, it has been estimated that more than 80 percent of the jails in which juveniles are confined are *un*suitable for adults, let alone children (NCCD, 1967:121). As a consequence, the results are sometimes deadly:

> In Iowa a girl is thrown into jail because she runs away to get married: she hangs herself. She is sixteen years old.
>
> In Missouri, a seventeen-year-old is homosexually assaulted and kicked to death by jail cellmates.
>
> Another seventeen-year-old is murdered in a Miami jail (Goldfarb, 1976:307–308).

In other cases, children suffer brutal treatment, if not death, at the hands of adult offenders. For example, three brothers, Billy, age 12, Brian, age 13, and Dan, age 14, were suspected of stealing some coins from a local store and placed in jail with adult prisoners:

> After the lights were out in the jail, the men ordered the boys to take off their clothes. When they refused . . . the men tore off the boys' clothing, and then, one by one, each of the men forcibly raped the three brothers. Pointing to a long electric cord hanging in the cell, one of the men warned the boys that if they uttered a sound . . . he would choke them to

death. . . . The boys obeyed . . . and were silent (Children's Defense Fund, 1976:1).

Finally, brutal treatment sometimes comes at the hands of authorities. Two 13-year-old boys, one white, the other black, were confined in a state hospital and were caught having homosexual relations with each other:

> Officials at the hospital . . . bound them to their beds for a period of seventy-seven and one-half hours, and they tied their hands and feet to the bedposts and spread-eagled them on the beds in such a position that the boys could only move their hands about three or four inches in each direction. They were allowed up only to shower (Goldfarb, 1976:308).

A comment by Patricia Wald (1976:124–125) sums up the opinions of most critics today regarding these practices. It is not much different from those made in 1899:

> There is no responsible evidence to indicate that we know how to predict dangerous or violent behavior in a juvenile any more than we do in an adult. Yet juvenile courts have operated on the premise that they are authorized to detain for possible future criminal behavior.
>
> [Equally as bad], status offenders are also held for the longest periods in detention. It is ironically and bitterly true that most lawbreakers can go back home but those who offend against their parents usually cannot.

Assembly-line justice

A fourth problem has to do with the possibility that the juvenile court is administering assembly-line justice. As originally conceived, judges and probation officers were to be mature and wise individuals who had access to a rich set of resources for helping children. How well have these objectives been realized?

First, it must be recognized that the structure of the juvenile court takes many different forms: In some states, it is a unit of county government; in others, there are statewide juvenile court systems; in others, juvenile matters are heard exclusively by family courts; in others, the court is a part of a broad based trial court system, either on the highest superior court level or on the municipal court level where lesser criminals are tried. In some instances, it is a part of a probate court where civil as well as criminal matters are heard. In short, there is no uniform system of juvenile justice (Rubin, 1976b:133–134).

Likewise, judges are not uniformly qualified. In 1963, a fifth of all judges had received no college education; almost half had not attained a college degree; and a fifth were not members of the bar. Rather than being selected for their unique knowledge of child psychology, three fourths of them had been elected to office. Indeed, almost two thirds were probably continuing political careers, having been previously elected to other offices (President's Commission, 1967a:6–7).

A survey in 1973 produced similar findings. Of 1,314 judges, only 12 percent were persons who devoted full time to juvenile matters. By contrast, over two thirds said they spent less than a quarter of their time on such matters, and almost nine out of ten said they spent half time or less (Smith, 1974:33). This state of affairs reflects the fact that the juvenile court has never attained much stature in our system of courts or in the legal profession. Few law schools even have courses on juvenile court law, and, in those jurisdictions where the juvenile court is a part of the superior or district court system, judges often feel that assignment to the juvenile division is an assignment to Siberia (Rubin, 1976b:135).

With all these problems, some juvenile courts operate a kind of assembly-line justice. For example, Cohen (1975b:13) discovered that in one court it took an average of 76 days for intake personnel to decide what should be done about a case; if it required judicial action, the waiting period was doubled to 130 days; and, if it was contested in court, the wait was 211 days. Furthermore, in congested courts of this type, the President's Commission (1967a:7) found that the average court hearing itself may last no longer than 10 or 15 minutes.

Intolerant communities.   Dedicated and competent judges are often hampered by intolerant communities. In one case, a judge who refused to transfer a murder case to adult court because he believed the young-ster involved could be rehabilitated better in the juvenile justice system was defeated for reelection for being too permissive. By contrast, another judge was very popular in his community because he believed that several nights in detention were good for any kid apprehended by the police, even if his case had to be dismissed later in court for insuffi-cient evidence (Rubin, 1967b:146).

Lack of resources.   A related problem has to do with the fact that most communities have not provided concerned judges with the resources they need to help juveniles. In Los Angeles, for example, the juvenile court handled 26,604 cases in 1972–73, or 83 more cases than the adult superior court. Yet, it had only half the judicial personnel (*Los Angeles Times*, June 19, 1974).

Probation was also to be "the cord upon which all the pearls of the juvenile court are strung." Yet, in 1965, one third of all full-time judges reported that they had no probation officers to assist them, and 83 percent said that they had no psychiatric or psychological assistance either (President's Commission, 1967a:6). Most states do make provision for probation services, and 74 percent of the nation's counties do have some probation officers, but their caseloads are high and their pay is low (President's Commission, 1967a:6). The average probation officer has between 75 and 80 delinquents to supervise, to say nothing of the social studies they are supposed to make of new cases coming before the court. Again, assembly-line justice is implied.

Justine Polier (1964:30), an eminent judge from the family court in New York maintains with considerable justification that the lack of resources is the juvenile court's greatest problem:

> The lack of appropriate services and facilities for delinquent children and to a much greater extent for neglected children has contributed more than any other single factor to negating the purpose of the court.
>
> The values of diagnostic studies and recommendations is too often reduced to a paper recommendation. In shopping for placement, probation officers are forced to lower their sights from what they know a child needs to what they can secure. Their sense of professional responsibility is steadily eroded. The judge, in turn, becomes the ceremonial official who in many cases approves a disposition which he knows is only a dead end for the child.

If adequate resources were provided, Judge Polier believes, many of the other charges levied against the court would seem much less important.

Scientific explanations and ideologies

Finally, the changing explanations and ideologies of science have also helped to tarnish the image of the juvenile court. Its rehabilitative ideology was built upon assumptions derived primarily from control theory—namely, the idea that delinquent behavior is due to the defective socialization of children and that in order to rehabilitate them they must be personally treated and cared for. But other bodies of theory have painted a much different picture.

From the cultural deviance theory of Shaw and McKay to the Marxian perspective of the radicals, each new body of scientific thought has added ammunition to the idea that delinquent behavior cannot be prevented and controlled by tinkering with the mind and morality of the delinquent. To do so is to treat symptoms, not causes. It is society that segregates people by age, class, and race, that produces delinquent subcultures among children, that defines rules favoring the powerful and then labels and stigmatizes the powerless who break them. It is society that is criminogenic, not individual families and children.

If that is the case, argued Lemert (1967:93), it is a "brave idea" indeed which suggests that the juvenile court can both prevent and remedy all youthful misbehavior by itself. Not only is such an idea contrary to most theories of delinquency, but it is contrary to the scientific study of law-violating behavior. Since hidden delinquent acts are high among all segments of the youth population, since most of these acts go unpunished and unacted upon, and since the police and courts release most of the juveniles whom they do catch, the juvenile court can have but small impact on youthful misbehavior. It has bitten off more than it can chew.

Beyond that, 20th century social science has constructed an ideological superstructure which has not only increasingly disavowed the optimistic assumption that the juvenile court can actually help juveniles, but it has seriously eroded the notion that there should be any special court at all for them. Except for serious juvenile criminals, their acts would be best dealt with by other than legal means—by means that reduce unemployment, enrichen slum schools, combat racial and economic segregation, reduce the generation gap, and give young people a stake in conformity. When such ideas are combined with those of other critics, therefore, one encounters some remarkable dilemmas in trying to draw some final conclusions about an appropriate role for the juvenile court.

Conclusions: Courts, critics, and dilemmas

The historical and ideological trends which led to the invention of the juvenile court have retained considerable vigor well into the 1970s:

The rate at which juveniles have been referred to court has been going up steadily since 1958. Females now constitute one fourth of these referrals and will likely become a larger part.

The juvenile court is still continuing to serve as a backup institution designed to enforce the moral rules governing childhood. This is indicated by the fact that the one type of offender most often referred to court is the status offender, followed closely by the property offender. Together, they comprise more than seven out of ten referrals.

Court personnel continue to exercise a great deal of informal discretion, particularly at the intake stage. This is revealed by a contradictory set of facts. On the one hand, intake personnel release at least half of all court referrals, using procedures much like those used by the police at an earlier stage in the process. On the other hand, these same officials confine far more juveniles in detention centers and jails at the intake stage than are ultimately sentenced to correctional facilities following formal consideration of their cases.

Though only a small fraction of all court referrals are finally confined in correctional institutions, status offenders are as likely to be sentenced to these facilities as are criminal property offenders and are exceeded proportionately only by serious personal offenders.

Figure 16–1 provides a graphic portrayal of these procedures. Like Figure 15–1 on the police processing of juveniles, it utilizes 1974 data. But, since it derives estimates on the routing of juveniles from a variety of sources, it serves better as a general, rather than a precise, illustration of how juveniles are handled. The lack of uniform annual data on the outcome of court decision making does not permit fully accurate estimates.

Critics

There has been something in the practices of the juvenile court for every critic: People who see the court as being too permissive advocate a more stern and punitive form of justice; people who see the court as possessing too much discretion advocate a more classical form of justice; social scientists who see society as criminogenic advocate a more liberal concept of justice; and radicals advocate revolution.

Dilemmas

Combined with the practices of the juvenile court, these criticisms are full of paradoxes. To begin with, there is support for the contention of social scientists that the court is not an effective device for controlling crime. Indeed, one could argue that its functions are primarily symbolic. Since only a small fraction of all law violators are discovered and

FIGURE 16–1
The juvenile court filtering process

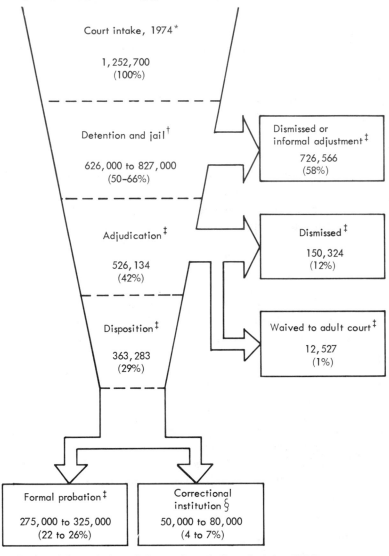

Court intake, 1974*

1,252,700
(100%)

Detention and jail†

626,000 to 827,000
(50–66%)

Dismissed or
informal adjustment‡
726,566
(58%)

Adjudication‡

526,134
(42%)

Dismissed‡
150,324
(12%)

Disposition‡

363,283
(29%)

Waived to adult court‡
12,527
(1%)

Formal probation‡

275,000 to 325,000
(22 to 26%)

Correctional
institution§
50,000 to 80,000
(4 to 7%)

* National Center for Juvenile Justice. Juvenile Court Statistics, 1977:14.

† Current censuses are conducted on a daily rather than annual basis. Annual estimates, therefore, vary widely. These estimates are based on President's Crime Commission, 1967c:121; Sarri, 1974:5 and 7.

‡ Estimates based on National Survey of Juvenile Courts. Cf. Sarri and Hasenfeld, 1976:69–70.

§ Estimates based on one-day censuses of correctional facilities and National Survey of Juvenile Courts. Cf. LEAA, 1974:7; Sarri and Hasenfeld, 1976:69–70.

since an even smaller number are ever tried in court and confined in an institution, the court does little more than indicate to juveniles that something bad *might* happen to them if they misbehave. Otherwise, the court does little to protect society.

But, while this argument has been used by people of liberal persuasion to support their contention that means other than the legal system means should be used to prevent delinquency, it could be used just as well by conservatives who argue that the juvenile court has been too permissive. Rather than being more lenient with juveniles, the police and courts should be tougher. Which of their solutions, therefore, shall be pursued—delinquency prevention or a war on crime?

In a similar way, court practices support the contention of either classical or labeling critics that the juvenile court has often been arbitrary, that detention has been used excessively, and that constitutional procedures have been lacking. Yet, it is equally clear that judges and probation officers, like the police, have been pragmatic labeling theorists. They release at least 50 percent of their referrals, without formal trial or placement, including many criminal as well as status offenders. What should policy makers make of this state of affairs? Is it best to tighten up procedures so that the juvenile court becomes more like an adult criminal court, or should officials be permitted to continue releasing large numbers of offenders on the assumption that informal discretion is needed to avoid labeling children unnecessarily?

Critics of liberal and labeling persuasion have also argued that status offenders should not be the concern of the juvenile court. Yet, many influential persons, representing views across the ideological spectrum, are ambivalent over this potential change: Most state laws still include status offenses as grounds for court intervention; parents, teachers, and the police continue to assert the need for a backup institution to deal with ungovernable children, school dropouts, and runaways; the Supreme Court demands that the juvenile court use procedures that insure fairness for children, yet it notes that guarantees of due process need not interfere with the traditional goals of the juvenile court; attorneys continue to play a reluctant role in juvenile court because they often share the belief that misbehaving children should not be permitted to violate the rules governing childhood; and some influential judges argue that the limitations of the juvenile court stem less from inherent weaknesses in its fundamental purposes than from a lack of adequate resources. For many people, in short, the traditional functions of the juvenile court continue to be important.

What it all means

It is clear that what we are confronted with is a host of dilemmas, not final answers. Indeed, society's social construction of delinquency is like a stalagmite on the floor of a cave. It is a structure that has been formed, not just by recent events and ideas, but by the constant drip of ideologically laden beliefs that stretch back for centuries. It should not be surprising, therefore, that contradictions are present.

When we examine the results of efforts to rehabilitate delinquents in the next chapter, we will find that there are even more dilemmas to consider. Hence, after all the dilemmas are in, we will return to this ideological potpourri in order to determine how it is likely to affect the future course of justice for juveniles.

References

Alexander, Paul W.
   1962   "Constitutional rights in the juvenile court." Pp. 82–84 in Margaret K. Rosenheim (Ed.), *Justice for the Child*. Chicago: University of Chicago Press.

Arnold, William R.
   1971   "Race and ethnicity relative to other factors in juvenile court dispositions." *American Journal of Sociology*, September, LXVII:211–227.

Axelrad, Sidney
   1952   "Negro and white male institutionalized delinquents." *American Journal of Sociology*, May, LVII:569–574.

Baker, Harvey H.
   1910   "Procedure for the Boston juvenile court." Pp. 318–327 in Hastings H. Hart (Ed.), *Preventive Treatment of Neglected Children*. New York: Charities Publication Committee.

Blumstein, Alfred and Stafford, Richard A.
   1974   "Application of the jussim model to a juvenile justice system." *Proceedings of the National Council of Juvenile Court Judges*, December: 60–84.

California Youth Authority
   1974   *Juvenile Probation in California, 1973*. Sacramento: California Youth Authority.

Carter, Robert M. and Gitchoff, G. Thomas
   1970   "An alternative to youthful mass disorder." *The Police Chief*, July, 37:52–56.

Chesney-Lind, Meda
  1977 "Judicial paternalism and the female status offender." *Crime and De-linquency*, April, 23:121–130.

Children's Defense Fund
  1976 *Children in Adult Jails*. New York: Washington Research Project, Inc.

Cohen, Lawrence E.
  1975a *Pre-Adjudicatory Detention in Three Juvenile Courts*. Law Enforce-ment Assistance Administration. Washington, D.C.: U.S. Govern-ment Printing Office.

  1975b *Juvenile Dispositions: Social and Legal Factors Related to the Processing of Denver Delinquency Cases*. Law Enforcement Assistance Adminis-tration. Washington, D.C.: U.S. Government Printing Office.

Creekmore, Mark
  1976 "Case processing: intake, adjudication; and disposition" Pp. 119–151 in Rosemary Sarri and Yeheskel Hasenfeld (Eds.), *Brought to Justice? Juveniles, the Courts, and the Law*. National Assessment of Juvenile Corrections. Ann Arbor: University of Michigan.

Eaton, Joseph W. and Polk, Kenneth
  1961 *Measuring Delinquency*. Pittsburgh: University of Pittsburgh Press.

Emerson, Robert M.
  1969 *Judging Delinquents: Context and Process in Juvenile Court*. Chicago: Aldine.

Fox, Sanford
  1970 "Juvenile justice reform: an historical perspective." *Stanford Law Re-view*, June, 22:1187–1239.

Gibbons, Don C. and Griswold, Manzer J.
  1957 "Sex differences among juvenile court referrals." *Sociology and Social Research*, November-December, XLII:106–110.

Goldfarb, Ronald
  1976 *Jails: The Ultimate Ghetto*. New York: Anchor Books.

Harpur, W. R.
  1899 *The Report of the Educational Commission of the City of Chicago*. Chicago: Lakeside Press.

Hasenfeld, Yeheskel
  1976 "Youth in the juvenile court: input and output patterns." Pp. 60–72 in Rosemary Sarri and Yeheskel Hasenfeld (Eds.), *Brought to Justice? Juveniles, the Courts, and the Law*. National Assessment of Juvenile Corrections. Ann Arbor: University of Michigan.

Hoffman, Edward
  1974 "The treatment of deviance by the educational system: history." Pp. 41–56 in William C. Rhoads and Sabin Head (Eds.), *A Study of Child*

Variance (Vol. 3). Ann Arbor: Institute for the Study of Mental Retardation and Related Disabilities, University of Michigan.

In re Gault
1967   387 U.S. 1, 18L. Ed.2d 527, 87 S. Ct. 1428.

In re Winship
1970   397 U.S. 358, 25L. Ed.2d 368, 90S.Ct. 1068.

Joint Commission on Correctional Manpower and Training
1968   *Offenders as a Correctional Manpower Resource.* Washington, D.C.: Joint Commission on Correctional Manpower and Training.

Kent v. *U.S.*
1966   383 U.S. 541, 16L. Ed.2d 84, 86 S.Ct. 1045.

Ketcham, Orman W.
1962   "The unfulfilled promise of the American juvenile court." Pp. 22–43 in Margaret K. Rosenheim (Ed.), *Justice for the Child.* New York: Free Press.

Lathrop, Julia
1916   "Introduction." Pp. 1–15 in Sophonisba P. Breckenridge and Edith Abbott, *The Delinquent Child and the Home.* New York: Survey Associates, Inc.

Law Enforcement Assistance Administration
1971   *National Jail Census, 1970: A Report on the Nation's Local Jails and Type of Inmates.* Washington, D.C.: U.S. Government Printing Office.

1974   *Children in Custody.* Washington, D.C.: U.S. Government Printing Office.

Lemert, Edwin M.
1967   "The juvenile court— quest and realities." Pp. 91–106 in President's Commission on Law Enforcement and Administration of Justice, *Juvenile Delinquency and Youth Crime.* Washington, D.C.: U.S. Government Printing Office.

1970   *Social Action and Legal Change: Revolution within the Juvenile Court.* Chicago: Aldine.

Lemert, Edwin M. and Rosberg, Judy
1948   "The administration of justice to minority groups in Los Angeles County." University of California, Publications in Culture and Society, *II:*1–28.

Lerman, Paul
1978   "Order offenses and juvenile delinquency." In LaMar T. Empey (Ed.), *Juvenile Justice: The Progressive Legacy and Current Reforms.* Charlottesville: University of Virginia Press.

Low, S.
>   1965   *America's Children and Youth in Institutions, 1959–1960–1964: A Demographic Analysis.* Children's Bureau. Washington, D.C.: U.S. Government Printing Office.

Mack, Julian W.
>   1910   "The juvenile court as a legal institution." Pp. 293–317 in Hastings H. Hart (Ed.), *Preventive Treatment of Neglected Children.* New York: Charities Publication Committee.

Mann, Dale
>   1976   *Intervening with Convicted Serious Juvenile Offenders.* National Institute of Juvenile Justice and Delinquency Prevention, LEAA. Washington, D.C.: U.S. Government Printing Office.

Mattick, Hans W. and Sweet, Ronald P.
>   1969   *Illinois Jails: Challenge and Opportunity for the 1970s.* Chicago: University of Chicago Law School.

Minnesota Department of Corrections
>   1970   *Characteristics of Institutional Populations, 1969–72.* St. Paul: Minnesota Department of Corrections.

National Center for Juvenile Justice
>   1977   *Juvenile Court Statistics, 1974.* Pittsburgh: National Council of Juvenile Court Judges.

National Commission on the Causes and Prevention of Violence
>   1969   *Crimes of Violence* (Vol. II). Washington, D.C.: U.S. Government Printing Office.

National Council on Crime and Delinquency
>   1961   *Standards and Guides for the Detention of Children and Youth* (2nd ed.). New York: National Council on Crime and Delinquency.

>   1967   "Correction in the United States." Pp. 115–212 in President's Commission on Law Enforcement and Administration of Justice. *Task Force Report: Corrections.* Washington, D.C.: U.S. Government Printing Office.

National Probation and Parole Association
>   1957   *Guides for Juvenile Court Judges.* New York: National Probation and Parole Ass.

Paulsen, Monrad G. and Whitebread, Charles H.
>   1974   *Juvenile Law and Procedure.* Reno: National Council of Juvenile Court Judges.

Pawlack, Edward J.
>   1977   "Differential selection of juveniles for detention." *Journal of Research in Crime and Delinquency,* July, 14:1–12.

Platt, Anthony M.
  1969   *The Child Savers.* Chicago: University of Chicago Press.

Polier, Justine W.
  1964   *A View from the Bench: The Juvenile Court.* New York: National Council on Crime and Delinquency.

President's Commission on Law Enforcement and Administration of Justice
  1967a *Juvenile Delinquency and Youth Crime.* Washington, D.C.: U.S. Government Printing Office.

  1967b *The Challenge of Crime in a Free Society.* Washington, D.C.: U.S. Government Printing Office.

  1967c *Task Force Report: Corrections.* Washington, D.C.: U.S. Government Printing Office.

Rothman, David J.
  1978   "The progressive legacy: American attitudes toward juvenile delinquency." Pp. 1–25 in LaMar T. Empey (Ed.), *Juvenile Justice: The Progressive Legacy and Current Reforms.* Charlottesville: University of Virginia Press.

Rubin, H. Ted
  1976a *The Courts: Fulcrum of the Justice System.* Pacific Palisades: Goodyear Publishing.

  1976b "The eye of the juvenile court judge: a one-step-up view of the juvenile justice system." Pp. 133–159 in Malcolm W. Klein (Ed.), *The Juvenile Justice System.* Beverly Hills, Ca.: Sage Publications.

Sarri, Rosemary C.
  1974a *Under Lock and Key: Juveniles in Jails and Detention.* Ann Arbor: University of Michigan, National Assessment of Juvenile Corrections.

  1974b "The detention of youth in jails and detention facilities." *Youth Reporter,* April, 5–8.

Sarri, Rosemary and Yeheskel Hasenfeld (eds.)
  1976   *Brought to Justice? Juveniles, the Courts and the Law.* National Assessment of Juvenile Corrections. Ann Arbor: University of Michigan.

Scarpitti, Frank R. and Stephenson, Richard M.
  1971   "Juvenile court dispositions: factors in the decision making process." *Crime and Delinquency,* April, *XVII*:142–151.

Schultz, J. Lawrence
  1974   "The cycle of juvenile court history." Pp. 239–258 in Sheldon Messinger et al. (Eds.), *The Aldine Crime and Justice Annual, 1973.* Chicago: Aldine.

Smith, D. C.
  1974   "A profile of juvenile court judges in the United States." *Juvenile Justice,* August, 25:27–38.

Sosin, Michael and Sarri, Rosemary
   1976   "Due process—reality or myth?" Pp. 176–206 in Rosemary Sarri and Yeheskel Hasenfeld (Eds.), *Brought to Justice? Juveniles, the Courts, and the Law.* National Assessment of Juvenile Corrections. Ann Arbor: University of Michigan.

Sumner, Helen
   1971   *Locking Them Up: A Study of Juvenile Detention Decisions in Selected California Counties.* New York: National Council on Crime and Delinquency.

Terry, Robert M.
   1967   "Discrimination in the handling of juvenile offenders by social control agencies." *Journal of Research in Crime and Delinquency,* July, 4:218–230.

United Nations
   1961   *Report prepared by the Secretariat.* New York: United Nations.

Wakin, Edward
   1975   *Children without Justice.* New York: National Council of Jewish Women.

Wald, Patricia M.
   1976   "Pretrial detention for juveniles." Pp. 119–137 in Margaret K. Rosenheim (Ed.) *Pursuing Justice for the Child.* Chicago: University of Chicago Press.

Wisconsin Division of Family Services
   1974   *Profile of Juveniles in Wisconsin: 1974.* Madison: Wisconsin Division of Family Services.

17

REFORMING DELINQUENTS: FROM OPTIMISM TO DISMAY

In the previous chapter, we learned that questions relative to the future of the juvenile court are filled with dilemmas. The same is true of society's efforts to prevent delinquency and to reform offenders. That history is characterized not just by rehabilitation, but by other methods that can be conveniently summarized as a series of four Rs: retribution, restraint, rehabilitation and reintegration. In this and the next chapter, therefore, we will be examining these four Rs, the theories that lie behind them, and the evidence regarding their effectiveness.

Retribution

Retribution refers to the dispensing of punishment according to the presumed desserts of the offender. It is justified on two grounds: (1) that suffering is fair recompense for a criminal act and (2) that if suffering is severe enough it might deter others from committing crime.

Despite the fact that the modern concept of childhood had grown rather pronounced by the 18th century, retribution was still the dominant response to young criminals at that time. Sometimes, they were put to death:

> Nicholas Carter, about fourteen Years of Age, was condemned [hanged] for robbery. He said, That his Father imployed him in sewing and making of gloves: But he being Idle, and regardless of his Parents Good Admonitions, ran away from them, and joyned himself to bad Company. . . . [T]he Boy, desired all Young People to take timely warning by his so sudden a Death (Sanders, 1970:25).

Although a few children, like Nicholas, were hanged, most of them received clemency after being sentenced to die (Sanders, 1970:21). In 17th century New England, for example, the laws of the colonies stated that children could be put to death for cursing or smiting their parents, for blasphemous treatment of the scriptures, for being stubborn or rebellious, or for committing other "notorious" crimes of this sort. In practice, however, punishments were usually less stringent. Consider the mercies of the court in the case of one Mistress How:

> The Court upon consideration of what is testified, ordered that for her swearing she pay ten shillings, and for her cursing speeches and rebellion to her mother, and profane speeches of the scriptures, tending to blasphemy, that she be corrected publicly by whipping, suitable to her years, and if this be not a warning but that she go on in these courses, it will come to higher censure (Bremner, 1970,I:38).

Besides whipping, other forms of corporal punishment were also common:

> William Carter a little Boy, about Ten Years of Age, was Indicted for stealing . . . two Gold rings . . ., a piece of Coined Gold, and Mony. . . . It was fully proved, so he was found Guilty [and sentenced to be burnt in the hand] (Sanders, 1970:25–26).

In North Carolina, a slave boy, Peter, confessed that he was present when his master was murdered by his brother:

> The Court haveing taken into consideration the youth of the said Peter and considering him under the Influence of his said older Brother Darby, have thought proper to pass his Sentence in the following words to wit.
>
> That the said Negro boy Peter be committed to Gaol and there to Remain under a Good Guard, till Tomorrow, and then between the Hours of one and four o'clock he be taken out thence and tied to a Post on the Court House lott and there to have one half of Each of his Ears cut off and be branded on Each Cheek with the letter M and Receive one hundred lashes well laid on his bare back and that the Sheriff See this order Executed (Sanders, 1970:324).

Finally, because disfigurement, death, and whipping were sometimes viewed as being too cruel or because they did not seem to deter crime, English reformers suggested that two additional forms of punishment might be tried:

> The methods now employed to dispose of delinquent children failing either to reform them or relieve society from their presence, it is certainly expedient a new experiment should be tried.

> Now it appears to us that it would be real humanity towards these unfortunate creatures to subject them to compulsory and perpetual exile from England. . . . Abroad, in New South Wales [Australia], they often become prosperous and useful citizens; but, at home, they seem incapable of resisting the temptations presented by a luxurious and refined community (Sanders, 1970:137).

The new idea, called "transportation," was accepted and widely used in England and France. The following is an example of its application to a young English girl:

> Susannah Tyrell, a Girl about Ten Years Old, was Indicted for stealing two Gold Rings . . . and 14 shillings. . . . The evidence was that she confest, That one Elizabeth Sallowes (Now in Newgate) did give her a key to open the Door. . . . So that upon the whole, she was found guilty to the value of 9 shillings. She was ordered to be transported (Sanders, 1970:26).

Some notion of the extent to which "transportation" was used in England can be gleaned by reports that were made to the House of Commons. Between 1787 and 1797, 93 children and 5,765 men and women were transported to Australia. Between 1812 and 1817, 780 males and 136 females, all of them under the age of 21, were similarly transported. Five of these were "infants" of 11, 7 were age 12, 17 were age 13, 32 were age 14, and 65 were 15 years of age (Sanders, 1970:69). Unlike the present, however, there were no program evaluators to determine how well the 11- and 12-year-olds enjoyed their trips abroad, but it is certain that they could no longer commit crimes in England.

A somewhat similar method, which was even older than transportation, involved the removal of children to the "hulks"—abandoned, rotting ships, unfit for service, that were anchored off shore in rivers, bays, and inlets. Sometimes children served out their sentences along with adult convicts on these airless, vermin-infested ships, working as tailors, shoemakers, carpenters, and bookbinders. In other cases, they were confined on the hulks awaiting transportation to Australia. The following is one witness's description of the methods that were used to move children, bound in chains, from the various gaols of England to the hulks:

> After having pined and rotted in their respective county gaols . . . which varies from three months to as many years, . . . some [prisoners] are chained on tops of coaches; others, as from London, travel in an open caravan, exposed to the inclemency of the weather, to the gaze of the idle and the taunts and mockeries of the cruel. . . . Men and boys, children just emerging from infancy, as young in vice as in years, are fettered together, and . . . paraded through the kingdom. . . . [They are] ragged and sickly and carrying in their countenance proofs of the miseries they had undergone (Sanders, 1970:70).

The significant thing about the use of hulks, along with capital punishment, branding, whipping, disfigurement, and transportation, was that these methods, rather than confinement in prison, were the primary forms of punishment prior to the 19th century. In virtually all Western countries, "prisons were uniformly considered to be merely places of safekeeping, that might serve a deterrent purpose but had no concern for the rehabilitation or reformation of those confined" (Sellin, 1964:xix). Gradually, however, the treatment of offenders was revolutionized.

Restraint

As Western societies turned the corner from the 18th to the 19th century, efforts to control crime concentrated increasingly upon the notion that lawbreakers, young or old, could be reformed by restraining them in prison. Stimulated by the Enlightenment philosophers and classical criminologists of France, England, and Italy and encouraged by their newly won independence, American reformers sought to reduce the cruelties of retributive punishments and to find alternative methods.

The Pennsylvania System

Pennsylvania led the way. In 1790, that state passed a law which led to one of the most significant innovations in penal history: the construction of a prison in which convicts could be confined in solitary cells as a method of reforming them (McKelvey, 1968:6). Led by the Quakers, by influential reform societies, and by such individuals as Benjamin

Franklin and William Bradford, reformers assumed that by segregating offenders from all corrupting influences and by denying them all but the physical necessities of life they would recognize the errors of their ways and would repent (Barnes, 1972:122). That is why prisons came to be called "penitentiaries." They dereived their meaning from the word "penitence"—meaning to experience remorse and contrition for sin and to choose the path of righteousness.

This method was first tried in the old Walnut Street Jail in Philadelphia, but it soon failed due to excessive overcrowding. Not to be deterred, however, reformers passed new legislation which permitted the construction of two entirely new prisons. The most famous was the Eastern State Penitentiary constructed at Cherry Hill, Pennsylvania, in 1829. Its design was one in which a series of seven massive stone corridors radiated like the spokes of a huge wheel from a central rotunda (Pettigrove, 1910). Each of the corridors contained a series of large cells, $8 \times 15 \times 12$ feet high, into which offenders were placed in solitary confinement. These long cell blocks were only one story high so that each offender could have access to a small outside exercise yard of his own, entirely walled off from all other inmates. Eventually, some offenders planted small gardens and communed with nature, such nature as they could create.

Meanwhile, several other states constructed prisons, but, lacking Pennsylvania's ingenuity, they housed prisoners in large dormitories rather than individual cells. As a result, serious overcrowding and a lack of discipline soon "converted all these prisons into riotous dens of iniquity and roused a wave of popular indignation" (McKelvey, 1968:7). By contrast, the ease with which discipline and control could be maintained under the Pennsylvania system roused the envy and interest of distraught reformers from other places, both here and abroad. Indeed, Pennsylvania authorities were so pleased with what they had wrought that they often worked themselves into a Neoplatonic ecstasy in describing it. The following are the remarks of a Pennsylvania prison inspector in 1854 (Cf. Barnes, 1972:130):

> Disease and mental imbecility so confidently predicted as necessarily incident to separate confinement have resulted in health and intellectual improvement. Depraved tendencies, characteristic of the convict, have been restrained by the absence of vicious association, and in the mild teaching of Christianity, the unhappy criminal finds a solace for an involuntary exile from the comforts of social life. . . . Shut out from the tumultuous world, he can indulge his remorse unseen and find ample

opportunity for reflection and reformation. His daily intercourse is with good men, who in administering to his necessities animate his crushed hopes and pour into his ear the oil of joy and consolation. He has abundance of light, air, and warmth; he has good and wholesome food; he has seasonable and comfortable clothing; he has the best of medical attendance; he has books to read, and ink and paper to communicate with his friends at stated periods; and weekly he enjoys the privilege of hearing God's holy word expounded by a faithful and zealous Christian minister (Barnes, 1972:130).

The Auburn (New York) System

Leaders in New York were dutifully impressed with Pennsylvania's theory of solitary confinement. Hence, in 1816, a law was passed permitting the construction of a prison at Auburn, New York, designed with individual cells in mind. But where the cells at Eastern State in Pennsylvania were large and permitted access to the outside, those in the new Auburn prison were nothing more than cages, $3\frac{1}{2} \times 7 \times 7$ feet high, with no outside access. The result was disaster. Locked in their tiny cells, left in complete idleness, and lacking any means for exercise or human contact, many Auburn prisoners became ill or mad. It took only two years, 1822–23, for officials to conclude that the experiment had been a hopeless failure. The consequence was the development of an alternative system of prison discipline called the "Auburn" system (Barnes, 1972:133–136).

Although inmates in the new Auburn prison were locked up in their cages at night, they were permitted to work together during the day. But, in order to forestall disobedience and opposition, officials hit upon some new methods of social control: complete silence at all times, the requirement that prisoners march in lockstep, that they keep their eyes downcast, and that they never approach each other face-to-face (McKelvey, 1968:8; Barnes, 1972:136). Coupled with these new means of maintaining order and the fact that working prisoners could help to pay for their own keep, Auburn officials, no less than those in Pennsylvania, waxed eloquent over their achievements:

It is not possible to described the pleasure which we feel in contemplating this noble institution. . . . We regard it as a model worthy of the world's imitation. . . .

The whole establishment, from the gate to the sewer, is a specimen of neatness. The unremitted industry, the entire subordination and subdued feeling of the convict, has probably no parallel among an equal number of criminals. In their solitary cells they spend the night with no other books but the Bible, and at sunrise they proceed, . . . in solid columns, with the block march, to their workship; thence, in the same order at the hour of breakfast, to the Common Hall, where they partake of their wholesome and frugal meal in silence. Not even a whisper is heard; . . . When they are done eating, at the ringing of a little bell, . . . they rise from the table, form the solid columns, and return . . . to the workshops. . . . [I]t is the testimony of many witnesses that they have passed more than 300 convicts, without seeing one leave his work, or turn his head to gaze at them. . . . At the close of the day, . . . the work is all laid aside at once, and the convicts return, . . . to their solitary cells, where they partake of the frugal meal. . . . After supper, they can read scriptures undisturbed and then reflect in silence on the errors of their lives (Louis Dwight, the foremost champion of the Auburn System, as quoted by Barnes, 1972:136–137).

Not included in this glowing statement, however, was the fact that, in addition to silence, the lockstep, and downcast eyes, whipping was also used to encourage prisoners to maintain order and to reflect on the errors of their ways (Barnes, 1972:136).

Conflicts between the two systems

So partisan were the protagonists of the Auburn and Pennsylvania systems that their conflicts dominated the development of penology, both here and abroad, for much of the 19th century (Cf. Henderson, 1910a). France, for example, sent two famous Frenchmen—Alexis de Tocqueville and Gustave de Beaumont—to inspect the two systems and to make recommendations as to which should be adopted by the French government. Though the two emissaries felt that the Pennsylvania system produced "the deepest impressions on the soul of the convict," they recommended that France adopt the Auburn plan because it was more "legal" and was cheaper to run. French officials, however, rejected the recommendation and adopted the Pennsylvania system (Barnes, 1972:142–143; Beaumont and Tocqueville, 1964:115–135). Other Europeans followed suit: "England adopted it in 1835; Belgium in 1838; Sweden, in 1840; Denmark, in 1846; Norway, in 1851; Holland, in the same year" (Barnes, 1972:144).

By contrast, the Auburn system became the dominant pattern in this country. The Pennsylvania system produced much better control over inmates, but its practice of keeping them in total idleness was terribly expensive. Hence, modifications introduced at Auburn were those that were copied (Henderson, 1910a). In summary, then, the remarkable invention of the prison as a place of reform is best remembered for two main features: (1) the segregation of convicts from the outside world and into separate, solitary cells; and (2) the development of methods for subduing and controlling large numbers of them while they toiled during the day. If nothing else, prisons became effective devices for incapacitating offenders for the duration of their sentences.

Restraint for juveniles

Institutions designed exclusively for juveniles followed the construction of prisons by several years. Until then, and after, many were confined in the Auburn, Pennsylvania, and other prisons. Although asylums and houses of refuges, run largely by private groups, began to appear about 1825, the first public reformatories and training schools were not built until almost 1850:

> The Lyman School for Boys opened in Westborough, Massachusetts, in 1846. Then came the New York State Agricultural and Industrial School in 1849 and the Maine Boys Training Center in 1853. By 1870, Connecticut, Indiana, Maryland, Nevada, New Hampshire, New Jersey, Ohio, and Vermont had also set up separate juvenile training facilities; by 1900, 36 states had done so (President's Commission, 1967a:141).

Just as the prison was viewed as a humane, forward-looking gesture, so was the development of these juvenile facilities. At the same time, the treatment of unruly and delinquent children did not suddenly partake of methods that we might consider enlightened or that were greatly different from the way adults were treated:

> Many of the juvenile reformatories were . . . , in reality, juvenile prisons, with prison bars, prison cells, prison garb, prison labor, prison punishments, and prison discipline. It was recognized as a legitimate part of the purpose of the institution to inflict upon the child punishment for his wrongdoing (Hart, 1910:11).

As the 19th century wore on, however, there were signs of significant change. Perhaps the most profound was the increasing preoccupation of society with the developmental needs of children: "Every child allowed to grow up in ignorance and vice and to become a pauper or criminal is liable to become in turn the progenitor of criminals" (Cf. Platt, 1969:130). To many Americans it seemed that, if their worst fears were to be avoided, all poor, uneducated, and parentless children had to be treated as well as disciplined.

Paradoxically, these concerns over children percolated upward and were expressed as concerns over adults. The reason was that the line between childhood and adulthood was becoming ever more blurred as the concept of adolescence began to develop and to extend further and further into the adult years. Hence, as Rothman (1971:76) suggests, 19th century Americans eventually became so sensitive to childhood that "they stripped away the years from adults and made everyone into a child." The Cincinnati Prison Congress of 1870, for example, suggested that great good could be accomplished if criminals were made "the objects of generous parental care." Instead of being sentenced to suffering in prison, they should be "trained to virtue" (Henderson, 1910c:40).

Rehabilitation

What was emerging, of course, was the concept of *rehabilitation*. Although reformers made scattered reference to it throughout the 19th century, it was not until the Cincinnati Prison Congress of 1870 that it was formally adopted as an ideology and embodied in a formal Declaration of Principles. The following statement, attributed to Enoch Wines, who also drafted the principles, constitutes a kind of preamble to them:

> A prison governed by force and fear is a prison mismanaged, in which hope and love, the two great spiritual, uplifting, regenerating forces to which mankind must ever look for redemption, are asleep or dead.
>
> Why not try the effect of rewards upon the prisoner? Rewards, as truly as punishments, appeal to the inextinguishable principle of self-interest in his breast (Wines, 1910:12).

The difference between this preamble and the punishment philosophies of the past is striking, but Wines was not content with being an idealist philosopher. His Declaration of Principles not only spelled out rehabilitation in abstract terms, but outlined the specific methods by which it should be accomplished. The following are excerpts from the more important ones (Cf. Henderson, 1910c:39–63):

1. *Rehabilitation.* Rehabilitation, not punishment, is the primary goal of penology:

> Whatever differences of opinion may exist among penologists on other questions . . . , there is one point on which there may be . . . almost

perfect unanimity, namely, that the moral cure of criminals, adult as well as juvenile, . . . is the best means of attaining the repression of crime; hence . . . reformation is the primary object to be aimed at in the administration of penal justice (p. 17).

2. *Treat criminals not crimes.* The Declaration of Principles directly opposed the premise of classical criminology that punishment and restraint should be allocated according to the seriousness of the criminal act. Instead, rehabilitation should be administered according to the needs of the offender:

> The treatment of criminals by society is for the protection of society. But since such treatment is directed to the criminal rather than to the crime, its great object should be his moral regeneration. Hence the supreme aim of prison discipline is the reformation of criminals, not the infliction of vindictive suffering (p. 39).

3. *The indeterminate sentence.* The practice of giving offenders a definite sentence, according to the seriousness of their criminal acts, should be replaced by sentences that are indefinite:

> Peremptory sentences ought to be replaced by those of indeterminate length. . . . Reformation is a work of time; and a benevolent regard to the good of the criminal himself, as well as to the protection of society, requires that his sentence be long enough for reformatory processes to take effect (pp. 40–41).

4. *Classification.* The practice of confining all prisoners together without regard to age, character, or sex should be eliminated. Prisons should be designed to meet the needs of different kinds of prisoners:

> Prisons, as well as prisoners, should be classified or graded so that there shall be prisons for the untried, for the incorrigible, and for other degrees of depraved character, as well as separate establishments for women and for criminals of the younger class (p. 41).

5. *Education.* Education is an indispensable element in rehabilitating offenders:

> Education is a vital force in the reformation of fallen men and women. Its tendency is to quicken the intellect, inspire self-respect, excite to higher aims, and afford a healthful substitute for low and vicious amusements (p. 40).

6. *Industrial training.* Occupational training is good both for practical and personal reasons:

Industrial training should have both a higher development and a greater breadth than has heretofore been, or is now, commonly given to it in our prisons. Work is no less an auxiliary to virtue than it is a means of support (p. 41).

7.   Rewards.   Rewards are far more salient in producing change than is the fear engendered by punishment:

Since hope is a more potent agent than fear, it should be made an ever-present force in the minds of prisoners, by a well-devised and skillfully applied system of rewards for good conduct, industry, and attention to learning. Rewards, more than punishments, are essential to every good prison system (p. 39).

8.   Self-respect.   Punishment only degrades; correctional practices should uplift:

The prisoner's self-respect should be cultivated to the utmost, and every effort made to give back to him his manhood. There is no greater mistake in the whole compass of penal discipline than its studied imposition of degradation as a part of punishment. Such imposition destroys every better impulse and aspiration. It crushes the weak, irritates the strong, and indisposes all to submission and reform. It is trampling where we ought to raise and is therefore as unchristian in principle as it is unwise in policy (pp. 40–41).

9.   Parole.   Treatment in an institution completes only half the task; offenders require help when they return to the community:

More systematic and comprehensive methods should be adopted to save discharged prisoners by providing them with work and encouraging them to redeem their character and regain their lost position in society. . . . And to this end it is desirable that state societies be formed, which shall cooperate with each other in this work (p. 42).

10.   Prevention.   Prevention is far more promising than is confinement after a crime has been committed:

Preventive institutions, such as truant homes, industrial schools, etc., for the reception and treatment of children not yet criminal, but in danger of becoming so, constitute the true field of promise in which to labor for the repression of crime.

It is our conviction that one of the most effective agencies in the repression of crime would be the enactment of laws by which the education of all the children of the state should be made obligatory. Better to force education upon the people than to force them to suffer for crimes (pp. 41–42; 44).

In summary, this Declaration of Principles is characterized by three outstanding features. The first is optimism. In contrast to the pessimistic and retributive features of prior penal philosophies, the rehabilitative philosophy was conceived in the belief that men and women, as well as children, could be reclaimed from evil. To be sure, the task would require extensive conditioning and programming, but rehabilitation should appeal to the self-interest of the offender as well as to that of the state. Furthermore, this point of view became even more optimistic with the invention of the juvenile court. By calling all problem children "delinquents" rather than "criminals" and by applying the principles of rehabilitation, the younger generation could be redeemed and future crime prevented.

The second feature of the rehabilitative philosophy is its singular focus upon the individual offender. It is his or her morals which require construction or regeneration; it is his or her particular characteristics for which classification, separate institutions, and the indeterminate sentence are required; it is his or her educational deficiencies which demand attention; and it is his or her character from which society needs protection. Indeed, nothing could be more democratic: Delinquency could be prevented and crime controlled if, without regard to the race or background of the person, he or she was treated and given a helping hand.

The final outstanding feature of the declaration was its reaffirmation of the idea that the institution is the most effective means for treating children not yet criminal, as well as for rehabilitating those who are. Although there were organized groups throughout the 19th century who were opposed to institutional confinement for children, they were in the minority. Thus, the idea prevailed that the best place for meeting the needs of deprived children was in self-sufficient correctional utopias which could provide everything an understanding family and well-organized community could provide, only better:

> In the ordinary family home the [delinquent] child is often at a great disadvantage. . . . The neighborhood may be thoroughly bad. The daily journey to and from school may lead past saloons. . . . The mother may be lazy, slatternly, and shiftless. The father may be drunken, vicious, improvident. . . . In the institution, however, we are able to control absolutely the child's environment. We can create ideal sanitary conditions. . . . We can select his school teacher and his Sunday School teacher. We can bring to bear upon him the most helpful and elevating influences. The [child] will never play truant, he will never be out with a gang, he will

never be late to school. Under these circumstances, why should we not be able to produce satisfactory results? (Hart, 1910:62).

Overall, then, the rehabilitative ideology was both seductive in its optimism and revolutionary in its impact. Z. R. Brockway, who was the first correctional administrator to apply the principles of rehabilitation in a youth reformatory, immodestly declared that they were "destined to change men's habits of thought concerning crime and the attitude of society toward criminals; to rewrite from end to end every penal code in Christendom; and to modify and ennoble the fundamental law of every state. It is a change from a plane where feeling sways to the loftier realm and reign of wisdom" (Brockway, 1910:93). Immodest or not, much of Brockway's prophecy came true.

The reformatory

It is significant that the first place in which the principles of rehabilitation were applied was in a revolutionary new reformatory constructed for boys and young men, ages 16 to 30. The tendency for 19th century Americans to "strip away the years" from adults was clearly evident. Contrary to the idea that young children should be punished like adults, the exact reverse was suggested. Young adults were to be treated and disciplined like children.

Once again the indefatigable Enoch Wines led the way. As leader of the New York Prison Association, he gained authorization in 1869 to plan for the new reformatory at Elmira, New York. The plant was completed about 1876, and Z. R. Brockway was chosen as its first superintendent (Brockway, 1910:88–107; Scott, 1910:95–98).

In 1877, Brockway drafted and gained the passage of an "organic" law designed to implement fully the principles of the Cincinnati Prison Congress: the use of the indeterminate sentence; a system of classification; a program of treatment, education, physical discipline, and work; and the granting of parole governed by parole board. The program and design of the new reformatory resembled a strict military school more than anything else. Although Brockway's conception of discipline was far more strict than that advocated by members of the helping professions today, his general approach has had lasting appeal: "To make a good boy out of his bundle of perversities, his entire being must be revolutionized. He must be taught self-control, industry, respect for himself and the rights of others" (Cf. Platt, 1969:52).

Reformatories for girls. The same was no less true for girls. According to Mrs. Frederick Wines, the daughter-in-law of Enoch Wines, female delinquents were characterized by the following list of problems, all requiring treatment and training:

> Neglect, brutality on the part of others; . . . disobedience, self-will, laziness, the love of dress, the want of education, poverty, animal appetites and passions cultivated; . . . curiosity to see life, social ambition, and the desire for a career; evil associations, the lack . . . of a good home, in general the want of training in the power of self-control (Barrows, 1910:147).

Given these problems, ideal reformatories for young females were said to operate like Brockway's for boys:

> There may be some difference in minor points, but in each one we find the graded system [classification], parole upon earning a certain degree of credit, industries that will be useful in the outer world, lighter employment as a means of recreation, physical drill in the gymnasium, with baths and scrupulous neatness of person and domicile, attention to music, . . . good academic schools, . . . outdoor work and recreation of all kinds. . . . Nowhere does the state do more than try to develop a religious and reverential atmosphere, and inculcate the belief that the noblest ideal of pure religion is to keep one's self unspotted from the world (Barrows, 1910:139).

In theory, then, the new scientific reformatory, created by Wines and Brockway, became the prototype for progressive penology throughout the country.

Industrial and training schools

Just as reformatories were built for older youth so industrial and training schools were first constructed for younger status offenders and delinquent children. New guidelines stressed the importance of locating both institutions in the country and reaffirmed the idea that they should emulate the character of the well-disciplined family. Hence, by the time the juvenile court was well-established, they were widespread, except in the South which had not yet constructed special institutions for juveniles (Bremner, 1970, I:672; Platt, 1969:61–62). Furthermore, as child-saving increased apace, it became steadily more difficult to distinguish among "industrial schools," "reformatories," or "training schools." As Hastings Hart put it in 1910 (p. 70), "Juvenile reformatories were first known as houses of refuge; when that term became opprobrious, they were called reform schools; when that term in turn became obnoxious, the name industrial school was used; and when that name became offensive, they were called training schools."

Likewise, it became increasingly difficult to distinguish among the types of children who were put into these institutions. Since, according to juvenile court law, the purpose of rehabilitation was to treat children, not crimes, there was little need to distinguish among them; all needed help. Furthermore, the growing influence of psychodynamic theory added the ominous note that serious criminal acts are inevitable unless the hidden drives and unconscious motives of problem children are unlocked and treated. Schooling, recreation, and job training will do little good unless these obstructions are eliminated first.

Dissatisfaction with institutions

Despite the constructions of all these institutions, a growing number of reformers began voicing opposition to them in the early 20th century. The difficulty with locking children up, said Hastings Hart, in 1910, is "institutionalism":

> In a great institution like the New York House of Refuge, with 700 boys, or Girard College, with 1,700 boys, or the Catholic Protectory, with 2,700 children, the child is lost in the mass. He is one of a multitude. It is almost impossible to give him that personal attention which is essential to the normal development of a child. . . . The child lacks initiative; he lacks courage; he lacks power to act for himself. In the institution someone else is doing his thinking for him, someone else is planning his life for him; and when he goes into the world, he goes at a disadvantage (p. 62).

Hart was voicing a complaint that has since become common; namely, that children who have been raised by the state are incapable of free and independent judgment; confinement becomes a way of life; they are comfortable only in a setting where all decisions are made for them.

> However good an institution may be, however kindly its spirit, however genial its atmosphere, however homelike its cottages, however fatherly and motherly its officers, however admirable its training, it is now generally agreed . . . that institutional life is at the best artificial and unnatural, and that the child ought to be returned at the earliest practicable moment to the more natural environment of the family (1910:12).

It was this line of reasoning which led many of the first juvenile court judges to argue that probation, and not institutions, should be the cord upon which all the pearls of the juvenile court are hung. For most juveniles, it was the preferable alternative: "When we have exhausted the resources of the home, the church, and juvenile court, the probation office, then we turn to the juvenile reformatory and ask of it success in dealing with the problem in whose solution all other agencies have failed" (Hart, 1910:11).

Probation

Actually, probation had roots that went far deeper than the first juvenile courts (Diana, 1960). It was first used in Boston in 1841 when a shoemaker, named John Augustus, began to provide bail for minor adult offenders, women, and children and to assist them following their court appearances. After Augustus died, the Boston Children's Aid Society and other volunteers continued his "rescue" work. Massachusetts formalized these volunteer activities in 1869 by appointing an agent of the State Board of Charities, a private agency, to investigate children's cases, to make recommendations to the criminal court, and to receive children for placement. In 1878, an additional law was passed permitting the employment of paid probation officers in Boston (United Nations, 1951:29–42). The laws of a few other states, as well as those in Great Britain, legalized probation late in the 19th century, permitting first-time offenders, in particular, to be released on good conduct (Tappan, 1960:422). But it was the juvenile court movement which really legitimated probation and gave it its impetus. By 1925, all states, except Wyoming, had legalized it. Thus, as we saw in the last chapter, the practice today has become so widespread that far more delinquents are placed on probation or are released informally without any court sanction than are confined in institutions.

Parole

Along with probation, another rehabilitative supplement which was gradually added to the array of rehabilitative techniques was parole (Cf. Carter and Wilkins, 1970:177–276). It will be recalled that parole was first suggested by the Cincinnati Prison Congress in 1870 and was first used at the Elmira Reformatory by Z. R. Brockway in about 1880. Like probation, parole has a dual purpose: casework assistance for the offender and protection of the community. But, unlike probation, parole is a community service that follows, rather than precedes, incarceration. The idea is that delinquents who have suffered "institutionalism" should not be suddenly released to the community without supervision and help. Instead, parole should be part of the indeterminate sentence. If delinquents are given help and can successfully adjust to the community, they will be permitted to remain there, but, if they seem unable to cope with its many demands, they will be returned to the institution for further rehabilitation. Hence, like other elements of the rehabilitative philosophy, parole was legalized in virtually every state as a part of the juvenile court movement.

Rehabilitation and the administration of justice

All of these developments are evidence in support of Z. R. Brockway's prophecy that the principles of rehabilitation would modify the laws of every state. So great has their impact been, in fact, that they have revolutionized the administration of American justice. Prior to the application of the methods and principles set down in 1870, the fate of an offender, juvenile or adult, was prescribed by law and decided by the judge once his or her guilt was established: imprisonment, hard labor, a fine, or some other penalty. But, once the rehabilitative revolution occurred, this power was greatly diminished and transferred elsewhere. In the juvenile court, for example, new laws permitted the court to defer sentencing until the offender could be studied and recommendations made to the judge. Probation officers, psychiatric consultants, and others shared and influenced the judge's dispositional decisions. But this was merely the beginning.

Once a dispositional decision was made, the court simply turned the offender over to probation or institutional personnel for imprecisely defined treatment. Responsibility and power were divided, not only among people close to the court, but, eventually, throughout the whole correctional system. The adoption of the indeterminate sentence and the classification of offenders lodged new power and responsibility in probation departments and state departments of correction. Their decisions, in turn, led to the construction of diagnostic centers and specialized institutions; reformatories, industrial schools, farms, probation camps, and cottage programs. Hypothetically, these were expected to respond to different classes of offenders, rather than to classes of crimes—first-time offenders, neglected children, hard-core delinquents, males and females.

The result was such specialized roles for correctional people as administration, care and feeding, custody supervision, casework, education, therapy, and vocational training. Then, following incarceration, the use of parole further divided power and responsibility and lodged them in parole boards and parole officers. They, rather than judges or correctional people, became the ones who decided when an offender would finally receive his or her freedom.

In short, the concept of rehabilitation totally altered the older, classical system of justice. As a result, the young delinquent was made to answer for his rehabilitation, not merely to a judge, but to a host of decision makers, all of whom were given a hand in deciding his fate and judging his performance. A crucial question, therefore, is how this revolution has worked out. Have its grand and optimistic hopes come true?

Dismay

For more than half of the 20th century, the belief that rehabilitation would work was not seriously challenged. The juvenile justice system operated in relative quietude with only occasional outcries from concerned legal or professional groups, from the National Council on Crime and Delinquency, academic criminologists, and other politically impotent groups (Cf. Tonry, 1976). But, during the past decade, dismay and cynicism have become the property of all Americans. The concept of rehabilitation is in a shambles.

Norman Carlson, director of the Federal Bureau of Prisons, described the shambles in an address to the American Academy of Psychiatry and the Law in 1975. His first step was to disavow the most fundamental premise of rehabilitation; namely, that delinquency is a disease for which specific causes can be isolated and a successful treatment administered. "We cannot diagnose criminality," he said, "we cannot prescribe a precise treatment, and we certainly cannot guarantee a cure" (p. 1). But that was not all. Carlson also attacked the notion that by applying the principles of rehabilitation the juvenile justice system could correct the worst consequences of such social ills as poverty, neglect, and racism and, thereby, save the younger generation from crime. "Neither you nor I," he told his audience, "can control unemployment, social inequity, racial discrimination, and poverty. Neither the psychiatrist nor the correctional officer can deal with broken families, poor neighborhoods, bad schools, and lack of opportunity" (p. 1). Solo efforts of this type are futile. If better results are desired, other methods will have to be found.

One obvious reason for Carlson's disillusionment has been the persistence of high rates of youth crime. The desirable outcomes so confidently predicted by Enoch Wines, Z. R. Brockway, and the founders of the juvenile court have not come to pass. But beyond that, his cynicism has also been generated by three other factors: (1) attacks on the concept of rehabilitation itself; (2) a lack of resources for fully implementing the methods of rehabilitation; and (3) the theories and findings of the scientific community.

Deficiencies in concept

Addressing a gathering of social scientists at Harvard in 1974, Rosemary Sarri, Robert Vinter and Rhea Kish declared that the juvenile justice system represents "the failure of a nation." That system, they maintained, "remains an anachronistic local-government vehicle, overwhelmed with the shortcomings of an entire society" (p. 1). Historically, the care and handling of children have been the responsibility of family, school, and community. More and more, however, those tasks have been turned over to policemen, judges, and correctional authorities. The juvenile justice system, as a result, is inundated with clients. It has been expected to solve problems which it cannot possibly hope to address.

These critical remarks seemed to suggest that the members of the juvenile justice system have been the unwilling victims of uncaring parents and communities. But, while there is no denying that such has often been the case, history indicates that it would be incorrect to assume that the practice of unloading unwanted children has been uninvited and unexpected. The reformers who wrote the Declaration of Principles in 1870 or who invented the juvenile court in 1899 argued that problem children *should* be turned over to the juvenile court; treatment *should* be left to experts. Hence, because many judges and correctional people have shared this belief, they have not merely been the victims of society; they have also been the victims of their own philosophy. By assuming that rehabilitation would be a panacea, they have tacitly encouraged community irresponsibility.

As a result, influential critics like Edwin Lemert (1967:96) have called for a marked change in philosophy. Rather than assuming that the rehabilitative ideology is a cure-all, judges and the helping professions should leaven their arrogance with humility and should lower their expectations:

> [I]t would be well to delete entirely from [the laws of the land] pious injunctions that the care, custody, and discipline of children under the control of the juvenile court shall approximate that which they would receive from their parents, which taken literally becomes meaningless either as ideal or reality. Neither the modern state nor an harassed juvenile court judge is a father; a halfway house is not a home; a reformatory cell is not a teenager's bedroom; a juvenile hall counselor is not a dutch uncle; and a cottage matron is not a mother (Lemert, 1967:92).

Rather than the medical model, a more realistic model for youth helpers would be "midwifery." Judges, probation officers, psychiatrists, and counselors must recognize that, like midwives, they do not have the precise knowledge by which to diagnose ills and to prescribe cures. At best, they can only assist the process of maturation and cannot, therefore, have much impact on its outcome. Hence, the only defensible philosophy for the juvenile justice system is one of "judicious nonintervention" (Lemert, 1967:96).

Lack of resources

In rebuttal to Lemert's critical remarks, many judges, correctional administrators, national commissions, and treatment personnel have maintained that correctional problems are due to a lack of resources, not to flaws in the concept of rehabilitation. Indeed, this theme has been a persistent one since juvenile courts first became widespread.

In the 1930s, two national commissions—the National Commission on Law Observance and Enforcement (1931) and the White House Conference on Child Health and Protection (1932)—noted the lack of support for rehabilitative facilities and programs: the continued detention of juveniles in jails; poorly paid and unqualified judges; inadequate numbers of probation officers; few psychiatric services, inadequate foster homes and institutional care; and the absence of an effective parole system (White House Conference, 1932:21).

But, while these national commissions lamented the lack of rehabilitative tools, their faith in the ideology of individualized treatment remained unflagging. Thus, their recommendations continued to stress what Tonry (1976:287), describes as a "familiar litany"; namely, that current problems would be solved if there were more rehabilitative programs and more, better paid and better qualified personnel. Indeed, this theme has persisted for almost half a century.

In 1967, the President's Commission on Law Enforcement and Administration of Justice continued to lament the lack of adequate resources. The average probation officer, for example, is expected to maintain a caseload of from 75 to 100 probationers, to conduct presentence investigations, to maintain extensive paper work, and to carry out other functions as well. As a result, there is little time for dealing with the actual problems that juveniles have:

> A probation officer has arranged a meeting with a 16-year-old boy on probation for car theft. . . . The boy begins to open up and talk for the first time. He explains that he began to "slip into the wrong crowd" a year or so after his stepfather died. He says that it would help to talk about it. But there isn't time; the waiting room is full, and the boy is not scheduled to come back for another 15-minute conference until next month (President's Commission, 1967a:5).

Though probation costs only about one tenth what it costs to keep delinquents in state training schools, many states have simply failed to provide the juvenile court with sufficient personnel to meet the demand.

The same is true of the nation's training schools. Too many of them are custodial institutions in which children are merely warehoused—isolated "from the outside world in an overcrowded, understaffed security institution with little education, little vocational training, little counseling or job placement, or other guidance or release" (President's Commission, 1967c:80).

When Sarri, Vinter and Kish (1974:3) added up all these problems, therefore, they questioned whether society really *likes* its children: It offers them minimal protection of their constitutional rights, it casts them aside, stigmatized but unaided; and it denies them other community services once they enter the juvenile justice system. "The expectation that [such a system] can offer effective remedial aid," they argued, "is as valid as an expectation that the highway department can resolve the energy crisis." Neither is likely to do much good.

The findings of science

Despite this catalog of complaints, many of which are scarcely new, the theories and findings of science may have been even more devastating in their impact. They have raised questions about both the concept of rehabilitation *and* the resources that have been supplied:

1.   Effects of institutional programs

Twentieth century sociologists have added volumes to Hastings Hart's original complaint about "institutionalism." Most of them question the effectiveness of institutional confinement even under the most ideal of conditions:

Opposition to authority. Most sociologists maintain that delinquents already share negative perceptions of authority when they enter an institution. Hence, the deprivation of liberty will only heighten their resistances to change. Indeed, even among people who do not have a delinquent history—that is, among those who are confined in mental hospitals, orphan asylums, or prisoner-of-war camps—captivity seems to generate an inmate code whose function is resistance to authority rather than cooperation with it (Bartollas, et al., 1976; Clemmer, 1940; Cressey, 1960; Schrag, 1954; Sykes, 1965; Sykes and Messinger, 1960).

Consider the statement of Jimmy Dunn, a young criminal who had already spent much of his life in juvenile institutions:

> The easiest way to get a bad name [in an institution] is to talk to bulls. That's one of the rules: you don't talk to bulls, and bulls include anyone . . . who doesn't have a number. The best way to get along in the joint is to completely ignore the staff (Mannochio and Dunn, 1970:38).

The argument is that places of captivity are caste systems (Barker and Adams, 1959; Bartollas, et al., 1976). Inmates and staff are divided into mutually exclusive groups. As a result, inmates like Jimmy Dunn play it cool and give an outward appearance of good behavior without ever becoming involved with treatment staff or trying to change (Ohlin and Lawrence, 1959).

Rejection and fear. Investigators also argue that institutional life is characterized by personal isolation and fear (Bartollas, et al., 1976; Clemmer, 1940; Glaser, 1964). Although inmates may stick together in resisting the efforts of staff members to change them, their own relationships are not sufficient to overcome the devastating effects of captivity. Even in cottage programs, to say nothing of training schools, there is a great deal of inmate predation upon inmate: homosexual rape, exploitation of the weak, and assault (Polsky, 1962). "Despite all the time I have spent in prison," Jimmy Dunn once said, "it is a terrifying place to me; it is hopeless." Yet, he went on, prisons are "cakewalks" when compared to juvenile reform schools. "For the rest of my life I'll never have half the trouble I had in the years I spent there. Reform school kids' idea of a little friendly fun is a race riot!'' (Manocchio and Dunn, 1970:158). Indeed, Dunn was nearly beaten to death himself when he first went to reform school at age 13.

Among imprisoned girls, some qualitatively different patterns occur. The deprivation of normal relationships seems to result in an artificial construction of all-female "families." These "families" not only produce homosexual relationships of a physical nature, but girls adopt the roles of various family members in order to find functional substitutes for the normal relationships which confinement denies them. Ironically, in pursuit of satisfying conventional roles, they end up playing roles that are deviant (Giallombardo, 1974).

Staff conflicts. The main idea that staff members have common rehabilitative goals is a myth (Schrag, 1961). Treatment staff are at odds with custodial staff; counselors compete with cottage parents; or work supervisors resent teachers (Bartollas, et al., 1976). New professionals and techniques are often grafted onto existing programs without any heed to the problems they create (Ohlin, 1958; Weber, 1957). Too often, as a result, conflict remains unresolved, and staff members become more concerned with protecting their own interests than with insuring the overall welfare of inmates.

Overall, then, most critics have concluded that even the most treatment-oriented of institutions are incapable of realizing desirable ends. They are so full of logical contradictions that, while they may suppress offenders, they can do little to rehabilitate them (Goffman, 1961). Indeed, some critics go much further. Bartollas, et al. (1976:259) say that "The juvenile correctional institution, not unlike every other type of total institution, is or can be far more cruel and inhumane than most outsiders ever imagine.

Recidivism rates. Such devastating critiques appeal to commonsense as well as to scientific theory. Since prisons were first built almost 200 years ago, the few original cynics have been joined by a swelling chorus of doubters, all of whom argue that under conditions of captivity people are not likely to change for the better. Yet, there are those who caution against excessive overgeneralization. Several studies suggest that group counseling, milieu therapy, and other techniques of this type, particularly in smaller institutions, are likely to improve institutional adjustment. The social distance between inmates and staff is decreased, and inmates are more manageable and cooperative (Lipton, et al., 1975:299–322; Street, 1965).

If that is the case, it would be reasonable to assume that once these inmates are released from confinement, they would be more likely to stay out of trouble. Most studies, however, do not support that assumption; recidivism is not markedly reduced, if at all (Kassebaum, et al., 1971; Lipton, et al., 1975:528–529; Seckel, 1965). For example, the most defensible study on the subject revealed precisely this outcome. According to the best ideals of the rehabilitative model, Karl Jesness (1970) carefully diagnosed delinquents and classified them into different "maturity" types—types that include both psychological and interactional dimensions. Then, he randomly selected among these inmate types, assigning one group to an experimental program in which each of them received the type of treatment that was best suited to his particular needs while a second group was assigned to the regular institutional program.

After treatment was completed, Jesness found that according to his theory the experimental group had shown greater psychological improvement. Yet, when these "improved" individuals were released to the community, their recidivism rates were not only high, but were identical to those of the control group who were not specially treated. Careful diagnosis, classification, and treatment, in short, had not produced lower rates of criminality. Thus, when the results of this and similar studies were added up, they were far from encouraging. Instead, they seemed to suggest that no matter what form rehabilitation takes in institutions it does not make a great deal of difference. The violation rates of inmates, whether in "enlightened" or "custodial" programs, remain about the same.

2. Effects of noninstitutional treatment

Such findings have helped to reinforce the arguments of early childsavers, like Hastings Hart, that the principles of rehabilitation, if they are to work, must be applied in the community. In fact, this argument has been so persuasive that probation long ago became the norm for convicted delinquents. By the mid-1960s, for example, five times more juveniles were placed on probation than were confined in institutions (President's Crime Commission, 1967a:133–143). The disparity is even greater today (Cf. Chapter 16). But this is not all.

Spurred by psychodynamic theory, the child guidance movement of the 1940s and 1950s led to a number of clinical programs for "predelinquents"—programs for the unruly children who in earlier times might have been placed in houses of refuge or industrial schools. Finally, in the 1960s, some intensive community programs were created to treat serious delinquents who had already failed on probation—delinquents for whom incarceration would ordinarily have been the only choice. How successful, then, have these programs been?

Probation.   We have already seen that probation usually represents little more than an occasional contact with an overworked probation officer. Yet, there is some evidence that it is a useful tool. In a summary analysis of 15 probation studies conducted in a variety of jurisdictions, Ralph England (1957) reported success rates that varied between 60 and 90 percent. A second survey by Max Grunhut (1948), covering such states as Massachusetts, California, New York, and a number of foreign countries, provided similar results with the modal success rate at about 75 percent. Surprisingly, however, such findings did not "prove" that probation rehabilitates. The reason is that most studies have not been designed to answer a crucial question: What if the offenders who were placed on probation had been released without any supervision whatsoever?

Before one can say that probation rehabilitates, one has to be able to answer such a question affirmatively. But, in order to do that, an experimental research design is required. The only way one can be certain whether one method of rehabilitation is more effective than another or is more effective than no service whatsoever is to have randomly selected experimental and control groups by which to compare the effects of different programs on delinquents. The experimental group is treated—in this case, assigned to probation—while the control group is not subjected to any treatment or is treated in some other fashion.

Unfortunately, studies of probation effectiveness which make use of experimental designs are rare. In fact, the most reliable studies of casework efforts began, not with probation but with parole. In 1953, the California Department of Corrections started a series of experiments to determine whether intensive supervision of adult parolees would reduce recidivism (Adams, 1970). Its goal, however, was not to determine whether parole was better than nothing, but whether the assumption was correct that more and better services would prove helpful. Thus, the department set up small, experimental caseloads of from 15 to 35 offenders, assigned them to selected parole officers, and, then, sought to determine whether their success rates would be superior to offenders who were placed in ordinary caseloads of from 72 to 90 persons. After 11 years of study, in which thousands of experimentally selected parolees were compared, few differences in outcome were observed. There was little evidence that lowered caseloads had had produced lower re-cidivism rates (Adams, 1970:722–723).

Despite this disappointing result, these initial efforts stimulated further studies of both probation and parole by the California Youth Authority, by the Los Angeles County Probation Department, and by the Federal Department of Probation. Briefly, the results were these (Adams, 1970:724–725; Lipton, et al., 1975).

> After two years, the California Youth Authority discontinued the use of smaller caseloads because of an apparent lack of positive results. There was little evidence that caseloads of only 36 delinquents did any better after receiving intensive supervision than did caseloads of 72.

> The Los Angeles County Probation Department reported better re-sults with juvenile probationers. Lowered caseloads and intensive supervision resulted in less time in detention, fewer court appear-ances, and fewer new arrests. This limited evidence was encouraging.

> The Federal Department of Probation used three caseload sizes to test probation effectiveness: regular caseloads of 85 persons; *ideal* caseloads of 50 persons; and *intensive* caseloads of only 25 persons. After two years of experimentation and random assignment, how-ever, the outcome did not favor the use of lowered caseloads. In-deed, while the *regular* caseloads of 85 persons and the *ideal* of 50 had violation rates of 22 and 24 percent respectively, the *intensive* caseloads of only 25 persons had a failure rate of 38 percent. Clearly, intensive supervision had resulted in higher rather than lower violation rates. The reason seems to have been that when probation officers on the *intensive* caseloads were able to monitor offenders more carefully they noted more instances in which pro-bationers did not live up to the conditions of their probation. Con-sequently, they were more inclined to define them as failures. Paradoxically, therefore, greater supervision led not to greater "success," but to greater "failure."

In summary, then, these findings produced two important outcomes. On the one hand, they tended to confirm nonexperimental studies of probation which indicate that about three quarters of all probationers do not become recidivists. On the other hand, they lent only partial support to the long-held assumption that, if probation officers could be given smaller caseloads, they could rehabilitate offenders more successfully. But, as important as these findings were, they still did not answer the fundamental questions that were raised earlier: Does probation rehabilitate? What if offenders were not assigned to probation at all? Would their violation rates be any higher?

Probation officers may be required to investigate cases prior to trial and to see that they are processed more quickly and fairly, but their services may not help to rehabilitate offenders. Indeed, there are hints that this may be the case. In their study of several hundred delinquents, McEachern and Taylor (1967) found that those offenders who were convicted and made wards of the court, but were *not* supervised by probation officers, had lower recidivism rates than those who were supervised. The same was true of delinquents who were treated informally and released at intake without actual conviction. Those who were *not* visited by probation officers did better than those who were.

Since this finding strikes so strongly against our traditional beliefs about the need for supervision, it must be treated with caution. Yet, there is additional evidence which tends to support it. It is derived from several studies of prevention programs which, like probation, utilize casework methods as a means of preventing truants, emotionally disturbed, or unruly children from becoming serious lawbreakers.

Prevention for predelinquents.   Perhaps the best known study of a prevention effort for "predelinquents" was the Cambridge-Somerville Youth Study which was conducted between 1936 and 1945 (Powers and Witmer, 1951; McCord and McCord, 1959). Seven hundred and fifty boys attending schools in Cambridge and Somerville, Massachusetts, were identified by teacher interviews, by psychiatric evaluations, and by psychological tests as troublemakers who were likely to become delinquent. Using random selection, 325 of the boys were then placed in an experimental group to receive services while the remaining 325 were placed in a control group for which nothing was done.

The experimentals received all of the services which ideally probationers are supposed to receive: individual counseling, family guidance, tutoring, medical treatment, recreational services, and even occasional financial assistance. This rich array of services, which would make the ordinary juvenile judge green with envy, then went on for an average of 5 years for each child. But, contrary to both theory and hope, repeated follow-up studies, made 5, 10 and 25 years after treatment, revealed no significant differences between the treated and untreated children. The numbers of children who were subsequently convicted of delinquent and criminal acts and the ages at which they were convicted did not differ for the two groups.

Prevention experiments since Cambridge-Somerville have used both similar and alternative methods: Some have identified first graders as "predelinquents" and then sought to treat their emotional and familial difficulties (Craig and Furst, 1965). Some have used nominations by teachers and principals to identify sixth graders who were "headed for trouble" and provided special role models and classes for them (Reckless and Dinitz, 1972). Some have sought out "high-risk" girls and boys in junior high schools and provided them with an array of individual and group services (Berleman and Steinburn, 1967; Meyer, et al., 1965). And some have used detached workers with delinquent gangs in an attempt to coalesce them around nondelinquent activities and, through agency coordination, to convert them into prosocial clubs (Miller, 1962; Klein, 1971). Yet, in all these efforts there is virtually no evidence that the provision of casework and group services has made a difference (Bereleman and Steinburn, 1969). Treatment programs that appeared to embody many of the ideals of rehabilitation were no more effective in preventing and controlling crime than no program at all. By implication, therefore, the same may be true of probation.

Community alternatives to incarceration. Though the inconclusive findings of other studies might have deterred the development of still more community alternatives, such has not been the case. The desire to get away from institutions has seemed all-pervasive. Hence, the late 1950s and early 1960s were marked by the development of community programs for serious convicted delinquents—young people who, for the most part, had already failed on probation and seemed headed for incarceration in a training school.

One of the first of these was Highfields (McCorkle, et al., 1958). Though it was not a community program in the truest sense, Highfields was scarcely a traditional, institutional program. A group of no more than 20 boys, ages 16 and 17, were sent to live with a small staff without guards and detailed routine on the old Lindbergh estate in New Jersey. The program continues today.

During the day, the boys work at a nearby mental hospital. In the evening, the total population is broken into two groups of ten, each of which then has a meeting. Formal rules are few. Control, instead, is exercised informally through the development of a group culture which presumably decreases distance between staff and offenders and sponsors the offender in a more active, reformation role. The idea is that individuals are best helped who themselves become the helpers of others.

In order to test the effectiveness of Highfields, its graduates were compared to a group of boys who had been committed to the New Jersey State Reformatory at Annandale (Weeks, 1958). A lower percentage of Highfields than of Annandale boys recidivated (37 versus 53 percent). However, the results of the comparison are questionable because both groups were not randomly selected under experimental conditions. For example, the Annandale boys tended to be a little older, perhaps more experienced in delinquency, and from poorer social backgrounds than the Highfields boys. As a consequence, the most appropriate conclusion is that Highfields has proven neither less nor more successful than incarceration. In terms of recidivism, at least, it would be difficult to argue that one method was superior to the other.

Yet, the findings at Highfields were significant nonetheless. The reason is that they seemed to indicate that Highfields was able to do just as well as total incarceration but at much less expense to the state and at much less personal cost to the delinquents involved. Delinquents stayed at Highfields only three or four months, as contrasted with many more months at Annandale. Still, they did just as well after release. Hence, a much cheaper form of community programming without the negative effects of confinement was just as successful as total incarceration.

A second, widely acclaimed project has been the Community Treatment Program of the California Youth Authority directed by Marguerite Q. Warren. Beginning in the early 1960s, this project utilized randomly selected experimental and control groups as a means of determining the effectiveness of programming in the open community as contrasted to total incarceration, or even "living-in," as at Highfields (Palmer, 1971; Warren, 1964; 1968).

The Community Treatment Program also hewed far more closely to the classical principles of rehabilitation than did Highfields. Each member of the experimental group was diagnosed and classified into one of several maturity types—types which indicate the individual's perception of himself and his typical way of interacting with others—that is, whether he is passive or aggressive, conformist or manipulator, neurotic or acting out. After classification, each delinquent was then assigned to a parole agent who was trained to treat the presumed needs of that particular delinquent.

The control group, by contrast, was assigned to one of the institutions of the California Youth Authority where after confinement its members were released on regular parole. While in the community, the caseloads in the experimental program were very small, from 9 to 10 offenders per agent, as compared to around 55 offenders per agent in the control program.

The outcome findings of this experiment have raised considerable controversy. The overall success rates reported by the project staff have favored the community program (Palmer, 1971:84). After following subjects for two years, 58 percent of the experimental boys and 66 percent of the girls were defined as successes because their paroles had not been revoked. By contrast, the success rates for the control boys and girls were much lower: 46 and 52 percent respectively. Furthermore, there was evidence that some of the maturity subtypes had done much better than others because of the special treatment they received.

It has been pointed out, however, that these differential rates of success may be a function more of the contrasting ways traditional parole agents and experimental staff handled their clients than the way clients actually behaved (Lerman, 1968; 1975: chap. 4). Warren and Palmer (1966), for example, noted that 68 percent of the failures among the control group were due to recommendations by their parole agents that parole be revoked, as contrasted with only 29 percent among the experimentals. Why did these great disparities occur?

The reason, apparently, is that regular parole agents were not as tolerant of new offenses among their parolees as were the experimental staff, particularly offenses that were of low and medium seriousness. Thus, they defined more of the control group parolees as failures even though their delinquent behaviors may not have been different from those of the experimentals. Indeed, the experimentals may have committed more offenses than controls. For example, the average number of new offenses per experimental boy was 2.8 versus only 1.6 per control boy—a difference that was highly significant (Lerman, 1968; Palmer and Warren, 1967:11–12). Consequently, most investigators have concluded that the evidence is not sufficient to warrant the claim of project staff that the Community Treatment Program was clearly superior to incarceration. Although it might have been more effective for selected types of offenders, it was not more effective overall.

In summary, then, the Community Treatment Program came out something like Highfields. While, on the one hand, it may have done approximately as well as incarceration, it was not clearly superior in reducing recidivism. It could not be said that, if applied to all delinquents, crime rates would be noticeably reduced. Indeed, this experiment, like most of those which preceded it, tended to reinforce the whole history of inconclusive scientific investigation. Whether the object of study has been the variation of treatment within institutions, or in the use of probation, parole, prevention, or intensive community programming, it has been difficult to demonstrate that one rehabilitative approach is consistently more successful than another.

From a scientific standpoint, such findings may simply mean that our methods of classifying offenders and of dealing with them are still in a primitive state. We do not know enough about either to make a difference. But, from a practical standpoint, the lack of conclusive findings has simply contributed to the shambles in which the concept of rehabilitation now finds itself. Indeed, as we will see in the next chapter, a new generation of reformers has arisen and revolutionary new methods for reforming offenders are being tried. But, before turning to those methods, it is important that we recall the important findings and implications of this chapter.

Summary and conclusions

There are three lessons in this chapter which, if kept in mind, may help us to evaluate the "revolution" in juvenile justice which we will be considering in the chapter to follow.

1.   The revolutionary epochs of correctional history

The major epochs thus far in our correctional history may be summarized as a succession of three R's:

Retribution.   Prior to the 19th century, society's efforts to control crime were dominated by a philosophy of *retribution.* Punishments were cruel but were justified on the grounds that suffering is fair recompense for criminal acts. Little thought was given to the idea of redeeming offenders, young or old.

Restraint.   In the first part of the 19th century, the retributive philosophy was gradually replaced by a philosophy of *restraint.* Offenders were confined in prisons and reformatories; length of stay was graded according to the seriousness of criminal acts; and reformers anticipated that inmates would experience remorse and would reform.

Rehabilitation.   Throughout the 19th century, people became increasingly sensitive to childhood, not only softening their attitudes toward children, but stripping the years away from adults. Toward the end of that century, therefore, these attitudes were crystallized into a complex philosophy of *rehabilitation*. By attending to the needs of the individual and by implementing complex programs of diagnosis and treatment, known offenders could not only be rehabilitated, but crime among dependent and unruly children could be prevented.

Despite marked differences in these philosophies, it is important to remember that each new epoch has not made a complete break from those that preceded it. When prisons and reformatories were built, for example, faith in retributive punishments did not suddenly disappear. For the most part, they just changed form and became less physical. Transportation, burning, branding, and disfigurement were replaced by solitary confinement, silence, the lockstep, and milder forms of flogging. These may have been somewhat less severe, but they were punishments nonetheless.

Equally obvious has been the overlap between restraint and rehabilitation. Rather than suggesting that rehabilitation might occur better elsewhere, the prophets of treatment merely argued that reformatories and training schools should be made into correctional utopias, not eliminated. It was not until the 20th century that this faith was gradually diluted. Nevertheless, elements of all these philosophies remain in our belief structures today and they continue to exert an influence.

2.   From optimism to dismay

Each new revolutionary epoch has begun with great optimism and has ended in dismay. When retributive punishments became too difficult for humanists to tolerate, the invention of prisons was not only hailed as a gesture befitting the most noble inclinations of humankind, but as a solution to the sufferings and horrors of criminal acts. The same was no less true of the rehabilitative epoch. Indeed, the idea is still unthinkable that concerted efforts should not be made to reclaim children from evil. People would still like to think that somewhere, under some set of circumstances, dedicated correctional workers can change young offenders for the better and can return them to society as healthy and productive citizens. Yet, in recent years, it has become increasingly unfashionable to think in such hopeful terms.

We have already read the pessimistic pronouncements of Norman Carlson, director of the Federal Bureau of Prisons, but Carlson does not stand alone. In 1966, the New York State Governor's Commission on Criminal Offenders commissioned a survey to determine the most effective means for rehabilitating criminals and delinquents. This important survey covered 231 evaluation studies conducted in this country and elsewhere between 1945 and 1967 (Lipton, et al., 1975). But, rather than coming up with promising guidelines for future programming, it provided the same kinds of baffling and inconclusive results that we have already examined in this chapter. Not only were the results of this study popularized in the national media and in prestigious public forums by Robert Martinson, one of the authors of the survey, but his message was that "With few isolated exceptions, the rehabilitative efforts that have been reported so far have had no appreciable effect on recidivism" (Martinson, 1974:25). Nothing works!

On the opposite side of the contintent in 1968, the Committee on Criminal Procedure of the California Legislature reached much the same conclusion, at least with respect to prisons: "There is no evidence," it said, "that more severe penalties deter crime more effectively than less severe penalties. There is no evidence that prisons rehabilitate most offenders" (Cf. Ward, 1972:200). This committee, however, offered a ray of hope. It suggested that if rehabilitative programs do not work the best that can be done is to save the taxpayers some money: "There is evidence that larger numbers of offenders can be effectively supervised in the community at insignificant risk and considerable savings in public expense" (Cf. Ward, 1972:200).

And that is what was done. A bill was passed by which county governments in California were subsidized to keep offenders, adult as well as juvenile, at home on probation rather than turning them over to the state for rehabilitation. As a result, correctional effectiveness was measured in terms of dollars saved rather than offenders "rehabilitated": "Between 1966 and 1972, California can demonstrate that it has saved $185,978,820 through cancelled construction, closed institutions, and new institutions not opened" (Smith, 1973:69). But, despite saving money, probation subsidy did not make noticeable reductions in recidivism (Center on Administration of Criminal Justice, 1977).

3.   Separating fact from ideology

All these changes suggest that, during the 1960s history had begun to repeat itself. A new generation of reformers, if not judges and correctional people, had become convinced that the principles of rehabilitation were dead and that alternative principles had to be found. Once again, a philosophy which had been introduced with great fanfare and which had captured the imaginations of a nation had ended in despair. But is that despair warranted? Is it based on fact or popular belief?

From a scientific standpoint, the support is probably more ideological and factual. There is no denying that an impossible burden has been laid upon the juvenile justice system. It cannot prevent all delinquency nor can it remedy the effects of poverty and discrimination. Likewise, the resources with which it has had to work are inadequate. But, beyond that, the evidence regarding its capacity to rehabilitate a more limited number of convicted offenders is inconclusive. Strictly speaking, its worth for this purpose is neither proven nor disproven.

One reason is that many of the studies upon which demands for change are based are faulty; their designs are primitive. In the large survey of correctional effectiveness conducted for the governor's commission in New York, for example, the authors had to evaluate the effectiveness of "treatment" which included anything from informal probation to total incarceration, anything from individual psychotherapy to skill development, anything from milieu therapy to leisure time activities (Lipton, et al., 1975). In all, 11 different "treatment" modalities were assessed, many of which were included in a single "rehabilitative" package and applied in settings that varied widely. From a scientific standpoint, therefore, the task of separating out and assessing the impact of these widely different combinations of methods on different groups of offenders under varying circumstances is profoundly difficult under the best of conditions. But given the kinds of evaluation studies with which the authors had to work, the task is a researcher's nightmare. It is impossible.

Contrary to the optimistic predictions of people like Z. R. Brockway and Enoch Wines, science has never yet been able to establish valid typologies which are used, first, to distinguish among types of offenders and, then, to design programs that will address their particular needs. It is entirely possible, therefore, that the findings of no difference between alternative kinds of programs are due, not to the fact that these programs had no impact, but because they were used indiscriminately on all people. Had different kinds of offenders been identified and then matched with programs appropriate to their problems, the results might have been different. The point is that at present we cannot discard this possibility because the necessary theoretical and research work has not been accomplished.

Were this not enough, the programs—the mysterious black boxes to which offenders were assigned—were rarely subjected to analyses which would permit us to know what actually went on in them. We do not know whether they conformed to design or not. Then, when offenders were released from these black boxes, the methods used to measure their effects upon offenders were ambiguous and tremendously varied. Some studies used psychological change; some used parole revocation; some used arrest; and some used reconviction. To make results even more questionable, many of these same studies did not make use of experimental designs by which valid comparisons in outcome could be made. Ambiguities were further compounded. Hence, until more of these problems are also addressed, the grounds for drawing final conclusions will remaim shaky indeed.

Finally, we will be unable to develop a valid body of knowledge about correctional effectiveness by simply summing up the results of a host of studies that vary in quality. Most of them, in fact, are practical ventures without the benefit of theoretical structure. Hence, it is difficult to treat them as contributors to one or more bodies of knowledge, to raise them to higher levels of abstraction, and to determine what they mean. They shed little new light on the control implications of different theories of delinquency or on broader theories concerned with the responses of individuals and organizations to different strategies of intervention.

In short, it is difficult to tell whether the inconclusive findings of correctional effectiveness are due to faulty programs, to faulty research, or to both. Likely, it is the latter. Social and cultural change, however, will not wait until all the evidence is in. High rates of crime and other problems, if nothing else, create their own demands for new ideas and new methods. Indeed, a new revolution has been taking place, one that is adding yet another "R"—*reintegration*—to those we have already discussed. We will examine it in the next chapter.

References

Adams, Stuart
    1970   "Correctional caseload research." Pp. 721–732 in Norman Johnston et al., (Eds.), *The Sociology of Punishment and Correction* (2nd ed.). New York: John Wiley.

Barker, Gordon H. and Adams, W. Thomas
    1959   "The social structure of a correctional institution." *Journal of Criminal Law, Criminology and Police Science*, January–February, XLIX:417–422.

Barnes, Harry Elmer
    1972 *The Story of Punishment* (Rev. ed.). Montclair, N.J.: Patterson-Smith.

Barrows, Isabel C.
    1910 "Reformatory treatment of women in the United States. Pp. 129–167
          in Charles R. Henderson (Ed.), *Penal and Reformatory Institutions.*
          New York: Charities Publication Committee.

Bartollas, Clemens, Miller, Stuart J. and Dinitz, Simon
    1976 *Juvenile Victimization: The Institutional Paradox.* New York: John
          Wiley.

Beaumont, Gustave de and Tocqueville, Alexis de
    1964 *On the Penitentiary System in the United States and Its Application in
          France.* Carbondale: Southern Illinois University Press. (1833).

Berleman, William C. and Steinburn, Thomas W.
    1967 "The execution and evaluation of a delinquency prevention pro-
          gram." *Social Problems,* Spring, 14:413–423.

    1969 "The value and validity of delinquent prevention experiments."
          Crime and Delinquency, October, 15:471–478.

Bremner, Robert H. (Ed.)
    1970 *Children and Youth in America: A Documentary History.* 2 vols. Cam-
          bridge: Harvard University Press.

Brockway, Z. R.
    1910 "The American reformatory prison system." Pp. 88–107 in Charles R.
          Henderson (Ed.), *Prison Reform and Criminal Law.* New York:
          Charities Publication Committee.

Carlson, Norman
    1975 "Giving up the medical model." *Behavior Today,* November, 6:1.

Carter, Robert M. and Wilkins, Leslie T.
    1970 *Probation and Parole.* New York: John Wiley.

Center on Administration of Criminal Justice
    1977 *An Evaluation of the California Probation Subsidy Program.* Vol. IV.
          Davis, Ca.: University of California.

Clemmer, Donald R.
    1940 *The Prison Community.* New York: Rinehart.

Craig, Maude M. and Furst, Philip W.
    1965 "What happens after treatment? A study of potentially delinquent
          boys." *Social Service Review,* June, 165–171.

Cressey, Donald R.
    1960 *The Prison.* New York: Holt, Rinehart and Winston.

Diana, Lewis
    1960 "What is probation?" *Journal of Criminal Law, Criminology, and Police
          Science.* July–August, 51:189–204.

England, Ralph
    1957   "What is responsible for satisfactory probation and post-probation outcome?" *Journal of Criminal Law, Criminology, and Police Science,* March–April, 47:667–677.

Giallombardo, Rose
    1974   *The Social World of Imprisoned Girls.* New York: John Wiley.

Glaser, Daniel
    1964   *The Effectiveness of a Prison and Parole System.* Indianapolis: Bobbs-Merrill.

Goffman, Erving R.
    1961   *Asylums.* New York: Doubleday.

Grunhut, Max
    1948   *Penal Reform.* New York: Clarendon Press.

Hart, Hastings
    1910   *Preventive Treatment of Neglected Children.* New York: Charities Publication Committee.

Henderson, Charles R. (ed.)
    1910a   *Penal and Reformatory Institutions.* New York: Charities Publication Committee.

    1910b   *Correction and Prevention.* New York: Charities Publication Committee.

    1910c   *Prison Reform and Criminal Law.* New York: Charities Publication Committee.

Jesness, Karl F.
    1970   "The Preston typology study." *Youth Authority Quarterly,* Winter, 23:26–38.

Kassebaum, Gene, Ward, David and Wilner, Dan
    1971   *Prison Treatment and Its Outcome.* New York: John Wiley.

Klein, Malcolm W.
    1971   *Street Gangs and Street Workers.* Englewood Cliffs, N.J.: Prentice Hall.

Lemert, Edwin M.
    1967   "The juvenile court—quest and realities." Pp. 91–106 in the President's Commission on Law Enforcement and Administration of Justice, *Juvenile Delinquency and Youth Crime.* Washington, D.C.: U.S. Government Printing Office.

Lerman, Paul
    1968   "Evaluating institutions for delinquents." *Social Work,* 13:55–64.

    1975   *Community Treatment and Social Control.* Chicago: University of Chicago Press.

Lipton, Douglas, Martinson, Robert and Wilks, Judith
   1975   *The Effectiveness of Correctional Treatment.* New York: Praeger Publishers.

Manocchio, Anthony J. and Dunn, Jimmy
   1970   *The Time Game.* Beverly Hills, Ca.: Sage Publications.

Martinson, Robert
   1974   "What works? Questions and answers about prison reform." *The Public Interest,* Spring, 35:22–54.

McCord, Joan and McCord, William
   1959   "A follow-up report on the Cambridge-Somerville youth study." *Annals of the American Academy of Political and Social Science,* March, 322:89–98.

McCorkle, Lloyd W., Bixby, Lovel F. and Elias, Albert
   1958   *The Highfields Story.* New York: Henry Holt.

McEachern, Alexander W. and Taylor, Edward M.
   1967   *The Effects of Probation.* Probation Project Report No. 2, Youth Studies Center. Los Angeles: University of Southern California.

McKelvey, Blake
   1968   *American Prisons* (Reprint ed.). Montclair, N.J.: Patterson-Smith.

Meyer, Henry J., Borgatta, Edgar F. and Jones, Wyatt C.
   1965   *Girls at Vocational High.* New York: Russell Sage Foundation.

Miller, Walter B.
   1962   "The impact of a 'total-community' delinquency control project." *Social Problems,* Fall, 10:168–191.

National Commission on Law Observance and Enforcement
   1931   *The Child Offender in the Federal System of Justice.* Washington, D.C.: U.S. Government Printing Office.

Ohlin, Lloyd E.
   1958   "The reduction of role conflict in institutional staff." *Children,* March–April, 5:65–69.

Ohlin, Lloyd E. and Lawrence, William C.
   1959   "Social interaction among clients as a treatment problem." *Social Work,* April, IV:3–13.

Palmer, Theodore B.
   1971   "California's treatment program for delinquent adolescents." *Journal of Research in Crime and Delinquency,* January, 8:74–92.

Palmer, Theodore B. and Warren, Marguerite Q.
   1967   *Community Treatment Project, CTP Research Report,* No. 8, Part I. Sacramento: California Youth Authority.

Pettigrove, Frederick G.
1910 "State prisons of the United States under separate and congregate systems." Pp. 27–67 in Charles R. Henderson (Ed.), *Penal and Reformatory Institutions*. New York: Charities Publication Committee.

Platt, Anthony M.
1969 *The Child Savers: The invention of Delinquency*. Chicago: University of Chicago Press.

Polsky, Howard W.
1962 *Cottage Six*. New York: Russell Sage.

Powers, Edwin and Witmer, Helen
1951 *An Experiment in the Prevention of Delinquency: The Cambridge-Somerville Youth Study*. New York: Columbia University Press.

President's Commission on Law Enforcement and Administration of Justice
1967a *Task Force Report: Corrections*. Washington, D.C.: U.S. Government Printing Office.

1967b *Task Force Report: Juvenile Delinquency and Youth Crime*. Washington, D.C.: U.S. Government Printing Office.

1967c *The Challenge of Crime in a Free Society*. Washington, D.C.: U.S. Government Printing Office.

Reckless, Walter C. and Dinitz, Simon
1972 *The Prevention of Juvenile Delinquency: An Experiment*. Columbus: Ohio State University Press.

Rothman, David J.
1971 *The Discovery of the Asylum*. Boston: Little, Brown.

Sanders, Wiley B.
1970 *Juvenile Offenders for a Thousand Years*. Chapel Hill: University of North Carolina Press.

Sarri, Rosemary, Vinter, Robert D. and Kish, Rhea
1974 "Juvenile justice: failure of a nation." Paper presented at the Annual Meeting of the Directors of Criminal Justice Research Centers. Cambridge: Harvard Law School. (Unpublished).

Schrag, Clarence
1954 "Leadership among prison inmates." *American Sociological Review*, February, *19*:37–42.

1961 "Some foundations for a theory of correction." Pp. 309–357 in Donald R. Cressey (Ed.), *The Prison*. New York: Holt, Rinehart and Winston.

Scott, Joseph F.
1910 "American reformatories for male adults." Pp. 89–120 in Charles R. Henderson (Ed.), *Penal and Reformatory Institutions*. New York: Charities Publication Committee.

Seckel, Joachim M.
  1965 *Experiments in Group Counseling at Two Youth Authority Institutions. Research Report No. 46.* Sacramento: California Youth Authority.

Sellin, Thorsten
  1964 "Introduction: Tocqueville and Beaumont and prison reform in France." Pp. xv–xl in Gustave de Beaumont and Alexis de Tocqueville, *On the Penitentiary System in the United States and its Application in France.* Carbondale: Southern Illinois University Press.

Smith, Robert L.
  1973 *A Quiet Revolution: Probation Subsidy.* Youth Development and Delinquency Prevention Administration, HEW. Washington, D.C.: U.S. Government Printing Office.

Street, David
  1965 "The inmate group in custodial and treatment settings." *American Sociological Review*, February, 30:40–55.

Sykes, Gresham M.
  1965 *The Society of Captives.* New York: Atheneum Press.

Sykes, Gresham M., and Messinger, Sheldon
  1960 "The inmate social system." Pp. 5–19 in *Theoretical Studies in Social Organization of the Prison.* Social Science Research Council, Pamphlet No. 15.

Tappan, Paul W.
  1960 *Crime, Justice and Correction.* New York: McGraw-Hill.

Tonry, Michael H.
  1976 "Juvenile justice and the national crime commissions." Pp. 281–298 in Margaret K. Rosenheim (Ed.), *Pursuing Justice for the Child.* Chicago: University of Chicago Press.

United Nations
  1951 *Probation and Related Measures.* New York: Department of Social Affairs.

Ward, David A.
  1972 "Evaluative research for corrections." Pp. 184–206 in Lloyd E. Ohlin (Ed.), *Prisoners in America.* Englewood Cliffs, N.J.: Prentice Hall.

Warren, Marguerite Q.
  1964 "An experiment in alternatives to incarceration for delinquent youth: recent findings in the community treatment project." *Correction in the Community: Alternatives to Incarceration.* Sacramento: Board of Corrections Monograph No. 4, June, 39–50.

  1968 "The case for differential treatment of delinquents." Sacramento: Center for Training in Differential Treatment. (Mimeo).

Warren, Marguerite Q. and Palmer, Theodore B.

  1966   *The Community Treatment Project after Five Years.* Sacramento: California Youth Authority.

Weber, George H.

  1957   "Conflicts between professional and nonprofessional personnel in institutional delinquency treatment." *Journal of Criminal Law, Criminology, and Police Science,* May–June, *XLVIII*:26–43.

Weeks, H. Ashley

  1958   *Youthful Offenders at Highfields.* Ann Arbor: University of Michigan Press.

White House Conference on Child Health and Protection

  1932   *The Delinquent Child.* New York: Century.

Wines, Frederick H.

  1910   "Historical introduction." Pp. 3–38 in Charles R. Henderson (Ed.), *Prison Reform and Criminal Law.* New York: Charities Publication Committee.

18

THE NEW REVOLUTION: REINTEGRATION

We are now in the early phases of a new revolution in juvenile justice, one which stresses *reintegration* for problem youth. But whereas prior philosophies of delinquency control have focused primarily on eliminating evil tendencies in the delinquent, this one suggests that delinquency is a two-sided coin.

On one side of the coin is illegal behavior. Except in rare cases, however, that behavior is not pathological and unique to delinquents. Like conformist behavior, instead it is a reflection of the myriad of social forces which play upon young people—their places in the class structure of society, the social groups to which they belong, our overall culture, and within it a host of dissonant subcultures. While this complex set of forces may cause some children to behave in a delinquent way, their behavior, in most instances, is not a reflection of mental illness or personal depravity. Rather, it represents an understandable pattern of a social adjustment to a given set of environmental forces.

On the other side of the coin is the way society defines and reacts to behavior. Delinquency is not merely what children do. Rather, it is society which defines rules, labels those who break rules, and prescribes ways for reacting to them. These processes of defining, labeling, and reacting, therefore, are often more important than actual behavior in determining (1) the social meaning and character of delinquency and (2) which children among a multitude of youthful lawbreakers will actually be defined as bad; and (3) how society will organize its reactions to official delinquents.

Given the two-sided nature of delinquency, it is obvious that it must be dealt with as an interactional, not a personal, phenomenon. Social as well as behavioral change is required. Of the two, in fact, social change is probably the more important. The reason is that behavior, delinquent or otherwise, is the product of the way society socializes its children, providing supports and opportunities for some but denying them to others. Hence, by changing the organization of society, marginal children can be more easily assimilated into conventional activities and institutions, and delinquency can be reduced. Indeed the control of delinquency is a task for the entire society, not just the juvenile justice system. Reintegration requires new patterns of interaction between children and others, new opportunities, and new social roles.

Roots of revolution

Like prior revolutionary approaches to the reformation of delinquents, the reintegrative philosophy was an outgrowth of two things: significant societal change and new theories of delinquency. Both came into the striking relief in the tumultuous decade of the 1960s.

The decade started on a buoyant note. John Kennedy had just been elected President, and Americans responded warmly to his charismatic leadership. After a decade of little growth and limited vision, he suggested it was time "to get the country moving again." Heroic undertakings were in order; America should continue to pursue its grand destiny.

No little part of that destiny, the new President maintained, lay with the nation's youth. The time had come when the burdens of inequality, racism, and delinquency should be lifted from the shoulders of poor and uneducated children. In order to help accomplish this task, therefore, Kennedy created the President's Committee on Juvenile Delinquency and Youth Crime and appointed his brother Robert, the Attorney General, as its Chairperson. Furthermore, other committee members were highly influential persons: the Secretary of Health, Education, and Welfare and the Secretary of Labor. This was to be a serious effort.

Strain and cultural deviance theory

True to the spirit of the times, new ways of viewing the delinquency problem also provided the rationale for the work of the President's Committee. As we learned in Chapter 11, the social programs of the committee were guided by the arguments of strain and cultural deviance theorists which suggested that the nation's poor and minority youth were not being effectively assimilated into the country's opportunity structure. The gates to success were closed. As a result, inherently social children were being forced to resort to desperately deviant measures in order to get ahead. Ironically, they were delinquent, not because they rejected America's cardinal virtue—the success ethic—but because they believed so strongly in it. The solution, therefore, was obvious: the nation had only to reopen the gates of opportunity in order to prevent crime and to redeem its prodigal children.

This arresting argument also seemed to indicate why the juvenile court had not successfully stemmed the tide of juvenile problems. It was not the court's intrepid efforts that were at fault but its ideological and theoretical underpinnings. Rehabilitation was too narrow a guiding principle. Dependency, neglect, and lawbreaking were due, not to intrafamily tensions and emotional disturbance, but to social inequality, disorganized neighborhoods, and the absence of legitimate opportunity. Indeed, the parents of delinquent children, as much as the children themselves, were the victims of social inequality.

Given this new definition of the problem, it was obvious that the nation's strategy should be one of reintegration and prevention, not rehabilitation. Racial and economic discrimination should be eliminated, hope instilled in the members of lower-class families, enriched schooling provided, and legitimate work opportunities made available. If the underclass children of the country were reintegrated into the mainstream of American life, their motives for committing delinquent acts would be removed and the worst features of delinquency eliminated.

So persuasive were these ideas that they led to the creation of the Office of Youth Development and Delinquency Prevention in the Department of Health, Education, and Welfare, to a modest federal program designed to assist local communities to bring more of their resources to bear on the delinquency problem, and to the creation of Mobilization for Youth in New York City (see Chapter 11). But such efforts as these were far too modest for the implied goals of the reintegrative philosophy. It demanded steps that were far more heroic. That is why, in keeping with its logic, it eventually contributed to the creation of the poverty and other Great Society programs of the late 1960s. Billions were spent in an endeavor to assimilate the poor into the opportunity structure of American society, to renew the cities, to achieve racial equality, and thereby to reduce delinquency and its attendant problems.

Destruction of morale

Yet, even as these unparalleled remedial programs were taking place, American morale began to hurtle down a psychic slide which eventually turned the grand aspirations of the early 1960s to ashes. President Kennedy was assassinated by Lee Harvey Oswald. Attempts to block integration were followed by civil disobedience, urban riots, and burning cities. Martin Luther King and Robert Kennedy, the two remaining symbols of earlier hopes, were themselves assassinated. Involvement in the Vietnam War continued to escalate, despite mounting opposition. More and more young people dropped out, turned to drugs, joined communes, ran away, marched on Washington, or found some other way to attack the "establishment." Crime rates rose and violence begat violence. Finally, the Vietnam War, along with the burglaries, the wiretaps, the perjuries, and the coverups of the Nixon administration spilled the crises of the 1960s over into the 1970s. Not only had American streets been filled with protest, disruption, and crime, but now they had reached the highest levels of American government. Thus, faith in the capacity of American institutions to insure tranquility and to implement reforms was at an all-time low. A period in history which had begun buoyantly and with great hope eventually ended in disillusionment, mutual distrust, and cynicism.

This gradual destruction of American morale had a discernible effect on the evolution of the reintegrative philosophy. Consider the impact of subsequent events on the form that it finally took.

The President's Commission

In response to the traumas of increasing unrest, President Lyndon Johnson, John Kennedy's successor, established a new Commission on Law Enforcement and Administration of Justice in 1965 (cf. President's

Commission, 1967a). The purpose of this commission was to take stock of rising crime rates and to recommend reforms. Significantly, the commission's recommendations, which were published in 1967, were overwhelmingly reintegrative in character. Yet, they were also characterized by a heavy reliance upon labeling, as well as strain, theory. Hence, some contrasting, partly inconsistent themes were built into them.

One theme was still heroic in character, reflecting the earlier emphasis upon delinquency prevention and large-scale social change. The second, by contrast, reflected the growing distrust of government and stressed a hands-off policy, particularly that of saving children from the stigmatizing and destructive effects of legal processing. Thus, while both themes tended to be reintegrative, they could eventually lead to sharply different social policies if they were not reconciled in some way or if one gained precedence over the other.

The heroic theme

We are already familiar with the heroic theme. It was drawn from cultural deviance and strain theories and suggested that the way to control delinquency was to change society—to eliminate poverty, to promote equality of opportunity, and thereby to eliminate the need for crime. Consider the commission's expression of this theme in its recommendations:

1. *A stake in conformity.* "It is inescapable," declared the President's Commission (1967a:57), "that juvenile delinquency is directly related to conditions bred by poverty." That is why reform is a community, not a court, function:

> The Commission doubts that even a vastly improved criminal justice system can substantially reduce crime if society fails to make it possible for each of its citizens to feel a personal stake in it—in the good life that it can provide and in the law and order that are prerequisite to such a life (1967a:58).

2. *Prevention.* "Once a juvenile is apprehended by the police and referred to the juvenile court, the community has already failed" (President's Commission, 1967a:58). Thus, it follows that the most promising method for dealing with crime is by eliminating the social conditions that drive young people to commit it. Indeed, prevention is most likely to succeed if it concentrates on children:

> They are not yet set in their ways; they are still developing, still subject to the influence of the socializing institutions that structure . . . their environment: family, school, gang, recreation program, job market. But that influence, to do the most good, must come before the youth has become involved in the formal criminal justice system (1967a:58).

3. *Creation of opportunity.* Since prevention is the most promising method for eliminating crime and since the juvenile justice system cannot provide poor children with equality of opportunity, then the responsibility falls on political, economic, and educational, not legal, institutions. Indeed, the crime commission recommended that steps be taken to provide a minimum family income for all Americans, to reduce unemployment, to foster activities which tie families together, to help slum children make up for inadequate preschool preparation, to raise their hopes and expectations for higher education, to develop job placement in the schools, to eliminate barriers to employment posed by discrimination, and to involve more young people in responsible community activities (President's Commission, 1967a:66; 69; 74; 77).

In summary, then, this set of recommendations was characterized by two distinguishing features. First, it was concerned with what strain and cultural deviance theorists would suggest are the "primary" sources of delinquent behavior: poverty, inequality, inadequate education, and lack of opportunity. Secondly, the heroic recommendations were concerned far more with reforming the political, economic, and social structures of American society than with reforming the juvenile justice system. Indeed, the commission seemed to be suggesting that the country should search out those factors which produce constructive legitimate behavior and, then, should restructure American institutions so that this kind of behavior, rather than which is delinquent, would be encouraged. In other words, what was needed was a *national youth policy* designed to produce legitimate behavior rather than a juvenile justice policy designed to punish or to undo the effects of illegitimate behavior.

The hands-off theme

The hands-off theme of the President's Commission was not necessarily inconsistent with its heroic theme, but it certainly represented a sharp change in emphasis. After implying that poverty, discrimination, and the lack of opportunity were the primary causes of the delinquency problem and that the protection of society, no less than the salvation of its children, required that these causes be eliminated, the commission then began to suggest that an even greater culprit might be the juvenile justice system.

This change in focus was stimulated by two things. The first was the presumed failures of the juvenile court—the continued detention of children in jails, assembly-line justice, the lack of due process, excessively large caseloads, crowded training schools, and a growing body of evidence that correctional programs, even under the best of circumstances, did not seem to make a difference. The juvenile court had not lived up to expectations; it was clearly not a panacea (cf. Chapter 16).

The second, and more important, source was the growing popularity of labeling theory in the mid- and late 1960s. It will be recalled that, according to labeling theory, really serious delinquent behavior is the product not of "primary" or "original" causes, like poverty or lack of opportunity, but of the way society reacts to youthful lawbreakers. It is these reactions which produce dangerous career behavior—what labeling theorists call "secondary" deviance (cf. Chapter 13). Thus, the failure of the juvenile court was used as evidence in support of labeling theory's basic argument: namely, that the process of identifying, labeling, and stigmatizing children had only made their problems worse, not better. Indeed, if labeling theory was correct, high rates of juvenile crime were due less to the failure of other social institutions than to the excessively zealous and moralistic interference of the juvenile court in the lives of children. Rather than leaving children alone, thus keeping them on the conventional path that leads from childhood to adulthood, the court had only made them more delinquent.

In an essay for the President's Commission, Edwin Lemert (1967:96) suggested what seemed to be the only logical solution. "If there is a defensible philosophy for the juvenile court," Lemert advised, "it is one of *judicious nonintervention* (emphasis added). Rather being allowed to monitor a widerange of youth behavior, the court "is properly an agency of last resort for children, holding to a doctrine analagous to that of appeals courts which require that all other remedies be exhausted before a case will be heard" (p. 96).

The President's Commission was obviously persuaded by this argument because virtually all of its remaining recommendations were predicted on the assumption that the juvenile court was a major, if not the primary, source of increasing delinquency rates. As a result, it recommended a series of reforms which may now be subsumed under a list of familiar catchwords: *decriminalization, diversion, due process* and *deinstitutionalization*. All of them were designed to limit severely the power and jurisdiction of the court.

1. *Decriminalization.* Contrary to society's traditional stance toward children this reform suggests that society should have no legal jurisdiction over the moral behaviors of children. All status offenses should be decriminalized. The term "juvenile delinquency" should be restricted solely to violations of the criminal law.

Two arguments were advanced in favor of this reform. First simple justice demands it: Juveniles should not be prosecuted for behavior which, if exhibited by adults, would not be prosecuted. Secondly, "individual morality has become functional rather than sacred or ethical in the older sense. [Hence], it has become equally or more important to protect children from the unanticipated and unwanted consequences of organized movements in their behalf than from the unorganized, adventious 'evils' which gave birth to the juvenile court" (Lemert, 1967:97). In short, said the commission, "Serious consideration should be given to complete elimination of the court's power over children for noncriminal conduct" (1967a:85).

2. *Diversion.* Diversion suggests that more first-time and petty, as well as status, offenders should be channeled away from legal processing and into community institutions. The juvenile court, Lemert argued (1967:97), is primarily a court of law. As such, it can only seek to redress harms, to enjoin offenders from further illegal behaviors, and to punish them for what they have done. "It cannot . . . make a father good, a mother moral, a child obedient, or a youth respectful of authority." Whenever it attempts these things, it only creates confusion and value conflict. Therefore, it should not attempt them.

As an alternative, the President's Commission (1967a:82) urged that there should be more warnings and station adjustments by the police, more screening out of offenders at the intake stage of court processing, more informal supervision by probation officers, and more referrals to nonlegal agencies in the community. Indeed, the commission recommended the creation of a Youth Service Bureau in each community which would coordinate all youth services and thus perform most of the functions that the juvenile court was originally intended to perform. The latter meanwhile should become a court of law.

3. *Due process.* The belief that the juvenile court should serve as a court of law, rather than as a substitute parent, was underscored by the decisions of the Supreme Court in the *Kent* (1966) and *Gault* (1967) cases.

The Supreme Court had agreed with labeling theorists that children had received the worst of two possible worlds—neither protection of their rights nor helpful and regenerative treatment.

Paying a great deal of attention to these decisions, the crime commission (1967a:87) reaffirmed the importance of insuring due process for juveniles: notice to parents well in advance of any legal proceeding by the court; the mandatory appointment of a defense lawyer; proper presentation of evidence, ruling out excessive informality, hearsay, or rumor; and a clear distinction between adjudicatory and dispositional hearings. The juvenile court, in short, should follow more closely the model of the adult criminal court.

4. *Deinstitutionalization.* Deinstitutionalization suggests that correctional programs should be removed from training schools and reformatories and located in open community settings. Like programs of diversion, their purpose should be to integrate the offender into the nondelinquent activities of the community, not into the routine of the reformatory.

> The correctional strategy that presently seems to hold the greatest promise, based on social science theory and limited research, is that of reintegrating the offender into the community. A key element in this strategy is to deal with problems in their social context, which means in the interaction of the offender and the community. It also means avoiding as much as possible the isolating and labeling effects of commitment to an institution. There is little doubt that the goals of reintegration are furthered much more readily working with an offender in the community than by incarcerating him (President's Commission, 1967b:28).

In summary, then, the hands-off recommendations of the President's Commission were similar to its heroic recommendations in the sense that they exhibited greater faith in the capacity of community institutions to solve youth problems than in the capacity of the juvenile court to do so. But, beyond this similarity, there were also some striking differences.

The heroic recommendations suggested that serious crime was due to inequality, discrimination, and poverty. What was required, therefore, was a national youth policy designed to open up educational, social, and work opportunities. In lieu of juvenile court processing, the ultimate goal would be give all children a greater stake in conformity.

The hands-off recommendations, by contrast, suggested that serious crime was due to "secondary" deviance—to the expression of delinquent identities and behavior by children who had been unnecessarily tagged, labeled, and treated as bad. In this instance, therefore, the foremost goal of policy should be to limit the power and jurisdiction of the juvenile court. Status offenses should be decriminalized, and criminal lawbreakers left alone wherever possible. Should intervention be necessary, diversion, due process, and deinstitutionalization should be applied in lieu of traditional justice procedures.

It is conceivable, of course, that both sets of recommendations might have been adopted and applied, despite their theoretical inconsistencies. As it turned out, however, a modified version of the hands-off recommendations proved the more attractive and became the core of the reintegrative philosophy. The heroic recommendations were gradually forgotten, while the four Ds—decriminalization, diversion, due process, and deinstitutionalization—became the hallmarks of reform. The change, however, was gradual.

Cementing the revolution

Following the recommendations of the President's Commission, the first action on the federal level was the passage of a new act by Congress—the Juvenile Delinquency Prevention and Control Act of 1968 (Law Enforcement Assistance Administration [LEAA], 1974). Interestingly, this new act stressed some of the more heroic features of the President's Commission. It was to be administered by the Youth Development and Delinquency Prevention Administration (YDDPA), which was located in the Department of Health, Education, and Welfare. It was to encourage the development of community based youth programs, as well as to assist the police, courts, and corrections in dealing with delinquents. By 1970, however, Congress apparently felt that the act was languishing in HEW. Nothing of a very heroic nature had happened. Consequently, in April 1971, Congressional pressure generated an agreement among various federal agencies that the YDDPA would concentrate all of its efforts on programs *outside* of the juvenile justice system, while the Law Enforcement Assistance Administration, a new agency within the Department of Justice, would focus on the juvenile justice system itself.

This agreement was then embodied in some new legislation—the Juvenile Delinquency Prevention Act of 1972. An attempt was made to increase the effectiveness of the federal effort by limiting the activities of the YDDPA strictly to prevention efforts, particularly to the creation of coordinated youth service system—youth service bureaus—in the nation's communities. This effort was short-lived, however, and was subsequently superceded by a new series of recommendations and political acts.

The National Advisory Commission on Criminal Justice Standards

One of these events was the creation of yet another national commission by the Nixon administration in 1973—the National Advisory Commission on Criminal Justice Standards and Goals. But, in contrast to encouraging the further development of a national youth policy, this commission was justice oriented. Paradoxically, however, it turned to labeling theory as the basis for its recommendations:

> [A] number of studies . . . suggest that many children mature out of delinquent behavior. If this is true, the question is whether it is better to leave these persons alone or put them into the formal juvenile justice system. . . . There is a substantial body of opinion which favors "leaving alone" *all except those who have had three or four contacts with the police* (National Advisory Commission, 1973a:109 emphasis added).

Thus, although this commission was comprised largely of criminal justice professionals and politicians, it followed the lead of the 1967 President's Commission and recommended a policy of decriminalization, diversion, due process, and deinstitutionalization (National Advisory Commission, 1973a; 1973b). These recommendations, in turn, were reflected in the legislation that now governs federal policy.

The Juvenile Justice Act of 1974

This legislation is the Juvenile Justice and Delinquency Prevention Act of 1974 (LEAA, 1974). This new act phased out the youth services activities of YDDPA and created a new office—the Office of Juvenile Justice and Delinquency Prevention. This new office, however, is located in the Law Enforcement Assistance Administration, not in the Department of Health, Education, and Welfare, a highly symbolic change.

Although the new act stresses "prevention," its major intent is to promote changes in the administration of juvenile justice, in particular to promote the four *D*s. As a result, any state which wishes to receive federal funds today has to meet several basic requirements:

> Federal funds must be used to develop or to maintain programs designed "to prevent delinquency, to divert juveniles from the juvenile justice system, and to provide community based alternatives to juvenile detention and correctional facilities" (LEAA, 1974:395).
>
> After two years, each state must guarantee that juvenile status offenders will not be confined in juvenile detention or correctional facilities. Deinstitutionalization for them must be complete. If such children have no place else to stay, communities should create new "shelters" for them. (LEAA, 1974:396).
>
> No delinquent can be detained or confined in any institution where he or she will have contact with adult offenders (LEAA, 1974:395).

Finally, the Office of Juvenile Justice and Delinquency Prevention is authorized to make grants designed to encourage the development of new techniques of rehabilitation, new community alternatives to incarceration, and new methods of diversion. New prevention efforts are also encouraged but not of the heroic society-changing variety. Rather the funds are to "improve the capability of public and private agencies . . . to provide services for . . . youth in danger of becoming delinquent"—better counseling methods, crisis intervention, family therapy, and other remedial activities of this type (LEAA, 1974:398).

Nothing was said about the need to coordinate delinquency prevention efforts with welfare and educational programs designed to raise minimum family incomes, to develop job placement services in the schools, or to raise the hopes and expectations of underclass children for higher education. Instead, the main message of current federal legislation in delinquency is that the juvenile court and its original child-saving principles are failures. When absolutely necessary, young criminals should be given a formal trial. Otherwise, every possible step should be taken to keep them free from the court's destructive and stigmatizing effects, even to the extent of giving them a free ride for their first two or three offenses.

Implementing the revolution

Since the reintegrative revolution is now based more upon the premises of labeling than of strain theory, a key question is how it is being implemented: Are the uses of decriminalization, diversion, due process, and deinstitutionalization reflective of a policy of *judicious nonintervention?* Are more children being left alone? Is the power of the juvenile court being diminished?

As it turns out, the use of the four *D*s has reduced the power of the juvenile court and is changing its practices, but children are not being left alone. Instead, a whole new child-saving bureaucracy seems to be developing which is dominated to a considerable degree by law enforcement personnel. As a result, it is questionable that Lemert's basic injunction is being followed: namely, that children should be protected "from the unanticipated and unwanted consequences of organized movements in their behalf." Rather, the reintegrative revolution is much like those that preceded it. People are still concerned with saving children, and, while they have introduced some practices that are new, their interventions heavily reflect past traditions and practices.

Decriminalization

The recommendation that juvenile status offenses should be decriminalized has had a mixed, but not a bandwagon, effect. In part, this is because, influential groups have defined "decriminalization" in different ways. For example, such prestigious groups as the International Association of Chiefs of Police, the National Council on Crime and Delinquency, and the framers of the Model Act for Family Courts have argued that the jurisdiction of the juvenile court over status offenders should be eliminated entirely (National Task Force, 1977:3). To these groups, "decriminalization" means that children who have not been charged with a crime should not be taken to court. Legally, at least, all status offenses would be defined out of existence.

Other prestigious groups, by contrast, have given "decriminalization" a different meaning. The National Advisory Commission on Corrections and the framers of the Uniform Juvenile Court Act argue that status offenders should simply be given a different, but less stigmatizing, name and left under the jurisdiction of the juvenile court (National Task Force, 1977:3). Their solution, in other words, would be euphemistic: Status offenders would no longer be called "delinquents," though they could be taken to court if necessary.

As it turns out, it is this kind of thinking that has dominated social policy and the making of legislation in most states. The movement actually began in California as early as 1961 when a new legal code defined status offenders as "601s," while criminal offenders were called "602s" (cf. Lemert, 1970). The following year, the state of New York created a somewhat similar child to the California 601 and called him or her "a person in need of supervision" (PINS). Then, the movement really gained steam, with different states creating new acronyms for the status offender: Illinois called him a "minor otherwise in need of supervision" (MINS); Colorado, "child in need of supervision" (CHINS); Florida (CINS); and Georgia, merely "unruly child" (UC) (Rubin, 1974:6-7). By 1973, 25 states had created a separate category for the status offender (Levin and Sarri, 1974:12). Undoubtedly, more states have done so today, although not a single one has freed status offenders entirely from juvenile court jurisdiction (National Task Force, 1977:2).

There are two things about this name-changing effort to which attention should be called. On the one hand, a euphemistic solution to youth problems is not new. What today's reformers forget is that the term "delinquent" was invented in 1899 to decriminalize *all* misbehaving children, criminal or not, and to distinguish them from adult criminals. Furthermore, it was intended that the juvenile court should treat all such children as *status,* not criminal, offenders. That is, the court should be concerned with correcting their problems, not punishing their acts. Now, however, we are reversing the process somewhat. In an endeavor to free status offenders from stigma, we are calling them *CHINS* or *UCs,* while the really "bad apples" will still be called *delinquents.*

On the other hand, today's reformers are faced with a slippery problem which labeling theory and a policy of nonintervention poses: namely, the implication that if the legal rules against status offenses no longer existed the behaviors they represented would either disappear or would no longer be grounds for concern. Such a notion, of course, is fallacious. There would still be children who refuse to go to school, who become homeless street people, or who seriously jeopardize their futures in some other ways. Thus, if society chose to ignore these children, it would be engaging in a legislative sleight-of-hand in which only the rules were changed, not the problems. Remediation of some type is still needed.

That remediation, of course, need not be legal, providing that children and parents are willing participants in it. But sometimes they are not. Sometimes the juvenile court is a useful backup institution. Hence, this may be one reason that all states have continued to permit the juvenile court to exercise some jurisdiction over status offenders. Yet, though they have done that, the influence of the court is declining, less because the laws of the various states require it than because of the increasing use of diversion, due process, and deinstitutionalization.

Diversion

Easily the most popular of the reforms now being promoted is *diversion*. Ostensibly, its purpose is to reduce the number of children being inserted into the juvenile justice system, but, again, this general purpose is overwhelmed by a host of ambiguous meanings. The reason is that diversion is being promoted by different people for different reasons (cf. Cressey and McDermott, 1973; Rutherford and McDermott, 1976):

> People of a labeling persuasion argue that, for the most part, diversion means "hands-off"—leaving children alone wherever possible (Schur, 1973:154–155).

> To others, diversion means just the opposite. It would involve the mobilization of greater, not fewer, programs in behalf of children, although legal processing would be excluded. To this group, such problems as running away, dropping out of school, or child prostitution cannot be ignored. Hence, diversion presents the opportunity to solve their problems without making them go to court.

> To still others, diversion is a means of freeing the juvenile justice system from petty, Mickey Mouse offenders so that the court can concentrate on controlling the "hustlers," the "punks," and the "muggers" who are the real threats to society.

> Finally, there are those who see diversion as a method of supervising and controlling the large numbers of juveniles who are now counseled and released by the police. Since a movement is afoot to decriminalize these kinds of troublemakers, diversion is an alternative means for keeping them under control.

Given these disparate interpretations of what diversion means, how widely has it been used, what forms has it taken, and what impact has it had?

1. *Extent of diversion.* First, let it be said that as a new "reform" diversion has not resulted in leaving kids alone, as labeling theorists have recommended. Rather, hundreds, if not thousands, of new programs have been set up to give juveniles even more, rather than less, "service." In California alone, there are between 150 and 200 diversion projects, some of them intensive programs where children are placed in full-time residential settings (Klein and Teilmann, 1976:1). Furthermore, a new association of professionals has developed—the California Association of Diversion and Youth Service Counselors. By 1975, in fact, they

had held their *third* annual conference (Klein, et al., 1976:111). In short, a whole new child-saving bureaucracy has developed (cf. Carter and Klein, 1976; Rutherford and McDermott, 1976).

2. *Control of diversion programs.*   Some of the new diversion programs are conceived and run by private agencies. Yet, despite the fact that diversion is supposed to be free from the control and influence of the justice system, the majority of these programs are either connected with, or run by, justice personnel (Klein and Teilmann, 1976; Baron, et al., 1973). The reasons are twofold: First, most referrals to diversion programs come from the police or the courts. Inevitably, therefore, the wishes of policemen and probation officers are important to the private agencies to whom referrals are made. Agencies that do not provide what officials require may no longer receive payments for the divertees referred to them. Secondly, many "diversion" programs are run by police or probation departments themselves. Rather than referring juveniles elsewhere, officials prefer to start their own "in-house" programs and to hire their own personnel (Klein, et al., 1976:104; Baron, et al., 1973). To the juvenile, therefore, "it must be clear that diversion has not meant 'escape' from the justice system" (Klein, et al., 1976:113).

3. *Program characteristics.*   According to the ideals of the reintegrative philosophy, diversion programs should be two-sided, just as delinquency is two-sided. One side should be concerned with changing offenders, while the other should be devoted to changing the opportunity structures of the community. Most programs, however, conform better to the rehabilitative than to the reintegrative model; that is, they are more concerned with changing offenders than with changing society. Consider some examples:

> The Alternative Routes Program received its referrals from the police, probation, schools, and other community agencies and sought to remedy their problems by short-term individual and group counseling (Carter and Gilbert, 1973).
>
> Youth in the Sacramento County 601 Diversion Project were referred by intake personnel in the juvenile court to a special unit of the probation department where they received family crisis therapy on a short-term basis (Baron, et al., 1973).
>
> The Pre-Trial Intervention and Diversion Project was designed to impart and to improve communication skills between parents and children (Binder, 1974).

A project conducted in a deprived, predominantly black area of a large eastern city concentrated on intensive counseling for youth and their parents (Elliott and Blanchard, 1975).

Finally, an exception to this pattern was Project Crossroads which provided employment services as well as counseling to first-time offenders (Lieberg, 1971).

These programs certainly conform to the notion that a short, helpful intervention is preferable to legal processing and supervision. In that sense, they may well be helpful. Yet, few of them have attempted to alter the way schools deal with their marginal children, to provide more work-study programs, or to mobilize support for a better integration of adult and youth roles. Hence, though they are located in the community, they have conformed more closely to the traditional treatment model of the juvenile court and of mental health agencies than to the heroic reintegrative model suggested by strain theorists.

4. *Reducing the official net.* No matter what means they use to change offenders, diversion programs are supposed to reduce the volume of cases being inserted into the juvenile justice system. In some ways, this is a large order to fill. It will be recalled that, for many years, the police have counseled and released about half of all the children they have taken into custody, to say nothing of those whom they have excused with a warning. Following that, intake personnel in the court release an additional number after lecturing them, warning them, or releasing them on "informal probation." As a result, only about one quarter of all children taken into custody are actually submitted to a formal trial. Diversion, in other words, is nothing new; we have just made a bigger thing of it today. Nonetheless, if "true" diversion is working, there should be a distinct reduction in the number of juveniles either referred to court or subjected to a formal hearing.

The available evidence suggests that reductions may not be taking place. In their study of two mammoth police departments—the Los Angeles City Police Department and the Los Angeles County Sheriff's Department—and of 35 smaller departments in surrounding cities, Klein and Teilmann (1976:1–14) found that the juveniles who were being referred to diversion programs were the younger, nonserious, nonrepeat offenders who in prior years would have been counseled and released anyway. Otherwise, the kinds and numbers of juveniles who were referred to court remained about the same. "If this pattern is continued," the authors note (p. 11), "it would suggest that 'true' diversion—turning offenders away from the justice system who would otherwise have been inserted into it—has been displaced by the provision of referral and treatment for offenders who otherwise would have simply been released." In short, the meaning of diversion has been shifted from diversion from the juvenile justice system to referral to some other agency (Klein and Teilmann, 1976:108).

5.   *Implications of the larger net.*   Diversion has apparently contributed to the development of a new system of social control for children and to a new bureaucracy to run it. With unbroken consistency, investigators suggest that this is the case (Blomberg, 1975; Graecen, 1975; Klein, et al., 1976; Kutchins and Kutchins, 1973; Mattingly and Katkin, 1975; Vorenberg and Vorenberg, 1973). These developments, of course, are greeted with mixed reactions.

To those who feel that our social services for discordant families, runaway youth, or unwed mothers are inadequate, they are welcome. Perhaps for the first time, help can be provided for children whom the juvenile court was unable to help. Other persons, however, worry about the coercive potential of the new system (Klein, et al., 1976:109; Nejelski, 1976). Assignment to a diversion program, as we have seen, does not mean that juveniles are now free from the controls of law enforcement authorities. Many of them attend diversion programs, not on a voluntary, but a conditional, basis. If they perform well and cooperate, they are told that no further legal action will be taken. But, if they are uncooperative, they can be returned for further processing (Lieberg, 1971; Klein, et al., 1976:112–114). Furthermore, assignment to a diversion program instead of court is not necessarily less stigmatizing, if people are worried about that. The child's undesirability is still made evident, and his or her social standing could suffer.

Given the coercive and stigmatizing potential of diversion, it is surprising that no legal challenges have yet been raised against it. It and other reforms were instituted because the juvenile court was accused of failing to insure constitutional protections for juveniles—advisement of their rights, the presence of defense counsel, a fair trial, and the right of appeal. Yet, few of these protections are available to children assigned involuntarily to diversion programs, despite the fact that they are only alleged, not convicted, offenders. It is entirely possible, therefore, that the constitutional rights of juveniles who are charged with crimes and referred to court will be better protected than those who are charged with less serious crimes and are diverted.

6. *Effectiveness of diversion.* It is to be hoped that diversion, with all its birth problems and limitations, will prove to be helpful reform. As yet, however, conclusive evidence is unavailable. In their examination of nine of the "better" evaluated programs, Gibbons and Blake (1976) found that while juveniles assigned to some diversionary projects had lower recidivism rates than those who were inserted into the juvenile justice system the same was not true of others. In one instance, Klein (1975) found that juveniles who had simply been counseled and released had lower official rearrest records than those who had either been assigned to a diversion program or referred to court. Yet, when he interviewed juveniles in all these groups, he found that their *self-reported* rates of delinquency did not differ; all were equally delinquent. His conclusion, therefore, was that it was not that the counseled and released group had actually committed fewer delinquent acts, only that the other juveniles, who had been diverted or legally processed, were more visible to the police and thus more likely to be picked up. Yet, even these results must be interpreted with caution because, like virtually all of the other studies, the findings were not based on the results of research in which experimental and control groups had been randomly selected or carefully matched before comparisons were made.

As a result, two conclusions by Cressey and McDermott (1973:59–60) summarize well the things we have learned about the actual practice of diversion:

1. The faddist nature of diversion has produced a proliferation of diversion units and programs without generating a close look at whether the juvenile subject to all this attention is receiving a better deal.

2. So far as we know, no one has shown that the juvenile offender and his family perceive their handling as materially different under the auspices of a diversion unit than under a more traditional justice agency. . . . For this reason, it seems crucial that in-depth qualitative and longitudinal studies be the first order of business for subsequent diversion research.

Due process

For over 60 years, juvenile court judges operated upon the assumption that honesty was good for the souls of children. Anything that discouraged them from making a clean breast of all their misdeeds could only defeat efforts to redeem them. The problem, however, was that children were not always aware of the consequences of making a confession and some judges took advantage of that fact. Consequently, the prescription today is for greater legal formality. The civil proceedings of the past should now take on the formal character of a criminal trial. Children charged with delinquent acts should have most of the rights afforded adults (Rubin, 1976:83). Furthermore, it is becoming steadily more apparent that parents, as well as children, will have the right of counsel to protect their rights in cases where they are charged with child neglect (Sutton, 1973). No longer will judges be empowered to remove children from their families in the absence of full due process procedures. Formality will rule where informality has operated for three quarters of a century.

But lest we assume that formality is somehow equitable with absolute "justice," or that it can magically unravel problems that would mystify Solomon, consider some of the issues that remain to be resolved:

1. *Assembly-line justice.* The juvenile court has already been accused of dispensing assembly-line justice, of expending too little time and attention on each case. But, if that is true of the juvenile court, it is no less true of adult criminal courts where formality is the rule. The reason is that due process procedures take more time, more personnel, and more resources than do informal procedures. As a result many criminal courts are characterized by a massive backlog of cases which take months, sometimes years, to resolve. If the juvenile court follows the lead of these courts, therefore, greater justice is by no means insured. Indeed, there is every chance that new forms of injustice will occur.

About 90 percent of all prosecutions in our criminal courts are now resolved by guilty pleas, many of them the result of plea bargaining, not adversary procedures and a careful analysis of the evidence (Lefcourt, 1971). For the most part, these guilty pleas are the result of the poverty and ignorance of accused persons. They cannot afford, or do not know about, the kinds of legal procedures that might be used in their behalf.

The same problems already are, or will be, characteristic of the juvenile court, unless a massive infusion of funds, facilities, and personnel are forthcoming. Constitutional safeguards depend heavily upon a family's capacity to hire expensive lawyers and other legal assistence. Poor parents and their children, however, usually must depend upon overworked and less skilled public defenders to handle their cases. In some jurisdictions, public defenders are not available while in others they may not even review the cases they are expected to try until a few minutes before they are to appear in court. As a result, the parents and children who can afford it least and often need it the most are the ones who do not have the means to guarantee that evidence in their behalf is capably presented and fairly judged.

2. *Treating offenses versus children.* Recent higher court decisions require that the evidence presented in court must be restricted to the offense alleged in the petition. Hence, the court is not permitted, as in the old days, to consider side issues that may prejudice the case against an offender or throw new light upon it. The child's offense, far more than his or her social conditions, is the focus of attention.

Justine Polier (1978), a former judge of the Family Court in New York, points out that this may have a paradoxical effect. For example, she cites a 1941 case in which a young girl was found guilty of a delinquent offense. However, the probation investigation revealed that the girl had been the subject of excessive abuse and neglect since the time of her mother's death. Consequently, the judge arbitrarily vacated the finding of delinquency and defined the girl as neglected. Such action today, says Judge Polier, could not be taken because any finding must be based solely on the offense presented in the petition. Due process procedures, in other words, may move us closer to a classical, than to an individualized, concept of justice.

Judge Polier (1978) also warns that today's emphasis upon due process is likely to throw the juvenile courts open to public exposure and to sensationalized reports by the media. Not only is this likely to label a child far worse than older practices ever did, but it threatens the independence of the judiciary. Since their reelections or reappointments may depend upon public support, their inclinations to treat criminal children in a way that is commensurate with their years is likely to be eroded. The net effect will be for the courts to submit to demands that criminals, no matter what their age, be treated more alike and perhaps more harshly.

3. *Due process and status offenders.* Status offenders present even more problems. On the one hand, the statutes of many states still prohibit such acts as "growing up in idleness or delinquency," "beyond the lawful control of parents," or "deportment endangering the morals, health, or general welfare of a child" (Rose, 1974). As a result, a few appeals courts have declared such laws unconstitutional. In *Gonzalez* v. *Maillard* (1971), a three-judge panel in California ruled that the phrase "in danger of leading an idle, dissolute, lewd, or immoral life" was too vague. "If the statute under which a juvenile is charged is so uncertain

and all-encompassing that the state need prove no specific crime . . ., defense counsel has little idea of what he must defend against." Due process cannot be insured.

On the other hand, the actual behaviors of some status offenders continue to present serious problems. As a result, most challenges to status offender laws *have not* been sustained by the higher courts (Paulsen and Whitebread, 1974). In a New York case, for example, an appeals court made the following ruling regarding a 13-year-old boy who would not go to school and who habitually stayed out until 2 or 3 A.M. against his parents' wishes:

> While the doctrine of *parens patriae* does not permit any unfairness in judicial procedure towards juveniles . . . [it is] this Court's opinion . . . that the State has the power to perform the parental role of insuring the child's education and training, when the parent is unable to control him sufficiently to perform it. If children were permitted the same freedom of choice as adults, they might well be unequipped when they attain adulthood to exercise *any* freedom of choice—specifically, without any education or training, they would be unable to choose to work in a job for which they in fact have the potential. Enforcement against the child of the compulsory school law appears still to be constitutional (Paulsen and Whitebread, 1974:46).

This case was relatively straight forward. Consider an additional one of the type which has convinced some judges that the juvenile court should continue to have jurisdiction over status offenders, despite due process questions. It involved a 15-year-old girl in Ohio (Paulsen and Whitebread, 1974:67). Technically, the girl was out of control of, and unresponsive to her, parents. But she was also unmarried and had just given birth to a baby. Thus, the court not only had a status offender on its hands but a potentially neglected or dependent infant. Furthermore, the court psychologist argued that the girl presented "a poor prognosis for successful self-management and even poorer prognosis for success as a mother."

How should due process operate in a case like this? What should the "offense" be? Should the court deal only with the charge that the girl was "beyond the control of her parents"? Or should it go further and define the new baby as "neglected" and take it from a mother who legally was still a child? Or should it define the baby as "dependent" and then attempt to supervise both the mother and baby? Or should the court have no jurisdiction at all in the case? And, if it had no jurisdiction, should the two children be ignored, or should some other agency make the necessary decisions—an agency from which there might be no legal appeal if the mother or her parents did not like its decision? In short, the matter of deciding what to do in cases like this does not readily lend itself either to formal procedures or to inaction. Neither will provide magical solutions.

4. *Spread of due process.* It is clear from the foregoing that formal procedures, as well as those that are informal, have their problems. As a consequence, the response of hundreds of juvenile courts to demands that they insure due process for children have not been swift and uniform. As we saw in Chapter 16, many of them have part-time, ill-trained judges who may not only be incompetent but who cling to the informal practices of the past. In such courts, the introduction of changes mandated by the Supreme Court has been slow indeed (Sosin and Sarri, 1976). Nonetheless, the handwriting is on the wall. Investigations have shown that conformity to the requirements of the *Gault* decision is growing (Ralston, 1971; Rubin, 1976); that lawyers are being seen more frequently in court (Reasons, 1970); and that many court personnel themselves support the introduction of due process standards (Franklin and Gibbons, 1973). Thus, it would seem to be only a matter of time until the old juvenile court is replaced by a court, or courts, where far more formality is the rule.

Deinstitutionalization

The fourth and final reform—*deinstitutionalization*—has been justified on three grounds: (1) the destructive impact of places of captivity on children; (2) the new reintegrative ideology which stresses the need for greater community tolerance and change; and (3) increased attention to the civil rights of children. The following statement by Senator Birch Bayh (1971) sums up these sentiments:

> Today, too many young people are thrown into custodial institutions who should be handled in the community. We want to find ways to establish meaningful alternatives to incarceration. . . . Punishment, isolation, neglect, and abuse seem to be the hallmarks of institutional life. This includes harassment, affront to human dignity, and the gross denial of human rights.

As Senator Bayh urges, therefore, deinstitutionalization has been widely advocated, not merely for status offenders but for serious criminal offenders as well.

1. *Deinstitutionalization for status offenders.*   The move to deinstitutionalize programs for status offenders has been supported by more than sentiment. The Juvenile Justice and Delinquency Prevention Act of 1974 requires that states receiving federal funds to support new community programs must agree to remove all status offenders from places of detention or incarceration within two years. Effective January 1, 1977, moreover, the laws of California were amended to conform to this provision of the federal law. Status offenders can no longer be confined in secure facilities of any type, either before or after a court hearing (California Welfare and Institutions Code, 1976).

2. *Types of status offender programs.*   Like diversionary programs, most alternatives to incarceration for status offenders conform more closely to the rehabilitative than to the ideal reintegrative model; that is, they stress diagnostic services, short-term crisis intervention, counseling, temporary placement in shelter care homes, or long-term placement in foster or group homes (National Institute for Juvenile Justice, 1977: 13–14). Except for efforts to improve family relations, therefore, relatively little attention is paid to changing the school, neighborhood, and community networks in which status offenders participate.

A possible exception is *Achievement Place*, a program for young "predelinquent" boys which has been applied in several communities in the Midwest (Phillips, 1968; Phillips, et al., 1971; Wolf, et al., 1974). Achievement Place is a family-style group home where, under the direction of a specially trained husband-and-wife team, five or six boys continue to participate in regular community schools and other youth activities as a part of the program strategy. In order to facilitate this participation, close relations are established with the boys' teachers, while the boys themselves are encouraged to do well in school, to develop their capacities for self-government, to change the behaviors that get them into trouble, and to cooperate in doing the necessary tasks of running a home and living together.

In order to induce these kinds of changes, the "parents" at Achievement Place, in cooperation with school personnel, have set up a "token economy" in which boys can earn or lose points which can be exchanged for conventional privileges: special advantages at home, going downtown to sports or other events, obtaining an allowance or acquiring savings that can be used to purchase special gifts. The point is that rewards or punishments are directly predicted on actual behavior. To the extent that a child acquires conventional skills and discards those that cause him difficulty, he receives direct and tangible rewards.

3. *Reactions to status offender programs.* The movement to deinstitutionalize programs for status offenders has met with both good and bad press. Most of the positive reactions have already been described: the idea that truants, runaways, and ungovernable children should not be treated like criminals, particularly the idea that they should not be locked up with "hard-core" delinquents in detention centers, adult jails, or training schools.

On the negative side, reactions usually have to do with the loss of institutionalization as a backup for parents, schools, and other community agencies. As one experienced and concerned probation administrator told this author: "We have given up trying to control status offenders. Since the threat of institutional placement no longer exists for them, there is nothing we or the court can do to, or for, them unless they will it."

A prime example is runaways who number in the hundreds of thousands. In order to control them, the courts, often at the request of parents, have customarily placed such children in detention pending a court hearing, particularly when they are picked up at night and have no place to stay. Under the new regulations, however, "secure" detention can no longer be used. As a consequence, many of the habitual runners simply run again. In a recent case, for example, a California judge tested the new state law which said he could no longer detain status offenders. When his appeal was rejected, the result was immediate: Twelve youngsters simply walked away from the "shelter" home to which they had been transferred (*Los Angeles Times,* May 7, 1977). A second example has to do with the schools:

> "This is war," says Jim Walsh, security director of George Washington High School in New York City, "and we need to keep every weapon in our defense arsenal. That means we have to be able to get the troublemakers out of school and into court fast when we need to. You know, it's the student who is unruly or disobedient today who'll mug you on the way out the door tomorrow" (*Los Angeles Times,* February 13, 1976).

A third issue has to do with the notion that status offenders should never be incarcerated, no matter what the quality of an institutional program might be. Policemen, judges, and probation officers are often confronted with the seamy side of juvenile life—13- and 14-year-old prostitutes, male and female, children on pills and alcohol, or youngsters who are defiant and uncontrollable at home and school. Since these children often come from homes where parents are cruel or uncaring and since they are unprepared to care for themselves, authorities do not always feel that incarceration is the worst of two possible worlds for them.

Indeed, the issues have been posed most clearly by Judge Margaret Driscoll, president of the National Council of Juvenile Court Judges, on the one hand, and Bob Smith, deputy director of the California Youth Authority, on the other. Judge Driscoll does not agree that status offenders should never be incarcerated and is even more critical of the idea that all their offenses should be decriminalized:

> If these children can't be brought to court, what on earth is going to happen to them? Are they seriously telling us that when all else has failed they are simply willing to leave 13- and 14-year-old girls out on the street to fend for themselves? (*Los Angeles Times*, February 12, 1976).

Mr. Smith, by contrast, argues that current changes are worth the risk:

> It is very harsh to say this and I know I am going to shock a lot of people, but in my mind, even these youngsters will be less damaged if left out on the street than if exposed to the downward spiral of our juvenile justice system. Unfortunately, history has shown that we too often have been the cause rather than the cure of juvenile crime. The answer is not to jail these kids but to provide more and better counseling agencies to which they can turn if they wish (*Los Angeles Times*, February 12, 1976).

Deinstitutionalization for criminal offenders

Paradoxically, programs of deinstitutionalization for criminal offenders, based on the reintegrative model, may have a longer history than those for status offenders. One of the first of these was the Provo Experiment which operated in Utah from 1960 to 1966 (Empey and Rabow, 1961; Empey and Erickson, 1972). It was designed deliberately for 15- to 18-year-old male offenders whose long records made them candidates for incarceration. Assumptions regarding the causes of their delinquency were derived largely from symbolic interactionist and strain theories:

> 1. that the greater part of delinquent behavior is not that of individuals engaging in highly secretive deviations, but is a group phenomenon—a shared deviation which is the product of a differential group experience in a particular subculture; and
>
> 2. that because most official delinquents tend to be the children of lower-class parents, their lives are characterized by learning situations which limit their access to success goals (Empey and Rabow, 1961:681).

Given these two assumptions, it was concluded that the success of any program would rest on its capacity to undo the ties of individual boys to their delinquent groups in the community and to provide legitimate alternatives to these delinquent ties. Hence, the program possessed three fundamental characteristics:

> The delinquents assigned to the program were permitted to continue living at home, although they were required by court order to attend the program daily. By allowing boys to remain in the community, their resistances to involvement in the program might not only be lessened by the conflicting loyalties and problems which they faced each day, but which would become the grist for the program mill. Real-life issues, rather than the artificial ones of an institution, would be those with which everyone would struggle.

> In order to analyze and to resolve these difficult issues, a daily group meeting was held in which the delinquent group itself became both the medium and the target of change. If delinquency was a group product, then means were required by which to change the adherence of delinquents to deviant group norms and to replace them with conventional values, beliefs, and rationalizations. Along with a single adult leader, therefore, two groups of ten boys each met five days a week to analyze the pros and cons of delinquency, to suggest solutions for their shared problems, to control further delinquent acts, and to make crucial decisions, including the decision as to when an individual was ready to be released from the program. Offenders, in short, were sponsored in an active reformation role. Any failures or successes would be those of the entire group, not just those of the group leader.

> Finally, the third program element was designed to open up conventional opportunities and experiences for the members of the groups. This was done by employing boys who were already school dropouts (about two thirds of them) in a city sponsored work program. Those who were still in school were encouraged to remain there but were employed on Saturdays, during the winter, and on weekdays during the summer.

A second experiment of this type—the Silverlake Experiment—was run in Los Angeles between 1964 and 1968 (Empey and Lubeck, 1971). Although this experiment operated on the same assumptions as the Provo Experiment, two basic changes were made in the program. Because Los Angeles was so large, boys could not continue living at home and yet attend daily meetings. Therefore, it was necessary to place them in a residential home located in a middle-class neighborhood where they lived during the week. (They could return home on weekends).

Secondly, experience in the Provo Experiment had indicated that decent jobs would be foreclosed to this population of boys unless they acquired more educational skills. As a result, negotiations were undertaken to permit them to attend the local high school, a task in which they were assisted by a tutor which the program provided. The daily group meetings, however, were held as before.

Even before the results of these and other experiments were known, however, the reintegrative ideology took root and was expressed in the recommendations of the various commissions about which we read earlier. The movement to deinstitutionalize correctional programs, therefore, was not based upon conclusive evidence that community programs would work any better. Instead, it was the product of the new reintegrative ideology.

1.   Closing juvenile institutions in Massachusetts.   The most striking result of the movement was the closing of all juvenile training schools in the state of Massachusetts. This was a radical step for Massachusetts because it had been the first state in the nation to open training schools—one for boys at Westboro in 1846 and one for girls at Lancaster in 1854 (Ohlin, et al., 1977:1). But, in 1972, after two years of "constant crisis, confrontation, and confusion," when he tried to reform these schools, Dr. Jerome Miller, the director of youth services in Massachusetts, decided to close them entirely (Ohlin, et al., 1977:4–12). Hereafter, all correctional programs would be located in the community. The new system would be as follows:

> It would involve the decentralization . . . of services into seven regions; the development of new court liaison staff . . . to coordinate detention, diagnostic, and referral policies . . .; a new network of community services including residential and nonresidential placements for individuals and small groups; and some centralized services for the institutional treatment of dangerous and disturbed offenders (Ohlin, et al., 1977:12–13).

Despite the radical step taken by Massachusetts, the development of community programs has been uneven throughout the country. In only a few states are there as many serious delinquents in new deinstitutionalized programs as in institutions (Vinter, et al., 1975:45–52). The reasons for this slow rate of change are several: traditional feelings that offenders should be punished, entrenched bureaucracies, political opposition, and fears for public safety. Hence, an important question is whether the evidence regarding the effectiveness of deinstitutionalized programs would warrant greater support for them. The evidence, pro and con, is as follows:

2. *Dangerousness to the community.* The public wants to be protected from young robbers, thieves, and muggers. One crucial question, therefore, is whether community programs reduce public protection while offenders are actually participating in them. At least when they are locked up, delinquents cannot harm others.

This question was carefully studied in the Provo Experiment (Empey and Erickson, 1972:73–94). Contrary to public fears, however, the evidence clearly indicated that boys in the community programs were significantly less delinquent *while they were under supervision* than were the members of a randomly selected group who had been placed on regular probation. Even more important, the experimental boys were no more delinquent than a matched group who were incarcerated in a state training school. Even though the latter were supposedly securely confined, they committed as much crime when they went home on short furloughs or when they escaped as the experimental group did while they remained free in the community. It should be noted, however, that the in-program rates for both groups were relatively low.

3. *Postprogram recidivism rates.* In the last chapter, we learned that few scientific studies have been able to show that one correctional approach is superior to another in terms of reducing postprogram recidivism rates after supervision is ended. The same is true of deinstitutionalization. The use of community programs for both status and criminal offenders has not increased postprogram recidivism rates, but it has not decreased them either (Ohlin, et al., 1977:55–79; Empey and Lubeck, 1971; Empey and Erickson, 1972; Wolf, et al. 1974). The best that can be said is that community programs do at least as well as training schools, but they are not superior as had been hoped.

4. *Humaneness.* Since community programs usually do at least as well as incarceration in controlling delinquency, it is often argued that they should receive preference because they are more humane. There are some additional grounds for this argument. One is that the length of stay for delinquents in many community programs is considerably shorter than it is for comparable groups who are incarcerated. At Silverlake, for example, the average stay was only half as long, 6 versus 13 months (Empey and Lubeck, 1971:309).

Even more to the point, a complex analysis in the Provo Experiment revealed that while the community program was not highly positive in its effects it was not destructive either. The opposite was true for incarceration; it made some boys more delinquent later on than they might have been otherwise. As a consequence, virtually all of the offenders in this study who eventually became serious adult felons were those who had been incarcerated, not those who had been left in the community. Within four years, the members of this group had committed murder, kidnap, rape, assault, robbery, and burglary (cf. Empey and Erickson, Chaps. 9 and 11). In the interest of community protection as well as offenders, therefore, community programming may be more humane.

5.   *Costs of programming.* Almost universally, community programs cost far less to operate than do institutional programs. Various studies indicate that the savings may be as much as 60 percent (Empey and Erickson, 1972:201; Empey and Lubeck, 1971:309; Ohlin, et al., 1977:30; Vinter, et al., 1975:45). At Silverlake, for example, a savings of $3 million could be realized for every 1,000 boys assigned to the community, rather than to the institutional, program. Hence, such findings suggest that without enlarging correctional budgets large sums could be freed for improving services and conducting better research if more community programs were used.

6.   *The negative side.* Deinstitutionalization also has its negative side. Despite the finding that community programs have not proven more dangerous overall than incarceration, there is still a small minority of offenders who continue to behave in a criminal way. Scull (1977:152–153), for example, maintains that such persons are likely to create "deviant ghettoes"—groups of offenders who join together to manipulate the system and to prey on others who are less powerful than they.

This is not an idle issue; one boy in the Provo Experiment showed up his first day carrying a pistol. Two others, along with an older convict, planned an attack on an opposing group using chains, brass knuckles, and a sawed-off shotgun (Empey and Erickson, 1972:68). In the Silverlake Experiment, a group of new boys joined together in their off-hours to prey on homosexuals, beating and robbing them after receiving pay to act as prostitutes for them (Empey and Lubeck, 1971:186–210). In all these instances, fortunately, serious acts were either prevented or brought to an end because of the courage of some prosocial offenders who brought them to light in the discussion groups. Nonetheless, prosocial offenders who take such actions are confronted with a cruel dilemma—a dilemma in which they might be losers no matter what they do. If they "rat" on other members of the group, they might be defined as "snitches" and either lose the respect of their peers or, worse still, be the objects of physical attack. But, if they do not discuss what is going on, their own desires to change might be frustrated. The program of which they are a part will come under the domination of hard-core delinquents, not those who want to behave legitimately.

As a result of problems like these, a group of adult ex-convicts, who are operating their own prevention and correctional program for juvenile gang members in Los Angeles, argue strenuously against any tendency to pretend that all delinquents are "good boys" at heart. It is their opinion that unless the small number of persistently deviant ones are sanctioned immediately a community program can easily become a "deviant ghetto." A small criminal minority will shoot dope, hide contraband, threaten others, and eventually will take control unless program leadership is vigilant. The implication, of course, is that the possibility of incarceration must be kept open for this criminal minority unless changes on their parts are forthcoming. If this minority could be identified in advance, the success of community programs might be improved, but, as yet, there is no scientific way for doing so.

By contrast, a second criticism of deinstitutionalization is that more community programs are simply widening the net of the new juvenile justice system. Based upon their national study of juvenile corrections, Vinter, et al. (1975:33, 77), maintain that the number of juveniles in training schools is not being greatly reduced. Instead, new community programs are simply being filled with juveniles who under ordinary circumstances would have been placed on probation or treated in some other way. Rather than emptying training schools, deinstitutionalization, like diversion, is being used to justify greater controls over a newer and larger group of youngsters, many of whom are petty offenders.

Finally, as we have seen, it is often difficult to distinguish "reintegrative" from "rehabilitative" treatment or "community" from "institutional" programs. This is due in part to the faddish nature of deinstitutionalization. Many delinquents are being placed into agencies which treated disturbed or "predelinquent" children heretofore and which are not doing any different now. The clientele has changed but the treatment practices have not. Similarly, many "community" programs involve full-time residence for youngsters in "group homes," "private shelters," or "ranches" in which they remain as isolated from family, friends, school, and neighborhood as if they were in a training school. Many new programs neither change community networks nor provide legitimate alternatives. They may be located in or near a community, but they are not a part of it.

In summary, the findings with respect to deinstitutionalization are much like those for decriminalization, due process, and diversion. Deinstitutionalization has been greeted with mixed attitudes; it may have widened the net of the juvenile justice system; and it has had mixed results. What conclusions, then, may be drawn about it and the other reforms of the reintegrative revolution?

Conclusions

The reintegrative revolution began on a buoyant note in the early 1960s. Based on strain theory, its early theme was a heroic one: the nation's strategy should be one of large-scale social change in the interest of delinquency prevention. But, as the movement progressed, American morale began to hurtle down a psychic slide. As it did so, a second reintegrative theme, based on labeling theory, began to emerge. This theme minimized such causes of delinquency as poverty and lack of opportunity and stressed the importance of leaving children alone. The nation's strategy should be one of judicious nonintervention and should concentrate on implementing four reforms: decriminalization, diversion, due process, and deinstitutionalization.

It was the second theme which tended to survive and to become the official ideology of the reintegrative movement. But this ideology notwithstanding, the revolution has not actually followed a policy of judicious nonintervention. The power of the juvenile court has been reduced somewhat; the application of due process will help to safeguard the rights of juveniles who are subjected to court proceedings; and community programs may be cheaper and more humane than incarceration. But the application of current reforms has not always meant less interference in the lives of children.

The goal of diversion was to reduce the number of juveniles being inserted into the juvenile justice system, but, rather than doing that, many diversion programs have become places of referral for offenders who otherwise would have been counseled and released. Meanwhile, others are being processed much as before. As a result, diversion has apparently contributed to the development of a new semilegal system of social control which is far from free from the influence of law enforcement and correctional, if not judicial, authorities.

The same may be true for deinstitutionalization. Juveniles who would have been treated informally or placed on probation in the past are now being referred to intensive community programs. Meanwhile, the number of offenders who are being institutionalized has not been greatly reduced, despite the likelihood that community programs are equally effective.

If these trends continue, the net effect will be to expand, rather than to contract, the number of juveniles who are subjected to the semilegal controls of new remedial programs. Although this development is contrary to the policy implications of labeling theory, many reformers are in favor of it. To them, it represents an opportunity to help many juveniles whom the juvenile court was unable to help in the past. Indeed, it may do that. But, if history is any criterion, optimism should be tempered with caution.

As yet, there is little evidence that the four *D*s have actually reduced delinquency rates. Little thought has been given to the constitutional rights of juveniles who are assigned to diversionary programs, despite the fact that they are only alleged, not convicted, offenders. And referral to a welfare or mental health program is not necessarily less stigmatizing than referral to the juvenile court.

Finally, and perhaps more important theoretically, is the fact that programs of diversion and deinstitutionalization seem to conform better to rehabilitative than to reintegrative ideals. A revolution which began by implying the need for a national youth policy designed to prevent delinquency has ended up by expanding the range of rehabilitative controls and services. Meanwhile, the schools, the neighborhoods, the peer networks, and the communities which socialize and shape children remain relatively unaffected.

These developments are ironic because the reintegrative revolution thus far is consistent neither with its original heroic goals nor with its later and more modest goal of leaving children alone. Instead, it is some nondescript combination of past and present, old and new. This outcome, however, should not surprise us. Our review of correctional history in the past two chapters has revealed that each so-called revolution—restraint and rehabilitation, as well as reintegration—is a long time in taking shape and inevitably becomes intertwined with older traditions and practices. Since such seems to be the nature of social evolution, it must always be remembered that any new reform, particularly in its early days, is better recognized by the ideals it proposes than by the actual practices that it disposes.

References

Baron, Robert; Feeney, Floyd; and Thornton, Warren
    1973   "Preventing delinquency through diversion: The Sacramento court 601 diversion project." *Federal Probation*, March, 37:13–18.

Bayh, Birch
    1971   Statement to U.S. Senate Committee on the Judiciary, Subcommittee to Investigate Juvenile Delinquency, 92d Congress, First Session, May 3–18.

Binder, Arnold
    1974   "Pretrial Intervention and Diversion," Project No. 1426 (mimeo).

Blomberg, T. G.
    1975   "Diversion: A Strategy of Family Control in the Juvenile Court Process." Tallahassee: School of Criminology, Florida State University (mimeo).

California Welfare and Institutions Code
    1976   Assembly Bill No. 3121. Chap. 1071:1–24.

Carter, Robert and Gilbert, John
    1973   *Alternate Routes: An Evaluation*. Sacramento: California Youth Authority.

Carter, Robert M. and Klein, Malcolm W.
    1976   *Back on the Street: The Diversion of Juvenile Offenders*. Englewood Cliffs, N.J.: Prentice-Hall.

Cressey, Donald R. and McDermott, Robert A.
    1973   *Diversion for the Juvenile Justice System*. National Assessment of Juvenile Corrections. Ann Arbor: University of Michigan.

Elliott, Delbert and Blanchard, Fletcher
    1975   "An impact study of two diversion projects." Paper presented at the Annual Meetings of the American Psychological Association. Chicago.

Empey, LaMar T. and Erickson, Maynard L.
    1972   *The Provo Experiment: Evaluating Community Control of Delinquency*. Lexington, Ky.: D.C. Heath.

Empey, LaMar T. and Lubeck, Steven
    1971   *The Silverlake Experiment: Testing Delinquecy Theory and Community Intervention.* Chicago: Aldine.

Empey, LaMar T. and Rabow, Jerome
    1961   "The Provo Experiment in delinquency rehabilitation." *American Sociological Review* 26 (October):679–695.

Franklin, Jerry and Gibbons, Don C.
    1973   "New directions for juvenile courts—probation officers' views." *Crime and Delinquency,* October, *19*:508–518.

In re Gault
    1967   387 U.S. 1, 18 L, Ed. 2nd 527, 87 S. Ct. 1428.

Gibbons, Don and Blake, Gerald F.
    1976   "Evaluating the impact of juvenile diversion programs." Paper presented at the Annual Meetings of the Pacific Sociological Association, San Diego.

Gonzalez v. Mailliard
    1971   Civ. No. 50424, N.D. Cal., 2/9/71. Appeal docketed, U.S. No. 70–120, 4/9/71.

Graecen, John M.
    1975   "Pitfalls and possibilities in juvenile justice reform." Paper presented at the National Conference on Juvenile Justice, Los Angeles.

Kent v. *United States.*
    1966   383 U.S. 541, 16 L. Ed. 2nd 84, 86S. Ct. 1045.

Klein, Malcolm W.
    1975   *Alternative Dispositions for Juvenile Offenders: An Assessment of the Juvenile Referral and Resource Development Program.* Social Science Development Program. Social Science Research Institute. Los Angeles: University of Southern California.

Klein, Malcolm W., et al.
    1976   "The explosion in police diversion programs." Pp. 101–120 in Malcolm W. Klein (Ed.), *The Juvenile Justice System.* Beverly Hills, Ca.: Sage Publications.

Klein, Malcolm W. and Teilmann, Kathie S.
    1976   *Pivotal Ingredients of Police Juvenile Diversion Programs.* Washington, D.C.: National Institute for Juvenile Justice and Delinquency Prevention.

Kutchins, H. and Kutchins, S.
    1973   "Pretrial diversionary programs: new expansion of law enforcement activity camouflaged as rehabilitation." Paper presented at the Annual Meetings of the Pacific Sociological Association, Hawaii.

Law Enforcement Assistance Administration
>   1974   Indexed legislative history of the "Juvenile Justice and Delinquency
>   Prevention Act of 1974." Washington, D.C.: Law Enforcement Assis-
>   tance Administration.

Lefcourt, Robert (Ed.)
>   1971   *Law against the People.* New York: Vintage Books.

Lemert, Edwin M.
>   1967   "The juvenile court—quest and realities." Pp. 91–106 in the Presi-
>   dent's Commission on Law Enforcement and Administration of Jus-
>   tice, *Task Force Report: Juvenile Delinquency and Youth Crime.* Wash-
>   ington, D.C.: U.S. Government Printing Office.
>
>   1970   *Social Action and Legal Change: Revolution within the Juvenile Court.*
>   Chicago: Aldine.

Levin, Mark M. and Sarri, Rosemary C.
>   1974   *Juvenile Delinquency: A Comparative Analysis of Legal Codes in the
>   United States.* University of Michigan: National Assessment of
>   Juvenile Corrections.

Lieberg, Leon
>   1971   *Project Crossroads: Final Report to the Manpower Administration, U.S.
>   Department of Labor.* Washington, D.C.: U.S. National Committee for
>   Children and Youth.

Mattingly, J. and Katkin, D.
>   1975   "The youth service bureau: a re-invented wheel?" Paper presented at
>   the Society for the Study of Social Problems, San Francisco.

National Advisory Commission on Criminal Justice Standards and Goals
>   1973a *A National Strategy to Reduce Crime.* Washington, D.C.: U.S. Gov-
>   ernment Printing Office.
>
>   1973b *Report on Courts.* Washington, D.C.: U.S. Government Printing
>   Office.

National Institute for Juvenile Justice and Delinquency Prevention
>   1977   *National Evaluation Design for the Deinstitutionalization of Status Of-
>   fender Programs.* Washington, D.C.: U.S. Government Printing
>   Office.

National Task Force to Develop Standards and Goals for Juvenile Justice and
Delinquency Prevention
>   1977   *Jurisdiction—Status Offenses.* Washington, D.C.: National Institute for
>   Juvenile Justice and Delinquency Prevention.

Nejelski, Paul
>   1976   "Diversion: the promise and the danger." *Crime and Delinquency,*
>   October, 22:393–410.

Ohlin, Lloyd E.; Miller, Alden D.; and Coates, Robert B.
1977 *Juvenile Correctional Reform in Massachusetts.* Washington D.C.: U.S. Government Printing Office.

Paulsen, Monrad G. and Whitebread, Charles H.
1974 *Juvenile Law and Procedure.* Reno: National Council of Juvenile Court Judges.

Phillips, Elery L.
1968 "Achievement Place: token reinforcement procedures in a home-style rehabilitation setting for 'predelinquent' boys." *Journal of Applied Behavior Analysis,* Fall, 1:213–223.

Phillips, Elery L., et al.
1971 "Achievement Place: the modification of the behaviors of predelinquent boys within a token economy." *Journal of Applied Behavior Analysis,* Spring, 4:45–59.

Polier, Justine Wise
1978 "Prescriptions for reform—doing what we set out to do?" in LaMar T. Empey (ed.), *Juvenile Justice: The Progressive Legacy and Current Reforms.* Charlottesville: University of Virginia Press.

President's Commission on Law Enforcement and Administration of Justice
1967a *The Challenge of Crime in a Free Society.* Washington, D.C.: U.S. Government Printing Office.

1967b *Juvenile Delinquency and Youth Crime.* Washington, D.C.: U.S. Government Printing Office.

Ralston, William H., Jr.
1971 "Intake: informal disposition or adversary proceeding?" *Crime and Delinquency,* April, 17:160–167.

Reasons, Charles E.
1970 "Gault: procedural change and substantive effect." *Crime and Delinquency,* April, 16:163–171.

Rose, Robert G.
1972 *Juvenile Statutes and Non-Criminal Delinquency: Apply the Void-for-Vagueness Doctrine.* Washington, D.C.: Office of Youth Development, HEW.

Rubin, Ted
1974 "Transferring responsibility for juvenile noncriminal misconduct from juvenile courts to nonauthoritarian community agencies." Phoenix: Arizona Conference on Delinquency Intervention (mimeo).

1976 *The Courts: Fulcrum of the Justice System.* Pacific Palisades: Goodyear Publishing.

Rutherford, Andrew and McDermott, Robert
    1976   Juvenile Diversion. Phase I Summary Report. Washington, D.C.: National Institute of Law Enforcement and Criminal Justice.

Schur, Edwin M.
    1973   *Radical Nonintervention: Rethinking the Delinquency Problem.* Englewood Cliffs, N.J.: Prentice-Hall.

Scull, Andrew
    1977   *Community Treatment and the Deviant—A Radical View.* Englewood Cliffs, N.J.: Prentice-Hall.

Sosin, Michael and Sarri, Rosemary
    1976   "Due process—reality or myth?" Pp. 176–206 in Rosemary Sarri and Yeheskel Hasenfeld (eds.), *Brought to Justice? Juveniles, the Courts, and the Law.* National Assessment of Juvenile Corrections. Ann Arbor: University of Michigan.

Sutton, Jean
    1973   *Parent's Right to Counsel in Dependency and Neglect Proceedings.* HEW Publication No. (OHD)—75–26037. Washington, D.C.: Department of Health, Education, and Welfare.

Vinter, Robert D.; Downs, George; and Hall, John
    1975   *Juvenile Corrections in the States; Residential Programs and Deinstitutionalization.* National Assessment of Juvenile Corrections. Ann Arbor: University of Michigan.

Vorenberg, Elizabeth W. and Vorenberg, James
    1973   "Early diversion from the criminal justice system: practice in search of a theory." Pp. 151–183 in Lloyd E. Ohlin (ed.), *Prisoners in America.* Englewood Cliffs, N.J.: Prentice-Hall.

Wolf, Montrose M.; Phillips, Elery; and Fixen, Dean L.
    1974   *Achievement Place: Phase II.* Department of Human Development. Manhattan, Kansas: University of Kansas.

19

CONCLUSIONS: CHILDHOOD, DELINQUENCY, AND THE FUTURE

Our review of recent history suggests that the current revolution in juvenile justice is part of a larger transitional phase in American life. Faith in prior beliefs and social arrangements has declined, and new alternatives are being sought. As a result, hope for the future is mixed: Optimists see the transition as the gateway to a better life; pessimists view it as a one-way street to disaster (Miller, 1973).

In light of these mixed feelings, it is important that we pay more than passing attention to the current revolution in juvenile justice. In what ways does it relate to other significant changes in the social order? Will it be any more effective in civilizing children than the prior revolutions about which we have already read: the revolution which led to the construction of houses of refuge and reformatories following the War of Independence or the revolution which contributed to the invention of the juvenile court a century later?

The current revolution can now be encapsulated into a list of familiar catchwords (the four Ds): decriminalization, diversion, due process, and deinstitutionalization. Efforts to implement these catchwords are not without opposition and certainly not without ambiguity, but the changes they symbolize, like other changes in American life, indicate a pervasive disillusionment with existing institutions and portend new ways for organizing the control and socialization of children.

563

This fact should give us pause. As David Rothman (1971:xiv–xv) has so cogently pointed out, there is a prevailing tendency to regard major societal innovations as "reforms"—as improvements over that which existed before. The reformatory, for example, was regarded as a humane improvement over prior methods of punishment and the juvenile court as an improvement over older methods of dealing with the problems of juveniles. Yet, it would be difficult to maintain, in the light of history, that either innovation was a pure and unmistakable step in the progress of humanity. To do so, Rothman suggests, would not only be bad logic but bad history.

If this is the case, how should today's innovations—the four Ds—be regarded? Are they progressive steps in the treatment of the young? Will they reduce delinquency? Let me paraphrase Rothman's answer (1971:xv): If we are to describe any or all of the four Ds as "reforms," we will be taking for granted precisely what should be the focus of investigation. Our innovations should be carefully scrutinized rather than accepted outright as improvements over existing practices. Otherwise, we will fall into the same trap as most of the reformers who have preceded us; namely, the tendency to equate change with effectiveness and to assume that good intentions are the same as helping children or protecting society.

There is no foolproof way for avoiding this trap, but we may be able to gain some useful insights by examining the following issues: (1) the relationship of current reforms in juvenile justice to other significant changes in the status of children; (2) the capacity of these reforms to take the place of the juvenile court in remedying such youth problems as truancy, incorrigibility, dependency, and neglect; (3) their ability to control youth crime; and (4) how adequate they seem to be as a strategy, not merely for undoing the effects of youth problems, but for civilizing youths in such a way that they are productive and creative citizens.

Changes in the status of children

As we began our study of childhood and delinquency, we discovered that in premodern times children were treated with indifference and were often exploited. With the discovery of "childhood," however, Western civilization became increasingly preoccupied with youth. During the past century, in particular, major bodies of knowledge and social institutions have been modified, and new ones erected, to take into account the assumption that children are qualitatively different from adults and must be carefully safeguarded. As a result, children have become both the most indulged and the most constrained segment of our society (Coleman, 1974:29). The "invention" of delinquency, the creation of the juvenile court, the drafting of child labor laws, legal requirements regulating the school-leaving age, pediatricians, child psychiatrists, and elementary and secondary school teachers are all a reflection of our modern construction of childhood. But, just as we are now changing our beliefs and practices with regard to juvenile justice so we are changing our beliefs and practices with regard to the treatment of children in general.

Children's rights

At the cutting edge is a small group of new, moralist reformers. Two of the most prominent, Richard Farson (1974) and John Holt (1974), would do away with childhood as we know it. Instead, they would enforce a new "Bill of Rights" for children. In addition to bringing about reforms in juvenile justice, they would permit youngsters *of all ages* to decide whether they wished to live with their parents, with someone else, or in state-run child care centers; to choose and to design their own educational programs, including the option not to attend school; to use alcohol or drugs and to experience sex with no more restrictions placed upon them than those placed upon adults; to obtain employment; to manage their own money; to own credit cards; to enter binding contracts; to vote; and to share completely in the political pro cess. In short, says Farson, "We are on the threshold of a new consciousness of children's rights, a dramatically new concept of childhood itself. The fundamental change will be a recognition of the child's right to live with the same guarantee of freedom that adults enjoy, the basic right being that of self determination" (*Los Angeles Times*, January 28, 1975).

As one might guess, Farson's conclusion has been greeted with disbelief and no little derision. "Can you imagine," asked James Dobson, a professor of pediatrics, "a 6-year-old girl driving her own car to an escrow office, where she and her preschool male friend would discuss the purchase of a new home over a martini or two?" (*Los Angeles Times*, October 18, 1975). Given our present beliefs, such an event would strain the imagination. Yet, changes have occurred during recent decades which would have strained the imaginations of our founding fathers or the childsavers who invented the juvenile court.

1. *Political suffrage.* Until 1920, adult women did not enjoy the right to vote, to say nothing of property less, dependent children. But, in 1944, Georgia lowered the voting age from 21 to 18. In 1955, President Eisenhower urged that Congress and the states pass a constitutional amendment establishing 18 as the voting age for the entire country. In 1960, the White House Conference on Children and Youth urged greater participation of the young in political affairs. Finally, in 1971, the 26th Amendment to the Constitution was ratified by the states granting full suffrage to young people 18 and older (Coleman, 1974:42).

2. *Free speech.* Children have customarily been denied the right to free speech because of their subordinate status and the belief that parents and principals know what is best for them. During the 1960s, however, a variety of higher court decisions supported their rights to freedom of speech.

In one case, where high school students were protesting the Vietnam War by wearing armbands, the Supreme Court held that children were "persons" under the Constitution, not mere chattel. Thus, their rights to express their opinions should not be constrained, except where those opinions might severely disrupt classwork or interfere with the rights of others (*Tinker* v. *Des Moines Independent School District,* 1969).

3. *The right to work.* Child labor legislation was originally written to protect children from exploitation in the sweatshops, the mines, and the factories of the 19th century. During the 20th century, even more restrictive legislation has had the effect of confining adolescents to low-paying, part-time or dead-end jobs without any career potential. In 1970, however, delegates to the White House Conference on Youth (1971), asserted that "earlier laws and conventions designed to 'protect' the weak (women and children) are increasingly viewed as constraints that must be cast aside." Other opponents to child labor legislation have voiced similar sentiments, suggesting that "protection from responsibility (in the guise of exclusions from the world of work and too-long exposure to the artificial atmosphere of the classroom) constitutes a deprivation of [children's] rights to participate in 'meaningful activity' " (Coleman, 1974:43).

Reacting to these criticisms, several states have relaxed the enforcement of mandatory schooling or have lowered the school-leaving age to 16. In the state of California, for example, 16-year-olds may leave high school by passing an "equivalency" test—an examination which, besides including some academic material, tests their ability to acquire a driver's license, to fill out a job application, to complete tax forms, and other practical tasks of this type. The assumption is that, if teenagers can read and can perform certain practical tasks at a minimal level, they should be liberated from public schooling, presumably to enter the job market.

4. *Sexual freedom.* Well into this century, children were expected to remain chaste and were warned about the sinful character of sexual license and the dangers of "masturbation insanity" (Skolnick, 1973:175). "The sexual secretions," it was said, "must be conserved, lest character and intellect be weakened or destroyed" (Hale, 1971:465). Today, by contrast, young people are besieged by the media with pictures, stories, and plays about the joys of sex and the rights of all people—young or old—to enjoy it without restraint. As Farson (1974) and Holt (1974) have suggested, children should have the right to conduct their sexual lives with no more restriction than adults.

This point of view is reinforced by the fact that today's youth reach physical maturity at a far earlier age than in generations past. For example, in 1900, boys did not reach their full growth until about age 23; now, they are fully mature at 17 and are capable of reproducing far earlier than that (Gillis, 1974:188). The same is true of girls. Formerly, they did not begin to menstruate until their late teens; now, they do so at a much younger age. Hence, ideological demands for greater sexual freedoms are reinforced by changing biological drives.

Finally, the Supreme Court has held that, as a matter of constitutional right, an unmarried, pregnant teenager has the option to decide whether to bear the child or to have it aborted. Neither parents nor boyfriend can veto her choice (*Los Angeles Times*, July 5, 1976). Such an option for a "child" would have been unthinkable a generation or two ago.

5. *Freedom without responsibility.* The protected, and increasingly affluent, status of middle- and upper-class youth has permitted them to enjoy an increasing number of freedoms which would have been unavailable to adults a few generations ago.

> Grand tours of foreign countries were once the exclusive prerogative of sons of noblemen; now a broad segment of middle-class youth enjoys foreign travel along with the ability to gratify its tastes in clothes, music, and a multitude of forms of entertainment. . . . Young people today are far more cosmopolitan in outlook than their predecessors (Coleman et al., 1974:128).

But this is not all. Freedoms previously associated with university age youth have been rapidly appropriated by adolescents in high school: handy vans, skiing vacations, or trips to Florida during Easter vacation. Furthermore, because of the anonymity of urban civilization, they have not had to account to their elders for their behavior. It is impossible to quarantine them from "evil" when both biological and social conditions render older methods of control obsolete.

In summary, then, the children's rights movement means that we are in a transitional phase in our beliefs about childhood. Reforms in juvenile justice are but the tip of an iceberg of much greater proportions. The "hands-off" ideology of the reintegrative movement and the four Ds are reflections of larger trends favoring greater freedoms for children and less interference in their lives by families, schools, and courts.

But this social movement is not the only rights movement of great significance, nor does it guarantee an idyllic existence for children in the future. Instead, children are in competition with other important segments of the population for scarce jobs, resources, and opportunities.

Changing population structure

This competition can be illustrated by paying attention to the changing population structure of society. Throughout the entire history of civilization, societies have been predominantly young. In the late 17th century, the average life expectancy at birth was 32 years in England, and about 27.5 years in Germany (Gillis, 1974:10). This meant that the ratio of young to old people was extremely high:

> It has been estimated that, in the English village of Stoke-on-Trent in 1701, 49 percent of the population were under 20 years of age. In Sweden in 1750 the ratio of those persons aged 15–29 years to every 100 persons aged 30 years and over was 63 percent. In France in 1776 the ratio was 65 percent; and as late as 1840 it was approximately 77 percent in England (Gillis, 1974:11).

In the United States, in 1900, the ratio of young people ages 14–24 to the population aged 25–64 was still about 52 percent. But, by 1970, it had declined to 45 percent, and by 1990 it will go down further to about 33 percent (Coleman et al., 1974:47).

The reasons are twofold: (1) a decline in the birth rate and (2) an increase in life expectancy. Since 1957, the fertility rate has dropped from a peak of 3.76 children per woman to a record low of 1.75 in 1976.

The United States may well be on its way to the goal of zero population growth (*Time*, February 28, 1977). Meanwhile, average life expectancy at birth has increased to about 68 years for men and 72 years for women.

The obvious consequence of both of these trends is a striking change in the population pyramid: Whereas it used to be exceedingly heavy with young people at the bottom, it is now growing heavier at the top with older people. For example, the growth in population from 1950 to 1970 was lowest for people under 45, 30.5 percent. By contrast, the population of people over 65 increased by 63 percent. Even more striking was the growth in the number of people over 75, 97 percent—from 3.9 million in 1950 to 7.6 million in 1970 (U.S. Department of Commerce, 1971). What, then, are some of the implications of these remarkable trends?

1. *The rights of the elderly.*   One obvious implication has to do with the character of a society whose population is growing progressively older. Current trends may hasten a decline in our protective stance toward the young and focus it, instead, on older populations. "By the year 2020 there will be almost twice as many people over 65 (43 million) as there are today, exerting immense new pressures on the Social Security, pension, and Medicare systems" (*Time*, February 28, 1977). Amitai Etzioni, a sociologist, says that "this means a less innovative society in which fewer people will have to attend, care, feed, house, and pay for a larger number" (*Time*, February 28, 1977). Children may enjoy the right to work, to enjoy sex, and to vote at young ages, but they may also be saddled with a great many more responsibilities. Ever larger numbers of older people will have to be supported by a proportionately smaller and youthful segment of the population.

Charles Westoff, a demographer, does not agree with Etzioni. He believes that a better life is in store for everyone, even if our population is growing older. "Zero population growth," he says, "will reduce pressures on the environment and resources. It will probably increase per capita income. It will reduce pressure on governmental services. And it will give society an opportunity to invest more in the quality rather than the quantity of life" (*Time*, February 28, 1977).

If Westoff is correct, it may well be that, a generation or two from now, lesser numbers of children will be highly treasured, and creative opportunities for them will be unprecedented. But what about the more immediate future? It may hold less promise. Consider the right to work. Because of the changing population pyramid, young people are in direct competition with the elderly for a scarce number of jobs. Fourteen states have already passed laws limiting the right of employers to force mandatory retirement on employees over age 65. By 1978, it appears that the Congress of the United States will have passed a similar law to cover the entire country. Indeed, the House of Representatives passed it, in 1977, by a whopping 359 votes to 4 (*Time*, October 10, 1977). As a result, jobs that might have gone to a growing number of teenage school-leavers may be held by the elderly instead.

2. *The rights of adult women.* In a similar way, the growing employment of adult women also places them in competition with the young. Between 1960 and 1974, the number of female workers rose by 50 percent, while that for males rose by only 17 percent. Thus, while the number of working women was less than one half the number of working men in 1960, it was nearly two thirds as great by 1974. Furthermore, virtually all of this increase occurred among married women, not among single teenagers (Carter and Glick, 1976:424).

The rise in employment among adult women, like the potential rise among the elderly, is obviously a serious obstacle to the fulfillment of the right to work for children. In 1933, when unemployment was high, a spokesman for the National Child Labor Committee declared that the employment of children had become an economic menace. "Children should be in school and adults should have whatever worthwhile jobs there are" (Coleman et al., 1974:35). Child advocates, notwithstanding, the same sentiment tends to prevail today. In a highly competitive job market, the preference is for supplying adults with jobs, not children. They rank at the bottom of the political and economic ladder.

As a result, almost half of the nation's unemployed in 1976 were between the ages of 16 and 24—3.5 million of them (National League of Cities, 1977:1). Economists are concerned that 17.5 percent of America's high school and college graduates cannot find a job (*Time*, October 10, 1977). But if unemployment is a problem for this group, consider the problems of the lesser educated school dropout or early school-leaver. Estimated unemployment rates for adolescents, in general, run anywhere from 20 to 40 percent, but for black teenagers in urban areas they may be as high as 60 percent (National League of Cities, 1977). "A generation of young people is moving into its 20s—the family forming years—without knowing how to work, since many have never held jobs" (*Time*, August 29, 1977).

What all of this means is that the movement to grant greater freedoms to children is not yet matched by a set of institutional arrangements by which rights can become a reality, particularly for those whose economic and social status is the lowest. The notion that children's rights should be equal with those of adults is relatively empty unless it is congruent with means by which they can become self-sufficient. "As yet, however, youth's right to work is much farther from realization than the child's right to protection against certain kinds of work at too early an age" (Coleman et al., 1974:40).

3.   *Desirability of children.*   It may be that in the present competition for individual liberties, children will become less desirable. Indeed, feelings of ambivalence are not new. For the past two centuries, adults have viewed them as fragile and in need of protection, on the one hand, but trying and bothersome, on the other. However, as they compete more and more with adults for scarce rights and resources, this ambivalence may well increase. Indeed, the declining birth rates mentioned earlier seem to imply that such is the case. First, the cost of raising children becomes increasingly onerous: "Inflation," says *Time* magazine (February 28, 1977), "has already made the cost of rearing a large family (now estimated at more than $250,000 for four children from cradle through college) all but prohibitive." This cost competes continually with adult desires for travel, a new house, or expensive hobbies.

Second, children now interfere not only with the professional aspirations of the father but those of the mother. As Judith Blake Davis, a demographer, puts it, "You won't find those sacrificial mothers any more" (*Time,* February 28, 1977). Women, as well as men, want to forge their own destinies, and children can be distinct hindrances to doing so. For example, abortion has become as commonplace today as infanticide and abandonment were in the Middle Ages. In some ways, history may be repeating itself. Furthermore, the issue has already been decided on legal grounds: The Supreme Court has ruled that a woman has the constitutional right to decide whether she shall bear a child. Neither the wishes of the father nor anyone else may supercede hers.

The moral issues, however, still provoke controversy—that is, whether abortion involves the killing of human beings and whether a clear line can be drawn between babies and fetuses. On the one hand, Karen DeCrow, president of the National Organization of Women, and leader of its radical wing, says, "Yes, we mean that we want abortion up to the ninth month" (*Los Angeles Times,* February 9, 1976). On the other hand, Right to Life advocates argue that aborting babies is murder, particularly those who are in the last half of the gestation period. As a result, the moral dilemmas that face us today are not unlike those that faced people in the 16th and 17th centuries when reformers sought to have infanticide and abandonment made illegal.

Those who favor abortion argue that its use will insure that only those children will be born whose parents really want them. Hence, they will be better off. Yet, this argument rings hollow in light of the fact that both the federal and most state legislatures have refused to provide public assistance to indigent mothers who want an abortion but cannot afford one. In other words, prejudice and economic considerations override the wishes of poor mothers and the welfare of their offspring. Thus, if the argument is valid that abortion is justified on the grounds that no child should be born who is not wanted, then society is doing an injustice to children who are born to parents who neither want them nor can afford to care for them. Indeed, such parents often abandon their children, psychologically if not literally.

It may be that contraception, instead of abortion, will eventually solve the problem for poor, as well as affluent, women. But that possibility aside, two trends already seem to be underway. First, we seem to be witnessing significant changes in the nature of family life. Some individual rights are being gained at the expense of interactional relationships and of family unions of long duration. Rates of divorce and single parenthood are at unprecedented proportions (Carter and Glick, 1976:392–394). One cannot "do one's own thing" without some reduction in one's capacity to sacrifice in the interests of others.

Second, these trends will be felt most keenly by people at the bottom of the economic heap. Without the economic resources to "do their own thing," and yet to provide care for their offspring, poor and minority parents are likely to have children who will suffer the most. Already, in fact, there is evidence that such is occurring:

> Over one third of all black children and 1 in 14 of all white children live in single-parent families. Over 2 million children live in single-parent (usually father absent) households, almost *double* the number of ten years ago. In 1950, 18 percent of black families were female-headed; in 1969 the proportion had risen to 27 percent; by 1973 it exceeded 35 percent. The average income for a single-parent family with children under six years of age was, in 1970, only $3,100, well below the official "poverty line" (Cf. Bronfenbrenner, 1974; Monahan, 1957; as cited by Wilson, 1975:231).

Since it is among these families where rates of school failure, venereal disease, unwanted teenage pregnancies, criminal victimization, and child abuse are the highest, it is obvious that there are glaring contradictions between the rhetoric of the children's rights movement and actual reality. Many problems remain. A basic question, therefore, is whether current reforms in juvenile justice will help to remedy them. Since the power of the juvenile court over status offenses and cases of dependency and neglect have been reduced, will decriminalization, diversion, due process, and deinstitutionalization serve as adequate substitutes?

Remedying youth problems

The opposing arguments with respect to this question are best understood in terms of two contrasting concepts of childhood, and the assumptions upon which they are based. When the juvenile court was invented, it was assumed: (1) that children are qualitatively different from adults; (2) that legal intervention in their lives is justified because of their dependent and protected status; and (3) that the goal of intervention is rehabilitation, not punishment. Based on these assumptions, therefore, children's rights were defined in terms of protecting them from parental neglect and abuse, immorality, excessive and dangerous work, and insuring that they attended school in order to prepare themselves for adulthood (Coleman et al., 1974:29–34).

Today, by contrast, we have not only grown disillusioned with our child-saving institutions but our concept of childhood is changing. More and more our assumptions about children take the following form: (1) that they are not qualitatively different from adults, at least not so much as we thought; (2) that their right to self-determination should prevent legal interference into their lives for behavior which, if exhibited by adults, would not be considered illegal; and (3) that children should be granted all the constitutional protections afforded adults, including the protection of their rights against parents, the school, or the legal system itself. The notion seems to be declining that children should be both protected and suppressed because they are socially and psychologically immature.

Although these newer assumptions are most evident in our treatment of teenagers, they are not accepted universally. Instead, we are in a transitional phase where conflicts are created between old and new beliefs. As a result, the arguments for and against the four Ds reflect this conflict. Indeed, whenever change occurs, some old problems may be eliminated, but new ones will present themselves. This case is no different; some obvious dilemmas are emerging.

Decriminalization

Decriminalization is clearly a reflection of the growing belief that children are less different from adults than previously thought, and that the legal system should be prohibited from censoring their moral conduct or challenging their right to leave school at an earlier age. But Herman and Julia Schwendinger (1978), who are radical theorists, argue that, while decriminalization may reduce the harrassment of working-class children by the police, it might also do lasting harm to them. Working-class families already have a difficult time controlling their children in the face of the poor public schools, meager family resources, and the attraction of neighborhood gangs. Hence, if decriminalization is combined with new laws granting children the right to leave school at an early age, it would simply be another example of benign neglect, justified by high-flown, but class-biased, principles. The chances of working-class children for integration into the opportunity structures of society would become even worse. Until equal opportunities are available to all, working-class, if not well-to-do, parents need the juvenile court as a back-up institution. Without it, their children will become even more disadvantaged.

A related problem is cited by former family court justice, Justine Wise Polier (1978)—a problem with which every police officer, judge, and correctional worker is familiar; namely, that such terms as "incorrigibility" or "ungovernability" usually cover a multitude of problems, as well as "sins." Desperate parents often come to officials asking for help, not only because their children are truant, stay out late, and get drunk but because they are drug users, gang members, or thieves. But, because these children are referred to officials by their parents, they have usually been defined legally as status offenders. If, however, all status offenses were decriminalized, officials could not take action, parental wishes notwithstanding. Lacking proof of criminal behavior, officials could not prefer charges against the children in question, and parental requests for help would have to be ignored.

The same sorts of dilemmas are associated with the runaway problem. In 1976 there were from 519,000 to 613,000 runaway children (*ORC Newsletter*, 1976). Concerned parents often implore officials for help in locating and controlling these children. But, to the degree that runaway behavior is decriminalized, officials lose their power to sustain these requests, at least by coercive means. In states like California, for example, it is illegal to detain runaways unless they have committed a crime.

They may be taken to "shelter" homes to get them off the streets, but unless they freely choose to remain, they cannot be forced to do so. When all these problems are added up, therefore, it is clear that while decriminalization helps to resolve some dilemmas, it creates others. Indeed, it is inherent in the libertarian concept of freedom that, if children are like adults, they should be free to do all the harm to themselves they want, so long as they do not injure others.

Diversion

Perhaps because of the dilemmas created by decriminalization, the practice of diversion represents an uneasy compromise between the older controls of the juvenile court and total freedom for children from moral constraints. We are disillusioned with the old but leery of the new. Hence, by providing community alternatives to court referral for status offenders and petty criminals, diversion is supposed to provide remedies without infringing excessively on the rights of children. But, like decriminalization, diversion creates some dilemmas of its own.

The most salient has to do with the enthusiastic acceptance and widespread application of diversion. Although its ostensible purpose was to reduce the number of juveniles being inserted into the juvenile justice system, it has apparently not done that (Cf. Chapter 18). Rather, it has produced a new semilegal, semiwelfare bureaucracy which has extended the net of social control and is collecting children who would otherwise have been warned and released. Thus, while diversion in the form of counseling, family therapy, and crisis intervention may be help ful to this new clientele, what about their legal rights? What about the juveniles who are still being referred to court? The evidence suggests that about as many are being processed as before.

Not only are these outcomes opposite to the injunction of labeling theorists "to leave children alone whenever possible" (Schur, 1973), but they are criticized as perpetuating many of the problems they were supposed to correct:

1. Children who are diverted to the new correctional bureaucracy do not have the same recourse to legal appeal and review that they would if they were referred to court.

2. History has come full circle: Whereas the juvenile court was invented to decriminalize all children, we have now returned to the practice of dividing them into two groups. Divertees are labeled as "good"

kids, while those who are sent to court are labeled as "bad." Thus, in seeking to decriminalize one group, we are recriminalizing another (Polier, 1978).

3. Diversion programs reflect this division because they prefer working with the "good" kids, not the "bad" ones. One national survey revealed that only 25 percent of the juveniles accepted by Youth Service Bureaus were in jeopardy of being sent to court anyway (Nejelski, 1976).

Radical theorists argue that these outcomes are but further examples of discrimination by a class-conscious society (Schwendinger and Schwendinger, 1978). Diversion programs have expanded rapidly, not because they are designed to improve the rights of working-class children but because they are adaptable to middle-class needs. The kinds of "diversion" programs which working-class children need are those which would provide a minimum family income, improve slum schools, and create jobs for working-class teenagers (Scull, 1977). Without them, these children will gain little and will continue to populate our courts and correctional institutions.

Indeed, this interpretation does point to a striking irony. The ideologies of both the children's rights movement and the reintegrative revolution suggest that the most important need for marginal children is assimilation into social institutions where conventional opportunities are available. Most diversionary programs, however, are more rehabilitative than reintegrative in character; that is, they concentrate far more upon traditional forms of counseling and therapy than upon combining these with changes in educational, political, and employment structures. As a result, Arthur Pearl argues that diversion programs will be losers unless they divert marginal youth to places of opportunity where they are able to function as participating and honored members of society (As quoted by Galvin et al., 1977). Without this opportunity, the battle in behalf of youth will not be won. Instead, age, class, and racial barriers will persist, and the rights of other groups will take precedence.

Due process

There is no belief in Anglo-American jurisprudence which has greater support than the belief that the rights of all litigants in a case should be protected by due process procedures. It should not be surprising, therefore, that this principle should now be extended to children. Indeed, the lack of due process in the juvenile court has not only done injustice to children but to their parents. That is why efforts are now being made to insure that the constitutional rights of both are protected. Yet, even this reform poses dilemmas.

On the one hand, various appeals courts have ruled that litigants must always have their day in court. For example, if parents are charged with child abuse or neglect, they have the right to know the sources of the charges against them, what those charges contain, and to hire a lawyer to present their cases. Such is only fair (Cf. Browne, 1973).

On the other hand, the formalities of due process—raised benches, judicial robes, codified procedures, and the presence of lawyers—do not always guarantee better solutions to youth problems (Polier, 1978). For example, consider the requirement that the issues in any case must be restricted to the charges that are alleged in a petition, and no others. Suppose that the petition accused a young girl of habitually staying out late and "being in danger of lewd conduct"—a coverup for prostitution. Yet, the girl may have gotten into trouble because her parents were rarely at home, abused her, and did not care what she did. In other words there might be as many grounds for charging the parents with neglect as with charging the child for being a status offender.

In the past, judges were expected and permitted to explore this possibility by examining the total circumstances of the family. Now, if that exploration goes beyond the charge and might reflect negatively upon the parents, it could be suppressed by the parents' lawyer. The focus today is upon proving the charge alleged in the petition, not upon exploring the social and psychological factors associated with it. Hence, the requirements of due process may rule out important information to which an informal juvenile court had access in the past.

A related problem has to do with instances in which parents are charged with neglect or child abuse. Sometimes the abuse might be physical; sometimes it might be psychological. But because psychological harm is so difficult to prove, the court is restricted more and more to cases in which the child has been battered, burned, or malnourished. The court is less able to give attention "to the erosive destruction wreaked upon children by continuing emotional injury or deprivation" (Polier, 1978). Furthermore, efforts to prove such injury are weakened by the disrepute into which psychiatric testimony and the medical model of the juvenile court have fallen. In short, the rights of parents in a case like this may have been gained at the expense of the child's.

In other cases, by contrast, dilemmas are posed when the newly found rights of children take precedence over those of their parents. In a recent case, Cynthia, a 15-year-old, initiated a petition claiming that she was "incorrigible" and should be placed in a foster home in order to avoid her parents' restrictions on her smoking, dating, and other activities. Although the juvenile court found that Cynthia's parents were fit to raise her, it ruled in her favor and placed her in a foster home. Furthermore, this decision was upheld by the Supreme Court of the state in which Cynthia lived (*Brigham Young University Law Review*, 1976). Hence, both courts apparently agreed with those child advocates who believe that children should have the right to live where they want and to be free of parental restrictions on their moral behaviors.

Deinstitutionalization

Like due process, deinstitutionalization is another reform which has been widely endorsed, at least for neglected children and status offenders, if not juvenile criminals. Indeed, the Juvenile Justice Prevention Act of 1974 requires that states cannot receive federal funds for the former groups unless programs for them are completely deinstitutionalized within a two-year period. The handwriting is on the wall.

Perhaps the most debatable aspect of this reform is its all-or-none character. By defining all "institutions" as bad, it condemns without distinction such diverse places as adult jails, archaic training schools, and huge prison-like edifices, on the one hand, and small public or private institutions and clinical treatment centers, on the other. Obviously, there are great differences among these types of "institutions." What is needed, therefore, are two things: (1) a clearer definition of the term "deinstitutionalization," and (2) an evaluation of any program to make sure that it serves important functions, whether it is residential or not. The goal of "deinstitutionalization" is to rid juvenile programs of social isolation, personal degradation, stultifying routines, and severe punishments, not to rid them of helpful services for children.

As programs are deinstitutionalized, one goal would be to avoid what Polier (1978) calls the "turnstyle" child—the child for whom a return to the community is ordered without that child having a suitable place to live. Some status offenders and neglected children are mentally ill, mentally retarded, or severely lacking in interpersonal and educational skills. All too often, they are persons who are difficult to place and difficult to help. Hence, if adequate provision is not made for them, they may be dumped from one foster or group home to another or returned to unfit family settings.

With respect to this issue, a recent national study of the educational levels of neglected children in state institutions revealed some striking disabilities (Bartell et al., 1977:38–40). Although 81 percent of these children were between the ages of 14 and 17, and presumably getting ready to enter the job market, only 7 percent could read at an eighth-grade level or higher. By contrast, one out of five could read no better than a second-grade child, and 80 percent no better than a fifth grader. And, since their abilities to do math were even lower, it was obvious that, without help, they could not become productive citizens.

Such findings do not justify keeping juveniles in institutions. Yet, the movement to provide alternatives has done little to increase the capacity and willingness of the schools and other socializing institutions to solve the problems of the educationally or culturally disadvantaged. Instead, a vacuum has been created in which deinstitutionalized children have neither the limited resources of the training school nor realistic community alternatives. As a result, this is one more instance in which the ideology of reform does not square with reality. It does little good to "deinstitutionalize" programs if children are left worse off than before.

Summary

Current reforms have reduced the power of the juvenile court over the status problems of juveniles and have led to the creation of a new, loosely constructed system of community programs to deal with children. This system may have solved some problems, but it has created others. Judge James W. Byers, president of the National Council of Juvenile Court Judges, argues that one of the greatest of these is the danger that overall responsibility for the protection of children will no longer be located in any single legal body (Byers, as quoted by Galvin et al., 1977:12).

> The "dream that social agencies will appear out of nowhere to provide for a 13-year-old child who is without food, clothing, or care because he has run away or because he cannot function in his home, or is truant from school . . . is an unrealistic view. There must be some place where the responsibility is fixed. . . .

Because of the need for such a place, Judge Byers argues that status offenders should be kept under the outer edge of the umbrella of the juvenile court. Even though they would appear in court only on rare occasions, overall responsibility for their welfare should remain there.

The Juvenile Justice and Delinquency Prevention Task Force of the National Advisory Commission on Criminal Justice Standards and Goals recently made a different proposal (LEAA Newsletter, 1977:1). It has proposed that a new Family Court be created and given jurisdiction over "families with service needs." This new court could deal with a child, its parents, and public institutions as well. A school, for example, could be ordered to provide remedial reading for a child. In short, the new family court would be empowered to deal, not only with the child and its family, but with the whole social context that affects both. But whether this model, or the older juvenile court model, is followed, it appears that sentiments still prevail for locating legal responsibility for the status problems of juveniles somewhere. While these problems will not be defined as delinquent, they will still be the object of legal attention.

Controlling juvenile crime

When the juvenile court was created, all children, criminal or otherwise, were to be treated the same. Our discussion of status offenders and neglected children, however, has revealed an increasing tendency to separate these children from those charged with crimes and to treat them in different ways. This has led to a bitter conflict over the future status of juvenile criminals.

On the one side is the crusading ideology upon which current reforms are based. This ideology, it will be recalled, suggests that the juvenile justice system rather than helping delinquents has made them more criminal (Cf. Miller, 1973:456).

1. *Overcriminalization.* No act is inherently delinquent. Instead, crime is created by moral entrepreneurs who, in legislating their own brand of morality, protect their own favored positions in society.

2. *Labeling and stigmatization.* The stigma of legal processing criminalizes misbehaving children and leads to secondary deviance—criminal careers based upon the adoption of a deviant identity.

3. *Overinstitutionalization.* Juveniles have been warehoused in adult jails, detention centers, and training schools which are nothing more than schools for crime.

4. *Overcentralization.* Too much power has been lodged in police, courts, and correction agencies. The solution is decentralization, community programs, and community control.

5. *Discriminatory bias.* Juveniles are often labeled as criminal more because of their age, sex, class level, and demeanor than because of the acts they have committed.

As we have seen, this set of crusading issues has contributed to significant changes in the treatment of juveniles: A marked increase in diversion programs for petty criminals, greater attention to the constitutional rights of those charged with crimes, experimental community programs for serious offenders, and the closing of training schools in Massachusetts. Furthermore, scientific studies have revealed that community programs for serious delinquents are apparently as effective in controlling recidivism as are training schools, that they usually operate at much less cost, and that they are probably more humane. But the persistence of high rates of youth crime has divided public opinion and promoted opposition to current reforms.

Youth crime

Most Americans are now well aware of the fact that traditional forms of crime are very much a youthful phenomenon, that delinquency hits its peak at about age 16 or 17, and declines thereafter. Furthermore, they are besieged with reports that rates of arrest among juveniles have gone up steadily for the past 15 years—the very years when current reforms were being instituted; that law violations among girls have been increasing at a striking rate; and that violent crimes, which used to be confined largely to older populations, are being committed at an increasing rate by the young. Assaults, rape, and murder, as well as property crimes, are moving down the ladder of age (Cf. Chapters 6–8).

Most citizens are also convinced that these rising crime rates have eroded the quality of American life (Hindelang, 1975). They are increasingly fearful because few segments of our population have been spared:

1. *Children.* The average person may not know that children are the most victimized segment of the population, but they are aware that many schools have become battlegrounds. A survey of U.S. school districts by the U.S. Senate Subcommittee on Delinquency (1977:9) revealed the following increases in school-related crimes, between 1970 and 1973:

Homicide 18.5%
Rape 40.1
Robbery 36.7
Assault on teachers 77.4
Assault on students 85.3
Burglary and larceny 11.8
Weapons seized 54.4
Drugs and alcohol 37.5

"Ten years ago," said Dr. Owen Kiernan, executive secretary of the National Association of Secondary School Principals, "violence and vandalism were remote problems. Occasionally, we would have a so-called blackboard jungle school, but this was quite unique. This is no longer the case" (U.S. Senate Subcommittee on Delinquency, 1977:7). "The past few years," agreed a teacher, "have seen violence and vandalism become an almost daily occurrence. . . . Students and school personnel have become numbed by these acts; a subdued anger, frustration, and acquiescence seem to pervade the system" (U.S. Senate Subcommittee on Delinquency, 1977:8).

2. The elderly. Most Americans hear a great deal about attacks on the elderly. Sometimes the consequences are almost unbelievable:

NEW YORK (AP)—Hans and Emma Kabel know they had become easy prey.

Twice in the last month, Kabel, 78, had been followed home and attacked and robbed in the neatly furnished apartment he had shared with his wife for 50 years.

In the more recent incident, the intruders had stabbed Mrs. Kabel with a fork to force her to tell them where she had hidden $275 from her husband's pension.

"We don't want to live in fear anymore," said a note found in the apartment after the elderly couple laid out burial clothes, slashed their wrists, and then hung themselves. . . .

Mrs. Kabel's body was found in the kitchen hanging from a doorknob by a short rope. The body of her husband was in the spare bedroom (*Los Angeles Times*, October 8, 1976).

3. The poor. What the average American may not know is that the most common victims of crime are not the affluent but people who are residents of our urban ghettoes. Indeed, the leading cause of death among young black men is not some dread disease but violent, intentional killing.

Researchers surveying homicides in Cleveland discovered that the overall rate had more than tripled between 1958 and 1974. They found that about 20 blacks were slain in the city for every white from 1958 to 1962, and 12 blacks for every white from 1963 to 1974. The study also showed that the ages of most victims had dropped from the early 40s to the late 20s. In Washington, a spokesman for the National Center for Health Statistics said that, nationally, homicides were the leading cause of death among black males 25 to 34 years (*Los Angeles Times*, September 1, 1977).

In Chicago, the age of greatest vulnerability has been even lower, ages 15–24 (Block and Zimring, 1973:5). The most dramatic single increase in murder victimization rates between 1965 and 1970 was among young, black males in this age range.

There are some signs that these high rates of victimization and slaughter may be leveling out and that the crime rate may not continue to increase each year (FBI, 1977; National Criminal Justice Information and Statistics Service, 1977). But such signs to many Americans are almost beside the point. Instead, the most salient is their growing awareness of the striking contrast between high juvenile crime rates and the ideology and nature of current reforms. It does not make much sense to many of them to suggest that the reasons juveniles commit heinous crimes is because they have been overly stigmatized and treated harshly by the juvenile court, and that they should be diverted from legal processing or assigned to a community program after committing a robbery, a burglary, or an assault. The time has come, many believe, when the protection of the community must take precedence over the protection of young, human predators.

Unanticipated consequences of current reforms

Paradoxically, the unanticipated consequences of current reforms may have contributed to these feelings. Their effects and ideology are often used as grounds for counterarguments. Consider the following:

1.   Child advocates suggest that children have the right to live with the same guarantees of freedom that adults enjoy. If that is the case, why should they not be subjected to the same responsibilities, including punishment for their crimes?

2.   If status offenders are different from young criminals, and are simply misbehaving youngsters who should be diverted or ignored, why not get tough with the real culprits—the young criminals? Why continue the outmoded philosophy that serious law violators should be treated the same as truants and runaways by a permissive juvenile court?

3.   If the juvenile court has not guaranteed the right of due process for young criminals, why not try them in adult court where they will

not only be given a fair trial but will be subjected to the same punishments as adults if they are guilty?

In short, the reintegrative revolution, along with high rates of juvenile crime, is generating a punitive counterrevolution—a movement which is advocating a return to former policies stressing punishment and deterrence.

The counterrevolution

Walter Miller (1973:454–455) has outlined the crusading issues of the counterrevolution:

Excessive leniency.   Current reforms have contributed to excessive leniency on the part of the legal system toward lawbreakers.

Denial of victim rights.   Every one of the four Ds grants rights to the offender at the expense of the victim. Law-abiding citizens also have rights, particularly protection of their lives and property from human predators.

Erosion of discipline and respect for authority.   The whole ideology of current reforms is an outgrowth of an increasingly permissive society. Discipline has been eroded, and youth no longer respect the authority of parents, schools, police, and courts.

Cost of crime.   Since the enormous costs of crime must be borne by hard-working, law-abiding citizens, reforms can no longer be justified in the name of protecting youthful lawbreakers.

Destruction of social order.   When one adds up the excessive leniency of our courts, the denial of victim rights, the erosion of discipline, and the cost of crime, one discovers that social order is being destroyed. This destruction, moreover, is aided by the decline in sexual morality, by excessive permissiveness in the schools, by the destruction of the American family, and by the granting of adult rights to children.

Based on these crusading issues, three major reforms of a counterrevolutionary nature have been instituted or are being advocated:

1.   *Lower the age of accountability.*   Consistent with the view that children should be treated more like adults, various states have lowered the age of accountability for crime from 18 to 16, and now require that juveniles charged with serious felonies be sent automatically to adult court (Cf. California Welfare and Institutions Code, 1976). It is no longer assumed that, because they are immature, they are not fully responsible for their acts.

This step is being taken despite the fact that the juvenile court in most states has long had the power to waive jurisdiction and to send a juvenile to adult court if it felt the gravity of the offense required it. But, because the juvenile court is now suspect, an increasing number of states do not trust it with that responsibility. All juveniles charged with serious felonies must automatically go to criminal court to be tried like adults.

2. *Abolish the juvenile court.* Now that the Supreme Court has ruled that the juvenile court must become more formal, some legalists have advocated an even more extreme step—doing away with the juvenile court altogether (Cf. McCarthy, 1977). It is a diseased organ that no longer performs any useful function. Neglected children, and perhaps status offenders, would be handled entirely by family courts, while young criminals, no matter what their ages, would be tried in criminal courts. Not only would the rights of such children be better protected, but they would gain a greater sense of the meaning of justice and of the gravity of their acts.

3. *Punish and incapacitate offenders.* Finally, a growing number of philosophers, social scientists, and legal scholars have suggested that justice demands an elimination of the individualized, rehabilitative approach to offenders and a return to punitive practices in which retribution and restraint are the governing principles (Morris, 1974; Wilks and Martinson, 1976; Wilson, 1975; van den Haag, 1975).

Significantly, these scholars dwell little on the need to separate adults from juveniles. Indeed, the policies they recommend would probably have greater impact on teenagers and on young adults than upon older persons because the young are the most criminal. Unless indicated otherwise, therefore, the points on which these scholars tend to agree are as follows:

The rehabilitative philosophy of the past century has been a failure. There is almost no evidence that we can successfully rehabilitate offenders.

It is futile to try to control crime by focusing on its causes. The justice system is unable to rectify many of them. Hence, its principal purpose should be that of insuring that punishment is swift, certain, and uniform.

While most people violate the law occasionally, the preponderant proportion of all crimes are committed by a small number of habitual offenders. Consequently, incarceration and isolation from the community must be used to minimize the chances that they will repeat their offenses.

The indeterminate sentence and parole boards should be abolished. All sentences should be of determinate length and should be based upon seriousness of offense and the offender's prior criminal history.

Each time an offender is reconvicted, the length of the sentence would be increased—doubled, perhaps, for a second offense or tripled for a third (van den Haag, 1975; Wilks and Martinson, 1976).

Since most criminals are adolescents or young adults, the goal of increasingly stringent sentences would be to immobilize young, repeat offenders until at least age 35. After that, the need for controls diminishes because the impulse to criminality drops sharply (van den Haag, 1975).

These punitive practices would do injustice to the 40 percent of all young offenders not likely to commit serious, particularly violent, crimes, again. But, since we cannot identify this 40 percent in advance, it is necessary to incarcerate them in the interest of sparing the victims of the remaining 60 percent (van den Haag, 1975).

In short, the primary purposes of penal sanctions are to punish and to incapacitate offenders. These purposes need not rule out efforts to assist their social adjustment, but such efforts are secondary to the goals of protecting victims, of deterring further crime, and of insuring that justice is uniform for all. All that remains to be decided for juveniles is after how many repeat offenses and at what age they would begin serving long terms of permanent incarceration.

Implications

There is no more evidence that punishment is more effective in deterring crime than other forms of intervention. Nonetheless, it is not likely that current reforms will remain unaffected by the punitive philosophy. It has been a part of our thinking for centuries, and its ressurgence in new dress is not going to decrease its attractiveness. Beyond that, it is important to keep in mind the growing precociousness of youth. Not only are they physically mature at an earlier age today, but their crimes during the past 15 years seem to have become steadily more adult. The law violations of juveniles ages 15–17, as a result, are much more like those of young adults ages 18–20 than like young teenagers ages 12–14. This is particularly true where violent crimes are concerned. Hence, when this precociousness is combined with liberal sentiments favoring the notion that juveniles should be treated more like adults, it also provides grounds for conservative beliefs that the age of accountability for crimes should be reduced. The traditional assumption that age 18 is a magic dividing line between childhood and adulthood is making less and less sense to people today.

Second, although the reintegrative and punitive ideologies are diametrically opposed in their policy implications, both have helped to discredit beliefs in the efficacy of rehabilitation. The fundamental premises upon which a century of court and correctional practices have been based are steadily being eroded. For example, while we are being urged to deinstitutionalize correctional programs for serious delinquents on the one hand, the indeterminate sentence and the use of parole—key elements in the rehabilitative philosophy—are being phased out on the other, at least for adults. Some states have already taken the latter step, and a bill has been introduced in the Congress to do so on the federal level (*Los Angeles Times*, September 27, 1977).

Should these trends become nationwide, what will happen to teenage criminals who continue to commit crime despite efforts to help them in community programs? If the rehabilitative ideology and its practices are phased out of institutional programs, there is every possibility that repeat offenders will be incarcerated in correctional settings where the punitive philosophy prevails. Their failure to respond to community intervention will be used to justify the use of determinate, and possibly longer, sentences for them. Given these possibilities, what issues emerge?

1. *Brutal pessimism.* Some people see current developments as evidence of a "brutal pessimism."

> Rehabilitation . . . should never have been sold on the promise that it would reduce crime. Recidivism rates cannot be the only measure of what is valuable in corrections. Whether in prison or out, every person is entitled to physical necessities, medical and mental health services, and a measure of privacy. Prisoners need programs to provide relief from boredom and idleness . . . libraries, classes, physical and mental activities (Bazelon, 1977:2).

Yet, efforts to improve either prisons or correctional practices, without resorting to current extremes, are undermined repeatedly. Each such effort, no matter how humane, is defined as "rehabilitative" and, therefore, unacceptable (Schwendinger and Schwendinger, 1978).

2. *Disuse of other theories.* A related issue has to do with the disuse of other theoretical approaches to the crime problem. Progressively over the past ten years, the crusading ideology provided by labeling theory,

and its punitive counterrevolution, have deflected the attention of scholars and policy makers away from the implications of control, cultural deviance, strain, radical, and other theories, and the need to improve and to assess these theories. Ways in which they might have tempered the current debate, and suggested other approaches, have largely been discredited or ignored.

3. *Population affected.* A third issue has to do with the population of young people most likely to be affected by current conflicts over the best way to control crime. For the most part, they are members of poor and minority groups. Police records show that arrest rates are higher for minorities than for whites, higher for low-income than for high-income persons, and higher in our urban centers than in the suburbs. Victimization studies, though they look at crime from a totally different perspective, paint an identical picture: blacks are more vulnerable than whites; poor people are more vulnerable than affluent people; and ghetto dwellers are more vulnerable than suburbanites.

As our review of American history indicated, the cycle for poor and minority people has been a vicious one. First, they were defined as inferior. Then, society was organized as though the definition were true; that is, ethnic minorities and poor people became a relatively permanent underclass that was isolated in impoverished cultural settings in which educational, economic, and social enrichment were lacking. Finally, when the consequences of this impoverishment led to violence and higher rates of crime, those rates were used as proof that these people were inferior. The prophecy was fulfilled. How likely, then, are current trends to disrupt the fulfillment of this prophecy in the future?

Our analysis in this chapter has revealed that the capacity of the four Ds to alter the prophecy is limited. While current reforms have provided help in the form of counseling, family therapy, or group homes for delinquents, they have done little to reduce the futility and disorganization of slum life, to change and improve ghetto schools, or to increase opportunities for youth employment. Perhaps it is asking far too much of the justice system that it remedy such complex problems. Perhaps the task should be left to other social institutions. It has already been proven that the juvenile court, by itself, can not achieve the broad goals originally set for it. But to their worst social critics, the four Ds represent but another instance of benign neglect for our most needy population.

The punitive approach would do even less to alter the self-fulfilling prophecy. While its advocates recognize that members of the lower class are those most likely to be affected by retributive policies, they argue that efforts to assist their social adjustment should be secondary to the goal of protecting victims, of deterring further crime, and of insuring that punishment is uniform for all. The justice system is incapable of, and should not be expected to, redress societal inequities.

If this is the case, a profound problem is posed: What is the ultimate goal of justice policy: repressive order or moral order (Bazelon, 1977)? If it is repressive order, then a punitive approach is appropriate. But, if it is moral order, then justice policy must be joined with other policies and a longer, more painful and more costly approach taken. Not only must victims be spared the horrors of crime but ways must be sought for altering the conditions which cause others to prey upon them.

4. *The forgotten element.* The final issue has to do with the forgotten element in our conflicted approach to crime control; namely, the massive amount of crime committed by the adolescent population at large. Recall what we learned in earlier chapters (6–8; 15–16):

Self-report studies indicate that juveniles from all social strata commit an enormous amount of undetected delinquency. Only about 10 percent of their delinquent acts are detected by the police.

Studies of the police indicate that, of that 10 percent, only a small proportion result in arrest.

Of this small proportion, about half are handled entirely by the police and are not referred to court for trial. This means that, at most, only 5 percent of all the acts remain in the system after detection. Likely, the figures is lower than that.

This small number if reduced even further by intake personnel in the court; less than half actually result in an appearance before a judge. At most, therefore, something less than 2.5 percent of all delinquent acts actually result in court action and conviction. What, then, are the implications?

The first has to do with the assumption that the primary cause of crime is poverty. Such an assumption is faulty. Although poor and minority youth are overrepresented in our courts and correctional agencies, the large amount of law violation by other segments of the population, even if proportionately smaller, still belies the notion that poverty is the singular cause. It cannot be; too many middle- and upper-class youth violate the law. Hence, while we must be concerned with the effects of both the reintegrative and punitive philosophies on the poor, we must also pay attention to other segments of the population if our goal is to reduce crime and to protect victims.

The second implication has to do with the capacity of both the punitive and the reintegrative approaches to reduce the degree of crime committed by the youth population at large. Those who advocate retribution and restraint, for example, suggest that the best approach is the suppression of chronic offenders. Although they do not commit all crime, they commit a disproportionate amount. Therefore, if they are immobilized, some reduction will be realized. But what if only 1, or 2, or even 10 percent of all criminal acts by juveniles come to the attention of officials?

The answer seems obvious. Although society might be better protected if all chronic offenders were locked up, many people would still be victimized. Furthermore, some of the same problems are inherent in reintegrative reforms. For the most part, they are organized to deal only with those juveniles who come to the attention of legal authorities. As a result, it seems likely that, if society wishes greater protection from juvenile crime, additional perspectives and approaches are required. More attention has to be paid to the costly process of promoting moral order and of preventing crime.

Crime prevention

In any consideration of crime prevention, one finding stands out above all others: Crime is predominantly a youthful phenomenon. It is concentrated so heavily in the adolescent and early adult years that it is obviously the function of a crucial phase in the life cycle. Hence, if that crucial phase could be affected in such a way that crime played a less important part in it, the results for society might be highly desirable.

Given this possibility, consider what we have learned about childhood and the changing status of children in American society.

1.   As a phase in the life cycle, childhood has become progressively longer during the past century. Except for contacts with their parents and teachers, children have been increasingly segregated from other adults and the responsibilities associated with adulthood. They have become the most indulged yet the most constrained segment of our society.

2.   The family and the school have been designated as the primary agents of socialization, but the prolongation of education has led to the creation of youth ghettos and dimunition in the effect of both home and school. Peers have become alternative sources of socialization. This is particularly true for those who are educationally disadvantaged and

who are residents of our slums. For many, youth gangs have superseded both the family and the school as a source of important values and social norms.

3. In recent years a movement in behalf of children's rights has been generated. The school-leaving age has been lowered, greater due process in the courts has been achieved, concern over teenage unemployment has increased, and children have been granted greater sexual, political, and legal freedoms.

4. The children's rights movement is not the only such movement, however. It now finds itself in competition with movements in behalf of women, the elderly, and minority groups. While these movements are obviously overlapping, they are not always mutually supportive and often create new and unanticipated consequences.

5. One such consequence is the changing nature of family life. More mothers are working; divorce rates are increasing; and single parent families are more common. The traditional role of the nuclear family as a socializing agent is not only undergoing change but is probably declining in effectiveness.

6. Another consequence is related to education. As it increases in importance as preparation for work in a highly technological society, the lowering of the school-leaving age has had the effect of freeing those who are probably the least capable of doing without it and of competing for a job; namely, poor and educationally disadvantaged youth who find school unbearable but who are not prepared to work.

In short, we are in a transitional period in American society where former controls over children have been decreased but where alternative sources of socialization have not yet been developed. While the definition of childhood has changed, children are not much closer to being accepted as adults or of having to assume the responsibility that goes with it. In a period of increasing instability, therefore, it should not be too surprising that crime rates have increased.

Principles of crime prevention

This state of affairs is all the more striking when one considers the ideology of current reforms in light of the task of crime prevention. The primary goal of prevention, it would seem, should be to develop a legitimate identity among young people and a belief in the importance of conforming to social rules. To seek only the avoidance of a deviant identity by refraining from the use of legal processing and stigma, by diverting juveniles, and even by deinstitutionalizing correctional programs is, in one sense, to approach prevention negatively. The more difficult and prior task is to insure that young people acquire a productive, satisfying, and legitimate self-concept. In support of that notion, consider the general principles that might govern the acquisition of such a concept:

1.   A legitimate identity among young people is most likely to occur if they have a stake in conformity (Toby, 1957); if, in other words, they develop a sense of competence, a sense of usefulness, a sense of belonging, and a sense that they have the power to affect their own destinies through conventional means (Polk and Kobrin, 1972:5).

2.   The cultivation in young people of a legitimate identity and a stake in conformity requires that they be provided with socially acceptable, responsible, and personally gratifying roles. Such roles have the effect of creating a firm attachment to the aims, values, and norms of basic institutions and of reducing the probability of criminal involvement (Polk and Kobrin, 1972:5).

3.   Since social roles are a function of institutional design and process, any strategy of delinquency prevention must address the present state of institutional instability and change. Means must be sought by which roles for children are more clearly defined, by which they are reinforced by significant others, and by which they expand the range of opportunities and responsibilities open to young people.

If followed, these principles imply a radical change in societal priorities—priorities that go far beyond either the reintegrative revolution or its punitive counterrevolution. Before the members of society and their elected representatives can prevent crime on any large scale, they will have to eradicate the poverty and ignorance that make life helpless for a significant minority of the American people and break the bonds that confine them to miserable and unacceptable conditions in our urban ghettos and rural slums. It is ludicrous to speak of fostering a legitimate identity or a stake in conformity among those for whom crime is one major way of alleviating unacceptable conditions and of realizing the American dream of getting ahead. Unless the necessary resources are forthcoming, such methods of intervention as family counseling or youth service bureaus can be little more than Band-Aids on a huge and gaping wound.

It would be a mistake, however, to suggest that all crime would be eliminated were poverty removed. That is too convenient a shibboleth. Many predatory law violators are relatively affluent young people who have not acquired a stake in conformity. One reason that many of them are inclined to leave the creature comforts of their homes and to escape through drugs or some other means, or to justify their acts of senseless vandalism, theft, and violence, is because they feel they have no power over, or stake in, what is happening to them. The childish self-indulgence that is so common among many reflects a loss of purpose and direction. Lacking institutional constraints of a rewarding kind, some young Americans behave in an immature and destructive way.

Crime prevention strategies

A fundamental question is whether America has the will or the knowledge to change its priorities in the interest of providing its young people with a greater stake in conformity. James Wilson (1975:198–9) contends that it would be foolhardy to assume that such is the case: "I argue for a sober view of man and his institutions that would permit reasonable things to be accomplished, foolish things abandoned, and utopian things forgotten." We neither understand the causes of crime nor are we capable of formulating governmental policies that would be effective in rooting it out.

Radical criminologists, by contrast, maintain that the only long-run alternative is to liberate children from the evils of the class struggle by overthrowing our capitalist system and installing a completely socialist alternative. Only if this is done will exploitation by white-collar criminals cease and the underclass in American society be freed from the degrading and hopeless conditions that continue to perpetuate violent, personal crimes (Cf. Chapter 15).

In between these two extremes are Galvin and his associates (1977) who suggest that what is required in the development of a national youth policy by which the billions now being spent for education, welfare, Medicare, job training, and juvenile justice might be used more effectively in a coherent plan for youth.

Though radical criminologists and those who advocate a national youth policy are more optimistic than is Wilson, he has much in favor of his position. Many social action programs—whether urban renewal, the poverty program, or remedial job training—have not had a noticeable effect on crime rates. Yet, the suggestion that no action should be taken is scarcely a palatable alternative either. Indeed, whether a coherent youth policy is formed or not, there is little doubt that America will continue to pour money into a wide variety of educational, welfare, and justice programs. Based on that fact alone, what are some of the things to which attention might be paid? How might we capitalize on programs and expenditures that are already ongoing?

1.   *Child care.*   An increasing number of Americans are unwilling to agree on the virtues of monogamous marriage and the nuclear family as the nursery for the next generation. Recognizing that trend, we might avoid the worst features of child abuse, neglect, and disease by pledging ourselves to the welfare of children directly, providing day care and communal child-rearing arrangements for children from any class or race whose parents cannot, or will not, provide a conventional, two-parent home. By no means would this include the majority of children, but it may help those whose futures are the most endangered.

By way of example, a movement started by Dr. Hermann Gmeiner, an Austrian, has resulted in the creation of children's villages, involving more than 10,000 children in 48 countries (Bourne, 1974). Unwanted or homeless youngsters are placed in family-size units with carefully selected "mothers"—women who are not only screened and carefully trained but many of whom have already raised children of their own. They are assisted in this task by a lesser number of resident males in the villages who help to supply a father image.

While these children are growing up, they participate in local community schools and other normal activities. When they reach the age of employment, they are then required to get jobs, to pay for their keep, and to put half of their savings into bank accounts. Then, when they are ready to move out, they are assisted in finding apartments, which they often share with each other. In short, a reasonable substitute for the traditional family may have been found and is being tried.

2.   *Schooling.*   The one institution in society that is supposed to resolve all class, ethnic, and other differences and to provide a uniform socialization for all children is the school. People expect it to provide equal opportunity for every child, and since it is the one major link between childhood and adulthood, any failure on its part has serious consequences. Yet, these expectations notwithstanding, the overall structure of the educational system, especially in our urban centers, is often ill-adapted to the different localities and subcultural groups to which it must relate. Its local branches, the neighborhood schools, usually operate on centralized policies set up and administered by people whose view of the world is often vastly different from those of the children and parents whom it is supposed to serve. This often results in lack of communication, conflict, and delinquent behavior.

If the school could do things like the following, its capacity to give the young a greater stake in conformity might be enhanced:

1.   It could do more to analyze the peculiar characteristics of any neighborhood in which it is located. Its curriculum, its organization, and its activities could then be tailored to fit better the needs of the clientele it is trying to serve.

2.   By facilitating its linkage with other legitimate institutions in the community, other school functions could also be performed more capably. For example, in an endeavor to upgrade the level of academic achievement in its schools, the Oakland School District recently took the following steps: It created a council of teachers and parents charged with establishing standards of achievement and with enforcing the pursuit of those standards; it tested students periodically to determine their progress; and it established a three-party learning contract to which parents, teachers, and pupils were signatories:

> Under this agreement, *the student* obligates himself to do homework in a quiet place for two hours each night, unaccompanied by television. *The parent*, in turn, agrees to provide an environment suitable for concentration to enforce the no-TV clause. *The teacher*, meanwhile, promises to insist on the daily completion of homework assignments, and vows to help each student reach the newly designated scholastic standards (*Los Angeles Times,* October 22, 1977).

The virtues of this approach lie not merely in its assistance to the educational process, but to the establishment of a network of social control comprised, not of law enforcement personnel, but of parents, teachers, and youth. What the Oakland School District is helping to do is to reestablish a coherent network of social relations and expectations that has been progressively lost in our increasingly anonymous, urban civilization. We have no modern equivalent of the tight-knit network of family, school, church, and community which characterized the small, New England towns of 18th century America. In that day, professional police forces were unknown because they were not needed. The program of the Oakland School District represents an effort to reestablish such a network. In seeking to improve education, however, it is also having the effect of defining and reinforcing appropriate roles for juveniles.

3.   This network of relationships, and its bridging of the gap between the generations, could be expanded even further. Traditionally, the school has failed to provide children with the kinds of experiences

that give adults a sense of usefulness and competence. Yet, there are any number of constructive roles which students do not now play but which could be sponsored by the school: *(a)* in conjunction with teacher-parent councils, analyses could be made of the school's tracking, stratification, and discipline systems to see if, in some way, these could be changed to enhance involvement rather than alienation; *(b)* tutorial programs could be organized so that students at all levels help others; *(c)* drug education programs, or programs designed to reduce racial conflict or conflict with the police, could be organized, and students given the chance to educate adults as well as the reverse; *(d)* the school could act as an advocate in behalf of its students so that it could contribute a youth perspective to the policy decisions made by many community groups and agencies; and *(e)* the school could make it possible for students to participate in constructive community programs—cleaning the environment, registering voters, participating in crisis-intervention and delinquency prevention programs, and so on.

Obviously the schools could not perform these functions without a significant enlargement of its mandate, a change in educational philosophy, and greatly increased resources. These are not forthcoming ordinarily because neither citizens nor the school see the role of the school as that of preventing delinquency. But this is because prevention has been defined in terms of controlling deviance rather than enhancing legitimacy. By reversing the definition, however, many of the foregoing could be justified. Citizens and policy makers need to recognize the social-psychological as well as the educational side of educational programs.

3. *Linking school and work.* Perhaps the most glaring omission in the socialization of youth has been the lack of a coherent link between the educational experience and the world of work. In recent years, however, the Comprehensive Employment and Training Act of 1973 (CETA), a federally sponsored program, has been used by various communities to establish this link (National League of Cities, 1977).

In Albuquerque, New Mexico, students have been discouraged from dropping out of school by providing them with economic incentives. CETA funds are used to place these students in subsidized positions within public and private agencies. In addition to working 12 hours per week, students receive general, remedial, and occupational education. Information and supportive assistance relative to work problems are also provided.

In Baltimore, an alternative school curriculum has been set up. First,

Baltimore's labor market projections are studied to identify current skill shortages and future occupational needs. Then, special schools are organized which offer nontraditional courses in the kinds of occupations that are open—business, health, communication, or community services. Students in health, for example, study medical history, laboratory techniques, and math, during which time they are also employed in these occupations. They receive both the minimum wage and academic credit for their work.

In these and other instances, then, the traditional practices of both the schools and employers have been enlarged and changed. By pursuing activities of this type on a more comprehensive basis, the socialization of youth and their commitment to conventional pursuits might be enhanced.

4. *Job creation.* Finally, more attention must be paid to the low status of the adolescent job applicant and to the shortage of career opportunities for the young in general. The most difficult policy decision relative to this issue is whether government should be the employer of last resort when jobs are unavailable in the private sector. Not only is job creation by government sometimes inflationary, but vested private interests often block legislation designed to provide jobs.

There are examples, however, of cases in which government and private funds have been used to support encouraging projects. One is the $4.3 million Maverick Corporation which runs a tire-recapping operation in Hartford, Connecticut (*Time,* August 29, 1977). Its purpose is to provide both work experience and an income until employees can be placed in better positions.

> Maverick employs 350 ghetto dwellers, including 100 people age 17 to 20. Typically, a worker is offered $2.50 an hour, and told that whoever shows up punctually will get $2.67 instead. Anyone who is so much as one minute late loses the bonus for the entire week. Morale is high, and last year 85 workers moved on to private jobs.

Again, it is significant that, like the Oakland School District, this program is designed to establish a network of social control that defines appropriate roles and provides rewards for constructive behavior rather than merely punishing young workers for deviant behavior. Whether any young person is lower, middle, or upper class, such forms of social control are both useful and productive.

By contrast, what is often overlooked when jobs are not available is the   incredible   cost—socially   and   emotionally,   as   well   as economically—of keeping youth in idleness. For example, the cost of incarcerating a delinquent today is in the neighborhood of $14,000 per person. Placement in a psychiatric hospital may be as much as $30,000. Too often, costs of this type are ignored in considering other alternatives. One or more young people could be sent to Harvard or Yale, or employed for a year, for the price it takes to confine, to feed, and to guard a delinquent. Jobs, in short, might not only be less costly in economic terms but in terms of the destruction wreaked on the unemployed in terms of a loss of self-esteem and self-worth. When these are lacking, young people have little to lose by becoming delinquet. That is why punishment alone is not likely to deter them from criminal behavior.

Conclusions

We have seen in this chapter that there are many reasons to regard current reforms in juvenile justice as something less than a panacea. While they are a part of a larger social movement designed to grant greater rights to children, their concentration upon avoiding the negative effects of legal processing and incarceration has led to many unanticipated consequences, all of which are not desirable in a democratic society. They have done little to rectify the ambiguous position of children in society, to remedy some of the worst features of neglect, poverty, and ignorance, and they have helped to foster a counterrevolution that favors a punitive reaction to juvenile criminals. And, while current reforms have helped to undo some of the worst features of the juvenile court, they have failed to address adequately the most significant feature of the delinquency problem, namely, the heavy concentration of criminal activities during the adolescent and early adult years. It would appear, therefore, that until ways are found to reorganize that crucial phase in the life cycle we call "childhood," and to give young people a greater stake in conformity, society will continue to bear the exhorbitant costs of crime.

References

Bartell, Ted, et al.
  1977 *Compensatory Education and Confined Youth.* Santa Monica, Ca: Systems Development Corporation.

Bazelon, David L.
    1977   "Crime and what we can do about it." *LEAA Newsletter,* September, 6:2.

Block, Richard, and Zimring, Franklin E.
    1973   "Homicide in Chicago, 1965–1970." *Journal of Research in Crime and Delinquency,* January 10:1–12.

Bourne, Eric
    1974   "Forging new families for homeless children." *Christian Science Monitor,* June 6:F–1.

Brigham Young University Law Review
    1976   "Status offenses and the status of children's rights: do children have the legal right to be incorrigible?" *Brigham Young University Law Review,* 3:659–691.

Bronfenbrenner, Urie
    1974   "The origins of alienation." *Scientific American,* August, 231:48–59.

Browne, Elizabeth W.
    1973   *Child Neglect and Dependency: A Digest of Case Law.* Reno: National Council of Juvenile Court Judges.

California Welfare and Institutions Code
    1976   Assembly Bill No. 3121. Chapter 1071:1–24.

Carter, Hugh, and Glick, Paul C.
    1976   *Marriage and Divorce: A Social and Economic Study* (rev. ed.). Cambridge: Harvard University Press.

Coleman, James S., et al.
    1974   *Youth: Transition to Adulthood.* Chicago: University of Chicago Press.

Farson, Richard
    1974   *Birthrights: A Bill of Rights for Children.* New York: MacMillan.

Federal Bureau of Investigation
    1977   *Crime in the United States, 1976.* Washington, D.C.: U.S. Government Printing Office.

Galvin, James L., et al.
    1977   *Youth and Delinquency, 1977.* San Francisco: National Council on Crime and Delinquency Research Center.

Gillis, John R.
    1974   *Youth and History.* New York: Academic Press.

Hale, N.
    1971   *Freud and the Americans.* New York: Oxford University Press.

Hindelang, Michael J.
    1975   *Public Opinion Regarding Crime, Criminal Justice and Related Topics.* Washington, D.C.: U.S. Government Printing Office.

Holt, John
    1974   *Escape from Childhood.* New York: Dutton and Co.

LEAA Newsletter
    1977   "Juvenile justice task force report recommends new family court."
            September, 6:1–5.

McCarthy, Francis B.
    1977   "Should juvenile delinquency be abolished?" *Crime and Delinquency,*
            23 (2):196–203.

Miller, Walter B.
    1973   "Ideology and criminal justice policy: some current issues." Pp.
            453–473 in Sheldon L. Messinger et al. (eds.), *The Aldine Crime and
            Justice Annual, 1973.* Chicago: Aldine.

Monahan, Thomas P.
    1957   "Family status and the delinquent child: a reappraisal and some new
            findings." *Social Forces,* March, 35:250–258.

Morris, Norval
    1974   "The future of imprisonment: toward a punitive philosophy."
            Michigan Law Review, 72:1161–1180.

National Criminal Justice Information and Statistics Service
    1977   *Criminal Victimization in the United States, 1972–1974.* Washington,
            D.C.: U.S. Government Printing Office.

National League of Cities
    1977   *CETA and Youth: Programs for Cities.* Washington, D.C.: National
            League of Cities and U.S. Conference of Mayors.

Nejelski, Paul
    1976   "Diversion: the promise and the danger." *Crime and Delinquency,* Oc-
            tober, 22:393–410.

Opinion Research Corporation
    1976   "Runaway incidence ascertained." *ORC Newsletter,* July,:1.

Polier, Justine Wise
    1978   "Prescriptions for reform—doing what we set out to do?" in Lamar
            T. Empey (ed.), *Juvenile Justice: The Progressive Legacy and Current
            Reforms.* Charlottesville: University of Virginia Press.

Polk, Kenneth, and Kobrin, Solomon
    1972   *Delinquency Prevention through Youth Development.* Washington,
            D.C.: U.S. Government Printing Office.

Rothman, David J.
    1971   *The Discovery of the Asylum.* Boston: Little, Brown and Co.

Schur, Edwin M.
    1973   *Radical Nonintervention: Rethinking the Delinquency Problem.* En-
            glewood Cliffs: Prentice-Hall.

Schwendinger Herman, and Schwendinger, Julia

  1978 "Delinquency and social reform: a radical perspective." In LaMar T. Empey (ed.), *Juvenile Justice: The Progressive Legacy and Current Reforms.* Charlottesville: University of Virginia Press.

Scull, Andrew

  1977 *Community Treatment and the Deviant—A Radical View.* Englewood Cliffs: Prentice-Hall.

Skolnick, Arlene

  1973 *The Intimate Environment: Exploring Marriage and the Family.* Boston: Little, Brown and Co.

Time Magazine

  1977 "Looking to the ZP Generation." February 28, 110:71.

  1977 "The American Underclass." August 29, 110:14–27.

Tinker v. *Des Moines Independent School District*

  1969 393 U.S. 503.

Toby, Jackson

  1957 "Social disorganization and a stake in conformity." *Journal of Criminal Law, Criminology and Police Science,* May–June, 48:12–17.

U.S. Department of Commerce

  1971 *Bureau of Census Reports, 1950–1970.* Washington, D.C.: U.S. Government Printing Office.

U.S. Senate Subcommittee on Delinquency

  1977 *Challenge for the Third Century: Education in a Safe Environment.* Washington, D.C.: U.S. Government Printing Office.

van den Haag, Ernest

  1975 *Punishing Criminals.* New York: Basic Books.

White House Conference on Youth

  1971 "Preamble." *Recommendations and Resolutions.* Washington, D.C.: U.S. Government Printing Office.

Wilks, Judith, and Martinson, Robert

  1976 "Is the treatment of criminal offenders really necessary?" *Federal Probation,* March, XXXX:3–8.

Wilson, James Q.

  1975 *Thinking about Crime.* New York: Basic Books.

Zimring, Franklin E.

  1975 *Dealing with Youth Crime: National Needs and Federal Priorities.* Chicago: Center for Studies in Criminal Justice, University of Chicago (Unpublished).

indexes

AUTHOR INDEX

SUBJECT INDEX

D

*This book has been set in 10 and 9 point Palatino,
leaded 3 points. Part numbers are in 30 point
Palatino italic and part titles are in 20 point
Palatino. Chapter numbers are in 72 point Caslon
italic and chapter titles are in 16 point Palatino.
The size of the type page is 27 by 45 picas.*